PLANNING LAW

A Practitioner's Handbook

PLANNING LAW

A Practitioner's Handbook

William Webster

Wildy, Simmonds & Hill Publishing

Contains public sector information licensed under the Open Government Licence v3.0

ISBN: 9780854902552

British Library Cataloguing in Publication Data

A catalogue record for this book is available from the British Library

First published in 2019 by

Wildy, Simmonds & Hill Publishing
Wildy & Sons Ltd
Lincoln's Inn Archway
Carey Street
London WC2A 2JD
www.wildy.com

Typeset by Heather Jones, North Petherton, Somerset.
Printed in Great Britain by CPI Antony Rowe, Chippenham, Wiltshire.

Contents

Foreword

In an area of the law that is constantly changing, and constantly growing in complexity, a new textbook will always be welcome – the more so if it is thorough, reliable and insightful. This one undoubtedly is.

The challenges facing an author who aims to reflect recent changes to the legislative regime for planning, and to record the work of the courts in developing and clarifying the law, are formidable. Gathering the various themes into a clear and usable guide is no easy task.

William Webster has managed to cover his subject fully, with a sure grasp of the law, and a facility to point out the salient principles where they occur. His discussion of the principles governing development control and plan-making, the interpretation of national planning policy, planning conditions and obligations, environmental impact assessment, the enforcement of planning control, listed buildings and conservation areas, town and village greens, the lawfulness of planning decisions, and a host of other topics, is thoughtful, lucid and comprehensive. The analysis is sound, and amply supported by relevant case law.

Practitioners looking for answers to the questions they meet in advising clients on the law, and when preparing argument in proceedings before the courts, can expect to find answers here. For judges too, both in the Planning Court and elsewhere, the text will be enlightening.

I wish this excellent book the success it deserves.

The Right Honourable Lord Justice Lindblom
Royal Courts of Justice
January 2019

Preface

Writing a planning textbook was always going to be a daunting task. It is very probably the most intensively regulated area of the law, in which the law, procedure and policy bristle with impending changes. Keeping up to date has, however, been the priority and this book endeavours to achieve this by introducing fresh material in the various fields which it covers.

Whilst I have attempted to state the law as at 24 July 2018, I readily apologise if events (such as appeals or other changes in law or planning policy/guidance) have clashed with the publishing process, although in some cases I did manage to persuade the publishers (even after typesetting) to make a number of alterations to the text.[1]

I began work on this book towards the end of 2017 and delivered the manuscript to the publishers in early July 2018. In the same month the Government published revisions to the National Planning Policy Framework (NPPF) issued in 2012. Rather than delay publication of the book, the references made herein to the NPPF are to the 2012 version and not the revised version whose layout differs from the earlier version. The main NPPF revisions are, however, covered in Chapter 24, 'Revisions to the National Planning Policy Framework (July 2018)', which reviews all the key changes introduced in the new version of the NPPF. It is hoped that this will help readers to understand what the material changes are, how they are intended to work in practice and where they can be found in the new NPPF, which can be downloaded online.

This book covers a wide range of well-known planning topics within a single volume. I sincerely hope that the book's layout provides a clear and intelligible narrative, with ample footnotes for readers looking for summaries of the more recent cases (and I have included as many as I can) and the various contemporary

---

1   For those looking for a truly up-to-date analysis of state of the law in this field at the date of publication of this work, I would recommend Christopher Young QC's paper given at the 46th Joint Annual Planning Law Conference entitled, 'Case Law Update in a Post "Suffolk" World', which the Chair rightly regarded as an essential reference document for practitioners in 2018–19. The paper has been published in the *Journal of Planning and Environment Law* at [2018] JPL, Issue 13.

statutory and other materials. Indeed, there is almost always a case which helps on the point you are considering. I also hope that the book will provide answers for busy planning professionals and others to the range of problems which commonly arise in day-to-day practice in either the public or private sectors or to readers with an interest in the subjects covered.

This book is not exclusively a planning text. I have also included sections on village greens and assets of community value, as well as a lengthy chapter on public rights of way. I have tried to ensure that the book will be of importance to practitioners who require guidance on the rights and obligations which exist in these areas where experience suggests that frequent problems arise. The book ends with a section on gypsies and travellers for those looking to access the relevant law within this discrete field (usually as a matter of some urgency).

I am indebted to Lord Justice Lindblom for kindly providing a Foreword and to Robert Weatherley for his assistance on the public rights of way chapter. I am also grateful to Andrew Riddoch of Wildy, Simmonds & Hill for his wise advice and support throughout. My thanks also go to my clerks at 3 Paper Buildings, most notably to Mark Heath, Robert Leonard and Joe Townsend, all of whom helped me cope with the demands of my practice in tandem with book writing. Lastly, I must thank my wife for putting up with my absence when writing, particularly as I struggled to complete the text in the final months.

All errors and omissions in this book are my own. Readers are, however, encouraged to get in touch with me directly (or with the publishers) if they spot any mistakes or wish to offer suggestions for the next edition.

William Webster
3 Paper Buildings
Temple
1 January 2019

List of Abbreviations

2007 Regulations	Commons (Registration of Town and Village Greens) (Interim Arrangements) (England) Regulations 2007
2008 Order	Town and Country Planning (Mayor of London) Order 2008
2008 Regulations	Commons Registration (England) Regulations 2008
2012 Regulations	Town and Country Planning (Tree Preservation) (England) Regulations 2012
2014 Regulations	Commons Registration (England) Regulations 2014
ACV	asset of community value
ACV Regulations	Assets of Community Value (England) Regulations 2012
AGLV	Area of Great Landscape Value
AOC	agricultural occupancy condition
AONB	Area of Outstanding Natural Beauty
AUV	alternative use value
Birds Directive	Council Directive 79/409/EEC of 2/4/1979 on the conservation of wild birds, replaced by the Council Directive 2009/147/EC of 30/11/2009 on the conservation of wild birds, as last amended by Council Directive 2013/17/EU of 10/6/2013
BOAT	byway open to all traffic
CA	Court of Appeal
CA 2006	Commons Act 2006
CIL	Community Infrastructure Levy
CILR	Community Infrastructure Levy Regulations 2010
CLEUD	certificate of lawfulness of existing use or development
CPR	Civil Procedure Rules
CPRE	Campaign to Protect Rural England
CRA 1965	Commons Registration Act 1965
CRG	CIL review group
DCLG	Department for Communities and Local Government
DCMS	Department for Digital, Culture, Media & Sport
Defra	Department of the Environment, Food and Rural Affairs
DHCLG	Department of Housing, Communities and Local Government

DMPO	Town and Country Planning (Development Management Procedure) (England) Order 2015
DMS	definitive map and statement
EA	Environment Agency
ECHR	European Convention for the Protection of Human Rights and Fundamental Freedoms 1950
ECJ	European Court of Justice
EIA	environmental impact assessment
EIA Regulations 2011	Town and Country Planning (Environmental Impact Assessment) Regulations 2011
EIA Regulations 2017	Town and Country Planning (Environmental Impact Assessment) Regulations 2017
EPA 1990	Environmental Protection Act 1990
ES	Environmental Statement
EUV	existing use value
EUV+	existing use value plus
EWCA	England and Wales Court of Appeal
EWHC	England and Wales High Court
EZ	Enterprise Zone
FFT	Friends Families and Travellers Action Group
GLA	Greater London Authority
GLAA 1999	Greater London Authority Act 1999
GLAA 2007	Greater London Authority Act 2007
GPDO	Town and Country Planning (General Permitted Development) (England) Order 2015
HA 1980	Highways Act 1980
Habitats Directive	Council Directive 92/43/EEC of 21/5/1992 on the conservation of natural habitats and of wild fauna and flora, as last amended by Council Directive 2013/17/EU of 10/6/2013
Habitats Regulations 2017	Conservation of Habitats and Species Regulations 2017
HCA	Homes and Communities Agency
HDT	Housing Delivery Test
HL	House of Lords
HMO	house in multiple occupation
HRA	Habitats Regulation Assessment
Inquiries Procedure Rules	Town and Country Planning (Hearings and Inquiries Procedure) (England) (Amendment) Rules 2013
LA 2011	Localism Act 2011
LBA 1990	Planning (Listed Buildings and Conservation Areas) Act 1990 (or Listed Buildings Act 1990)
LBC	local borough council
LGA	Local Government Act 1972
LIT	Local Infrastructure Tariff
LNR	Local Nature Reserve
LPA	local planning authority

LRR 2003	Land Registration Rules 2003
MCZ	Marine Conservation Zone
MHCLG	Ministry of Housing, Communities and Local Government
MNR	Marine Nature Reserve
MOL	Metropolitan Open Land
MPA	mineral planning authority
MPG	Minerals Policy Guidance Note
MPS	Minerals Policy Statement
NERC 2006	Natural Environment and Rural Communities Act 2006
NFDC	New Forest District Council
NGO	non-governmental organisation
NIA	Nature Improvement Area
NNR	National Nature Reserve
NPPF	National Planning Policy Framework 2012
NPPG	National Planning Practice Guidance
NSIP	Nationally Significant Infrastructure Project
OSA 1906	Open Spaces Act 1906
PCPA 2004	Planning and Compulsory Purchase Act 2004
PHA 1875	Public Health Act 1875
PINS	Planning Inspectorate
PiP	permission in principle
PPA	planning performance agreement
PPG	Planning Policy Guidance Note
PPG2	Planning Policy Guidance 2: Green belts, January 1995, amended March 2001
PPS	Planning Policy Statement
PSI	potential strategic importance
RIGS	Regionally Important Geological and Geomorphological Sites
RUPPs	roads used as public paths
SAC	Special Area of Conservation
SANGS	suitable alternataive natural greenspaces
SEA	Environmental Assessment of Plans and Programmes Regulations 2004 (or 'Strategic Environmental Assessment Regulations')
SEA Directive	European Directive 2001/42/EC
SHMA	Strategic Housing Market Assessment
SLA	Special Landscape Area
SMA	Sensitive Marine Area
SPA	Special Protection Area
SPD	supplementary planning document
SSCLG	Secretary of State for Communities and Local Government
SSSI	Site of Special Scientific Interest
TCPA 1990	Town and Country Planning Act 1990

TPO	Tree Preservation Order
TVG	town or village green
UDA	Urban Development Area
Use Classes Order 1987	Town and Country Planning (Use Classes) Order 1987 (SI 1987/764) (as amended)
UKHL	United Kingdom House of Lords
WCA 1981	Wildlife and Countryside Act 1981
WMS	Written Ministerial Statement

Table of Cases

References are to page numbers.

Table of Statutes

References are to page numbers.

Table of Statutory Instruments

References are to page numbers.

Table of EU and International Material

References are to page numbers.

Table of Other Material

References are to page numbers.

Chapter 1

Administration of Planning Law

INTRODUCTION

1.1   Responsibility for the administration of town and country planning falls under two heads, namely central government and local planning authorities (LPAs). Since 2006 the Department for Communities and Local Government (DCLG) (renamed in January 2018 as the Department of Housing, Communities and Local Government (DHCLG)) has been primarily responsible for planning in England.[1] In Wales, since 1999 planning has been the responsibility of the Welsh Assembly.[2] The Department for Digital, Culture, Media & Sport (DCMS) is responsible for the listing of historic buildings and the scheduling of ancient monuments.[3]

THE SECRETARY OF STATE

1.2   The Secretary of State has a number of powers and duties under town planning legislation.[4]

Delegated legislation in the form of orders and regulations made by the Secretary of State

1.3   Under the Use Classes Order 1987,[5] certain uses of land are deemed not to constitute development at all and will not require planning permission. Further,

---

[1]   At the time of writing, the Secretary of State is the Rt Hon James Brokenshire MP.

[2]   The functions of the Secretary of State are vested in the National Assembly for Wales (SI 1999/ 672).

[3]   At the time of writing, the Secretary of State is the Rt Hon Matt Hancock MP.

[4]   Clearly, most decisions are made on behalf of the Secretary of State by senior civil servants and, in the case of planning appeals, the decision will have been delegated to a planning inspector.

[5]   The Town and Country Planning (Use Classes) Order 1987 (SI 1987/764) (as amended) (Use Classes Order 1987).

the Town and Country Planning Act 1990 (TCPA 1990) provides a means whereby the Secretary of State can grant planning permission for various classes of development by means of a General Permitted Development Order.[6] Such development is known as a 'permitted development right' and there have been a number of such orders over the years. The various permissions granted are subject to limitations, conditions and exceptions. Permitted development rights may also be withdrawn under a condition imposed on a grant of planning permission or as a result of what is termed an 'article 4 direction'.[7] Also relevant to development is the power of the Secretary of State (or the Welsh Assembly) to make building regulations.[8]

Confirmation of orders made by a local planning authority

1.4   These range from orders for the revocation or modification of a planning permission[9] to orders requiring that any use of land should be discontinued,[10] and to compulsory purchase and various highways orders.[11] Further, orders which make provision for the designation of areas of special control (in which only certain classes of outdoor advertisements may be displayed) only become effective after confirmation by the Secretary of State.[12]

Supervisory (including quasi-judicial) functions

1.5   The Secretary of State may call in unitary development plans, structure plans and local plans for approval.[13] There is also a right of appeal against planning decisions and a failure to take such decisions.[14] Appeals against

---

[6]   TCPA 1990, ss 58(1)(a) and 59. See the Town and Country Planning (General Permitted Development) (England) Order 2015 (SI 2015/596) (GPDO). The GPDO grants planning permission in art 3 for the classes of development mentioned in Sch 2.

[7]   This is a direction made by the Secretary of State or by the LPA under the GPDO, art 4. An art 4 direction operates to restrict permitted development granted by art 3 in which event the relevant development may not be carried out without planning permission.

[8]   Building Act 1984, Pt 1.

[9]   TCPA 1990, ss 97, 98.

[10]   TCPA 1990, s 103.

[11]   TCPA 1990, s 226; Acquisition of Land Act 1981, s 13; TCPA 1990, Pt X.

[12]   The Town and Country Planning (Control of Advertisements) (England) Regulations 2007 (SI 2007/783) make provision for the designation of areas of special control. For instance, a conservation area or an Area of Outstanding Natural Beauty (AONB) may be designated as an area of special *control*.

[13]   TCPA 1990, ss 18, 35A and 44.

[14]   TCPA 1990, s 78. It should be noted that although decisions of the Secretary of State are not precedents in the formal sense (in contrast to decisions of a court of law), they nonetheless remain indicative of the policy of the Secretary of State in future cases.

enforcement notices are also determined by the Secretary of State.[15] In the case of appeals against a refusal by an LPA to grant a certificate of lawful use or of proposed use,[16] the Secretary of State is being asked to certify the lawfulness of the use or proposed use or operations on land, which is a purely judicial decision in which questions of planning policy and the public interest do not arise. Similarly, on appeals against enforcement notices,[17] the Secretary of State may have to decide whether, as a matter of law, the activity of which complaint is made gives rise to a breach of planning control.

Original jurisdiction

1.6   The Secretary of State is authorised to call in planning applications for determination by him.[18] He also has a reserve power to serve a completion notice,[19] or to make a revocation or modification order,[20] or to make a Tree Preservation Order (TPO),[21] or to acquire land compulsorily,[22] or to require the acquisition or development of land.[23] It should also be noted that whilst the majority of planning appeals are dealt with by the Planning Inspectorate (PINS), the Secretary of State retains powers to 'recover' a planning appeal which has been submitted to PINS. A 'recovered inquiry' is basically a planning appeal (against an LPA's decision) which the Secretary of State can decide for himself, rather than allowing one of his inspectors to take the final decision, as is the normal process.[24]

---

[15]   TCPA 1990, s 174.

[16]   TCPA 1990, ss 191,192.

[17]   TCPA 1990, s 174.

[18]   TCPA 1990, s 77 (he may make a direction to this effect so that he may make a decision on the application instead of the LPA – such directions may relate either to a particular application or to applications of a class specified in the direction).

[19]   TCPA 1990, s 96. A completion notice may be served by an LPA under s 94 but s 96 is a default power enabling the Secretary of State to serve a completion notice himself to the same effect. A completion notice arises in circumstances where a planning permission lapses if development is not begun within a period specified in a condition, or if approval of reserved matters is not applied for within a specified period. A completion notice authorises the termination of permission in the case of the relevant permission which has not yet been completed. The notice provides (and if served by an LPA will be subject to confirmation by the Secretary of State) that the permission ceases to have effect by a specified date other than in relation to operations carried out by then.

[20]   TCPA 1990, s 100.

[21]   TCPA 1990, s 202.

[22]   TCPA 1990, s 228.

[23]   TCPA 1990, s 231.

[24]   The law stems from TCPA 1990, s 79. As with called-in planning applications, an inspector will write a report to the Secretary of State which will make a recommendation on how the appeal should be determined. The Secretary of State will then take the final decision on the appeal. Recovery of an appeal can occur at any stage of the appeal process, even following an inquiry

Framing of national policy

1.7   In addition to his other functions, the Secretary of State is in pole position to shape planning policy through the provision of advice and information from the DHCLG setting out the Government's planning policies for England and how these are expected to be applied.

1.8   In addition to planning circulars sent to LPAs (which were usually available to the public as well and which provide non-statutory advice and guidance on particular issues to expand on subjects referred to in legislation), prior to 2012, policy, information and advice were conveyed through Planning Policy Guidance Notes (PPGs). The tendency was for advice on law and procedure to be contained within circulars, with PPGs being the main source of guidance on policy. However, PPGs were progressively replaced by Planning Policy Statements (PPSs). The Secretary of State also issued Minerals Policy Guidance Notes (MPGs) and Minerals Policy Statements (MPSs). It should be added that the Secretary of State is also responsible for national policy statements under the quite separate development consent system for Nationally Significant Infrastructure Projects (NSIPs) introduced in the Planning Act 2008.

1.9   In 2010 the Government decided to set out its national policy objectives in a single document which became known as the National Planning Policy Framework (NPPF) which came into effect on 27/3/2012 and which replaced over a thousand pages of pre-existing national policy.[25] Planning law requires that applications for planning permission must be determined in accordance with the development plan which includes the local plan and neighbourhood plans that have been made in relation to the area unless material considerations indicate otherwise.[26] The NPPF must now be taken into account in the preparation of local and neighbourhood plans, and is also a material consideration in planning

---

being held, but it cannot be done after the inspector has issued his/her decision. The Secretary of State has a wide discretion about when to recover an appeal. It is usually because the development is of strategic importance or has significant implications for national policy or raises novel issues.

[25]   NPPF, Annex 3 sets out a total of 44 PPGs, PPSs and MPGs, one Circular and a number of letters to Chief Planning Officers which were replaced by the NPPF. However, the NPPF does not contain specific policies for NSIPs for which particular considerations apply. These are determined in accordance with the decision-making framework set out in the Planning Act 2008 and relevant national policy statements for major infrastructure, as well as any other matters that are considered both important and relevant. Nor does the NPPF contain specific waste policies, since national waste management planning policy in England is contained in the Waste Management Plan for England published on 12/12/2013 which brings current and planned waste management policies together under the umbrella of one national plan and fulfils the mandatory requirements of the revised Waste Framework Directive, Art 28.

[26]   Planning and Compulsory Purchase Act 2004 (PCPA 2004), s 38(6), and TCPA 1990, s 70(2).

decisions.[27] Relevant policies must also reflect and, where appropriate, promote relevant EU obligations and statutory requirements.

1.10 In association with the NPPF there is the National Planning Practice Guidance (NPPG), which was published online on 6/3/2014 and contains 41 categories from Advertisements through to Water Supply. As part of the Government's initiative to cut down the quantity of guidance, the NPPG was accompanied by a long list of cancelled circulars, policy and practice guidance, but in turn is still a lengthy document. The NPPG was accompanied on the same date by a new PINS guidance on planning appeals, call-ins and enforcement. The NPPG has not been published officially in a single format or in print format as it is intended to be accessed online. The online version, comprising over 600 web pages, is not always straightforward to use and contains numerous hypertext links signposting the NPPF and other materials. The paragraph numbering, which does not follow in numerical form the alphabetical order of subjects on the website, is not always easy to follow.[28]

Challenges to decisions of the Secretary of State/propriety in decision-making by Planning Ministers

1.11 Decisions of the Secretary of State are subject to appeal in the High Court. He is also answerable to Parliament for the way in which he and the DHCLG discharge their planning functions. Complaint may also be made to the Parliamentary Commissioner for Standards (or 'Ombudsman') who can investigate complaints from members of the public who believe they have suffered injustice because of maladministration (as opposed to questioning a decision on its merits). Complaints must be directed through an MP and the complainant must first have put their grievance to the department concerned in order to allow officials to respond before taking the matter further.[29]

---

[27] PCPA 2004, ss 19(2)(a) and 38(6), and TCPA 1990, s 70(2). In relation to neighbourhood plans, under PCPA 2004, s 38B and C and Sch 4B, para 8(2) (inserted by Localism Act 2011 (LA 2011), s 116 and Schs 9 and 10), the independent examiner will consider whether, having regard to national policy, it is appropriate to make the plan.

[28] The *Encyclopedia of Planning Law and Practice* (Sweet & Maxwell, looseleaf) (*Encyclopedia of Planning*) (Vol 7) reproduces, as closely as possible, the text of the NPPG. For the benefit of print *Encyclopedia* users, where the absence of a hyperlink might hinder a proper understanding of the text, explanatory footnotes have been inserted. Quite how this online-only format resource will develop in practice is hard to say, but the NPPG is by no means convenient for practitioners to use, although it is possible to print off individual sections.

[29] The Parliamentary Ombudsman's powers and responsibilities are set out in the Parliamentary Commissioner Act 1967. The Ombudsman's powers are limited in that he cannot, in the absence of special reasons, investigate matters in respect of which the complainant could take action in

1.12   Guidance was issued in 2012 and was directed to 'Planning Ministers', which referred collectively to the Secretary of State and other ministers in the DHCLG exercising planning decision-making responsibilities on his behalf. The guidance raises a number of general principles (viz: avoiding conflicts between public duties and private interests, behaving fairly, avoiding bias and approaching matters with an open mind).[30]

LOCAL PLANNING AUTHORITIES

1.13   In the general run of cases, to find out who your LPA is you need only go onto the Planning Portal.[31]

1.14   Identifying an LPA and the bodies exercising the various functions under the TCPA 1990 can sometimes be tricky.[32] Part 1 of the TCPA 1990 explains which local authorities are to be treated as the LPA. The basic position is as follows:

(a)   Within Greater London, the council of a London borough is the LPA and the mineral planning authority (MPA) for the borough.[33]

(b)   The Greater London Authority (GLA) is not an LPA but the Mayor has some powers in relation to planning.[34]

---

the courts. Decisions of the Ombudsman are subject to judicial review (see by way of example, *R v Parliamentary Commissioner for Administration ex parte Balchin* [1997] JPL 917.

[30]   *Guidance on Planning Propriety Issues*, DCLG, February 2012. It is perhaps worth mentioning that at para 7 the following is stated: '7. The overall objective of this guidance is to help Planning Ministers ensure that decisions are properly taken and to avoid, as far as possible, the risk of successful legal challenge of decisions. However, no set of principles or guidance is a substitute for common sense.'

[31]   Which is a joint venture between TerraQuest and the DCLG which provides an overview of the planning system in England. Indeed, around 80% of planning applications are now submitted online and it is now possible to apply to every LPA in England and Wales through the Planning Portal.

[32]   TCPA 1990, s 1 and the following sections within Pt 1. There is a very helpful analysis of this in the *Encyclopedia of Planning* starting at P1.03.

[33]   TCPA 1990, s 1(2) and (4). The relevant LPAs within London are the 32 borough councils, the Common Council of the City of London, the London Legacy Development Corporation, and the Old Oak & Park Royal Development Corporation.

[34]   The Mayor is consulted on all planning applications that are of potential strategic importance (PSI) to London. These are commonly known as 'referred' applications. An application is referable if it meets the criteria set out in the Town and Country Planning (Mayor of London) Order 2008 (SI 2008/580) (the 2008 Order). Under the legislation establishing the GLA, the Mayor has to produce a spatial development strategy for London – which has become known as the London Plan – and to keep it under review. The development plans of the boroughs have to be in general conformity with the London Plan.

(c) For metropolitan areas in England outside London, the metropolitan district council is both the LPA and the MPA.[35]

(d) For non-metropolitan areas (i.e. the English 'shire counties'): (i) where there is a two-tier local government structure, the functions of the LPA are shared by the district council (as district planning authority) and the county council (as county planning authority);[36] and (ii) where a unitary council has been created,[37] that council is to be treated as both a county council and a district council,[38] with the result that a unitary council will be the LPA for its area for all purposes.

(e) In Wales, the LPA is the county council or county borough council for each area (except in National Parks where the National Park Authority is the LPA for all purposes).[39]

1.15 There are, however, some exceptions to the basic position explained above in cases where statute provides for a transfer of functions which are set out in the *Encyclopedia of Planning* at P1.04. However, some analysis is required in the case of the allocation of functions between county and district councils in *non-metropolitan* (or former shire county) areas.

(a) Structure planning is a function of county planning authorities[40] (although in Greater London and metropolitan areas, structure plans are being succeeded by unitary development plans). In most areas where unitary authorities have been created, structure plans are being maintained through joint arrangements between these authorities and the former county councils.

(b) District councils are responsible for preparing local plans for their area, whereas county councils deal with minerals and waste local plans.[41] It is, however, open to the Secretary of State to set up joint planning boards to act as a united planning county or district for the areas or parts of the areas of any two or more county councils or district councils.[42]

---

[35] TCPA 1990, s 1(2) and (4).

[36] See TCPA 1990, Sch 1, for the distribution of functions most of which are allocated to the district councils whereas waste and minerals planning is allocated to county councils (as the MPA).

[37] Under the Local Government Act 1992.

[38] Local Government Changes for England Regulations 1994 (SI 1994/867), reg 5(6), with the result that a unitary council is the LPA for its area for all purposes under TCPA 1990, s 1(1).

[39] Local Government (Wales) Act 1994; also see TCPA 1990, Sch 1A, for distribution of LPA functions in Wales.

[40] TCPA 1990, Sch 1, para 2.

[41] TCPA 1990, ss 30, 37, 38 (in Greater London and the metropolitan areas the local plan function is currently vested in the London boroughs and the metropolitan districts). County councils are required to prepare a Minerals and Waste Development Scheme for their area.

[42] TCPA 1990, s 2.

(c)   In National Parks in England, the responsibility for preparing local plans vests in the National Park Authority for the area.[43] National Park Authorities in Wales are required to prepare unitary development plans rather than structure plans and local plans. In the Broads (comprising the area of the Norfolk and Suffolk Broads) the function rests with the Broads Authority which has many of the functions of an LPA.

(d)   Development control[44] is a function of district planning authorities, unless it relates to a county matter (i.e. waste or minerals).

Internal political management

1.16   The Local Government Act 2000 required local authorities to shift from their traditional committee-based system of decision-making to an executive model, possibly with a directly elected Mayor (subject to approval by referendum), and with a cabinet executive of ruling party group members. However, with effect from 3/12/2011,[45] the permitted forms of governance are (currently) executive arrangements and a committee system in the case of those local authorities which do not operate executive arrangements in connection with the discharge of its functions.[46] Functions related to town and country planning and development control are executive functions and accordingly fall to be discharged by the authority through delegation to a committee, a sub-committee or an officer of the authority (such as a chief planning officer in the case of planning applications),[47] whereas the formulation of planning policy will be the responsibility of the executive.

---

[43]   A National Park Authority is the sole planning authority for all the purposes of the TCPA 1990 for the area of the park (except for those functions identified in TCPA 1990, s 4A(4) which are exercised concurrently with the district council). It needs to be noted that permitted development is limited in National Parks which is art 2(3) land within the meaning of the GPDO (see *Encyclopedia of Planning* at 3B-1012.2).

[44]   Under TCPA 1990, Part III.

[45]   Local Government Act 2000, s 9B (as amended by LA 2011, Sch 2(1), para 1).

[46]   The allocation of functions between an authority's executive and non-executive branches are dealt with in the Local Authorities (Functions and Responsibilities) (England) Regulations 2000 (SI 2000/2853) as amended by the Local Authorities (Functions and Responsibilities) (England) (Amendment) Regulations 2001 (SI 2001/2212).

[47]   Local Government Act 1972 (LGA 1972), s 101. Officers must act within the terms of their delegated powers (see *R (Carlton-Conway) v Harrow LBC* [2002] JPL 1216; *R (Technoprint plc) v Leeds City Council* [2010] EWHC 581 (Admin); *R (Friends of Hethel) v South Norfolk DC* [2011] JPL 192. It should be noted that a number of cases have considered whether the private law concept of an estoppel arises in planning law. Since *R (East Sussex County Council) ex parte Reprotech (Pebsham) Ltd* [2002] JPL 821, a decision of the House of Lords, this is no longer considered feasible. The issue has frequently arisen in the past because of statements made to developers by officers which, if binding on the LPA, might otherwise hinder it in the performance of its functions. In *Reprotech* the HL considered estoppel to be an unhelpful concept in planning

MISCELLANEOUS PLANNING POWERS

Simplified Planning Zones

1.17   A Simplified Planning Zone is an area where the need to apply for planning permission for certain types of development is removed so long as the development complies with the details and guidance set out in the scheme.[48] These schemes operate in a similar way to a special or general development order made by the Secretary of State. Developers are accordingly able to carry out development as of right up to the tolerances specified by the scheme without requiring further planning permission.

Enterprise Zones

1.18   Within such areas, the Enterprise Zone (EZ) will be the LPA to the extent mentioned in the order designating the EZ.[49] A designation order has effect to grant planning permission for development specified in the EZ scheme prepared by the LPA for the area and approved by the Secretary of State.

Urban Development Areas

1.19   Within such areas, the Urban Development Area will be the LPA.[50]

Regeneration under the Housing and Regeneration Act 2008

1.20   Where an area is designated for development under the Housing and Regeneration Act 2008, the Secretary of State may make an order designating the Homes and Communities Agency (HCA) to be the LPA for the whole or part of the area if he thinks that it would improve the effectiveness with which the HCA carries out its functions.[51]

---

law. The position is much the same in the case of the public law concept of legitimate expectation (*Henry Boot Homes Ltd v Bassetlaw DC* [2002] EWCA Civ 983).

[48]   TCPA 1990, ss 82–87.

[49]   TCPA 1990, s 6. The designation of an EZ is made by order under Local Government, Planning and Land Act 1980, Sch 32, para 5.

[50]   TCPA 1990, s 7. The designation is made by order under the Local Government, Planning and Land Act 1980, s 149(1).

[51]   Housing and Regeneration Act 2008, ss 13–15.

Housing Action Trust areas

1.21   Where a Housing Action Trust has been established for any area, the Secretary of State may make an order[52] designating the trust as the LPA for various purposes.[53]

Town planning involving compulsory purchase for planning purposes

1.22   Compulsory purchase powers (subject to authorisation by the Secretary of State) are conferred on local authorities authorising them to purchase land in their area for planning and public purposes.[54] A local authority may also exercise its power of compulsory purchase to acquire: (a) any land adjoining the main land which is to be the subject of the compulsory purchase; or (b) any exchange land in the case of the acquisition of land forming part of a common or open space, or fuel or field garden allotment.[55]

1.23   Two other powers should be mentioned under this head: (a) the power of disposal by local authorities of land held for planning purposes;[56] and (b) the

---

[52]   Housing Act 1988, s 67.

[53]   Including under TCPA 1990, Pt III, the Planning (Listed Buildings and Conservation Areas) Act 1990 (LBA 1990), and in relation to the kinds of development specified in the order made by the Secretary of State.

[54]   TCPA 1990, s 226. The power under s 226 authorises the compulsory purchase of land: (a) whose acquisition is suitable for and would be required in order to secure the carrying out of development, redevelopment or improvement of such land; or (b) which is required for a purpose which it is necessary to achieve in the interests of proper planning of an area in which the land is situated. In the case of acquisitions under (a), the authority must not exercise its powers unless it thinks that the development, redevelopment or improvement is likely to contribute to the provision or improvement of the economic well-being of the area, or of its social well-being or of its environmental well-being (see subsection 1A). The s 226 power does not extend to: (i) the GLA which has independent compulsory purchase powers for the purposes of housing and regeneration under the Greater London Authority Act 1999 (GLAA 1999), at ss 333ZA to 333ZD; or (ii) the HCA (see para 1.20) which has such power under the Housing and Regeneration Act 2008; or (iii) to urban development corporations which are given such power under Local Government, Planning and Land Act 1980, s 142; or (iv) to Mayoral Development Corporations which are given such power under LA 2011, s 207; or (v) the Secretary of State for DHCLG who has a separate power in the TCPA 1990, at s 228, and a reserve power under s 231 which authorises him to require land to be acquired by an authority in the interests of the proper planning of an area in which the land is situated. Reference should also be made to the current guidance in England for the disposal of surplus land acquired by, or under the threat of, compulsion: Compulsory purchase process and the Crichel Down Rules: guidance Oct 2015; and similarly for Wales in NAFWC 14/2004 – Revised Circular on compulsory purchase orders.

[55]   TCPA 1990, s 226(3).

[56]   TCPA 1990, s 233, which is in addition to the general power of a local authority to dispose of land under LGA, s 123.

power of an authority to develop land itself which has been acquired or appropriated for planning purposes and which continues to be held for these purposes.[57]

Challenges to validity on the ground of the authority's powers

1.24   The validity of any permission, determination or certificate granted, made or issued by an LPA may not be called in question on the ground that it should have been granted, made or given by some other LPA.[58]

Discharge of the functions of one local authority by another

1.25   A local authority may arrange for the discharge of any of its functions by any other local authority.[59] Further, two or more authorities may discharge any of their functions jointly and they may arrange for the discharge of those functions by a joint committee or by an officer of one of them.[60]

Duty of an LPA to co-operate with neighbouring LPAs

1.26   An LPA is under a duty to co-operate with neighbouring LPAs in relation to strategic cross-border issues.[61]

---

[57]   TCPA 1990, s 235.

[58]   TCPA 1990, s 286. See *Co-Operative Retail Services Ltd v Taff-Ely BC* (1981) 42 P & CR 1.

[59]   TCPA 1990, s 101(1).

[60]   TCPA 1990, s 101(5)(a).

[61]   PCPA 2004, s 33A (introduced by LA 2011, s 110(1), following the abolition of regional spatial strategies and the return of spatial planning powers to LPAs). See *R (St Albans City and District Council) v Secretary of State for Communities and Local Government* [2017] EWHC 1751 (Admin), a case where the court rejected a challenge to an inspector's finding (arising from his examination of a draft local plan) that the claimant's plan could not be found to be sound as it had failed to give adequate consideration to helping meet the development needs of other nearby authorities and had thereby not met its duty to co-operate. It was a case where (as the inspector found) the claimant should have given detailed and rigorous consideration to strategic cross-boundary matters and priorities and drawn robust conclusions with regards to whether or not any of those priorities could be delivered in a sustainable way within its district, bearing in mind the environmental and other constraints that existed. Sir Ross Cranston, sitting as a Judge of the High Court, refused the claimant's challenge. He found that the inspector's conclusion on the soundness of the draft plan was correctly reached as a matter of planning judgment and was neither irrational nor unlawful. He ruled: (a) that what measures of constructive engagement should take place and the nature and extent of any co-operation in order to meet the s 33A duty were matters of planning judgment for an LPA and the court should allow the authority a substantial margin of appreciation or discretion (*Barker Mill Estates Trustees v Test Valley BC* [2016] EWHC 3028 (Admin) applied); (b) that it was for an inspector to conduct a rigorous examination of all the evidence received so as to enable him to reach a planning judgment on

PLANNING ADMINISTRATION IN GREATER LONDON[62]

1.27   The Greater London Authority Act 1999 (GLAA 1999) created a GLA which is the top-tier administrative body for Greater London. It consists of a Mayor[63] and an elected 25-member London Assembly with scrutiny powers. The authority was established in 2000 and derives most of its powers from the 1999 Act and the Greater London Authority Act 2007 (GLAA 2007).

1.28   Strategic planning in London is the shared responsibility of the Mayor of London, the 32 London boroughs and the Corporation of the City of London. The

---

whether there had in fact been an active and ongoing process of co-operation (*R (Central Bedfordshire Council) v Secretary of State for Communities and Local Government* [2015] EWHC 2167 (Admin) applied); (c) that in reviewing an inspector's decision regarding an LPA's performance of its s 33A duty, the court's role was limited to considering whether he/she had acted rationally and lawfully; it was a matter of judgment for an inspector and a more intensive review would undermine the Parliamentary intention behind that provision (*Zurich Assurance Ltd v Winchester City Council* [2014] EWHC 758 (Admin) and *Barker Mill Estates* applied); (d) that the duty to co-operate was not a duty to agree – the duty to co-operate was active and ongoing even when discussions seemed to have hit the buffers (*Central Bedfordshire Council* applied); and (e) that in reaching an overall judgment on an LPA's compliance with its s 33A duty, an inspector was not required to balance those matters where there was co-operation against those where it was absent. It should also be noted that, under s 33A(7), LPAs are required to have regard to any guidance given by the Secretary of State about how their duty is to be complied with. Such guidance as is material to the s 33A duty is contained in the NPPF, paras 156, 178, 181 and 182. Examination of a local plan for soundness is covered in para 182. Essentially the plan is to be examined by an inspector whose role is to assess whether the plan has been prepared in accordance with the duty to co-operate, legal and procedural requirements and whether it is sound. Whether it is sound involves consideration as to whether it is positively prepared (including unmet requirements from neighbouring authorities where it is reasonable and consistent with achieving sustainable development); justified; effective (the plan, *inter alia*, should be based on effective joint working on cross-boundary strategic priorities); and consistent with national policy. As to housing needs, see NPPF, para 47.

62   This chapter deals with mayoral planning powers in Greater London but not elsewhere. For example, in May 2017, six new metropolitan Mayors were elected to lead combined authorities in England. These new leaders wield varying degrees of planning power depending on the scope of the powers which they have been given. For instance, the Greater Manchester Mayor, Andy Burnham, has the authority to draw up a statutory spatial plan for the city-region, and to introduce a mayoral Community Infrastructure Levy (CIL) and can also compulsorily purchase land. The Liverpool City Region Mayor and the West of England Mayor also have powers to produce statutory plans, with the Mayor of Rotherham having the right to call in planning applications. Some new Mayors have less power than is imagined. Andy Burnham's spatial framework cannot go ahead without the unanimous vote of the Mayor's cabinet, which includes representatives from all Greater Manchester's districts. Further, those Mayors who have call-in powers can only exercise them with the consent of the relevant planning authority. Several Mayors are able to set up Mayoral Development Corporations but they have to secure the agreement of the relevant boroughs in order to do so. The West Midlands Mayor has no strategic planning powers at all. A full analysis of the planning powers of Mayors outside Greater London is beyond the scope of this book.

63   Currently Sadiq Khan since May 2016.

Mayor is responsible for producing a spatial development strategy (also known as the 'London Plan').[64] The development plan documents of the London boroughs (or of neighbourhood plans) must be in general conformity with the London Plan (which is required to be kept under review), whose policies must be taken into account in planning decisions. However, neither the Mayor nor the GLA is a planning authority and development control functions remain largely with the London boroughs.

Mayoral planning powers

1.29   The Mayor has powers to direct the LPA of a London borough: (a) to consult with him before granting or refusing an application for planning permission; or (b) to refuse an application for planning permission of a prescribed description in any particular case.[65]

1.30   These powers arise in the case of what are termed 'PSI' applications[66] which concern applications of potential strategic importance which must be forwarded by the relevant LPA to the Mayor in order that he may determine whether the application complies with the spatial development strategy.[67] If the Mayor considers that to grant planning permission on a PSI application would be contrary to the spatial development strategy or otherwise contrary to good strategic planning in London, he may direct the LPA to refuse the application.[68]

---

[64]   The current London Plan was adopted in March 2016. The Mayor also issues planning guidance (viz: Mayor's (i) Housing Supplementary Planning Guidance (March 2016) which provides further guidance on London Plan policies for housing; and (ii) his Affordable Housing and Viability Supplementary Planning Guidance (September 2017), which is intended to raise the amount of affordable housing coming through the planning system ahead of the new London Plan in 2019).

[65]   TCPA 1990, ss 74(1B) and (1C) (inserted by GLAA 1999, s 344). The Secretary of State prescribes which applications are subject to these powers (see 2008 Order, arts 4–6, as amended by the Town and Country Planning (Mayor of London) (Amendment) Order 2011 (SI 2011/550)). Housing and Planning Act 2016, s 149 amends these powers, including the power to call in a planning application under TCPA 1990, s 2A, and the 2008 Order at art 7 enabling the Secretary of State to prescribe these applications by reference to the Mayor's spatial development strategy under GLAA 1999, Pt 8, or the London borough development plan documents adopted or approved under the PCPA 2004. Section 149 also allows the Secretary of State, by a development order, to authorise the Mayor to direct a London borough to consult the Mayor before granting or refusing an application for planning permission for development described in the direction. Similar directions are currently given by the Secretary of State under existing powers and are used, in conjunction with the Mayor's power to direct refusal of planning applications in prescribed circumstances, to restrict development which might have an impact on wharves on the River Thames or key London 'sightlines'.

[66]   See para 1.32 for meaning of a PSI application.

[67]   2008 Order, arts 4 and 5.

[68]   2008 Order, art 6. Before giving such direction on the ground that the application is contrary to good strategic planning in Greater London, the Mayor is required to have regard to those matters

Power is also conferred on the Mayor to enter into section 106 planning obligations which will be enforceable by him and by the LPA.[69]

1.31   With regard to PSI applications, the Mayor is also able to direct that he is the LPA for the application (in effect, to call in for his own decision).[70] Before deciding a planning application himself, the Mayor must give the applicant and the LPA an opportunity to make oral representations and must also publish a document dealing with the formalities in relation to public hearings and public access to documents.[71]

What are 'PSI' applications?

1.32   A 'PSI' application means any application for planning permission which the LPA considers falls within any of the four categories mentioned in the Schedule to the 2008 Order (in which event the LPA must notify the Mayor of its potential strategic importance).[72] However, for the purposes of the power of the Mayor to make a section 2A direction,[73] a PSI application means any application for planning permission for development which the LPA considers falls within a category set out in Parts 1 and 2 of the Schedule to the 2008 Order. If the LPA receives an application for planning permission for development which they

---

identified in art 6(2) so far as material to the application. Subject to any further direction, the LPA must refuse the application (arts 6(7) and (8)).

69   TCPA 1990, s 2E (inserted by GLAA 2007, s 32).

70   This he may do by giving a direction under TCPA 1990, s 2A, if he considers (see 2008 Order, art 7) that: (a) the development or any issues raised by the development to which the PSI application relates is of such a nature that it would have a significant impact on the implementation of the spatial development strategy; (b) the development or any of the issues raised by the development to which the application relates has significant effects that are likely to affect more than one London borough; and (c) there are sound planning reasons for issuing a direction. By virtue of TCPA 1990, s 2B(2), the Mayor is also required to have regard to guidance issued by the Secretary of State. The Mayor will also be the LPA for the purpose of determining any connected application, including applications for listed buildings consent (including an application for the variation or discharge of conditions subject to which listed building consent has been granted) or conservation area consent (see TCPA 1990, s 2A(5)). By 2008 Order, art 3 (as amended by the Town and Country Planning (Mayor of London) (Amendment) Order 2011), certain land is excluded from the application of s 2A, namely land that is in the following areas: (a) the planning functions area referred to in London Thames Gateway Development Corporation (Planning Functions) Order 2005 (SI 2005/2721), art 3(1), as substituted by London Thames Gateway Development Corporation (Planning Functions) (Amendment) Order 2011 (SI 2011/549), art 4; or (b) the development area referred to in Olympic Delivery Authority (Planning Functions) Order 2006 (SI 2006/2185), art 3(1).

71   TCPA 1990, s 2F (inserted by GLAA 2007, s 35); 2008 Order, art 9 (access to representation hearings and documents).

72   2008 Order: see arts 4–6 and Sch, para 1(1).

73   I.e. under TCPA 1990, 2A, whereby the Mayor may direct that he is to be the LPA for the purposes of determining the application.

consider forms part of a more substantial proposed development, on the same land or adjoining land, they must treat that application as an application for planning permission for the more substantial development.

1.33   The Schedule to the 2008 Order contains four parts.

Part 1 – Large scale development

Category 1A

1.34   Development which comprises or includes the provision of more than 150 houses, flats, or houses and flats.[74]

Category 1B

1.35   Development (other than development which only comprises the provision of houses, flats, or houses and flats) which comprises or includes the erection of a building or buildings: (a) in the City of London[75] and with a total floor space of more than 100,000 square metres; (b) in Central London (other than in the City of London) and with a total floor space of more than 20,000 square metres; or (c) outside Central London and with a total floor space of more than 15,000 square metres.

Category 1C

1.36   Development which comprises or includes the erection of a building in respect of which one or more of the following conditions is met: (a) the building is more than 25 metres high and is adjacent to the River Thames;[76] (b) the building is more than 150 metres high and in the City of London; or (c) the building is more than 30 metres high and outside the City of London.

---

[74]   The Mayor may also issue his own planning guidance to the London Plan which he is able to enforce on applications for more than 150 homes which will be a material consideration in planning decisions made by him through the call-in process. For instance, the Mayor published guidance in August 2017 which confirmed his intention, in cases not involving public subsidy, where developers provide 35% or more affordable housing on schemes in the capital to avoid having to provide a viability appraisal. Those seeking to provide lower levels will be subject to both detailed appraisals and additional reviews during the build out of the scheme to assess whether more affordable housing might be provided.

[75]   See definition of geographic extent in para 2 of Category 1B.

[76]   See para 2 of Category 1C for the circumstances in which a building is adjacent to the River Thames for the purposes of this category.

Category 1D

1.37 Development which comprises or includes the alteration of an existing building where: (a) the development would increase the height of the building by more than 15 metres; and (b) the building would, on completion of the development, fall within a description set out in paragraph (a) to Category 1C.

Part 2 – Major infrastructure

Category 2A

1.38 Development which comprises or includes mining operations where the development occupies more than 10 hectares.

Category 2B

1.39 Waste development to provide an installation with capacity for a throughput of more than: (a) 5,000 tonnes per annum of hazardous waste; or (b) 50,000 tonnes per annum of waste, in each case produced outside the land in respect of which planning permission is sought.

Category 2C

1.40 Development to provide: (a) an aircraft runway; (b) a heliport (including a floating heliport or a helipad on a building); (c) an air passenger terminal at an airport; (d) a railway station or tram station; (e) a tramway, an underground, surface or elevated railway, or a cable car; (f) a bus or coach station; (g) an installation for use within Class B8 (storage or distribution) of the Schedule to the Use Classes Order 1987 where the development occupies more than 4 hectares; (h) a crossing over or under the River Thames; or (i) a passenger pier on the River Thames.

1.41 Development to alter an air passenger terminal to increase its capacity by more than 500,000 passengers per year.

1.42 Development for a use which includes the keeping or storage of buses or coaches where: (a) it is proposed to store 70 or more buses and/or coaches; or (b) the part of the development that is to be used for the keeping or storage of buses and/or coaches occupies more than 0.7 hectares.

1.43 For the purposes of point (b) above, the area used for keeping or storing buses and/or coaches includes the area occupied by maintenance, administrative, and staff facilities connected with such use.

Category 2D

1.44   Waste development which does not accord with one or more provisions of the development plan in force in the area in which the application site is situated and which falls into one or more of these subcategories: (a) it occupies more than 0.5 hectares; (b) it is development to provide an installation with a capacity for a throughput of more than: (i) 2,000 tonnes per annum of hazardous waste; or (ii) 20,000 tonnes per annum of waste.

Part 3 – Development which may affect strategic policies

Interpretation

1.45   Part 3 of the Schedule to the Order states:

In this part, land shall be treated as used for a particular use if—

(a)   it was last used for that use; or
(b)   it is allocated for that use in—

    (i)   the development plan in force in the area in which the application site is situated;
    (ii)   proposals for such a plan; or
    (iii) proposals for the alteration or replacement of such a plan.

Category 3A

1.46   Development which would be likely to: (a) result in the loss of more than 200 houses, flats, or houses and flats (irrespective of whether the development would entail also the provision of new houses or flats); or (b) prejudice the residential use of the land which exceeds 4 hectares and is used for residential use.

Category 3B

1.47   Development which: (a) occupies more than 4 hectares of land which is used within Class B1 (business), B2 (general industrial) or B8 (storage and distribution) of the Use Classes Order 1987; and (b) is likely to prejudice the use of that land for any such use.

Category 3C

1.48   Development which is likely to prejudice the use as a playing field of more than 2 hectares of land which: (a) is used as a playing field at the time of the relevant planning application; or (b) has been used as such at any time in the preceding five years.

Category 3D

1.49   Development: (a) on land allocated as a Green Belt or Metropolitan Open Land in the development plan, in proposals for such a plan, or in proposals for the alteration or replacement of such a plan; and (b) which would involve the construction of a building with a floor space of more than 1,000 square metres or a material change in the use of such a building.

Category 3E

1.50   Development which: (a) does not accord with the development plan; and (b) comprises or includes the provision of more than 2,500 square metres of floor space for a use or uses falling within one of the following classes in the Use Classes Order 1987: (i) class A1 (retail); (ii) class A2 (financial and professional); (iii) class A3 (food and drink); (iv) class A4 (drinking establishments); (v) class A5 (hot food takeaways); (vi) class B1(business); (vii) class B2 (general industrial); (viii) class B8 (storage and distribution); (ix) class C1 (hotels); (x) class C2 (residential institutions); (xi) class D1 (non-residential institutions); or (xii) class D2 (assembly and leisure).

Category 3F

1.51   Development for a use, other than a residential use, which includes the provision of more than 200 car-parking spaces in connection with that non-residential use.

Category 3G

1.52   Development: (a) which involves a material change of use; (b) which does not accord with the development plan; (c) where the application site is used or designed to be used wholly or mainly for the purpose of treating, keeping, processing, recovering, or disposing of refuse or waste materials; and (d) where the application site: (i) occupies more than 0.5 hectares; or (ii) contains an installation with a capacity for a throughput of more than 2,000 tonnes per annum of hazardous waste; or (iii) contains an installation with a capacity for a throughput of 20,000 tonnes per annum of waste.

Category 3H

1.53   Development which: (a) comprises or includes the provision of houses and/or flats; (b) does not accord with the development plan; and (c) is on a site that is adjacent to land used for treating, keeping, processing, recovering, or disposing of refuse or waste materials with a capacity for a throughput of more than: (i) 2,000 tonnes per annum of hazardous waste; or (ii) 20,000 tonnes per annum of waste.

Category 3I

1.54   Development which: (a) involves a material change of use; (b) does not accord with the development plan; and (c) is either: (i) on a site that is used for keeping or storing 70 or more buses and/or coaches; or (ii) on a site on which the area of over 0.7 hectares is used for keeping or storing buses and/or coaches, which area includes the area occupied by maintenance, administrative and staff facilities connected with such use.

Part 4 – Development on which the Mayor must be consulted by virtue of a direction of the Secretary of State

Category 4

1.55   Development in respect of which the LPA is required to consult the Mayor by virtue of a direction given by the Secretary of State under art 10(3) of the Town and Country Planning (General Development Procedure) Order 1995.[77]

---

[77]   SI 1995/419.

Chapter 2

Development Plans and Plan-making

INTRODUCTION

2.1   Before dealing with plan-making, it should be noted at the outset that the following factors are core elements of modern planning law:

- the concept of development;
- the requirement of planning permission;
- the control over the grant of planning permission which derives from national and local policy frameworks;
- that in dealing with an application for planning permission, the local planning authority (LPA) must always have regard to the provisions of the development plan,[1] unless material considerations indicate otherwise.[2]

---

[1]   The Town and Country Planning (Local Planning) (England) Regulations 2012 (SI 2012/767) revive the term 'Local Plan'. Under the regulations, 'Local Plan' means any document of the description referred to in reg 5 at paras (1)(a)(i), (ii) or (iv), or in paras (2)(a) or (b). Regulation 5 prescribes the documents which are to be prepared as local development documents for the purposes of the Planning and Compulsory Purchase Act 2004 (PCPA 2004). The expression 'Local Plan' is therefore used in place of the expression 'development plan document' in the above 2012 Regulations. A 'supplementary planning document' (SPD) means any local development document of a description referred to in reg 5(1) and (2) (with the exception of an adopted policies map or a Statement of Community Involvement), which is not a local plan.

[2]   Town and Country Planning Act 1990 (TCPA 1990), s 70(2); PCPA 2004, s 38(6). The s 38(6) duty to have regard to the development plan unless material considerations indicate otherwise drives the 'plan-led' system of development control. It embodies a 'presumption in favour of the development plan', as Lord Hope described it in his speech in *City of Edinburgh Council v Secretary of State for Scotland* [1997] 1 WLR 1447 (at p 1449H), and, as Lord Clyde said in the same case (at p 1458B), 'a priority to be given to the development plan in the determination of planning matters'. The nature of the duty and the effect of the presumption in s 38(6) has recently been distilled in the Court of Appeal in *Secretary of State for Communities and Local Government v BDW Trading Ltd (t/a David Wilson Homes (Central, Mercia and West Midlands))* [2016] EWCA Civ 493. The key points to note are, first, that the s 38(6) duty is a duty to make a decision by giving the development plan priority, but weighing all other material considerations in the balance to establish whether the decision should be made in accordance with the plan. Secondly, the s 38(6) duty is not displaced or modified by government policy in the National Planning Policy

2.2   'Development', for these purposes, means 'the carrying out of building, engineering, mining or other operations in, on, over or under land,[3] or the making of any material change[4] in the use of any buildings or other land'.[5] This provision is important as it defines the scope of planning control.

2.3   Planning permission is required for the carrying out of any development. Permission may be the result of a specific application to an LPA and may relate to proposed or past development and, in the case of the latter, may retrospectively validate development which has already taken place without the requisite planning permission. Sometimes, permission may be granted by a development order made by the Secretary of State (known as permitted development rights)[6] or by virtue of a local development order made by the LPA.

NATIONAL PLANNING POLICY FRAMEWORK

2.4   In England and Wales, the current planning system is underpinned by policy considerations at both the national and local level. At the national level, most policy is now contained in the National Planning Policy Framework 2012

Framework 2012 (NPPF). Such policy does not have the force of statute. Nor does it have the same status in the statutory scheme as the development plan. Under TCPA 1990, s 70(2), and PCPA 2004, s 38(6), its relevance to a planning decision is as one of the other material considerations to be weighed in the balance (see judgment of Richards LJ in *R (Hampton Bishop Parish Council) v Herefordshire Council* [2014] EWCA Civ 878 at [30]). It is, for instance, for the decision-maker to decide what weight should be given to NPPF policy in so far as it may be relevant to the proposal. However, because this is government policy, it is likely to command significant weight, but the court will not intervene unless the weight given to it by the decision-maker can be said to be unreasonable in the *Wednesbury* sense (see *R (Cala Homes (South) Ltd) v Secretary of State for Communities and Local Government* [2011] 1 P & CR 22 (at [50]); *Bloor Homes East Midlands Ltd v Secretary of State for Communities and Local Government and Hinckley and Bosworth Borough Council* [2014] EWHC 754 (Admin) (at [46]); and *Crane v Secretary of State for Communities and Local Government* [2015] EWHC 425 (Admin) (at [62] and [70]). Planning policies and decisions must also reflect and, where appropriate, promote relevant EU obligations and statutory requirements. The NPPF also sets out that decision-takers may give weight to relevant policies in emerging plans according to their stage of preparation, the extent to which there are unresolved objections to relevant policies and their degree of consistency with policies in the NPPF (see National Planning Practice Guidance (NPPG) at Paragraph: 019 Reference ID: 12-019-20140306).

[3]   Which is termed 'operational development'.

[4]   Which is termed 'change of use'. A material change in the use of land has to be the result of a definable change in the character of the use made of the land (*Hertfordshire CC v Secretary of State for Communities and Local Government* [2012] EWHC 277 (Admin)).

[5]   TCPA 1990, s 55(1). Although there are exceptions: see s 55(2).

[6]   The Town and Country Planning (General Permitted Development) (England) Order 2015 (GPDO) grants permission for a number of minor forms of development. If a person is dissatisfied with the scope of his permitted development rights, he should obtain an express planning permission.

(NPPF), which was issued in March 2012 and sets out the Government's planning policies for England and how these are expected to be applied.[7] Although the guidance within the NPPF must now be taken into account in the preparation of local and neighbourhood plans, and is a material consideration in planning decisions,[8] it does not change the statutory primacy of the development plan as the starting point for decision-taking.[9] In the circumstances, proposed development that accords with an up-to-date local plan should be approved and proposed development that conflicts with it should be refused unless other material considerations indicate otherwise. It is, therefore, obviously desirable that LPAs should have an up-to-date plan in place.[10]

Presumption in favour of sustainable development

2.5   Central to the NPPF is the presumption that development should be sustainable, which, as it states in paragraph 14, should be seen 'as a golden thread running through both plan-making and decision-taking'.[11]

2.6   Paragraph 14 provides:

For **plan-making** this means that:

- [LPAs] should positively seek opportunities to meet the development needs of their area;
- local plans should meet objectively assessed needs, with sufficient flexibility to adapt to rapid change, unless:

---

[7]   The NPPF is divided into three main parts: 'Achieving sustainable development' (paras 6–149), 'Plan-making' (paras 150–185) and 'Decision-taking' (paras 186–207). According to NPPF, para 6, the purpose of the planning system is to contribute to the achievement of sustainable development and that the policies in paras 18–219, taken as a whole, constitute the Government's view of what sustainable development in England means in practice for the planning system. At para 7, it is stated that there are three dimensions to sustainable development: an economic role, a social role and an environmental role (each is defined within para 7). It is said in para 8 that in order to achieve sustainable development, economic, social and environmental gains should be sought jointly and simultaneously through the planning system, which should play an active role in guiding development to sustainable solutions.

[8]   NPPF, para 13.

[9]   PCPA 2004, ss 19(2)(a) and 38(6), and TCPA 1990, s 70(2). In relation to neighbourhood plans, under ss 38B and C and 2004 Act, Sch 4B, para 8(2) (inserted by LA 2011, s 116 and Schs 9 and 10) the independent examiner will consider whether, having regard to national policy, it is appropriate to make the neighbourhood plan. NPPF, para 11 provides that planning law requires that applications for planning permission must be determined in accordance with the development plan unless material considerations indicate otherwise.

[10]   NPPF, paras 11 and 12.

[11]   NPPF, paras 14 and 17 (viz: core planning principles) deal with plan-making and decision-taking. Although this chapter deals with development plans and plan-making, it is considered appropriate to deal fully with the guidance provided under both these paragraphs.

– any adverse impacts of doing so would significantly and demonstrably outweigh the benefits, when assessed against the policies [in the NPPF] taken as a whole; or

– specific policies [in the NPPF] indicate that development should be restricted.[12]

For **decision-taking** this means:[13]

▪ approving development proposals that accord with the development plan without delay; and

▪ where the development plan is absent, silent or relevant policies are out-of-date, granting permission unless:

– any adverse effects of doing so would significantly and demonstrably outweigh the benefits, when assessed against the policies [in the NPPF] taken as a whole; or

– specific policies [in the NPPF] indicate that development should be restricted.[14]

2.7   The NPPF requires all local plans to be based upon and reflect the presumption in favour of sustainable development, with clear policies that will guide how the presumption should be applied locally.[15]

2.8   The presumption also impacts on neighbourhood planning. The NPPF at paragraph 16 states that neighbourhoods should:[16]

▪ develop plans that support the strategic development needs set out in local plans, including policies for housing and economic development;

▪ plan positively to support local development, shaping and directing development in their area that is outside the strategic elements of the local plan; and

▪ identify opportunities to use neighbourhood development orders to enable developments that are consistent with their neighbourhood plan to proceed.[17]

---

[12] For example, those policies relating to sites protected under the Birds and Habitats Directives (see NPPF, para 119) and/or designated as Sites of Special Scientific Interest (SSSIs); land designated as Green Belt, Local Green Space, an Area of Outstanding Natural Beauty (AONB), Heritage Coast or within a National Park (or a Broads Authority); designated heritage assets; and locations at risk of flooding or coastal erosion. These are the specific examples set out in the fn to NPPF, para 14.

[13] Unless material considerations indicate otherwise.

[14] See fn 12.

[15] NPPF, para 15.

[16] NPPF, para 16.

[17] Neighbourhood development orders can grant planning permission for specified developments in a neighbourhood area (TCPA 1990, s 61E(2) (as inserted by LA 2011, Sch 9)). This topic is dealt with in Chapter 3 'Neighbourhood Planning'.

Core planning principles

2.9   The NPPF at paragraph 17 lays down 'a set of 12 core land-use planning principles' applicable to both plan-making and decision-taking. These principles are that planning should:

- be genuinely plan-led, empowering local people to shape their surroundings, with succinct local and neighbourhood plans setting out a positive vision for the future of the area. Plans should be kept up to date and be based on joint working and co-operation to address larger than local issues. They should provide a practical framework within which decisions on planning applications can be made with a high degree of predictability and efficiency;
- not simply be about scrutiny, but instead be a creative exercise in finding ways to enhance and improve the places in which people live their lives;
- proactively drive and support sustainable economic development to deliver their homes, business and industrial units, infrastructure and thriving local places that the country needs. Every effort should be made objectively to identify and then meet the housing, business and other development needs of the area and respond positively to wider opportunities for growth. Plans should take account of market signals, such as land prices and housing affordability, and set out a clear strategy for allocating sufficient land which is suitable for development in their area, taking account of the needs of the residential and business communities;
- always seek to secure high quality design and a good standard of amenity for all existing and future occupants of land and buildings;
- take account of the different roles and the character of different areas, promoting the vitality of our main urban areas, protecting the Green Belts around them, recognising the intrinsic character and beauty of the countryside and supporting thriving rural communities within it;
- support the transition to a low-carbon future in a changing climate, taking full account of flood risk and coastal change, and encourage the reuse of existing resources, including the conversion of existing buildings, and encourage the use of renewable resources (for example, by the development of renewable energy);
- contribute to conserving and enhancing the natural environment and reducing pollution. Allocations of land for development should prefer land of less environmental value, where consistent with other policies in this Framework;
- encourage the effective use of land by reusing land that has been previously developed (brownfield land), provided that it is not of high environmental value;
- promote mixed-use developments and encourage multiple benefits from the use of land in urban and rural areas, recognising that some open land

can perform many functions (such as for wildlife, recreation, flood risk mitigation, carbon storage or food production);

▪ conserve heritage assets in a manner appropriate to their significance, so that they can be enjoyed for their contribution to the quality of life of this and future generations;

▪ actively manage patterns of growth to make the fullest possible use of public transport, walking and cycling, and focus significant development in locations which are or can be made sustainable; and

▪ take account of and support local strategies to improve health, social and cultural wellbeing for all, and deliver sufficient community and cultural facilities and services to meet local needs.

2.10   The NPPF does not contain policies for nationally significant infrastructure projects for which particular considerations apply. These are determined in accordance with the decision-making framework set out in the Planning Act 2008 and relevant national policy statements for major infrastructure, as well as any other matters that are considered both important and relevant (including policies within the NPPF). Nor does the NPPF contain specific waste policies, and national waste planning policy is now contained in the Waste Management Plan for England, issued in December 2013. Lastly, the NPPF does not contain specific policies on gypsy and traveller sites, which are dealt with separately in *Planning Policy for Traveller Sites* (March 2012), which is to be read with the NPPF. On 6/3/2014 the National Planning Practice Guidance (NPPG) (which is subject to frequent amendment) was launched online and, together with the NPPF, is now the bedrock of government policy and guidance (although the Government still provides policy guidance from time to time by means of ministerial statements).

A NEW SYSTEM OF DEVELOPMENT PLANS ARISING FROM THE PLANNING AND COMPULSORY PURCHASE ACT 2004 AND THE LOCALISM ACT 2011

2.11   At the local level, the Planning and Compulsory Purchase Act 2004 (PCPA 2004) (Parts 1 and 2)[18] introduced a new system of development plans for England and Wales and was later reformed by the Localism Act 2011 (LA 2011). The 2004 Act abolished the former structure, local and unitary plans system.[19] What took

---

[18]   Which came into force on 28/9/2004.

[19]   Structure plans were written statements of the LPA's general policies and proposals. They were adopted by the LPA after an examination in public conducted by a person or persons selected by the Secretary of State. It was a feature of structure plan inquiries that no one had any right to be heard and the emphasis was very much on a broad examination of the strategic issues for the area. Structure plans were supplemented by local plans which set out detailed policies and proposals

their place was a system of development plans for England and Wales which comprised (outside Greater London) a mix of regional spatial strategies[20] (for each of the eight regions – Wales was dealt with separately – which were not planning authorities as such, but merely regional plan-making authorities) and development plan documents for each LPA. The regional authorities and the system of regional planning in force from 2004 (i.e. regional spatial strategies)[21] were abolished by the LA 2011.[22] The removal of the regional tier of the planning system has, to an extent, been offset by the statutory duty on LPAs (and county councils) to co-operate on various matters, which include the preparation of development plan documents.[23]

---

for the use of the land in the area and informed day-to-day planning decisions. However, local plan-making was purely discretionary and until 1991 did not even have to extend to the whole of an LPA's area. Local plans (which were required to conform to the structure plan for the area) incorporated a written statement and a proposals map containing the various policies and other illustrative or explanatory matter prescribed by the Secretary of State or as the LPA sought fit to include on it. Local plans could not be adopted until after an inquiry had been held by an inspector who would consider objections and report back with recommendations to the LPA. In Greater London (in the case of each local borough council (LBC)) and the Metropolitan Counties (in the case of each of the metropolitan district councils), authorities were required to prepare unitary development plans instead of structure and local plans. In Wales, the Local Government (Wales) Act 1994 required each unitary council to prepare a unitary development plan to replace existing structure and local plans. The preparation and adoption of unitary development plans were very similar to local plans and subject to powers of call-in.

20 Spatial planning is not defined in the PCPA 2004, but has been described as something going beyond traditional land use planning, bringing together and integrating land use policies with other policies and programmes which influence the nature of places and how they function (see RMC Duxbury (ed), *Telling and Duxbury's Planning Law and Procedure* (Oxford University Press, 15th edn, 2013) at para 4.27).

21 It is considered unnecessary to deal with regional spatial strategies in any detail. Suffice to say, regional spatial strategies were intended to provide a broad development strategy for each of the eight regions. The emphasis was on matters of regional importance, and the regional spatial strategy was effectively the responsibility of the regional planning bodies for the various regions. With the change of government in 2010, the focus involved the promotion of decentralisation and democratic engagement and an end to what was termed 'top-down' government, which resulted in new powers being given to local communities and the abolition of regional spatial strategies.

22 Under the PCPA 2004 in Greater London, the development plan is the Mayor's spatial development strategy (the London Plan), together with the adopted or approved development plan documents for each LBC. In Wales, PCPA 2004, Pt 6 provides for a Wales spatial plan, along with local area development plans. LA 2011, s 109 provides for the abolition of statutory regional planning by repealing Local Democracy, Economic Development and Construction Act 2009, Pt 5.

23 PCPA 2004, s 33A (introduced by the LA 2011, s 110). The duty is one that requires an LPA to co-operate with other LPAs, county councils and other prescribed bodies (which include the Environment Agency (EA), English Heritage, Natural England, the Mayor of London, the Civil Aviation Authority, the HCA, each Primary Care Trust, the Office of Rail Regulation, Transport for London, each integrated transport authority, each highway authority and the Marine Management Organisation) in maximising the effectiveness with which duties within s 33A(3)

2.12   Other important elements of the PCPA 2004 reforms:

(a)   For the first time, those engaged in the formulation of development plan documents are required to exercise the function with the objective of contributing to the achievement of sustainable development.[24]

(b)   An LPA is required to carry out a sustainability appraisal of the proposals in a local plan during its preparation.[25] Its object is to promote sustainable

---

are undertaken, which, by s 33A(3)(a), includes the preparation of development plan documents (in so far as they relate to what is termed 'a strategic matter'), along with other activities that can reasonably be considered to prepare the way for the preparation of such documents (s 33A(3)(d)). 'Strategic matters' include sustainable development or the use of land having a significant impact on more than one planning area, especially in relation to strategic infrastructure, and sustainable development or use of land in a two-tier area if the development or use is a county matter (s 33A(4)). The engagement required includes considering whether to consult on, prepare, enter into and publish agreements on joint approaches to the undertaking of the activities mentioned in s 33A(3) (including the preparation of development plan documents and other local development documents) and, in the case of LPAs, considering whether to agree under s 28 to prepare joint local development plan documents. LPAs must also have regard to any guidance of the Secretary of State on how their duty is to be complied with (s 33A(7)). Whenever an LPA submits their local plan for independent examination, they will be expected to provide evidence that their s 33A duty has been complied with, otherwise they risk it being rejected by the examiner.

[24]   PCPA 2004, s 39(2). For the purposes of s 39(2), the person or body must in particular have regard to the desirability of achieving good design (s 39(2A)). Section 39(3) also requires regard to be had to national policies and advice contained in guidance issued by the Secretary of State and the National Assembly for Wales. NPPF, para 14 provides that there is a presumption in favour of sustainable development running through both plan-making and decision-taking (see paras 2.6 and 2.7). NPPF, para 15 goes on to provide that:

'Policies in Local Plans should follow the approach of the presumption in favour of sustainable development so that it is clear that development which is sustainable can be approved without delay. All plans should be based upon and reflect the presumption in favour of sustainable development, with clear policies that will guide how the presumption should be applied locally.'

[25]   PCPA 2004, s 19. More generally, s 39 requires that the authority preparing a local plan must do so 'with the objective of contributing to the achievement of sustainable development'. A sustainability appraisal applies to any of the documents that can form part of a local plan, including core strategies, site allocation documents and area action plans, and should only focus on what is needed to consider the likely significant effects of the local plan. The appraisal does not need to be done in any more detail, or using more resources, than is considered to be appropriate for the content and level of detail in the local plan. Sustainability appraisals incorporate the requirements of the Environmental Assessment of Plans and Programmes Regulations 2004 (SI 2004/1633) (commonly referred to as the 'Strategic Environmental Assessment Regulations') (SEA), which implement the requirements of the European Directive 2001/42/EC (the SEA Directive) on the assessment of the effects of certain plans and programmes on the environment. Sustainability appraisal ensures that potential environmental effects are given full consideration alongside social and economic issues. In short, strategic environmental assessment considers only the environmental effects of a plan, whereas sustainability appraisal considers the plan's wider economic and social effects in addition to its potential environmental impacts. Sustainability appraisals should meet all the requirements of the 2004 Regulations with the result that a separate strategic environmental assessment should not normally be required.

development by assessing the extent to which the emerging plan, when judged against reasonable alternatives, will help achieve relevant environmental, economic and social objectives. The process is therefore an opportunity to consider ways by which the local plan can contribute to improvements in environmental, social and economic conditions, as well as a means of identifying and mitigating potential adverse effects that the plan might otherwise have. It can be used to test evidence underpinning the plan and to help demonstrate how the tests of soundness have been met.

(c)   Development plans also have to meet the requirements of the Strategic Environmental Assessment Directive (the 'SEA Directive'), which is intended to provide a high level of protection for the environment and to contribute to the integration of environmental considerations into the preparation and adoption of plans and programmes which are likely to have significant effects on the environment.[26] A development plan or programme cannot be adopted or submitted for adoption unless it has been subjected to an environmental assessment by the responsible authority. Where an assessment is required, the responsible authority must prepare an environmental report.

Local development documents (comprising the local plan for the area)

2.13   Part 2 of the PCPA 2004 shifts from regional strategy to local planning in England. It establishes a new framework by replacing the former structure plans, local plans and unitary development plans with the preparation by LPAs and unitary authorities[27] of their local development scheme, which is their overall plan

---

Strategic environmental assessment alone can, however, be required in some limited situations where sustainability appraisal is not needed. This is usually only where neighbourhood plans or SPDs could have significant environmental effects.

[26]   The SEA Directive requires environmental considerations to be taken into account in plan-making and programmes in other fields such as energy, transport and telecommunications. In England the SEA Directive is implemented into law by the Strategic Environmental Assessment Regulations. There are separate regulations for Wales, namely the Environmental Assessment of Plans and Programmes (Wales) Regulations 2004 (SI 2004/1656).

[27]   Plan-making is the responsibility of district, London borough, metropolitan district, unitary and National Park authorities. LPAs with minerals and waste planning authorities (including county councils in respect of any part of their area for which there is a district council, London borough, metropolitan district, unitary and National Park authorities) should also produce plans to provide a framework for decisions (which can include combined minerals and waste plans). See NPPG at Paragraph: 006 Reference ID: 12-006-20140306.

for the preparation of development plan documents for the area.[28] These documents make up the local development framework which is effectively a folder of local development documents for delivering the spatial planning strategy for the area.[29]

2.14   The local development scheme is required to specify: (a) the local development documents which, when prepared, will comprise the local plan for the area;[30] (b) the subject matter and geographical area to which each development plan document relates;[31] (c) which development plan document (if any) is to be prepared jointly with one or more LPAs;[32] (d) any matter or area in respect of which the LPA has agreed or proposes to agree to the constitution of a joint committee;[33] and (e) a timetable for the preparation and revision of the development plan documents.[34] If an LPA has not prepared a local development scheme, the Secretary of State or the Mayor of London (in the case of the London boroughs) may prepare a local development scheme and direct the LPA to bring that scheme into effect.[35] An LPA must also revise its local development scheme whenever directed to do so by the Secretary of State or the Mayor of London.[36]

2.15   A local development scheme must be made available publicly and kept up to date. It is also important that local communities and interested parties can keep

---

[28]   PCPA 2004, s 15.

[29]   PCPA 2004, s 13: each LPA is required to 'keep under review the matters which may be expected to affect the development of their area or the planning of its development' and (s 15) to prepare a 'local development scheme' which (*inter alia*) specifies the local development documents which are to be 'development plan documents'. The authority's local development documents 'must (taken as a whole) set out the authority's policies (however expressed) relating to the development and use of land in their area' (s 17). 'Local development documents' are defined by regulations made under s 17(7). In short, they are documents which contain statements as to the development and use of land which the authority wishes to encourage, the allocation of sites for particular types of development and development management and site allocations policies intended to guide determination of planning applications. Together, they comprise the 'development plan' or 'local plan' for the area (Town and Country Planning (Local Planning) (England) Regulations 2012, regs 5 and 6).

[30]   PCPA 2004, s 15(2)(a).

[31]   PCPA 2004, s 15(2)(b).

[32]   PCPA 2004, s 15(2)(d).

[33]   PCPA 2004, s 15(2)(e) and s 29 (in conjunction with Local Government Act 1972 (LGA 1972), s 101). This is a mechanism whereby county councils can combine with LPAs, with the joint authority becoming the joint LPA for an area or for defined purposes (such as might arise in the case of minerals and waste planning, which are county matters).

[34]   PCPA 2004, s 15(2)(f).

[35]   PCPA 2004, s 15(3A).

[36]   PCPA 2004, ss 15(8)–(8F).

track of its progress. LPAs should publish their local development scheme on their website.[37]

NATIONAL PLANNING PRACTICE GUIDANCE

2.16 The following paragraphs (aided by footnotes) are taken from the NPPG: '1. Local Plans – Key Issues':[38]

What is the role of a Local Plan?[39]

National planning policy places Local Plans at the heart of the planning system so it is essential that they are in place and kept up-to-date.[40] Local Plans set out a vision and a framework for the future development of the area, addressing needs and opportunities in relation to housing, the economy, community facilities and infrastructure – as well as a basis for safeguarding the environment, adapting to climate change and securing good design. They are also a critical tool in guiding decisions about individual development proposals, as Local Plans (together with any neighbourhood plans which have been brought into force)[41] are the starting point for considering whether applications can be approved.[42]

National planning policy sets clear expectations as to how a Local Plan must be developed in order to be justified, effective, consistent with national policy and

---

[37] See NPPG at Paragraph: 009 Reference ID: 12-009-20140306.

[38] What follows is as found in the NPPG, except for the use of the expression 'LPAs' as a shorthand for local planning authorities and 'NPPF' as a shorthand for the National Planning Policy Framework. The numbering of the paragraphs in the text is *not* taken from the NPPG, but is used herein for ease of reference to the text in the NPPG.

[39] NPPG at Paragraph: 001 Reference ID: 12-001-20140306. Updated on 28/7/2017. See also NPPF, para 150.

[40] Local plans can be reviewed in whole or in part to respond to changing circumstances. LPAs should review the relevance of the local plan at regular intervals to assess whether some or all of it may need updating. Most local plans are likely to require updating in whole or part at least every five years. Reviews should be proportionate to the issues in hand. Indeed, local plans may be found sound, conditional upon a review in whole or part within five years of the date of adoption (see Paragraph: 008 Reference ID: 12-008-20140306 – updated on 6/3/2014). The NPPF also makes it clear that relevant policies for the supply of housing should not be considered up to date if the authority cannot demonstrate a five-year supply of deliverable housing sites (NPPF, para 47).

[41] See Chapter 3, which is devoted to neighbourhood planning. Neighbourhood plans can be developed before, after or in parallel with a local plan, but they must be in conformity with the strategic policies in the adopted local plan for the area (and any other strategic policies in the statutory development plan where relevant, such as the London Plan). Where a neighbourhood plan has been made, the LPA should take it into account when preparing their local plan strategy and policies and avoid duplicating policies that are in the neighbourhood plan (see NPPG at Paragraph: 013 Reference ID: 12-013-20170728 – updated on 28/7/2017).

[42] Planning decisions must be taken in accordance with the development plan, unless material considerations indicate otherwise (PCPA 2004, s 38(6), and NPPF, para 150).

positively prepared to deliver sustainable development that meets local needs and national priorities.[43]

What should a Local Plan contain?[44]

The Local Plan should make clear what is intended to happen in the area over the life of the plan, where and when this will occur and how it will be delivered.[45] This can be done by setting out broad locations and specific allocations of land for different purposes; through designations showing areas where particular opportunities or considerations apply (such as protected habitats);[46] and through criteria-based

---

[43] Local plans must be prepared with the objective of contributing to the achievement of sustainable development (PCPA 2004 at s 39(2)) and to this end, should be consistent with the principles and policies set out in the NPPF, including the presumption in favour of sustainable development (see NPPF, para 151). Local plans should be aspirational, but realistic. They should address the spatial implications of economic, social and environmental change. Local plans should set out opportunities for development and clear policies on what will or will not be permitted and where. Only policies that provide a clear indication of how a decision-maker should react to a development proposal should be included in the plan (see NPPF, para 154). NPPF, para 155 promotes the need for early consultation with neighbourhoods, local organisations and businesses so that local plans reflect a collective vision and a set of agreed priorities for the sustainable development of the area, including those contained in any neighbourhood plans that have been made.

[44] NPPG at Paragraph: 002 Reference ID: 12-002-20140306. Updated on 6/3/2014.

[45] For how detailed a local plan should be, see NPPG at Paragraph: 010 Reference ID: 12-010-20140306. For instance, in drafting policies, the LPA should avoid undue repetition, for example, by using generic policies to set out principles that may be common to different types of development. Nor should there be any need to reiterate policies that are already set out in the NPPF. Where sites are proposed for allocation, sufficient detail should be given to provide clarity to developers, local communities and other interests about the nature and scale of the development (addressing the 'what, where, when and how' questions). It is clearly vital for an LPA to be realistic about what can be achieved and when, particularly in relation to the level of infrastructure and services required for planned development (at least in the first five years of the local plan), which may need to be funded and brought on stream at an appropriate time if development is to be viable. Where the deliverability of critical infrastructure is uncertain, then the consequences of this should be addressed in the draft plan. The detail concerning planned infrastructure provision can be set out in a supporting document (such as an infrastructure delivery programme) that can be updated regularly. However, key infrastructure requirements on which delivery of the plan depends should be contained in the local plan itself. Where LPAs intend to bring forward a CIL regime, then this should be done in parallel with producing the local plan, as this allows questions about infrastructure funding and the viability of policies to be addressed in a comprehensive and co-ordinated way. See NPPG at Paragraph: 018 Reference ID: 12-018-20140306 – updated on 6/3/2014.

[46] The local plan may also require a Habitats Regulation Assessment (HRA), as set out in the Conservation of Habitats and Species Regulations 2017, if it is considered likely to have significant effects on European habitats or species located in the LPA's area or in its vicinity. Put simply, LPAs are required to carry out these assessments to make sure plans or projects affecting sites in and around EU-designated Special Areas of Conservation (SACs) or Special Protection Areas (SPAs) have no harmful effects on them. An assessment has two stages: a screening stage and then a full 'appropriate assessment'. Established practice following *R (Hart DC) v Secretary of State for Communities and Local Government* [2008] EWHC 1204 (Admin) has been that proposals to mitigate any negative impacts of a proposed plan or project, such as the provision of

policies to be taken into account when considering development. A policies map must illustrate geographically the application of policies in a development plan. The policies map may be supported by such other information as the LPA sees fit to best explain the spatial application of development plan policies.[47]

---

suitable alternative natural greenspaces (SANGS), can be considered at the screening stage. If the promoter can persuade the decision-maker at this point that negative impacts will be mitigated effectively, the requirement for an appropriate assessment is avoided. However, in a recent ECJ judgment on 12/4/2018, namely *People Over Wind and Peter Sweetman v Coillte Teoranta* (C-323/17) EU:C:2018:244, the CJEU ruled (in a case concerning the Habitats Directive and not the EIA Directive, namely Directive 2011/92/EU on the assessment of the effects of certain public and private projects on the environment) that the former approach was wrong and that mitigation measures which are intended to avoid or reduce the negative effects of development should be assessed at the stage of the appropriate assessment and that it is not permissible to take account of measures intended to avoid or reduce harmful effects of the plan or project on a European site at the screening stage. The Planning Inspectorate (PINS) has written to planning inspectors to provide guidance on the issue warning that both local plans and individual projects could fall foul of the ruling. The PINS guidance note says that inspectors should review local plans going through the examination process and ongoing appeal casework for compliance with the ruling. According to the note, inspectors should ask plan-making authorities to confirm the extent to which they consider their HRA assessment report is legally compliant with the ECJ decision and ask them to revisit the screening assessment in doing so. If a revised screening assessment concludes that an appropriate assessment is required, the guidance concludes that this should be carried out. PINS advises that further consultation may be required on any revised screening assessment or appropriate assessment. It is reported in *Planning* on 15/6/2018 that the ruling's focus on appropriate assessment carries significant planning implications. First, consultation with the statutory agency Natural England is mandatory when undertaking an appropriate assessment whereas it is merely optional at the screening stage. Secondly, appropriate assessments set a more stringent test. At the screening stage, promoters and LPAs must establish that a site allocation or project will have 'no significant effect' upon protected sites 'on the basis of objective information'. Lastly, NPPF, para 119 makes it clear that the 'tilted balance' in favour of sustainable development for councils lacking a five-year housing land supply does not apply where development requiring appropriate assessment is being considered, planned or determined. Experts agree that local plans in progress are potentially affected and it is likely that LPAs will ask consultants to reassess the local plan's HRA to ensure that it will pass the higher bar of 'appropriate assessment', and will then reconsult with Natural England which may no doubt be facing several consultation requests. On the other hand, other experts predict that the overall impact on plan-making may be limited and will merely require the reassessed HRA to be submitted during the plan's public examination, rather than involving resubmission of the entire plan. That this may only be a procedural issue is echoed in the PINS guidance note, which says that 'if avoidance and reduction measures are adequate to exclude adverse effects on European sites' integrity, the approach required is primarily a procedural one'. It is suggested that in many cases, LPAs may be able to simply re-present existing screening HRAs as full appropriate assessments. See the article 'Mitigation Measures and Appropriate Assessments: A Change in the Wind from Luxembourg: *People over Wind v Teoranta*' by Stephen Tromans QC and Victoria Hutton in the *Journal of Planning and Environmental Law* (2018; issue 8 at p 896). The revised NPPF does not take account of the European Court of Justice (ECJ) ruling and the government says that it is still examining the implications of the judgment.

[47] The policies map should illustrate geographically the policies in the local plan and be reproduced from, or based on, an Ordnance Survey map. If the adoption of a local plan would result in changes to a previously adopted policies map, when the plan is submitted to PINS for examination an up-to-date submissions policies map should also be submitted, showing how the adopted policies

Local Plans should be tailored to the needs of each area in terms of their strategy and the policies required.[48] They should focus on the key issues that need to be addressed and be aspirational but realistic in what they propose.[49] The Local Plan should aim to meet the objectively assessed development and infrastructure needs of the area,[50]

---

map would be changed as a result of the new plan. The PCPA 2004, s 19 sets out specific matters to which the LPA must have regard when preparing a local plan. Regulations 8 and 9 of the Town and Country Planning (Local Planning) (England) Regulations 2012 prescribe the general form and content of local plans and the adopted policies map, while reg 10 states what additional matters LPAs must have regard to when drafting their plans.

[48]   NPPF, para 156 requires LPAs to set out the strategic priorities for the area in the local plan. It states that strategic policies should deliver: (i) the homes and jobs needed in the area; (ii) the provision of retail, leisure and other commercial development; (iii) the provision of infrastructure for transport, telecommunications, waste management, water supply, wastewater, flood risk and coastal change management, as well as the provision of minerals and energy (including heat); (iv) the provision of health, security, community and cultural infrastructure and other local facilities; and (v) climate change mitigation and adaptation, conservation and enhancement of the natural and historic environment, including landscape. NPPF para 158 also stipulates that LPAs should ensure that local plans are based on adequate, up-to-date and relevant evidence about the economic, social and environmental characteristics and prospects of their areas. Para 158 onwards sets out the types of evidence that may be required for these purposes. The evidence should be focused tightly on supporting and justifying the particular policies in the local plan. Such evidence should be appropriate and proportionate for producing a sound local plan. NPPG at Paragraph: 014 Reference ID: 12-014-20140306 – updated on 6/3/2014 – mentions that evidence of co-operation and considering different options for meeting development needs will be key for this process. The NPPG goes on to say that the evidence needs to inform the plan and shape its development rather than being collected retrospectively. It should also be kept up to date so that where key studies are reliant on data that is a few years old, they should be updated to reflect the most recent information available. LPAs should also publish documents that form part of the evidence base as they are completed, rather than waiting until options are published or a local plan is published for representations. This will help local communities and other interests to consider the issues and engage with the LPA at an early stage in developing the local plan. It will also help communities, who may be able to use such evidence to inform the development of their own plans, bring forward neighbourhood plans.

[49]   LPAs should seek opportunities to achieve each of the economic, social and environmental dimensions of sustainable development, and net gains across all three. Significant adverse impacts on any of these dimensions should be avoided, and, whenever possible, alternative options which reduce or eliminate such impacts should be pursued. Where adverse impacts are unavoidable, measures to mitigate the impact should be considered. Where adequate mitigation measures are not possible, compensatory measures may be appropriate (NPPF, para 152).

[50]   NPPF, para 157 states that local plans should: (i) plan positively for the development and infrastructure required in the area to meet the objectives, principles and policies of the NPPF; (ii) be drawn up over an appropriate time scale, preferably a 15-year time horizon, take account of longer term requirements, and be kept up to date; (iii) be based on co-operation with neighbouring authorities, public, voluntary and private sector organisations; (iv) indicate broad locations for strategic development on a key diagram and land-use designations on a proposals map; (v) allocate sites to promote development and flexible use of land, bringing forward new land where necessary, and provide detail on form, scale, access and quantum of development where appropriate; (vi) identify areas where it may be necessary to limit freedom to change the uses of buildings, and support such restrictions with a clear explanation; (vii) identify land where development would be inappropriate, for instance, because of its environmental or historic

including unmet needs of neighbouring areas where this is consistent with policies in the NPPF as a whole. Local Plans should recognise the contribution that Neighbourhood Plans can make in planning to meet development and infrastructure needs.

How should LPAs express the need for different types of housing in their local plan?[51]

LPAs should ensure that the policies in their Local Plan recognise the diverse types of housing needed in their area and, where appropriate, identify specific sites for all types of housing to meet their anticipated housing requirements. This should include sites for older people's housing including accessible mainstream housing such as bungalows and step-free apartments, sheltered or extra care housing, retirement housing and residential care homes. Where LPAs do not consider it appropriate to allocate such sites, they should ensure that there are sufficiently robust criteria in place to set out when such homes will be permitted. This might be supplemented by setting appropriate targets for the number of these homes to be built. Reference should also be made to guidance in relation to housing and economic needs assessment and to housing and economic land availability assessment.[52]

How is a Local Plan produced?[53]

LPAs develop a Local Plan by assessing the future needs and opportunities of their area, developing options for addressing these and then identifying a preferred approach.[54] This involves gathering evidence, carrying out a sustainability appraisal

---

significance; and (viii) contain a clear strategy for enhancing the natural, built and historic environment, and supporting Nature Improvement Areas where they have been identified.

[51] NPPG at Paragraph: 006 Reference ID: 12-002-20150320. Updated on 20/3/2015. See also consultation proposals for the NPPG issued by the Department of Housing, Communities and Local Government (DHCLG) in March 2018 which, at pp 52–56, deal with the promotion by LPAs (as part of their plan-making process) of build to rent as a distinct asset class within the private rented sector and of how it can meet the housing needs of different demographic and social groups.

[52] See Housing and Economic Needs Assessments in NPPG at Paragraph: 001 Reference ID: 2a-001-20140306 through to Paragraph: 037 Reference ID: 2a-037-20140303. See guidance on Housing and Economic Land Availability Assessment in NPPG at Paragraph: 001 Reference ID: 3-001-20140306 through to Paragraph: 043 Reference ID: 3-043-20140306. Lastly, see guidance on the approach to assessing local housing need in the Draft PPG issued by DHCLG in March 2018 (at pp 24–32) which sets out the three standard steps: (a) setting the baseline; (b) making adjustments to take account of market signals; and (c) capping the level of any increase (although there may be circumstances where it is justifiable to identify need above the need figure identified by the standard method).

[53] NPPG at Paragraph: 003 Reference ID: 12-003-20140306. Updated on 6/3/2014; NPPF, para 158.

[54] With effect from 31/1/2018, LPAs are now required to identify the strategic priorities of the development and use of land in their area (bringing into force Neighbourhood Planning Act 2017, ss 8(1) and (3)). Under these provisions, LPA's monitoring reports must make clear the extent to which they are relying on policies in a spatial development strategy to deliver their strategic priorities and where the relevant policies are to be found.

to inform the preparation of the Local Plan and effective discussion and consultation with local communities, businesses and other interested parties.[55]

There is considerable flexibility open to LPAs in how they carry out the initial stages of plan production, provided they comply with the specific requirements in regulation 18 of the Town and Country Planning (Local Planning) (England) Regulations 2012 ('the Local Plan Regulations') on consultation, and with the commitments in their Statement of Community Involvement. Consultation exercises on emerging options are often termed 'issues and options', 'preferred options' or 'pre publication'. LPAs should always make clear how any consultation fits within the wider Local Plan process.[56]

LPAs must also publicise their intended timetable for producing the Local Plan. This information is contained within a Local Development Scheme, which LPAs should publish on their web site and must keep up to date. Up-to-date and accessible reporting on the Local Development Scheme in an Authority's Monitoring Report is an important way in which LPAs can keep communities informed of plan making activity.

What is the role of the examination?[57]
Having received any representations on the publication version of the plan, the LPA should submit the Local Plan and any proposed changes it considers appropriate along with supporting documents to the Planning Inspectorate for examination on behalf of the Secretary of State.

The examination starts when the Local Plan is submitted to the Planning Inspectorate and concludes when a report to the LPA has been issued. During the examination a planning Inspector will assess whether the Local Plan has been prepared in line with

---

[55] LPAs need to engage at an early stage with local groups who may be affected by its proposals. Communities contemplating or pursuing a neighbourhood plan will be particularly interested in the emerging plan, which will provide the strategic framework for their neighbourhood plan policies. The LPA will also need to ensure that it works proactively with other authorities on strategic cross-boundary issues in line with the duty to co-operate. Town and Country Planning (Local Planning) (England) Regulations 2012, reg 18 sets out specific bodies or persons that an LPA must notify and invite representations from in developing its local plan. The LPA must take into account any representations made and will need to set out how the main issues raised have been taken into account. It must also consult the Strategic Environmental Assessment consultation bodies on the information and level of detail to include in the sustainability appraisal report (see para 2.12(b) and (c)). PCPA 2004, s 18 also requires LPAs to produce a Statement of Community Involvement (which should be published on the LPA's website), which should explain how they will engage local communities and other interested parties in producing their local plan and determining planning applications. See NPPG at Paragraph: 017 Reference ID: 12-017-20140306 – updated on 6/3/2014.

[56] With effect from 31/7/2018, LPAs are required to set out policies for involving interested parties in the preliminary stages of plan-making in their Statements of Community Involvement (bringing into force Neighbourhood Planning Act 2017, s 13(2)).

[57] NPPG at Paragraph: 004 Reference ID: 12-004-20160519. Updated on 19/5/2016; NPPF, paras 178 and 182.

the relevant legal requirements (including the duty to co-operate)[58] and whether it meets the tests of 'soundness' contained in the National Planning Policy Framework.

The Inspector should work proactively with the LPA. Underpinning this is the expectation that:

- issues not critical to the plan's soundness or other legal requirements do not cause unnecessary delay to the examination of the plan
- inspectors should identify any fundamental concerns at the earliest possible stage in the examination and will seek to work with the LPA to clarify and address these
- where these issues cannot be resolved within the examination timetable, the potential of suspending the examination should be fully considered, with the LPA having an opportunity to assess the scope and feasibility of any work needed to remedy these issues during a period of suspension, so that this can be fully considered by the Inspector
- consideration should be given to the option of the LPA making a commitment to review the plan or particular policies in the plan within an agreed period, where this would enable the Inspector to conclude that the plan is sound and meets other legal requirements
- if necessary, the Inspector may be asked by the LPA to recommend modifications to the Local Plan that would address any issues with soundness or procedural requirements that are identified during the examination.[59] The

---

[58] *R (St Albans City and District Council) v Secretary of State for Communities and Local Government* [2017] EWHC 1751 (Admin); LPAs must engage actively and constructively and on a continuing basis with neighbouring authorities. In this case, the authority refused to participate in a joint Strategic Housing Market Assessment (SHMA) with its neighbours after defining its own housing market area, and its plan did not list any strategic cross-boundary matters or priorities. The decision of the local plan examiner that the LPA had failed in its duty to co-operate was upheld. The Secretary of State now has the power to direct two or more LPAs to prepare a joint development plan document; provision is also made for the exercise of default powers by county councils in relation to development plan documents where districts are failing to co-operate effectively (see amendments made to the PCPA 2004, by various provisions contained in Neighbourhood Planning Act 2017, ss 9 and 10 and Sch 2).

[59] An example of how this might work in practice can be seen from the way in which an examining inspector concluded that the Mid Sussex District Plan 2014–2031 provided an appropriate basis for the planning for the district, provided a number of modifications were made to it. These modifications included an increased housing target and a commitment to work proactively with other LPAs in the future to address unmet housing need. The LPA had initially proposed a housing allocation of 13,600 dwellings to be provided at an average rate of 80 per year. However, the inspector said that the figure should be increased to a minimum of 16,390 dwellings over the 17-year plan period, representing an increase of 2,790 dwellings or just over 20%. The inspector said that concerns about housing affordability and employment growth meant that the housing need for the district was 14,892 dwellings, or 876 homes a year. As he put it: 'conditions therefore justified an adjustment to the objectively assessed need in Mid Sussex in response to market signals, the need to ensure the adequate provision of new affordable housing delivery and the need for sufficient housing to support the forecast growth in employment'. In addition, Mid Sussex were also required to accommodate 1,498 homes of 'unmet need' from the North Western Sussex Housing Market area (principally Crawley). The result of all this was an overall housing

Inspector can only recommend modifications if they are asked to do so by the LPA itself. If, in doing so, the Inspector identifies any fundamental issues with the plan, they may recommend that the plan should not be adopted by the LPA. The LPA will then need to consider whether to withdraw the plan and prepare a new document for submission. In this situation, any existing Local Plan policies will remain in force while a new plan is prepared, although some of those existing policies are likely to become increasingly out-of-date.

2.17   The following paragraphs (aided by footnotes) are taken from the NPPG: '2. Preparing a Local Plan':[60]

Who is responsible for preparing a Local Plan?[61]
Those LPAs responsible for 'district matters' should prepare and maintain an up-to-date Local Plan for their area: this includes district, London borough, metropolitan district, unitary, and national Park authorities.

Those LPAs with minerals and waste planning responsibilities should also produce plans to provide a framework for decisions involving these uses (this includes county councils in respect of any part of their area for which there is a district council, London borough, metropolitan district, unitary and National Park authorities). LPAs can produce combined minerals and waste plans and, where relevant, may also prepare one Local Plan combining policies on minerals, waste and other planning matters.

The Marine Management Organisation is producing a series of marine plans to cover the English marine (off shore) area. Coastal LPAs will need to take these into account when preparing their Local Plans, insofar as they have implications for on-shore activities.

Can an LPA produce a joint Local Plan with another authority or authorities?[62]
Section 28 of the Planning and Compulsory Purchase Act 2004 enables two or more LPAs to agree to prepare a joint Local Plan, which can be an effective means of

---

requirement of 'a minimum of 16,390 dwellings between 2014 and 2031'. The inspector added that 'The requirement should be delivered as an average of 876 [dwellings per annum (DPA)] to 2023/24 and an average of 1,090 dpa in the last seven years of the plan, reflecting the timing of Crawley's unmet need'. The revised plan also included a controversial site allocation for around 500 homes in Hassocks. The inspector said that both the increased housing need figure and site allocation were 'essential to ensure the plan makes adequate provision for new housing and are therefore necessary for soundness' (details taken from *Planning* 14/3/2018).

[60]   As before, what follows is as found in the NPPG except for the use of the expression 'LPAs' as a shorthand for local planning authorities and 'NPPF' as a shorthand for the National Planning Policy Framework. See also consultation proposals for the NPPG issued by the DHCLG in March 2018, which deal extensively with plan-making at pp 37–51 (under the headings: (a) Statutory duty and role of plans; (b) Tests of soundness; (c) Statement of common ground; (d) Evidence base; and (e) Plan review guidance.)

[61]   NPPG at Paragraph: 006 Reference ID: 12-006-20140306. Updated on 6/3/2014.

[62]   NPPG at Paragraph: 007 Reference ID: 12-007-20140306. Updated on 6/3/2014.

addressing cross-boundary issues, sharing specialist resources and reducing costs (e.g. through the formation of a joint planning unit).

The duty to cooperate requires LPAs and certain other public bodies to cooperate with each other in preparing a Local Plan, where there are matters that would have a significant impact on the areas of two or more authorities.[63] A joint Local Plan is one means of achieving this and those preparing Joint Plans will wish to consider a joint evidence base and assessment of development needs. Less formal mechanisms can also be used. In particular, LPAs should consider opportunities for aligning plan timetables and policies, as well as for sharing plan-making resources.[64]

How often should a Local Plan be reviewed?[65]
To be effective plans need to be kept up-to-date. Policies will age at different rates depending on local circumstances, and the LPA should review the relevance of the Local Plan at regular intervals to assess whether some or all of it may need updating. Most Local Plans are likely to require updating in whole or part at least every five years. Reviews should be proportionate to the issues in hand. Local Plans may be found sound conditional upon a review in whole or part within five years of the date of adoption.

The NPPF makes clear that relevant policies for the supply of housing should not be considered up-to-date if the authority cannot demonstrate a five-year supply of deliverable housing sites. LPAs should also consider whether plan-making activity by other authorities has an impact on planning and the Local Plan in their area. For example, a revised Strategic Housing Market Assessment will affect all authorities in that housing market area, and potentially beyond, irrespective of the status or stage of development of particular Local Plans.

There are requirements for a LPA to support neighbourhood planning. Further detail is provided in Neighbourhood Planning guidance.

An LPA must set out the timetable for producing or reviewing its Local Plan in its Local Development Scheme.

---

[63] With effect from 16/1/2018, power is conferred on the Secretary of State to direct pairs or groups of local authorities to take over plan-making functions from districts (bringing into force Neighbourhood Planning Act 2017, ss 9 and 10).

[64] See fn 58 for *R (St Albans City and District Council) v Secretary of State for Communities and Local Government* [2017] EWHC 1751 (Admin) and the default powers of the Secretary of State where neighbouring LPAs are not co-operating in the preparation of joint development plan documents and to allow county councils to create a strategic plan in areas where districts are failing to co-operate effectively and where the county council's involvement would help.

[65] NPPG at Paragraph: 008 Reference ID: 12-008-20140306. Updated on 6/3/2014. See NPPF, para 47.

What should the Local Development Scheme contain?[66]
A Local Development Scheme is required under Section 15 of the Planning and Compulsory Purchase Act 2004 (as amended by the Localism Act 2011). This must specify (among other matters) the documents which, when prepared, will comprise the Local Plan for the area. It must be made available publicly and kept up-to-date. It is important that local communities and interested parties can keep track of progress. LPAs should publish their Local Development Scheme on their website.

How detailed should a Local Plan be?[67]
While the content of Local Plans will vary depending on the nature of the area and issues to be addressed, all Local Plans should be as focused, concise and accessible as possible. They should concentrate on the critical issues facing the area – including its development needs – and the strategy and opportunities for addressing them, paying careful attention to both deliverability and viability.

In line with the NPPF, the Local Plans should be clear in setting out the strategic priorities for the area and the policies that address these, and which also provide the strategic framework within which any neighbourhood plans may be prepared to shape development at community level.

In drafting policies the LPA should avoid undue repetition, for example by using generic policies to set out principles that may be common to different types of development. There should be no need to reiterate policies which are already set out in the NPPF.

Where sites are proposed for allocation, sufficient detail should be given to provide clarity to developers, local communities and other interests about the nature and scale of the development (addressing the 'what, where, when and how' questions).

The policies map should illustrate geographically the policies in the Local Plan and be reproduced from, or based on, an Ordnance Survey map. If the adoption of a Local Plan would result in changes to a previously adopted policies map, when the plan is submitted to the Planning Inspectorate for examination an up-to-date submission policies map should also be submitted, showing how the adopted policies map would be changed as a result of the new plan.

Section 19 of the Planning and Compulsory Purchase Act 2004 sets out specific matters to which the LPA must have regard when preparing a Local Plan. Regulations 8 and 9 of the Town and Country Planning (Local Planning) (England) Regulations 2012 prescribe the general form and content of Local Plans and adopted policies map, while regulation 10 states what additional matters LPAs must have regard to when drafting their plans.

---

[66] NPPG at Paragraph: 009 Reference ID: 12-009-20140306. Updated on 6/3/2014.
[67] NPPG at Paragraph: 010 Reference ID: 12-010-20140306. Updated on 6/3/2014. See also NPPF, para 156.

How should a Local Plan reflect the presumption in favour of sustainable development?[68]
Paragraphs 14 and 15 of the NPPF indicates that Local Plans should be based upon and reflect the presumption in favour of sustainable development. This should be done by identifying and providing for objectively assessed needs and by indicating how the presumption will be applied locally.

Should all the Local Plan policies be contained in one document?[69]
The NPPF makes clear that the Government's preferred approach is for each LPA to prepare a single Local Plan for its area (or a joint document with neighbouring areas). While additional Local Plans can be produced, for example a separate site allocations document or Area Action Plan, there should be a clear justification for doing so.

What is the relationship between the Local Plan and Neighbourhood Plans?[70]
Neighbourhood plans, when brought into force, become part of the statutory development plan for the area that they cover.

They can be developed before, after or in parallel with a Local Plan, but the law requires that they must be in general conformity with the strategic policies in the adopted Local Plan for the area (and any other strategic policies that form part of the statutory development plan where relevant, such as the London Plan).

Neighbourhood plans are not tested against policies in an emerging Local Plan although the reasoning and evidence informing the Local Plan process may be relevant to the consideration of the basic conditions against which a neighbourhood plan is tested.

There are requirements for an LPA to support neighbourhood planning. Further detail is provided in the Neighbourhood Planning guidance.

Where a neighbourhood plan is brought forward before an up-to-date Local Plan is in place the LPA should take a proactive and positive approach, working collaboratively with a qualifying body. This could include sharing evidence and seeking to resolve any issues to ensure the draft Neighbourhood plan has the greatest chance of success at independent examination.

Where a neighbourhood plan has been brought into force, the LPA should take it into account when preparing the Local Plan strategy and policies, and avoid duplicating the policies that are in the neighbourhood plan.

---

[68] NPPG at Paragraph: 011 Reference ID: 12-011-20140306. Updated on 6/3/2014. See also NPPF, paras 14 and 15.

[69] NPPG at Paragraph: 012 Reference ID: 12-012-20140306. Updated on 6/3/2014.

[70] NPPG at Paragraph: 013 Reference ID: 12-013-70728. Updated on 28/7/2017. See also the section on neighbourhood plans in consultation proposals for the NPPG issued by the DHCLG in March 2018 at pp 33–36, which includes guidance on housing requirements and allocations in designated neighbourhood areas and when neighbourhood plans are protected from the presumption in favour of sustainable development.

What evidence is needed to support the policies in a Local Plan?[71]

Appropriate and proportionate evidence is essential for producing a sound Local Plan, and paragraph 158 onwards of the NPPF sets out the types of evidence that may be required. This is not a prescriptive list; the evidence should be focused tightly on supporting and justifying the particular policies in the Local Plan. Evidence of cooperation and considering different options for meeting development needs will be key for this process.

The evidence needs to inform what is in the plan and shape its development rather than being collected retrospectively. It should also be kept up-to-date. For example, when approaching submission, if key studies are already reliant on data that is a few years old, they should be updated to reflect the most recent information available (and, if necessary, the plan adjusted in the light of this information and the comments received at the publication stage).

LPAs should publish documents that form part of the evidence base as they are completed, rather than waiting until options are published or a Local Plan is published for representations. This will help local communities and other interests consider the issues and engage with the authority at an early stage in developing the Local Plan. It will also help communities bringing forward neighbourhood plans, who may be able to use this evidence to inform the development of their own plans.

Can LPAs in the process of plan making use the same approaches that have been accepted as sound in other Local Plans adopted since the introduction of the NPPF?[72]

Local authorities can consider following approaches established in local plan examinations that have been undertaken since the NPPF was introduced, provided they are both relevant and appropriate.

What roles do Sustainability Appraisal and Habitats Assessment play?[73]

Every Local Plan must be informed and accompanied by a Sustainability Appraisal. This allows the potential environmental, economic and social impacts of the proposals to be systematically taken into account, and should play a key role throughout the plan-making process. The Sustainability Appraisal plays an important part in demonstrating that the Local Plan reflects sustainability objectives and has considered reasonable alternatives. The Sustainability Appraisal should incorporate a Strategic Environmental Assessment to meet the statutory requirement for certain plans and programmes to be subject to a process of 'environmental assessment'.

The Local Plan may also require a Habitats Regulation Assessment as set out in the Conservation of Habitats and Species Regulations 2010 (as amended) if it is

---

[71] NPPG at Paragraph: 014 Reference ID: 12-014-20140306. Updated on 6/3/2014. See NPPF, para 158.

[72] NPPG at Paragraph: 015 Reference ID: 12-015-20140306. Updated on 6/3/2014.

[73] NPPG at Paragraph: 016 Reference ID: 12-016-20140306. Updated on 6/3/2014.

considered likely to have significant effects on European habitats or species, located in the LPA's area or in its vicinity.

Who should be involved in preparing a Local Plan?[74]

LPAs will need to identify and engage at an early stage with all those that may be interested in the development or content of the Local Plan, including those groups who may be affected by its proposal but who do not play an active part in most consultations. Those communities contemplating or pursuing a Neighbourhood plan will have a particular interest in the emerging strategy, which will provide the strategic framework for the neighbourhood plan policies. The LPA will also need to ensure that it works proactively with other authorities on strategic cross boundary issues in line with the duty to cooperate.

Regulation 18 of the Town and Country Planning (Local Planning) (England) Regulations 2012 sets out specific bodies or persons that an LPA must notify and invite representations from in developing its Local Plan. The LPA must take into account any representation made, and will need to set out how the main issues have been taken into account. It must also consult the Strategic Environmental Assessment consultation bodies on the information and level of detail to include in the sustainability appraisal report.

Section 18 of the Planning and Compulsory Purchase Act 2004 requires LPAs to produce a Statement of Community Involvement, which should explain how they will engage local communities and other interested parties in producing their Local Plan and determining planning applications. The Statement of Community Involvement should be published on the LPA's website.

How can the LPA show that a Local Plan is capable of being delivered including provision for infrastructure?[75]

A Local Plan is an opportunity for the LPA to set out a positive vision for the area, but the plan should also be realistic about what can be achieved and when (including in relation to infrastructure). This means paying careful attention to providing an adequate supply of land, identifying what infrastructure is required and how it can be funded and brought on stream at the appropriate time; and ensuring that the requirements of the plan as a whole will not prejudice the viability of development.

Early discussion with infrastructure and service providers is particularly important to help understand their investment plans and critical dependencies. The LPA should also involve the Local Enterprise Partnership at an early stage in considering the strategic issues facing the area, including the prospects for investment in infrastructure.

The Local Plan should make clear, for at least the first five years, what infrastructure is required, who is going to fund and provide it, and how it relates to the anticipated

---

[74] NPPG at Paragraph: 017 Reference ID: 12-017-20140306. Updated on 6/3/2014.

[75] NPPG at Paragraph: 018 Reference ID: 12-018-20140306. Updated on 6/3/2014.

rate and phasing of development. This may help in reviewing the plan and in development management decisions. For the later stages of the plan period less detail may be provided as the position regarding the provision of infrastructure is likely to be less certain. If it is known that a development is unlikely to come forward until after the plan period due, for example, to uncertainty over deliverability of key infrastructure, then this should clearly be stated in the draft plan.

Where deliverability of critical infrastructure is uncertain then the plan itself should address the consequences of this, including possible contingency arrangements and alternative strategies. The detail concerning planned infrastructure provision can be set out in a supporting document such as an infrastructure delivery programme that can be updated regularly. However the key infrastructure requirements on which delivery of the plan depends should be contained in the Local Plan itself.

The evidence which accompanies an emerging Local Plan should show how the policies in the plan have been tested for their impact on the viability of development, including (where relevant) the impact which the Community Infrastructure Levy is expected to have. Where LPAs intend to bring forward a Community Infrastructure Levy regime, there is a strong advantage in doing so in parallel with producing the Local Plan, as this allows questions about infrastructure funding and the viability of policies to be addressed in a comprehensive and coordinated way.

What weight does an emerging local plan carry in decision-making?[76]
The NPPF sets out that decision-takers may give weight to relevant policies in emerging plans according to their stage of preparation, the extent to which there are unresolved objections to relevant policies, and their degree of consistency with policies in the NPPF.

2.18   The following paragraphs (aided by footnotes) are taken from the NPPG: '3. Publication and examination of a Local Plan':[77]

What happens when a Local Plan is published?[78]
The publication stage plan should be the document that the local authority considers ready for examination. This plan must be published for representations by the LPA, together with other 'proposed submission documents', before it can be submitted to the Planning Inspectorate for examination. This provides a formal opportunity for the local community and other interests to consider the Local Plan, which the LPA would like to adopt. The specific publication requirements are set out at Regulations 17, 19 and 35 (and 21) of the Town and Country Planning (Local Planning) (England) Regulations 2012.

---

[76]   NPPG at Paragraph: 019 Reference ID: 12-019-20140306. Updated on 6/3/2014. See NPPF, para 216.

[77]   As before, what follows is as found in the NPPG, except for the use of the expression 'LPAs' as a shorthand for local planning authorities and 'NPPF' as a shorthand for the National Planning Policy Framework.

[78]   NPPG at Paragraph: 020 Reference ID: 12-020-20140306. Updated on 6/3/2014.

What should the LPA do when submitting a Local Plan for examination?[79]

Having received any representations on the publication version of the plan, the LPA should submit the Local Plan and any proposed changes it considers appropriate along with supporting documents to the Planning Inspectorate for examination on behalf of the Secretary of State. A Statement of Representations Procedure should be published alongside the submission version of the Local Plan.

The submitted documents should include those that were made available at the publication stage (updated as necessary), including details of who was consulted when preparing the Local Plan (at Regulation 18 stage) and how the main issues raised have been addressed. The LPA must also include details of the representations made following publication of the Local Plan and a summary of the main issues raised – see Regulation 22 of the Town and Country Planning (Local Planning) (England) Regulations 2012.

What happens if the Inspector has significant concerns about a submitted Local Plan before the hearings begin?[80]

The Inspector will make an initial assessment of the Local Plan once it has been submitted for examination. If the Inspector forms an early view that the submitted Plan may have serious shortcomings, the Inspector will raise this with the LPA at an early stage.

Where any major concerns are identified, in relation to the duty to cooperate, other procedural requirements or the soundness of the plan, the Inspector will write to the LPA setting these out. Where the issues cannot be addressed through correspondence the Inspector may arrange for an exploratory meeting to take place. The Inspector will give the LPA every opportunity to respond to any concerns and address key issues that may lead the Inspector to conclude that the plan is not sound or that a legal requirement has not been met.

Where the Inspector has significant concerns about the soundness of a submitted plan, the Inspector may consider that the examination cannot be completed without additional work being undertaken. This may require consideration of a suspension or partial suspension of the examination process to give the LPA time to undertake further work to address the issues raised. Inspectors should make every effort to engage fully with the LPA in meaningful discussions to determine the scope and feasibility of any additional work needed.

Who is involved and what is discussed in a hearing session?[81]

Anyone who has made representations seeking to change a published Local Plan must, if they request, be given the opportunity of attending a hearing (Section 20(6) of the Planning and Compulsory Purchase Act 2004). The LPA will liaise with those

---

[79] NPPG at Paragraph: 021 Reference ID: 12-021-20140306. Updated on 6/3/2014.

[80] NPPG at Paragraph: 022 Reference ID: 12-022-20140306. Updated on 19/5/2016. See NPPF, para 182.

[81] NPPG at Paragraph: 023 Reference ID: 12-023-20140306. Updated on 6/3/2014.

who have asked to appear at the hearing to arrange attendance, including whether interested groups wish to nominate a representative to put forward their views.

The LPA is required to publicise details of the hearing sessions at least 6 weeks before they are scheduled to take place – under regulation 24 of the Town and Country Planning (Local Planning) (England) Regulations 2012.

The appointed Inspector may hold a pre-hearing meeting, the purpose of which is to clarify the critical issues to be considered at the hearing sessions, and to explain the procedures to be followed. Where no pre-hearing meeting is held these matters will be dealt with through a written note from the Inspector.

The subject of the hearings is determined by the Inspector based on the documents submitted by the LPA and the representations that have been made. During the hearings the Inspector may ask participants to provide additional information by set deadlines. Such requests will be circulated to all those attending by the Programme Officer (an independent official who provides administrative support to the Inspector).

What modifications are required to make a submitted Local Plan sound?[82]

The Inspector can recommend 'main modifications' (changes that materially affect the policies) to make a submitted Local Plan sound and legally compliant only if asked to do so by the LPA under section 20(7C) of the 2004 Planning and Compulsory Purchase Act as amended.[83] The council can also put forward 'additional modifications' of its own to deal with more minor matters.

Where the changes recommended by the Inspector would be so extensive as to require a virtual re-writing of the Local Plan, the Inspector is likely to suggest that the LPA withdraws the plan. Exceptionally, under section 21(9)(a) of the Planning and Compulsory Purchase Act 2004, the Secretary of State has the power to direct an LPA to withdraw its submitted plan.

Inspectors will require the LPA to consult upon all proposed main modifications. Depending on the scope of the modifications, further Sustainability Appraisal work may also be required. The Inspector's report on the plan will only be issued once the

---

82 NPPG at Paragraph: 024 Reference ID: 12-024-20140306. Updated on 6/3/2014.

83 In other words, an LPA does not have to implement the recommendations of the inspector. However, the authority will only be able to adopt the plan if the inspector recommends that it be adopted. LPAs therefore have a choice to make if the inspector does not recommend adoption: it must either accept the inspector's proposed modification or make its own modifications and re-submit the draft plan for examination. However, an LPA is free to make non-material modifications of its own before adoption (PCPA 2004, s 23(2), (2A) and (3)). It is also the case that an LPA may withdraw a draft plan at any time before it has finally been adopted (PCPA 2004, s 22). This could arise where policies in the draft plan have been superseded by changes in national policies such that the LPA may need to reconsider its own policies rather than submit to modifications through the examination process.

LPA has consulted on the main modifications and the Inspector has had the opportunity to consider the representations on these.

Whether to advertise any 'additional modifications' is at the discretion of the LPA, but they may wish to do so at the same time as consulting on the main modifications.

What happens if a Local Plan is found unsound?[84]

Where the Inspector concludes that the duty to cooperate or other basic procedural requirements have not been met, or there are issues regarding the soundness of the plan that cannot be addressed through modifications, it will be recommended that the submitted plan is not adopted. In these circumstances the LPA will be unable to adopt the Local Plan and it should be withdrawn in accordance with regulation 27 of the Town and Country Planning (Local Planning) (England) Regulations 2012.

Speedy withdrawal of a Local Plan from examination in such circumstances provides certainty to the local community, applicants and other interests about the status of the planning framework in the area. Until a revised plan is brought forward to adoption, any existing Local Plan will remain in place.

Following withdrawal of a Local Plan from examination an LPA should consider whether to republish under Regulation 19 or reconsult under Regulation 18 of the Town and Country Planning (Local Planning) (England) Regulations 2012 and what matters this republication or reconsultation should address.

2.19   The following paragraphs (aided by footnotes) are taken from the PPG: '4. Local Plans – Adoption, monitoring and supplementary planning documents':[85]

What needs to be done to formally adopt a Local Plan?[86]

Once the examination process is complete, adoption is the final stage of putting a Local Plan in place. This requires confirmation by a full meeting of the LPA (regulation 4(1) and (3) of the Local Authorities (Functions and Responsibilities) (England) Regulations 2000). On adopting a Local Plan, the LPA has to make publicly available a copy of the plan, an adoption statement and Sustainability Appraisal in line with regulations 26 and 35 of the Town and Country Planning (Local Planning) (England) Regulations 2012.

While the LPA is not legally required to adopt its Local Plan following examination, it will have been through a significant process locally to engage communities and other interests in discussions about the future of the area, and it is to be expected that the authority will proceed quickly with adopting a plan that has been found sound.

---

[84]   NPPG at Paragraph: 025 Reference ID: 12-025-20140306. Updated on 6/3/2014.

[85]   As before, what follows is as found in the NPPG, except for the use of the expression 'LPAs' as a shorthand for local planning authorities and 'NPPF' as a shorthand for the National Planning Policy Framework.

[86]   NPPG at Paragraph: 026 Reference ID: 12-026-20140306. Updated on 6/3/2014.

What is the role of the Authority Monitoring Report?[87]

LPAs must publish information at least annually that shows progress with Local Plan preparation, reports on any activity relating to the duty to cooperate and showing how the implementation of policies in the Local Plan is progressing and are encouraged to report as frequently as possible on planning matters to communities. This is important to enable communities and interested parties to be aware of progress. LPAs can also use the Authority Monitoring Report to provide up-to-date information on the implementation of any neighbourhood plans that have been brought into force, and to determine whether there is a need to undertake a partial or full review of the Local Plan.

This information should be made available publicly. Regulation 34 of the Town and Country Planning (Local Planning) (England) Regulations 2012 sets out what information reports should contain, although there is other useful information that can be set out. In particular, the reports can highlight the contributions made by development, including section 106 planning obligations, Community Infrastructure Levy and New Homes Bonus payments, and how these have been used.

Are Supplementary Planning Documents needed?[88]

Supplementary planning documents [SPDs] should be prepared only where necessary and in line with paragraph 153 of the NPPF.[89]

---

87   NPPG at Paragraph: 027 Reference ID: 12-027-20170728. Updated on 28/7/2017. See PCPA 2004, s 35.

88   See NPPG at Paragraph: 028 Reference ID: 12-028-20140306. Updated on 6/3/2014, and NPPF, para 153. SPDs are not development plan documents and do not need to be submitted to the Secretary of State for independent examination. The LPA should, however, screen such documents to ensure that an assessment is not required under the SEA Directive. The function of an SPD is to provide further detail to policies in a development plan document (i.e. design guides, area development briefs, masterplan or issue-based documents). SPDs should obviously be compatible with national and local policies. SPDs may be adopted by an LPA by resolution. Before an SPD is adopted, the LPA must prepare a 'consultation statement' which, along with the SPD, must be available for public inspection in the manner specified under the Town and Country Planning (Local Planning) (England) Regulations 2012, reg 35, and representations may be made by any person within a period of four weeks (see regs 12 and 13, which deal with public participation and representations on SPDs). The Secretary of State may also direct an LPA not to adopt an SPD until he decides to give a direction under PCPA 2004, s 21(1), requiring the authority to modify the document.

89   *William Davis Ltd v Charnwood BC* [2017] EWHC 3006 (Admin); an LPA's 'housing mix' policy was quashed on the basis that it had been published as an SPD rather than as a local development plan document. The policy regulated the development of land and, by virtue of Town and Country Planning (Local Planning) (England) Regulations 2012, reg 5(1)(a)(i) and (iv), was a local development document. Charnwood BC's local plan envisaged the construction of 13,940 homes between 2011 and 2028. The policy was formulated on the basis that there would be a growing need for smaller households due to greater longevity and the fact that couples bore children later in life. In May 2017, Charnwood BC published a housing SPD that addressed the mix of homes of particular sizes to be built over the next 25 years. As an SPD, it was not subject to independent scrutiny by the Secretary of State as a development plan document would have been. The document sought to set aside up to 45% of the total build over the period for one- and two-bedroom homes, 45–55% for three-bedroom homes and 10–20% for four-bedroom homes.

They should build upon and provide more detailed advice or guidance on the policies of the Local Plan. They should not add unnecessarily to the financial burdens on development.

Regulations 11 to 16 of the Town and Country Planning (Local Planning) (England) Regulations 2012 set out the requirements for producing Supplementary Planning Documents.

In exceptional circumstances a Strategic Environmental Assessment may be required when producing a Supplementary Planning Document.

CHALLENGING A LOCAL PLAN

2.20 An adopted plan may be challenged on legal grounds by an application made to the High Court made within six weeks of the date of adoption, but not otherwise.[90] The Secretary of State also has default powers in cases where he thinks that an LPA is not making progress with the adoption of a plan. In such a case, he may take over the task of plan-making at the expense of the authority.[91]

It also sought to lay down that 60–70% of the one- and two-bedroom homes would be affordable. Five developers sought a judicial review on the ground that the document was far too prescriptive and addressed topics that were not appropriate for an SPD. The court agreed, holding that an SPD was not an appropriate vehicle for dealing with issues of such strategic importance. The overall mix of housing across the authority's area should have been subjected to independent scrutiny.

[90] PCPA 2004, s 113. *Woodfield v JJ Gallagher Ltd* [2016] EWCA Civ 1007; where it was found that a judge had not exceeded her powers under s 113(7) by remitting a policy in a local development plan to the Secretary of State; directing him to appoint a planning inspector who would recommend adoption of the policy subject to a specified modification; and directing the LPA to adopt the policy subject to that modification. This case involved a very late in the day and minor legal error, and to have required further environmental assessment would have been disproportionate. As Lindblom LJ made clear, the statutory development plan-making process had run its course, and during that process, the public had been fully involved. It is plain that sub-sections (7A), (7B) and (7C) are widely drawn and afford an ample range of remedies. The amended regime does not, however, allow the court to stray into the planning merits. Basically, the court has great flexibility to tailor the remedy to fit the breach.

[91] PCPA 2004, s 27. If the LPA is not making progress, the Secretary of State may take over the task of plan-making. On 16/11/2017 the Secretary of State threatened to take over plan-making in the case of 15 authorities, one of whom, York, had last produced a full plan in 1954. According to research by Savills, it was also reported on 20/12/2017 that only 46% of LPAs in England had a post-NPPF (i.e. March 2012) local plan in place. The 56% which did not have an up-to-date post-NPPF plan were found to be at various stages of the plan-making process, with 7% yet to begin initial preparation of a post-NPPF plan. It is also worthy of note that in the year to November 2017, 18% of LPAs had a lack of five-year housing supply confirmed on appeals. Of these LPAs, more than half (58%) believed that they had identified an adequate supply of land, whereas a further 18% had a published figure of under five years.

DEVELOPMENT PLANS IN WALES

2.21   Wales has its own National Development Framework which sets out the National Assembly's policies in relation to the use and development of land in Wales.[92] Provisions exist dealing with the preparation of the Framework, its review and revision.[93] Power also exists to designate strategic planning areas and to establish strategic planning panels.[94]

Local development plans in Wales

2.22   Every LPA in Wales must also prepare a local development plan which should set out the authority's objectives in relation to the development and use of land in its area and its general policies for the implementation of those objectives. The plan may also set out specific policies in relation to any part of the area of the authority.[95] Such plans must be in general conformity with the National Development Framework for Wales and the strategic development plan for any strategic planning area that includes all or part of the area of the LPA.[96] The LPA must also carry out an appraisal of the sustainability of the plan and prepare a report of the findings of the appraisal.[97]

2.23   The LPA must submit its local development plan to the National Assembly for independent examination.[98] It is the responsibility of the Assembly to cause an examination to be held, and the examiner's recommendations become effectively binding upon the LPA.[99] In considering a plan submitted to it, the Assembly may take account of any matter it thinks is relevant.[100] The Assembly may approve, approve subject to specified modifications or reject a plan submitted to it, giving reasons.[101] An LPA is also required to carry out a review of its local development plan whenever it thinks its plan should be reviewed or at such times as the Assembly prescribes.[102] The LPA must also prepare a revision of its local development plan if the Assembly directs it to do so or if, following a review, it thinks the plan should be revised.

---

[92]   PCPA 2004, Part 8 – Wales.

[93]   PCPA 2004, ss 60A–60C.

[94]   PCPA 2004, ss 60D–60J.

[95]   PCPA 2004, s 62(1)–(3).

[96]   PCPA 2004, s 62(3A).

[97]   PCPA 2004, s 62(6).

[98]   PCPA 2004, s 64(1).

[99]   PCPA 2004, s 64(4)–(8).

[100]   PCPA 2004, s 64(7).

[101]   PCPA 2004, s 65(9).

[102]   PCPA 2004, s 69.

STRATEGIC PLANNING IN GREATER LONDON

2.24   Reference has already been made to the Mayor's planning powers.[103] As previously mentioned, the Greater London Authority Act 1999 (GLA 1999) made significant amendments to the planning regime regarding London. It provided for the establishment of a Greater London Authority (GLA) comprising a directly elected executive Mayor and an elected Assembly. These bodies have planning functions, including in relation to spatial planning.[104]

2.25   The Mayor is required to prepare and publish a document called a spatial development strategy (which is called the 'London Plan'), which must contain a statement formulating the Mayor's strategy for spatial development in Greater London.[105]

2.26   The spatial development strategy will include the Mayor's general policies in respect of the development and use of land in Greater London, although dealing only with matters which are of strategic importance.[106] The spatial development strategy must also include statements of other specified strategies or policies involving spatial development, whether or not they relate to the development or use of land.[107] The spatial development strategy must contain a reasoned justification of the Mayor's strategy and a key diagram.[108] The Mayor must also have regard to the Secretary of State's waste policies, the prevention of major accidents and the need to maintain appropriate space between buildings.[109]

2.27   The procedures for preparing and revising the spatial development strategy are drawn from the legislation relating to structure plans.[110] They establish the

---

[103]   See para 1.29.

[104]   GLAA 1999, Part 8.

[105]   GLAA 1999, s 334. The current London Plan was adopted in March 2016. A draft new London Plan was published for consultation on 1/12/2017, setting out the Mayor's new strategic directions for planning in London until 2041 (final publication is expected in autumn 2019). The Mayor also issues planning guidance viz: Mayor's: (a) Housing Supplementary Planning Guidance (March 2016), which provides further guidance on London Plan policies for housing; and (b) his Affordable Housing and Viability Supplementary Planning Guidance (September 2017), which is intended to raise the amount of affordable housing coming through the planning system ahead of the new London Plan in 2019.

[106]   GLAA 1999, ss 334(1)–(4).

[107]   GLAA 1999, s 334(4); see various duties of the Mayor to which he is to have regard in formulating strategy prescribed in ss 41(4)–(6).

[108]   GLAA 1999, s 334(7) and Town and Country Planning (London Spatial Development Strategy) Regulations 2000, regs 4 and 5.

[109]   GLAA 1999, s 342(1). There is a useful summary of the matters to which the Mayor is to have regard in formulating the spatial development strategy in the *Encyclopedia of Planning* at 2-4229.1.

[110]   GLAA 1999, s 335; see also Town and Country Planning (London Spatial Development Strategy) Regulations 2000: Part 1 deals with form and content of the spatial development strategy; Part II

relationship between the spatial development strategy and unitary development plans and the right of public participation in the spatial development strategy policy-making process. It is, however, important to remember that whereas detailed planning still remains the preserve of the London LPAs, the spatial development strategy (as a spatial development plan dealing with the implications of the other strategies formulated by the Mayor, as well as his other policies) is intended to focus on major development and infrastructure requirements. Two further points should be noted: first, the development plans of the London boroughs must still be in general conformity with the spatial development strategy; and secondly, the spatial development strategy must be kept under review by the Mayor and may be altered by him or by direction of the Secretary of State.[111]

CORRECT APPROACH TO THE INTERPRETATION OF A LOCAL PLAN

2.28   The interpretation of a development plan is a matter of law for the court and not for the LPA to determine as it pleases within the limits of rationality.[112]

---

deals with procedure; Part III deals with availability of documents; and Part IV deals with conformity and conflict between unitary development plans and the spatial development strategy.

[111] GLAA 1999, ss 339–341.

[112] *Tesco Stores Ltd v Dundee City Council (ASDA Stores Ltd Intervening)* [2012] UKSC 13. The legal principles, when addressing questions involving the meaning of a planning policy, are usefully set out by Dove J in *Richborough Estates Ltd v Secretary of State for Housing, Communities and Local Government* [2018] EWHC 33 (Admin) at [39], where he stated as follows:

'39. The legal principles when addressing a question of this kind are as follows: (i) The question of the interpretation of a planning policy is a question of law for the court: see *Tesco Stores v Dundee City Council* [2012] UKSC 13; [2012] PTSR 983. (ii) The task of interpretation should not be undertaken as if the planning policy were a statute or a contract; the approach must recognise that planning policies will contain broad statements of policy which may, superficially, conflict and require to be balanced in reaching a decision: see *Hopkins Homes* (in the Supreme Court) at paragraph 25. Planning policies are designed to shape practical decision-making and they should be interpreted with that practical purpose clearly in mind. They have to be applied by planning professionals and the public for whose benefit they exist, and are primarily addressed to that audience. (iii) It is important that the language of the policy is read in its proper context when textual interpretation is required: see *Tesco Stores* at paragraphs 18 and 21. That context will include the subject matter of the policy and its planning objectives. It will also include the wider policy framework within which the policy sits and to which it relates. (iv) Often policies will call for judgment to be exercised as to how they apply in the particular factual circumstances of the case: see paragraphs 19 and 21 of *Tesco Stores*. It is important to distinguish between the interpretation of policy which requires judicial analysis, and the exercise of judgment in the application of policy which is a matter for the decision-maker: see *Hopkins Homes* (in the Supreme Court) at paragraph 26'.

(The reference to *Hopkins Homes* is a reference to *Secretary of State for Communities and Local Government v Hopkins Homes Ltd* [2017] UKSC 37.)

The same applies to the interpretation of the NPPF.[113] However, even where there are disputes over interpretation, they may well not be determinative of the outcome. It has been stressed that the courts should respect the expertise of specialist planning inspectors and start at least from the presumption that they will have understood the policy framework correctly.[114]

Housing delivery and the relevance of policy in plan-making

2.29   It has already been indicated that each LPA is required to keep under review matters which may be expected to affect the development of its area.[115] Within their development plan documents, LPAs must set out their policies relating to the development and use of land in their area. In preparing such documents, the LPA must have regard to national policies and advice contained in guidance issued by the Secretary of State.[116] Further, every development plan document must be submitted to the Secretary of State for independent examination, one of whose purposes is to determine whether it complies with the relevant statutory requirements, including the requirement that it should have regard to national policies and guidance issued by the Secretary of State.[117]

2.30   Any person or body exercising any function in relation to local development documents must exercise it 'with the objective of contributing to the achievement of sustainable development' and for that purpose must have regard to 'national policies and advice contained in guidance issued by the Secretary of State'.[118] Here, then, we have statutory force being given to the concept of 'sustainable development' (which is not defined).

'presumption in favour of sustainable development'

2.31   It will be recalled that the 'presumption in favour of sustainable development' is said to be 'at the heart of' the NPPF and should be seen as 'a golden thread running through both plan-making and decision-taking' (NPPF, paragraph 14). In the case of plan-making, it will be recalled that the 'presumption in favour of sustainable development' should be taken to mean: (a) that LPAs 'should positively seek opportunities to meet the development needs of their

---

[113]   *R (Hunston Properties Ltd) v Secretary of State for Communities and Local Government* [2014] JPL 599. See also *Hopkins Homes* (fn 112) at [23]–[26] (per Lord Carnwath).

[114]   *Hopkins Homes* (fn 112) (Lord Carnwath at [19]–[21] and [25]–[26]). It is important to note that a distinction is to be drawn between issues of interpretation of policy, appropriate for judicial analysis, and issues of judgment in the application of that policy.

[115]   PCPA 2004, Part 2.

[116]   PCPA 2004, s 19(2).

[117]   PCPA 2004, s 20(1), (5)(a).

[118]   PCPA 2004, s 39.

area'; and (b) that 'Local Plans should meet objectively assessed needs' 'unless
any adverse impacts of doing so would significantly and demonstrably outweigh
the benefits, when assessed against the policies (within the NPPF) taken as a
whole', or where 'specific policies (within the NPPF) indicate that development
should be restricted'.[119] However, it has been made plain in the Supreme Court[120]
that NPPF, paragraph 14 cannot detract from the priority given by statute to the
development plan.[121]

2.32   Accordingly, NPPF, paragraph 14 gives rise to significant new guidance
when it comes to plan-making with attention focused on the need for local plans
to identify and provide for the objectively assessed needs of their area.[122]

---

[119] In this regard, see fn 9 to NPPF, para 14, which lists the following examples: (i) policies relating
to sites protected under the Birds and Habitats Directives and/or designated as SSSIs; (ii) land
designated as Green Belt, Local Green Space, an AONB, Heritage Coast or within a National
Park (or a Broads Authority); (iii) designated heritage assets; and (iv) locations at risk of flooding
or coastal erosion. These are examples, and the list is not intended to be exhaustive.

[120] *Hopkins Homes* (fn 112) (Lord Carnwath at [14]).

[121] TCPA 1990, s 70(2), and PCPA 2004, s 38(6) (in which, in the case of decision-taking, LPAs are
required to have regard to the provisions of the development plan unless material considerations
indicate otherwise as, for instance, where a policy in the development plan is outdated or has been
superseded by more recent guidance). An appeal against a refusal of planning permission lies to
the Secretary of State, who is subject to the same duty in respect of the development plan (TCPA
1990, ss 78 and 79(4)). In *St Modwen Developments Ltd v Secretary of State for Communities
and Local Government* [2016] EWHC 968 (Admin), Ouseley J stated that the NPPF is not to be
construed like a statute or contract. However, the NPPG will be relevant as an aid to interpretation
of the NPPF by the court (see [36]).

[122] The Court of Appeal has recently provided some welcome clarity on the correct approach to
NPPF, para 14 and how it related to the presumption in favour of the development plan, in
*Barwood Strategic Land II LLP v East Staffordshire Borough Council and Secretary of State for
Communities and Local Government* [2017] EWCA Civ 893 (this decision followed *Hopkins
Homes* in the Supreme Court). The case involved a developers' appeal against the quashing of
outline planning permission for a residential development and how the NPPF presumption
operated in cases where an LPA had failed to demonstrate a five-year supply of deliverable
housing sites. Although *Barwood Strategic Land* is of crucial importance to decisions on planning
applications (rather than in its application to plan-making), it is, nonetheless, considered
appropriate, within this chapter, to deal with the up-to-date jurisprudence affecting NPPF,
para 14 to its fullest extent and, where material, the same principles will be covered in later
chapters. Lindblom LJ laid down the following principles at [35]: (1) The 'presumption in favour
of sustainable development' in the NPPF, unlike the presumption in favour of the development
plan in PCPA 2004, s 38(6), is not a statutory presumption. It is only a presumption of planning
policy, which requires of a planning decision-maker an exercise of planning judgment within the
balancing exercise mandated under s 38(6). (2) NPPF, para 14 describes what the 'presumption
in favour of sustainable development' means, explaining in clear and complete terms the
circumstances in which, and the way in which, it is intended to operate. The presumption, as
described in para 14, is the so-called 'golden thread running through both plan-making and
decision-taking'. There is no other 'presumption in favour of sustainable development' in the
NPPF, either explicit or implicit, and no other 'golden thread'. (3) When the s 38(6) duty is

Other policies in NPPF which impact on housing provision in plan-making

2.33   One turns next to other important policies within the NPPF that impact directly on housing provision in plan-making.

2.34   NPPF, Section 6 (paragraphs 47 to 55) is entitled, 'Delivering a wide choice of high quality homes'. Paragraph 47 states that to boost significantly the supply of housing, LPAs should:

- use their evidence base to ensure that their Local Plan meets the full, objectively assessed needs for market and affordable housing in the housing market area, as far as is consistent with the policies set out in [the NPPF], including identifying key sites which are critical to the delivery of the housing strategy over the plan period;

---

lawfully performed, a development which does not earn the 'presumption in favour of sustainable development' – and does not, therefore, have the benefit of the 'tilted balance' – may still merit the grant of planning permission. On the other hand, a development which does have the benefit of the 'tilted balance' may still be found unacceptable, and planning permission for it refused. This is the territory of planning judgment, where the court will not go except to apply the relevant principles of public law. The 'presumption in favour of sustainable development' is not irrebuttable. Thus, in a case where a proposal for development of housing is in conflict with a local plan whose policies for the supply of housing are out of date, the decision-maker is left to judge, in the particular circumstances of the case at hand, how much weight should be given to that conflict. The absence of a five-year supply of housing land will not necessarily be conclusive in favour of the grant of planning permission. This is not a matter of law. It is a matter of planning judgment. (4) The operation of the 'tilted balance' (and the primary purpose of NPPF, para 49 – in which relevant policies for the supply of housing will not be considered up to date where the LPA cannot demonstrate a five-year supply of deliverable housing land – is that it will trigger the operation of the 'tilted balance' under para 14) involves a planning judgment being made in relation to the two exceptions relevant to a case where the 'development plan is absent, silent or relevant policy made under para 14 (namely (i) where the adverse impacts of granting planning permission would 'significantly and demonstrably outweigh the benefits' of granting permission, or (ii) where specific policies within the NPPF indicate that development should be restricted). However, planning permission will not be withheld simply because the second of these two exceptions applies'. Lindblom LJ stated at [22](2) that:

'the second of these two exceptions does not "shut out" the "presumption in favour of sustainable development" simply because any of the "specific policies" – of which examples are given in footnote 9 – is in play (see paragraph 45 of my judgment in *Watermead Parish Council v Crematoria Management Ltd* [2017] EWCA Civ 152). Once identified the specific policy in question has to be applied – and, where that specific policy requires it, a planning judgment exercised – before the decision-maker can ascertain whether the "presumption in favour of sustainable development" is available to the proposal in hand'.

- identify and update annually a supply of specific deliverable[123] sites sufficient to provide five years' worth of housing against their housing requirements with an additional buffer of 5% … to ensure choice and competition in the market for land. Where there has been a record of persistent under delivery of housing, local planning authorities should increase the buffer to 20% … to provide a realistic prospect of achieving the planned supply and to ensure choice and competition in the market for land;
- identify a supply of specific, developable[124] sites or broad locations for growth, for years 6–10 and, where possible, for years 11–15;

---

[123] See NPPF, para 47, fn 11: to be considered *deliverable*, sites should be available now, offer a suitable location for development now and be achievable with a realistic prospect that housing will be delivered on the site within five years and in particular that development of the site is viable. Sites with planning permission should be considered deliverable until permission expires, unless there is clear evidence that schemes will not be implemented within five years, for example, they will not be viable, there is no longer a demand for the type of units or sites have long term phasing plans. In *St Modwen Developments Ltd v Secretary of State for Communities and Local Government* [2017] EWCA Civ 1643, the Court of Appeal explained the proper approach to NPPF, para 47. This was a case where the developer claimed that the Inspector had misinterpreted para 47 when concluding that an LPA had properly refused planning permission for a large housing development on the basis that it had in fact demonstrated the existence of a five-year supply of housing land. The decision was upheld by the judge, and the appeal to the Court of Appeal was dismissed. Lindblom LJ ruled that the definition of the word 'deliverable' in the first part of the footnote to para 47 went to a site's capability of being delivered within five years, not to the certainty or probability that it actually would be. The second part of the definition (which referred to sites with planning permission) clearly implied that, to be considered deliverable and included in the five-year supply, a site did not necessarily have to have planning permission already granted for housing development on it. Sites might be included in the five-year supply if the likelihood of housing being delivered on them within the five-year period was no greater than a 'realistic prospect', being the third element of the definition. That did not mean that for a site properly to be regarded as 'deliverable', it had necessarily to be certain or probable that housing would in fact be delivered upon it, or delivered to the fullest extent possible, within five years. There is then a distinction to be made between deliverability and actual delivery, and that under para 47, deliverability entailed only a 'realistic prospect' of the site being delivered. In other words, the fact that a particular site was capable of being delivered within five years did not mean that it necessarily would be. For instance, the landowner or housebuilder might choose to hold the site back. The developer in *St Modwen* had argued that the inspector had misinterpreted para 47 by failing to carry out an assessment of what would probably by delivered in terms of the supply of housing land, an approach which the Court of Appeal rejected. This is because the argument misses the essential distinction between the concept of deliverability, in the sense in which it was used in the policy, and the concept of an 'expected rate of delivery', which is not the same thing as deliverability. The decision in *St Modwen* is helpful to LPAs in that they now have a clearer idea of where they stand when it comes to their five-year supply calculations. It is understood that *St Modwen Developments*, which (at the time of the book going to press) is evidently seeking permission to appeal to the Supreme Court, will be arguing that the Court of Appeal's formulation sets the bar too low and that delivery of identified sites should be 'probable' within five years if the test is to have any force in boosting supply.

[124] To be considered *developable*, sites should be in a suitable location for housing development and there should be a reasonable prospect that the site is available and could be viably developed at the point envisaged.

- for market and affordable housing, illustrate the expected rate of housing delivery through a housing trajectory for the plan period and set out a housing implementation strategy for the full range of housing describing how they will maintain delivery of a five-year supply of housing land to meet their housing target; and
- set out their own approach to housing density to reflect local circumstances.

2.35 NPPF, paragraph 49 also contains this important policy:

49. Housing applications should be considered in the context of the presumption in favour of sustainable development. Relevant policies for the supply of housing should not be considered up-to-date if the local planning authority cannot demonstrate a five-year supply of deliverable housing sites.[125]

2.36 NPPF, paragraphs 150 to 185 deal specifically with plan-making. Reference should be made to paragraph 159 under the heading 'Housing', which states as follows:

Housing
159. Local planning authorities should have a clear understanding of housing needs in their area. They should:

- prepare a Strategic Housing Market Assessment to assess their full housing needs, working with neighbouring authorities where housing areas cross administrative boundaries. The Strategic Housing Market Assessment should identify the scale and mix of housing and the range of tenures that the local population is likely to need over the plan period which:

  − meets household and population projections, taking account of migration and demographic change;

---

[125] In *Hopkins Homes*, the Supreme Court ruled that the words 'policies for the supply of housing' indicated the category of policies with which para 49 was concerned, namely housing supply policies. Although other groups of policies, such as policies for the protection of the countryside, could affect the operation of housing policies, that did not make them policies for the supply of housing. In so far as the objectives in para 47 were not met by housing supply policies, it was natural to describe those policies as out-of-date for the purposes of para 49. There was no need for a legalistic exercise to decide whether individual policies came within 'policies for the supply of housing'. The important question was whether the result was a five-year supply in accordance with the para 47 objectives (*Bloor Homes East Midlands Ltd v Secretary of State for Communities and Local Government* [2014] EWHC 754 (Admin) applied). The Supreme Court ruled that the primary purpose of para 49 was to act as a trigger to the operation of the 'tilted balance' under para 14. In the absence of relevant or up-to-date development plan policies, the balance was tilted in favour of granting permission, except where the benefits were significantly and demonstrably outweighed by the adverse effects, or where specific policies indicated otherwise. See *Barwood Strategic Land II LLP* (fn 122) at [22], where Lindblom LJ notes the five basic points which are to be taken from *Hopkins Homes*.

- addresses the need for all types of housing, including affordable housing and the needs of different groups in the community (such as, but not limited to, families with children, older people, people with disabilities, service families and people wishing to build their own homes; and
- caters for housing demand and the scale of housing supply necessary to meet this demand;

- prepare a Strategic Housing Land Availability Assessment to establish realistic assumptions about the availability, suitability and the likely economic viability of land to meet the identified need for housing over the plan period.

2.37   NPPF, paragraph 213 provides that where necessary, plans should be revised as quickly as possible to take account of the policies 'through a partial review or by preparing a new plan'.[126]

2.38   NPPF, paragraph 215 provides that due weight is to be given to relevant policies in existing plans according to their degree of consistency with the NPPF and the closer the policies in the development plan to the policies in the NPPF, the greater the weight that may be given to them.

NATIONAL PLANNING PRACTICE GUIDANCE

Strategic Housing Market Assessment

2.39   Guidance exists to support LPAs in objectively assessing and evidencing development needs for housing (both market and affordable) and economic development.[127] The primary objective of identifying need is to identify the future quantity of housing needed, including a breakdown by type, tenure and size, and to provide an indication of gaps in current land supply.[128]

---

[126]   See the Town and Country Planning (Local Planning) (England) (Amendment) Regulations 2017 (SI 2017/1244), which came into force on 15/1/2018, apart from reg 4, which came into force on 6/4/2018. These regulations require all LPAs to have up-to-date plans (and Statements of Community Involvement) and commence the statutory duty for LPAs to identify their strategic priorities and the policies to address them. Additional powers are also provided for the Secretary of State to intervene in plan-making where authorities are not planning effectively for the needs of communities. The regulations introduce a requirement to review local plans/Statements of Community Involvement at least every five years from adoption.

[127]   NPPG at Paragraph: 001 Reference ID: 2a-001-20140306 through to Paragraph: 037 Reference ID: 2a-037-20140306. Most of this guidance dates back to 6/3/2014. The assessment of housing and economic development needs includes the SHMA requirement set out in NPPF, para 159 (first bullet).

[128]   NPPG at Paragraph: 002 Reference ID: 2a-002-20140306. Updated on 6/3/2014. The guidance affects both housing and economic development needs assessments. Only housing need will be addressed in this part.

2.40   Need for housing in the context of the guidance refers to the scale and mix of housing and the range of tenures that is likely to be needed in the housing market area over the plan period and should also cater for the housing demand of the area and identify the scale of housing supply necessary to meet that demand. Need for all land uses should address both the total number of homes or quantity of economic floor space needed based on quantitative assessments and also on the understanding of the qualitative requirements of each market segment. Assessing development needs should be proportionate and does not require LPAs to consider purely hypothetical future scenarios, only future scenarios that could be reasonably expected to occur.[129]

2.41   In relation to the guidance for the assessment of housing and economic development needs, it is noted[130] that there is no one methodological approach or use of a particular dataset(s) that will provide a definitive assessment of development need. However, the use of the standard methodology[131] set out in the guidance is recommended, as it ensures that the assessment findings are transparently prepared. It is stated that if LPAs wish to depart from the methodology contained in the guidance, they should explain why their particular local circumstances have led them to adopt a different approach.

2.42   The guidance requires the LPA to carry out its assessment of housing need within what is termed the 'Housing Market Area', which is a geographical area defined by household demand and preferences for all types of housing, reflecting the key functional linkages between places where people live and work. The extent of the housing market areas identified will vary, and many will cut across LPA boundaries, and LPAs should accordingly work alongside other constituent authorities under the duty to co-operate. Where there is a joint plan, housing requirements and the need to identify a five-year supply of sites can apply across the joint plan area.[132]

Strategic housing land availability assessment

2.43   Guidance also exists to support LPAs in identifying a future supply of land which is suitable, available and achievable for housing and economic development uses over the plan period. The assessment of land availability includes the

---

[129]   NPPG at Paragraph: 003 Reference ID: 2a-003-20140306. Updated on 6/3/2014.

[130]   NPPG at Paragraph: 005 Reference ID: 2a-005-20140306.

[131]   Which begins at Paragraph: 014 Reference ID: 2a-014-20140306.

[132]   NPPG at Paragraph: 008 Reference ID: 2a-008-20140306 through to Paragraph: 011 Reference ID: 2a-011-20140306 (these paras are all dated 6/3/2014).

preparation of the Strategic Housing Land Availability Assessment.[133] The assessment of land availability is an important step in the preparation of local plans.

2.44   The NPPF identifies the advantages of carrying out land assessments for housing and economic development as part of the same exercise in order that sites may be allocated for the use which is most appropriate. An assessment should: (a) identify sites and broad locations with potential for development; (b) assess their development potential; (c) assess their suitability for development; and (d) assess the likelihood of development coming forward.[134]

2.45   The assessment forms a key component of the evidence base to underpin policies in development plans for housing and economic development, including supporting the delivery of land to meet identified need for these uses. From the assessment, plan-makers will then be able to plan proactively by choosing sites to go forward into their development plan documents to meet objectively assessed needs.[135]

SUMMARY

2.46   At present, the NPPF and national planning guidance require each LPA to define a Housing Market Area and to identify the 'objectively assessed need' for market and affordable housing within this area. The guidance sets out a recommended method for doing so, using the latest national statistics for projected household formation as a starting point. This is then adjusted to take account of a range of issues, including employment growth and market signals.

REFORM

New Housing Delivery Test

2.47   A new standardised approach to assessing housing delivery comes into force in November 2018, with the aim of providing a boost to housing delivery.[136]

---

[133] As set out in NPPF, para 159 (second bullet). The guidance is extensive and runs between NPPG at Paragraph: 001 Reference ID: 3-001-20140306 and NPPG at Paragraph: 043 Reference ID: 3-043-20140306. Most of this guidance dates back to 6/3/2014.

[134] NPPG at Paragraph: 001 Reference ID: 3-001-20140306. Updated on 6/3/2014.

[135] NPPG at Paragraph: 002 Reference ID: 3-002-20140306. Updated on 6/3/2014.

[136] The methodology for calculating the Housing Delivery Test (HDT) measurement is set out in the Housing Delivery Test Measurement Rule Book. The Secretary of State will publish annually the HDT result for each LPA in England in November.

The test assesses housing delivery by comparing official figures for the number of new homes delivered over a three-year period to the authority's requirements during the same period.[137] Sanctions are to be imposed on those authorities (which face the prospect of having the NPPF's presumption in favour of sustainable development being applied in their areas) if housing delivery falls below 25% from November 2018, below 45% from November 2019 and below 75% from November 2020. The presumption in favour of sustainable development will remain in place until subsequent Housing Delivery Test (HDT) results demonstrate that delivery exceeds the required rate of delivery in the following year.[138]

2.48   The proposal is to measure delivery against the housing requirement for the previous three years. From November 2018, where the test indicates delivery of below 95%, the draft NPPG says an LPA should prepare an action plan 'to assess the causes of under-delivery and identify actions to increase delivery in future years'. Also from November 2018, where delivery falls below 85%, the draft NPPG says that authorities must plan for an additional 20% buffer on their housing land supply.

2.49   The revised NPPF and NPPG also provide that for authorities with an adopted local plan which is less than five years old, the housing requirement figure is to be the target figure in their plan. Where there is no up-to-date plan, authorities must use a local housing need figure which is based on the Government's household growth projections up to 2017/18. After April 2018, this figure would be calculated by using the Government's new standard housing need assessment method. For delivery figures, the new test will utilise the Government's net additional dwellings figure, but authorities will be able to count net additions arising from certain kinds of communal accommodation, such as student housing, towards their housing delivery figures which, in some areas, could well result in an increase in housing delivery figures.

2.50   In calculating their own housing requirements, authorities must also take into account any unmet need in neighbouring authorities which it has agreed to take on.

2.51   In a very helpful article by Adam Branson in the *Planning* magazine published on 20/4/2018, it is said that research suggests that only three authorities

---

[137] The HDT is, in effect, the annual measurement of housing delivery performance in the plan-making authority area. The HDT does not apply to National Park authorities or to development corporations without full plan-making and decision-making powers. Put simply, the HDT is the percentage measurement of the number of net homes delivered over a rolling three-year period against the number of homes required over a three-year period in the plan-making authority area. The DHCLG has prepared a draft methodology to calculating the HDT.

[138] Reference should be made to the consultation proposals for the NPPG issued by DHCLG in March 2018 at pp 20–23 (Housing Delivery Test).

(two in Lancashire and one in London) currently have delivery rates below the 25% threshold, but around 54% of all English authorities would currently face some sort of penalty. The Local Government Association is reported as saying (*Planning* online on 25/5/2018) that, using the Government's new HDT methodology, 42% of authority areas will fall under the 75% threshold by 2020. Notwithstanding this, planning permissions were granted for more than 350,000 homes in England in 2017 – the most for more than ten years according to housebuilders[139] – and this is no doubt the result of government policy changes and market forces. The increase between 2016 and 2017 was in fact 16%. It was also reported in *Planning* (in the issue dated 18/5/2018) that a study by consultants found that for the Government to reach its target of 300,000 homes per annum, it would require in excess of 400,000 permissions[140] per annum, partly because not all permissions are built out, and partly because the larger sites deliver homes more slowly.[141] The complaint is that it is unfair to impose targets on local communities which can only be met by private developers and then to penalise those communities if those builders do not deliver.

2.52   The Department of Housing, Communities and Local Government (DHCLG) takes the view that the current process leaves substantial room for interpretation and has given rise to LPAs incurring excessive cost in employing experts to come up with a housing need figure. It is suggested that it can cost LPAs around £50,000 to prepare a Strategic Housing Market Assessment (SHMA). The view is taken that LPAs, developers and local communities often engage in disputes on the method used, which delays the process (by around six

---

[139]   As against this, statistics show that in the first quarter of 2018, new build dwelling starts in England were estimated at 39,350, a 5% decrease on the same period in 2017. Annual new build dwelling starts totalled 157,480 in the year to March 2018, down by 3% in the previous year. Completions totalled 160,470 in the year to March 2018, an increase of 8% compared with 2016/17. This is still well below the Government's target of 300,000 new homes per annum. Separate statistics also revealed that the number of new affordable homes in England in 2017 rose to 42,220, although social home completions fell for the fourth consecutive year (figures taken from *Planning* dated 27/6/2018).

[140]   DHCLG statistics show that in the year to 31/3/2018 permission was granted for 347,000 homes compared to 314,000 in the previous 12 months. However, the statistical bulletin reveals no change in the speed of decision-making performance over the same period.

[141]   It is claimed that housebuilders operating on large sites avoid triggering drops in local market prices by carefully controlling the type and pricing of the homes they build. This is alleged to be the most important factor limiting the build-out of permissions. On top of this, it is also accepted that small builders need a more plentiful supply of small sites if they are to make a bigger contribution to meeting housebuilding targets. There is clearly a need for a better mix to overcome the dependence of local plans on a handful of large sites to meet housebuilding targets. Hence the draft NPPF revisions, which say that LPAs should ensure that at least 20% of the sites identified for housing in their plans are half a hectare or less. This is a controversial solution to the problem of large site housing allocations in local plans.

months) and adds cost. Moreover, few methods take significant account of the affordability of housing in their areas.

2.53   The result is a standardised approach to the assessment of local housing need which, it is claimed, will be simpler and more easy to understand, would be based on publicly available data and would be more realistic in so far as it would reflect the actual need for homes in each area, taking into account the affordability of homes locally. The DHCLG considers that high house prices indicate a relative imbalance between supply and demand for new homes and makes housing less affordable. It says that the affordability of new homes is the best evidence that supply is not keeping up with demand. In addition, the DHCLG considers that any approach must also allow an understanding of the minimum number of homes that are needed across England as a whole.

Chapter 3

Neighbourhood Planning

INTRODUCTION

3.1 The neighbourhood planning system was introduced by the Localism Act 2011 (LA 2011).[1] Its function is to give communities a much stronger say in shaping development and growth within their local areas. This is because a neighbourhood plan forms part of the local development plan and sits alongside the local plan prepared by the local planning authority (LPA). It means that decisions on planning applications will be made using both the local plan and the neighbourhood plan, in conjunction with any other material considerations.

3.2 Neighbourhood planning: (a) allows local communities to set planning policies through a *neighbourhood plan* that will be used in the determination of planning applications by the LPA; and (b) facilitates the grant of planning permission for specific development through a *neighbourhood development order* within a particular neighbourhood area.

3.3 Neighbourhood planning is not a legal requirement but a right which communities in England can choose to use (unless they decide that they could achieve the outcomes they want to see through other planning routes, such as incorporating their proposals for their neighbourhood into the local plan).

3.4 Neighbourhood planning is becoming very popular. As at 3/8/2017, a total of 328 neighbourhood plans had been adopted in England.

---

[1]   LA 2011, Pt 5, Ch 3 and Schs 9–11. Schedule 9 inserts new sections into the TCPA 1990 at ss 61E–61Q. Schedules 10 and 11 also insert new Schs 4B and 4C into the same Act. These sections allow for planning permission to be granted through neighbourhood development orders. Schedule 9, Pt 2 amends PCPA 2004 to provide for a neighbourhood development plan. The Neighbourhood Planning (General) Regulations 2012 (SI 2012/637) provide for procedural matters in connection with neighbourhood planning.

3.5   To help deliver neighbourhood plans, communities drawing up a neighbourhood plan or order which secures the consent of local people in a referendum will benefit from 25% of the revenues from the Community Infrastructure Levy (CIL) arising from the development that takes place in their area.[2]

3.6   It is also worth noting that the National Planning Policy Framework 2012 (NPPF)[3] says that LPAs should:

> take a proactive and positive approach to proposals (for neighbourhood development orders and community right to build orders), working collaboratively with community organisations to resolve any issues before draft orders are submitted for examination. Policies (in the NPPF) that relate to decision-taking should be read as applying to the consideration of proposed neighbourhood development orders, whenever this is appropriate given the context and relevant legislation.

NEIGHBOURHOOD DEVELOPMENT ORDERS

3.7   A neighbourhood development order can grant planning permission for specific types of development in a specific neighbourhood area.[4] Any qualifying body[5] may initiate the process to require an LPA (in England) to make a

---

[2]   Parish and town councils (which are parish councils serving a town which have the same powers, duties and status as parish councils) are the lowest tier of local government. The funding for parish councils is allocated by the district council and is called an annual precept. The income and expenditure for the next financial year are calculated in the form of estimates, and this amount is added to the local council tax and is then returned to the parishes in two yearly instalments. They can also apply for UK grants and EU money. Receipts of levy from CIL therefore represent significant additional revenue for smaller parish councils which have allocations for significant residential development within their neighbourhood plan areas. There is therefore a tension between LPAs and parishes in those cases where the former seek to adjust neighbourhood area boundaries in order to secure levy for themselves in the case of large developments which they consider are functionally part of their areas and inappropriate to be included within the neighbourhood plan area. For instance, in February 2017, a Cheshire LPA amended a parish council's proposed neighbourhood plan area to exclude a new garden village. The parish was expected to earn an estimated £2.5 million in CIL payments from the garden village.

[3]   At para 202.

[4]   TCPA 1990, s 61E(2). A 'neighbourhood area' is defined in s 61G as an area which has been designated as such by an LPA on the application of a parish council or neighbourhood forum. See fn 1 for regulations dealing with procedures involved on applications for the designation of neighbourhood areas by qualifying bodies.

[5]   TCPA 1990, s 61E(6). A 'qualifying body' means a parish council, or an organisation or body designated as a neighbourhood forum, authorised to act in relation to a 'neighbourhood area' (the meaning of this expression will be found in s 61G) as a result of TCPA 1990, s 61F. The LPA has a discretion to designate an organisation or body as a neighbourhood forum if it is satisfied that it meets the conditions laid down in s 61F(5) and (6), namely: (a) if the organisation or body is established for the express purpose of promoting or improving the social, economic and

neighbourhood development order. An LPA to whom a proposal for the making of a neighbourhood development has been made must make the order as soon as reasonably practicable after a referendum has been held where more than half those voting have voted in favour of the order.[6]

Authority to initiate the process

3.8   Only a parish council is authorised to act in relation to a neighbourhood area if the area includes the whole or any part of the area of the council.[7] If that area also includes the area of another parish council then the parish council is only authorised to act if the other parish council for the neighbourhood area has given its consent.[8]

3.9   In areas where there is no parish council only an organisation or body which has been designated by the LPA as a *neighbourhood forum* for the neighbourhood area may put forward proposals.[9] In determining an application the LPA must have regard to the desirability of designating the whole of the area of the parish council as a neighbourhood area; and the desirability of maintaining the existing boundaries of areas already designated as neighbourhood areas. In practice, neighbourhood areas will usually follow the boundaries of existing parish councils unless the LPA considers that some other area would be more appropriate. Once an LPA designates an area as a neighbourhood area it must publicise this fact on its website and in such other manner it considers appropriate in order to bring the designation to the attention of those who live, work and carry

---

environmental wellbeing of an area that consists of or includes the neighbourhood area concerned; (b) its membership is open to individuals who live or work within the neighbourhood area concerned and individuals who are elected members of a county council or London borough any of whose area falls within the neighbourhood area; (c) its membership includes a minimum of 21 individuals, each of whom lives or works in the neighbourhood area or is an elected member of a county council, district council or London borough whose area falls within the neighbourhood area concerned; (d) it has a written constitution. A designation ceases to have effect after five years (s 61F(8)). The LPA may also withdraw an organisation or body's designation (s 61F(9)). Regulations concerning the process to be followed concerning the designation of neighbourhood areas can be found in Neighbourhood Planning (General) Regulations 2012, Pt 2. Regulations concerning the process to be followed concerning the designation of neighbourhood forums can be found in Pt 3. The above 2012 Regulations have been subject to amendments by the Neighbourhood Planning (General) (Amendment) Regulations 2015 (SI 2015/20) and the Neighbourhood Planning (General) and Development Management Procedure (Amendment) Regulations 2016 (SI 2016/873). The meaning and relationship between s 61F (authorisation to act in relation to neighbourhood areas) and s 61G (the meaning of a neighbourhood area) was considered in R (Daws Hill Neighbourhood Forum) v Wycombe District Council [2014] EWCA Civ 228.

6   TCPA 1990, s 61E(4).

7   TCPA 1990, s 61F(1).

8   TCPA 1990, s 61F(2).

9   TCPA 1990, s 61F(3)–(7).

on business in the area. If, however, it refuses to designate a neighbourhood area then it must similarly publicise this fact to people living and working in the area. The LPA must also give reasons for its refusal and make the document setting out its reasons available for public inspection.[10] The LPA should also consider whether it should designate the area as a 'business area' where it considers that the area is wholly or predominantly business in nature.[11]

Contents of a neighbourhood development order

3.10   There is a wide ambit to what the order can do. It can grant planning permission (with or without conditions or limitations)[12] in relation to some or all of the land in the neighbourhood area[13] although it cannot grant planning permission for excluded development[14] which includes: (a) county matters (waste and minerals); (b) development falling within the Town and Country Planning (Environmental Impact Assessment) Regulations 2017[15] which revoked the 2011 Regulations (EIA Regulations 2017); (c) development consisting of a nationally significant infrastructure project (within the meaning of the Planning Act 2008); (d) prescribed development or development of a prescribed description; and (e) development within a prescribed area or an area of prescribed description.[16]

Process of making of neighbourhood development orders

3.11   The process is a rigorous one and is set out in Schedule 4B to the TCPA 1990, to which reference should be made in view of its length and complexity. However, having satisfied itself that the application is duly made, the LPA is required to submit the draft neighbourhood development order and such other documents as may be prescribed, for independent examination.[17] The LPA may, with the consent of the qualifying body, appoint an appropriate independent person to carry out the examination; or, if he considers it expedient, the Secretary of State may appoint a person. The matters which the examiner must consider include whether the draft order meets what are termed 'the basic conditions'[18] which concern the appropriateness of making the order having regard: (a) to policy

---

[10]   Neighbourhood Planning (General) Regulations 2012, reg 7.
[11]   TCPA 1990, s 61H.
[12]   TCPA 1990, s 61L.
[13]   TCPA 1990, s 61J(1).
[14]   TCPA 1990, s 61J(2).
[15]   SI 2017/1012.
[16]   TCPA 1990, s 61K (no development, development of a prescribed description, area or area of a prescribed description has yet been prescribed for the purposes of (d) and (e)).
[17]   TCPA 1990, Sch 4B, para 7.
[18]   TCPA 1990, Sch 4B, para 8(2).

guidance; (b) to the desirability of preserving any listed building or its setting or of preserving or enhancing the character or appearance of any conservation area; (c) to the achievement of sustainable development; (d) to its conformity with strategic policies in the development plan; (e) to its compatibility with EU regulations; and (f) to its compliance with regulations made by the Secretary of State.

3.12 Examination of the issues will normally take the form of considering written representations, although the examiner may cause a public hearing to be held to give interested parties a fair chance to put their cases.[19] The examiner must make a report on the draft order which must recommend that the draft order is submitted to a referendum, or that it is modified as may be specified before being submitted to a referendum, or that the proposal is refused.[20] The LPA must consider the examiner's report and decide what action to take on each of the recommendations made by the report.[21] If the LPA is satisfied that the order meets the 'basic conditions' and the other specified criteria, a referendum must be held on the making of a neighbourhood development order.[22] If, however, the LPA proposes to make a decision that differs from that recommended by the examiner and the reason for this is attributable to new evidence or a new fact or a different view taken by the LPA as to a particular fact, it may refer the issue to independent examination.[23] The Secretary of State also has important powers where the qualifying body asks him to intervene.[24]

3.13 Where a referendum is to be held, the relevant council[25] must make the arrangements for it and local residents will be entitled to vote.[26] Where the draft order relates to a neighbourhood development order which has been designated as a 'business area'[27] an additional referendum must be held on the making of the order. In such a case non-domestic ratepayers in the referendum area are entitled to vote. The LPA may make a neighbourhood development order if there is a vote in favour of the order in only one of the two applicable referendums. In the result, there are two referendums: one for local residents and one for non-domestic ratepayers in the referendum area. Once it has decided to make a neighbourhood development order, or to refuse to make it, the LPA's decision must be publicised

---

19   TCPA 1990, Sch 4B, para 9.
20   TCPA 1990, Sch 4B, para 10. Provisions for the holding of a referendum are contained in the Neighbourhood Planning (Referendums) Regulations 2012 (SI 2012/2031).
21   TCPA 1990, Sch 4B, para 12(2).
22   TCPA 1990, Sch 4B, para 12(4).
23   TCPA 1990, Sch 4B, para 13(1) and (2).
24   TCPA 1990, Sch 4B, para 13B.
25   TCPA 1990, Sch 4B, para 14(3). This will be the district council; a London borough council; a metropolitan district council; or a county council.
26   TCPA 1990, Sch 4B, para 14(2) and (4).
27   TCPA 1990, s 61H(1) and (3); Sch 4B, para 15.

on its website. Details of where the relevant decision document may be inspected must be provided and the LPA must also send a copy of such document to the qualifying body and any person who asked to be notified of the decision. Similar requirements are imposed on the LPA once the neighbourhood development order has been made.[28]

Community right to build orders

3.14   A community right to build order is a form of neighbourhood development order that can be used to grant planning permission for small-scale development with community benefit on a specific site or sites in a neighbourhood area. For example, such an order can be used to approve the building of homes, shops, business premises, affordable housing for rent or sale, community facilities or playgrounds. Where a community organisation wishes to develop the land itself (subject to acquiring the land if appropriate), the resulting assets can only be disposed of, or improved or developed in a manner which the organisation considers benefits the local community or a section of it.[29]

Other provisions concerning neighbourhood development orders

3.15   The Secretary of State and the LPA (with the consent of the former) may revoke a neighbourhood development order. The LPA may also modify an order for the purpose of correcting errors.[30] There are also provisions in relation to publicity and notification in the case of modification or revocation.[31]

3.16   LPAs are also required to have regard to any guidance issued by the Secretary of State in the exercise of their functions relating to neighbourhood development orders.[32] Provision is also made as to the making of regulations which deal with the arrangements of an LPA for the making of any prescribed decision in the case of neighbourhood development orders.[33]

3.17   Any legal challenge in the case of a neighbourhood development order should be brought by way of judicial review within six weeks beginning on the day after the day on which the decision is published.[34]

---

[28]   Neighbourhood Planning (General) Regulations 2012, regs 26 and 27.

[29]   TCPA 1990, Sch 4C. See also Neighbourhood Planning (General) Regulations 2012, Pt 4, which contains the prescribed conditions for community right to build organisations.

[30]   TCPA 1990, s 61M(1), (2), (4).

[31]   Neighbourhood Planning (General) Regulations 2012, Pt 8, which, in dealing with procedures, also makes specific reference to the revocation and modification of community right to build orders.

[32]   TCPA 1990, s 61O.

[33]   TCPA 1990, s 61P.

[34]   TCPA 1990, s 61N.

NEIGHBOURHOOD DEVELOPMENT PLANS

Introduction

3.18   In contrast to neighbourhood development orders, a neighbourhood development plan does not grant planning permission. Instead, its function is to set out policies[35] in relation to the development and use of land in the area of the

---

[35]   There are no prescribed restrictions on what can be included in a neighbourhood development plan (*R (Larkfleet Homes Ltd) v Rutland County Council* [2015] PTSR 589 (see para 22) and in the Court of Appeal at [2015] PTSR 1369 (see para 21)). For instance, a neighbourhood development plan can include site allocation policies for housing in the absence of a development plan document setting out strategic policies on housing issues (see *R (Gladman Developments Ltd) v Aylesbury Vale DC* [2015] JPL 656); although, having said that, a qualifying body should carry out an appraisal of the options and an assessment of individual sites against clearly identified criteria for housing and economic land availability assessment; see NPPG at Paragraph: 001 Reference ID: 3-001-20140306, and for viability see NPPG at Paragraph: 001 Reference ID: 10-001-20140306). In *Crane v Secretary of State for Communities and Local Government* [2015] EWHC 425 (Admin), the court held that the Secretary of State had not erred in law when upholding the refusal of planning permission for a housing development in a village. He had been correct to conclude that the development would conflict with a neighbourhood development plan which had allocated other sites for development. It was held that there was nothing wrong with the conclusion that although the policies for the supply of housing in the development plan were not up to date, and although the claimant's development would add to the supply of housing in the district, the proposal's conflict with the neighbourhood plan was in itself a powerful and decisive factor against granting planning permission. The court found that such a conclusion was not beyond the range of reasonable planning judgment allowed to a decision-maker when undertaking the balancing exercise required by NPPF, para 14, which involved considering whether the harm associated with the proposed development would 'significantly and demonstrably' outweigh the likely benefits (see Lindblom J at [42], [46], [72] and [78]). Reference should also be made to *R (DLA Delivery Ltd) v Lewes District Council* [2015] EWHC 2311 (Admin) (applying *Woodcock Holdings Ltd v Secretary of State for Communities and Local Government* [2015] EWHC 1173 (Admin)), where it was found that the absence of a local plan did not preclude the preparation and formal approval of a neighbourhood development plan. It was also held in *DLA Delivery Ltd* that a neighbourhood development plan could include policies dealing with the use and development of land for housing before the appropriate local plan was adopted, although the weight to be attached to it if it was adopted before the local plan, or was divergent from it, would be a matter for planning judgment. See NPPG at Paragraph: 009 Reference ID: 41-009-20140306 (updated on 11/2/2016), where it is stated that where a neighbourhood plan is brought forward before an up-to-date local plan is in place, the qualifying body and the LPA should discuss and aim to agree the relationship between policies in (i) the emerging neighbourhood plan; (ii) the emerging local plan; and (iii) the adopted development plan with appropriate regard to national policy and guidance. The NPPG encourages LPAs to work with a qualifying body to produce complementary plans, including policies for housing supply. This is because PCPA 2004, s 38(5) requires that the conflict must be resolved by the decision-maker favouring the policy which is contained in the last document to become part of the development plan. It is further said that neighbourhood plans should consider providing indicative delivery timetables and allocating reserve sites to ensure that emerging evidence of housing need is addressed. This will help minimise conflicts and will ensure that policies within the neighbourhood plan are not overridden by a new local plan.

neighbourhood development plan.[36]

3.19   The NPPF, paragraph 16, states that neighbourhoods should: (i) develop plans that support the strategic development needs set out in local plans, including policies for housing and economic development; (ii) plan positively to support local development, shaping and directing development in their area that is outside the strategic elements of the local plan; and (iii) identify opportunities to use neighbourhood development orders to enable developments that are consistent with their neighbourhood plan to proceed.

3.20   A neighbourhood plan must therefore address the development and use of land in the area of its operation. This is because, if successful at examination and referendum, the neighbourhood plan will become part of the statutory development plan once it has been brought into force by the LPA.[37] Because applications for planning permission are required to be determined in accordance with the development plan (unless material considerations indicate otherwise),[38]

---

[36]   PCPA 2004, s 38A(2) (as inserted by the LA 2011). The process for the making of neighbourhood development orders contained in TCPA 1990, Sch 4B (including the provision for independent examination of orders proposed by qualifying bodies and provision for the holding of referendums on orders proposed by those bodies) also applies in relation to the making of neighbourhood development plans, subject to the modifications set out in PCPA 2004, s 38C(5). The procedural requirements for making neighbourhood development plans are contained in Neighbourhood Planning (General) Regulations 2012, Pt 5, regs 14–20. On 1/10/2016, reg 17A was inserted into these regulations, setting out a timetable for decisions following an examiner's recommendations. The procedure for referendums is set out in the Neighbourhood Planning (Referendums) Regulations 2012.

[37]   As indicated, a 'made' neighbourhood development plan constitutes part of the development plan for the purposes of TCPA 1990, s 70 and PCPA 2004, s 38(5) and (6). A neighbourhood development plan may still be accorded significant weight in the planning judgment even when it is out of date (*Crane v Secretary of State for Communities and Local Government* [2015] EWHC 425 (Admin)). See *Crane* at [71] where Lindblom J said that neither NPPF, para 49 nor para 14 prescribes the weight to be given to policies in an out-of-date plan, although one may infer from para 49 that in the Government's view the weight to be given to out-of-date policies 'for the supply of housing' will normally be less, often considerably less, than the weight due to policies which provide fully for the requisite supply. The weight to be given to out-of-date policies will vary according to the circumstances, including, for example, the extent to which the policies actually fall short of providing for the required five-year supply and the prospect of development soon coming forward to make up the shortfall. In *Crane*, it was the finding of Lindblom J that the Secretary of State had not erred in law when upholding the refusal of planning permission for a housing development in a village. He had been correct to conclude that the development would conflict with a neighbourhood plan which had allocated other sites for development.

[38]   PCPA 2004, s 38(6).

policies contained in a neighbourhood plan accordingly assume considerable importance in the planning process.[39]

3.21   Except in one instance,[40] an LPA must make a neighbourhood development order where it has been passed by a majority voting in a referendum unless it gives rise to a breach of EU or human rights law. In such a case the LPA must make the plan as soon as reasonably practicable after the referendum has been held.[41]

Making a neighbourhood development plan[42]

3.22   The process is much the same as in the case of a neighbourhood development order. The process is begun by a qualifying body (i.e. a parish council or a body designated as a neighbourhood forum) and the procedure is generally the same as that in the case of neighbourhood development orders.[43]

3.23   A neighbourhood plan must specify the period for which it is to have effect, may not include provision about development that is excluded development and may not relate to more than one neighbourhood area.[44] If a policy contained in a neighbourhood plan conflicts with any other statement or

---

[39]   NPPG at Paragraph: 006 Reference ID: 41-006-20170728 (updated on 28/7/2017) states that 'A neighbourhood plan attains the same status as the local plan once it has been agreed at a referendum. At this point it comes into force as part of the statutory development plan. Applications for planning permission must be determined in accordance with the development plan, unless material considerations indicate otherwise (see s 38(6) of the Planning and Compulsory Purchase Act 2004)'.

[40]   PCPA 2004, s 38A(5). An LPA does not have to make a neighbourhood development order if there is a vote in favour of the order in one (but not the other) of the referendums held in a business development area.

[41]   PCPA 2004, s 38A(4), (6).

[42]   NPPG deals with neighbourhood plan-making at Paragraph: 040 Reference ID: 41-001-20160211 through to Paragraph 064: Reference ID: 41-064-20170728. See summary of key stages at NPPG at Paragraph: 080 Reference ID: 41-080-20170728, and an outline of the basic conditions that a draft neighbourhood plan or order must meet if it is to proceed to referendum at NPPG at Paragraph: 065 Reference ID: 41-65-20140306.

[43]   TCPA 1990, Sch 4B. The procedure for making neighbourhood development plans is set out in Neighbourhood Planning (General) Regulations 2012, regs 14–20 (as amended by the Neighbourhood Planning (General) (Amendment) Regulations 2015 and in the Neighbourhood Planning (General) and Development Management Procedure (Amendment) Regulations 2016). The detailed arrangements in relation to the holding of a referendum are also the same (Neighbourhood Planning (Referendums) Regulations 2012). A helpful summary of the process for making a neighbourhood development plan will be found in *R (Kebbell Developments Ltd) v Leeds City Council* [2016] EWHC 2664 (Admin) at [12].

[44]   PCPA 2004, s 38B(1).

information in the neighbourhood plan, the conflict must be resolved in favour of the policy.[45]

3.24   Once a neighbourhood plan is made, a number of provisions relating to neighbourhood development orders apply to the former with necessary modification. For instance: (a) revocation and modification of neighbourhood plans;[46] (b) challenge by a claim for judicial review brought within six weeks;[47] and (c) guidance issued by the Secretary of State.[48]

Environmental assessment

3.25   A neighbourhood plan must comply with the provisions of the Conservation of Habitats and Species Regulations 2017 (formerly the 2010 regulations as amended) and the EIA Regulations 2017.[49] In summary, a neighbourhood plan should not have a significant effect on a European site,[50] nor should a neighbourhood development order grant planning permission for development which is likely to have a significant effect on a European site.[51] Where the development proposed in a neighbourhood development order is EIA development[52] it should be subjected to an environmental impact assessment (EIA).

3.26   Reference should also be made to the requirements of the Environmental Assessment of Plans and Programmes Regulations 2004 (commonly referred to as the 'Strategic Environmental Assessment Regulations' or 'SEA') which implement the requirements of the European Directive 2001/42/EC (the 'SEA

---

[45]   PCPA 2004, s 38B(3). This is consistent with s 38(5), which provides that where there is a conflict between components of the development plan, the conflict must be resolved in favour of the policy which is contained in the last document to become part of the development plan.

[46]   PCPA 2004, s 38C(2)(c).

[47]   PCPA 2004, s 38C(2)(d). See *R (Oyston Estates Ltd) v Fylde BC* [2017] EWHC 3086 (Admin), which concerned time limits for the judicial review of a neighbourhood development plan where Kerr J considered the different stages of making a neighbourhood plan. Once the six-week period for challenging each stage has passed, it is immune from challenge. Flaws in the examiner's report may be relied on in a challenge by way of judicial review brought within six weeks of publication of the LPA's decision to hold a referendum.

[48]   PCPA 2004, s 38C(2)(e).

[49]   This is provided for in Neighbourhood Planning (General) Regulations 2012, Schs 2 and 3 (see regs 32–33).

[50]   Neighbourhood Planning (General) Regulations 2012, Sch 2, para 1.

[51]   Neighbourhood Planning (General) Regulations 2012, Sch 2, paras 2 and 3, which inserts a new reg 78A into the Conservation of Habitats and Species Regulations 2010 (SI 2010/490).

[52]   Namely EIA development within the meaning of the EIA Regulations 2017.

Directive') on the assessment of the effects of certain plans and programmes on the environment. SEA covers an area of strategic planning not covered by the EIA Regulations 2017 by requiring assessment of the environmental effects of plans which are likely to have significant effects on the environment. SEA requires an assessment by the responsible authority, before adoption, of the environmental implications of the plans and policies which form the basis of future development consents.

IMPACT OF NPPF ON NEIGHBOURHOOD PLANNING

3.27 As previously indicated, policies within the NPPF are a material consideration. Paragraph 14 explains that at the heart of the NPPF is a presumption in favour of sustainable development which should be seen as 'a golden thread running through both plan-making and decision-taking'. Paragraphs 183 to 185 deal specifically with neighbourhood plans:

> 183. Neighbourhood planning gives communities direct power to develop a shared vision for their neighbourhood and deliver the sustainable development they need. Parishes and neighbourhood forums can use neighbourhood planning to:
>
> - set planning policies through neighbourhood plans to determine decisions on planning applications; and
> - grant planning permission through Neighbourhood Development Orders and Community Right to Build Orders for specific development which complies with the order.
>
> 184. Neighbourhood planning provides a powerful set of tools for local people to ensure that they get the right types of development for their community. The ambition of the neighbourhood should be aligned with the strategic needs and priorities of the wider local area. Neighbourhood plans must be in general conformity with the strategic policies of the Local Plan. To facilitate this, local planning authorities should set out clearly their strategic policies for the area and ensure that an up-to-date Local Plan is in place as quickly as possible. Neighbourhood plans should reflect these policies and neighbourhoods should plan positively to support them. Neighbourhood plans and orders should not promote less development than set out in the Local Plan or undermine its strategic policies.
> 185. Outside these strategic elements, neighbourhood plans will be able to shape and direct sustainable development in their area. Once a neighbourhood plan has demonstrated its general conformity with the strategic policies of the Local Plan and is brought into force, the policies it contains take precedence over existing non-strategic policies in the Local Plan for that neighbourhood, where they are in conflict. Local planning authorities should avoid duplicating planning processes for non-strategic policies where a neighbourhood plan is in preparation.

Weight to be attached to an emerging neighbourhood plan in decision-making

3.28   Weight may be given by decision-makers to an emerging neighbourhood development plan. NPPF, paragraph 216, deals with the factors which are relevant in the case of emerging plans generally: (a) the stage of preparation of the emerging plan (the more advanced the stage of preparation, the greater the weight that may be given); (b) the extent to which there are unresolved objections to relevant policies (the less significant the unresolved objections, the greater the weight that may be given); and (c) the degree of consistency of the relevant policies in the emerging plan to the policies in the Framework, the greater the weight that may be given.

3.29   Accordingly, an emerging neighbourhood plan may well be a material consideration. Whilst a referendum ensures that the community has the final say on a neighbourhood plan, decision-makers should normally respect evidence of local support prior to the referendum when seeking to apply weight to an emerging neighbourhood plan. The consultation statement submitted with the draft neighbourhood plan should reveal the quality and effectiveness of the consultation that has informed the plan proposals.[53]

3.30   Selected provisions of the Neighbourhood Planning Act 2017 are now in force[54] which deal with the status of post-examination neighbourhood development plans and approved neighbourhood development plans. Further, with effect from 31/1/2018, under regulations made under the 2017 Act,[55] LPAs are now under a duty to notify neighbourhood planning groups in the advanced stage of developing a neighbourhood plan (i.e. where a neighbourhood development plan has been adopted or examined) of any upcoming planning applications (including applications for approval of reserved matters under an outline planning permission or alterations to those applications which have been accepted by the LPA) which could impact on the emerging neighbourhood plan (unless the qualifying body has confirmed in writing to the LPA that it does not

---

[53]   NPPG at Paragraph: 007 Reference ID: 41-007-20170728.

[54]   With effect from 19/7/2017 (Neighbourhood Planning Act 2017 (Commencement No 1) Regulations 2017, reg 2).

[55]   Neighbourhood Planning (General) and Development Management Procedure (Amendment) Regulations 2017 (which came into force on 31/1/2018). These regulations update notification of planning application requirements to neighbourhood planning qualifying bodies; introduce flexibility into the process for modifying neighbourhood plans that are intended to keep them up to date, so the process is proportionate to the changes being proposed; and facilitate the modification of a neighbourhood area and provide for what is to happen to a neighbourhood development plan or order that is already in force in that area.

wish to be so notified).[56] The regulations also implement a new streamlined procedure for the modification of a neighbourhood plan.[57] This procedure applies where a proposed modification to a plan already in force would materially affect the policies in the plan but which would not be so significant or substantial as to change the nature of the plan. Under the new procedure, once the modifications have been considered by an independent examiner, the recommendations will, in most cases, be binding and there will be no requirement for a referendum before the modified plan comes into force.

3.31 With effect from 31/7/2018, LPAs are also required to set out their policy for discharging their duty to give advice or assistance to qualifying bodies to facilitate proposals for neighbourhood development plans or neighbourhood development orders, including proposals for the modification of the former.[58]

3.32 An LPA is now required to have regard to a post-examination neighbourhood plan.[59] In practice, once an LPA has made a decision[60] that a referendum should be held on the draft plan, regard should be had to such plan in dealing with applications for planning permission in the area of the neighbourhood, so far as material to the application. Consistently with this, prior to the making of a neighbourhood plan, but following its approval at a referendum, it is deemed to form part of the development plan for that area. This

---

[56] Bringing into force reforms contained in the Neighbourhood Planning Act 2017, s 2, which operate to amend TCPA 1990, Sch 1, by the introduction of the amendments at paras 8 and 8A.

[57] Bringing into force reforms contained in Neighbourhood Planning Act 2017, s 4, which operate to effect amendments to PCPA 2004, ss 38A and 38C, and also introduce a new Sch A2 to that Act which deals with the procedure where a proposal is made for the modification of a neighbourhood development plan by the LPA.

[58] Bringing into force the reforms contained in Neighbourhood Planning Act 2017, s 6.

[59] Neighbourhood Planning Act 2017, s 1 amends TCPA 1990, s 70 (determination of applications for planning permission: general considerations), by the insertion into subsection (2) of (aza) which requires an LPA to have regard to a post-examination plan, so far as material to the application. A post-examination plan is one where: (a) an LPA has made a decision that a referendum or referendums are to be held on the draft plan; (b) the Secretary of State has directed that a referendum should be held; (c) an examiner has recommended that an LPA should make the draft plan; or (d) an examiner has recommended that an LPA should make the draft plan with modifications (unless in the case of (c) or (d) the LPA makes the draft plan with or without modifications, or decides not to make the draft plan), in which case the LPA must take the plan into account, as it would be if modified in accordance with the recommendations. A draft neighbourhood plan *ceases* to be a post-examination draft neighbourhood plan if the LPA is under no duty to make a neighbourhood development plan or if the draft plan would breach any EU obligation or infringe the Human Rights Act 1998, or if a single referendum is held on the draft plan and half or fewer of those voting in the referendum vote in favour of the plan or where two referendums are held on the plan (i.e. where the plan relates to a neighbourhood area designated as a business area under TCPA 1990, s 61H) and half or fewer of those voting in each of the referendums vote in favour of the plan.

[60] Under TCPA 1990, Sch 4B, para 12(4).

ceases to be the case where (rarely) the LPA decides not to make the neighbourhood plan.[61]

What if there is an emerging neighbourhood plan but the LPA cannot show a five-year supply of deliverable housing sites?

3.33   Decision-makers will still have to give weight to relevant policies in the emerging neighbourhood plan even though these policies should not be considered up to date. Documentation produced in support of, or in response to, emerging neighbourhood plans may also be of assistance to decision-makers.[62]

What if there is a neighbourhood plan in force in the LPA's area but the LPA cannot show a five-year supply of deliverable housing sites?

3.34   A Written Ministerial Statement (WMS) on 12/12/2016 dealt with decision-making on planning applications and appeals in cases where the LPA could not demonstrate a five-year supply of housing land, but where there was a neighbourhood plan in force. The WMS provided that neighbourhood plans should not be deemed to be out of date (under NPPF, paragraph 49) if: (a) the WMS is less than two years old or where the neighbourhood plan had been part of the development plan for two years or less;[63] (b) the neighbourhood plan allocated sites for housing (although the WMS did not specify the minimum number of allocations for the policy to apply); and (c) the LPA could demonstrate a three-year supply of housing land as against its five-year housing requirement.[64]

---

[61]   Neighbourhood Planning Act 2017, s 3.

[62]   NPPG at Paragraph: 082 Reference ID: 41-082-20160211.

[63]   On 7/2/2017 the Secretary of State for Housing, Communities and Local Government published a Housing White Paper, consulting on a wide variety of issues, including proposed changes to housing policy and guidance. It contained a commitment to continue to provide for protection of neighbourhood plans as set out in the WMS and sought views on how housing need could be met.

[64]   See *Richborough Estates Ltd v Secretary of State for Housing, Communities and Local Government* [2018] EWHC 33 (Admin), where a legal challenge to the WMS failed. What it means is that added weight may be given to neighbourhood plans in those cases where the LPA has less than a five-year supply of housing land. See Dove J at [44]–[46], where he said that it was obvious that the purpose of the WMS, and the subsequent addition to the NPPG, was to change national policy in relation to housing applications in areas with a recently made neighbourhood plan. NPPF, para 49 continues to apply as a trigger for the 'tilted balance' in accordance with *Hopkins Homes* [2017] UKSC 37. The effect of the WMS and the NPPG is that when assessing the 'tilted balance', significant weight should be given to the neighbourhood plan if the three criteria in the WMS and the NPPG apply. The *Richborough Estates* case had been stayed pending the Supreme Court's decision of the *Hopkins Homes* case. In that case, Lord Carnwath emphasised that the NPPF was no more than 'guidance' and as such a 'material

3.35   Subsequently, the Supreme Court in *Secretary of State for Communities and Local Government v Hopkins Homes Ltd*[65] has determined that weight remains a matter of planning judgment. In the circumstances, where the development plan is absent or silent, or relevant policies are out of date, NPPF, paragraph 14, states that permission should be granted unless the adverse impacts of doing so would significantly and demonstrably outweigh the benefits when assessed against the policies within the NPPF as a whole (or restrictive policies in the NPPF indicate that development should be restricted). It follows that decision-makers (in dealing with applications under this head) should give specific consideration to policies in the NPPF which are concerned with neighbourhood planning. Reference has already been made to NPPF, paragraphs 184 and 185. Reference should also be made to paragraph 198, which provides that where a planning application conflicts with a neighbourhood plan, planning permission should not normally be granted. Clearly decision-makers must take into account the impact of granting permission in the case of an application which conflicts with a neighbourhood plan. It follows that where the criteria in the WMS apply, decision-makers should still give significant weight to the neighbourhood plan despite the fact that the LPA cannot demonstrate a five-year supply of deliverable housing land.[66]

THE COST OF NEIGHBOURHOOD PLANNING

3.36   It will be up to the parish or town council or neighborhood forum to pay for the preparation of a neighbourhood plan. The LPA has a duty to pay the costs of the examination and referendum. The cost of producing a neighbourhood plan will depend largely on the scope, complexity and size of the plan. The latest government estimates suggest that plans could cost between £20,000 and £86,000 and take up to one to two years to prepare.

---

consideration' for the purposes of TCPA 1990, s 70(2) and did not displace the primacy given by statute to the statutory development plan. Thus, it must be exercised consistently with, and not so as to displace or distort, the statutory scheme. In *Hopkins Homes* the Supreme Court examined the relationship between paras 14 and 49 of the NPPF. The Supreme Court clarified that the absence of a five-year housing land supply triggered the NPPF, para 14, presumption. It was a matter of planning judgment as to whether or not policies for the supply of housing were out of date under NPPF, para 49, which, following *Hopkins Homes*, is construed narrowly.

[65]   [2017] UKSC 37.

[66]   NPPG at Paragraph: 007 Reference ID: 41-007-20170728 (updated on 28/7/2017). See also the section on neighbourhood plans in consultation for the NPPG issued by DHCLG in March 2018 at pp 33–36, which includes guidance on housing requirements and allocations in designated neighbourhood areas and when neighbourhood plans are protected from the presumption in favour of sustainable development.

Chapter 4

Development Control

BASIS OF DEVELOPMENT CONTROL

4.1   The basis of development control is that planning permission is required for the carrying out of any development of land.[1] The term 'development'[2] means:

(a)   the carrying out of:

    (i)   building,[3]

---

[1]   TCPA 1990, s 57(1). This section lays out the basis for development control.

[2]   TCPA 1999, s 55.

[3]   The term 'building operations' is defined in TCPA 1990, s 55(1A) as including: (a) the demolition of buildings; (b) rebuilding; (c) structural alterations or additions to buildings; and (d) any other operations normally undertaken by a person carrying on business as a builder (it is clear that this definition will include almost any substantial work on land – the test is whether the physical character of the land is altered (*Cheshire CC v Woodward* [1962] 2 QB 126)). Clearly, issues of size (see *Buckinghamshire County Council v Callingham* [1952] 1 All ER 1166 – where an enforcement notice requiring the removal of a model village was upheld); degree of permanence (see *Measor v Secretary of State for the Environment, Transport and Regions* [1998] 4 PLR 93 – where the court held that the stationing of 18 mobile and touring caravans for residential use did not constitute 'buildings on the ground that they lacked the degree of permanence and attachment to constitute buildings'); and physical attachment to the site (see *Tewkesbury Borough Council v Keeley* [2004] EWHC 2594 (QB) – where it was held that sheds on wheels did not constitute buildings) will be crucial. Clearly, if a structure is not a building, then there could be no building operation in relation to it. See also *Skerritts of Nottingham Ltd v Secretary of State for the Environment, Transport and Regions (No 2)* [2000] 2 PLR 102, where the erection and siting of a large marquee in the grounds of an hotel for nine months of the year was found to constitute development, as was the erection of substantial polytunnels for growing fruit in *R (Hall Hunter Partnership) v First Secretary of State* [2006] EWHC 2482 (Admin). The term 'building' is defined in s 336(1) as including 'any structure or erection, and any part of a building, as so defined, but does not include plant or machinery comprised in a building'. This is a wide definition and would include structures which would not ordinarily be described as buildings, but as chattels, such as the heavy, but movable, poultry units in *R (Save Woolley Action Group Ltd) v Bath and North East Somerset Council* [2012] EWHC 2161 (Admin).

(ii)   engineering,[4]

(iii) mining or other operations,[5]

in, on, over or under land (which is described as 'operational development');[6] or

(b)   making any material change in the use of any buildings or other land. Where development is carried out in breach of planning control, it is unlawful and may be the subject of enforcement action by the local planning authority (LPA).[7]

4.2   Planning law is therefore concerned with either: (a) operational development, or (b) making a material change of use of any building or other land. The former is concerned with the physical alteration of the land, whereas the latter is concerned with activity taking place on the land, but which does not alter its physical characteristics.[8] In some cases they overlap, as where a building is to be erected or converted for the purposes of an entirely new use.[9] Further,

---

4   The term 'engineering operations' will include the formation or laying out of means of access to highways (s 336(1)) and will no doubt also cover works which are designed by and/or supervised by civil or traffic engineers (see *Fayrewood Fish Farms Ltd v Secretary of State for the Environment* [1984] JPL 267).

5   The term 'other operations' is not to be treated as *eiusdem generis* with the operations which precede this expression, even if (doubtfully) there was a class or genus to such operations (*Coleshill and District Investment Co Ltd v Minister of Housing and Local Government* [1969] 2 All ER 525) and is therefore not limited to building, engineering or mining operations. It was, for instance, found to be wide enough to include other significant operations affecting land, such as the placement of the movable poultry units in *R (Save Woolley Action Group Ltd) v Bath and North East Somerset Council* [2012] EWHC 2161 (Admin), or the removal of topsoil.

6   *Beronstone Ltd v First Secretary of State* [2006] EWHC 2391 (Admin), where a local authority issued an enforcement notice in a case where, within the Green Belt and an AONB, 554 wooden posts had been laid out so as to define the boundaries of 40 plots of land and a network of accessways, without planning permission. The inspector, having taken account of the extent, visibility, grid-like patterns and degree of permanence of the posts, found that they had a detrimental effect on the land and were of sufficient substance, scale and type to amount to 'development' within the meaning of TCPA 1990, s 55, and the enforcement notice was accordingly upheld. The court upheld the inspector's decision, holding that the issue of development was one of fact and degree based on the individual circumstances of the case. The term 'development' in TCPA 1990, s 55 will also include the formation and laying out of means of access to highways and will no doubt cover works which are designed by and/or supervised by civil or traffic engineers (see *Fayrewood Fish Farms Ltd v Secretary of State for the Environment* [1984] JPL 267).

7   TCPA 1990, s 172. The county planning authority may also be an appropriate authority to issue an enforcement notice in its capacity of mineral planning authority (Sch 1, paras 1 and 11).

8   *Parkes v Secretary of State for the Environment* [1979] 1 All ER 211 at 213.

9   Reference should be made to TCPA 1990, s 75(2) and (3), which provides that a planning permission may (in the terms of the grant or as a condition) specify the purpose for which a new building may be used (or even exclude the operation of the Town and Country Planning (Use Classes) Order 1987 (SI 1987/764) (as amended) (Use Classes Order 1987) or restrict future use

development projects may be large enough to involve more than one operation or use which cannot reasonably be regarded as being ancillary to the other and which may well require separate consents.[10]

OPERATIONS WHICH DO NOT CONSTITUTE DEVELOPMENT

4.3   There are exceptions to the system such that certain operations or uses will *not* be taken to involve development of the land, in which case no planning permission is required. For instance, works of maintenance, improvement or other alteration of any building which affect only the interior of the building or which do not materially affect the external appearance of a building, will not constitute development.[11]

---

in a case where planning permission may not even be required), but if it does not, then it is implied that the building may be used for the purpose for which it is 'designed' which, for these purposes, means was intended as reflected by the terms of the application and any terms of limitation contained in the grant such that a change to any other use (provided it constitutes development within the meaning of s 55) would require permission. See *Wilson v West Sussex County Council* [1963] 2 QB 764; *East Suffolk County Council v Secretary of State for the Environment* (1972) 70 LGR 595; *Kwik Save Discount Group Ltd v Secretary of State for Wales* [1981] JPL 198 at 201–202; *Harding v Secretary of State for the Environment* [1984] JPL 503; *Barnett v Secretary of State for Communities and Local Government* [2010] 1 P & CR 8; *Peel Land and Property Investments Plc v Hyndburn Borough Council* [2013] EWCA Civ 1680.

10   In *West Bowers Farm Products v Essex County Council* (1985) 50 P & CR 368, a development involving the extraction of minerals on a substantial scale in the course of engineering operations on agricultural land involved two activities and could not be described solely as engineering operations for the purposes of agriculture. This meant that the claimants were unable to rely on permitted development rights, but as operations for those purposes and partly of working and winning minerals. See also *R v Durham City Council ex parte Lowther* [2002] P & CR 22; *R (Edwards) v Environment Agency (No 2)* [2006] EWCA Civ 877 (affirmed by the House of Lords in [2008] UKHL 22).

11   TCPA 1990, s 55(2)(a); although planning permission will be required: (a) for increases of floor space of more than 200 square metres where the building is used for the retail sale of goods other than hot food (s 55(2A)); (b) where the building is a listed building (LBA 1990, s 9); or (c) in the case of internal works which are part and parcel of, or integral to, a material change of use, for which planning permission is required (*Somak Travel Ltd v Secretary of State for the Environment* [1987] JPL 630). The impact of works which may affect the external appearance of a building is a subjective one, and the exemption was made out in *Kensington and Chelsea Royal London Borough Council v CG Hotels* (1980) 41 P & CR 40, where the work involved in installing floodlights in the basement area and on the first floor balconies of an hotel was not an operation amounting to development. In *Burroughs Day v Bristol City Council* [1996] 1 PLR 78, the court held that to materially affect the external appearance of a building, the alterations had to be judged by reference to the building as a whole. The test was not whether the works merely affected the exterior of the building, but whether they materially affected its 'external appearance'. In this case, the roof alterations were not visible from any of the surrounding streets, and the court held

4.4   It should be noted that deemed permission is granted: (a) for works of enlargement, improvement or other alteration of a dwelling-house (subject to certain limitations);[12] (b) for other specified building operations including works reasonably necessary for the purposes of agriculture within an agricultural unit;[13] and (c) for non-domestic alterations or extensions, etc. (again subject to specified limitations).[14]

4.5   Other exceptions to development (and the need for planning permission) include:

(a)   the carrying out on land by a local highway authority within the boundaries of a road any works required for the maintenance or improvement of the road (but, in the case of any such works which are not exclusively for the maintenance of the road, not including any works which may have significant adverse effects on the environment);[15]

---

that they did not therefore constitute development. The courts will also be astute to ensure that alterations are not on such a large scale that they go beyond maintenance or improvement and amount to the reconstruction of a building, particularly where work is carried out in stages (see *Street v Essex County Council* (1965) 193 EG 537, DC; *Larkin v Basildon District Council* [1980] JPL 407; *Hewlett v Secretary of State for the Environment* [1983] JPL 105).

12   GPDO, art 3, Sch 2, Pt 1.

13   GPDO, art 3, Sch 2, Pt 6.

14   GPDO, art 3, Sch 2, Pt 7.

15   TCPA 1990, s 55(2)(b). The creation of a 'cycle super-highway' in London was not 'development' within the meaning of TCPA 1990, s 55(1) and did not require planning permission. The construction works were works of improvement carried out by a highway authority within the boundaries of a road and were therefore exempted by s 55(2)(b) (see *R (Licensed Taxi Drivers Association) v Transport for London* [2016] EWHC 233 (Admin)). See also *R (Dillner) v Sheffield City Council* [2016] EWHC 945 (Admin), where the felling of roadside trees by a highway authority as part of its duties under the Highways Act 1980 was found not to be 'development' for the purposes of s 55 and accordingly did not require planning permission. Gilbart J found that the 1980 and 1990 Acts drew a clear distinction between maintenance (including repair), which it was the authority's duty to perform, and improvement, which it had a power to carry out. The duty to maintain was directed at the fabric of the highway and the interests of passage and re-passage, not at retaining the trees growing within it. Provided tree felling was carried out under a duty to maintain, no consent under s 211 of the 1990 Act was needed. The requirement in the Town and Country Planning (Tree Preservation) (England) Regulations 2012 (SI 2012/605) for environmental assessment applied only to projects of deforestation on sites of at least one hectare in size, which was not the case in this instance. At most, the fact that a tree could contribute to the appearance and character of a conservation area could be a material consideration, but there was no evidence that the authority or their contactors had failed to take it into account. Furthermore, it was also found that the EIA Regulations 2011, now superseded by the EIA Regulations 2017 (which deal with the necessity for an environmental assessment in the case of development which may have significant adverse effects on the environment), are not directed at highway maintenance or repair but are only applied where a feature of the road was replaced by something different. Removing a tree from a highway did not amount to such a change. It followed that as the works did not amount to development within the

(b) works by local authorities or statutory undertakers in connection with sewers, mains, pipes, cables or other apparatus, including the breaking open of any street or other land;[16]

(c) the use of any buildings or other land within the curtilage of a dwelling-house for any purpose incidental to the enjoyment of the dwelling-house;[17]

(d) the use of any land for the purposes of agriculture or forestry and the use of any building occupied together with land so used;[18]

(e) no development is involved by a change of use from one purpose to another within one of the use classes specified in an order made by the Secretary of State under this section;[19]

(f) the demolition of any description of a building specified in a direction given by the Secretary of State to LPAs or to a particular LPA.[20]

---

meaning of s 55, and as no environmental impact assessment was required, there was held to be no duty of consultation at any point. There are also permitted development rights under the GPDO (art 3, Sch 2, Pt 9, Classes A–E) for works carried out by, respectively, highway authorities outside but adjoining the boundary of an existing highway (provided they are required or incidental to the maintenance or improvement of the highway) and whoever undertakes works in relation to unadopted streets and private ways.

[16] TCPA 1990, s 55(2)(c). There are also unrestricted development rights under the GPDO (art 3, Sch 2, Pt 10) for the same operations. Further, Pipe-Lines Act 1962, s 5(2) provides that work on pipe-lines is also deemed not to involve development.

[17] TCPA 1990, s 55(2)(d); s 55(3) provides for the avoidance of doubt: (a) that the use as two or more separate dwelling-houses of any building previously used as a single dwelling-house involves a material change of use of the building and of each part of it which is so used (i.e. no sub-division without planning permission – nor are there any permitted development rights which would permit this); and (b) the deposit of refuse or waste on land also involves a material change of use notwithstanding that the land is comprised in a site already used for that purpose if: (i) the superficial area of the deposit is extended; or (ii) the height of the deposit is extended and exceeds the level of the land adjoining the site. Similarly, s 55(5) also provides (without prejudice to any regulations relating to the control of advertisements) that the use for display of advertisements on any external part of a building which is not normally used for that purpose shall be treated as involving a material change of use of that part of the building.

[18] TCPA 1990, s 55(2)(e).

[19] TCPA 1990, s 55(2)(f); the current Use Classes Order was made in 1987, replacing that made in 1972.

[20] TCPA 1990, s 55(2)(g). Despite the introduction of s 55(1A) (which includes demolition as a 'building operation'), s 55(2)(g) still leaves it open to the Secretary of State to exclude the demolition of certain types of building from the scope of development. This he did in the Town and Country Planning (Demolition – Description of Buildings) Direction 1995, contained in the (now cancelled) Circular 10/95. By virtue of para 2(1), the Direction excluded from the definition of development the demolition of any building which was listed, or in a conservation area or which was a scheduled monument and any building other than a dwelling-house or a building adjoining a dwelling-house. However, these provisions were ruled unlawful in *Save Britain's Heritage v Secretary of State for Communities and Local Government* [2011] EWCA Civ 334, which meant that planning permission was required for demolition in such cases. These difficulties were, however, overcome by the Town and Country Planning (Description of Buildings) Direction 2014, which preserves the position in two cases of demolition under 1995 Direction, para 2(1), namely: (a) any building with a cubic content of less than 50 cubic metres

A MATERIAL CHANGE IN THE USE OF ANY BUILDINGS OR OTHER LAND

4.6   Buildings or land (described as the 'planning unit' which is a judge-made concept for deciding whether there has been a material change of use) may have more than one use.[21] Some activities may be ancillary to the primary use of the land (such as storage space in a retail unit or offices attached to a manufacturing

---

measured externally; and (b) the whole or part of any gate, fence, wall or other means of enclosure unless in a conservation area, neither of which will constitute development. However, it should be noted that the GPDO (art 3, Sch 2, Class B of Pt 11) now provides for demolition, subject to the limitations and conditions of that Part. Demolition will not be permitted: (a) if the building has been rendered unsafe or otherwise uninhabitable by the action or inaction of any person with an interest in the land on which the building stands and it is practicable to secure safety or health by works or repair or works for affording temporary support; (b) in the case of the demolition of an unlisted building in a conservation area; or (c) if the building is used for a purpose falling within Class A4 (i.e. a drinking establishment) and is a listed community asset or in relation to which the LPA has notified the developer of a nomination to list the building as a community asset. In most cases, therefore, there will be no need to apply for planning permission to demolish a building unless the LPA has made an art 4 direction restricting the permitted development rights that apply to the demolition. Although a planning application to demolish a listed building is not normally needed, listed building consent may well be required if the building is in a conservation area. Demolition is also dealt with under the Building Act 1984 (s 80 deals with the requirement of notice to a local authority of intended demolition except for demolition: (a) in pursuance of a demolition order or obstructive building order; or (b) of an internal part of a building, where the building is occupied and it is intended that it should continue to be occupied; (c) of a building that is (measured externally) no more than 1,750 cubic feet; or (d) in the case of a greenhouse, conservatory, shed or prefabricated garage forming part of a larger building; or (e) of an agricultural building unless it is contiguous to another building that is not itself an agricultural building – it is an offence under s 80(4) to begin a demolition unless a s 80 notice has been given and either the local authority has given notice under s 81 or a period of six weeks has elapsed from the giving of the s 80 notice to which the local authority has not responded (or such longer period as the person who gave the s 80 notice may allow)). The local authority's s 81 notice may specify conditions which need to be met, which may include precautions to protect adjoining properties and the public. Demolition work must also comply with the Construction (Design and Management) Regulations 2015 (SI 2015/51). Building regulations relating to site preparation and resistance to contaminants and moisture will also need to be met once the preparation work starts on site.

21   *Burdle v Secretary of State for the Environment* [1972] 1 WLR 1207, where Bridge J said at p 1212 that it would be 'a useful working rule to assume that the unit of occupation is the appropriate planning unit, unless and until some smaller unit can be recognised as the site of activities which amount in substance to a separate use both physically and functionally'. See also *South Staffordshire DC v Secretary of State for the Environment* [1987] JPL 635 at 639, where it was said by Glidewell LJ that the phrase 'planning unit' was a useful shorthand to describe the area of land or part of a building or group of buildings to which an LPA should have regard when considering whether there had been a material change in the use of any buildings or other land. It was thus the appropriate area to consider in order to decide whether land has an established use; see also *R (Sellars) v Basingstoke and Deane BC* [2013] EWHC 3673 (Admin), where the identification of the relevant planning unit was considered to be a material consideration on an application for a certificate of lawful use under TCPA 1990, s 191.

facility) and will not require a separate planning permission, provided they can reasonably be said to be linked with the primary use of the planning unit. On the other hand, when the primary use of the planning unit comes to an end, the ancillary use ends with it.[22] The ancillary link may also be lost where it is functionally severed from the primary use[23] or where it ceases to be ancillary and becomes a primary use in its own right (i.e. an ancillary use cannot be converted into an independent primary use).[24] It is also possible that a change of ownership or in the identity of the person carrying out the ancillary activity may give rise to a material change in use. The result in all these cases is to sever the ancillary use from the primary use, and thereby give rise to a new primary use for which a separate planning permission would be required. It would thus mean that the land has a mixed or dual use or it may even have been split into two separate planning units.

4.7   In considering whether there has been a material change of use, the starting point is to look at the existing primary use of the planning unit and the ancillary uses which are incidental to it. If the use proposed is significant and falls within neither of these categories there is likely to have been a material change of use.[25]

---

[22]   *David W Barling v Secretary of State for the Environment and Swale District Council* [1980] JPL 594, where land was used for the storage of building materials in connection with the building of two houses. An enforcement notice was served when the storage use was continued in connection with a general building business. It was held that when storage became independent of the building operations, it constituted a material change of use.

[23]   *Peake v Secretary of State for Wales* (1971) 70 LGR 98 (repairs carried out on a private car in a domestic garage but where the ancillary link is severed when cars belonging to others come to be repaired on a commercial basis); *Wood v Secretary of State for the Environment* [1973] 1 WLR 707 at 709 (sale of farm produce from a farm regarded as an ancillary activity, but that status may be lost if produce imported from outside is sold); *Lloyd-Jones v Minister of Housing and Local Government* (1967) 204 EG 1200; *Bromley London Borough Council v Hoeltschi (George) and Son Ltd* (1977) 244 EG 49.

[24]   *Trio Thames Ltd v Secretary of State for the Environment* [1984] JPL 183, where, in a case involving a building with planning permission for a restaurant with dine and dance facilities which was being used as a night club and restaurant, the Divisional Court held that the Secretary of State was right to regard the planning permission as one for a primary use for a restaurant and thus not authorising a dual or mixed use for a restaurant and night club. See also *G Percy Trentham Ltd v Gloucestershire County Council* [1966] 1 All ER 702; *Brazil (Concrete) Ltd v Amersham Rural District Council and Minister of Housing and Local Government* (1967) 18 P & CR 396. *Percy Trentham* was a case where the previous use of the building was for housing farm machinery, and the issue was whether a successor could use it for storing building materials. It was held that the farm unit had to be looked at as a whole and the building in question could not be severed from the rest of the farmhouse and buildings. *Brazil (Concrete) Ltd* was another case where the former primary use had ended and was unable to support a change of use to a different class of primary use under the Use Classes Order 1987.

[25]   The question is whether a new use is substantially different in nature from the former use: for instance, has there, as a matter of fact and degree, been a change in the character of the use? (See *Birmingham Corp v Minister of Housing and Local Government* [1964] 1 QB 178; *Blackpool BC v Secretary of State for the Environment* (1980) 40 P & CR 104; *Clarke v Minister of Housing*

It is, of course, easy to recognise that the conversion of a single dwelling-house into flats will constitute a material change of use,[26] as will a change from residential to industrial use, but it becomes more difficult, for instance, when an existing use has merely been intensified.[27] Essentially, it is a matter of fact and degree for the LPA (or Secretary of State) to determine whether an established use remains substantially unchanged,[28] although in most cases one need look no further than the categories of use within the Use Classes Order 1987 (where a change of use for another purpose within the same use class will not constitute development) where the intensification of a use within a particular category of use is such as to take the use outside that category altogether.[29]

4.8   Certain elements of use may be indicative of a material change of use:

---

and Local Government 64 LGR 346.) A useful example is *Harrods Ltd v Secretary of State for the Environment, Transport and the Regions* [2002] EWCA Civ 412, which involved an appeal against a decision upholding the refusal of an application for a certificate of lawful use in relation to the proposed use of the roof of the London store for helicopter landing solely by the owner of Harrods in connection with his position as chairman and his work in directing the day-to-day operations within the department store, involving no more than ten landings per week, on the basis that the proposed use would be incidental or ancillary to the use of Harrods as a department store. The inspector thought it was, as it were, a car parking area, but the court concurred with the Secretary of State in rejecting that approach. The Court of Appeal dismissed the owner's appeal, holding that where an application is made for a certificate of lawful use under TCPA 1990, s 192, the test to be applied was whether the proposed use was 'ordinarily incidental' or ancillary to the primary use of the planning unit. The introduction of a helicopter landing pad to the roof of Harrods store amounted to a change of use which was not ordinarily incidental to its primary retail use. Schiemann LJ said at [23] that:

'A person who moves next door to a shop can expect normal shopping activities to go on there without there being a requirement for planning permission. A person who moves next door to Harrods can expect things which are normal there and in other emporia of that size. But if what an appellant wants to introduce is not generally associated with what goes on in shops then it seems probable that Parliament intended that neighbours should have the chance to object to the grant of planning permission and thus force the owner to go through the appropriate procedures to get his planning permission. And it is probably a fair comment (although legally irrelevant) that the fact that this appeal is being pursued through one court after another is an indication that Harrods are not particularly hopeful of actually getting a planning permission. In any event, they have chosen not to apply. They may turn out to have been unduly pessimistic. That is not for this court to judge.'

Sedley LJ considered that the sole question was 'what activities legitimately form part of the extant shop use'.

26   TCPA 1990, s 55(3)(a).

27   In cases where there has been a change in the character of the use, it is more likely that there will have been a material change of use.

28   *Westminster City Council v British Waterways Board* [1985] AC 676.

29   *Brooks and Burton Ltd v Secretary of State for the Environment* [1977] 1 WLR 1294.

(a) Alteration in the character of the land and buildings.[30]

(b) Intensification in the existing use or activity taking place on the land.[31]

(c) Discontinuance of use for a lengthy period followed by a resumption of such use.[32]

(d) Where the change of use materially affects the land for other reasons, such as its impact on local amenities.[33]

(e) If the change is *de minimis* it will not be material.

---

[30] *Guildford Rural District Council v Penny* [1959] 2 QB 112, where the use of a field for stationing caravans had increased from eight to 27 was found not to constitute a material change of use, as the land continued to be used as a caravan site. In other words, the character of the land was unchanged. See also *East Barnet Urban District Council v British Transport Commission* [1962] 2 QB 484, where there had been no material change of use, as the land had always been used as a storage and transport depot, even though what was stored and by whom had changed.

[31] *Brooks and Burton Ltd v Secretary of State for the Environment* [1977] 1 WLR 1294; *Birmingham Corporation v Minister of Housing and Local Government and Habib Ullah* [1964] 1 QB 178 (two single dwelling-houses used by several families); *Peake v Secretary of State for Wales* (1971) 22 P & CR 889 (use of private garage intensified to full-time vehicle repairs). It is plain that a mere increase in use will not give rise to a material change of use. What matters is whether the intensification of use has brought about a definable change in the character of the use made of the land (*Hertfordshire County Council v Secretary of State for Communities and Local Government* [2012] EWHC 277 (Admin) at [35]–[40] (which was largely upheld in the Court of Appeal at [2012] EWCA Civ 1473, see also *R (Reed) v Secretary of State for Communities and Local Government* [2014] EWCA Civ 241 at [26])). In short, the mere intensification of use will not of itself give rise to a material change of use. See *Royal London Borough of Kensington and Chelsea v Secretary of State for the Environment* [1981] JPL 50, where the authority alleged a breach of planning control by the use of a garden as an extension to the restaurant. There was an existing permitted use for a restaurant and as the planning unit consisted of the restaurant plus garden, there was no breach of planning control. In other words, additional tables in the garden did not give rise to a material change of use by intensification of the restaurant use. Also see *Blum v Secretary of State for the Environment* [1987] JPL 278 (to cross the permitted line, any intensification of use must also be accompanied by a material change in the character of a use of the planning unit, as may well arise in circumstances where there has been a substantial intensification of a use).

[32] The question is whether a reasonable person would consider that the former use had been abandoned, such that if it is resumed after a lengthy period, a decision-maker would be entitled to find that there will have been a material change of use requiring planning permission (*Hartley v Minister of Housing* [1970] 1 QB 413; *Maddern v Secretary of State for the Environment* [1980] JPL 676; *Secretary of State for the Environment v Hughes* (2000) 80 P & CR 397, CA).

[33] Where the nature of the use has changed such as where the number of people using the land increases, where it is likely to cause more noise or where it otherwise impacts on the neighbourhood. See *Devonshire County Council v Allens Caravans (Estates) Ltd* (1962) 14 P & CR 440 at 441; *Williams v Minister of Housing and Local Government* (1967) 18 P & CR 514 (owner of nursery garden using timber building to sell not only home grown produce, but imported fruit as well); *Blum (Lilo) v Secretary of State for the Environment and Richmond London Borough Council* [1987] JPL 278 (livery stables being used as a riding school).

(f)	Where the planning unit has been divided into two or more units. This is already the case in relation to a dwelling-house,[34] but may also arise in other cases which are not covered by the Use Classes Order 1987.

Identifying primary uses or changes of use

4.9	Identifying primary uses or changes of use is never easy. The following are examples of this:

(a)	There is, for instance, a distinction between temporary car parking and commercial storage.[35]

(b)	In the case of caravans stationed on land, in assessing whether there has been a material change of use, the questions to ask are: (i) what is the use of the planning unit; (ii) whether the effect of the introduction of the caravans, and the use to which they are put, affected the use of the planning unit; and (iii) whether there had been a material change of use (or, put another way, did the purpose for which the caravan was to be used fit in with the existing use of the land).[36] It follows that if the use of a residential caravan is wholly unconnected with the primary or ancillary uses of the planning unit, there will have been a material change of use, such as the use of residential caravans stationed on agricultural land as holiday accommodation.

(c)	In the case of housing, there are a number of examples such as the change of use of a single dwelling-house to a dwelling-house in multiple occupation where lodgers or tenants have their own rooms.[37] A change of use may occur when a property already in multiple occupation comes to be used as a guest house[38] or as a hostel for the homeless,[39] or where a seasonal caravan site is used for permanent residential purposes.[40] Although the relationship

34	TCPA 1990, s 55(3)(a).

35	*Crawley Borough Council v Hickmet Ltd* [1998] JPL 210. This was a case where the first instance court had found that the use of land for airport parking constituted commercial storage for which there was an established use which meant that there had been no change of use. The appeal was allowed on the basis that these were separate uses.

36	*Deakin v First Secretary of State* [2006] EWHC 3402 (Admin) (applying *Wealden District Council v Secretary of State for the Environment* (1988) 56 P & CR 286). See also *Restormel Borough Council v Secretary of State for the Environment and Rabey* [1982] JPL 785.

37	*Birmingham Corporation v Habib Ullah* [1964] 1 QB 178; *Clarke v Minister of Housing and Local Government* (1966) 18 P & CR 82; *Hammersmith London Borough Council v Secretary of State for the Environment* (1975) 73 LGR 288; *Mornford Investments Ltd v Minister of Housing and Local Government* [1970] 2 All ER 253; *Mayflower (Cambridge) Ltd v Secretary of State for the Environment* (1975) 30 P & CR 28; *Duffy v Pilling* (1977) 33 P & CR 85; *Lipson v Secretary of State for the Environment* (1976) 33 P & CR 95.

38	*Winmill v Secretary of State for the Environment* [1982] JPL 445.

39	*Panayi v Secretary of State for the Environment* [1982] 50 P & CR 109.

40	*Forest of Dean District Council v Secretary of State for the Environment* [1995] JPL 937.

between residents living in the same dwelling-house is clearly material as to whether they are in fact living together as a single household, this is not necessarily conclusive.[41] It is also clear that in determining whether a unit of residential accommodation was in use as a single dwelling-house, regard should be had as to whether the unit provided the facilities required for normal private domestic life. There was no requirement for the unit to be used as a permanent home. This meant that residential accommodation does not necessarily lose its characteristic of a single dwelling-house if it was used as holiday accommodation, although a material change of use would always be a question of fact and degree in each case, depending on whether the character of the use had changed.[42]

Activities which do not constitute a material change of use

4.10   Reference is now made to certain uses which do not constitute development:

(a)   use within the curtilage of a dwelling-house for any purpose incidental to the enjoyment of the dwelling-house;[43]
(b)   the use of land for the purposes of agriculture or forestry;[44]
(c)   use of buildings or land for a purpose of any class specified in the Use Classes Order 1987.[45]

4.11   These excluded uses will now be addressed in turn.

Use not involving development within the curtilage of a dwelling-house for any purpose incidental to the enjoyment of the dwelling-house as such

4.12   This section is concerned with use rather than operational development. In other words, even though a change of use is permitted, any necessary building work may require planning permission. Subject to specified exceptions and subject to various conditions, certain development is permitted within the curtilage of a dwelling-house under article 3 of, and Part 1 (Classes A–H) of Schedule 2 to, the GPDO.

---

[41]   *R (Hossack) v Kettering Borough Council* [2002] EWCA Civ 886.

[42]   *Moore v Secretary of State for the Environment, Transport and the Regions* [1998] 2 PLR 65; *Blackpool Borough Council v Secretary of State for the Environment* [1980] JPL 527.

[43]   TCPA 1990, s 55(2)(d).

[44]   TCPA 1990, s 55(2)(e).

[45]   TCPA 1990, s 55(2)(f).

4.13   The curtilage of a dwelling-house is normally a small area of land attached to and containing a dwelling-house.[46] Nor is it necessarily coincident with the extent of the owner's legal estate or relevant planning unit. This explains why land beyond the extent of a maintained garden which does not serve the dwelling-house in any necessary or meaningful way will very probably not fall within its curtilage for planning purposes.[47] The use of the curtilage buildings or land must reasonably be for a purpose incidental to the enjoyment of the dwelling-house as a dwelling-house.[48]

Use of land or buildings not involving development for the purposes of agriculture[49] or forestry

4.14   This exception to development is consistent with the latitude accorded to land[50] used for agriculture or forestry in the case of permitted development under article 3 of, and Part 6 (Classes A–E) of Schedule 2 to, the GPDO, subject to the limitations and conditions mentioned. Although the definition of agriculture is wide, it does not include the breeding and keeping of horses otherwise than for use in agriculture.[51] Ancillary use can, for example, also include the use of a caravan to store and mix animal feed,[52] but a material change of use to a leisure use will arise when there has been sub-division of grazing land into 490 plots and where one or more of the plots were being used for the stationing of caravans.[53]

4.15   Whereas the sale of farm produce is an ancillary use, this will not be the case if the produce has been imported or processed elsewhere before being offered for sale on the farm. Similarly, where animals from various farms are kept in a special place before being removed from the farm, the use will not be an ancillary

---

[46]   *McAlpine v Secretary of State for the Environment* [1995] 1 PLR 16; *Dyer v Dorset County Council* [1989] 1 QB 346.

[47]   *Collins v Secretary of State for the Environment* [1989] EGCS 15.

[48]   *Croydon London Borough Council v Gladden* [1994] 1 PLR 30.

[49]   The term 'agriculture' is defined by TCPA 1990, s 336(1). The definition is very wide and includes:

> 'horticulture, fruit growing, dairy farming, the breeding and keeping of livestock (including any creature kept for the production of food, wool, skins or fur, or for the purpose of its use in the farming of land), the use of land as grazing land, meadow land, market gardens and nursery grounds, and the use of land for woodlands where that use is ancillary to the farming of land for other agricultural purposes, and "agriculture" shall be construed accordingly.'

[50]   'land' includes 'a building' in TCPA 1990, s 336(1).

[51]   *Belmont Farm v Minister of Housing and Local Government* (1962) 13 P & CR 417. In this case, it was found that the minister was correct to decide that breeding and training horses for international show jumping on a farm and the erection of an aircraft hangar on it were not an agricultural use and so required planning permission.

[52]   *Wealden District Council v Secretary of State for the Environment* [1988] JPL 268.

[53]   *Pitman v Secretary of State for the Environment* [1989] JPL 831.

use.[54] Further, in circumstances where: (a) land is used for growing grapes to produce wine; (b) there is public viewing of the wine-making process; and (c) wine is also offered for sale to the public along with light refreshments, the use of the land for the production of wine will be an agricultural use and thus exempted from planning controls. The other activities are merely incidental to the growing of grapes and the production of wine, and would be comparable to the making of cider or apple juice by apple farmers and a normal incident of agriculture.[55] Similarly, where timber is felled and stockpiled on land before being removed from the land, the place where the felled timber was stored would be treated in the same way as the place where the standing timber was grown, and both places would be exempted from planning controls.[56] It is worth mentioning under this head that paragraph 28 of the National Planning Policy Framework 2012 (NPPF) in the section 'Supporting a prosperous rural economy' states that planning policies should promote the development and diversification of agricultural and other land-based businesses.

Town and Country Planning (Use Classes) Order 1987 (as amended)[57]

4.16   Where buildings[58] or other land are used for the purpose of any class specified in the Use Classes Order 1987, the use of those buildings or land (or any part) for another purpose within the same use class will not constitute development with the result that there will be no requirement for planning permission.[59] The following points should, however, be noted at the outset:

(a)   it does not necessarily follow that any change of use which is not authorised by the Use Classes Order 1987 will require planning permission as it may be that there has been no material change of use;[60]

(b)   even if permission is not needed for a change of use, the change might still involve building and other works which require permission;

(c)   a permissible change of use under the Use Classes Order 1987 might still involve a breach of condition in a planning permission previously granted;

---

[54]   *Warnock v Secretary of State for the Environment* [1980] JPL 690.

[55]   *Millington v Secretary of State for the Environment* [1999] 3 PLR 118.

[56]   *Farleyer Estate v Secretary of State for Scotland* [1992] 2 PLR 123.

[57]   TCPA 1990, s 55(2)(f).

[58]   A reference to a building includes references to land occupied with the building and used for the same purposes (Use Classes Order 1987, art 3(2)).

[59]   Use Classes Order 1987, art 3(1).

[60]   Conversely, where the change of use is from one to another within the same class, then, whether the use is material or not, the Use Classes Order 1987 still gives permission for the change of use.

(d) not all uses fall within one of the use classes contained in the Schedule to the Use Classes Order 1987;[61]

(e) the Use Classes Order 1987 applies in the case of sub-division of the planning unit with the exception of dwelling-houses;[62]

(f) not all uses of land fall within the specified uses but it may be possible to include unusual uses on the basis that they are *sui generis* to a use within a particular class;[63]

(g) it is always necessary to determine whether the use under examination is in fact ancillary to a primary use which is the true focus of the Use Classes Order 1987;[64]

(h) the right to make a change of use within one of the use classes only arises when the premises have actually been used for a use within that class;[65]

(i) it does not matter that the initial use may have been unlawful.

---

[61] Some uses are specifically excluded by Use Classes Order 1987, art 3(6); these include: (a) use as a theatre; (b) use as an amusement arcade or centre, or a funfair; (c) use as a launderette; (d) for the sale of fuel for motor vehicles; (e) for the sale or display for sale of motor vehicles; (f) for a taxi business or business for the hire of motor vehicles; (g) use as a scrapyard, or a yard for the storage or distribution of minerals or the breaking of motor vehicles; (h) for any work registrable under the Alkali, etc. Works Regulation Act 1906; (i) use as a hostel; (j) use as a waste disposal installation for the incineration, chemical treatment (as defined in Council Directive of 15/7/1975 on waste (75/442/EEC) [1975] OJ L194/39, Annex IIA, heading D9) or landfill of waste to which Council Directive 91/689/EEC of 12/12/1991 on hazardous waste [1991] OJ L377/20 applies; (k) use as a retail warehouse club, being a retail club where goods are sold, or displayed for sale, only to persons who are members of that club; (l) use as a night club; (m) use as a casino; (n) use as a betting office; and (o) use as a pay day loan shop.

[62] Use Classes Order 1987, art 4. In other words, rights conferred by the Use Classes Order 1987 and the exemption from development control apply not only to the whole of the planning unit, but also to any part of the buildings or other land to which it was applicable (i.e. with the exception of dwelling-houses – see TCPA 1990, s 55(3)(a)).

[63] *Tessier v Secretary of State for the Environment* [1975] JPL 39; *Forkhurst Ltd v Secretary of State for the Environment* (1982) 46 P & CR 89; *Kuxhays v Secretary of State for the Environment* [1986] JPL 675; *Wolff v Enfield London Borough Council* (1987) 281 EG 1320; *Farm Facilities Ltd v Secretary of State for the Environment* [1981] JPL 42; the Use Classes Order 1987 effectively declares a number of *sui generis* uses: see art 3(6)(b) (amusement arcade or funfair); (f) (taxi business or business for hire of motor vehicles); and (k) and (l) (warehouse clubs and nightclubs).

[64] For instance, commercial property within Class B1 may have a staff canteen (a Class A3 use), but as an ancillary use it would not constitute a separate use within Class A3 and could be changed at any time without permission, provided any new use was ancillary to the primary use (*Brazil Concrete Ltd v Amersham Rural District Council* (1967) 18 P & CR 396). Another example would be where a Class A1 use as a shop was also used for ancillary purposes as offices (a B1 use). However, the Class B1 ancillary use would not make it a building (for instance) within Class B1 (light industrial use). To cover this situation, Use Classes Order 1987, art 3(3) provides that 'A use which is included in and ordinarily incidental to any use in a class specified in the Schedule is not excluded from the use to which it is incidental merely because it is specified in the Schedule as a separate use'. See *Vickers-Armstrong Ltd v Central Land Board* (1957) 9 P & CR 33, where offices in an administration block within an aviation works were found to be incidental to the use of a general industrial building.

[65] *Kwik Save Discount Group Ltd v Secretary of State for the Environment* (1980) 42 P & CR 166.

Use Classes[66]

PART A

CLASS A1 (SHOPS)[67]

4.17   Use for all or any of the following purposes where the sale, display or services is to visiting members of the public:[68]

(a)   for the retail sale of goods other than hot food;[69]
(b)   as a post office;
(c)   for the sale of tickets or as a travel agency;
(d)   for the sale of sandwiches or other cold food for consumption off the premises;
(e)   for hairdressing;
(f)   for the direction of funerals;
(g)   for the display of goods for sale;
(h)   for the hiring out of domestic or personal goods or articles;
(i)   for the washing or cleaning of clothes or fabrics on the premises;
(j)   for the reception of goods to be washed, cleaned or repaired;
(k)   as an internet café; where the primary purpose of the premises is to provide facilities for enabling members of the public to access the internet.

CLASS A2 (FINANCIAL AND PROFESSIONAL SERVICES)

4.18   Use for the provision of the following services where the services are provided principally to visiting members of the public:

(a)   financial services;
(b)   professional services (other than health or medical services);
(c)   any other services which it is appropriate to provide in a shopping area.

---

[66]   In which material changes of use between categories of use within the same class will be taken not to have involved the carrying out of development. The various Use Classes are set out in the Schedule to the 1987 Order (the contents of this chapter contain the latest amendments to the Use Classes).

[67]   The term 'shop' is restricted in its scope to uses which take place in buildings and does not authorise retail uses on open land (*Cawley v Secretary of State for the Environment* [1990] 2 PLR 90). See also *R v Kensington and Chelsea London Borough Council ex parte Europa Foods Ltd* [1996] EGCS 5, where Macpherson J said that the word 'shop' was used as a convenient generic term for activities carried on in a typical high street.

[68]   Hence a retail warehouse club is not a shop (*R v Thurrock Borough Council ex parte Tesco Stores Ltd* [1994] JPL 328).

[69]   Any mixed use involving other activities which are not comprised within the Class A1 use would take it outside the class (*Lydcare v Secretary of State for the Environment and Westminster City Council* (1984) 49 P & CR 186 – retail sales and the viewing of films in coin-operated booths). Clearly, any ancillary use for storage, etc. would be ancillary to the primary use, and the building would still be Class A1.

CLASS A3 (FOOD AND DRINK)

4.19   Use for the sale of food or drink for consumption on the premises.[70]

CLASS A4 (DRINKING ESTABLISHMENTS)

4.20   Use as a public house, wine-bar or other drinking establishment.

CLASS A5 (HOT FOOD TAKEAWAYS)

4.21   Use for the sale of hot food for consumption off the premises.

PART B

CLASS B1 (BUSINESS)

4.22   Use for all or any of the following purposes, being a use which can be carried out in any residential area without detriment to the amenity of that area by reason of noise, vibration, smell, fumes, smoke, soot, ash, dust or grit:

(a)   as an office other than a use within Class A2 (financial and professional services);
(b)   for research and development of products or processes; or
(c)   for any industrial process.[71]

4.23   The points to note on Class B1 are these:

(a)   it represents a merger of offices and light industrial use and would include, for instance, computer development and manufacture and pharmaceutical research and manufacture;
(b)   the expression 'any residential area' is general and is not confined to the area surrounding the land;[72]
(c)   the definition focuses on the impact of the use on the amenity of the area so that efforts made to mitigate the impact of the use (such as noise insulation and dust extraction) may involve a change of use from general (i.e. Class B2 use) to light industrial.[73]

---

[70]   This includes only restaurants and cafés.
[71]   The term 'industrial process' is defined in Use Classes Order 1987, art 2 and is very broad. It is also something which must be carried on in the course of a trade or business (other than agriculture) and not for pleasure (*Newbury District Council v Secretary of State for the Environment* [1981] AC 578 at 614). See *Rael-Brook Ltd v Minister of Housing and Local Government* [1967] 2 QB 65, where a centre for the production of school meals was found to be industrial, which meant that a change of use to shirt-making did not require planning permission.
[72]   *W.T. Lamb Properties Ltd v Secretary of State for the Environment* [1983] JPL 303.
[73]   *Blight & White Ltd v Secretary of State for the Environment* [1993] 1 PLR 1.

CLASS B2 (GENERAL INDUSTRIAL)[74]

4.24   It should be noted that where B1 (light industrial) and B2 (general industrial) uses occur within a single site or on adjacent sites used as part of the same undertaking, those classes may be treated as a single class, provided the area occupied for general industrial purposes is not substantially increased. What this means is that changes of use (i.e. from light industrial to general industrial) may occur within buildings or on lands comprised within the same undertaking without any need to obtain planning permission.[75]

4.25   Classes B3–B7 involve specialist industrial processes and are not covered in this book.

CLASS B8 (STORAGE OR DISTRIBUTION)

4.26   Use for storage or as a distribution centre.[76]

PART C

CLASS C1 (HOTELS)

4.27   Use as a hotel or as a boarding or guest house where, in each case, no significant element of care is provided.[77]

CLASS C2 (RESIDENTIAL INSTITUTIONS)

4.28   Use for the provision of residential accommodation and care to people in need of care[78] (other than a use within Class C3 (dwelling-houses)). Use as a hospital or nursing home. Use as a residential school, college or training centre.

---

[74] Although any change of use to use for the purposes of a waste disposal installation for the incineration, chemical treatment or landfill of hazardous waste will give rise to a material change of use (as reinforced by Town and Country Planning (Environmental Impact Assessment) Regulations 2017, Sch 1, para 9).

[75] Use Classes Order 1987, art 3(4).

[76] This use will not include on-site retail use such as a 'cash and carry warehouse' (*LTSS Print and Supply Services Ltd v London Borough of Hackney* [1976] QB 663). The storage may also include the storage of electronic data.

[77] A change of use from a dwelling-house or block of flats to use as a hotel or hostel, or from a hotel to bed-sitting rooms, is capable of constituting a material change of use for which planning permission is required (*Birmingham Corp v Habib Ullah* [1964] 1 QB 178; *Panayi v Secretary of State for the Environment* [1985] JPL 783; *Mayflower Cambridge Ltd v Secretary of State for the Environment* (1975) 30 P & CR 28).

[78] The term 'care' is defined in Use Classes Order 1987, art 2 as meaning 'personal care for people in need of such care by reason of old age, disablement, past or present dependence on alcohol or drugs or past or present mental disorder, and in Class C2 also includes the personal care of children and medical care and treatment'.

CLASS C2A (SECURE RESIDENTIAL INSTITUTIONS)

4.29   Use for the provision of secure residential accommodation, including use as a prison, young offenders institution, detention centre, secure training centre, custody centre, short-term holding centre, secure local authority accommodation or as military barracks.

CLASS C3 (DWELLING-HOUSES)

4.30   Use as a dwelling-house (whether or not as a sole or main residence) by:

(a)   a single person or by people to be regarded as forming a single household;
(b)   not more than six residents living together as a single household where care is provided for residents; or
(c)   not more than six residents living together as a single household where no care is provided to residents (other than a use within Class C4).[79]

CLASS C4 (HOUSES IN MULTIPLE OCCUPATION)

4.31   Use as a dwelling-house by not more than six residents[80] as a house in multiple occupation (HMO).[81] What this means is that a material change of use

---

[79]   The term 'single household' in Class C3(a) is to be construed in accordance with Housing Act 2004, s 258. This class facilitates the change of use from a single-family home to sharing by up to six unrelated persons living together as a single household (see *R (Hossack) v Kettering Borough Council* [2002] EWCA Civ 886 – clearly, the fewer the residents living in the same house, the more likely it is that they will be living together as a single cohesive household) and will include small community care homes consisting of up to six people living together under arrangements for providing care and support within the community (see Circular 13/87, para 27; *R (Crawley Borough Council) v First Secretary of State* [2004] EWHC 160 (Admin)). Even if more than six unrelated people live together in a single household, it will not necessarily constitute a material change of use, although it would if the use fell into Class C1 (hotels). Nor will the Use Classes Order 1987 apply where there is a planning condition which restricts the use of the property (*R (Tunbridge Wells Borough Council) ex parte Blue Boys Development* (1990) 59 P & CR 315), nor where the existing use, prior to any change of use to bring it within this class, was outside the scope of the class (*Richmond London Borough Council v Secretary of State for Environment, Transport and the Regions* [2000] EGCS 47), in which event permission is still needed (i.e. conversion of a house comprising seven flats (which was outside Class C3) into a single-family dwelling-house which is a Class C3(a) use). It should be noted that in London, this use class will be subject to the Greater London Council (General Powers) Act 1973, which provides that planning permission is required for a change of use from residential to temporary sleeping accommodation (*Hyde Park Residence Ltd v Secretary of State for the Environment, Transport and Regions* [1999] 3 PLR 1).

[80]   Which can include minors (*Paramaguru v Ealing LBC* [2018] EWHC 373 (Admin)).

[81]   A house in multiple occupation does not mean a converted block of flats within the meaning of Housing Act 2004, s 257, but otherwise has the same meaning as in s 254 of the 2004 Act. We are dealing here with properties consisting of multiple units of living accommodation where the occupants are not living together as a single household, but who nonetheless share one or more of the basic amenities, such as a toilet or kitchen.

from Class C3 to C4 (involving a conversion of a single dwelling-house into two or more separate dwellings) will require planning permission.

PART D

CLASS D1 (NON-RESIDENTIAL INSTITUTIONS)

4.32   Any use not including a residential use:

(a)   for the provision of any medical or health services except the use of premises attached to the residence of the consultant or practitioner;
(b)   as a crèche, day nursery or day centre;
(c)   for the provision of education;
(d)   for the display of works of art (otherwise than for sale or hire);
(e)   as a museum;
(f)   as a public library or public reading room;
(g)   as a public hall or exhibition hall;
(h)   for, or in connection with, public worship or religious instruction;
(i)   as a law court.

CLASS D2 (ASSEMBLY AND LEISURE)

4.33   Use as:

(a)   a cinema;
(b)   a concert hall;
(c)   a bingo hall;
(d)   a dance hall;
(e)   a swimming bath, skating rink, gymnasium or area for other indoor or outdoor sports or recreations, not involving motorised vehicles or firearms.

Chapter 5

Permitted Development

INTRODUCTION

5.1   There are special provisions involving land on 1/7/1948 which had both a normal use and a temporary use for which planning permission is not required, even if development is involved.[1] Nor is permission necessary where:

(a)   planning permission has been granted for a limited period, or by a development order subject to limitations, and there is a resumption of the normal use of the land before that permission was granted (provided the previous use was not begun in contravention of planning control);[2] or

(b)   there is a resumption of the previous lawful use of the land where an enforcement notice has been served in respect of an unauthorised use.[3]

5.2   Other than in these cases, planning permission is required for any development of land.[4]

5.3   Planning permission may be granted in a number of ways such as where planning permission is deemed to have been granted by virtue of a development order made by the Secretary of State or by virtue of a local development order made by a local planning authority (LPA).[5] A development order may be made either as a general order affecting all land (except so far as the order otherwise provides) or as a special order applicable only to such land or descriptions of land as may be specified in the order.[6] This chapter is concerned primarily with

---

[1]   TCPA 1990, Sch 4, paras 1–3, and s 57(7).

[2]   TCPA 1990, s 7(2), (3) and (5).

[3]   TCPA 1990, s 57(4).

[4]   TCPA 1990, s 57(1).

[5]   TCPA 1990, ss 58(1)(a) and 59.

[6]   TCPA 1990, s 59(3).

permission granted under the Town and Country Planning (General Permitted Development) (England) Order 2015 (GPDO).[7]

THE GPDO

5.4   The GPDO is highly technical and detailed. The various permissions granted are subject to limitations, conditions and exceptions which, in the case of limitations and conditions, are separately defined for each class of permitted development and, of course, any significant departure from the scope of the permitted development may well justify an enforcement notice in order to remedy what would be a breach of planning control.

Article 4 directions

5.5   Rights under the GPDO may also be withdrawn by virtue of a direction made by the Secretary of State or by an LPA. These are known as 'article 4 directions' which operate to restrict permitted development granted by article 3 (other than in the case of the use of land for mineral exploration or the removal of material from mineral-working deposits), in which case the relevant development may not be carried out unless permission has been granted for it on an application.[8] The article 4 direction may apply to all or any development of the relevant part, class or paragraph which is specified in the direction or to any particular part, class or paragraph which is specified in the direction. There are various developments which are excluded from the scope of article 4.[9] Where

---

[7]   SI 2015/596, and made pursuant to the powers of the Secretary of State under TCPA 1990, ss 58–71. This order consolidates the Town and Country Planning (General Permitted Development) Order 1995 (SI 1995/418) and the 22 instruments which have amended that Order and also includes a number of new policy changes in England.

[8]   Where permitted development rights are withdrawn, an application must be made for planning permission for the relevant operation or change of use. The guidance for when it is appropriate to make art 4 directions can be found in the NPPG at Paragraph: 038 Reference ID: 13-038-20140306 (Circular 9/95 (App D) is retained in Wales) and in NPPF, para 200. The removal of permitted development rights is an exceptional step and should only be done where this is necessary to protect local amenity or the wellbeing of an area. It might arise in the case of development within conservation areas or where an LPA wishes to strictly control the change of use of dwellings to houses in multiple occupation (HMOs), such as where the character of an area was changing through a proliferation of HMOs driven by the need for student accommodation. It might also arise where the change of use of an HMO from a single dwelling was impermissible because it was in an area covered by an art 4 direction specifically controlling HMOs (although a lack of identifiable harm might well be a material consideration outweighing the conflict with adopted local plan policy).

[9]   GPDO, art 4(2)(a)–(f).

permitted development rights have been withdrawn,[10] any person prejudicially affected by the withdrawal may seek compensation for abortive expenditure. There is a pre-condition, namely that an application for planning permission should first have been made and refused or otherwise granted subject to conditions which differ from those arising under the development order.[11] Applications for compensation should be made within 12 months from the date of the refusal of permission for development which was once permitted development.[12]

Permitted development – planning conditions

5.6   A planning condition could exclude planning permission granted by the Secretary of State by means of the GPDO. For instance, a condition which stated that the property could be used for 'no other purpose whatsoever, without express planning consent from the Local Planning Authority first being obtained' was sufficient to exclude the operation of the GPDO.[13]

---

[10] By revocation or amendment of the development order itself or by virtue of the issue of directions under powers conferred by the order withdrawing permission under the order.

[11] TCPA 1990, s 108(1); s 108(2) requires that the application for planning permission is made within 12 months of the date when the withdrawal of permission came into operation.

[12] Town and Country Planning General Regulations 1992 (SI 1992/1492), reg 12. See *Pennine Raceway Ltd v Kirklees Metropolitan Borough Council* [1984] RVR 85 and *Carter v Windsor and Maidenhead Royal Borough Council* [1988] 3 PLR 6, for the assessment of compensation which mirrors that arising under TCPA 1990, s 107, which concerns compensation where planning permission is revoked or modified. It should be noted that the Town and Country Planning (Compensation) (England) Regulations 2015 (SI 2015/598) make provision to ensure that no compensation arises where adequate notice has been given of the removal of planning permission granted under a development order, local development order or neighbourhood development order. The GPDO also amends procedures in relation to art 4. It is now the case that an art 4 direction cannot prevent the carrying out of development which had prior approval before the date when the art 4 direction came into force. This protection will, however, only exist for three years following the date when prior approval had been granted, at which point any development must have been completed.

[13] *Dunnett Investments Ltd v Secretary of State for Communities and Local Government* [2017] EWCA Civ 192 (following *Trump International Golf Club Scotland Ltd v Scottish Ministers* [2016] 1 WLR 85). In interpreting a planning condition which was said to exclude the operation of the GPDO, the following themes could be discerned from the authorities: (a) a planning condition could exclude the GPDO; (b) exclusion might be express or implied, however, a grant for a particular use could not in itself amount to an exclusion; (c) to exclude the application of the GPDO, the words used in the relevant condition, taken in their full context, must clearly evince an intention on the part of the LPA to make such an exclusion; and (d) it is also material to consider the context which includes the planning history of the site which might well indicate that the LPA was anxious to maintain close control over its planning use and wanted to consider the merits of any proposal in light of the site's character and location.

Scope of permitted development – overview

5.7   Article 3 of the GPDO gives effect to the permitted development rights contained in Schedule 2.[14] If a person is dissatisfied with the scope of his permitted development rights, he should obtain an express planning permission.

5.8   Certain elements of article 3 of the GPDO should be noted:

(a)   Nothing in the GPDO permits development contrary to any condition imposed by an express grant of planning permission.[15]

(b)   Rights under the GPDO will not validate unlawful building operations in the case of an existing building (although operations which were undertaken unlawfully will become lawful once the time has elapsed for taking enforcement action against them),[16] nor will a permission granted in the case of an existing use validate that use where the use is unlawful.[17]

(c)   The GPDO does not (with limited exceptions)[18] authorise any development which involves the formation, laying out or material widening of a means of access to an existing highway which is a trunk road or classified road, or which creates an obstruction to the view of persons using any highway used by vehicular traffic, so as to be likely to cause danger to such persons.[19]

(d)   The GPDO does not permit the laying or construction of a notifiable pipe-line (except for works by statutory undertakers under Part 15, Class A) where the appropriate procedure is laid down under the Pipe-Lines Act 1962.[20]

(e)   The GPDO does not permit demolition except as provided for in Part 11, Classes B and C.[21]

(f)   Nor is development permitted where the application for development is one which requires an environmental impact assessment (EIA) unless the LPA has adopted a screening opinion[22] that the development is not an EIA

---

[14]   Made pursuant to TCPA 1990, s 58(1)(a), which provides for the grant of planning permission by a development order.

[15]   GPDO, art 3(4). *East Barnet Urban District Council v British Transport Commission* [1962] 2 QB 484; *Newbury District Council v Secretary of State for the Environment* [1981] AC 578; *Adur District Council v Secretary of State for Environment, Transport and the Regions* [2000] 1 PLR 1.

[16]   TCPA 1990, s 191(2), which is four years from the time of the substantial completion of the operations (s 171B(1)).

[17]   GPDO, art 3(5). Where a particular use or operation is subject to an enforcement notice, permitted development rights will not operate to override the notice (*Masefield v Taylor* [1987] JPL 721).

[18]   Schedule 2, Pt 9, Classes A, B, D and E and Pt 18, Class A.

[19]   GPDO, art 3(6).

[20]   GPDO, art 3(8).

[21]   GPDO, art 3(9).

[22]   Under EIA Regulations 2017, reg 5.

development[23] or where the Secretary of State has made a screening direction that the development is not an EIA development,[24] or where the Secretary of State has given a direction that the development is exempted from the application of the regulations.[25] Development excluded from the GPDO under this head is, however, subject to a number of exceptions such as arise in the case of development which consists of the carrying out by a drainage body of improvement works.[26]

(g)   The GPDO is also subject to various restrictions contained in the Conservation of Habitats and Species Regulations 2017.[27]

5.9   The GPDO provides a different regime in the case of the use of land for mineral exploitation (Part 17, Class K) and the removal of material

---

[23]   GPDO, art 3(10)(a).

[24]   Under EIA Regulations 2017, reg 7(5) or reg 6(4); GPDO, art 3(10)(b).

[25]   Under EIA Regulations 2017, reg 63; GPDO, art 3(10)(c). Where, however, an LPA has adopted a screening opinion that the development is EIA development and the Secretary of State has made a screening opinion to the contrary, but has not directed that the development is exempted from the application of EIA Regulations 2017, reg 63 (or has otherwise directed that the development is in fact EIA development), that development shall be treated as development which is not permitted by the GPDO (art 3(11)).

[26]   GPDO, art 3(12)(a): 'Improvement works' for these purposes means works within the meaning of the Environmental Impact Assessment (Land Drainage Improvement Works) Regulations 1999 (SI 1999/1783) (as amended).

[27]   SI 2017/1012. See GPDO, art 3(1), which expressly provides that permitted development rights were to be subject to the former 2010 Regulations at regs 73–76 (now 2017 Regulations, regs 75–78). The matter was considered by Patterson J in *Stevens (t/a KCS Asset Management) v Blaenau Gwent County Borough Council* [2015] EWHC 1606 (Admin), who summarised these regulations at [64]. The regulations provide that where it is intended to carry out permitted development which is likely to have a significant effect on a European site or a European offshore marine site and is not directly connected with or necessary to the management of the site, it must not be begun until the developer has received written notification of the approval of the LPA under reg 75. By reg 74, an opinion may be sought from the local nature conservation body as to whether the proposed development is likely to have a relevant effect. Where the nature conservation body has enough information to conclude on the effect of the development, it must notify the applicant and the LPA in writing. An application to the LPA for approval under the GPDO must be accompanied by a copy of any relevant notification by the appropriate nature conservation body. If the nature conservation body states its opinion is that the development is not likely to have a significant environmental effect then that opinion (which is conclusive of that question for the purpose of reliance on the planning permission granted by the GPDO – reg 74(6)) has to be sent to the applicant by the LPA (reg 75(4)). The LPA must otherwise take account of any representations made by the appropriate nature conservation body and must make an appropriate assessment of the implications of the development for the European site or European offshore marine site in view of that site's conservation objectives. In light of the conclusions of the assessment, the LPA may approve the development only after having ascertained that it will not adversely affect the integrity of the site.

working-deposits other than a stockpile (Part 23, Class B).[28] These classes require notification to be made to the mineral planning authority of the intention to carry out the development, and the authority has the power to make a direction excluding permitted development rights (which the Secretary of State has power to disallow). The justification for the removal of such rights is subject to specified criteria such as whether the development is to be carried out in a National Park, an Area of Outstanding Natural Beauty (AONB), a site of archaeological interest or a site of Special Scientific Interest, or where there is a risk of serious detriment being caused to the amenity of the area or where the development would constitute a serious nuisance to local residents or to a hospital or a school.[29]

Contents of GPDO – overview

5.10   Put shortly, article 3(1) of the GPDO grants planning permission for the classes of development described in Schedule 2, subject to the very detailed limitations and conditions applicable to each class of development, which should be studied with care, as the scope of this book is no more than an overview of the rights conferred by the GPDO.

5.11   Schedule 2 to the GPDO is broken down into 19 Parts but only Parts 1 to 7 are considered herein (although a number of new development rights under the GPDO are highlighted). Reference should be made to the GPDO for fuller details which are beyond the scope of this book.

Schedule 2
Part 1 Development within the curtilage of a dwelling-house.
Part 2 Minor operations.
Part 3 Changes of use.
Part 4 Temporary buildings and uses.
Part 5 Caravan sites and recreational campsites.
Part 6 Agricultural and forestry.
Part 7 Non-domestic extensions, alterations, etc.
Part 8 Transport related development.
Part 9 Development relating to roads.
Part 10 Repairs to services.
Part 11 Heritage and demolition.
Part 12 Development by local authorities.
Part 13 Water and sewerage.
Part 14 Renewable energy.
Part 15 Power related development.

---

[28]   See GPDO, art 5.
[29]   GPDO, art 5(2).

Part 16 Communications.[30]
Part 17 Mineral and mining exploration.
Part 18 Miscellaneous development.
Part 19 Development by the Crown or for national security purposes.

Part 1 – Development within the curtilage of a dwelling-house

5.12   Class A – the enlargement, improvement or other alteration of a dwelling-house.[31]

5.13   Class B – the enlargement of a dwelling-house consisting of an addition or alteration to its roof.

5.14   Class C – any other alteration to the roof of a dwelling-house.

5.15   Class D – the erection of a porch outside any external door of a dwelling-house.

5.16   Class E – the provision within the curtilage of a dwelling-house of: (a) any building or enclosure, swimming or other pool required for a purpose incidental[32] to the enjoyment of the dwelling-house as such, or the maintenance, improvement or other alteration of such a building or enclosure; or (b) a container used for domestic heating purposes for the storage of oil or liquid petroleum gas.

---

[30]   *R (Mawbey) v Lewisham LBC* [2018] EWHC 263 (Admin); for the purposes of Part 16, Class A, para A.1(2)(c), the term 'mast' included a central support pole holding antennae that transmitted and received radio waves. The term was broad enough to cover both ground-based and building-based structures and did not specify characteristics such as height, scale, design and directional array. The court ruled that the GPDO was to be construed in a broad and common-sense manner by ascertaining the ordinary meaning of the language used (*Evans v Secretary of State for Communities and Local Government* [2014] EWHC 4111 (Admin), considered). However, where the language used was ambiguous and where the interpretations of the legislation were conflicting, it would be appropriate to rely on external aids to construction to assist in identifying the ordinary meaning of the language used, to shed light on the purpose of the legislation and to ascertain the mischief which the legislation was intended to address and the legislative remedy.

[31]   A permitted development right extends the current right for larger household rear extensions for a further three-year period until 30/5/2019. If any neighbour raises objections when he is notified of the proposal, the right is subject to a prior approval as to the impact on the amenity of the adjoining premises.

[32]   *Emin v Secretary of State for the Environment* (1989) 58 P & CR 416; the correct approach is to consider whether the proposed use was subordinate to the use of the house as a dwelling-house. In order to form a conclusion, the nature and scale of the proposed activities had to be considered in which the size of the buildings was relevant but in no way decisive. In other words, regard should be had to the use to which it is proposed to put a building and to consider the nature and scale of that use in the context of whether it was a purpose incidental to the enjoyment of the dwelling-house.

5.17   Class F – development consisting of: (a) the provision within the curtilage of a dwelling-house of a hard surface for any purpose incidental to the enjoyment of the dwelling-house as such; or (b) the replacement in whole or part of such a surface.

5.18   Class G – the installation, alteration or replacement of a chimney, flue or soil and vent pipe on a dwelling-house.

5.19   Class H – the installation, alteration or replacement of a microwave antenna on a dwelling-house or within the curtilage of a dwelling-house.

Part 2 – Minor operations

5.20   Class A – gates, fences, walls or other means of enclosure.

5.21   Class B – means of access to a highway.

5.22   Class C – painting of the exterior of any building or work.

5.23   Class D – CCTV cameras.

Part 3 – Changes of use

5.24   Whereas the Use Classes Order 1987 makes provision for changes of use within specified classes (and is clearly advantageous in cases where the relevant change of use is material) which will be deemed not to constitute development (and as a result do not require planning permission), the GPDO adds to this by permitting development in the case of material changes of use from one class to another or to a use which is *sui generis*.[33]

5.25   Part 3 is looked at more closely because of its relationship with the Use Classes Order 1987.

5.26   The use changes under Part 3 are substantial and are summarised below.

5.27   Development is permitted in so far as it consists of a change of use as follows (it should be noted that Classes C, J, M, N, O, P, Q, R, S and T require a prior approval process which is prescribed by paragraph W and each Class prescribes the criteria relevant to this process).

---

[33]   It will be recalled that the Town and Country Planning (Use Classes) Order 1987 (SI 1987/764) (as amended) (Use Classes Order 1987) permits changes of use from one class to another. A use which is *sui generis* (meaning 'of its own kind') concerns uses which do not fall within any particular class of use under the Use Classes Order 1987.

5.28 Class A – restaurants, cafés or takeaways to retail:

- Restaurants and cafés (A3) or hot food takeaways (A5) to a use falling within A1 (shops) or A2 (financial and professional services).

5.29 Class AA:

- Drinking establishments (A4) to drinking establishments (A4) with restaurants and cafés (A3) (i.e. drinking establishments with expanded food provision).
- Drinking establishments with expanded food provision to drinking establishments (A4).[34]

5.30 Class B – takeaways to restaurants and cafés:

- Hot food takeaways (A5) to a use falling within A3 (restaurants and cafés).

---

[34] Town and Country Planning (General Permitted Development) (England) (Amendment) (No 2) Order 2017, art 3 removed permitted development rights allowing the change of use of a building falling within Class A4 (drinking establishment) of the Schedule to the Use Classes Order 1987 to a building within Classes A1 (shops), A2 (financial and professional services) and A3 (restaurants and cafés) and to a temporary flexible use or a state-funded school for up to two academic years. Art 4 also removed permitted development rights allowing for the demolition of buildings used for a purpose within Class A4 (drinking establishments). In 2015, permitted development rights were removed from public houses listed as Assets of Community Value (ACVs), and even public houses nominated to become ACVs required planning permission for a change of use. The position now, in light of the changes made under the 2017 development order (which implemented the measures contained in s 15 of the Neighbourhood Planning Act 2017, which was in response to growing concerns over closures of many public houses and the limited opportunities for local communities to have a say in the process without recourse to the AVC process and art 4 directions), is that, in the case of public houses, permitted development rights for changes of use to a shop, restaurant or café or demolition have, since 23/5/2017, been withdrawn with the result that developers now need to go through the planning application process to secure redevelopment. The new development order includes a new limited permitted development right which allows public houses to change use to what is known as a 'drinking establishment with expanded food provision' (which is a new permitted development right allowing an A4 public house to convert to an A3 restaurant and café and an A4 drinking establishment and back again), which enables a more extensive food offer to be introduced without any controls which may not entirely be protecting the inherent public house use. It means that the pressure to list public houses as ACVs is no longer as great as it once was, although the fact that a public house may be listed as an ACV is more than likely to be considered by the LPA as a material consideration whose effect may well preclude its eventual redevelopment for housing or other purposes. On the other hand, the new measures cannot force landowners to keep open public houses which are no longer viable. In such cases, premises will remain closed while the landowner seeks consent for redevelopment.

5.31   Class C – retail, betting office or pay day loan shop[35] or casino to restaurant or café:

- Change of use from shops (A1), financial and professional services (A2), a betting office or pay day loan shop or casino to a use within A3 (restaurants and cafés); and development consisting of building or other operations for the provision of facilities for ventilation and extraction (including the provision of an external flue) and the storage of rubbish reasonably necessary to use the building for a use within A3 (restaurants and cafés).[36]

5.32   Class D – shops to financial and professional:

- Shops (A1) to financial and professional services (A2).[37]

---

[35]   Betting offices and pay day loan shops are removed from Class A2 use and become *sui generis*. They will continue to benefit from the permitted development rights to change to Class A1 or Class A2 uses. They will also benefit from the permitted development right to temporarily change use for a period of two years (GPDO, Sch 2, Pt 4, Class D), after which they can revert to their previous use or change to Class A1 or Class A2 uses. Premises that have changed use to a betting office or pay day loan shop under the Class D temporary permitted development right retain their original use class and will revert to that at the end of the two-year period.

[36]   This is new. Up to 150 square metres of floor space will be able to change use, and the right is subject to a prior approval process covering noise, smell/odours, transport and highways, hours of opening as well as siting and design in relation to extraction, ventilation, waste management, storage and undesirable impacts on shopping facilities. Shopping impacts will be assessed in relation to the effect of the development on the sustainability of key shopping centres and the provision of services. This is intended to enable LPAs to protect successful retail provision in key shopping areas, such as town centres, while underused shop units are kept in use outside those areas. LPAs may consider the impact of the development on the provision of important local services, such as post offices, though only if there is a reasonable prospect of the premises being occupied by another retail use. Premises may revert from Class A3 use to their original use class if that was Class A1 (shops) or Class A2 (financial and professional services) under existing permitted development rights. A planning application will be required for change of use from Class A3 to a betting office or pay day loan shop. The existing permitted development right for the temporary change of use from Class A1 and Class A2 to Class A3 for a period of two years will remain. The right does not apply to land within the curtilage of listed buildings or scheduled monuments, to SSSIs, safety hazard areas and military explosives storage areas. See also minor amendments in General Permitted Development (England) (Amendment) Order 2018, arts 6–8, with effect from 6/4/2018.

[37]   This is also new. The rights will also apply equally to premises that have changed to a shop (Class A1) following planning permission granted by an LPA, or by exercising a permitted development right.

5.33   Class E – financial and professional or betting office or pay day loan shop to shops:

- Development consisting of a change of use of a building with a display window at ground floor level from a use within A2 (financial and professional services) or a use as a betting office or a pay day loan shop to a use within A1 (shops).

5.34   Class F – betting offices or pay day loan shops to financial and professional:

- Use of premises as a betting office or pay day loan shop to a use falling within Class A2 (financial and professional services).

5.35   Class G – retail or betting office or pay day loan shop to mixed use:

- From use within A1 (shops) to a mixed use for any purpose within A1 (shops) and as up to two flats.
- From use within A1 (shops) to a mixed use for any purpose within A2 (financial and professional services) and as up to two flats.
- From use within A2 (financial and professional services) or as a betting office or pay day loan shop to a mixed use within A2 (financial and professional services) and as up to two flats.
- From a building with a display window at ground floor level, from a use for any purpose within A2 (financial and professional services) or as a betting office or pay day loan shop to a mixed use for any purpose within A1 (shops) and as up to two flats.
- From a use as a betting office or a pay day loan shop to a mixed use as a betting office or a pay day loan shop and as up to two flats.

5.36   Class H – mixed use to retail:

- From a mixed use for any purpose within A1 (shops) and as up to two flats to A1 (shops).
- From a mixed use for any purpose within A1 (shops) and as up to two flats to A2 (financial and professional services).
- From a mixed use for any purpose within A2 (financial and professional services) and as up to two flats or as a betting office or pay day loan shop and as up to two flats to A2 (financial and professional services).
- Where the building has a display window on the ground floor, from a mixed use for any purpose within A2 (financial and professional services) and as up to two flats or as a betting office or pay day loan shop and as up to two flats to use within A1 (shops).
- From a mixed use as a betting office or pay day loan shop and as up to two flats to a use as a betting office or pay day loan shop.

5.37   Class I – industrial and general business conversions:

- From use within B2 (general industrial) or B8 (storage or distribution) to a use within B1 (business).
- From use within B1 (business) or B2 (general industrial) to a use within B8 (storage or distribution).

5.38   Class J – retail or betting office or pay day loan shop to assembly and leisure:

- From A1 (shops) or A2 (financial and professional services) or as a betting office or pay day loan shop to D2 (assembly and leisure).[38]

5.39   Class K – casinos to assembly and leisure:

- From use as a casino to D2 (assembly and leisure).

5.40   Class L – small houses in multiple occupation (HMOs) to dwelling-houses and vice versa:

- From C4 (HMOs) to C3 (dwelling-houses).
- From C3 (dwelling-houses) to C4 (HMOs).

5.41   Class M – retail or betting office or pay day loan shop to dwelling-houses:

- Change of use of a building from A1 (shops) or A2 (financial and professional services) or from use as a betting office or pay day loan shop or a mixed use combining use as a dwelling-house with: (a) use as a betting

---

[38] This is new, with an upper threshold of 200 square metres of total floor space. The right applies to premises that were in Class A1 or Class A2 use on 5/12/2013. However, the right would not apply to premises that have changed to Class A1 or Class A2 under other permitted development rights after 5/12/2013, until they have been in use for a period of five years. This right is subject to a prior approval process covering transport and highways, hours of opening, noise impacts of the development and undesirable impacts on shopping facilities. Shopping impacts will be assessed in relation to the effect of the development on the sustainability of important shopping centres and the provision of services. This is intended to enable LPAs to protect successful retail provision in key shopping areas, such as town centres, while underused shop units are kept in use outside those areas. LPAs may consider the impact of the development on the provision of important local services, such as post offices, though only if there is a reasonable prospect of the premises being occupied by another retail use. The permitted development right does not apply in conservation areas, National Parks, AONBs, the Broads and World Heritage Sites. Nor do they apply to land within the curtilage of listed buildings, scheduled monuments, SSSIs, safety hazard areas or military explosives areas. Permitted development rights to convert a Class D2 premises to a registered nursery or state-funded school do not apply to premises that change to Class D2 use under these rights.

office, pay day loan shop or launderette; or (b) a use within A1 (shops) or A2 (financial and professional services), to a use within C3 (dwelling-houses); and building operations reasonably necessary to convert the above building to a use within C3 (dwelling-houses).[39]

5.42 Class N – specified *sui generis* uses to dwelling-houses:

- Development consisting of a change of use of a building and any land within its curtilage from use as an amusement arcade or centre or a casino (i.e. as *sui generis* uses which do not sit within any specific use class) to use within C3 (dwelling-houses), along with building operations reasonably necessary to convert a building to that use.[40]

5.43 Class O – offices to dwelling-houses:

- Change of use from B1(a) (offices) to C3 (dwelling-houses).[41]

5.44 Class P – storage or distribution centre to dwelling-houses:

---

[39] See also minor amendments in General Permitted Development (England) (Amendment) Order 2018, arts 6–8, with effect from 6/4/2018.

[40] This is new. The aim is that this will enable re-use of existing buildings, support high streets and increase housing supply. Up to 150 square metres of floor space will be able to change to residential use. The right is subject to a prior approval process covering transport and highways, flooding, contamination and, where building works are to be carried out under the permitted development right, design. The right does not apply in National Parks, AONBs, the Broads and World Heritage Sites, nor to land within the curtilage of listed buildings or scheduled monuments, or SSSIs, safety hazard areas and military explosives storage areas. After changing use to a residential use, existing permitted development rights for dwelling-houses (Class C3) will not apply. See also minor amendments in General Permitted Development (England) (Amendment) Order 2018, arts 6–8, with effect from 6/4/2018.

[41] This class (which was introduced in 2013) involves a prior approval process. Put shortly, development under Class O will not be permitted unless the LPA makes a determination on traffic impacts, contamination risks, flooding risks and impacts on noise from commercial premises on the intended occupiers of the site. Furthermore, development is not permitted by Class O if the building was not used for Class B1(a) (i.e. offices) on 29/5/2013 or in the case of a building which was in use before that date but was not in use on that date, when it was last in use. This form of development is very attractive to developers in the case of vacant office stock and large numbers of new homes are being created by this route. The critics argue that many of the homes that are built under the prior approval process are well below the space and design standards that would normally be expected, although a number of such schemes are admittedly aimed at young professionals more concerned about price and location than floor plans. Moreover, in removing the need for planning permission, the government also removed the LPA's ability to obtain contributions from developers for affordable housing or infrastructure by way of planning obligations. There is also concern at the loss of employment space in town centres and its impact on rents in areas of shortage.

- Change of use from B8 (storage or distribution centre) to C3 (dwelling-houses).[42]

5.45   Class Q – agricultural buildings to dwelling-houses:

- A change of use from an agricultural building and any land within its curtilage to Class C3 (dwelling-houses), along with building operations reasonably necessary to convert a building to that use. The agricultural-to-residential permitted development right has aroused great interest since its introduction in 2015.[43] The permitted development is limited to building

---

[42]   This is also new and, following an amendment with effect from 6/4/2018, extends the existing temporary right to change the use of a building from a storage or redistribution centre to a dwelling-house (Sch 2, Pt 3, Class P) for a further period. Development under Class P is permitted provided that the prior approval date (defined in Sch 2, Pt 3, para X) falls before 10/6/2019 and the change of use is completed within three years of the prior approval date. Up to 500 square metres of floor space will be able to change use to residential. The right is subject to a prior approval process covering transport and highways, air quality impacts on intended occupiers, noise impacts of the development, risks of contamination, flooding and the impact the change of use would have on existing industrial uses. If the site is under an agricultural tenancy, then the consent of both the landlord and the tenant will be needed for any development to be permitted. The right only applies to buildings that were last used or were in use as storage or distribution (Class B8) on or before 19/3/14. This would include former businesses in an office use (Class B1) or general (Class B2) buildings that have changed use to storage or distribution (Class B8) use under existing permitted development rights, provided that they were in such uses on 19/3/14. However, there is an additional requirement that a building seeking to change use must have been in Class B8 use for a period of at least four years before the date development begins. The new right does not apply in National Parks, AONBs, the Broads and World Heritage Sites, listed buildings or land within the curtilage of listed buildings, scheduled monuments, or in SSSIs, safety hazard areas and military explosives storage areas. After changing use to a residential use, existing permitted development rights for dwelling-houses (Class C3) will not apply.

[43]   It has been reported that in the second quarter of 2017, nearly two-fifths of prior approval applications were refused. While this is less than the refusal rate from late 2014 (when it neared 60%) it has remained at around 40% since the second quarter of 2015. In comparison, the average refusal rate for all types of permitted development prior approval applications stood at just 19% in the second quarter of 2017, less than half the rate for Class Q applications, and has remained at about the same level for the past three years. Having said that, it seems that a number of agricultural-to-residential prior approval refusals are being allowed on appeal. The difficulties concern the complexity of the rules, and the most common reasons for refusal involve siting and location, structural integrity and the use of the site (the right does not apply where the site was not solely in agricultural use at the cut-off date of 20/3/2013, or, if earlier, when it was last in use). With effect from 6/4/2018, art 10 of the General Permitted Development (England) (Amendment) Order 2018 extends Sch 2, Pt 3, Class Q (agricultural buildings to dwelling-houses) to increase the number of dwelling-houses permitted from three to a maximum of five (including any previous development under Class Q). The existing floor space limitation on agricultural buildings that may change use under Class Q is extended from 450 square metres to 465 square metres for larger dwelling-houses. Including any previous development under Class Q, up to three larger dwelling-houses are permitted with a maximum floor space of 465 square metres, and up to five smaller dwelling-houses with each having no more than 100 square metres of floor space. These changes (defined in art 2)introduce definitions of smaller and larger dwelling-houses, with

operations reasonably necessary to convert the building to a Class C3 use which would necessarily exclude a rebuild. It is a matter of planning judgment as to where the line is drawn, although it seems plain that it will be harder for agricultural buildings with few structural elements to win approval for conversion to housing.[44]

---

the former having no more than 100 square metres of floor space in use as a dwelling-house and the latter having between 100 square metres and 465 square metres of floor space in use as a dwelling-house. Article 10 of the amending Order provides that development under para Q (b) is permitted provided that it takes place together with development permitted by para Q (a).

[44] *Hibbitt v Secretary of State for Communities and Local Government* [2016] EWHC 2853 (Admin), which concerned the refusal by an LPA (which was upheld by an inspector) to approve the conversion of an open-sided steel-framed barn into an automatically approved dwelling under Class Q. The court agreed with the inspector that the works went a long way beyond what might reasonably be described as a conversion. The development was in all practical terms starting afresh, with only a modest amount of help from the original agricultural building. The court stated that the case raised an issue about the need to 'avoid in the countryside' new isolated homes. A balance had to be struck between automatic approval and detailed assessment of applications. These considerations militated in favour of only approving clear-cut cases and against a wide construction of Class Q. A proper balance was struck by ensuring that only genuine conversions and not fresh or rebuilds were automatically cleared.

See also *East Hertfordshire DC v Secretary of State for Communities and Local Government* [2017] EWHC 465 (Admin), which concerned one of the conditions which had to meet with the approval of the LPA, namely, as to whether the location or siting of the building made it otherwise impractical or undesirable for the building to change from agricultural to a Class C3 use (see Q.2(1)(e)). Dove J held that the purpose of Class Q was clearly to deliver more homes and to increase housing supply. It was intended to lead to the development of residential uses in locations which would not ordinarily be contemplated by the undiluted application of policies in the NPPF relating to location (such as para 55, which states that LPAs should avoid new isolated homes in the countryside unless there were special circumstances). Dove J ruled that whether a development was 'undesirable' called for the exercise of a planning judgment by the decision-maker in the particular context in which it arose. He said that to apply the NPPF's policies with the same rigour in respect of accessibility of residential development to the Class Q prior approval process as would be applied to an application for planning permission for residential use would potentially frustrate the purpose of the introduction of Class Q, namely, to increase the supply of housing through the conversion of agricultural buildings which by definition would very frequently be in the countryside. Whilst accessibility was not an irrelevant consideration when considering Q.2(1)(e), the bar in relation to the test of unacceptability would necessarily be set significantly higher than it would be in the context of an application for planning permission. The fact that an agricultural building was in a location where planning permission would not normally be granted for accessibility reasons would not amount to a sufficient reason for refusing prior approval. In *East Hertfordshire DC*, the challenge of the claimant LPA to decisions of the inspector to allow an appeal against the refusal of prior approval to convert a barn to residential use failed. (Indeed, under the NPPG, the fact that the agricultural building was in a location where planning permission would not normally be granted for a new dwelling was not in itself a sufficient reason for refusing prior approval.)

5.46   Class R – agricultural buildings to a flexible commercial use:

- Development consisting of a change of use of an agricultural building to a flexible use falling within A1 (shops), A2 (financial and professional services), A3 (restaurants and cafés), B1 (business), B8 (storage or distribution), C1 (hotels) or D2 (assembly and leisure).

5.47   Class S – agricultural buildings to state-funded school or registered nursery:

- Development consisting of a change of use of a building and any land within its curtilage from use an agricultural building to use as a state-funded school or registered nursery.

5.48   Class T – business, hotels, etc. to state-funded school or registered nursery:

- Development consisting of a change of use of a building and any land within its curtilage from a use within C1 (hotels), C2 (residential institutions), C2A (secure residential institutions) or D2 (assembly and leisure) to use as a state-funded school or a registered nursery.

5.49   Class U – return to previous use from a converted state-funded school or registered nursery:

- Development consisting of a change of use of land from a use permitted by Class T above to the previous lawful use of the land.

5.50   Class V – Changes of use permitted under a permission granted on an application:

- Development consisting of a change of use of a building or other land from a use permitted by planning permission granted on an application, to another use which that permission would have specifically authorised when it was granted.

Part 4 – Temporary buildings and uses

5.51   Class A – temporary buildings and structures:

- The provision on land of buildings, movable structures, works, plant or machinery required temporarily in connection with and for the duration of operations being or to be carried out on, in, under or over that land or on land adjoining that land.

5.52   Class B – temporary use of land:

- The use of any land for any purpose for not more than 28 days in total in any calendar year, of which not more than 14 days in total may be for the purposes of: (a) holding a market; (b) motor car and motor cycle racing including trials of speed, and practising for these activities, and such permitted use.

5.53   Class C – use as a state-funded school for two academic years.

5.54   Class D – shops, financial, cafés, takeaways etc. to temporary flexible use:

- Change of use falling within A1 (shops), A2 (financial and professional services), A3 (restaurants and cafés), A5 (hot food takeaways), B1 (business), D1 (non-residential institutions) and D2 (assembly and leisure) or use as a betting office or pay day loan shop to a flexible use falling within A1 (shops), A2 (financial and professional services), A3 (restaurants and cafés) or B1 (business) for a single continuous period of up to two years.

5.55   Class E – temporary use of buildings or land for film-making purposes.[45]

Part 5 – Caravan sites and recreational campsites

5.56   Class A – use of land, other than a building, as a caravan site:

- Development under this head is permitted subject to the condition that the use is discontinued when the circumstances specified in A.2 cease to exist, and all caravans on the site are removed as soon as reasonably practical. The circumstances are those specified in paragraphs 2 to 10 of Schedule 1 to the Caravan Sites and Control of Development Act 1960 (cases where a caravan site licence is not required), but in relation to those mentioned in paragraph 10 do not include use for winter quarters.

---

[45]   This is also new and allows for temporary filming and the associated operational development for the sole purpose of commercial film making. The right would not cover filming which is ancillary or related to another enterprise. Where the right is used, the existing permitted development right for temporary use of land for 28 days (14 days for some uses) will not apply. The new right allows filming inside existing buildings and outside on sites of up to 1.5 hectares (including buildings and land) and also allows the construction and removal of associated sets. Use of the land or buildings under the new right cannot exceed nine months in any 27-month rolling period. Prior approval is required for each filming period in relation to transport and highways, noise, filming dates, hours of working, flooding and the impact of light on neighbouring land. The right does not apply in conservation areas, National Parks, AONBs, the Broads and World Heritage Sites. Nor does it apply to listed buildings, scheduled monuments, SSSIs, safety hazard areas or military explosives storage areas.

5.57   Class B – development on a caravan site required by conditions:

- Permitted development is that required by the conditions of a site licence
  in force under the Caravan Sites and Control of Development Act 1960.

5.58   Class C – use of land by members of certain recreational organisations:

- The use of land by members of a recreational organisation for the purposes
  of recreation or instruction, and the erection or placing of tents on the land
  for the purposes of the use. The term 'recreational organisation' means an
  organisation holding a certificate of exemption under section 269 of the
  Public Health Act 1936 (power of local authority to control the use of
  movable dwellings).

Part 6 – Agricultural and forestry

5.59   Class A – agricultural development on units of 5 hectares or more:

- The carrying out on agricultural land comprised in an agricultural unit of
  5 hectares or more of: (a) works for the erection, extension or alteration of
  a building; or (b) any excavation or engineering operations, which are
  reasonably necessary for the purposes of agriculture within that unit.

5.60   Class B – agricultural development on units of less than 5 hectares:

- The carrying out on agricultural land comprised in an agricultural unit of
  not less than 0.4 but less than 5 hectares, of development consisting of:

  - the extension or alteration of an agricultural building;
  - the installation of additional or replacement plant or machinery;
  - the provision, rearrangement or replacement of a sewer, main, pipe,
    cable or other apparatus;
  - the provision, rearrangement or replacement of a right of way;
  - the provision of a hard surface;
  - the deposit of waste; or
  - the carrying out of any of the following operations in connection with
    fish farming, namely, repairing ponds and raceways; the installation of
    grading machinery, aeration equipment or flow meters and any
    associated channel; the dredging of ponds; and the replacement of
    tanks and nets,

  where the development is reasonably necessary for the purposes of
  agriculture within the unit.

5.61   Class C – mineral working for agricultural purposes:

- The winning and working on land held or occupied with land used for the purposes of agriculture of any minerals reasonably necessary for agricultural purposes within the agricultural unit of which it forms part. Such development is not permitted within 25 metres of a trunk road or classified road. No mineral extracted is to be moved to any place outside the land from which it was extracted, except to land which is held or occupied with that land and is used for the purposes of agriculture.

5.62   Class E – forestry developments:

- The carrying out on land used for the purpose of forestry, including afforestation, of development reasonably necessary for those purposes consisting of:

    – works for the erection, extension or alteration of a building; the formation, alteration or maintenance of private ways;
    – operations on that land, or on land held or occupied with that land, to obtain the materials required for the formation, alteration or maintenance of such ways;
    – other operations (not including engineering or mining operations).

Part 7 – Non-domestic extensions, alterations, etc.

5.63   Class A – extensions, etc. of shops or financial or professional premises.

5.64   Class B – construction of shop trolley stores.

5.65   Class C – click and collect facilities.[46]

5.66   Class D – modification of shop loading bays.[47]

---

[46]   This is new and allows retailers to erect click and collect facilities within the curtilage of their existing shop, such as in car parks. One facility per retail premises may be erected. Any buildings will be limited to 4 metres in height and a gross floor space of up to 20 square metres. Prior approval is required covering the impact of the development in respect of design, siting and external appearance of the new structure. The right does not apply in conservation areas, National Parks, AONBs, the Broads and World Heritage Sites. Nor does it apply to land within the curtilage of listed buildings or scheduled monuments, or SSSIs.

[47]   This is a new permitted right allowing retailers to modify the size of their existing shop loading bay by up to 20% in any dimension. The right does not apply in conservation areas, National Parks, AONBs, the Broads and World Heritage Sites. Nor does it apply to land within the curtilage of listed buildings or scheduled monuments, and SSSIs. There is also a condition that requires any materials to be of a similar appearance to those used in the existing building.

5.67   Class E – hard surfaces for shops, catering or financial or professional premises.

5.68   Class F – extensions, etc. of office buildings.

5.69   Class G – hard surfaces for office buildings.

5.70   Class H – extensions, etc. of industrial buildings or warehouses.[48]

5.71   Class I – developments relating to an industrial process:

- Development carried out on industrial land for the purposes of an industrial process consisting of:

  - the installation of additional or replacement plant or machinery; the provision, rearrangement or replacement of a sewer, main, pipe, cable or other apparatus; or the provision, rearrangement or replacement of a private way, private railway, siding or conveyor.

5.72   Class J – hard surfaces for industrial and warehouse premises:

- Development consisting of:

  - the provision of a hard surface within the curtilage of an industrial building or warehouse to be used for the purpose of the undertaking concerned; or the replacement in whole or part of such a surface.

5.73   Class K – waste deposits from an industrial process:

- The deposit of waste material resulting from an industrial process on any land comprised in a site which was used for that purpose on 1/7/1948 whether or not the superficial area or the height of the deposit is extended as a result.

5.74   Class L – development at waste management facilities:

- Development carried out on land used for the purposes of a waste management facility consisting of:

---

[48]   There is now a permitted development right which makes permanent the time-limited increased permitted development rights introduced in May 2013 for extensions to shops, offices, industrial and warehouse development, and establishments providing catering, financial or professional services. These rights do not apply in conservation areas, National Parks, AONBs, the Broads and World Heritage Sites, or in SSSIs, or within the curtilage of a listed building.

- the extension or alteration of a building; and the installation of replacement plant or machinery.[49]

5.75 Class M – the erection, extension or alteration of a school, college, university or hospital building.

5.76 Class N – hard surfaces for schools, colleges, universities or hospitals:

- Development consisting of:

  - the provision of a hard surface within the curtilage of any school, college, university or hospital to be used for the purposes of that school, college, university or hospital; or the replacement in whole or part of such surface.

CONCLUSIONS ON PERMITTED DEVELOPMENT

5.77 Permitted development rights granted by the GPDO involve essentially minor development. It is clearly desirable, in order to support growth in the economy, that a mechanism is available which dispenses with the necessity for formal application to be made for planning permission in cases which are unlikely to be contentious. It is also clearly helpful to have, within Part 3 (Changes of use), a further means of expanding development rights in addition to that contained in the Use Classes Order 1987.

5.78 It has also been said that where a proposal for development exceeds the threshold for permitted development, the fact that a level of development is allowed at all will undoubtedly be of value in negotiations with the planning authority. It is also important to remember that the Secretary of State and LPA have powers to make directions under article 4 of the GPDO the effect of which will be to remove permitted development rights generally or in specific cases (such as in conservation areas). Persons concerned in the development of land who believe that an express planning permission is not required should always

---

[49] A new permitted development right allows waste operators for *sui generis* waste management facilities to replace any plant or machinery and buildings on land within the curtilage of a waste management facility, and which is ancillary to the main waste management operation. The permitted development right allows minor works to take place where equipment is being replaced and there is no more than a 15% increase in the floor space occupied by the plant or machinery that is being replaced; nor should the replacement building, plant and machinery exceed the existing facilities on site by more than 50% or 100 square metres, whichever is smaller. These rights do not apply in National Parks, AONBs, the Broads, conservation areas, World Heritage Sites, land within the curtilage of listed buildings and scheduled monuments or SSSIs.

take care to check whether development proposed is in fact affected by such a direction.

5.79   Lastly, this section only deals in detail with Parts 1 to 7 of Schedule 2 to the GPDO which are mainly concerned with limited development. Developers should always consult the GPDO in detail to ensure that the proposed development is not caught by exclusions and conditions which could result in conflict with the LPA, which may well be entitled to take enforcement action to secure compliance with an operative condition. Indeed, in some cases, permitted development is subject to a condition that a developer must apply for a determination as to whether prior approval is required for certain impacts before the development can begin.

Chapter 6

Planning Permission

INTRODUCTION

6.1   This chapter is concerned with the procedure relating to applications for planning permission and their consideration by the local planning authority (LPA).[1] It deals with the law associated with grants of planning permission, not least in relation to scope, meaning and duration of grants. It also includes discussion of the application of the development plan and considers the importance of housing land supply and its impact on decision-taking under the National Planning Policy Framework 2012 (NPPF) issued by the Department for Communities and Local Government (DCLG) on 27/3/2012 and soon to be revised. Planning conditions, planning obligations, the revocation or modification

---

[1]   In England, the application will usually be made: (a) in the case of land in Greater London, to the relevant borough council (unless it is an application of potential strategic importance, in which case the Mayor of London may direct that he is to be the LPA for the purposes of determining the application (TCPA 1990, ss 2A–2F, added by the Greater London Authority Act 2007)); (b) in metropolitan county areas, to the metropolitan district council; (c) in the case of unitary councils in non-metropolitan county areas, to the relevant unitary council; (d) in National Parks, to the National Park authority for the area of the Park; and (e) in other cases, to the relevant district council as district planning authority. The Broads Authority is the sole district planning authority for its area. See Town and Country Planning (Development Management Procedure) (England) Order 2015, art 11, regarding general provisions relating to applications and to which bodies they must be made. In Wales, it will be: (f) the relevant National Park authority; or (g) the county council or county borough council. County matters in England are now confined to applications in relation to minerals, waste disposal and operational development of land partly within and partly outside National Parks – for a list of county matters, see TCPA 1990, Sch 1, para 1, and Town and Country Planning (Prescription of County Matters) (England) Regulations 2003 (SI 2003/1033), reg 2. Certain applications are made directly to the Planning Inspectorate (PINS): (i) applications for development consent for nationally significant infrastructure; (ii) applications for urgent Crown development; and (iii) applications for major development under TCPA 1990, s 62A, where the LPA has been designated by the Secretary of State and the applicant has chosen to submit an application to PINS. The Department of Energy and Climate Change administers the provisions of the Electricity Act 1989 for developers seeking consents from the Secretary of State.

of planning permissions and environmental impact assessments (EIAs) are considered in the following chapters.

APPLICATIONS FOR EXPRESS PERMISSION – PROCEDURE

6.2   Applications for planning permission and their handling are governed by a combination of Part III of the Town and Country Planning Act 1990 (TCPA 1990) (see s 62) and subordinate legislation consisting of the Town and Country Planning (Development Management Procedure) (England) Order 2015 (DMPO)[2] (which came into force on 15/4/2015) and the Town and Country Planning (Development Management Procedure) (Wales) Order 2012.[3] There is also a wealth of guidance to be found in the National Planning Practice Guidance (NPPG) which was issued on 6/3/2014,[4] and in the revised versions of the four procedural guides on: (a) planning appeals; (b) called-in planning applications; (c) enforcement notice appeals; and (d) lawful development certificate appeals, published by the Planning Inspectorate (PINS) on 23 March 2016.

PRE-APPLICATION CONSULTATION

6.3   The NPPF[5] and the NPPG encourage pre-application engagement between applicants and the LPA, statutory and non-statutory consultees, elected members and the local community. Where the application is going to be large and/or complex, applicants and LPAs may sometimes enter into a planning performance agreement (PPA) with a view to agreeing timescales, actions and resources for handling the application. Such agreements can be a useful focus for pre-application discussions about the issues which will need to be addressed.

6.4   Pre-application consultation is compulsory in the case of a development involving the installation of more than two wind turbines or where the hub height of any turbine exceeds 15 metres.[6]

---

[2]   SI 2015/595.

[3]   SI 2012/801.

[4]   Available at http://planningguidance.communities.gov.uk.

[5]   NPPF, paras 188–195.

[6]   DMPO, arts 3 and 4.

APPLICATIONS

6.5   Any person may apply for planning permission[7] whether he owns the land or not, although the owner must be notified of any application affecting his land (and this includes any tenants of agricultural holdings on such land).[8] Applications are made on a standard application form and must contain the prescribed information.[9] The application must be accompanied[10] by: (a) a certificate of ownership in which the applicant certifies that he has satisfied the requirement in relation to the notification of owners;[11] (b) a Design and Access Statement (if required);[12] (c) a statement as to pre-application consultation (if

---

[7]   Applications may be made for: (a) full planning permission; (b) outline planning permission (which means planning permission for the erection of a building, subject to a condition requiring the subsequent approval of the LPA with respect to one or more of the following reserved matters, namely access, appearance, landscaping, layout and scale; (c) reserved matters application (these are defined in DMPO, art 2); an LPA cannot refuse final permission on other grounds which they could have taken into account on the outline application; any such application must be within the ambit of the outline planning permission but whether or not a departure is so significant as to require a fresh application for permission is a question of fact and degree (see *R v Hammersmith and Fulham LBC ex parte GLC* (1985) 51 P & CR 120, CA); such applications normally have to be made within three years from the date when outline planning permission was granted (see TCPA 1990, s 92); (d) for the discharge or modification of a planning condition (whereby application may be made for planning permission for the development of land without complying with the conditions subject to which a previous planning permission was granted); (e) for non-material changes to an existing planning permission; (f) lawful development certificates; (g) prior approval for some permitted development rights; (h) listed building consent (see Listed Building Act 1990, s 9); and (i) non-planning consents (namely, consents that may have to be obtained alongside or after, and separate from, planning permission) such as advertisement consent, consent required under a Tree Preservation Order and hazardous substances consent.

[8]   DMPO, art 13 deals with the giving of notice to an owner or tenant of the land (additional steps need to be taken in the case of minerals applications).

[9]   See NPPG and DMPO, art 7.

[10]   DMPO, art 11(2), which sets out what has to be lodged with an LPA in the case of applications: (a) for outline planning permission (art 5); (b) for approval of reserved matters (art 6); and (c) those applications mentioned in art 7 (i.e. mining operations).

[11]   DMPO, art 14. The notice requirement is mandatory so that once an application has been submitted without due notice to an owner, the requisite notice to the owner could not be fulfilled (*R (Pridmore) v Salisbury DC* [2005] 1 P & CR 32, where there had been deliberate non-compliance and the resulting planning permission had been quashed).

[12]   DMPO, art 9, which sets out the requirements for a Design and Access Statement where it is needed, namely, in cases of major development (as defined in DMPO, art 2) or development within a World Heritage Site, a conservation area or in the case of applications for listed building consent, although a Design and Access Statement will not be required in those cases mentioned in art 9(4) (as where an application involves a material change in the use of land or buildings). See Design and Access Statements in NPPG at Paragraphs: 029 Reference ID: 14-029-20140306 through to 033 Reference ID: 14-033-20140306.

required);[13] (d) any particulars or evidence required by the LPA;[14] and (e) the appropriate fee.[15] Slightly different requirements apply in the case of certain applications (i.e. for listed building consent, mining operations, minerals development or hazardous substances consent).

6.6   Decisions on an application can sometimes be made by the Secretary of State who may decide to 'call in' an application, in which case the applicant or the LPA has a right to be heard at a public inquiry or other hearing.[16] The discretion will only usually be exercised in circumstances where the application involves issues of more than local significance.[17]

---

13   DMPO, art 4.

14   DMPO, art 11(2)(e) (3).

15   DMPO, art 11(2)(f).

16   *R (Save Britain's Heritage) v Secretary of State for Communities and Local Government* [2017] EWHC 3059 (Admin), where it was held that the Secretary of State is under no duty to give reasons for a decision not to call in a planning application under TCPA 1990, s 77. This is because a call-in decision is a very different type of decision to a decision by an LPA to grant planning permission. A call-in decision is, in essence, a procedural decision by the Secretary of State on whether to intervene in the planning process; it does not result in the grant of any substantive rights. Unlike an inspector's or Secretary of State's decision letter after an inquiry, it is not a reasoned letter which must deal adequately with the principal issues in dispute between the parties at an inquiry.

17   TCPA 1990, s 77. See *R (Persimmon Homes Ltd) v Secretary of State* [2008] JPL 323; *R (Hadfield) v Secretary of State* [2002] EWHC 1266 (Admin); *Lakin v Secretary of State for Scotland* 1988 SLT 780. Where the Town and Country Planning (Consultation) (England) Direction in Circular 02/09 applies (and where the LPA is minded to grant planning permission), the authority is required to send details of the application to the Secretary of State and may not itself determine the application for 21 days in order that the Secretary of State may decide whether to call in the application for his own determination (or issue a holding direction under DMPO, art 31). The cases falling within the direction involve: (a) inappropriate development in the Green Belt where the floor space to be created is 1,000 square metres or more or any other development which would have a significant impact on the openness of the Green Belt; (b) development outside town centres (involving floor space exceeding 5,000 square metres) which is not in accordance with the development plan; (c) development affecting a World Heritage Site, including any buffer zone, to which English Heritage has objected; (d) development on publicly owned playing fields to which the English Sports Council has objected; and (e) major development in a flood risk area to which the Environment Agency (EA) has also objected (major development is defined as development involving ten or more dwellings or where the site area is 0.5 hectare or more or, in the case of non-residential development, where the new floor space to be provided is 1,000 square metres or more or where the site area is 1 hectare or more). See also the position in Wales under the Notification Direction (Welsh Government Circular 07/12), where LPAs are required to refer applications to the Welsh Ministers where they are considering the grant of planning permission in the case of certain types of development.

MULTIPLE APPLICATIONS

6.7   It should be noted that more than one application may be made for planning permission in relation to the same land. However, where two planning permissions exist, both cannot be implemented if they are mutually inconsistent.[18] There are, however, limits to this latitude. To avoid abuse of the system a planning authority may decline to determine an application where, in the previous two years, either the Secretary of State has dismissed an appeal against a refusal of a similar application (meaning, for these purposes, where the development and the land to which the applications relate are the same or substantially the same), or where the LPA has refused more than one similar application and there has been no appeal to the Secretary of State against any such refusal, and the authority considers that there has been no significant change in the relevant considerations since the refusal of the similar application or dismissal of the appeal.[19] There are

---

[18]   *Pilkington v Secretary of State for the Environment* [1973] 1 WLR 1527. Here, an owner of land obtained and implemented a planning permission for the erection of a bungalow on site B on the condition that no other dwelling would be erected on the land. However, the owner subsequently discovered an earlier planning permission for the erection of a bungalow on another part of the land, i.e. on site A, which permission contemplated the use of the remaining land as a smallholding. When the owner started building on site A, he was served with an enforcement notice requiring the restoration of site A to its original condition. The enforcement notice was upheld. It was found that the earlier permission was incapable of implementation as it was physically impossible in the light of the erection of the bungalow on site B (*Ellis v Worcestershire County Council* (1961) 12 P & CR 178 approved). In *Staffordshire County Council v NGR Land Developments Ltd* [2002] EWCA Civ 856, it was held that where two planning permissions existed in different terms in relation to the same land, the correct test for determining whether the earlier permission was still valid was whether it remained physically possible to carry out the permitted development in accordance with the terms of the earlier permission. If not, then the second permission can be regarded as an alternative rather than as cumulative.

[19]   TCPA 1990, s 70A. See *R (Gill) v Central Bedfordshire Council* [2015] EWHC 3458 (Admin); when exercising its power under s 70A to decline to determine a subsequent application for planning permission for a garage at a residential property, an LPA had taken into account an irrelevant consideration, namely, its finding that the application would have the effect of altering an enforcement notice which required the demolition of the garage. The LPA's decision would be quashed so that the application could be reconsidered on a lawful basis. However, the court found that the fact that the proposed garage shared with the constructed garage characteristics that had been judged fatal to the success of the previous application was a relevant factor in determining whether the developments were similar, which the LPA was entitled to take into account (*R (Harrison) v Richmond-upon-Thames LBC* [2013] EWHC 1677 (Admin), considered).

similar powers enabling an LPA to decline to determine overlapping[20] or retrospective[21] applications.

VALIDATION AND TIME LIMITS FOR DECISIONS

6.8   Once the relevant planning authority[22] has received the relevant documentation and fee it must send an acknowledgement of the application to the applicant.[23] Applications for minor and small-scale development should be validated within three to five working days, and applications for major development within ten working days after receipt of the application. There is a right of appeal to the Secretary of State where the LPA has failed to determine the application within the requisite time limits.[24] These are 13 weeks in the case of major development[25] and eight weeks in all other cases (unless these periods have been increased by consent) – these periods run from the day immediately following the date on which the application was received by the LPA.[26] However, decisions in the case of applications for non-material changes to an existing planning permission must be made within 28 days (or such longer period as may

---

[20]   TCPA 1990, s 70B. This is where similar applications are made at the same time, or where an application is made at a time when the earlier application is still under consideration either by the LPA or by the Secretary of State (on appeal or call-in), or in a case where there has been no determination of the earlier application and the time for appeal has not yet elapsed. We are dealing here with what is known as twin-tracking. This is where two applications are made at the same time, yet only one is appealed, which will enable a developer to continue discussions with the LPA without losing his place in the queue of appeals. There is also a concern that an authority might change its mind on the second application.

[21]   TCPA 1990, s 70C. This section was inserted into the TCPA by LA 2011, s 123(2) and came into force on 6/4/2012. It provides a power for an LPA to decline to determine an application for planning permission which would involve granting permission, whether for the 'whole or any part of the land', for 'the whole or any part of the matters specified in the enforcement notice as constituting a breach of planning control'. This arises where, if a second application is allowed, it would conflict with matters contained in an extant enforcement notice as constituting a breach of planning control. See *R (Banghard) v Bedford BC* [2017] EWHC 2391 (Admin), where the limits of the power were identified.

[22]   DMPO, art 11(1).

[23]   DMPO, arts 11 and 39: the form of letter used must be the same or substantially the same as the standard form in Sch 1, which should also be used in applications for a certificate of lawful use or development.

[24]   TCPA 1990, s 78(2)(a).

[25]   Defined in DMPO, art 2(1) (for England and Wales) (and includes where the development involves ten or more dwelling-houses or where the floor space to be created by the development is 1,000 square metres or more).

[26]   Time limits for decisions can be found in DMPO, art 34(2).

be agreed)[27] and in the case of applications requiring environmental assessment, the period is 16 weeks.

6.9   The validation requirements are set out in the NPPG.[28]

PLANNING PERFORMANCE AGREEMENTS AND EXTENSION OF TIME AGREEMENTS

6.10   There has been a sharp increase in the use of PPAs[29] under which, in cases involving major planning applications, applicants pay for agreed processing milestones and service levels to be met. LPAs clearly benefit from revenue from PPAs while developers like the certainty which they provide.

6.11   What happens is that LPAs and developers agree at pre-application stage certain milestones for processing applications outside the statutory time limits. LPAs are able to charge for this service.[30] A similar type of arrangement is what is known as an extension of time agreement, which is where the applicant and the LPA agree that the application can be determined beyond the legal deadline, albeit at no extra charge for applicants. Such applications are agreed after submission of the application (with no extra charge for applicants) and commits an applicant not to appeal against non-determination of an application for a specified period.

6.12   The rise in PPA usage is due to LPA resourcing pressures and to pressure within the industry for greater certainty over timescales (not least when applications will be determined) for which developers are prepared to pay. Further benefits provided by PPAs include consistency of staff handling the application and more flexibility in allowing proposals to be altered during the planning process.

---

[27]   DMPO, art 10, which deals with procedure in the case of such applications.

[28]   Starting at Paragraph: 016 Reference ID: 14-016-20140306.

[29]   Which were first introduced into the planning system in April 2008. See PPAs in NPPG at Paragraph: 016 Reference ID: 20-016-20150326.

[30]   In the edition of *Planning* for 23/2/2018, it was reported that Westminster City Council was charging £26,000 plus VAT for major application PPAs and £15,000 plus VAT for other applications involving complex issues (raising some £2 million per annum, which was said to be sufficient to support 17 professional planners in a 50-strong department), whereas Stratford-on-Avon DC was not charging for PPAs.

PUBLICITY

6.13   Applications for planning permission must be publicised by the LPA.[31] The methods involve a site notice, publication of a notice in a local newspaper, neighbour notification and information which has to be published on the authority's website. The appropriate methods will be referable to whether the application involves major or minor development, is an EIA application, does not accord with the relevant development plan or affects a public right of way. For instance, in the case of minor development, the authority must display a site notice on or near the land for not less than 21 days or serve notice on the adjoining occupier or owner.[32] Any failure to publicise the application in the appropriate manner may afford grounds for quashing any decision to grant planning permission.[33] Attention is also drawn to the statutory publicity requirements for planning and heritage applications in the NPPG in the section 'Consultation and pre-decision matters'.[34]

PLANNING REGISTERS

6.14   Every LPA is required to keep a planning register.[35] Part I of the register contains a copy of every application (and associated plans, drawings or other documents such as any planning obligation or highways agreement proposed or entered into in connection with the application) for planning permission (thereby

---

[31]   This is dealt with fully in DMPO, art 15.

[32]   DMPO, art 15(5).

[33]   *R (Wembley Fields Ltd) v Brent London Borough Council* [2005] EWHC 2978 (Admin); *R (Gavin) v Haringey Borough Council* [2003] EWHC 2591 (Admin).

[34]   NPPG at Paragraph: 029 Reference ID: 15-029-20170728 at Table 1.

[35]   DMPO, art 40 requires each LPA to maintain a register of planning applications in relation to their area. It is for the LPA to decide what information beyond the statutory minimum should be included on the statutory register. Each LPA is to have regard to the Code of Recommended Practice for Local Authorities on Data Transparency, which sets out the government's expectations for the publication of public data. In addition, LPAs are expected to have regard to their obligations under the (now) Data Protection Act 2018 and to consider whether redactions are appropriate before publishing personal information on the register. It was reported in May 2017 that Basildon Borough Council was fined £150,000 by the Information Commissioner's Office for breaching the Data Protection Act 1998 after it published sensitive personal information in the form of a written statement in support of a householder's planning application in relation to proposed works in the Green Belt. It was reported that the statement contained sensitive personal data relating to a static traveller family which had been living on the site for many years. In particular, it referred to the family's disability requirements, including mental health issues, the names of all the family members, their ages and the location of their home. It was reported that the breach arose when an inexperienced council officer did not notice the personal information in the statement and there was no procedure in place for a second person to check it before the personal data was inadvertently published online.

giving the public notice of pending applications), including applications for approval of reserved matters (i.e. those not yet disposed of). Part II contains a record of all applications and the decisions taken on them (along with associated plans, drawings and other documents).[36] Part II must also contain information in connection with any decision by the Secretary of State on a deemed application for planning permission arising from an enforcement appeal or in relation to applications for lawful development certificates or in relation to Simplified Planning Zone schemes. Separate registers also exist for minerals applications, Tree Preservation Orders, enforcement notices and stop notices, notices under section 211 of the TCPA 1990 (preservation of trees in conservation areas), and applications for hazardous substances consent. The NPPG also deals with planning registers.[37]

POST-APPLICATION CONSULTATION

6.15   After a planning authority has received a planning application, it will undertake a period of consultation where views on the proposed development can be expressed and taken into account. The main types of consultation are: (a) public consultation (the period for making comments will be not less than 21 days or 14 days where a notice is published in a newspaper); (b) statutory consultees (who are under a duty to respond to consultations within 21 days); see list of statutory consultees in the case of applications for planning permission and heritage applications in the NPPG in the section 'Consultation and pre-decision matters'[38] (including government departments and other authorities at local and national level); (c) any consultation required by a direction (i.e. where the Secretary of State directs LPAs that additional consultation must take place in specific local circumstances); and (d) non-statutory consultees where there are planning policy reasons to engage other consultees who are likely to have an interest in the proposed development (who should respond within the period specified by the LPA); reference should also be made to the list of non-statutory consultees in the NPPG.[39] A planning application may be amended in appropriate circumstances but this not does mean that an applicant for permission or an LPA would be entitled to side-step ordinary procedural requirements.[40]

---

[36]   TCPA 1990, s 69 and DMPO, art 40. The register must be kept available for public inspection at all reasonable hours. Where the register is kept using electronic storage, the authority may make the register available for inspection online (art 40(14)).

[37]   NPPG at Paragraph: 062 Reference ID: 14-062-20140306 through to 14-064-20140306.

[38]   NPPG at Paragraph: 030 Reference ID: 15-030-20170728, Table 2, first column.

[39]   NPPG at Paragraph: 031 Reference ID: 15-031-20140306, Table 3, first column.

[40]   *R (Holborn Studios Ltd) v Hackney LBC* [2017] EWHC 2823 (Admin), where the court quashed a planning permission granted without further consultation following the amendment of the

APPLICATIONS FOR OUTLINE PLANNING PERMISSION[41]

6.16   An application may be made for outline planning permission. This is where the applicant is looking for a decision in principle only and will not involve detailed plans. Such an application would be granted subject to a condition specifying reserved matters for the authority's subsequent approval.[42]

6.17   It is acceptable for an applicant to make more than one application for the approval of reserved matters covering the same ground, and approval may also be

---

application. The court considered the circumstances in which planning permission might be granted for a development other than one for which an application was initially made, and the test to be applied when reviewing the grant of such a permission. The question whether further consultation was required following changes to the planning proposal depended upon, *inter alia*, the nature and extent of those changes and the potential significance to those who might be consulted. Although an LPA had a discretion as to whether to accept an amendment to a planning application and grant permission, the question of what fairness might require it to do in the circumstances was ultimately one for the court to determine. It was not the court's function merely to review the reasonableness of an LPA's judgment of what fairness required. The test for reviewing the grant of permission for alternative development without further consultation was whether the process had been so unfair as to be unlawful. In *Holborn Studios*, the decision in *Bernard Wheatcroft Ltd v Secretary of State for the Environment* (1982) 43 P & CR 233 was doubted.

41   See DMPO, art 5 and also art 6 for applications for approval of reserved matters (setting out what such application requires). Article 7(3) provides that an application for outline permission only does not need to give details of any reserved matters (although this could be useful in the case of applications for development in the Green Belt where issues of openness arise where illustrative drawings may well be of value to the applicant).

42   DMPO, art 2(1) defines 'reserved matters' in relation to an outline planning permission to mean any of the following matters in respect of which details have not been given in the application (other definitions within art 2(1) are also added for ease of reference): (a) access (meaning the accessibility to and within the site for vehicles, cycles and pedestrians in terms of the positioning and treatment of access and circulation routes and how these fit into the surrounding access network); (b) appearance (meaning the aspects of a building or place within the development which determines the visual impression the building or place makes, including the external built form of the development, its architecture, materials, decoration, lighting, colour or texture); (c) landscaping (meaning the treatment of land (other than buildings) for the purpose of enhancing or protecting the amenities of the site and the area in which it is situated and includes: (i) screening by fences, walls or other means; (ii) the planting of trees, hedges, shrubs or grass; (iii) the formation of banks, terraces or other earthworks; and (iv) the laying out or provision of gardens, courts or squares, water features, sculpture or public art and the provision of other amenity features); (d) layout (meaning the way in which buildings, routes and open spaces within the development are provided, situated and orientated in relation to each other and to buildings and spaces outside the development); and (e) scale (meaning the height, width and length of each building proposed within the development in relation to its surroundings).

sought in stages (provided they are made prior to the expiry of the time limit for making such application).[43]

6.18   The following are important elements which apply in the case of outline grants:

(a)   The LPA cannot refuse approval of reserved matters because it no longer considered that the development would be desirable.[44]

(b)   Approval of reserved matters could not be used to alter the nature of the development for which outline permission had been given.[45]

---

[43]   *Heron Corp Ltd v Manchester City Council* [1978] 1 WLR 937. In other words, an applicant might have a choice of approvals, although the authority might grant a subsequent approval on the condition that an earlier approval was not proceeded with.

[44]   *Thirkell (Lewis) v Secretary of State* [1978] JPL 844. In this case, the authority had recognised that urbanisation was inevitable when it granted outline permission, and it could not resile from this.

[45]   *R v Castle Point District Council ex parte Brooks* [1985] JPL 473. This was a case where the applicant obtained outline permission to build a bungalow for the better management of his fruit farm. He later applied for approval of reserved matters, showing plans for a very substantial house for which approval was given. A neighbouring owner successfully applied to quash this decision on the basis that approval of reserved matters could not be used to alter an original planning permission. In *R (Morland) v West Wiltshire District Council* [2006] EWHC 1243 (Admin), the application for approval of reserved matters also failed to fall within the scope of the relevant permission and was invalid. Here the application for approval of reserved matters included the building of 71 dwellings on a site which had been set aside for a district centre on the masterplan attached to the original outline planning permission. The outline permission to which the application related, and the original permission which the later permission varied, contained similar conditions, providing that the district centre could include an element of ancillary residential development. The applicant contended that the masterplan was purely indicative, that the parent permission permitted both the district centre and residential development without fixing the location of either, and that he had been entitled to submit an application for approval of reserved matters showing residential development within the area set aside on the masterplan for the district centre. The authority's decision to register an application for approval of reserved matters in these circumstances was quashed. It was held that although the masterplan was illustrative, it was still intended to indicate something. Whereas minor revisions of boundaries and realignments of the highway layout would undoubtedly be within the scope of such an illustrative plan, a significant amount of non-ancillary residential development within the broad area set aside for the district centre was not. The appropriate way to seek an increase in the amount of residential development permitted within the district centre was to submit a new outline application. In *R v Hammersmith and Fulham London Borough Council ex parte Greater London Council* [1986] JPL 528, it was said to be a question of fact as to whether a detailed plan lodged in support of an application for approval of reserved matters was within the ambit of the outline permission. In this case, the authority had been entitled to conclude that the departure from the outline permission was insufficient to require a fresh application; see also *Centre Hotels (Cranston) Ltd v Secretary of State for the Environment* [1982] JPL 108; *Calcaria Construction Co Ltd v Secretary of State for the Environment* (1974) 27 P & CR 435; *Shemara v Luton Corporation* (1967) 18 P & CR 520.

(c) Where details in relation to aspects of reserved matters have been advanced at the outline stage, it is not open to the LPA to grant outline permission subject to the later approval of these matters. If an LPA wishes to limit the size of a development at the outline stage, then it should impose a condition which would have this effect.[46]

(d) It is open to an LPA to decide that an application for outline permission should not be considered separately from all or any of the reserved matters, in which case the LPA must, within one month after receipt of the application, notify the applicant that it is unable to determine it unless further details are submitted, specifying the details which it requires. The applicant is then free to provide such details or else appeal to the Secretary of State.[47]

(e) An application for full planning permission may take effect as an application for approval of reserved matters even if it is made out of time.[48]

APPLICATIONS FOR PERMISSION IN PRINCIPLE

6.19   This is a new concept and was introduced by the Housing and Planning Act 2016.[49]

---

[46] *R v Newbury District Council ex parte Chieveley Parish Council* [1999] PLCR 51; DMPO, art 2, which provides that there is no power to reserve matters of which details have been given in the outline application, though it is open to the applicant to amend the application by withdrawing the details, and it is open to the LPA to require further details, nor is there any objection either to the practice of including details 'for illustrative purposes only'.

[47] DMPO, art 5(2).

[48] *Cardiff Corpn v Secretary of State for Wales* (1971) 22 P & CR 718.

[49] Housing and Planning Act 2016, s 150, for the introduction of the grant of permission in principle (PiP) for housing-led development in England in TCPA 1990, s 58A; and s 151 for the power of the Secretary of State in a new s 14A in PCPA 2004, Pt 2, to make regulations requiring an LPA to prepare, maintain and publish registers of particular kinds of land within an LPA's area. The result of this was the Town and Country Planning (Brownfield Land Register) Regulations 2017 (SI 2017/403) (which came into force on 16/4/2017), which place a duty on LPAs to prepare, maintain and publish registers of brownfield land which is suitable for residential development. The Town and Country Planning (Permission in Principle) Order 2017 (SI 2017/402) (which came into force on 15/4/2017) provides that sites entered in Part 2 of the new brownfield registers will be granted PiP and is stated to be subject to review by 15/4/2022. LPAs are also expected to have compiled their brownfield registers by 31/12/2017. Reference should also be made to the NPPG, which provides guidance about PiP (revision date 28/7/2017), essential extracts of which are set out in the following paragraphs. The Town and Country Planning (Permission in Principle) (Amendment) Order 2017 (SI 2017/1309) (which came into force on 1/6/2018) also contains regulations enabling applications for PiP to be made for minor, housing-led development (applying to schemes of up to nine dwellings, commercial floor space of up to 1,000 square metres or in relation to sites of less than one hectare). The NPPG confirms that non-residential development can receive PiP, providing housing occupies the majority of the floor space in the case of the overall scheme. It also allows PiP to be sought in relation to part only of a larger site

6.20   The permission in principle (PiP) consent route is an alternative way of obtaining planning permission which separates the consideration of matters of principle for proposed development from the technical detail of the development. The PiP consent route has two stages. The first stage (or PiP stage) establishes whether a site is suitable in principle for residential development (i.e. development in which the residential use occupies the majority of the floor space). The second stage (or technical details consent stage) occurs when the detailed development proposals are assessed.[50]

6.21   LPAs can enter suitable sites in Part 2 of their brownfield land registers (subject to undertaking the necessary requirements for publicity, notification and consultation) which will trigger a grant of PiP.[51] Once the necessary secondary legislation has been introduced, it will also be possible to obtain PiP through

---

where the proposal does not constitute major development or another form of exempt development. Where PiP is granted by application, the permission should last for three years compared to five years for sites granted PiP via a brownfield land register. LPAs receiving PiP applications should also make a decision within five weeks. The Secretary of State can also call in PiP applications. On 28/6/2018, *Planning* reported that take-up under the new scheme is very low indeed and there seems to be little enthusiasm for this means of obtaining planning permission. It is, however, very early days. It is suggested that the process is more costly (even the Government's own impact assessment says that it is likely to cost around £800 more on average) and will take significantly longer, as it is a two-stage process. On the face of it, as a typical brownfield site is likely to secure planning permission anyway, developers will no doubt submit outline applications. It is also said that PiP consents are insufficiently detailed to give developers financial security.

[50]   NPPG at Paragraph: 001 Reference ID: 58-001-20170728.

[51]   An LPA may grant PiP if it fulfils the requirements set out in regs 6–13 of the Town and Country Planning (Brownfield Land Register) Regulations 2017 for entering a site in Part 2 of its brownfield land register, which will trigger a grant of PiP for that land. LPAs should consider the suitability of all relevant sites on their brownfield land registers for the grant of PiP, taking into account relevant policies in the development plan and other material considerations. There may be cases where other routes to planning permission (i.e. outline permission) are more appropriate. Land will be entered in Part 1 of the register where it meets the criteria in reg 4(1) and in Part 2 where it has also been allocated by the LPA for residential development following mandatory publicity (as set out in regs 6–9) and consultation procedures (as set out in regs 10–13). Where land is entered in Part 2 of the register, it will be granted PiP under TCPA 1990, s 59A. PiP and its effect are described in ss 58A, 59A and 70(2ZZAC) to (2ZZC) of that Act. These sections were inserted by Housing and Planning Act 2016, s 150. Regulations 14–18 make provision for exemptions, information which must be included for each entry in the register, public inspection of the register, review and revision of the register and provision of a power for the Secretary of State to be able to require LPAs to give the Secretary of State information in relation to their registers.

the local site allocation process[52] or by an application for non-major development.[53]

6.22   Following a grant of PiP, the site must receive a grant of technical details consent before development can proceed. The granting of technical details consent has the effect of granting planning permission for the development and other statutory requirements may apply at this stage (i.e. in relation to protected species or listed buildings). Technical details consent can be obtained following submission of a valid application to the LPA. An application for technical details consent must be in accordance with the PiP that is specified by the applicant in the technical details consent application form.[54]

6.23   PiP may be granted for residential development (i.e. development in which the residential use occupies the majority of the floor space). Non-residential development should be compatible with the proposed residential development. Appropriate non-residential uses may include, for example, a small proportion of retail, office space or community uses. The following types of development are specifically exempt from inclusion in a grant of PiP:

(a)   development consisting of the winning and working of minerals;
(b)   development falling within Schedule 1 Environmental Impact Assessment development;
(c)   development that is Schedule 2 Environmental Impact Assessment development and has been screened as Environmental Assessment development;
(d)   development that would be prohibited under the habitats protection legislation.[55]

6.24   Other factors should also be borne in mind:

(a)   It is not possible for conditions to be attached to a PiP and its terms may only include the site location, the type of development and amount of development.[56]

---

[52]   Site allocations in existing local or neighbourhood plans do not have a grant of PiP. However, planning applications should be decided in accordance with those site allocations unless material considerations indicate otherwise.

[53]   NPPG at Paragraph: 002 Reference ID: 58-002-20170728.

[54]   NPPG at Paragraph: 003 Reference ID: 58-003-20170728. Separate technical details consent applications cannot be made for different phases of the development. It is also open to LPAs to consider non-material changes to a grant of PiP. LPAs can also modify or revoke a grant of technical details consent.

[55]   NPPG at Paragraph: 004 Reference ID: 58-004-20170728.

[56]   NPPG at Paragraph: 020 Reference ID: 58-020-20170728.

(b) It will be possible for the LPA to attach planning conditions to a technical details consent provided they meet existing requirements around the use of conditions.[57]

(c) There is no right of appeal where the LPA decides not to enter a site in Part 2 of a brownfield land register and trigger the grant of PiP. A person with an interest in a site always has the option of submitting a planning application.[58]

(d) An application for technical details consent may be appealed on grounds of non-determination or refusal or against any condition imposed.[59]

(e) If the technical details consent application is refused, the PiP is unaffected and (subject to the powers of an LPA to decline to consider repeat applications) the applicant has the option to submit a new technical details consent application. It should be noted that a PiP granted through the allocation of land on a brownfield land register lasts for five years, whereas a PiP granted by application lasts for three years. A technical details consent application cannot be made if the PiP has expired.[60]

(f) The removal of a site from a brownfield land register does not revoke PiP previously granted to that land. LPAs have power to modify or revoke a grant of PiP. Compensation may be payable and such powers should only be exercised in exceptional circumstances, and where there is no other alternative course of action.[61]

(g) The Secretary of State has no power to call in a decision on whether to enter a site in Part 2 of a brownfield land register and trigger the grant of PiP.[62] However, the Secretary of State does have the power to call in applications for technical details consent.[63]

DETERMINATION OF APPLICATIONS

6.25 Before dealing with specific matters, it is as well to begin by reminding ourselves about the basics of the planning code when it comes to decision-making (whether the decision-maker is the LPA at first instance, and then the Secretary of State, on a called-in application[64] or by him or one of his inspectors on

---

[57] NPPG at Paragraph: 021 Reference ID: 58-021-20170728.

[58] NPPG at Paragraph: 024 Reference ID: 58-024-20170728.

[59] NPPG at Paragraph: 025 Reference ID: 58-025-20170728.

[60] NPPG at Paragraph: 026 Reference ID: 58-026-20170728.

[61] NPPG at Paragraph: 027 Reference ID: 58-027-20170728.

[62] NPPG at Paragraph: 028 Reference ID: 58-028-20170728.

[63] NPPG at Paragraph: 029 Reference ID: 58-0298-20170728.

[64] Under TCPA 1990, s 77.

appeal).[65] These are helpfully addressed in outline by Gilbart J in *William Davis Ltd & Others v Charnwood Borough Council*.[66] In particular, he noted as follows at [18]–[19]:

> 18. The law on decision making in the Planning Code is now well settled … The significance of the development plan is readily apparent from the relevant principles. In determining a planning application, the LPA or SSCLG [Secretary of State for Communities and Local Government] must act as follows. (In the case of LPAs, while reasons to grant permission are generally not given, the principles also apply to the deliberations by which it reached its conclusion; typically, the reasoning will be in the officer's report, and/or in the Minutes of the relevant committee.) The decision maker must:
>
> i)   have regard to the statutory development plan (see TCPA 1990 s.70(2));
> ii)   have regard to material considerations (TCPA 1990 s.70(2));
> ii)   determine the proposal in accordance with the development plan unless material considerations indicate otherwise (PCPA 2004 s.38(6));
> iv)   apply national policy unless he gives reasons for not doing so: see Nolan LJ in *Horsham DC v Secretary of State for the Environment* (1992) 63 P. & C.R. 219; [1992] 1 P.L.R. 81; [1992] J.P.L. 334 following Woolf J in *EC Gransden & Co Ltd v Secretary of State for the Environment* (1987) 54 P. & C.R. 86; [1986] J.P.L. 519 and see Lindblom J in *R. (on the application of Cala Homes (South) Ltd) v Secretary of State for Communities and Local Government* [2011] EWHC 97 (Admin); [2011] J.P.L. 887 at [50];
> v)   consider the nature and extent of any conflict within the development plan; *Tesco Stores Ltd v Dundee CC* [2012] UKSC 13 at [22] per Lord Reed;
> vi)   consider whether the development accords with the development plan, looking at it as a whole; see *R. v Rochdale MBC Ex p. Milne (No.2)* [2000] EWHC 650 (Admin); [2001] Env. L.R.22; (2001) 81 P. & C.R.27 per Sullivan J at [46]– [48]. There may be some points in the plan which support the proposal but there may be some considerations pointing in the opposite direction. It must assess all of these and then decide whether in the light of the whole plan the proposal does or does not accord with it; per Lord Clyde in *Edinburgh CC v Secretary of State for Scotland* [1997] 1 W.L.R. 1447; 1998 S.C. (H.L.) 33 cited by Sullivan J in *R. v Rochdale MBC Ex p.Milne (No.2)* at [48].
>
> 19. The interpretation of policy is for the court, but its application to the context of a particular proposal is for the decision maker.

---

65   Under TCPA 1990, s 78.
66   [2017] EWHC 3006 (Admin) at [15]–[29].

6.26   The LPA may grant permission[67] conditionally or unconditionally or it may refuse planning permission.[68] In dealing with an application, the authority shall have regard to: (a) the provisions of the development plan (so far as is material to the application);[69] (b) any local finance considerations (so far as is

---

[67]   Local Government Act 1972, s 101, allows the LPA to arrange for the discharge of its functions by a committee, a sub-committee, an officer or any other LPA. It is in the public interest for the LPA to ensure that it has effective delegation arrangements in place so that decisions on planning applications that raise no significant planning issues are made quickly and that resources are appropriately concentrated on applications of greatest significance to the local area. LPA delegation arrangements may include conditions or limitations as to the extent of the delegation, or the circumstances in which it may be exercised. Local authority members must maintain an open mind when considering planning applications. Where members take decisions on planning applications, they must do so in accordance with the development plan unless material considerations indicate otherwise. Members must only take into account planning considerations which can include public views where they relate to relevant planning matters. Local opposition or support for a proposal is not in itself a ground for refusing or granting planning permission, unless it is founded upon material planning reasons. Under LA 2011, Pt 1, each local authority is required to adopt a local code of conduct that sets out the expectations as to the conduct of members in carrying out their official duties. The local authority must also keep a register of members' interests. The DCLG publication 'Openness and transparency on personal interests: a guide for councillors' (2013) gives practical information about members' personal interests and standard arrangements introduced by the LA 2011. Section 25 of the 2011 Act clarifies that a member is not to be regarded as being unable to act fairly or without bias if they participate in a decision on a matter simply because they have previously expressed a view or campaigned on it. Members may campaign and represent their constituents and then speak and vote on those issues without fear of breaking the rules on pre-determination. Members may also speak with developers and express positive views about development. A distinction may be drawn between pre-determination and pre-disposition. Members must not have a closed mind when they make a decision, as decisions taken by those with pre-determined views are vulnerable to successful challenge. At the point of making a decision, members must carefully consider all the evidence that is put before them and be prepared to modify or change their initial view in the light of the arguments and evidence presented. Then, they must make their final decision at the meeting with an open mind based on all the evidence.

[68]   TCPA 1990, s 70(1).

[69]   This provision should be read with Planning and Compulsory Purchase Act 2004 (PCPA 2004), s 38, which defines the term 'development plan' (which sets out policies for the development and use of land) for the purpose of planning law which comprises development plan documents which have been adopted or approved for the area (i.e. local plan and neighbourhood plans and the London Plan). NPPF, paras 150–185 contain guidance in relation to the making of local plans and neighbourhood plans. PCPA 2004, s 38(6) provides that if regard is to be had to the development plan for the purpose of any determination to be made under the Planning Acts, the determination must be made in accordance with the plan unless material considerations indicate otherwise. In discharging these requirements, reference to policies is not of itself sufficient. An LPA must interpret the policies correctly and, given the duty imposed by s 38(6), as a general rule, it must also determine: (a) whether the individual material policies support or count against the proposed development or are inconsistent with it; and (b) whether the proposed development is in accordance with the development plan as a whole (*Tesco Stores Ltd v Dundee CC* [2012] UKSC 13 per Lord Reed at [17]–[19] and [22]; also *R (Hampton Bishop Parish Council) v Herefordshire Council* [2014] EWCA Civ 878, [2015] 1 WLR 2367 per Richards LJ at [28] and [32]–[33]). A useful recent case on s 38(6) is *R (Lensbury Ltd) v Richmond-Upon-Thames* [2016] EWCA Civ

material to the application) (this provision does not apply in Wales);[70] and (c) any other material consideration.[71]

6.27 The authority is also required to take into account representations made to it where notice of, or information about, the application has been: (a) given by site display under articles 13 and 15 of the DMPO (within 21 days of the date when the notice was first displayed); (b) served on an owner of the land or a tenant of an agricultural holding under article 13; (c) served on an adjoining owner or occupier under article 15; (d) served on an infrastructure manager under article 16 (in the case of representations received within 21 days of the date when the notice was served on that person under paragraphs (b)–(d)); or (e) where the notice of or information about the application has been published in a newspaper under articles 13 and 15 or on a website under article 15 (in the case of representations received within 14 days of the date on which such notice or information was published).[72]

814, in which, at [5]–[8], the Court of Appeal deals with the legal framework in relation to claims involving an alleged breach of duty on the part of an LPA to have regard to a policy in a development plan or to interpret it properly. Where it is considered that the development proposal does not accord with the development plan, it is necessary for the LPA to understand the nature and extent of the departure from the plan which the grant of consent would involve in order to consider on a proper basis whether such a departure is justified by other material considerations (*Tesco Stores Ltd v Dundee CC* at [22]). In *Lensbury Ltd*, an appeal was allowed where an LPA had failed to assess whether a planning application for a hydro-electric generating facility in an area designated as metropolitan open land (MOL) was 'inappropriate development' under local policy. It consequently failed to ask itself the critical question of whether 'very special circumstances' existed which justified the grant of planning permission for a hydro-electric generating facility. The appellant had successfully argued that the LPA had failed to take into account a policy which stated that 'the strongest protection should be given to the MOL and inappropriate development refused, except in very special circumstances, giving the same level of protection as in the Green Belt', and was therefore in breach of s 38(6). MOL is specific to London and is covered by the London Plan, which says that it should have the same protection as the Green Belt and applies the NPPF's Green Belt policies to MOL. This raised the question of 'inappropriate development', which no one had suggested to the LPA. The Court of Appeal considered that it was incumbent on the LPA, in these circumstances, to identify the correct approach to be applied under the relevant policy framework, even if those supporting and opposing the scheme had not done so.

70   The term 'local finance consideration' means: (a) a grant or other financial assistance that has been, or will or could be, provided to a relevant authority by a minister of the Crown; or (b) sums that a relevant authority has received, or will or could receive, in payment of CIL. See TCPA 1990, s 70(4).

71   TCPA 1990, s 70(2).

72   TCPA 1990, s 71(2)(a) (consultations in connection with determinations under s 70) and DMPO, art 33, which also provides (at art 33(2)) that an LPA must give notice of its decision to every owner of the land or tenant of an agricultural holding. The provisions as to representations to be taken into account under art 33(1) and (2) also apply in the case of applications referred or made to, or in the case of appeals to, the Secretary of State (art 33(3)) as if references to an LPA were to the Secretary of State.

PROVISIONS OF THE DEVELOPMENT PLAN (AND MATERIAL CONSIDERATIONS)

6.28   There are, in effect, two presumptions. The first is that applications for planning permission must be determined in accordance with the development plan[73] unless material considerations indicate otherwise.[74] The second is that arising under the NPPF which is now a material consideration in planning decisions.[75] The presumption under the NPPF is that in favour of sustainable

---

[73] *Tesco Stores Ltd v Dundee City Council* [2012] 2 P & CR 9 at [18], where Lord Reed said that:

'The development plan is a carefully drafted and considered statement of policy, published in order to inform the public of the approach which will be followed by planning authorities in decision-making unless there is good reason to depart from it. It is intended to guide the behaviour of developers and planning authorities. As in other areas of administrative law, the policies which it sets out are designed to secure consistency and direction in the exercise of discretionary powers, while allowing a measure of flexibility to be retained.'

[74] TCPA 1990, s 70(2) and PCPA 2004, s 38(6). The NPPF stresses the importance of having a planning system that is genuinely plan-led. When a proposal accords with an up-to-date development plan, it should be approved without delay, as is required by NPPF, para 14. Where the development plan is absent or silent, or where policies are out of date, NPPF para 14 requires the application to be determined in accordance with the presumption in favour of sustainable development, unless otherwise specified.

[75] NPPF, para 196. See paras 11–16, which deal with the presumption of sustainable development. Decision-makers are required to focus upon all of the so-called three dimensions to sustainable development (namely economic, social and environmental – see paras 7–10) rather than one at the expense of the others, see *Fordent Holdings Ltd v Secretary of State for Communities and Local Government* [2014] 2 P & CR 12. See also *Dartford Borough Council v Secretary of State for Communities and Local Government* [2016] EWHC 649 (Admin), where, at [42], Gilbart J stated that *Secretary of State for Communities and Local Government v Hopkins Homes Ltd* [2016] EWCA Civ 168, had:

'laid to rest several disputes about the interpretation of NPPF, both as to the particular paragraphs it addressed, but generally. For those of us who have swum for several years in the waters of Town and Country Planning, it has been striking that NPPF, a policy document, could sometimes have been approached as if it were a statute, and as importantly, as if it did away with the importance of a decision maker taking a properly nuanced decision in the round, having regard to the development plan (and its statutory significance) and to all material considerations. In particular, I would emphasise this passage in Lindblom LJ's judgment, which restates the role of a policy document, and just as importantly how it is to be interpreted and applied:

"[42]. The NPPF is a policy document. It ought not to be treated as if it had the force of a statute. It does not, and could not, displace the statutory 'presumption in favour of the development plan', as Lord Hope described it in *City of Edinburgh Council v Secretary of State for Scotland* [1997] 1 WLR at 1450B–G). Under s 70(2) of the 1990 Act and s 38(6) of the 2004 Act, government policy in the NPPF is a material consideration external to the development plan. Policies in the NPPF, including those relating to the 'presumption in favour of sustainable development', do not modify the statutory framework for the making of decisions on applications for planning permission. They operate within that framework – as the NPPF itself acknowledges, for example, in paragraph 12 (see paragraph 12 above). It is for the decision-maker to decide what weight should be given to NPPF policies in so far

development which affects both plan-making and decision-taking.[76] For decision-taking this means:[77]

- approving development proposals that accord with the development plan without delay; and
- where the development plan is absent or silent, or relevant policies are out of date, granting permission unless:

  - any adverse impacts of doing so would significantly and demonstrably outweigh the benefits, when assessed against the policies in the NPPF taken as a whole; or
  - specific policies in the NPPF indicate development should be restricted.[78]

---

as they are relevant to the proposal. Because this is government policy, it is likely always to merit significant weight. But the court will not intervene unless the weight given to it by the decision-maker can be said to be unreasonable in the *Wednesbury* sense.

[43]. When determining an application for planning permission for housing development the decision-maker will have to consider, in the usual way, whether or not the proposal accords with the relevant provisions of the development plan. If it does, the question will be whether other material considerations, including relevant policies in the NPPF, indicate that planning permission should not be granted. If the proposal does not accord with the relevant provisions of the plan, it will be necessary to consider whether other material considerations, including relevant policies in the NPPF, nevertheless indicate that planning permission should be granted ..."

[43]. NPPF is not to be used to obstruct sensible decision making. It is there as policy guidance to be had regard to in that process, not to supplant it.'

In *Secretary of State for Communities and Local Government v Hopkins Homes Ltd* [2017] UKSC 37, Lord Carnwath considered the status of the NPPF. He said (at [20]) that the NPPF is no more than 'guidance' and as such a 'material consideration' for the purposes of TCPA 1990, s 70(2) (see *R (Cala Homes (South) Ltd) v Secretary of State for Communities and Local Government* [2011] EWHC 97 (Admin) at [50] per Lindblom J), and that it could not displace the primacy given by statute and policy to the statutory development plan. He said that statements in development plans had to be read as statements of policy, not as statutory texts.

76 NPPF, para 14, where it is said that the presumption in favour of sustainable development 'should be seen as a golden thread running through both plan-making and decision-taking'.

77 NPPF, para 14.

78 For example, those policies relating to sites protected under the Birds and Habitats Directives or designated as Sites of Special Scientific Interest (SSSIs) or land designated as Green Belt, Local Green Space, an AONB, Heritage Coast, within a National Park (or the Broads Authority), or designated as heritage assets and locations at risk of flooding or coastal erosion. The position is the same in plan-making where, in NPPF, para 15 it is provided that policies in local plans should follow the approach of the presumption in favour of sustainable development so that it is clear that development which is sustainable can be approved without delay. All plans should be based upon, and reflect, the presumption in favour of, sustainable development, with clear policies that will guide how the presumption should be applied locally.

HOW SHOULD THE DEVELOPMENT PLAN BE APPLIED?

6.29   Although the presumption in favour of the development plan is a statutory requirement, the weight to be given to different considerations in deciding whether a proposed development was compatible with the local plan is fundamentally a matter for the planning authority and not one for the court.[79] The function of the court is to see whether the decision-maker has had regard to the presumption in favour of the development plan, rather than to assess the weight which should be given to it in light of other material considerations. This will be particularly relevant:

(a)   where the plan is out of date or contains no policies at all in relation to a proposed development;

(b)   where policies have been superseded by more up-to-date planning guidance;

(c)   where circumstances have changed, which means that certain policies may no longer be relevant;

(d)   where regard must be had to emerging plans;[80] or

(e)   whether policies in older plans are consistent with the NPPF.

---

[79]   *R v Leominster District Council ex parte Pothecary* [1998] JPL 335 (following *Edinburgh City Council v Secretary of State for Scotland* [1997] 1 WLR 1447). In *Secretary of State for Communities and Local Government v Hopkins Homes Ltd* [2017] UKSC 37, Lord Carnwath re-stated that the correct approach to the interpretation of a statutory development plan was discussed in *Tesco Stores Ltd v Dundee CC (ASDA Stores intervening)* [2012] UKSC 13, [2012] 2 P & CR 9 at [18]–[19], where Lord Reed said that policy statements in the development plan should be interpreted objectively in accordance with the language used, read as always in its proper context and should not be construed as if they were statutory or contractual provisions. He said that many of the provisions of a development plan were framed in language whose application to a given set of facts required the exercise of judgment by the planning authorities which could only be challenged on grounds of irrationality or perversity.

[80]   These involve new plans in the course of preparation or proposals for amending existing adopted plans, such as how many new homes will be provided and where these will be allocated or in the identification of new Green Spaces, new schools or improved infrastructure. See *R v City of London Corpn ex parte Allen* (1980) 79 LGR 223, where the court held that the authority was entitled to have regard to publicised proposals in a draft plan, although the authority should always consider objections to new proposals and should also consider whether the application should in fact be dismissed on the ground that it would be premature until the new proposals were adopted. Note the following cases on prematurity: *Arlington Securities Ltd v Secretary of State and Crawley Borough Council* [1989] JPL 166; *Larkfleet Ltd v Secretary of State for Communities and Local Government* [2012] All ER (D) 207 (Dec); *Truro City Council v Cornwall Council* [2013] All ER (D) 108 (Aug); *Davies v London Borough of Hammersmith* [1981] JPL 682. It is plain in all these cases that an emerging plan may be accorded weight and that prematurity (namely where an application should be refused on the ground that it predetermines or pre-empts a decision which ought to be taken in the development plan process as, for instance, where by reason of its scale, location and/or nature there is a risk that it might do so) may be a material consideration which would justify the refusal of planning permission. However, prematurity is in truth no more than one relevant consideration amongst others and is certainly not a bar to the grant of planning permission. The NPPG also confirms that in view of the principle of sustainable

6.30   In such cases, it will be a balancing exercise between the provisions of the plan and other material considerations which lend themselves to the proposed development. In other words, if there are material considerations which suggest that a particular policy ought not to be applied to the development, then the over-arching presumption in favour of the plan need not be applied.[81] The development plan should also be looked at as a whole rather than piecemeal. For instance, some policies may be more relevant to a particular development than others.[82] On the other hand, where a development plan is more recent, its policies will undoubtedly be more compelling than those which were out of date or which had been overtaken by events.[83]

---

development, arguments on prematurity are unlikely to be successful unless the development is so substantial, or its cumulative effect would be so significant, that to grant planning permission would be to undermine the plan-making process by pre-determining decisions about the scale, location or phasing of new development that are central to the local plan or neighbourhood planning, and that the emerging plan is at an advanced stage but is not yet formally part of the development plan for the area. The NPPF has added helpful guidance under this head (particularly in relation to emerging policies): (a) at para 211: policies in a local plan (and in the London Plan) should not be considered out of date simply because they were adopted prior to the publication of the NPPF; (b) at para 212: policies contained in the NPPF are expressed to be material considerations which LPAs should take into account (the NPPF should also be taken into account in the preparation of plans); (c) at para 213: plans may need to be revised to take account of policies in the NPPF; (d) at para 215: due weight is now required to be given to existing plans according to their degree of consistency with the NPPF (the closer the policies in the plan to the policies in the NPPF, the greater the weight they may be given); and (e) at para 216: (unless material considerations indicate otherwise) decision-makers may also give weight to relevant policies in emerging plans according to: (i) the stage of preparation of the emerging plan (i.e. the more advanced the preparation, the greater the weight that may be given); (ii) the extent to which there are unresolved objections to relevant policies (the less significant the unresolved objections, the greater the weight that may be given); and (iii) the degree of consistency of the relevant policies in the emerging plan to the policies in the NPPF (the closer the policies in the emerging plan to the policies in the NPPF, the greater the weight that may be given).

[81]   *R (Cala Homes (South) Ltd v Secretary of State for Communities and Local Government* [2011] JPL 1458 at 1450B–D per Lord Hope and 1458E–F per Lord Clyde; see also *Tesco Stores Ltd v Dundee CC (ASDA Stores intervening)* [2012] UKSC 13, [2012] 2 P & CR 9 at [18] (fn 80).

[82]   *Stratford-on-Avon District Council v Secretary of State for Communities and Local Government* [2014] JPL 104.

[83]   A similar situation arises in the case of emerging development plans. This is where a plan is under preparation or review and is going through the statutory procedures. Sometimes, a planning application will be refused on the grounds of prematurity as, for instance, where the proposed development would prejudice elements within the new or replacement plan or might prejudice the outcome of the plan process by predetermining decisions that ought really to be taken following full consideration of the relevant issues in the context of a public inquiry. This might involve decisions about the nature, scale, location or phasing of new development, which would result in an adverse impact on an environmental asset which the emerging plan is seeking to protect or where an application undermines a proposed Green Belt or countryside policy area designation which is proposed in the emerging plan. Clearly, the weight to be attached to policies in emerging plans will depend upon the stage of plan preparation or review. Where a plan is at

MATTERS TO BE TAKEN INTO ACCOUNT IN THE CASE OF CERTAIN DEVELOPMENT PROPOSALS

6.31   Special attention should be given to applications involving the following:

(a)   environmental assessment;[84]
(b)   habitats protection;[85]
(c)   waste planning;[86]
(d)   listed buildings and conservation areas;[87]
(e)   flood risk assessment;[88]

---

the draft stage, but no objections have been lodged to the relevant proposals, then considerable weight should be attached to those proposals because of the strong possibility that they will be adopted and replace those in the existing plan. On the other hand, where there are objections to relevant policies, then lesser weight may be attached. Much will depend on the nature of the objections and whether there are representations in support of particular policies. Other than in the circumstances described above, refusal of planning permission on grounds of prematurity will not usually be justified, although clearly each case will need to be judged on its merits.

[84]   The Town and Country Planning (Environmental Impact Assessment) Regulations 2017 (SI 2017/571) (EIA Regulations 2017) (which, subject to transitional provisions, revoked the EIA Regulations 2011 (which themselves had superseded the original EIA regulations made in 1988, and which transposed into the law of England and Wales the original requirements of Council Directive 85/337/EEC)) apply to development which is given planning permission under TCPA 1990, Pt III. These regulations apply the amended Directive 2014/52/EU on the assessment of the effects of development on the environment. The EIA Regulations 2017 only apply to certain types of development (i.e. development, other than exempt development, of a description mentioned in Sch 1 and also where development is found to be qualifying EIA development by virtue of factors such as its nature, size or location within the meaning of Sch 2, and can even apply to permitted development). They do not apply to development given consent under other regimes which are subject to separate EIA regulations.

[85]   The Conservation of Habitats and Species Regulations 2017 (SI 2017/1012) (see requirement for assessment of negative implications for European sites and European offshore sites in decision-taking by a competent authority contained in reg 63); NPPF, paras 109 and 116.

[86]   The Waste (England and Wales) Regulations 2011 (SI 2011/988) (regs 18–20), and the Controlled Waste (England and Wales) Regulations 2012 (SI 2012/811).

[87]   Planning (Listed Buildings and Conservation Areas) Act 1990 (LBA 1990), ss 66–67.

[88]   The NPPF sets out strict tests to protect people and property from flooding, which all LPAs are expected to follow: see paras 100–104. Technical guidance on flood risk published alongside the NPPF sets out how the policy in para 100 should be implemented (this policy provides that inappropriate development in areas at risk of flooding should be avoided by directing development away from areas at highest risk, but where development is necessary, making it safe without increasing flood risk elsewhere). When these tests are not met, national policy is clear that new development should not be allowed. The main steps to be followed are set out in the NPPG at Paragraph: 001 Reference ID: 7-001-20140306. In summary, they are designed to ensure that if there are better sites in terms of flood risk, or if a proposed development cannot be made safe, it should not be permitted. The main steps to be followed are these: (a) Assess flood risk: (i) LPAs must undertake a Strategic Flood Risk Assessment to fully understand the flood risk in the area to inform local plan preparation. (ii) In areas at risk of flooding or for sites of one hectare or more, developers should undertake a site-specific flood assessment to accompany applications for planning permission

(f)   air quality.[89]

(or prior approval for certain types of permitted development). (b) Avoid flood risk: (i) In plan-making, LPAs apply a sequential approach to site selection so that development is, as far as is reasonably possible, located where the risk of flooding (from all sources) is lowest, taking account of climate change and the vulnerability of future uses to flood risk (see NPPG at Paragraph: 018 Reference ID: 7-018-20140306 to Paragraph: 027 Reference ID: 7-027-20140306). (ii) In decision-taking, LPAs also apply the sequential approach for specific development proposals and, if needed, the exception test in order to steer development to areas with the lowest probability of flooding. (c) Manage and mitigate flood risk: (i) Where development needs to be in locations where there is a risk of flooding as alternative sites are not available, LPAs and developers must ensure that development is appropriately flood resilient and resistant, is safe for its users for the development's lifetime and will not increase flood risk overall. (ii) LPAs and developers should seek flood risk management opportunities (e.g. safeguarding land) and reduce the causes and impacts of flooding (e.g. through the use of sustainable drainage systems in developments). The NPPG also deals with the requirement to consult the EA on applications where there is a risk of flooding. The NPPG provides extensive guidance on planning and flood risk which is beyond the scope of this book. The guidance will be found within the section 'Planning Practice Guidance: Flood Risk and Coastal Change' at Paragraph: 001 Reference ID: 7-001-20140306 through to Paragraph: 078 Reference ID: 7-078-20140306. The sections dealing with flood zones and flood risk tables (Paragraph: 065 Reference ID: 7-065-20140306 to Paragraph: 067 Reference ID: 7-067-20140306) and the model checklist for a site specific flood risk assessment at Paragraph: 068 Reference ID: 7-068-20140306, are particularly useful.

[89]   Air quality is covered in the NPPF, para 24 and in the NPPG at Paragraph: 001 Reference ID: 32-001-20140306 through to Paragraph: 009 Reference ID: 32-009-20140306. See also draft Clean Air Strategy 2018, which outlines Defra's ambitions relating to reducing air pollution in the round, making the air healthier to breathe, protecting mature and boosting the economy. Action to manage and improve air quality is largely driven by EU legislation. The Ambient Air Quality Directive sets legally binding limits for concentrations in outdoor air of major air pollutants that impact on public health. The local air quality management regime requires every district and unitary authority to regularly review and assess air quality in their area. These reviews identify whether national objectives have been, or will be, achieved at relevant locations, by an applicable date. If national objectives are not met, or are at risk of not being met, the local authority concerned must declare an air quality management area and prepare an air quality action plan. This identifies measures that will be introduced in pursuit of the objectives and can have implications in planning. Local plans can affect air quality in a number of ways, including through what development is proposed and where, and the encouragement given to sustainable transport. Therefore, in plan-making it is important to take into account air quality management areas and other areas where there could be specific requirements or limitations on new development because of air quality. Air quality is a consideration in the Strategic Environmental Assessment, and sustainability appraisal can be used to shape an appropriate strategy, including through establishing the 'baseline' appropriate objectives for the assessment of impact and proposed monitoring. Air quality could be relevant to planning decisions. Whether this is the case will depend on the proposed development and its location. Concerns could arise if the development is likely to generate air quality impact in an area where air quality is already known to be poor. They could also arise where the development is likely to adversely impact upon the implementation of air quality strategies and action plans and/or, in particular, lead to a breach of EU legislation (including that applicable to wildlife). When deciding whether air quality is relevant to a planning application, considerations could include whether the development would: (a) Significantly affect traffic in the immediate vicinity of the proposed development site or further afield. This could be by generating or increasing traffic congestion; significantly changing traffic volumes, vehicle speed or both; or significantly altering the traffic composition on local roads. Other matters to

OTHER MATERIAL CONSIDERATIONS

6.32   It is a matter entirely for the decision-maker to attribute to the material consideration such weight as he thinks fit, and the court will not interfere unless the decision-maker has acted irrationally or unreasonably in the *Wednesbury* sense.[90] It is, however, necessary for the material consideration, if it is to serve a

consider include whether the proposal involves the development of a bus station, coach or lorry park; adds to turnover in a large car park; or results in construction sites that would generate large HGV flows over a period of a year or more. (b) Introduce new point sources of air pollution. This could include furnaces which require prior notification to local authorities; or extraction systems (including chimneys) which require approval under pollution control legislation or biomass boilers or biomass-fuelled CHP plant; centralised boilers or CHP plant burning other fuels within or close to an air quality management area or introduce relevant combustion within a Smoke Control Area. (c) Expose people to existing sources of air pollutants. This could be by building new homes, workplaces or other development in places with poor air quality. (d) Give rise to potentially unacceptable impact (such as dust) during construction for nearby sensitive locations. (e) Affect biodiversity: in particular, is it likely to result in deposition or concentration of pollutants that significantly affect a European-designated wildlife site and is not directly connected with or necessary to the management of the site, or does it otherwise affect biodiversity, particularly designated wildlife sites (see NPPG at Paragraph: 006 Reference ID: 32-006-20140306)? Where there are concerns about air quality, the LPA may seek further information including to establish the need and, where appropriate, scope of any assessment that is needed to support the application. The following could figure in assessments and be usefully agreed at the outset: (i) a description of the baseline conditions and how these could change; (ii) relevant air quality concerns; (iii) the assessment methods to be adopted and any requirements around verification of modelling air quality; (iv) sensitive locations; (v) the basis for assessing impact and determining the significance of an impact; (vi) construction phase impact; and/or (vii) acceptable mitigation measures (see NPPG at Paragragh: 007 Reference ID: 32-007-20140306 and Paragraph: 008 Reference ID: 32-008-20140306 (dealing with how an impact on air quality can be mitigated)). In *Wealden DC v Secretary of State for Communities and Local Government* [2017] EWHC 351 (Admin), a local authority and National Park authority's decision to adopt a joint care strategy was found to be flawed by their acceptance of erroneous advice from Natural England that planned development was unlikely to have a significant impact on the Ashdown Forest Special Area of Conservation (SAC) arising from the impact on air quality from increased traffic flows. The case was concerned with the preparation of development plan documents in neighbouring local authority areas and how potential developments in the future would, in combination with another plan, impact on the air quality of the SAC. It would, however, be permissible to disregard very low impacts. See ministerial planning decision of *Willson Developments Ltd v Bracknell Forest BC* (Land south of Foxley Lane, Binfield, Berkshire, 26/2/2018: APP/R0335/W/17/3177088), reported in JPL [2018] at p 718, where the inspector considered *Wealden DC*.

[90]   A consideration would be material if, viewed objectively, it was a factor which, when placed on the decision-maker's scales, would tip the balance to some extent, one way or another; in other words, it had to be a factor which had some weight, although it need not be determinative (see *R (Leckhampton Green Land Action Group Ltd) v Tewkesbury BC* [2017] EWHC 198 (Admin) (a case demonstrating the importance the court will afford to a planning officer's report which, in this instance, had advised the local authority's planning committee that they should be satisfied that the proposed development's benefits should be greater than the identified impacts on heritage assets, despite an examining inspector's preliminary findings about landscape impact), following *R (Kides) v South Cambridgeshire DC* [2002] EWCA Civ 1370).

planning purpose, to relate to the character of the use of the land.[91] The following are examples of factors which may or may not, in the particular circumstances of the case, be regarded as material considerations:

(a) Planning obligations[92] (material).

(b) The promotion of healthy eating in the context of planning permission for a fast food takeaway (material).[93]

(c) Financial considerations (which may be regarded as material) such as:

    (i)   viability and whether the development would even be carried out;[94]

    (ii) enabling development, namely development of one site in order to generate funding to carry out development on another (material);[95]

    (iii) off-site benefits, provided there is a real connection between the benefits and the development;[96]

---

[91] *Westminster City Council v Great Portland Estates Plc* [1985] AC 661; *Stringer v Minister of Housing and Local Government* [1971] 1 All ER 65 at 77.

[92] *Tesco Stores Ltd v Secretary of State for the Environment* [1995] 2 All ER 636. In this case, the court determined that if a planning obligation has some connection with a proposed development (and in this instance the obligation involved an agreement to fund a link road), it is a material consideration (as was found in this case even though the connection between the road and the development was considered to be slight).

[93] *R (Copeland) v Tower Hamlets London Borough Council* [2010] EWHC 1845 (Admin).

[94] *Sovmots Investments Ltd v Secretary of State for the Environment* [1977] QB 411; *Niarchos (London) Ltd v Secretary of State for the Environment* (1977) 35 P & CR 259; *Sosmo Trust Ltd v Secretary of State for the Environment and London Borough of Camden* [1983] JPL 806. See also *Parkhurst Road Ltd v Secretary of State for Local Communities and Local Government and Islington LBC* [2018] EWHC 991 (Admin) in which the judgment of Holgate J contains important guidance on valuation evidence in connection with viability assessments.

[95] *R v Westminster City Council ex parte Monahan* [1989] JPL 107, where permission for offices on a site in close proximity to the Royal Opera House, Covent Garden, was granted in order to fund improvements at the Opera House. See also *R (Derwent Holdings Ltd) v Trafford Borough Council* [2011] NPC 78, where planning permission was granted on a joint application involving the development of a superstore which would fund the development of local cricket club grounds – the sites were in close proximity and had reasonably been included in a single application – see [18]–[19] per Carnwath LJ for arguments about the legality of enabling developments. See also *R (Salford Estates (No 2) Ltd v Durham City Council* [2013] JPL 293 and NPPF, para 140 in relation to enabling development in the context of the conservation of heritage assets.

[96] *R v Plymouth City Council ex parte Plymouth and South Devon Cooperative Society Ltd* (1994) 67 P & CR 78; *Tesco Stores Ltd v Secretary of State for the Environment* [1995]1 WLR759; *R (Sainsbury's Supermarkets Ltd) v Wolverhampton City Council* [2011] 1 AC 437 (where the authorities on the issue of financial considerations as material considerations were reviewed by the Supreme Court (see [69]–[70] per Lord Collins). In *Forest of Dean DC and Resilient Energy Severndale Ltd v R (Peter Wright)* [2017] EWCA 2102 at [27], Hickinbottom LJ helpfully set out a number of cases dealing with the question as to what amounts to a material consideration. At [28] he set out the principle:

    'For a consideration to be material, it must have a planning purpose (i.e. it must relate to the character or the use of the land, and not be solely for some other purpose no matter how

(iv) the cost to the public in granting or refusing planning permission (such as the liability to pay compensation).[97]

(d) Planning Policy Statements other than those contained in development plans (mainly circulars) (material).[98] For instance, ministerial statements are an expression of government policy and should be followed unless there is good reason for not doing so.[99]

(e) Whether the development is needed (such as in the case of additional farm dwellings) (material).

---

well-intentioned and desirable that purpose may be); and it must fairly and reasonably relate to the permitted development (i.e. there must be a real – as opposed to a fanciful, remote or trivial or *de minimis* – connection with the development).'

The Court of Appeal dismissed an appeal from a decision of Dove J at [2016] EWHC 1349 (Admin), where the court had quashed a grant of planning permission for a wind turbine. The LPA had granted permission for it to be erected on agricultural land. The turbine was to be run by a community benefit society, and the permission was subject to a condition (consistently with a promise contained in the application) that the development would be undertaken by the society with, as part of the scheme, an annual donation being made to a local community fund based on 4% of turnover from the turbine's operation over its projected 25-year life. The permission was quashed on the basis that the donation was not a material planning condition and the LPA had acted unlawfully in taking it into account. The court found that there was no contradiction between, on the one hand, the NPPF, para 97 and the NPPG, which encourages the use of renewable energy, and particularly community-led activities in that regard, and, on the other, the legal requirements in regard to material considerations which would not favour unrestricted gifts of money to the local community. At the end of the day, the Court of Appeal found that a donation would only be material if it satisfied the criteria laid down in *Newbury District Council v Secretary of State for the Environment* [1981] AC 578 and that the concept of materiality, although broad, was not without limit. Davis LJ noted that the fact that desirable objects and worthy causes were involved 'cannot of themselves mandate a departure from the usual principles with regard to material considerations'. In other words, this was a case where the developer was simply choosing to spend some of the proceeds locally in circumstances where there was no connection with the planning purposes of the scheme.

[97] *Health and Safety Executive v Wolverhampton City* Council [2012] UKSC 34, [2012] 1 WLR 2264; *R (Samuel Smith Old Brewery Tadcaster) v Selby District Council* [2013] EWHC 1159 (Admin), [2013] All ER (D) 160 (May).

[98] Proper regard must be given to the relevant policy, and the reasons for decisions which depart from it must be clearly explained (see *Gransden (E.C.) & Co Ltd v Secretary of State for the Environment* [1986] JPL 519; upheld on appeal at [1987] 1 PLR 365).

[99] Recent noteworthy examples of a Written Ministerial Statement include: (a) the joint statement on energy policy issued on 17/5/2018 by Greg Clark, Business Secretary and James Brokenshire, the Housing, Communities and Local Government Secretary, that minerals local plans should not set restrictions or thresholds across their plan area that limit shale development without proper justification; and (b) the ministerial statement made by the then-Secretary of State for Communities and Local Government (Greg Clark) on 18/6/2015 in relation to on-shore wind turbine approvals, which set out new considerations to be applied in the case of proposed wind energy development.

(f)   Previous grants or refusals of planning permission (material).[100]
(g)   Matters of personal hardship (material although probably of limited weight where there are substantial planning objections).[101]

---

[100]   *North Wiltshire District Council v Secretary of State for the Environment* (1992) 65 P & CR 137 (at [145]); *R (Havard) v South Kesteven District Council* [2006] JPL 1734 (at [12]–[18]); *Bibb v Bristol City Council* [2012] JPL 565. Consistency in decision-making is important (see *Pertemps Investments Ltd v Secretary of State for Communities and Local Government* [2015] EWHC 2308 (Admin); *R (Milton (Peterborough) Estates Co (t/a Fitzwilliam (Malton) Estate) v Ryedale District Council* [2015] EWHC 1948 (Admin)). See also *R (Tate) v Northumberland CC* [2018] EWCA Civ 1519. In this case, the Court of Appeal found that it was well established that previous appeal decisions were capable of being material considerations in planning decisions in view of the importance of consistency in decision-making (following *DLA Delivery Ltd v Baroness Cumberlege of Newick* [2018] EWCA Civ 1305). The Court of Appeal ruled that the planning officer should have recognised that the LPA was dealing with a like case (following *North Wiltshire v Secretary of State for the Environment*, above). The LPA's appeal against a decision that it had erred in granting permission for the construction of a house in a Green Belt village by failing to give reasons for its decision that the development would be 'limited infilling' (within the meaning of NPPF, para 89) was rejected by the Court of Appeal as it was found to be contrary to an inspector's view in a previous appeal decision. Although the LPA was not bound to adopt the same approach as the inspector, if it was to take a different approach, it needed to acknowledge that difference and explain the inconsistency. Although that point had been made by the respondent in his letter of objection, the planning officer did not tackle it, and it was not entirely clear what approach he had adopted. No reasons were given in his report, in the minutes of the committee meeting or in the decision notice itself. The need for reasons to be given to explain such an inconsistency was not removed by the fact that the planning judgment involved was relatively straightforward (*North Wiltshire* (above), *Oakley v South Cambridgeshire DC* [2017] EWCA Civ 71, [2017] 1 WLR 3765 and *Dover DC v Campaign to Protect Rural England (Kent)* [2017] UKSC 79, [2018] 1 WLR 108 followed). Accordingly, the grant of permission was vitiated by a plain error of law inherent in which there was substantial prejudice to the respondent and to other members of the public affected by the grant (*Save Britain's Heritage v Number 1 Poultry Ltd* [1991] 1 WLR 153 followed).

[101]   *Tameside Metropolitan Borough Council v Secretary of State for the Environment and GA Myatt* [1984] JPL 180, *Great Portland Estates Plc v Westminster City Council* [1985] AC 661. Planning is, of course, concerned with land use from the point of view of the public interest and is not concerned with purely private interests, although personal circumstances are capable of being a material consideration, such as was the case in *Basildon District Council v Secretary of State for Environment, Transport and Regions* [2001] JPL 1184 (cited with approval in *South Bucks District Council v Porter (No 1)* [2003] UKHL 26, [2003] 2 AC 558 (at [31])), where the needs of gypsy families were relevant as the application involved the grant of planning permission for the stationing of caravans on three adjacent plots in the Green Belt. See also *South Bucks District Council v Porter (No 2)* [2004] UKHL 33, [2004] 1 WLR 1953 and *New Forest District Council v Owen* [2013] EWHC 265 (QB). Generally, an applicant's personal circumstances will not carry much weight, as the planning system is based on development plans where the focus is on the use and development of land rather than on the personal characteristics of the owner or occupier of land. This is particularly apposite when one remembers that planning permissions generally run with the land. However, it should not be overlooked that the relevance of personal circumstances may well also engage European Convention for the Protection of Human Rights and Fundamental Freedoms 1950, Art 8 (a right to respect for private and family life and home) and Children Act 2004, s 11, which gives effect in England and Wales to UN Convention on the Rights of the Child 1989, Art 3. Section 11(1) applies s 11 to local authorities in England and to a district council

(h) Whether a grant of planning permission would create a precedent (material).[102]

(i) Public opposition (material but there must be evidence to justify the public's concern).[103]

(j) Public concern about safety and health risks (material).[104]

---

which is not such an authority. Section 11(2)(a) provides that relevant bodies need to discharge their functions having regard to the need to safeguard and promote the interest of children. See *ZH (Tanzania) v Secretary of State for the Home Department* [2011] UKSC 4, [2011] 2 AC 166 (an immigration case in which the Supreme Court held that s 11 amounted to a duty on the part of decision-makers), a decision which has been held to apply to planning cases (see *Stevens v Secretary of State for Communities and Local Government* [2013] EWHC 792 (Admin), where it was said that where the Art 8 rights were those of children, their interests were a primary consideration, but the best interests of the children were not determinative of the planning issue. However, no other consideration was more important or to be given greater weight and those best interests had to be kept at the forefront of the decision-maker's mind in the balancing process under TCPA 1990, s 70 (it may be, of course, that temporary or personal permissions would suffice, or at least should be considered as a possibility, when the LPA is considering an applicant's personal circumstances, at least where there were children involved).

[102] *Collis Radio Ltd v Secretary of State for the Environment* (1975) 73 LGR 211; *Anglia Building Society v Secretary of State for the Environment* [1984] JPL 175; *Poundstretcher Ltd v Secretary of State for the Environment* [1989] JPL 90; *Rumsey v Secretary of State for the Environment, Transport and Regions* (2001) 81 P & CR 32; *R (Holland) v Secretary of State for Communities and Local Government* [2009] EWHC 2161 (Admin); *R (Sainsbury's Supermarkets Plc) v Local Government* [2009] EWHC 1501 (Admin).

[103] *West Midland Probation Committee v Secretary of State for the Environment* [1998] JPL 388 (permission refused for bail hostel upheld); *Smith v First Secretary of State* [2005] EWCA Civ 859 (gypsy caravan site – refusal of permission set aside; public concern of crime did not rest wholly on extrapolation from past events, but partly on assumptions which were not supported by evidence as to the characteristics of future occupiers. The evidence has to establish a real concern before that concern could enter the planning judgment). Public opposition unrelated to the character of the use of the land will never be enough. The public's fears must be objectively justified. Clearly, if the proposed development was likely to introduce an increased risk of danger, then that would need to be weighed in the balance.

[104] *Gateshead Metropolitan Borough Council v Secretary of State for the Environment* (1996) 71 P & CR 350. Refusal of permission quashed in the case of a clinical waste incinerator plant. Issues of emissions, pollution and acceptable limits raised in the application for planning permission were matters within the competence of HM Inspectorate of Pollution, and the Secretary of State was justified in concluding that those issues could properly be decided by the Inspectorate whose powers were adequate to deal with such concerns. If, for instance, at the inquiry it had been plain that discharges from the plant were bound to be unacceptable so that a refusal by the Inspectorate to authorise the incineration process under Environmental Protection Act 1990, Pt 1 would be the only proper course, then planning permission could have been refused by the Secretary of State. In short, although pollution was always capable of being a material consideration, the existence of dedicated controls under the 1990 Act was something which could be taken into account in planning decision-making. See also *R v Bolton Metropolitan Council ex parte Kirkman* [1998] JPL 787. But see *Harrison v Secretary of State for Communities and Local Government* [2009] EWHC 3382 (Admin). This was a case where an inspector upheld an enforcement notice and refused permission for a change of use from agriculture to a mixed use involving the processing of animal by-products, and where the landowner's challenge failed. It was held that the planning system, which had to determine whether a development was acceptable in the light of the impact

(k)   Alternative development proposals advanced by an opponent of planning permission (material but only in exceptional circumstances).[105]

(l)   The existence of alternative sites (material but only in an appropriate case).[106]

---

of the change of use, was distinct from the integrated pollution prevention and control regime under the Pollution Prevention and Control Act 1999 and the Pollution Prevention and Control (England and Wales) Regulations 2000 (SI 2000/1973). Even where a site had changed its use from agricultural to the processing of animal by-products and had been granted a conditional integrated pollution prevention and control permit, a planning inspector was entitled to reach his own conclusions as to the impact of the proposed development on amenity, particularly the effect of odour emissions, and whether the site under consideration was in fact the appropriate location for such development. See also NPPG at Paragraph: 001 Reference ID: 39-001-20140306 and Paragraph: 003 Reference ID: 39-03-20150415, and NPPF, paras 2.110, 172 and 194, and where material in Annex 2.

[105]   *Mount Cook Land Ltd v Westminster City Council* [2003] EWCA Civ 1346. Only in exceptional circumstances would it be relevant to consider alternative development proposals which were not the subject of the planning application, and even then the alternative would have to be at least a likelihood or real possibility in the foreseeable future in the event that the application was refused. *Mount Cook* was considered in *Lisle-Mainwaring v Carroll* [2017] EWCA Civ 1315, where it was said that even in an exceptional case, if the alternative proposal was to be a material consideration, it could not be incohate or vague, and there had to be a real possibility of it being implemented in the foreseeable future if it was to justify the refusal of planning permission. However, the status of an alternative use as a material consideration did not depend on the consequences of the alternative use not being brought about. The notion that it did would be inimical to the principles set out in *Mount Cook*. Essential to those principles was that a comparison between the development actually proposed and an alternative development was not generally a necessary or relevant exercise. If a proposed development was inherently acceptable because it would do little or no harm, it would not normally be necessary to go further and consider whether some other proposal might be even more acceptable.

[106]   The law under this head was considered in *Trusthouse Forte Hotels Ltd v Secretary of State for the Environment* [1986] JPL 834 (and at 53 P & CR 293), where planning permission for a hotel on Green Belt land was refused. The inspector had recommended that the need for hotel accommodation could be met on other sites without specifying them. The appeal was rejected. Although it was said to be desirable in many cases, it was not essential when rejecting an application on the ground that alternative sites existed to specify them. *R (Chelmsford Car & Commercial Ltd) v Chelmsford Borough Council* [2005] EWHC 1705 (Admin) involved two applications for planning permission in the Green Belt, and each site was competing for the same very limited and highly localised need for social housing. It was claimed by the owner (C) of the competing site which had failed to obtain planning permission that the authority, in determining the two applications, should have carried out a comparative assessment of the planning merits of the two rival sites on the entire criteria for development in the Green Belt and not just a comparison of the criterion that tended to favour the successful site. The court held that it was clear that in the circumstances, a comparison of the merits of the two proposed sites was a material consideration. The decision on each proposed development did not depend simply on which site provided the best relationship with the edge of the existing developed area. Nor did it depend on the fact that one proposed site was immediately adjacent to an existing development and one was not. There were a number of other factors to be considered. The authority had made a comparison between the successful site and that proposed by C for permission when the comparison led to the former site being more favourable under only one of the authority's criteria for development in the Green Belt. However, the authority had failed to make a similar comparison with regard to

GRANT OF PLANNING PERMISSION – PROCEDURE AND DURATION

6.33   In the case of major development, the LPA must determine applications[107] and give notice of its decision[108] to the applicant within 13 weeks beginning with the day immediately following that on which the application was received by the LPA, otherwise the time limit is eight weeks, although it is open to the applicant and the authority to agree an extended period (unless the applicant has already given notice of appeal to the Secretary of State).[109] Where a valid application has

---

the other criteria when the comparison would have led to C's application being more favourable. *R (Bovale Ltd) v Secretary of State for Communities and Local Government* [2008] EWHC 2538 (Admin) concerned a case where planning permission was sought for the development of a 'total care village' for the elderly. It was said that the facility would create jobs and be a visual improvement to the area. The inspector decided that these factors were not sufficient to overcome the fact that the proposal did not retain the site for employment development or make provision for affordable housing. He decided that this conflicted with the policies in the development plan. He also stated that the need for the development of these facilities could be met by other sites in the area. The application to quash the decision of the inspector was refused. It was said that each case turned on its particular facts and in some cases it would not be necessary to consider the possibility of alternative sites, but in this case it was plainly relevant to consider whether there were other sites on which the alleged need could be met. However, the application to quash was nonetheless refused as the proposal conflicted with the development plan. In *Derbyshire Dales District Council v Secretary of State for Communities and Local Government* [2009] EWHC 1729 (Admin), it was held that a planning inspector had not erred in law by deciding that he did not need to consider alternative sites for a wind turbine development. There was nothing in the relevant legislation and policies which required him to consider alternative sites. However, the availability of alternative sites will be a material consideration in the case of telecommunications masts (*Phillips v First Secretary of State* [2004] JPL 613; *St Leger-Davey v First Secretary of State* [2004] EWCA Civ 1612). *R (Langley Park School for Girls) v Bromley London Borough Council* [2009] EWCA Civ 734 involved a local authority's failure to consider alternative siting options when considering whether to grant planning permission to rebuild a school on MOL. It was held that this amounted to a failure to take account of a material consideration (the planning committee should have been advised to consider whether the injury to the MOL required an examination of the alternatives), and the grant of planning permission was quashed.

[107]   There is no general duty requiring an LPA to afford a hearing to an applicant or an objector, although in particular circumstances an authority may have raised an expectation that in the interests of fairness, this will occur (*R v Monmouth District Council ex parte Jones* (1985) 53 P & CR 108; *R v Kensington and Chelsea Royal London Borough Council ex parte Stoop* [1992] 1 PLR 58 and *R v Alnwick District Council ex parte Robson* [1997] EGCS 144).

[108]   The permission is given when notice of the decision to grant permission was issued (*R (Burkett) v Hammersmith and Fulham London Borough Council (No 1)* [2002] UKHL 23). It is also the duty of LPAs to give reasons if conditions are imposed on a grant or where the application is refused (DMPO, art 35). Where permission is granted, the minutes of the planning committee may disclose that its decision was flawed and liable to be quashed (*R v Newbury District Council ex parte Blackwell* [1998] JPL 680; *R v Rochdale Metropolitan Borough Council ex parte Brown* [1997] JPL 337).

[109]   See DMPO, arts 2 (definition of major development), 34(2)(a) and 32(2)(b) and (c). For Wales, see Town and Country Planning (Development Management Procedure) (Wales) Order 2012

not been determined within the relevant statutory period (or such other period as has been agreed in writing between the LPA and the applicant) the applicant has a right of appeal to the Secretary of State against non-determination. An LPA will be justified in refusing permission where an applicant causes deliberate delay and has been unwilling to agree to an extension of time.

6.34   The decision on the application will either be the grant of a conditional or unconditional planning permission or else it will be a refusal.[110] Conditions will be dealt with separately, but the discretion of the LPA to impose conditions is a wide one and conditions may regulate the development or the use of the land, provided they are referable to the intended development. They may also relate to the removal of any building or works authorised by the permission or the discontinuance of the use of any land and its reinstatement at the end of a specified period (this is known as a planning permission granted for a limited period).[111]

6.35   Planning permission shall be granted or deemed to be granted subject to a condition that the development to which it relates must be begun not later than three years from the date permission is granted, otherwise it will lapse, unless the LPA imposes a longer or shorter period.[112] In the case of an outline permission, application for approval of reserved matters must be made not later than three years (or such other period as the LPA may stipulate) from the date of the grant of outline permission, and any development to which the permission relates must be begun not later than two years after the final approval of reserved matters (or when any appeal from a decision of the LPA is determined).[113]

WHEN IS DEVELOPMENT 'BEGUN' FOR THE PURPOSES OF TIME-LIMITING CONDITIONS?

6.36   If the development consists of the carrying out of operations, the relevant date is the earliest date when any material operation comprised in the development begins to be carried out. In the case of a change of use, it is when the new use is instituted or, if the development comprises both, it will be the

---

(SI 2012/801). In a case falling within the scope of the EIA Regulations 2017, the period allowed for decision is 16 weeks from the submission of the Environmental Statement and accompanying documents under reg 61.

[110]   TCPA 1990, s 70(1).

[111]   TCPA 1990, s 72(1) and (2).

[112]   TCPA 1990, s 91(1) (subject to the exceptions in s 91(4)).

[113]   TCPA 1990, ss 92 and 93(2).

earlier of these events.[114] Where development has begun but where the LPA is satisfied that it is unlikely to be completed within a reasonable period,[115] it may serve a notice stating that the planning permission will cease to have effect at the end of a further period of not less than 12 months after the notice has taken effect.[116] However, the notice will not take effect unless and until it has been confirmed by the Secretary of State who may substitute a longer period.[117]

SCOPE AND MEANING OF A PLANNING PERMISSION

6.37   An LPA is not permitted to grant a permission which effects a substantial alteration in what had been proposed by the application but if, for instance, the decision-maker is considering granting an applicant less than what he was applying for, the applicant should normally be invited to make representations in relation to such a decision. However, a decision-maker should not take this step if there is any possible prejudice to those who might otherwise have raised objections.[118]

6.38   In construing a planning permission which is clear and unambiguous on its face, regard could only be had to the permission itself, including the conditions on it and the express reasons for those conditions. No regard could be had to the planning application or other extrinsic evidence, unless:

(a)   the permission incorporated the application by reference;[119] or
(b)   the permission itself is ambiguous;[120] or

---

[114]   TCPA 1990, s 56. By s 56(4), a material operation means any work of construction in the course of erection of a dwelling, any work of demolition, the digging of a trench which is to contain the foundations, the laying of any underground main or pipe to the foundations or any operation in the construction of a road and any change in the use of land which constitutes material development. The test is an objective one: has work been done under a planning permission which is not *de minimis* (the question being one of fact and degree)? See *East Dunbartonshire Council v Secretary of State for Scotland* [1999] 1 PLR 53; *Riordan Communications Ltd v South Bucks District Council* [2000] 1 PLR 45; *R (Ashfield) v National Assembly for Wales* [2003] EWHC 3309 (Admin).

[115]   TCPA 1990, s 96; the Secretary of State may also serve a completion notice.

[116]   TCPA 1990, s 94.

[117]   TCPA 1990, s 95.

[118]   *Granada Hospitality Ltd v Secretary of State for Environment, Transport and the Regions* [2001] PLCR 81. See also *R (Holborn Studios Ltd) v Hackney LBC* [2017] EWHC 2823 (Admin).

[119]   *R v Ashford Borough Council ex parte Shepway District Council* [1999] PLCR 12.

[120]   *R (Campbell Court Property) v Secretary of State for the Environment, Transport and Regions* [2001] EWHC 102 (Admin). In cases of ambiguity in a planning permission, it is permissible to look at the extrinsic evidence, including the application and the documentary evidence; *R v Ashford Borough Council ex parte Shepway District Council* [1999] PLCR 12; *Trump International Golf Club Scotland Ltd v Scottish Ministers* [2015] UKSC 74; *Wood v Secretary of*

(c)   there was an absence of authority or mistake.[121]

State for Communities and Local Government [2015] EWHC 2368 (Admin); *University of Leicester v Secretary of State for Communities and Local Government* [2016] EWHC 476 (Admin). In this instance, the university sought a lawful use certificate in relation to the mixed use of halls of residence for student accommodation and for conferences, whereas the planning permissions referred only to 'student accommodation'. However, a s 106 agreement and other extrinsic evidence referred to intended conference use. The LPA refused to grant a certificate because the permissions did not expressly permit conference use. On appeal, the university's project manager gave unchallenged evidence that conference use had always been intended. The inspector accepted that the permissions were ambiguous and so considered extrinsic evidence (i.e. the original applications). The inspector considered that the project manager's evidence was unhelpful to an interpretation of the planning permissions and he, too, refused to grant a certificate on the basis that the permitted use was for student accommodation alone and that neither application for planning permission referred to conference use. The university's appeal was upheld, as the inspector had erred in limiting his consideration of the extrinsic material to the applications for permission. If he had considered the other relevant material, he would have inevitably concluded that the use permitted was not just for accommodation for students, but was for a mixed use that included conference use.

[121] *Norfolk County Council v Secretary of State for the Environment* [1973] 1 WLR 1400. For construing a planning permission and implied terms, see *Lambeth LBC v Secretary of State for Communities and Local Government* [2018] EWCA Civ 844; in this case an LPA had intended to exclude the sale of food when varying a planning permission concerning the use of a DIY retail unit, but that restriction had not been incorporated into the permission. It was found that it was not possible to apply a corrective interpretation so as to add a planning condition to that effect, nor to add such a condition by implication. The court held that the current approach to the interpretation of planning permissions and similar documents had been considered by the Supreme Court in *Trump International Golf Club Scotland Ltd v Scottish Ministers* [2015] UKSC 74, [2016] 1 WLR 85. The process of interpreting a document was not materially different from that appropriate to other legal documents; although, because they affected third parties in a way that many legal contracts did not, there was only limited scope for the use of extrinsic material in their interpretation. Having regard to the more limited range of material that could be taken into account in ascertaining the meaning of words used in a planning decision, the ultimate question was still the same, namely, what a reasonable reader would understand the words to mean when reading the condition in the context of the other conditions and of the consent as whole. Whilst *Trump* did not concern planning permission, so that the court's observations were *obiter*, they had since been applied in the Court of Appeal and could therefore be taken as representing the law (see *R (Skelmersdale Ltd Partnership) v West Lancashire BC* [2016] EWCA Civ 1260 and *Dunnett Investments Ltd v Secretary of State for Communities and Local Government* [2017] EWCA Civ 192). The court went on to deal with implying conditions into a planning permission. It was held that although it was possible to imply words into a public document such as a planning permission, the court had to exercise great restraint in doing so, given the possibility of criminal sanctions (*Trump* applied). The limited range of available extrinsic evidence was a critical factor. In the case of private contract, recourse to the background facts might be the reason for implying a term, but that was not possible in a public document. There were, in essence, two routes to the implication of a term in private contracts: either the term had to be necessary to give business efficacy to the contract or it had to be so obvious that it went without saying (*Impact Funding Solutions Ltd v Barrington Support Services Ltd (formerly Lawyers at Work Ltd)* [2016] UKSC 57, [2017] AC 73 considered). Given the public and permanent nature of a planning permission, those tests required some modification. Whilst the 2014 permission had not achieved the local authority's intention, it had not, as a document, lacked practical or commercial coherence, and although a reasonable reader might wonder whether the local authority had made a mistake in not

6.39   The fact that an activity which was said to give rise to a nuisance had the benefit of planning permission would normally be of no assistance to the defendant in a claim brought by a neighbour who claimed that the activity caused a nuisance to his land in the form of noise or other loss of amenity.[122]

DUTY OF LPA TO GIVE REASONS

6.40   The Supreme Court in *Dover District Council v Campaign to Protect Rural England (Kent)* has recently explained the extent of the duty on an LPA to give reasons for its decisions. It also explained the legal consequences of a breach of that duty.[123]

---

re-stating the conditions attached to the previous permissions, that was not so obvious that it went without saying. It followed that it was not possible to imply the imposition of a condition in the 2014 permission preventing the sale of food.

[122]   *Coventry v Lawrence* [2014] UKSC 13.

[123]   [2017] UKSC 79. See also *R (Pearl) v Maldon District Council* [2018] EWHC 212 (Admin), where a neighbour's challenge to an LPA's decision to approve an application for reserved matters was upheld. The complaint was that the detailed plans differed from the building proposed when outline consent was granted (bigger footprint and location nearer the neighbouring property). As the LPA had no head of planning services, the authority's chief executive gave the final approval on the application. All she did was to 'endorse' the officers' recommendations without giving any reasons of her own, whereas her duty obliged her to give 'intelligible' reasons for her decision. It was found that in the 'absence of any reasoned explanation for her decision', the chief executive had had 'no regard' to the neighbour's objections. The court accordingly ruled that the authority had 'failed to comply with its obligation to provide a written record of the decision, including the reasons for it'. The decision was quashed and the application for approval of reserved matters was duly remitted for reconsideration by the LPA. *Dover DC v CPRE (Kent)* was also followed in *R (Steer) v Shepway DC* [2018] EWHC 238 (Admin), where a planning permission was quashed, as the committee, which was not following the recommendation in the Officer's Report in an application which concerned a protected AONB, had failed to provide adequate and intelligible reasons for its decision to grant planning permission. The court held that the defect in reasons went to the heart of the justification for the planning permission and undermined its validity. The court was also unable to conclude under s 31(2A) of the Senior Courts Act 1981 that it was highly likely that the outcome would not have been substantially different if the committee had addressed its mind properly to the reasons for rejecting the matters raised in the Officer's Report and by the objectors, and to the application of the NPPF. In *Oakley v South Cambridgeshire DC* [2017] EWCA Civ 71, the proposed development's 'significant and lasting impact on the local community' was seen as one of the factors giving rise to the LPA's duty to give reasons ([52]). Elias LJ also pointed out in *Oakley* at [62] that the duty to give reasons was also consistent with the UK's obligations under the Aarhus Convention (see Lord Carnwath's judgment in *Walton v Scottish Ministers* [2012] UKSC 44 at [100]). In *R (Rogers) v Wycombe DC* [2017] EWHC 3317 (Admin) Lang J stated that it is prudent for officers acting under delegated powers to set out their reasons for granting planning permission rather than merely relying on the contents of a report. See also *R (Tate) v Northumberland CC* [2018] EWCA Civ 1519 (mentioned at fn 101), where a decision granting permission was vitiated by the LPA's error in failing to give reasons for its departure from the approach of an inspector in a previous appeal decision in a 'like' case.

6.41   The case involved an application for outline permission for a scheme including 521 dwellings in the Kent Downs AONB west of Dover. The LPA gave permission (rejecting the planning officers' recommendation to reduce the number of dwellings) and the Campaign to Protect Rural England (CPRE) (Kent) challenged this on a number of grounds. CPRE's appeal was dismissed in the High Court. In the Court of Appeal the focus was on the adequacy of the LPA's reasons for granting permission. The court quashed the permission, ruling that the LPA had failed to sufficiently explain its views on how much harm the scheme would cause to the Area of Outstanding National Beauty (AONB), or whether it could be modified to mitigate the harm without becoming unviable.

6.42   The LPA appealed to the Supreme Court on the ground that, although its reasons had not complied with the former Town and Country Planning (Environmental Impact Assessment) Regulations 2011 (former EIA Regulations 2011) (it was EIA development as it included over 500 dwellings), the breach could have been remedied by a declaration that it had not complied with its EIA duty, with reasons to be supplied retrospectively. The appeal was dismissed.[124] The court found that where the Secretary of State or a planning inspector had made a decision following an inquiry or hearing, the decision-maker had to notify

---

[124] It was found that no attempt had been made to formulate reasons since permission was given. The defect in reasons went to the heart of the justification for permission (which was quashed – it was found that where there is a defect in the reasoning this was the appropriate remedy). It is then plain that even though LPAs need only give brief summaries of their reasons for granting permission, there are circumstances where a heightened duty arises. In *Dover District Council*, planning officers had warned the LPA that binding agreements should be reached with the developers to ensure that the development brought economic benefits to the area and that the hotel and conference centre were actually built. An officer's report also described the harm to the AONB from the development as 'significant', but expressed the view that the public interest was 'finely balanced' in favour of the development. Lord Carnwath also noted that at a planning meeting in June 2013, three members stated that harm to the AONB could be 'minimised' by 'effective screening' of the development from the surrounding area. This was contrary to the officer's report, which stated that screening would be 'largely ineffective'. The committee had met again in December 2013 with an updated officer's report which pointed out that there was no agreement in place that would guarantee the construction of the hotel and conference centre. However, following the signing of a s 106 agreement, permission was formally granted in April 2015. In these circumstances, Lord Carnwath had said that the essence of the LPA's duty was to provide sufficient information so that members of the public would be left with 'no room for genuine doubt' as to the reasons why permission was granted. Lord Carnwath also found that as the LPA had breached its duty under the former EIA Regulations 2011 to give reasons, a mere declaration that it had done so was insufficient in that in the three years since the consent was granted, the LPA had made no attempt to give further reasons for its decision. He said that records of the committee meeting left it unclear as to why members had seen fit to 'reject the views of their own advisers without further investigation'. He said that the lack of any legal mechanism to ensure that the hotel and conference centre were built required explanation. He also said that it was unclear why some members had believed that harm to the AONB could be minimised by screening when this was in direct conflict with the officer's report.

their decision, and their reasons for it, in writing to all persons entitled to appear who had appeared and any other attendee who had asked to be notified. There was no corresponding statutory rule applying to decisions following a written representations appeal. However, there was a duty to give a full reasoned decision. LPAs had to give reasons for refusing permission or imposing conditions. Regarding grants of permission, between 2003 and 2013 LPAs were required to include in the notice of the decision a summary of their reasons. That duty had been repealed by the Town and Country Planning (Development Management Procedure) (England) (Amendment) Order 2013,[125] art 7. Since 2014, local authority officers making any decision involving the grant of a permission or licence have been required to produce a written record of the decision and the reasons for it under the Openness of Local Government Bodies Regulations 2014, regulation 7.[126] Special duties arose in the case of EIA development. Under regulation 3(4) of the former EIA Regulations 2011 (see now regulation 3 of the EIA Regulations 2017), decision-makers are required to state in their decision that they had taken environmental information into consideration. Under regulation 24(1)(c) (now regulation 30(1) of the EIA Regulations 2017), where an LPA determined an EIA application, it had to inform the public of the decision and make available a statement containing the main reasons on which the decision was based.

---

[125] Now replaced by the Town and Country Planning (Development Management Procedure) (England) Order 2015 (SI 2015/595).

[126] See *South Buckinghamshire DC v Porter (No 2)* UKHL 33, [2004] 1 WLR 1953 for guidance on the intelligibility and adequacy of reasons (which was explained and followed in *R (Campaign to Protect Rural England) v Dover District Council*) which was found to apply as much to decisions of LPAs as it did to those of the Secretary of State or inspectors. In *Dover District Council*, it was held that where there was a legal requirement to give reasons, an adequate explanation was needed. If an LPA accepted an officers' report, no reasons further than those in the report might be needed. Even if it was not accepted, it might normally be enough for the committee's statement of reasons to be limited to the points of difference. The essence of the duty was the same: whether the information provided left room for doubt about what had been decided and why (applying *Clarke Homes Ltd v Secretary of State for the Environment* [2017] PTSR 1081). Although public authorities were under no general common law duty to give reasons, fairness in some cases required it (*R v Secretary of State for the Home Department ex parte Doody* [1994] 1 AC 531). *Oakley v South Cambridgeshire DC* [2017] EWCA Civ 71, [2017] 1 WLR 3765, was approved in *Dover District Council* where a duty to give reasons had been found where a committee had disagreed with the officer, notwithstanding the 2013 abrogation of the statutory duty to give reasons for granting permission. *Dover District Council* held that the existence of the common law duty to give reasons, supplementing the statutory rules, was consistent with the 2013 abrogation. See also *R (Midcounties Cooperative Ltd) v Forest of Deane DC* [2017] EWHC 2056 (Admin), where a decision to grant planning permission for an out-of-town retail development was quashed because it had failed to consider the retail impact or harm to the viability of the town centre and had also failed to explain its reasons for granting permission, despite the LPA having refused an application for a similar development a year earlier.

APPARENT BIAS IN DECISION-MAKING (INCLUDING ADVICE AND ASSISTANCE IN CONNECTION WITH PROPOSALS FOR NEIGHBOURHOOD PLANS)

6.43   The approach to a complaint of apparent bias requires regard to be had to the following factors:[127]

(a)   LPA officers are public officials who have a responsibility to take account of legitimately expressed interests raised with them by members of the public whom they are employed to serve. It is part and parcel of their role to have a listening ear to representations that are made to them, although from time to time there will be a necessity to turn representations away such as where they are illegal or vexatious.

(b)   As democratically elected representatives, councillors are expected to receive and consider representations and lobbying from those interested in the issues which they are determining. Evidence of political affiliation or of the adoption of policies towards a planning proposal will not for these purposes by itself amount to an appearance of bias. Something more is required, in the sense of the local member having abandoned the obligation at the point of decision-making to address planning issues fairly and on their merits, even though the member may have previously expressed a predisposition in relation to that decision.

(c)   In cases involving the process of the making of neighbourhood plans (where the LPA is under a duty to give such 'advice and assistance' to qualifying bodies as, in all the circumstances, it considers appropriate for the purpose of, or in connection with, facilitating the making of proposals for such plans),[128] the well-informed and fair-minded observer would have an appreciation of the obligation on LPAs in such circumstances. The statutory provisions are in relatively broad terms and reflect the fact that the LPA is well equipped with experienced professional officers to provide a range of expertise to support a qualifying local body (which may very well be without such resources of its own) in the making of its neighbourhood plan. That said, the statutory duty does not require the LPA to support the proposals of a neighbourhood plan come what may, or whatever may be its views of the merits of the neighbourhood plan. The LPA has important tasks within the statutory framework in terms of appraising the merits of a neighbourhood plan against the specific tests set out in the legislation. The duty to provide 'advice and assistance' does not, however, require uncritical and unthinking support. What it does require is relatively close engagement with the qualifying body to facilitate the making of the neighbourhood plan. It is

---

[127]   *R (Legard) v The Royal Borough of Kensington and Chelsea* [2018] EWHC 32 (Admin).
[128]   TCPA 1990, Sch 4B, para 3(1).

clearly a question of fact whether, in a particular case, the procedure throughout the process up to the decision of the LPA to send a neighbourhood plan to a referendum involved unfairness to the complainant's interests.

PRESUMPTION OF SUSTAINABLE DEVELOPMENT AND THE 'TILTED BALANCE' UNDER NPPF, PARAGRAPH 14, AND ITS IMPACT ON DECISION-TAKING

6.44   Paragraph 14 of the NPPF deals with the 'presumption in favour of sustainable development'[129] which, for decision-taking, means in those cases where the development plan is absent or silent, or where relevant policies are out of date, granting permission *unless* the two exceptions in the second stage of paragraph 14 apply, namely: (a) where the adverse impacts of granting permission would significantly and demonstrably outweigh its benefits, when assessed against the NPPF's policies taken as a whole; and (b) where specific policies in the NPPF indicated that development should be restricted.[130] These two exceptions to the presumption in favour of sustainable development are alternatives: the satisfaction of either one would be sufficient to disapply the presumption.[131]

---

[129]   NPPF, para 6 states that the 'policies in paras 18 to 219, taken as a whole, constitute the Government's view of what sustainable development in England means in practice for the planning system'; para 7 states that there are three dimensions to sustainable development, 'an economic role', 'a social role' and 'an environmental role'; para 8 explains that '[these] roles should not be undertaken in isolation, because they are mutually dependent'.

[130]   In terms of policies where development should be restricted, NPPF, para 14, fn 4 specifically refers to those policies relating to sites protected under the Birds and Habitats Directives or designated as SSSIs; land designated as Green Belt, Local Green Space, an AONB, Heritage Coast or within a National Park (or the Broads Authority); or designated heritage assets; and locations at risk of flooding or coastal erosion. NPPF, para 134 provides that, 'Where a development proposal will lead to less than substantial harm to the significance of a designated heritage asset, this harm should be weighed against the public benefits of the proposal, including securing its optimum viable use'. This is a policy indicating that development should be restricted. See also Green Belt policy in paras 79–92 and those policies in paras 115–116 which are concerned with conserving and enhancing the natural environment in National Parks, the Broads and AONBs.

[131]   *Forest of Dean DC v Secretary of State for Communities and Local Government* [2016] EWHC 421 (Admin). Reference should also be made to the important decision of the Court of Appeal in *Barwood Strategic Land II LLP v East Staffordshire BC* [2017] EWCA Civ 893, in which Lindblom LJ considered the meaning and scope of the presumption in favour of sustainable development in the NPPF and how it related to the presumption in favour of the development plan in PCPA 2004, s 38(6). The court found that planning policies were suitable for judicial interpretation, but they were not statutory or contractual provisions as such. The application of such policies involved an exercise of planning judgment, with which the court would not generally interfere. A decision-maker's failure to properly apply relevant policy would constitute

6.45   The position is reinforced in the section 'Determining applications' where NPPF, paragraph 197, states that '[in] assessing and determining development proposals, LPAs should apply the presumption in favour of sustainable development'. This consideration assumes very considerable importance in decision-making in the case of housing applications. This is because NPPF, paragraph 49, provides that relevant policies for the supply of housing should not be considered up to date if the LPA cannot demonstrate a five-year supply of deliverable housing sites.[132] If the LPA is able to demonstrate a five-year housing supply then it would engage the first stage of NPPF, paragraph 14, in which the presumption in favour of sustainable development means (assuming that the development proposals accord with the development plan) that permission should be granted. On the other hand, if there is no five-year housing supply then the so-called 'tilted balance' in the second stage of NPPF, paragraph 14, comes into play.[133]

6.46   In *Secretary of State for Communities and Local Government v Hopkins Homes Ltd* the Supreme Court considered how NPPF, paragraphs 14 and 49, should be interpreted.[134] The court considered that the primary purpose of paragraph 49

---

a failure to have proper regard to a material consideration (*Bloor Homes East Midlands Ltd v Secretary of State for Communities and Local Government* [2014] EWHC 754 (Admin) approved and *Secretary of State for Communities and Local Government v Hopkins Homes Ltd* [2017] UKSC 37, followed). The s 38(6) duty was to ensure that planning determinations accorded with the development plan. It involved weighing all other material considerations in the balance. The duty was not displaced or modified by the NPPF, which was merely guidance for decision-makers (*Edinburgh City Council v Secretary of State for Scotland* [1997] 1 WLR 1447 and *BDW Trading (t/a David Wilson Homes (Central, Mercia and West Midlands)) v Secretary of State for Communities and Local Government* [2016] EWCA Civ 493 applied.

[132] NPPF, para 47 (first bullet), makes plain that LPAs must ensure that their local plans meet 'the full, objectively assessed needs for market and affordable housing in the housing market area'. To achieve this (second bullet), LPAs must identify and update annually not only five years' worth of deliverable housing sites but, in addition, an additional buffer of 5% (moved forward from later in the plan period) to ensure choice and competition in the market for land, but where there has been a record of persistent under-delivery of housing, LPAs should increase the buffer to 20% to provide a realistic prospect of choice and competition in the market for land.

[133] NPPF, para 6 states that the 'policies in paragraphs 18 to 219, taken as a whole, constitute the Government's view of what sustainable development in England means in practice for the planning system'; para 7 states that there are three dimensions to sustainable development, 'an economic role', 'a social role' and 'an environmental role'; para 8 explains that '[these] roles should not be undertaken in isolation, because they are mutually dependent'.

[134] [2017] 1 WLR 1865. In *Barwood Strategic Land II LLP v East Staffordshire BC* [2017] EWCA Civ 893, at [22]–[23], Lindblom LJ considered that there were five basic points to be taken from *Hopkins Homes* which disclosed how the NPPF presumption in favour of sustainable development in para 14 was to be engaged and how it operated where the LPA had failed to demonstrate a five-year supply of deliverable housing sites (indeed, Lindblom LJ said that these points also provided the context in which the court had to consider the opposite case, namely, whether the LPA had done what the NPPF required it to do, in other words, whether it had put in place an up-to-date plan and was also able to demonstrate the necessary five-year supply). The five basic points are these: (a) the primary purpose of the policy in NPPF, para 49, is to act as a trigger to the operation of the 'tilted balance' under

was to act as a trigger for the operation of the 'tilted balance' under paragraph 14. In the absence of relevant or up-to-date development plan policies, the balance was tilted in favour of granting permission, except where the benefits were significantly and demonstrably outweighed by the adverse effects, or where specific policies indicate otherwise.[135] The court also stated that paragraph 49 indicated the category of policies with which the paragraph was concerned, namely housing supply policies. Although other groups of policies, such as policies for the protection of the countryside, could affect the operation of housing policies, that did not make them policies for the supply of housing. In so far as the objectives in paragraph 47 were not met by housing supply policies (and the objective of paragraph 47 is to boost significantly the supply of housing) it was only natural to describe those policies as out of date for the purposes of paragraph 49.

---

para 14; (b) the weight to be given to other restrictive non-housing policies under para 14 is always a matter of planning judgment for the decision-maker subject, where applicable, to the 'tilted balance' which involves two specific exceptions relevant to a case where the development plan is absent or silent, or where relevant policies are out of date. The second of those policies (i.e. where specific policies in the NPPF indicate that development should be restricted) will not necessarily shut out the presumption in favour of sustainable development simply because any of the specific policies (of which examples are given in fn 9) are in play (see *Watermead Parish Council v Crematoria Management Ltd* [2017] EWCA Civ 152 at [45]). Once identified, the specific policy has to be applied and a planning judgment exercised before the decision-maker can ascertain whether the presumption in favour of sustainable development is available to the proposal in hand; (c) the important question is whether the LPA can show a five-year housing supply in accordance with the objectives set by para 47. This shortfall is enough to trigger the operation of the second part of para 14 (and not para 49) which provides the substantive advice by reference to which the development plan policies and other material considerations relevant to the application are expected to be assessed; (d) the correct approach is one which shifts the emphasis to the exercise of a planning judgment under para 14. To achieve that, it is unnecessary to treat restrictive policies (such as policies for the Green Belt or for an AONB) as notionally out-of-date. Any relevant restrictive policy is to be brought back into para 14 as a specific policy under fn 9 and the weight to it remains a matter for the decision-maker in accordance with ordinary principles; (e) the rigid enforcement by LPAs of restrictive policies may prevent an LPA from meeting its requirement to meet a five-year supply. If an LPA, in default of the requirement of a five-year supply, were to continue to apply its environmental and amenity policies with full rigour, then the objectives of the NPPF will be frustrated. In those circumstances, it is reasonable for the guidance in NPPF, para 49 to suggest that development plan policies for the supply of housing, however recent they may be, should not be considered up to date. In such cases, the focus shifts to other material considerations and the wider view of the development plan policies has to be taken, and the decision-maker should be disposed to grant the application unless the presumption in favour of sustainable development can be displaced. In summary: *Barwood* takes a narrow view when it comes to the meaning of the expression 'relevant policies for the supply of housing' under NPPF, para 49, dealing essentially with numbers and distribution of homes as opposed to policies dealing with the disposition or restriction of new development. However, such policies can still be given less weight (which is a matter of planning judgment) in the application of the 'tilted balance' required by NPPF, para 14, seeing as boosting the supply of new housing and overcoming the housing deficit is the central theme of the NPPF.

[135] Applying *Bloor Homes East Midlands Ltd v Secretary of State for Communities and Local Government* [2014] EWHC 754 (Admin).

THE NPPF AS A MATERIAL CONSIDERATION IN PLANNING DECISIONS

6.47   Paragraph 11 of the NPPF in the section 'Conserving and enhancing the natural environment' also refers to the requirement in the Planning and Compulsory Purchase Act 2004 (PCPA 2004) that applications for planning permission must be determined in accordance with the development plan unless material considerations indicate otherwise. Paragraph 12 states that the NPPF 'does not change the statutory status of the development plan as the starting point for decision making' and emphasises the importance of LPAs having 'an up-to-date plan in place'. Paragraph 157 in the section of the NPPF dealing with plan-making states that 'Local Plans should be drawn up over an appropriate timescale, preferably a 15-year time horizon, take account of longer term requirements and be kept up to date'.[136] In the context of development control, paragraph 196 states:

> The planning system is plan-led. Planning law requires that applications for planning permission must be determined in accordance with the development plan, unless material considerations indicate otherwise. This Framework is a material consideration in planning decisions.

6.48   To complete the picture, in Annex 1 to the NPPF, which deals with 'Implementation', paragraph 214 states that '[for] 12 months from the date of publication,[137] decision-takers may continue to give full weight to relevant policies adopted since 2004, even if there is a limited degree of conflict with this Framework'. Paragraph 215 states that:

> [in] other cases and following this 12-month period, due weight should be given to relevant policies in existing plans according to their degree of consistency with this framework (the closer the policies in the plan to the policies in the Framework, the greater the weight that may be given).

THE NECESSITY TO PAY CLOSE SCRUTINY TO HOUSING NEEDS IN PLAN-MAKING AND DECISION-TAKING

6.49   NPPF, paragraph 159, in the section dealing with 'Plan-making', states that LPAs should have 'a clear understanding of housing needs in their area'. To

---

[136]   As Males J said in *Tewkesbury Borough Council v Secretary of State for Communities and Local Government* [2013] EWHC 286 (Admin) at [13] 'The weight to be given to a development plan will depend on the extent to which it is up to date. A plan which is based on outdated information, or which has expired without being replaced, is likely to command little weight'.

[137]   The NPPF (containing the Government's policy for planning in England) was published on 27/3/2012.

this end, they are required to prepare a Strategic Housing Market Assessment (SHMA) to assess their full housing needs and the scale of housing supply necessary to meet local demand, working with neighbouring authorities where housing market areas cross administrative boundaries.

6.50   The NPPF, paragraph 47, in the section 'Delivering a wide choice of high quality homes', provides as follows:

> To boost significantly the supply of housing, local authorities should:
>
> - use their evidence base to ensure that their local plan meets the *full, objectively assessed needs for market and affordable housing in the housing market area* [emphasis added], as far as consistent with the policies set out in this Framework, including identifying key sites which are critical to the delivery of the housing strategy over the plan period;[138]
> - identify and update annually a supply of specific deliverable[139] sites sufficient to provide five years' worth of housing against their housing requirements with an

---

[138] *Jelson Ltd v Secretary of State for Communities and Local Government* [2018] EWCA Civ 24. In this case, the Court of Appeal held that a planning inspector who dismissed an appeal against an LPA's refusal of outline permission for housing development did not err in identifying the 'full, objectively assessed needs' for housing in the area. It was held that the inspector's conclusions were coherent and well within the bounds of reasonable planning judgment. Lindblom LJ made it plain that appeals on such matters were unlikely to succeed. He said that responsibility for the assessment of housing need lies with the decision-maker and that it was no part of the court's role in reviewing the decision. Although the decision-maker is clearly expected to establish, at least to a reasonable level of accuracy and reliability, a level of housing need that represents the *full, objectively assessed needs* as a basis for determining whether a five-year supply exists, this is not an exact science. It is an evaluation that involves the decision-maker's exercise of planning judgment on the available material which may not be perfect or complete (see judgment of Lang J in *Shropshire Council v Secretary of State for Communities and Local Government* [2016] EWHC 2733 (Admin) at [27]). The scope for a reasonable and lawful planning judgment in such cases is broad (see judgment of Hickinbottom J in *Stratford-on-Avon DC v Secretary of State for Communities and Local Government* [2013] EWHC 2074 (Admin) at [43]). Often there may be no single correct figure representing the *full, objectively assessed needs* for housing in the relevant area. More than one figure may be reasonable to use. It may even be sensible to adopt a range, rather than trying to identify a single figure. The court stated that unless relevant policy in the NPPF or guidance in the NPPG had plainly been misunderstood or misapplied, the crucial question will always be whether planning judgment has been exercised lawfully, on the relevant material, in assessing housing need in the relevant area.

[139] In the footnote to this reference in the NPPF it is said that:

> 'To be deliverable sites should be available now, offer a suitable location for development now, and be achievable with a realistic prospect that housing will be delivered on the site within five years and in particular that development of the site is viable. Sites with planning permission should be considered deliverable until permission expires, unless there is clear evidence that schemes will not be implemented within five years, for example they will not be viable, there is no longer a demand for the type of units or sites have long term phasing plans'.

In *St Modwen Developments Ltd v Secretary of State for Communities and Local Government and East Riding of Yorkshire Council* [2017] EWCA Civ 1643, the Court of Appeal applied a

additional buffer of 5% (moved forward from later in the plan period) to ensure choice and competition in the market for land. Where there has been a record of persistent under delivery of housing, local planning authorities should increase the buffer to 20% (moved forward from later in the plan period) to provide a realistic prospect of achieving the planned supply and to ensure choice and competition in the market for land;

- identify a supply of specific, developable sites or broad locations for growth, for years 6–10 and, where possible, for years 11–15;
- for market and affordable housing, to illustrate the expected rate of housing delivery through a housing trajectory for the plan period and set out a housing implementation strategy for the full range of housing describing how they will maintain delivery of a five-year supply of housing land to meet their housing target; and
- set out their own approach to housing density to reflect local circumstances.

6.51   Crucially, NPPF, paragraph 49, provides that:

Housing applications should be considered in the context of the presumption in favour of sustainable development. *Relevant policies for the supply of housing should not be considered up-to-date if the local planning authority cannot demonstrate a five-year supply of deliverable housing sites* [emphasis added].

6.52   In dealing with plan-making, LPAs are, at paragraph 156, required to:

… set out the *strategic priorities* [emphasis added] for the area in the local plan. This should include strategic policies to deliver:

- the homes and jobs needed in the area;

6.53   NPPF, paragraph 159, goes on to provide in detail that:

LPAs should have a clear understanding of housing needs in their area. They should:

- prepare a [SHMA] to assess their full housing needs, … [which] should identify the scale and mix of housing and the range of tenures that the local population is likely to need over the plan period which:

  - meets household and population projections, taking account of migration and demographic change;
  - addresses the need for all types of housing, including affordable housing and the needs of different groups in the community (such as, but not limited to,

---

wide meaning to the term 'deliverable'. Lindblom LJ ruled that the definition of the word 'deliverable' in the first part of the footnote to para 47 went to a site's capability of being delivered within five years, not to the certainty or probability that it actually would be. In other words, it needs to be shown that delivery could happen at the site, based on evidence including local plans.

families with children, older people, people with disabilities, service families and people wishing to build their own homes); and
- caters for housing demand and the scale of housing supply necessary to meet this demand;

- prepare a Strategic Housing Land Availability Assessment to establish realistic assumptions about the availability, suitability and the likely economic viability of land to meet the identified need for housing over the plan period.'

6.54 Accordingly, LPAs responsible for preparing local plans are required to carry out a SHMA to assess (NPPF, paragraph 47) the *full, objectively assessed needs* of their area for market and affordable housing unless (NPPF, first part of paragraph 14) any adverse impacts of doing so would significantly and demonstrably outweigh the benefits, when assessed against the policies in the NPPF taken as a whole, or where specific policies indicate that development should be restricted. These policies in the NPPF do not apply to the preparation of a neighbourhood plan. In other words, the qualifying body is not responsible for preparing strategic policies in its neighbourhood plan to meet objectively assessed development needs across a local plan area.[140] However, a neighbourhood plan may include policies on the use of land for housing and locations for housing development and may also address local needs within its area.

St Albans City and District Council v Hunston Properties Ltd[141]

6.55 The above policies were considered in this case which involved a refusal of outline planning permission for a development in the Green Belt. Planning permission for 116 dwellings, a care home and associated facilities on agricultural land had been refused on the ground that virtually all of the site was within the Green Belt. The inspector found that there were no very special circumstances that might have justified what would otherwise have been inappropriate development within the Green Belt. The inspector had considered the shortfall in housing land supply in the district, but concluded that there was no shortfall on the basis of housing requirement figures contained in a revoked regional strategy (an up-to-date local plan containing housing requirements for a five-year period did not even exist when the inspector made her decision).

6.56 The developer appealed on the ground that the inspector had failed to identify the *full objectively assessed needs* for housing in the district as required by paragraph 47 of the NPPF. The judge at first instance found that the inspector had been wrong in law as he could not see how it could be open to an inspector

---

[140] *R (Crownhall Estates Ltd) v Chichester District Council* [2016] EWHC 73 (Admin).
[141] [2013] EWCA Civ 1610.

to reach a conclusion by reference to a figure contained in a revoked plan. The Court of Appeal agreed, holding that it was not for the inspector to carry out some sort of local plan process so as to arrive at a housing requirement figure. The court found that, using the correct policy approach, there was such a shortfall in housing land supply. The inspector had gone wrong by adopting a figure for housing requirements which was below the *full objectively assessed needs* figure until such time as the local plan process came up with a constrained figure. This had led her to find that there was no shortfall in housing land supply in the district. If she had followed the correct approach, she would have found that there was such a shortfall because the supply fell below the objectively assessed five-year requirement.

6.57   The inspector also had to determine whether very special circumstances could be demonstrated which overrode the Green Belt objection.[142] A consideration in this regard was the scale of any shortfall in housing land supply in the district and the planning context for this which involved the existence of policies protecting much or most of the undeveloped land from development except in exceptional or very special circumstances. In such circumstances, it was hardly surprising that there was no five-year supply of housing land. This affected the weight which might be attached to the housing land shortfall in circumstances where the Green Belt element meant that very special circumstances had to be shown if development was to take place at all. The court found that this was the approach which took proper account of the need to read the NPPF as a whole,[143] and the inspector's decision was quashed as she relied on a figure for housing land supply which departed from the correct approach in the NPPF.

Tewkesbury Borough Council v Secretary of State for Communities and Local Government[144]

6.58   The policies in the NPPF, paragraphs 47 and 49, and its relevance to the presumption of sustainable development in paragraph 14, were considered in this case where Males J stated as follows:[145]

> 20. Accordingly, both before and after the issue of the NPPF, the need to ensure a 5 year supply of housing land was of significant importance. Before the NPPF the absence of such a supply would result in favourable consideration of planning

---

[142]   NPPF, paras 87–88.

[143]   NPPF, para 14 reads, 'where the development plan is absent, silent or relevant policies are out-of-date, granting permission unless: – any adverse impacts of doing so would significantly and demonstrably outweigh the benefits, when assessed against the policies in this Framework taken as a whole; or …'.

[144]   [2013] EWHC 286 (Admin).

[145]   [2013] EWHC 286 (Admin) at [20]–[21].

applications, albeit taking account also of other matters such as the spatial vision for the area concerned. After the NPPF, if such a supply could not be demonstrated, relevant policies would be regarded as out of date, and therefore of little weight, and there would be a rebuttable presumption in favour of the grant of planning permission. All of this would have been well understood by local planning authorities. An authority which was not in a position to demonstrate a 5 year supply of housing land would have recognised, or ought to have recognised, that on any appeal to the Secretary of State from a refusal of permission there would be at least a real risk that an appeal would succeed and permission would be granted.

21. That is not to say, however, that the absence of a 5 year housing land supply would be conclusive in favour of the grant of planning permission. It may be that the NPPF, with its emphasis in paragraph 47 to the need 'to boost significantly the supply of housing', placed even more importance on this factor than PPS3 had done, but whether or not that is so, in both regimes the absence of such a supply was merely one consideration required to be taken into account, albeit an important one.

Solihull Metropolitan Borough Council v Gallagher Homes Ltd (the process leading to the adoption of local plans)[146]

6.59   *St Albans City and District Council v Hunston Properties Ltd*[147] was followed in the Court of Appeal in *Solihull MBC* which involved a challenge to the adoption of a local plan which allocated two sites in the Green Belt, which meant that development would almost certainly be refused. The developers' claim was upheld at first instance and the local plan was not adopted, but ordered to be remitted for re-examination by a different inspector (on appeal, it was agreed that the right order would have been to remit the defective parts of the local plan to the council).

6.60   The LPA challenged this finding on two grounds. First, whether paragraph 47 of the NPPF effected a radical policy change in respect of housing provision so as to undermine the inspector's treatment of this in his report following the examination in public of the draft local plan. Secondly, whether exceptional circumstances existed to justify the alteration of the boundaries of the Green Belt in the district to accommodate the above allocations.[148] The case was complex, but the fundamentals of the decision (in which the LPA's appeal was dismissed) were as set out below in so far as it concerned housing land supply policies under the NPPF.

6.61   The appeal was concerned with plan-making and development plan documents whose adoption is constrained by the requirements of the PCPA 2004

---

[146]   [2015] JPL 713.

[147]   [2013] EWCA Civ 1610.

[148]   NPPF, para 83.

which involves an examination in public by an inspector appointed by the Secretary of State, who has to determine: (a) whether the plan complies with various procedural requirements; (b) whether it is 'sound'; and (c) whether it is reasonable to conclude that the LPA has complied with any duty to co-operate. If the inspector is satisfied about points (a) and (b), he must recommend adoption of the plan and the authority may adopt the plan. If he is not satisfied as to points (a) and (b) and is not satisfied that the authority has complied with its duty to co-operate, he must recommend non-adoption and the authority must not adopt the plan. If he is not satisfied as to points (a) and (b), but is satisfied that the authority has complied with its duty to co-operate, he must recommend non-adoption but, on the authority's request, he must also recommend modifications to the plan that would make it satisfy those two requirements, in which event the authority may then adopt the plan with those modifications. It was against this background that the Court of Appeal had to consider NPPF, paragraph 47, and the steps which an LPA is now required to take (in furtherance of the presumption in favour of sustainable development in NPPF, paragraph 14) in order to 'ensure that their Local Plan meets the *full, objectively assessed needs for market and affordable housing in the housing market area*' [emphasis added].

6.62   Consistently with the decision in *St Albans City and District Council v Hunston Properties Ltd*[149] (involving a planning application rather than plan-making), it was emphasised in *Solihull MBC* that the making of the objectively assessed needs for market and affordable housing is an exercise which is prior to, and separate from, the application to that assessment of the impact of other relevant NPPF policies (i.e. a two-step approach in which housing need has first to be ascertained and to which effect must be given save only to the extent that that would be inconsistent with other NPPF policies). In other words, it is incorrect, for NPPF purposes, for all material considerations (including housing need, demand and other relevant policies) simply to be weighed together in the balancing exercise (as had been the case pre-NPPF). Nor is it sufficient to determine the maximum housing supply available and to constrain housing provision targets to that figure. NPPF, paragraph 47, requires full housing needs to be objectively assessed and then a distinct assessment made as to whether (and, if so, to what extent) other policy factors dictate otherwise or justify restraint. In other words, is any housing shortfall going to be outweighed by policies in the local plan or NPPF which will operate to preclude the development?

6.63   The process by which the inspector came to adopt the local plan in the *Solihull MBC* case did not meet the requirements of the NPPF. This was because neither the inspector nor the LPA had undertaken, as a separate and prior exercise, a full and objective assessment of housing need before going on to consider

---

[149]   [2013] EWCA Civ 1610.

constraints on meeting that need by the impact of other policies, from which it followed that the inspector's recommendation was legally flawed.

6.64   What this means in practice is that in the case of decision-making in housing applications, close scrutiny should always be paid to housing needs within the district. In the case of decision-making, the presumption in favour of sustainable development means that where relevant policies are out of date (i.e. no five-year supply of deliverable housing sites), planning permission should be granted unless any adverse impacts of doing so would significantly and demonstrably outweigh the benefits when assessed against the policies in the NPPF as a whole or where specific policies restrict development.[150]

Secretary of State for Communities and Local Government v Hopkins Homes Ltd (and the 'tilted balance')

6.65   Reference has already been made to the decision of the Supreme Court in *Hopkins Homes*.[151] It will be recalled that this case dealt with NPPF, paragraph 14 and its relation with paragraph 49. It was the view of Lord Carnwath[152] that the primary purpose of paragraph 49 (and the necessity for LPAs to demonstrate a five-year supply of deliverable housing sites) is simply enough to act as a trigger to the operation of the 'tilted balance' under the second part of paragraph 14. The effect of this is that in the absence of relevant or up-to-date policies in the development plan, the balance is tilted in favour of the grant of permission, except where the benefits are 'significantly and demonstrably' outweighed by the adverse effects, or where special policies indicate otherwise (such as those in relation to the Green Belt or for an AONB – see footnote 9 to paragraph 14 which gives examples of such restrictive policies). Paragraph 14 is not concerned solely with housing policy and can work for other forms of development covered by the development plan. For instance, policies for employment land or transport may also be found to be out of date for other reasons so as to trigger the paragraph 14 presumption. The only difference is that in those cases there is no equivalent test to that of the five-year supply for housing in NPPF, paragraph 49. In neither case is there any reason to treat the shortfall in the particular policies as rendering out of date other parts of the plan which serve a different purpose. The weight to be attached to such policies will be a matter of planning judgment for the decision-maker in accordance with ordinary principles.

---

[150]   NPPF, paras 14, 47 and 49.

[151]   [2017] 1 WLR 1865.

[152]   [2017] 1 WLR 1865 at [53]–[61].

Barwood Strategic Land II LLP v East Staffordshire BC

6.66   Reference should again be made[153] to *Barwood*,[154] where the Court of Appeal considered the meaning and scope of the presumption of sustainable development in NPPF, paragraph 14, and how it related to the presumption in favour of the development plan in section 38(6) of the PCPA 2004. The judgment of Lindblom LJ confirms that there is no scope for a policy presumption in favour of planning permission outside that contained in NPPF, paragraph 14, in those cases where the proposed development is not in accordance with the development plan.

6.67   The view taken by the court was that the section 38(6) duty was a statutory duty (or presumption) to ensure that planning determinations accorded with the development plan. It involved weighing all other material considerations in the balance. The duty was not displaced or modified by the presumption in favour of sustainable development in the NPPF, paragraph 14, which was merely guidance for decision-makers and was not a statutory presumption. For instance, when the section 38(6) duty was lawfully performed, a development which did not earn the sustainable development presumption, and which did not, therefore, have the benefit of the 'tilted balance' in paragraph 14, might still merit the grant of planning permission. A development not having the benefit of the paragraph 14 'tilted balance' might still be found unacceptable. The presumption in favour of sustainable development was not irrebuttable; where there was conflict between a proposal and a development plan, the decision-maker had to judge how much weight to give to that conflict. It was a matter of planning judgment, not a matter of law. It has since been said that, in future, reference to pre-*Barwood v East Staffordshire* authorities on the meaning and operation of the presumption in NPPF paragraph 14 should be avoided.[155]

CALCULATING THE SUPPLY OF HOUSING LAND – CAN THE LPA DEMONSTRATE A FIVE-YEAR SUPPLY OF DELIVERABLE HOUSING SITES UNDER NPPF, PARAGRAPH 49?[156]

6.68   The process starts with the housing targets contained in the local plan. Are they up to date or are there more up-to-date projections available and, if there are,

---

153   See fn 123.

154   [2017] EWCA Civ 893 (Lindblom LJ).

155   *Mansell v Tonbridge and Malling BC and others* [2017] EWCA Civ 1314 at [61].

156   What follows is subject to the new Housing Delivery Test (HDT) and the introduction of the new standardised approach to assessing housing need – see paras 2.47–2.53.

are they more reliable? Are the figures too constrained? Clearly, the LPA's evidence base needs to ensure that its local plan meets the *full, objectively assessed needs for market and affordable housing in the housing market area* as far as is consistent with policies set out in the NPPF.[157] It may be that an emerging local plan is underpinned by a fairly recent SHMA which is an update on an earlier assessment for the area which pre-dated the NPPF. Advice may always be had from other sources, including the Planning Advisory Service guidance,[158] or the LPA may even have commissioned an independent review of the housing requirements contained in its SHMA.

6.69   The LPA may eventually settle on an annual figure of X dwellings over the next five years which may even be the figure relied on in the emerging local plan. This begs the question as to whether a housing requirement of X dwellings is too low. What if a planning appeal falls to be determined before the local plan examination? In such circumstances, the authority's forecast can only be given limited weight. NPPF, paragraph 17 (third bullet), in the section 'Achieving sustainable development', refers to the fact that plans should take account of market signals, such as land prices and housing affordability, and should also set out a clear strategy for allocating sufficient land which is suitable for development in the LPA's area. In many parts of the country, it is the inability of people to access the private rented or owner-occupied market sectors (because of high house prices and rental levels relative to income) which can reflect a shortage of supply, and in some areas (no doubt in most) the problem may even be worsening. Clearly, the private sector will play an important role in affordable housing provision where the problem is all too often so large that it is unlikely to be eradicated in the short to medium term, and it must surely be sensible that a serious attempt should be made at tackling the issue to prevent the problem from getting progressively worse. Assumptions will, of course, need to be made to determine how many affordable homes can be generated from existing deliverable sites and whether this is likely to address the issue of affordability in any meaningful way. It may be that there is also insufficient housing to accommodate employees, which will be likely to deter new investment and have a deleterious effect on the economic growth forecast in the emerging local plan. One might ask what the annual housing requirement is likely to be on the basis of existing job levels and existing levels of migration into the district. What if these are set to increase when account is taken of predicted employment allocations in the emerging local plan? No doubt the SHMA will identify these and other relevant factors which comprise the evidence base which will enable the local plan to meet

---

[157]   NPPF, para 47 (first bullet).

[158]   Planning Advisory Service, *Ten Key Principles for Owning your Housing Number – Finding your Objectively Assessed Needs* (Local Government Association, July 2013).

'the full, objectively assessed needs for market and affordable housing in the housing market area'.[159]

6.70   When looked at in the round, it may be that the LPA's forecast of a housing need of X dwellings per annum over five years is woefully inadequate to meet projected local housing needs within the same period.[160] Might it be, perhaps, that the LPA has failed to take sufficient account of market signals such as higher land prices and housing affordability, factors which will obviously underscore the importance of a buoyant supply of housing land? On the other hand, the decision-maker may feel pre-disposed to accept the authority's figure of X dwellings, but only as a constrained figure which would provide only the very minimum requirement at the present time.

DEALING WITH HOUSING BACKLOG – *SEDGEFIELD* OR *LIVERPOOL* AND ADDITION OF BUFFER?[161]

6.71   To be added to the mix will be any backlog that has not been delivered against local plan requirements. One would need to know how many completions there have been since the end of the last plan period and, of course, whether the housing requirement figure needs to be modified to allow for modifications to the earlier targets. It may well be said that in order to meet *objectively assessed needs* and to deliver a choice of high quality homes, it makes sense to rectify any historic under-delivery as soon as possible. This is the so-called 'Sedgefield approach',[162]

---

[159]   NPPF, para 47 (first bullet).

[160]   It is perhaps worth noting what Lindblom J said at [105] in *Bloor Homes East Midlands Ltd v Secretary of State for Communities and Local Government and Hinckley and Bosworth Borough Council* [2014] EWHC 754 (Admin):

> 'Because the business of calculating the supply of housing land involves assumptions and judgment there will sometimes not be a single right answer to the question "Can the local planning authority demonstrate a five-year supply?" Often it will be perfectly clear what the answer is, even if there is a margin of dispute between applicant and authority. But since this question has considerable significance for the application of government policy in the NPPF, a robust calculation is essential. And in cases such as this, where the LPA's ability to show a five-year supply depends on several variables, any one of which could make a decisive difference to the outcome if an assumption or judgment contrary to the authority's were accepted, the need for clarity and precision will be vital'.

> And as Hickinbottom J said in *Stratford-upon-Avon District Council v Secretary of State for the Environment, Transport and Regions* [2013] EWHC 2074 (Admin) at [25]: the calculation of housing need 'is not the product of a mathematical exercise alone; it involves a series of planning judgments weighing a complex of material factors on the basis of all the available evidence, including (where available) projections from different models'.

[161]   Again, subject to the new HDT – see paras 2.47–2.53.

[162]   The so-called 'Sedgefield approach' seeks to ensure that housing shortfall from previous years is addressed promptly in that it places the shortfall into the next five years' supply. It is argued with

which seeks to deal with backlog over the next five years of the local plan rather than spreading it over the remainder of the plan period.[163] NPPF, paragraph 47, in the section 'Delivering a wide choice of high quality homes', indicates that a buffer should also be added to the housing requirement to ensure choice and competition in the market for land. This should normally be 5%, but where there is a persistent record of under-delivery it should be raised to 20%.[164] There is no definitive guidance as to the delivery period to be considered, but the NPPF does require an assessment of future housing delivery over the next five years, and it seems reasonable to assess past delivery over a similar period of time.

FINAL QUESTIONS IN ASSESSING FIVE-YEAR HOUSING SUPPLY (INCLUDING DELIVERY DISCOUNT IN ORDER TO REDUCE OVERALL SUPPLY FIGURE AND PLANNING JUDGMENT)

6.72   Taking all these factors into account, the decision-maker must decide what the total requirement should be over the next five years. To such figure will have to be applied the deliverable supply of housing sites over the same period. This figure, too, is almost certain to be the subject of fierce debate, such as the measure of discounting delivery (or the reasonableness of the so-called 'lapse rate' as it has been put)[165] in the case of the number of permitted new homes on the larger

some force that this approach is in tune with the NPPF which implies dealing with backlog expeditiously from which it follows that the backlog should be added to the five-year requirement.

[163] This is the so-called 'Liverpool (residual) method'. In *Bloor Homes East Midlands Ltd v Secretary of State for Communities and Local Government and Hinckley and Bosworth Borough Council* [2014] EWHC 754 (Admin) at [107]–[118], Lindblom J did not interfere with the adoption by the inspector in that case of the Liverpool approach. He said that the inspector was free to come to his own judgment about this and that it lay within the territory of planning judgment with which the court would not interfere (even though other inspectors may have disagreed with him in the same circumstances). Until we have firm policy guidance on the correct approach to the assessment of housing land supply, the choice between Sedgefield or Liverpool remains open to debate. At any rate, the emphasis in the NPPF on boosting the supply of housing surely points towards the choice of the Sedgefield approach unless, of course, there is a strong local reason for doing otherwise. For instance, the argument that the backlog in housing delivery should be met over the following five-year period may, in local circumstances, be unachievable given doubt over delivery of permitted and allocated schemes, in which case a longer period for addressing backlog may be more realistic.

[164] The NPPF does not elaborate on this concept, which is therefore a matter of planning judgment for the inspector who hears the appeal.

[165] Lewis J said in *Cotswold District Council v Secretary of State for Communities and Local Government* [2013] EWHC 3719 (Admin) at [71], that the question of the '10% lapse rate' was 'essentially a matter of judgment for the inspector', a judgment which in that case the inspector had made. It is worth noting that in *Bloor Homes East Midlands Ltd v Secretary of State for Communities and Local Government and Hinckley and Bosworth Borough Council* [2014]

sites, with a view (if the discount is a high one) to reducing the LPA's overall supply figure.[166] It may be, of course, that the LPA and the applicant for permission agree that whatever the figure for housing land supply, it is still appreciably less than five years. If the appeal scheme is a large one, the developer may be confident of delivery within the five-year period and may even be agreeable to a planning condition that would considerably reduce the period for implementation. In light of all this, the decision-maker may well be justified in coming to the view that the proposed development would make an important contribution towards the reduction of a serious housing deficit in the district, which is likely to weigh significantly in favour of the grant of planning permission.

AN LPA'S DUTY OF CARE IN DEALING WITH PLANNING APPLICATIONS

6.73   The general rule is that an LPA does not owe a duty of care to those affected by the performance of their statutory functions.[167] On the other hand, it

---

EWHC 754 (Admin), Lindblom J allowed Bloor's appeal and remitted the case for redetermination by the Secretary of State on the ground that the inspector had simply failed to deal with the case that there should be a discount in the case of permitted housing on the larger sites. The importance of this omission was that even on the most favourable view of the authority's case, the five-year supply was tight (5.02 years) and a discount of 10% would have meant that the housing land supply would have fallen below five years.

[166]   A 10% discount is supported by the paper *Housing Land Availability* (Department of the Environment, 1995). The NPPF requires sites to be deliverable and achievable, yet there may be inevitable difficulties in bringing all sites forward in the remainder of the plan period. For instance, permissions may lapse and viability issues will change. Development may either not occur or else be delayed for all manner of reasons, such as problems with ownership or difficulty with access or because of land conditions. Some sites may only have gained planning permission purely as a valuation exercise with no intention of being built, particularly in the case of the smaller sites. Furthermore, in a weak market, buildings may need to be redesigned to improve viability or the market for apartments may weaken with a change to larger houses and gardens, bringing about a reduction in density. The thinking is that it is quite ambitious to be thinking in terms of developing a large number of houses on larger sites in a five-year period. There may also be a considerable difference between the number of houses for which outline permission has been granted and the eventual density allowed following reserved matters approval. At the end of the day, the question of whether there is a five-year supply of housing land may well turn on only three matters, namely: (a) discounts on large sites; (b) Sedgefield or Liverpool; or (c) a 5% or 20% buffer, or perhaps on only one of these for it to be shown that the LPA has less than a five-year supply of deliverable housing land. (LPAs will obviously be seeking to rely on the Liverpool or residual method and no, or only a 5%, buffer.)

[167]   *Strable v Dartford BC* [1984] JPL 329; *Ryeford Homes Ltd v Sevenoaks DC* [1990] JPL 36 and *Murphy v Brentwood DC* [1990] 2 All ER 908; *Tidman v Reading BC* [1994] 3 PLR 72 and *Haddow v Secretary of State for the Environment* [2000] Env LR 212; *Fashion Brokers Ltd v Clarke Hayes (a firm)* [2000] PNLR 473; *R v South Norfolk District Council ex parte Pelham Homes Ltd* [2001] JPL 230; and *M R Dean v First Secretary of State* [2007] 2 P & CR 6.

has been held that a local authority could be liable to a claim in negligence where it had permitted the opening of a public footpath prior to the completion of necessary road or sightline improvements, without which it was aware there was a danger.[168]

---

[168] *Kane v New Forest DC* [2001] EWCA Civ 878, [2002] 1 WLR 312. In allowing the claimant's appeal, the court found that NFDC owed a duty to those who might have wanted to use the footpath, to ensure that it was not opened until the sightline dangers were removed. It was clear that NFDC had been aware of the danger but that only preliminary steps had been taken to remove it. Whilst the ordinary exercise of a statutory power to grant or refuse planning consent would not create a duty of care at common law, this did not confer a blanket immunity on LPAs if they permitted or required the construction of a potentially dangerous footpath, or if they failed when granting permission to impose a condition forbidding the opening of the footpath until the necessary sightlines had been cleared. And irrespective of any such condition, the LPA should have ensured that the footpath was not used until it was safe.

Chapter 7

Power to Make Non-material Changes to, or Otherwise Revoke or Modify, Existing Planning Permissions and the Liability of a Local Planning Authority to Pay Compensation

POWER TO MAKE NON-MATERIAL CHANGES TO PLANNING PERMISSION

7.1 The local planning authority (LPA) has power to make non-material changes to a planning permission.[1] This includes power to impose new conditions and to remove or alter existing conditions. An application must be made by or on behalf of a person with an interest in the land. There is no definition of the term 'non-material' but the LPA must be satisfied that the amendment sought is non-material in order to grant the application the effect of which is to amend the permission.[2]

---

[1] TCPA 1990, s 73 (applications to develop land without compliance with conditions previously attached) and s 96A (power to make non-material changes to planning permission or permission in principle). See NPPG, Reference ID: 17a-002-20140306 to 17a-019-20140306. See also Town and Country Planning (Development Management Procedure) (England) Order 2015 (DMPO), art 10. As by definition the changes sought will be non-material, it is unlikely that there will be effects which would need to be addressed under the Town and Country Planning (Environmental Impact Assessment) Regulations 2017.

[2] An application under TCPA 1990, s 73 will give rise to a wholly new planning permission, whereas s 96A does not result in a new permission but amends an existing permission (s 96A does not leave the option available under s 73 of implementing the unamended permission since there is only one permission, rather than a second permission which results from s 73). Under s 73, the LPA will only be considering the question of conditions subject to which planning permission should be granted. The authority may decide that permission should be granted subject to conditions differing from those to which the previous permission was granted, or that it should be granted unconditionally, or it may even decide that planning permission should be granted subject to the same conditions as before, in which event the application under s 73 will be refused. This provision will not apply to the extent that it has effect to change a condition subject to which

7.2   Where new issues arise after planning permission has been granted which require modification of the approved proposals, if they are fundamental or substantial then a new planning application will need to be submitted. Where less important changes are proposed, a developer has the following options for amending a proposal that has planning permission: he may either apply to make a non-material amendment; or he may seek to amend the conditions attached to the planning permission, including seeking to make minor material amendments.

REVOCATION OR MODIFICATION OF PLANNING PERMISSIONS

7.3   The LPA also has power to revoke or modify a planning permission to such extent as it considers expedient, having regard to the development plan and to any other material considerations.[3] No order can, however, be made after the relevant building operations have been completed or any relevant change of use has taken place, and the revocation will not affect any building operations which have previously been carried out.[4] In opposed cases, an order made will not take effect unless it is confirmed by the Secretary of State, who may confirm the order either without modification or subject to such modification as he considers expedient.[5] A mechanism exists whereby, in uncontested cases, an order may be made and in such a case it will be unnecessary for the Secretary of State to confirm the order, although the procedure will not be available in cases where planning permission has been granted or deemed to be granted by the Secretary of State or in relation to the modification of time-limiting conditions.[6] A default power also exists enabling the Secretary of State himself to make a revocation or

the previous planning permission was granted by extending the time within which a development must be started or an application for approval of reserved matters must be made.

[3]   TCPA 1990, s 97(1) and (2). In the exercise of powers under this section, the LPA is able to have regard, as a material consideration, to its potential liability for compensation and whether it is proportionate to the aim to be achieved (*R (Health and Safety Executive) v Wolverhampton City Council* [2012] 1 WLR 2264; see also *R (Usk Valley Conservation Group) v Brecon Beacons National Park Authority* [2010] EWHC 71 (Admin), where the judge held that the authority's decision to take enforcement proceedings rather than make a discontinuance order (on the basis that no compensation was payable in respect of the former) was lawful). Unless an order under this section is questioned by way of an application to the High Court within six weeks of its confirmation by the Secretary of State, it may not otherwise be questioned in any legal proceedings whatsoever (TCPA 1990, s 284(1)(e) – there is now a requirement for permission for s 288 applications).

[4]   TCPA 1990, s 97(3) and (4).

[5]   TCPA 1990, s 98.

[6]   TCPA 1990, s 99.

modification order (i.e. if the LPA will not make it), which will have the same effect as if it had been made by the LPA and confirmed by the Secretary of State.[7]

7.4   Because a planning permission usually confers a valuable substantive right which runs with the land, it can only be modified or revoked under the foregoing provisions.[8] Where this occurs it gives rise to a right to compensation for abortive expenditure or other loss, such as diminution in value, shown to be directly attributable to the revocation or modification.[9] No compensation is payable in respect of work done or loss arising out of anything done or omitted to be done before the grant of the planning permission which is revoked or modified (other than for diminution in value).[10] Claims for compensation should be made to the LPA within 12 months of the date of the relevant decision (unless the Secretary of State agrees to extend time)[11] and any dispute will be referred to and determined by the Upper Tribunal.[12]

DISCONTINUANCE ORDERS

7.5   Compensation for loss also arises in a case where the LPA considers it expedient (having regard to the development plan and to any other material considerations) in the interests of the proper planning of its area (including the interests of amenity):

(a)   that any use of land should be discontinued, or that any condition should be imposed on the continuance of a use of the land; or

---

[7]   TCPA 1990, s 100.

[8]   TCPA 1990, ss 97–100; otherwise there is no right to compensation for the loss of planning permission.

[9]   TCPA 1990, s 107. The entitlement to compensation is extended by s 108 to the withdrawal of permitted development rights under GPDO, arts 4–6, although in such a case a right to compensation only crystallises after an express application has been refused or granted subject to conditions, other than those prescribed by the development order. Provision is also made for compensation in the case of discontinuance orders under s 102. There is also provision: (a) for the apportionment of compensation for depreciation (s 109); (b) for the registration by the Secretary of State (as a local land charge) of compensation for depreciation and any apportionment which has been made in the case of the land, or any part of the land, in respect of which the compensation relates and for the recovery of compensation; and (c) for the recovery of compensation under s 111 in the case of subsequent development before it can be carried out, although there are exceptions to this (s 111(3)–(5)). See *Hobbs (Quarries) Ltd v Somerset County Council* (1975) 30 P & CR 286, LT, where compensation was awarded for loss of anticipated future business profits. Also see *Colley v Canterbury City Council* (1992) 64 P & CR 275, CA (which was upheld in the House of Lords at [1993] 1 All ER 591).

[10]   TCPA 1990, s 107(3).

[11]   Town and Country Planning General Regulations 1992 (SI 1992/1492), reg 12.

[12]   TCPA 1990, s 118.

(b)   that any buildings or works should be altered or removed, in which case the LPA may:

(i)   require the discontinuance of that use; or

(ii) impose such conditions as may be specified in the order on the continuance of it; or

(iii) require such steps as may be specified to be taken for the alteration or removal of the buildings or works, as the case may be.[13]

7.6   If the LPA is prepared to allow some alternative use of the land then a discontinuance order may also grant planning permission for these purposes.[14] A discontinuance order does not take effect unless confirmed by the Secretary of State who will give persons an opportunity of being heard by a person appointed by him before making his determination.[15] The Secretary of State may himself make such order should the LPA be unwilling to do so.[16] Non-compliance with a discontinuance order is an offence and is not dependent on enforcement action.[17] Furthermore, if steps required to be taken to remove buildings, etc. have not been taken, the LPA may enter the land and do the work itself and recover any expenses reasonably incurred by it in doing so.[18]

[13] TCPA 1990, s 102(1). Claims for compensation may be made by any person and it is not limited to persons with an interest in the land, although in such cases compensation would be limited to disturbance in the enjoyment of land and for works carried out (s 115(2)(b) and (3)). Provision is also made in s 115(4) for a deduction to be made from any compensation for the value of any timber, apparatus or other materials removed from the land for the purposes of complying with an order under s 102. Claims for compensation in the case of discontinuance orders must be in writing and served on the LPA within 12 months of the date of the order made under s 102 unless the Secretary of State extends time (Town and Country Planning General Regulations 1992 (SI 1992/1492), reg 12).

[14] TCPA 1990, s 102(2).

[15] TCPA 1990, s 103(1) and (3)–(6).

[16] TCPA 1990, s 104(1).

[17] TCPA 1990, s 189. It will, however, be a defence for the person charged with the offence to prove that he took all reasonable measures and exercised all due diligence to avoid commission of the offence by himself or by any person under his control (s 189(4)). The penalty is a fine, either on summary conviction (not exceeding the statutory maximum) or on conviction on indictment (s 189(3)).

[18] TCPA 1990, s 190.

Chapter 8

Planning Conditions

WHY ARE PLANNING CONDITIONS IMPOSED?

8.1   Planning guidance on the use of conditions is found in the National Planning Practice Guidance (NPPG) in the section, 'Use of Planning Conditions'.[1] It is made plain that planning conditions are imposed to enhance development where it would otherwise have been necessary to refuse permission by mitigating the adverse effects of the development. It is said that the objectives of planning are best served when the power to attach conditions to a planning permission is exercised in a way that is clearly seen to be fair, reasonable and practicable. It is also important to ensure that conditions are tailored to tackle specific problems, as opposed to being standardised or used to impose broad and unnecessary controls.

WHAT ARE THE MAIN POWERS RELATING TO THE USE OF CONDITIONS?

8.2   In granting planning permission local planning authorities (LPAs) are authorised to impose 'such conditions as they think fit'.[2] Government policy on

---

[1]   NPPG at Paragraph: 001 Reference ID: 21a-001-20140306 to 21a-034-20140306.

[2]   TCPA 1990, s 70(1)(a). The principal powers for the imposition of conditions can be found in TCPA 1990, ss 70 and 72 (s 72(1)(a) enables an LPA to impose conditions regulating the development or use of land under the control of the applicant even though it is outside the site which is the subject of the application); s 73 (which provides for applications for planning permission to develop land without complying with conditions previously imposed on a planning permission); s 73A (which provides, amongst other things, for retrospective planning applications to be made in respect of development which has been carried out without permission, and for applications for planning permission to authorise development which has been carried out without complying with some planning condition to which it was subject); and Sch 5. Sections 91 and 92 require the imposition of time-limiting conditions on grants of planning permission. Powers to impose conditions are also conferred on the Secretaries of State or their inspectors under ss 77, 79 and 177, and Sch 6. Unless the condition provides otherwise, planning permission runs with

the use of conditions is to be found in the National Planning Policy Framework 2012 (NPPF) at paragraphs 203 and 206 in the section 'Decision-taking'. Paragraph 203 states that LPAs 'should consider whether unacceptable development could be made acceptable through the use of conditions'. Paragraph 206 states that planning conditions 'should only be imposed where they are necessary, relevant to planning, and to the development to be permitted, enforceable, precise, and reasonable in all other respects'.[3]

8.3   These are the so-called six tests which must all be satisfied each time a decision to grant planning permission subject to conditions is made. These tests are set out alongside what are described as the key questions in the NPPG in the section, 'Use of Planning Conditions'.[4]

8.4   For instance: (a) in relation to the test of whether the condition is relevant to the development to be permitted, the key considerations are: (i) it is not sufficient that a condition is related to planning objectives: it must also be justified by the nature of the impact of the development permitted; and (ii) a condition cannot be imposed in order to remedy a pre-existing problem or issue not created by the proposed development; and (b) in relation to whether a condition is reasonable, the key considerations are: (i) whether the condition place an unjustifiable and disproportionate burden on an applicant; and (ii) an unreasonable condition cannot be used to make development that is unacceptable in planning terms acceptable.

WHAT APPROACH SHOULD BE TAKEN TO IMPOSING CONDITIONS?

8.5   The NPPG in the section, 'Use of Planning Conditions', states[5] that conditions should *not* be used in the following circumstances:

(a)   conditions which unreasonably impact on the deliverability of a development;

---

the land, and any conditions imposed on the permission will bind successors in title. In some areas, there may also be powers under local Acts which complement or vary the powers contained in the 1990 Act.

3   In *Aberdeen City and Shire Strategic Development Planning Authority v Elsick Development Company Ltd* [2017] UKSC 66, the Supreme Court reaffirmed the three-fold test that conditions: (a) must serve a planning purpose; (b) must be fairly and reasonably related to the development; and (c) must not otherwise be unreasonable in the *Wednesbury* sense.

4   NPPG at Paragraph: 004 Reference ID: 21a-004-20140306.

5   NPPG at Paragraph: 005 Reference ID: 21a-005-20140306.

(b)   conditions reserving outline application details;[6]
(c)   conditions requiring the development to be carried out in its entirety;[7]
(d)   conditions requiring compliance with other regulatory requirements (e.g. Building Regulations, Environmental Protection Act 1990);[8]
(e)   conditions requiring land to be given up or ceded to other parties, such as the highway authority;
(f)   positively worded conditions requiring payment of money or other consideration.[9]

8.6   For non-outline applications, other than where it will clearly assist with the efficient and effective delivery of development, it is important that the LPA limits the use of conditions requiring its approval of further matters after permission has been granted. This may be justified, for instance, in the case of aspects of the development that are not fully described in the application, such as the provision of car parking spaces.[10]

8.7   Conditions which prevent the carrying out of any development authorised by the planning permission until the condition has been complied with should only be used with care and where the LPA is satisfied that the requirements of the condition are so fundamental to the permitted development that it would have been otherwise necessary to refuse the whole permission. Clearly, development carried out without having complied with a condition precedent would be unlawful and may be the subject of enforcement action.[11]

---

[6]   Where details have been submitted as part of an outline planning application, they must be treated by the LPA as forming part of the development for which the application is being made. Conditions cannot be used to reserve these details for subsequent approval. The exception is where the applicant has made it clear that the details have been submitted for illustrative purposes only.

[7]   Such a condition will fail the test of necessity by requiring more than is needed to deal with the problem it is designed to solve. Such a condition is also likely to be difficult to enforce due to the range of external factors that can influence a decision as to whether to carry out and complete a development.

[8]   Conditions requiring compliance with other regulatory regimes will not meet the test of necessity and may not be relevant to planning.

[9]   Although it may be possible to use a negatively worded condition to prohibit development authorised by a planning condition until a specified action has been taken (e.g. the entering into of a planning obligation requiring the payment of a financial contribution towards the provision of supporting infrastructure).

[10]   NPPG at Paragraph: 006 Reference ID: 21a-006-20140306.

[11]   NPPG at Paragraph: 007 Reference ID: 21a-007-20140306. Problems arise where operations are carried out in breach of a condition precedent which prevent them from qualifying as commencing development (see *F.G. Whitley & Sons v Secretary of State for Wales* (1992) 64 P & CR 296). There are recognised exceptions to this rule, and it now appears to be settled law that even if one of the special circumstances' exceptions cannot be relied on, a developer might still be able to

8.8   Where the circumstances make this necessary and the six tests are met, conditions can be imposed to ensure that a development proceeds in a certain sequence.[12]

8.9   Conditions requiring works on land which is not controlled by the applicant, or which require the consent or authorisation of a third party, often fail the tests of reasonability and enforceability. It may, however, be possible to achieve a similar result using a condition worded in a negative form (known as a *Grampian* condition),[13] namely prohibiting development authorised by the planning permission or other aspects linked to the planning permission (e.g. the

---

argue that a decision by the LPA to bring enforcement proceedings would be open to judicial review on grounds of irrationality. See *R (Hammerton) v London Underground Ltd* [2002] EWHC 2307 (Admin) (endorsed in the Court of Appeal in *R (Prokopp) v London Underground Ltd* [2004] 1 P & CR 31 and (*obiter*) by Court of Appeal in *Norris v First Secretary of State and Stoke on Trent CC* [2006] JPL 1574) and *R (Hart Aggregates Ltd) v Hartlepool BC* [2005] EWHC 840 (Admin), where most of the authorities are reviewed. See also the sequential test advanced in the *Encyclopedia of Planning* at the end of P56.13.6.

12   NPPG at Paragraph: 008 Reference ID: 21a-008-20140306.

13   The principle of a negative condition was approved by the HL in *Grampian Regional Council v City of Aberdeen District Council* (1983) 47 P & CR 633, where planning permission for industrial development was granted subject to a condition that the developer was not to proceed until a nearby road had been closed. If the works fall within an existing highway or require the use of land which is not owned by the developer (or both), the highway authority will often agree to execute the works pursuant to Highways Act 1980, s 278 (provided the 'public benefit' test is made out). In its capacity as an LPA, it may, through a planning obligation, secure the payment of the money against any land of the developer that may benefit from the works, and/or obtain the benefit of a *Grampian*-style condition precedent preventing the development from being commenced or occupied until any agreed highway works have been completed. TCPA 1990, s 72 specifically authorises the imposition of a condition affecting other land under the control of the applicant. There is no absolute rule that the existence of difficulties for the developer in meeting conditions imposed, even if apparently insuperable, must automatically lead to a refusal of permission (*British Railways Board v Secretary of State for the Environment* [1994] 02 EG 107 at [109]–[110], where the court held that it would not be irrational to grant permission subject to a condition even if the condition related to land outside the ambit of the permission applied for which the applicant did not own). See also *Davenport v Hammersmith and Fulham LBC* (1999) 78 P & CR 421, where the condition provided that no vehicles in the control of the applicant for permission for a related business use were to be stored or parked on the adjoining highway. An issue arose on a case stated appeal arising out of enforcement proceedings as to whether the condition was *ultra vires* as it related to the use of land beyond the control of the applicants for permission. The court held that the TCPA 1971 had a wide power to grant planning permission either unconditionally or subject to conditions and there was nothing restricting an authority's power to impose negative conditions of the kind imposed in this instance which related to land outside the application site (it was found that the condition was reasonable as it was imposed in order to avoid obstruction of the highway and to safeguard the amenities of adjacent premises and, as such, was imposed for a proper planning purpose as a condition of allowing the applicants for permission to carry on their business). The power to impose such conditions was only limited by reference to the general principle that an authority could not lawfully impose a condition requiring an applicant to obtain a result that did not lie within his own power to obtain (applying *Mouchell Superannuation Fund Trustees v Oxfordshire CC* [1992] 1 PLR 97).

occupation of premises) until a specified action has been taken, such as the provision of supporting infrastructure. Such conditions should not be used where there are no prospects at all of the action in question being performed within the time limit imposed by the permission.[14]

8.10   Planning permission should not be granted subject to a positively worded condition which requires the applicant to enter into a planning obligation[15] or an agreement under other powers. Such a condition is unlikely to be enforceable. A negatively worded condition limiting the development which can take place until a planning obligation or other agreement has been entered into is also unlikely to be appropriate in the majority of cases. The sensible course is for the LPA to ensure that any planning obligation is entered into before granting planning permission. The advantage of this is that it encourages the parties to finalise the planning obligation or other agreement in a timely manner.[16] It may, however, be necessary, in exceptional circumstances, for a negatively worded condition requiring a planning obligation to be entered into before certain development can commence, such as in the case of a complex and strategically important development where there is evidence that the delivery of the development would otherwise be at serious risk, although in such cases the six tests should still be met.[17]

8.11   It may be possible to overcome a planning objection to a development proposal equally well by imposing a condition on the planning permission or by entering into a planning obligation. In such cases, the LPA should use a condition rather than seeking to deal with the matter by means of a planning obligation.[18]

8.12   It may be possible to impose a condition to modify plans and other details submitted with an application. If a detail in a proposed development, or the lack of it, is unacceptable in planning terms, the best course of action will be for the applicant to be invited to revise the application; but where this involves making significant changes, this may result in the need for a fresh planning application.

---

[14]   NPPG at Paragraph: 009 Reference ID: 21a-009-20140306.

[15]   TCPA 1990, s 106.

[16]   NPPF, para 204 provides that planning obligations should only be used where it is not possible to address unacceptable impacts through a planning condition.

[17]   NPPG at Paragraph: 010 Reference ID: 21a-010-20140306.

[18]   NPPG at Paragraph: 011 Reference ID: 21a-011-20140306. This is because the imposition of restrictions by means of a planning obligation deprives the developer of the opportunity of seeking to have the restrictions varied or removed by an application or an appeal if they are or become too onerous. It should, however, be noted that TCPA 1990, s 106A allows a developer to apply to the LPA to discharge or modify a planning obligation after the expiry of five years after the obligation is entered into.

However, it may be possible for the LPA to impose a condition making only a minor modification to the permitted development.[19]

8.13   Conditions may be used to limit the grant of planning permission to only part of the proposed development. Express powers to issue split decisions are given to the Secretary of State and inspectors.[20] In cases where the LPA considers part of the development to be unacceptable, it will normally be best for it to seek amended details from the applicant prior to a decision being made. In exceptional circumstances, it may be appropriate to use a condition to grant permission for only part of the development. Such conditions should be used only where the acceptable and unacceptable parts of the proposal are clearly distinguishable, and with the agreement of the applicant.[21]

8.14   An LPA may grant planning permission for a specified temporary period only.[22] It should be noted, however, that a temporary permission will rarely pass the test of necessity where the proposed development complies with the development plan, or where material considerations indicate that planning permission should be granted. A temporary permission may well be *suitable* in the following cases:

(a)   where a trial run is needed in order to assess the effect of the development on the area;
(b)   where it is expected that planning circumstances will change in a particular way at the end of the temporary period;
(c)   in the case of vacant land/buildings, to enable use prior to any longer-term regeneration plans coming forward;
(d)   to encourage empty property to be brought back into use so as to benefit an area by increasing activity;
(e)   it will rarely be justifiable to grant a second temporary permission, and such applications should either be granted permanently or refused if there is a clear justification for doing so.[23]

8.15   Unless the condition otherwise provides, planning permission runs with the land, and it is rarely appropriate for a condition to provide otherwise.[24] There may be exceptional circumstances where granting planning permission for development that would not normally be permitted on the site could be justified on planning grounds. For example, conditions limiting the benefits to a particular

---

[19]   NPPG at Paragraph: 012 Reference ID: 21a-012-20140306.
[20]   TCPA 1990, s 79.
[21]   NPPG at Paragraph: 013 Reference ID: 21a-013-20140306.
[22]   TCPA 1990, s 72.
[23]   NPPG at Paragraph: 014 Reference ID: 21a-014-20140306.
[24]   NPPG at Paragraph: 030 Reference ID: 21a-030-20140306.

class of people, such as new residential accommodation in the open countryside for agricultural or forestry workers, may be justified on the grounds that an applicant has successfully demonstrated an exceptional need. A condition used to grant planning permission solely on the grounds of an individual's personal circumstances will scarcely ever be justified in the case of permission for the erection of a permanent building, but might, for example, result from enforcement action which would otherwise cause individual hardship. A condition limiting the benefit of a permission to a company is inappropriate as its shares can always be transferred to other persons.[25]

8.16   Statutory consultees may suggest conditions which mitigate impacts and make the development more acceptable in planning terms. However, where third parties suggest conditions to the LPA, it will be essential for them to consider whether the six tests will be met on a case-by-case basis with reference to the facts of the proposal under consideration. It would clearly be unacceptable to require a condition that a development/requirement should be carried out to the satisfaction of a third party as this decision rests with the LPA.[26]

8.17   Conditions restricting the future use of permitted development rights or changes of use will rarely pass the test of necessity and should only be used in exceptional circumstances, and will need to be precisely described so that it is clear which rights have been limited or withdrawn.[27] Blanket removal of freedom

---

[25]   NPPG at Paragraph: 015 Reference ID: 21a-015-20140306.

[26]   NPPG at Paragraph: 016 Reference ID: 21a-016-20140306.

[27]   A recent case dealing with the specific exclusion of GPDO rights by way of a planning condition is that of *Dunnett Investments Ltd v Secretary of State for Communities and Local Government* [2017] EWCA Civ 192. The condition stated that the buildings should be used for Class B1 business 'and for no other purpose whatsoever' without express planning consent. The claimants applied for a lawful development certificate confirming that a change of use to Class C3 residential would not require planning permission. The authority refused the certificate, and its position was supported on appeal. The High Court subsequently ruled that the condition was sufficiently clear to exclude the operation of the GPDO. In the Court of Appeal, the claimants argued that the phrase 'express planning consent' was just as applicable to permission granted through the GPDO as to that granted following a planning application. Patten LJ reasoned that planning applications can exclude the application of GPDO permitted development rights. He held that such an exclusion may be express or implied, but a grant for a particular use cannot in itself amount to an exclusion. Lastly, he ruled that to exclude the application of the GPDO, the words used in the condition must clearly evince an intention on the LPA's part to make such an exclusion. He ruled that the natural and ordinary meaning of the words used meant the condition permitted other uses, but only subject to express permission. In the view of the court, the condition excluded planning permission granted under the terms of the GPDO. In the result, the court held that the phrase 'and for no other purpose whatsoever' was a clear and specific exclusion of GPDO rights.

to carry out small-scale domestic alterations is unlikely to meet the test of reasonableness and necessity.[28]

8.18   LPAs and applicants for planning permission are encouraged to liaise at an early stage about matters which may need to be subject to conditions and with a view to keep the number of conditions to a minimum. A planning performance agreement may be used to set a timetable for when discussions about conditions should take place.[29]

8.19   LPAs are encouraged to use the suggested models of acceptable conditions in the interests of consistency, although such conditions will, where appropriate, need to be devised or adapted to meet the particular circumstances of the case and, of course, to ensure compliance with the six tests.[30]

8.20   LPAs need to give reasons on the decision notice for imposing planning conditions.[31] Conditions relating to anything other than the matters to be reserved can only be imposed when outline planning permission is granted. The only conditions which can be imposed when reserved matters are approved are conditions which relate directly to those reserved matters.[32]

OCCUPANCY RESTRICTIONS[33]

8.21   LPAs are able to restrict the occupancy of market housing to local people. LPAs need this power as it means that local people are more likely to have access to housing which remains affordable and which serves local needs. This lends itself to sustaining a resident population within the area and balanced working communities, rather than enabling the very limited level of affordable housing to be taken by those with externally derived needs, be it people retiring to the area or looking to acquire a second home or holiday accommodation.

8.22   There are three main methods available to LPAs to restrict housing to local occupancy. They arise: (a) in the case of former council houses, as a result of the right-to-buy legislation;[34] or (b) as a consequence of affordable housing

---

[28]   NPPG at Paragraph: 016 Reference ID: 21a-017-20140306.

[29]   NPPG at Paragraph: 016 Reference ID: 21a-018-20140306 to 21a-020-20140306.

[30]   NPPG at Paragraph: 016 Reference ID: 021-20140306 and Circular 11/95: Use of Conditions in planning permission (see App A).

[31]   NPPG at Paragraph: 016 Reference ID: 21a-023-20140306 and 21a-024-20140306.

[32]   NPPG at Paragraph: 016 Reference ID: 21a-025-20140306.

[33]   *RLT Built Environment Ltd v Cornwall Council* [2016] EWHC 2817 (Admin).

[34]   Although not within the scope of this book, it is nonetheless helpful to note that Housing Act 1985, s 157 deals with the sale of public sector dwelling-houses in National Parks, Areas of

provision;[35] or (c) in the case of new properties or residential conversions of old buildings, as a result of planning conditions.

8.23   As already indicated, LPAs may grant planning permission subject to such conditions as it thinks fit.[36] It is not uncommon nowadays for LPAs to impose local occupancy conditions on the grant of planning permissions in relation to new-builds or residential conversions.

Outstanding Natural Beauty and areas designated as rural areas for these purposes by the Secretary of State (and there are a great many). In such cases, the selling authority is authorised to include within the conveyance or long lease to its former tenant a covenant which prohibits later disposals without the authority's consent which will not be withheld where the disposal is to a person satisfying certain conditions (or in the case of a disposal to more than one person, that at least one of them has satisfied the relevant conditions). These conditions broadly require a three-year-long connection with the area in question, either for work or for principal home purposes, otherwise consent is discretionary. The writer is aware of one authority whose policy is to give consent only to those who intend to use the property as their principal residence or in the case of current or past members of the armed forces. Restrictions under s 157 run with the land seeing as they will be entered against the property on the land register as a restriction on disposing of the land. If there is such a disposal in breach of the operative restrictions, the sanction is that it would be a nullity. The object of such restrictions is to enable selling authorities to keep some form of continuing control over their former housing stock.

[35]   Arising from planning obligations or unilateral undertakings under TCPA 1990, s 106. As is widely known, LPAs have policies whereby new development may be subject to the provision of on-site affordable housing provision of up to 40–50% of the number of new units. LPAs can achieve the same outcome as an occupancy condition (to which reference is made below) by way of an occupancy covenant made under s 106, whereby the LPA and the developer can come to terms about this as a planning obligation made with the LPA (or even offered as a unilateral undertaking in the form of a planning obligation by the developer) as an incident to the grant of planning permission. Planning obligations assist in mitigating the impact of development and usually operate to confer benefits on local communities (such as in the provision of affordable housing) and to support the provision of local infrastructure. A planning obligation may only constitute a reason for granting planning permission where the obligation can be said to be reasonably necessary to make the development acceptable in planning terms. Such obligations run with the land no matter who is the owner and are registered as a local land charge. For instance, provision may be made for on-site affordable housing provision which can include shared equity housing and other low cost homes for sale or at intermediate rents above those of social rent but below market rents. It can also include a new-build property or a private sector property that has been purchased for use as an affordable home. We are dealing here with housing provided to specified eligible households whose needs are not met in the market and will usually be owned and managed by local authorities or registered social landlords. In such cases, the affordable housing will be earmarked by the local authority for persons who are unable to compete in the local housing market who are in need of housing and who are resident or permanently employed in the local area or who used to live in the local area and wish to return for reasons of employment or family connections. Arrangements are normally made with the LPA to ensure that the benefit of affordable housing is enjoyed not only by the initial occupiers of the dwellings provided, but also by their successors through the management of the property by a registered landlord, a trust or similar through the use of planning conditions or a s 106 agreement.

[36]   TCPA 1990, s 70(1).

8.24   The justification for such conditions lies in the policies in either local or neighbourhood plans. The High Court has recently upheld a draft neighbourhood plan policy intended to halt the spread of second homes at St Ives in Cornwall.[37] As previously indicated, the neighbourhood plan process involves sequential requirements for independent examination and a local referendum. The law enables a qualifying neighbourhood body (say a town or parish council) to initiate a process for the purpose of requiring the LPA to make a neighbourhood plan setting out policies in relation to the use of land in a particular neighbourhood area. In this instance, a draft neighbourhood development plan, known as the St Ives Area Neighbourhood Plan, was found to comply with the relevant statutory requirements and was duly accepted by the LPA (Cornwall Council) following a public examination as to its soundness. Thereafter it was set to become the subject of a local referendum with a view to its adoption as formal planning policy in the area of the neighbourhood.

8.25   The claimant in the case was a company specialising in residential development design and they applied to the High Court to judicially review the decision of the LPA to hold a local referendum on the making by the LPA of a neighbourhood development order in what is a popular tourist resort. In fact, St Ives has one of the highest proportions of second homes and holiday lets in Cornwall and the proportion of dwellings occupied other than by a resident householder has substantially increased in recent years.

8.26   The draft neighbourhood plan included a policy (Policy H2) which was designed to address the housing needs of local people and the perceived problem of uncontrolled growth of dwellings used as second or holiday homes by requiring new open-market housing to be restricted to occupancy as a principal residence. An independent examiner concluded that due to the adverse impact on the local community/economy of the uncontrolled growth of second homes, the restriction in the case of further second homes in Policy H2 meant that the draft neighbourhood plan would contribute to achieving sustainable development.

8.27   Amongst other things, the claimant seeking judicial review argued: (a) that the LPA had failed to consider the provision of more market housing as a reasonable alternative to restricting the terms of occupancy of new homes pursuant to Policy H2; and (b) that there was a real risk that Policy H2 would interfere with rights under Article 8 of the European Convention for the Protection of Human Rights and Fundamental Freedoms 1950 (ECHR), namely that the policy would interfere with the rights of future homeowners which, if correct, meant that the LPA was obliged to justify it as a matter of law.

8.28   The outcome before the High Court was that the developers' challenge to neighbourhood Policy H2 failed. The court found that the aim of this policy was

---

[37]   *RLT Built Environment Ltd v Cornwall Council* [2016] EWHC 2817 (Admin).

to safeguard the sustainability of the settlements in the neighbourhood plan area by meeting the housing needs of local people and strengthening the local community and economy. The court accepted the evidence that the demand for second homes in the area was increasing with the result that any increase in market housing would not meet the policy objective behind Policy H2 of reducing the proportion of dwellings without permanent residents.

8.29   The objection on human rights grounds was also rejected. Whilst the court accepted that a draft neighbourhood plan could not be progressed to a referendum unless the LPA was satisfied that it was compatible with rights under the ECHR, it nonetheless found that: (a) it was questionable whether a policy such as Policy H2 might give rise to future circumstances in which Article 8 was infringed; (b) the claimant's interest was purely a commercial one; and (c) no one else had complained of a risk that their convention rights might be breached. The view was taken by the court that Policy H2 was justified on the evidence and lawful and that the LPA had properly concluded that further development in the area was unsustainable without it. Anyone buying a dwelling subject to the Policy H2 restriction would know that he would have to sell the property if he moved away.

8.30   On the face of it, the practical consequence of the neighbourhood policy in the St Ives case is that it makes it plain to purchasers of properties subject to occupancy conditions that if they do not live at the property or choose to move away, for whatever reason, then the restriction will require them to sell the property and it is this which will have the effect of decreasing the incidence of second homes in accordance with the aims of the Policy H2.

8.31   In the normal run of cases in areas where there is a limited stock of low-cost or affordable housing, it is likely to be difficult to overcome the imposition of an occupancy condition. For instance, in a recent appeal involving property in the Snowdonia National Park, the inspector had to consider whether a planning obligation restricting the occupancy of an affordable dwelling to persons employed in the local area was unnecessary and unreasonable. The obligation restricted occupancy of the affordable dwelling to persons employed within a 30-mile radius. The inspector had to consider whether, in terms of housing need in the area, it still served a useful purpose. The property in question had been granted planning permission as an affordable dwelling and the National Park's policy aimed to allow only new dwellings that met the needs of local people and should remain so in perpetuity. The inspector held that these objectives were still relevant to avoid speculative development in the National Park. Although the appellant argued that the 30-mile radius element was not in fact specifically referred to in the local plan and was accordingly unreasonable, the inspector nonetheless held that the specific radius requirements supported the policy objectives of meeting the needs of 'local communities' and supported the protection of the cultural and linguistic characteristics of the Snowdonia National Park which were different from other National Parks. He also found that the property in question could be considered affordable to local people provided the value was discounted by one-third to take account of the obligation. The inspector accordingly concluded that the obligation was necessary and reasonable and complied with Welsh Circular 13/97 and Planning Policy Wales.

8.32   In another recent planning appeal in the Lake District, local policy aimed at restricting open market housing to people with a local connection led to the dismissal of two schemes to convert and extend a shop and flat to create three flats. The appellant had argued that the policy had no regard to scheme viability and was inconsistent with paragraph 173 of the NPPF which stresses the need for development to be relieved of policy burdens which diminish viability and thus threaten the deliverability of the proposed development. The inspector disagreed, finding support in paragraph 54 of the NPPF (the need for LPAs in rural areas to be responsive to local circumstances and to plan housing development to reflect local needs – an example of this might be where a condition requiring a dwelling to be used for holiday letting purposes only should be deleted on the ground that that use was no longer viable) and circular advice on National Parks issued in 2010 for limiting housing in such areas to meet local needs. The inspector considered that viability issues did not outweigh the harm of allowing unfettered open market housing with the potential to become second homes, making no contribution at all to local housing needs.

8.33   The importance of the St Ives case is that it will encourage more local communities to draw up neighbourhood plans under the reforms introduced in the Localism Act 2011. They will do this in order to address the needs of local people who require ready access to affordable housing in areas of high value, not least in those parts of the United Kingdom which attract second-home ownership and in the case of market activity driven by retirement.

8.34   The downside to all this is that if there is a reduction in the stock of new market homes as a result of the imposition of occupancy conditions, it risks squeezing up prices in the *existing* housing stock which could well find its way into the hands of those living outside the local community wanting second homes or involved in the holiday letting business. Moreover, there is a real risk that developers may not be as interested in new market development if they see that LPAs' planning policies favour the imposition of occupancy conditions, and opportunities for new housing (with linked affordable housing) may very well be lost.

AGRICULTURAL OCCUPANCY CONDITIONS

8.35   Agricultural occupancy conditions (AOCs) are common in the countryside. An AOC arises typically where the condition restricts the occupancy of the residential use permission at a farm to a worker who is solely or mainly employed (or formerly employed or is the widow or widower of such person) in agriculture or forestry. Development plan policies commonly provide that development outside settlement limits would not be acceptable unless essential to the maintenance or enhancement of a sustainable farming enterprise. It is open to question whether the objectives of the local plan would be undermined by an AOC where there was no evidence to show that the farming business warranted a full-time worker or where the removal of the condition was justified to generate additional income to sustain the maintenance and enhancement of the farm. If such a condition is no longer necessary or unreasonable in the particular circumstances, then a case exists for its removal.[38]

8.36 It has been found that where a development does not comply in a material respect, or to a material extent, with a permission granted, an AOC attached to that permission cannot apply to the unauthorised development.[39]

CONDITIONS RELATING TO TIME LIMITS

8.37 As explained above, where an LPA grants planning permission, it is subject to a condition which specifies a time limit within which the development is to be begun, which is three years from the date when permission is granted or such longer or shorter period as the LPA may impose such as, in the case of a shorter period, where it has become appropriate to encourage development or, in the case of a longer period, where the development is complex and where there is

---

[38] The first option for getting an AOC removed (and an AOC can reduce the value of the affected property by as much as 30%) is to make a planning application after first demonstrating that there is no demand for a property with such a condition and that the AOC no longer serves any useful purpose. This can involve marketing it (usually for 12 months) at a price which reflects the AOC in order to find potential buyers who meet the eligibility criteria. The LPA may also require evidence that local farmers have been surveyed to see if they have an interest in the property. The second option is to apply for a certificate of lawfulness of existing use or development (CLEUD) if it can be shown that the AOC has been breached for a continuous period of at least ten years. If such a certificate is granted, the AOC restrictions will be suspended, preventing the LPA from bringing enforcement proceedings.

[39] *Handoll and Suddick v Warner Goodman and Streat* (1995) 70 P & CR 627. In this case, planning permission had been obtained for a dwelling subject to an AOC. However, a bungalow was subsequently built some 90 feet from the approved site, which the claimants subsequently purchased having been allegedly unaware of the AOC. In proceedings against their solicitors, vendors and the LPA, there was a trial of a preliminary issue as to whether the bungalow was subject to the occupancy condition. At first instance (applying *Kerrier District Council v Secretary of State for the Environment* (1981) 41 P & CR 284), it was found that the occupancy condition was enforceable even though the bungalow did not comply with the permission granted. On appeal, it was found that *Kerrier* had been wrongly decided and that an occupancy condition could not apply where it attached to development which did not comply in a material respect, or to a material extent, with the permission granted.

evidence that three years will not be long enough to allow all the necessary preparations to be completed before the development can start.[40]

8.38   In the case of outline planning permission, permission should be made subject to conditions imposing two types of time limit, one within which applications must be made for the approval of reserved matters and a second within which the development must be started. If justified on planning grounds, longer or shorter periods may be imposed.[41] If the decision notice omits to mention a time limit within which the development was supposed to have started, the permission is deemed to be granted subject to a condition that the development to which it relates must be begun not later than the expiry of three years from the date when permission was granted. In the case of an outline permission, the period is three years for the submission of all reserved matters and for development to begin within two years of the date on which the final reserved matters are approved.[42]

COMPLETION NOTICES

8.39   Where a planning permission has not lapsed because the work has begun within a specified period but has not been completed within a reasonable period, it is open to an LPA to serve a completion notice stating that the planning permission will cease to have effect at the expiration of a further period specified in the notice (except in relation to the development carried out by then). Such notices are subject to confirmation by the Secretary of State. A notice must allow at least 12 months after it takes effect for the development to be completed. Any period specified by the LPA for the completion of the development may be extended by the Secretary of State.[43]

---

[40]   TCPA 1990, s 91. See also NPPG at Paragraph: 027 Reference ID: 21a-027-20140306.

[41]   NPPG at Paragraph: 028 Reference ID: 21a-028-20140306.

[42]   NPPG at Paragraph: 029 Reference ID: 21a-029-20140306.

[43]   TCPA 1990, ss 94–96 (the Secretary of State has a default power and can also serve a completion notice himself should the LPA fail to do so). The completion notice will not affect the lawfulness of any development carried out before the planning permission becomes invalid at the end of the period specified in the notice (whether the original period specified or any longer period substituted by the Secretary of State). It follows that the local authority is unable to issue an enforcement notice to require demolition, no matter how unsightly the incomplete development might be (*Cardiff City Council v National Assembly for Wales and Malik* [2007] JPL 60; *Claude Rapose v Wandsworth LBC* [2011] JPL 600 at [37]).

CONSTRUING PLANNING CONDITIONS

8.40   In construing conditions, the following *dictum* of Patterson J in *Dunnett Investments Ltd v Secretary of State for Communities and Local Government* provides a useful overview of the law in this field:[44]

> 36. In construing conditions on a planning permission, although the Supreme Court were clear that the situation in *Trump* (supra)[45] was dealing with a different statutory regime, the judgments of Lord Hodge and Lord Carnwath are of assistance in defining where the law on planning conditions is now. They have moved the law on in relation to implied conditions and may have reformulated some of the previously accepted principles but, otherwise, in my judgment, the situation in construing planning conditions is not dissimilar to how it was.
>
> 37. From their judgments I distil the present position to be as follows:
>
> (i)   planning conditions need to be construed in the context of the planning permission as a whole;
>
> (ii)   planning conditions should be construed in a common sense way so that the court should give a condition a sensible meaning if at all possible;
>
> (iii) consistent with that approach a condition should not be construed narrowly or strictly;
>
> (iv)   there is no reason to exclude an implied condition[46] but, in considering the principle of implication, it has to be remembered that a planning permission

---

[44] [2016] EWHC 534 (Admin) at [36]–[37], where the condition 'without express planning consent from the Local Planning Authority first being obtained' was found to be sufficiently specific and unequivocal to exclude the 2015 GPDO (then the Town and Country Planning (General Permitted Development) (Amendment) (England) Order 2013 (SI 2013/1101)). See also *R (XPL Ltd) v Harlow Council* [2016] EWCA Civ 378, where a breach of condition notice requiring a bus company to cease running bus engines at its depot outside permitted hours referred to the 'industrial or commercial activities' prohibited outside those hours by a condition to its planning permission. The *eiusdem generis* principle could not be used to narrow the scope of the words 'industrial or commercial activities'. The principle had no place in the interpretation of planning conditions.

[45] *Trump International Golf Club Scotland Ltd v Scottish Ministers* [2015] UKSC 74, [2016] 1 WLR 85 (where the Supreme Court provided extensive guidance on interpreting planning permission).

[46] *Lambeth LBC v Secretary of State for Communities and Local Government* [2017] EWHC 2412 (Admin); this case involved an LPA which, when varying the conditions attached to an existing planning permission for a DIY retail store, had intended to impose a condition restricting the range of goods that could be sold to non-food goods, the proposed wording setting out that restriction had not been incorporated into the conditions. It was held that the conditions could not be interpreted as including the restriction, nor could it be implied as an additional free-standing condition. To imply a term, it was insufficient that it had probably reflected the local authority's intended purpose, or that it would be fair between the parties. It was not necessary to imply the term in order to give the permission business efficacy: the permitted use was retail subject to appropriate conditions. That outcome did not lack commercial or practical coherence (applying *Marks & Spencer Plc v BNP Paribas Securities Services Trust Co (Jersey) Ltd* [2015] UKSC 72, [2016] AC 742). Because the earlier permission was explicit as to the three conditions it imposed

(and its conditions) is 'a public document which may be relied upon by parties unrelated to those originally involved';

(v)   the fact that breach of a planning condition may be used to support criminal proceedings means that 'a relatively cautious approach' should be taken;

(vi) a planning condition is to be construed objectively and not by what the parties may or may not have intended at the time but by what a reasonable reader construing the condition in the context of the planning permission as a whole would understand;

(vii) a condition should be clearly and expressly imposed;

(viii) a planning condition is to be construed in conjunction with the reason for its imposition so that its purpose and meaning can be properly understood;

(ix) the process of interpreting a planning condition, as for a planning permission, does not differ materially from that appropriate to other legal documents.

DISCHARGING AND MODIFYING CONDITIONS ONCE PLANNING PERMISSION IS GRANTED

8.41   Conditions will affect future purchasers of the land as planning permission runs with the land and will bind future owners. If an owner does not wish to be subject to a condition he can:

(a)   apply to the LPA for the removal or alteration of some or all of the conditions by way of an application for planning permission to develop land without compliance with conditions previously attached;[47]

(b)   appeal to the Secretary of State against the decision of the LPA to grant planning permission subject to conditions;[48]

(following *France v Kensington and Chelsea RLBC* [2017] EWCA Civ 429, [2017] 1 WLR 3206), no other condition could be implied.

[47]   TCPA 1990, s 73; this will not involve a wholesale reconsideration of the application and the LPA will only consider the disputed conditions (do the extant conditions impact on the viability of the development and/or have they become unnecessary and unreasonable and/or is revision necessary in light of a change of circumstances?); nor is the section available in order to change a condition by extending the time within which a development must be started or an application for approval of reserved matters should be made (s 73(4)). The original planning permission will continue to exist whatever the outcome of the application under s 73. In granting permission under s 73, the LPA may also impose new conditions provided they do not materially alter the development that was subject to the original permission and are conditions which could have been imposed on the earlier planning permission. An LPA's decision to refuse an application under s 73 can be appealed to the Secretary of State, who will also only consider the condition/s in question.

[48]   An appeal must be received within 12 weeks of the date of the decision notice for householder planning applications and six months for other planning decision types. The inspector will re-determine the whole application (not only the decision to impose the conditions), which may produce unwanted consequences, such as the refusal of planning permission.

(c)   seek retrospective planning permission in cases where development has
      already taken place without planning permission or without complying with
      a condition subject to which planning permission was granted (which is
      clearly at risk of local authority enforcement action).[49]

8.42   The scope for an LPA to waive by non-statutory means the need to comply
with a condition is extremely limited. A legitimate expectation arising from the
conduct of an LPA could only occur in exceptional circumstances such as where
there was no third party or public interest.[50]

REFORM IN THE CASE OF PRE-COMMENCEMENT CONDITIONS

8.43   The concern of developers is that LPAs impose too many pre-
commencement conditions. The Government's response has been to prescribe
that LPAs can only impose such conditions if the applicant for permission has
agreed to them.[51] Such a provision does not prevent the prospect of prolonged

---

[49]   TCPA 1990, s 73A. See NPPG at Paragraph: 031 Reference ID: 21a-031-20140306. See also
       Lawson Builders Ltd v Secretary of State for Communities and Local Government [2015] EWCA
       Civ 122, where it was held that in an appropriate case an LPA considering an application under s
       73 for planning permission to proceed with a development without complying with conditions
       attached to an existing permission might grant, under s 73A, retrospective permission for a
       development already carried out, subject to conditions imposed under s 70. Reference should be
       made to *South Bucks District Council v Porter (No 2)* [2004] UKHL 33, where the HL upheld the
       retrospective grant of a limited personal planning permission by an inspector for the retention of
       a gypsy's mobile home on a site in the Green Belt as there were (as the inspector had found) very
       special circumstances which outweighed the environmental harm involved. The decision is also
       useful in that the HL held that wherever an occupier sought to rely upon the very fact of his
       continuing use of land, it must be material to recognise any unlawfulness of that use as a
       consideration operating to weaken his claim.

[50]   *Henry Boot Homes Ltd v Bassetlaw District Council* [2002] EWCA Civ 983, where no such
       exceptional circumstances were found. It had been brought to the appellant's attention on at least
       two occasions that the works carried out on the site might not be regarded as a valid
       commencement of the development and that there had been no lawful waiver of the appellant's
       failure to commence the development by the specified date (owing to the appellant's failure to
       satisfy certain conditions of the planning permission). The appellant had argued that it had a
       legitimate expectation that the works carried out on site in breach of condition would be regarded
       by the LPA as a valid commencement of the development. The appellant argued that there had
       been a waiver by the LPA of the need for compliance with the conditions of the planning
       permission and that development could lawfully commence without compliance. In dismissing
       the appeal, the court held that given that planning law was contained in a comprehensive statutory
       code, the scope for an LPA to waive by non-statutory means the need to comply with a condition
       was extremely limited.

[51]   TCPA 1990, s 100ZA, inserted by Neighbourhood Planning Act 2017, s 14(1). This section is not
       yet in force, other than from 19/7/2017 for the purpose of making regulations.

negotiations over pre-commencement conditions. To avoid this the Government intends to introduce a notice procedure which will force applicants to lay their cards on the table and to say whether or not they accept conditions proposed by the LPA, in which event permission can be granted on this basis. Should applicants say that they do not accept the conditions proposed or simply do not respond, they risk the prospect of their application for permission being refused, along with the uncertainty and cost of an appeal. It is, though, open to applicants merely to provide comments which will trigger negotiations and potentially a further notice period.

8.44   In January 2018 the Government issued draft regulations which will give applicants just ten working days to respond to proposed pre-commencement conditions. On the face of it, allowing applicants only ten days to make the 'substantive response' required by the draft regulations is somewhat unfair. The chances are that developers will respond to the proposed new regime by accepting the proposed conditions and obtaining planning permission with a view to applying to discharge or vary objectionable conditions later on. Applicants should also bear in mind that if they refuse to accept the conditions proposed, it is still open to inspectors on appeal to impose the LPA's proposed conditions. LPAs should always use the notice provisions with care and they need to be sure that proposed pre-commencement conditions can be defended on appeal.[52]

---

[52]   Stop press. On 1/10/2018 The Town and Country Planning (Pre-commencement Conditions) Regulations 2018 (SI 2018/566) came into force. TCPA 1990, s 100ZA, which was inserted by Neighbourhood Planning Act 2017, s 14, provides that planning permission for the development of land may not be granted subject to a pre-commencement condition (as defined in TCPA 1990, s 100ZA(8)) without the written agreement of the applicant to the terms of the condition. This requirement is subject to such exclusions as may be prescribed by the Secretary of State (see section 100ZA(6)). Regulation 2 provides that planning permission may be granted to a pre-commencement condition without the applicant's written agreement if the applicant has been notified of the intention to impose a pre-commencement condition but has not responded by the date specified in the notice. The provisions made in the Regulations apply only to conditions on a grant or modification of planning permission granted or modified after the coming into force of the Regulations. In practice, the new regulations will allow developers to refuse the imposition of pre-commencement conditions which they do not consider are warranted. It may, however, lead to protracted discussion and negotiation before permission can be granted, whereas it had been the government's intention to reduce delays between the grant of planning permission and work starting on-site. In addition, applicants will need to be careful that any notices from the LPA are dealt with with quickly (namely within ten working days beginning with the day after the date on which the notice is given) in order to avoid deemed consent being given to the imposition of the pre-commencement condition. LPAs will be subjected to an additional burden as a result of these regulations although, having said that, they are already subject to requirements under the Town and Country Planning (Development Management Procedure) (England) Order 2015 to include in their decision notices the reasons for imposing conditions.

Chapter 9

Planning Obligations

NATURE OF A PLANNING OBLIGATION[1]

9.1   A planning obligation[2] may be made with a local planning authority (LPA) or offered as a unilateral undertaking by a developer as an incident to the grant of planning permission.[3] Planning obligations assist in mitigating the impact of development and usually operate to confer benefits on local communities and to support the provision of local infrastructure. A planning obligation may, however, only constitute a reason for granting planning permission if it satisfies all of the following tests:

(a)   it should only be sought where it is not possible to address unacceptable impacts through a planning condition;[4] and
(b)   where the obligation is:

      (i)   necessary to make the development acceptable in planning terms;[5]

---

[1]   NPPG at Paragraph: 001 Reference ID: 23b-001-20150731 to 23b-11-20150814.

[2]   TCPA 1990, s 106(9): the planning obligation must be entered into by an instrument executed as a deed and must contain those particulars mentioned in s 106(10) and shall also be a local land charge under s 106(11). A s 106 agreement is subject to the usual rules of contract law with the result that invalid provisions may be severed leaving the remainder of the agreement enforceable (see *R v Somerset County Council ex parte Dixon* (1998) 75 P & CR 175 at 187).

[3]   TCPA 1990, s 106 (planning obligations), s 106A (modifications and discharge of planning obligations) and s 106B (modification or discharge of affordable housing requirements).

[4]   NPPF, para 203.

[5]   Obligations to transfer land to the local authority (such as land intended to be used as public open space) could follow from a s 106 obligation (*R v South Northamptonshire District Council ex parte Crest Homes Plc* [1994] 3 PLR 47). In *Jelson Ltd v Derby City Council* [2000] JPL 203, it was held that a s 106 agreement should not impose an obligation to transfer land to a social landlord unless the latter was also a signatory to the agreement and thus complied with Law of Property (Miscellaneous Provisions) Act 1989, s 2 (which did not arise in *Jelson* as no housing association could be nominated until after the development had begun, which meant that there was no signature to the s 106 agreement from any housing association). This decision (which has not been overruled but was not followed in *Milebush Properties Ltd v Tameside MBC* [2010] JPL

(ii)   directly related to the development;[6] and

(iii) fairly and reasonably related in scale and kind to the development.

COMMUNITY INFRASTRUCTURE LEVY REGULATIONS 2010, REGULATION 122

9.2   The tests under 9.1(b) above are given statutory force by regulation 122 of the CILR, which applies to all planning permissions and was intended to clarify the role of section 106 agreements following the introduction of the Community Infrastructure Levy (CIL). CIL is intended to have a much wider reach when it comes to the funding of infrastructure in a district, whereas section 106 agreements are necessarily more site-specific.[7]

9.3   There are a number of helpful cases on regulation 122. In *R (Welcome Break Group Ltd) v Stroud District Council*,[8] Bean J said that:

> An offered planning obligation which has nothing to do with the proposed development apart from the fact that it is offered by the developer is plainly not a material consideration and can only be regarded as an attempt to buy planning permission. However, if it has some connection with the proposed development which is more than *de minimis* then regard must be had to it. The extent, if any, to which it affects the decision is a matter entirely within the discretion of the decision-maker.

1303) would not prevent the imposition of a restriction whereby a specified proportion of the general market housing could not be occupied unless the affordable housing had been built and transferred to a registered housing association. It should be noted that *Jelson* was decided before the coming into force on 1/5/2000 of the Contracts (Rights of Third Parties) Act 1999 whereby identified third parties or persons of a particular description may sue on contracts that are expressly made for their benefit (there being no necessity that the third party was actually in existence at the time the contract was made for their benefit).

6   For instance, it was held by the Supreme Court in *R (Derwent Holdings Ltd) v Trafford Borough Council* [2011] All ER (D) 216 that for an off-site benefit to be material, it had to be related or connected to the development and that that connection had to be real rather than fanciful or remote. In *R (Thakenham Village Action Ltd) v Horsham District Council* [2014] JPL 772, the court reviewed the case law relating to when financial contributions may be directly related to a development. See also *Good Energy Generation Ltd v Secretary of State* [2018] EWHC 1270 (Admin) where it was held (following *Forest of Dean DC v Wright* [2017] EWCA Civ 2102 and *R (Sainsbury's Supermarkets Ltd) v Wolverhampton City Council* [2010] UKSC 20) that a developer's unilateral undertaking under s 106 proposing a community investment scheme and a reduced energy tariff for local residents, as part of its application for planning permission for a wind farm development, was not capable of being a material consideration as it failed to meet the requirements of the CILR 2010, reg 122.

7   See also NPPF, paras 204 and 206, which mirror the statutory tests in reg 122.

8   [2012] EWHC 140 (Admin) at [50].

9.4   See also *R (Mid-Counties Co-operative Ltd) v Forest of Dean District Council*[9] and *R (Mid-Counties Co-operative Ltd) v Forest of Dean District Council*,[10] both of which cases involved planning permissions (both of which were quashed) for an out-of-town retail store supported by planning obligations which required the developer to pay substantial contributions towards the enhancement of the town centre. Both cases were followed by *R (Tesco Stores Ltd) v Forest of Dean District Council*.[11] This case again involved the construction of a retail store on the outskirts of a town where the developer had put forward a section 106 planning obligation offering a package of financial contributions in order to help mitigate the adverse impacts associated with the proposed development. The planning application was recommended for refusal, but the LPA resolved to grant permission, subject to conditions, on the basis that the proposal would safeguard existing jobs at a site which was going to be demolished and rebuilt, that it would create new jobs and that the impact arising from the proposal would be mitigated by the section 106 agreement. The application to quash this decision failed, first, as it was found by Patterson J that the committee members were entitled to disagree with the recommendation of planning officers, provided they had a reasonable basis for doing so. Members were clearly entitled to give greater weight to employment considerations than the officers did, and the weight to be given to such a material consideration was entirely for the decision-maker. Secondly, it was said that it was axiomatic that an LPA had to apply the CILR to its decision-making process. That meant, in relation to a section 106 obligation which had been offered by a developer, that a decision-maker had to approach its assessment to the statutory tests with appropriate rigour. What was appropriate would vary with the circumstances of each case. The committee members had first to consider whether there was sufficient information available to them to take the section 106 agreement into account, and then to be aware of, and apply, the statutory tests. That was not something which, in the circumstances of the instant case, had to be applied with mathematical exactitude. The starting point for the committee members was an acceptance of harm to the city centre. It could be inferred that the members were satisfied that they had sufficient information to be able to take the section 106 agreement into account. They were looking for a partial amelioration of harm. The presumption in favour of refusal, applying the National Planning Policy Framework 2012 (NPPF) (the proposal was contrary to the NPPF and policy CSP.12 of the core strategy as there was insufficient need for a store of the size proposed and, due to its scale, it would have a significant impact on the vitality and viability of the town centre, and the proposed section 106 agreement also failed to make provision for the necessary contributions to mitigate the impact on the town centre), was capable of being overcome by the weight that members attached to the material consideration of

---

employment, and taking into account what was offered in the section 106 agreement. The committee members' decision accorded with their view that the benefits were sufficient to mitigate the residual harm caused by the development, at least in part, and they were content to accept harm to the retail centre of the Lydney town centre. That was a matter of planning judgment entirely for the members who took the decision to grant planning permission. This case is useful as it not only considered the two *Mid-Counties* cases referred to above, but also made it plain that the members were entitled to disagree with their planning officers and to give greater weight to what they considered was the most significant material consideration, namely that the development would safeguard existing jobs at the site and would also create new jobs.

9.5   In *Borough of Telford and Wrekin v Secretary of State for Communities and Local Government*[12] Sullivan LJ also spoke of the requirement for rigour when considering whether the regulation 122 tests are met. It was said at first instance, in this case by Turner J,[13] that the policy behind regulation 122 was 'to inhibit developers from "buying" planning permission with the promise of wide ranging largesse'. In *R (Working Title Films Ltd) v Westminster City Council*[14] Gilbart J said that the tests in regulation 122 were not a codification of the tests developed by case law, but rather the incorporation into the law of what previously were policy tests. The assessment of whether a section 106 obligation was necessary was a matter of planning judgment for the decision-maker. This case involved a section 106 agreement obliging a developer to build a community hall within a mixed use development which it was found did not breach regulation 122(2)(a). This was because the obligation was necessary as the benefits brought by the hall would compensate for the fact that the percentage of affordable housing on the development would be lower than that sought by the LPA's informal policy. The developer failed in its argument that the section 106 agreement breached the CILR as it considered that it was unnecessary to provide a community hall to make the development acceptable in planning terms. It was argued that the local authority should not be allowed to generate revenue from a community hall which could be used by anyone (although Gilbart J considered that no objection could be taken to a community hall, as throughout the country there were community facilities owned by local authorities that could be hired out for community events involving a whole range of activities that could properly take place). Gilbart J attached weight to the fact that, applying the legal test, the planning officer's report showed that he had approached the question of whether the community hall was necessary on the basis that its benefit to the community would compensate for the lower percentage of affordable housing. The officer had noted that only 27% of the housing would be affordable, whereas the LPA's

12   [2014] EWCA Civ 507 at [70].
13   [2013] EWHC 1638 (Admin) at [88].
14   [2017] JPL 173 at [22].

informal policy sought a 35% provision which, for economic viability reasons, could not be achieved without removing the community hall and public parking. It was the view of the officer that it would be more beneficial to provide the community hall and parking, with the reduced amount of affordable housing, with a view to providing a better overall development. Accordingly, planning permission was granted for the development of a neighbouring site subject to a section 106 agreement which obliged the developer to adhere to the community hall proposal. The developer sought judicial review of the LPA's decision. The view taken by Gilbart J was that the approach of the LPA as to whether the community hall was necessary was on the basis that its benefit to the community would compensate for the lower percentage of affordable housing. He said that was a planning judgment which the LPA was entitled to make. In the sense used in regulation 122(2)(a), the section 106 obligation was necessary as it provided a countervailing benefit to set against the disadvantage of the lesser provision of affordable housing and was acceptable in planning terms.

9.6   Where planning obligations are being sought or revised, LPAs should take account of changes in market conditions over time and, wherever appropriate, be sufficiently flexible to prevent planned development being stalled.[15]

9.7   It has been said that the tests for the validity of a planning condition[16] apply equally to a planning obligation.[17]

9.8   A planning obligation may operate to:

(a)   restrict the development or use of land in any specified way;[18]

---

[15]   NPPF, para 205.

[16]   *Newbury District Council v Secretary of State for the Environment* [1981] AC 578.

[17]   *R v Plymouth City Council ex parte Plymouth and South Devon Co-operative Society* (1994) 67 P & CR 78.

[18]   TCPA 1990, s 106(1)(a). A restriction may be for a specified period or may be indefinite. It may also be lifted under s 106A if it no longer serves any useful purpose. A restriction in a s 106 agreement is capable of overriding planning-use rights protected by a planning permission, an interim development order or a certificate of lawful use and a planning obligation is an appropriate mechanism for surrendering such rights. The Court of Appeal considered the scope of s 106(1)(a) in *R (Khodari) v Royal Borough of Kensington and Chelsea* [2017] EWCA Civ 333. In this case, a requirement in a planning permission that a developer enter into an obligation that future occupiers of a building would not apply for a residential parking permit was found not to be capable of being a planning obligation. It would, however, as the court found, be an enforceable obligation under s 16 of the Greater London Council (General Powers) Act 1974, a provision enabling a landowner to enter into a covenant 'in connection with the land', and the court held that there would indeed be a connection between the application site and the availability of parking permits, as these are only available to residents of the relevant London borough where the property is situated (for this provision to apply, the s 106 agreement must expressly include s 16 as an enabling power). The view taken by the court was that the term 'land' in s 106 meant the

(b)   require specified operations or activities to be carried out in, on, under or over the land;[19]

(c)   require the land to be used in any specified way;[20] or

(d)   require a sum to be paid to the authority on a specified date or dates or periodically.[21]

9.9   A planning obligation may:

(a)   be unconditional or subject to conditions;[22]

(b)   impose any restriction or requirement under paragraph 9.8 (a)–(c) either indefinitely or for such period or periods as may be specified;[23] and

(c)   if it requires a sum or sums to be paid, require the payment of a specified amount or an amount determined in accordance with the instrument by

---

land in which the person making the agreement was interested. It could be land other than that covered by the permission, provided there was a direct relationship between the two, but the person entering into the s 106 agreement still had to have an interest in that land. In this instance, the only land identified was the building itself and the use which the local authority wished to prevent was not use of any particular flat in the building, but rather, was use of the highway for parking. That was not a use of the property which meant that the parking obligation was incapable of being a planning obligation under s 106. In the result, a s 106 agreement will not usually be an appropriate way for imposing off-site obligations as with the exception of monetary obligations, the scope of s 106 is limited to the application land. An appeal from this decision was dismissed ([2017] EWCA Civ 333). It is now uncertain whether LPAs outside London will be in any position to secure permit-free development. Possible solutions could involve a resort to the subsidiary powers of local authorities under Local Government Act 1972, s 111, or to the exclusion of new dwellings from instruments creating parking schemes. In *R (AS Property Investments Ltd) v Hounslow LBC* [2008] EWHC 1631 (Admin), the developer was unwilling to enter into a planning obligation preventing the grant of parking permits to residents of new flats, but a solution was found by the exclusion of each new flat from the schedule of streets in the statutory instrument that created the Controlled Parking Zone. This solution was upheld by Sullivan J.

19   TCPA 1990, s 106(1)(b). The operations may be for a specified period or be indefinite. See *South Oxfordshire Borough Council v Secretary of State for the Environment* [1994] 1 PLR 72 (involving an undertaking to carry out specified operations). It is useful to note that other powers exist enabling local authorities to enter into and enforce positive covenants against successors of the original covenantor, namely, Local Government (Miscellaneous Provisions) Act 1982, s 3, Greater London Council (General Powers) Act 1974, s 16, Highways Act 1980, s 278 and Housing Act 1980, s 609.

20   TCPA 1990, s 106(1)(c).

21   TCPA 1990, s 106(1)(d).

22   TCPA 1990, s 106(2)(a). A planning obligation may be conditional in the *Grampian* sense, in other words, where it prevents the commencement of development until a condition precedent is satisfied. See *R v Canterbury City Council ex parte Springimage Ltd* [1993] 3 PLR 58 (involving the requirement of an obligation for the requisitioning of off-site sewage for drainage purposes before development could take place).

23   TCPA 1990, s 106(2)(b).

which the obligation is entered into and, if it requires the payment of periodic sums, require them to be paid indefinitely or for a specified period.[24]

9.10   A planning obligation is enforceable by the LPA identified in the agreement by whom the obligation is enforceable, against: (a) any person entering into the obligation; and (b) any person deriving title from that person.[25]

9.11   A restriction or requirement imposed under a planning obligation is enforceable by injunction.[26] In a case where there is a breach of a requirement to carry out any operations in, on or over the land, the authority by whom the obligation is enforceable may enter the land and carry out those operations and recover any expenses reasonably incurred by it in doing so from the person or persons against whom the obligation is enforceable.[27]

SCOPE OF TCPA 1990, SECTION 106

Aberdeen City and Shire Strategic Development Planning Authority v Elsick Development Co Ltd[28]

9.12   In the *Aberdeen City* case supplementary planning guidance required developers to enter into a planning obligation to contribute to a fund to be spent on transport infrastructure in and around Aberdeen. It involved the pooling of the contributions and no one developer was liable for the costs of any of the specified transport 'interventions'. The obligation to contribute to the fund was in addition to the requirement that a developer mitigated impacts specific to its development. The contributions from residential developers were fixed at a sum per residential unit. The payments were not tied to the impact of a particular development on the transport network. The planning authority had resolved to grant planning permission for a proposed development by the respondent but to issue that permission only after the respondent had entered into an obligation to contribute to the fund. The parties agreed that no contributions would have to be paid if the supplementary guidance was found to be invalid. The respondent asserted that the

---

24   TCPA 1990, s 106(2)(c).

25   TCPA 1990, s 106(3); although the instrument by which the planning obligation is entered into may provide that a person shall no longer be bound by the obligation in respect of any period during which he no longer has an interest in the land (s 106(4)).

26   TCPA 1990, s 106(5).

27   TCPA 1990, s 106(6): although before an authority exercises its power to carry out works itself, it must give not less than 21 days' notice of its intention to do so to any person against whom the planning obligation is enforceable (s 10(7)). Any person who wilfully obstructs a person acting in the exercise of his power to enter the land and carry out operations shall be guilty of an offence (s 106(8)).

28   [2017] UKSC 66.

contribution asked of it was out of all proportion to the demands which its development would make on the transport infrastructure for which the fund had been set up. The respondent successfully appealed to the Inner House against the decision of the planning authority to adopt the supplementary guidance. The appeal from this decision by the planning authority was dismissed, as the Inner House had found that the connection between certain developments, including the respondent's, and some of the transport interventions which the pooled fund was intended to finance, was at best trivial. The unlawfulness of the scheme did not arise from its non-compliance with the relevant ministerial guidance on planning obligations, which required, amongst other things, obligations which 'fairly and reasonably related in scale and kind to the proposed development'. That guidance was simply a material consideration which the planning authority had to take into account when deciding whether to grant planning permission. The weight which the planning authority attached to such guidance was a matter of planning judgment. The scheme of the supplementary guidance and the planning obligations which it promoted were unlawful for two separate reasons. First, the requirement imposed on a developer to contribute to the pooled fund, which was to finance the transport infrastructure needed to make acceptable all of the developments which the development plan promoted, entailed the use of a developers' contribution on infrastructure with which its development had no more than a trivial connection; the requirement was thus not imposed for a purpose in relation to the development and use of the burdened site.[29] Further, the planning authority did not include any provision in the planning obligation restricting the development of the respondent's site until a contribution was made. Instead, it resolved to grant planning permission for the development but to issue that permission only after the respondent had entered into the obligation. The planning obligation was therefore neither 'restricting nor regulating' the development of the site and so was outside the ambit of section 75. Secondly, following *Tesco Stores Ltd v Secretary of State for the Environment*,[30] it was established that for a planning obligation, which was to contribute funding, to be a material consideration in the decision to grant planning permission, there had to be more than a trivial connection between the development and the intervention or interventions which the proposed contributions would fund. It was held that the planning obligation which the respondent had entered into could not be a relevant consideration in the grant of planning permission. It was not within the power of an LPA to require a developer to enter into such an obligation, which would be irrelevant to its application for permission. If planning authorities in Scotland wished to establish a local development land levy in order to facilitate development, then legislation would have to be enacted to enable them to do so.

---

[29]   As was required by Town and Country Planning (Scotland) Act 1997, s 75, which is the equivalent of s 106 in Scotland.

[30]   [1995] 1 WLR 759.

9.13   The importance of the *Aberdeen City* case is that it emphasises the distinction between planning conditions and planning obligations whereby the latter are not required to relate to the development, whereas planning conditions must serve a planning purpose and must fairly and reasonably be related to the development and must not otherwise be *Wednesbury* unreasonable. However, a planning obligation (and one can enter into a planning obligation without having to be an applicant for planning permission) must be for a planning purpose and must restrict or regulate the development or use of land and must not be *Wednesbury* unreasonable. The decision in the *Aberdeen City* case was to the effect that the obligation must serve a purpose related to the site and cannot be for an ulterior purpose such as new infrastructure. To be lawful (and as a section 106 agreement to be a material consideration in the decision whether to grant permission), the obligation must have a connection with the proposed development. The court also made it clear that decision-makers must have regard to relevant guidance, although the weight to be attached to such guidance is a matter of planning judgment with which the court will be loath to interfere.

OFF-SITE COMMUNITY BENEFITS

9.14   See also *Forest of Dean DC v R (Peter Wright)*[31] where, on an application for planning permission for a wind turbine development which was to be undertaken by a community benefit society, a promised donation to a local community fund of a proportion of the turnover derived from the turbine (4%) was found not to be a material planning consideration. The court rejected the argument that the donation was a material consideration because, although it was an off-site benefit, it had a planning purpose and a real connection with the turbine. The Court of Appeal found that the judge at first instance had been entitled to conclude that the promised donation was an untargeted contribution of off-site community benefits which was not designed to address a planning purpose and had no real connection with the turbine. In the result, the donation was not a material consideration and the LPA had not been entitled to take it into account. In *Good Energy Generation Ltd v Secretary of State for Communities and Local Government*,[32] it was also held that a developer's unilateral undertaking under section 106 proposing a community investment scheme and a reduced energy tariff for local residents, as part of its application for planning permission for a wind farm development, was not capable of being a material consideration, as it failed to meet the requirements of regulation 122 of the CILR. It was said that there had to be a real rather than fanciful or remote connection between the benefit and the development if the benefit was to be treated as a consideration

---

[31]   [2017] EWCA Civ 2102.
[32]   [2018] EWHC 1270 (Admin).

weighing in favour of the grant of planning permission (*R (Sainsbury's Supermarkets Ltd) v Wolverhampton City Council*[33] followed). In this case the local tariff was considered to be a nebulous proposal which did not meet that requirement. It was essentially an inducement to make the proposal more attractive to local residents and to the LPA. The scheme was not necessary to make the development acceptable in planning terms.

BENEFITS OFFERED BY SUPERMARKETS IN CONNECTION WITH THE GRANT OF PLANNING PERMISSION

9.15   The benefits offered by supermarkets feature in cases on section 106 of the Town and Country Planning Act 1990 (TCPA 1990). In one case,[34] a proposal for planning permission by Sainsbury's included the construction, on site, of a tourist information centre, a bird-watching hide overlooking a river and a static art feature, whilst off-site, though in close proximity, there was to be a park-and-ride facility together with the offer of up to £1 million towards the cost of providing the necessary highway and drainage infrastructure for a nearby industrial site. The package proposed by Tesco for a second supermarket at the same out-of-town location included a financial contribution to the provision of a crèche, a wildlife habitat on a site contiguous to the development, a moving water sculpture on site and the sale to the council of a site for park-and-ride facilities. Each proposal was accompanied by offers to enter into section 106 agreements. Meanwhile the Co-op applied for permission to erect a supermarket about 3 miles away from the other sites and, although it was granted permission, it applied to quash the decisions granted to Sainsbury's and Tesco on the ground that only community benefits necessary to overcome or remedy planning objections could be taken into account as 'material considerations',[35] and that the authority had erred in taking into account the various community benefits proposed by Sainsbury's and Tesco. Co-op's appeal from the dismissal of its application was dismissed. The view taken by the Court of Appeal was that each and every one of the obligations offered by Sainsbury's and Tesco, whether on-site or off-site, were capable of being regarded as having a planning purpose and being related to the permitted development. In another case, the House of Lords held that an offer by Tesco to fund a link road under a section 106 agreement was found to be acceptable. It was held that a planning obligation under section 106 was a 'material consideration', and that although the link between the road and the development was slight, it

---

[33]   [2010] UKSC 20, [2011] 1 AC 437.

[34]   *R v Plymouth City Council ex parte Plymouth and South Devon Co-operative Society* (1994) 67 P & CR 78.

[35]   Within the meaning of TCPA 1990, s 70(2).

was nonetheless relevant. It was, however, held that the weight to be given to relevant considerations was entirely a matter for the decision-maker (which in this case was the Secretary of State, the application having been called in, who had rejected Tesco's application for permission) to attribute to the relevant considerations such weight as he thought fit, and the court would not interfere unless the decision-maker had acted unreasonably in the *Wednesbury* sense.

UNILATERAL UNDERTAKINGS

9.16   Unilateral undertakings in the form of a planning obligation may be accepted by an inspector on an appeal if he thinks it might accommodate the objections of the LPA.[36] They should not, however, be regarded as a convenient substitute for an agreement with the local authority if this is feasible.

OVERAGE

9.17   A planning obligation may not include a provision for overage. In *McCarthy & Stone Retirement Lifestyles Ltd v South Bucks DC*[37] it was determined that it would be impossible to include overage within a section 106 planning obligation. The LPA had requested an overage clause to be included within a unilateral undertaking which would require a viability review to take place and an additional contribution to be paid to the authority should the viability review demonstrate an increase in the viability of the development. The developer had argued that this request was neither reasonable nor necessary and was also contrary to regulation 122 of the CILR. The LPA accepted that the requirement for overage was not part of the development plan. The National Planning Practice Guidance (NPPG) also makes it clear that viability in decision-taking should be linked to current costs and values. The only exception to this is where a scheme required phased delivery over the medium to longer term. In this case, however, the developer was looking at a single phase development. In the event, the authority had to make do with a single contribution of £0.25 million for off-site affordable provision. It will, however, be possible for a seller to recoup from the buyer to whom land has been sold with the benefit of planning permission a share of any refunded section 106 payments or reduction in the level of any phased section 106 payments.

---

[36]   Examples of undertakings provided subsequent to an appeal hearing (with the agreement of both parties) might involve the provision of mitigation measures relating to the effect of housing on a Special Protection Area, highways, ecology and landscaping measures, securing the provision of open space or land for community purposes, including a school, the provision of surface water drainage and a specified level of affordable housing.

[37]   Planning Appeal: Decision Letter dated 12/2/2015: Appeal Ref: App/N0410/A/14/2228247.

USE OF DEVELOPER CONTRIBUTIONS

9.18   LPAs are expected to use all the funding received by way of planning obligations in order to make development acceptable in planning terms. Agreements will normally include provisions stating by when the funds will be used and how the funds will be used, and allow for their return, after an agreed period of time, where they are unspent.[38]

9.19   It is also worth mentioning that as set out in the Starter Homes Written Ministerial Statement of 2/3/2015, starter homes exception sites should not be required to make affordable housing or tariff style section 106 contributions.

MODIFICATION AND DISCHARGE OF PLANNING OBLIGATIONS

9.20   In the absence of consent, an application may be made to modify or discharge the planning obligation after the expiry of the period of five years from the date on which the obligation was entered into.[39] The main criterion for discharge is that the planning obligation no longer serves a useful purpose.[40] If the obligation does, however, continue to serve a useful purpose, but would serve that purpose equally well if it had effect subject to the proposed modification, then it shall have effect subject to those modifications.[41] It is also of some importance to note that the provisions of section 84 of the Law of Property Act 1925 (whereby restrictions, arising under covenant or otherwise, on the use of land or the building thereon may be discharged or modified by the Upper Tribunal) do not apply to planning obligations.[42] It should also be noted that it is government policy that where planning obligations are being sought or revised, LPAs should take account of changes in market conditions over time.[43]

---

[38]   PPG at Paragraph: 010 Reference ID: 23b-010-20140306.

[39]   TCPA 1990, s 106A(3) and (4), although with effect from 28/2/2013, in the case of planning obligations entered into on or before 6/4/2010, the five-year period is shortened to one month (see Town and Country Planning (Modification and Discharge of Planning Obligations) (Amendment) (England) Regulations 2013 (SI 2013/147), reg 3, which inserts a new reg 2A into the Town and Country Planning (Modification and Discharge of Planning Obligations) Regulations 1992 (SI 1992/2832) (which deals with the procedure for making such applications under s 106A) – the 2013 amendment does not apply in Wales).

[40]   TCPA 1990, s 106A(6)(b).

[41]   TCPA 1990, s 106A(6)(c).

[42]   TCPA 1990, s 106A(10).

[43]   NPPF, para 205.

PUBLICITY

9.21   A copy of any planning obligation proposed or entered into must be included in the register kept by the LPA.[44]

EXTENT OF DUTY TO NEGOTIATE

9.22   There are limits on the freedom of contract of an LPA in cases where the public interest has already been tested through the planning process.[45]

CONSULTATION

9.23   LPAs must act fairly and should take steps to consult in cases where planning obligations have a wider reach, such as where obligations are shared or directly or indirectly affect others.[46]

FORMALITIES

9.24   A planning obligation is required to be by deed stating that it is to be a planning obligation. It must also identify the land and the person entering into the obligation, along with his interest in the land and the LPA by whom the obligation is to be enforceable.[47] The planning obligation is also registrable as a local land charge.

---

[44]   Town and Country Planning (Development Management Procedure) (England) Order 2015 (DMPO), art 40.

[45]   *R v Warwickshire County Council ex parte Powergen Plc* [1997] 3 PLR 62; *R v Cardiff County Council ex parte Sears Group Properties Ltd* [1998] 3 PLR 55; *Mayor of London v London Borough of Enfield* [2008] Env. LR 33.

[46]   *Jelson Ltd v Derby City Council* [2000] JPL 203; *R v Litchfield District Council ex parte Litchfield Securities Ltd* [2001] 3 PLR 33; *R (Police and Crime Commissioner for Leicester) v Blaby District Council* [2014] All ER (D) 14 (Jun); *R (Wet Finishing Works Ltd) v Taunton Deane Borough Council* [2017] EWHC 1837 (Admin), where an LPA materially changed the mechanism by which restoration of a listed mill was to take place when it entered into a new s 106 agreement which excluded the mill owner, a party to an earlier s 106 agreement, and removed an obligation to pay it a heritage contribution. The court found that the owner had a legitimate expectation to be notified of the proposed new agreement which brought about material changes in the terms of the two agreements and to be given an opportunity to comment upon it before the new agreement was to be entered into, and the LPA had failed in that duty. Accordingly, there was a breach of procedural fairness and the later planning permission was quashed. The case contains a useful review of the authorities.

[47]   See formalities mentioned in TCPA 1990, s 106(9).

ENFORCEMENT

9.25   Once an obligation has become binding it cannot be challenged by the developer or his successor on the ground that it lacks sufficient nexus with the proposed development.[48] It is only the LPA which is entitled to enforce the obligation.[49] The LPA has a discretion whether to enforce the agreement and cannot be compelled to act.[50] There are statutory powers of enforcement, namely:

(a)   injunction;[51]
(b)   entry upon the land to carry out any operations in, on, under or over the land to which the planning obligation relates and recovery of costs;[52]
(c)   under regulations which are yet to be made, provision is made for the entry of a charge on the land of any sum or sums required to be paid under a planning obligation or for any costs incurred by the authority in carrying out operations on the land.[53]

---

[48]   See *Tesco Stores Ltd v Secretary of State for the Environment* [1995] 1 WLR 759; *R (Millgate Development Ltd) v Wokingham District Council* [2012] JPL 258, where the Court of Appeal confirmed the liability of a developer to make contributions under a s 106 agreement (which came into force on the grant of planning permission) remained valid despite an inspector's conclusion that the contributions were not justified.

[49]   TCPA 1990, s 106(3).

[50]   *Milebush Properties Ltd v Tameside MBC* [2011] PTSR 1654.

[51]   TCPA 1990, s 106(5). See *Newham LBC v Ali* [2014] EWCA Civ 676 at [20]–[23]. In the absence of special circumstances that would, on normal equitable principles, lead to the denial of an injunction (as, for instance, where the authority has acted in a way which justifies the withholding of relief, although the fact that there is an outstanding planning appeal will usually be irrelevant), where there has been a substantial breach of a planning obligation under s 106, the discretion to grant an injunction conferred by s 106(5) should normally be exercised in favour of the grant of an injunction. If a person wishes to contend that a planning obligation no longer serves a planning purpose, then it should seek to discharge or modify the obligation under s 106A or s 106B.

[52]   TCPA 190, s 106(6). The authority's expenses are recoverable from the person against whom the obligation is enforceable, which will include not only the present owner, but also the original covenantor and all intervening owners of his interest (unless the s 106 agreement provides that a person shall not be bound by the obligation in respect of any period during which he no longer has an interest in the land under s 106(4)), including any person deriving title from that person, such as a subsequent mortgagee (see s 106(3)).

[53]   It is unclear whether this is to be implemented by way of an entry in the local land charges register or along the lines of a charging order entered in the Register of Land Charges.

VAT TREATMENT OF DEVELOPERS' CONTRIBUTIONS

9.26   HMRC provides guidance on the VAT treatment of contributions made under planning obligations and other agreements. The current guidance is to be found in Notice 742 Land and Property (June 2012).

OLD PLANNING AGREEMENTS

9.27   Agreements entered into before 25/10/1991 under TCPA 1971, section 52, continue to be governed by the old law.

Chapter 10

Community Infrastructure Levy

INTRODUCTION (AND THE PROSPECT OF REFORM)

10.1   The future of the Community Infrastructure Levy (CIL) is in doubt. The Government's CIL review group (CRG) reported to the Government in October 2016[1] recommending that it should replace CIL with a twin-track system involving the introduction of a broad and low level Local Infrastructure Tariff (LIT) (which will *not* need to be set in a manner that involves setting a precise relationship between the quantum of infrastructure need and the amount of LIT that is charged, thus simplifying the charge-setting process) with section 106 being utilised for larger developments. It is the view of the CRG that this recommendation (along with others) will provide a fairer system for ensuring that all development, whether big or small, makes some contribution to cumulatively required infrastructure, whilst at the same time recognising the needs of larger more complex sites. It is also thought that this approach will raise more money for infrastructure by optimising LIT and developer contributions under section 106 agreements.

10.2   Under the proposal all developments, almost without exception, would be subject to LIT. Larger developments, which require direct mitigation to make them acceptable in planning terms or very specific major infrastructure on or close by the development, including infrastructure delivered up front, would be subject to an additional contribution under section 106 (strictly in accordance with tests under regulation 122 of the Community Infrastructure Levy Regulations 2010 (CILR). To the extent that the obligations cover financial contributions, these

---

[1]   'A New Approach to Developer Contributions', a report by the CIL Review Team submitted to the Minister in October 2016. The CIL Review Team was asked to look at the relationship between CIL and TCPA 1990, s 106 in the delivery of infrastructure, the impact of CIL on development viability, exemptions and reliefs from CIL, the administrative arrangements and governance associated with charging collecting and spending CIL, the ability of CIL to fund and deliver infrastructure, the impact of the neighbourhood portion on local communities' receptiveness to development and the geographic scale at which CIL is collected and charged. The report runs to 42 pages.

would continue to be collected by the relevant local authority and, where appropriate, passed to the body that provides the relevant infrastructure.

10.3   In light of the fact that CIL reform is on the cards, it has been reported that the ensuing uncertainty has brought work on introducing the levy almost to a standstill.[2]

10.4   The main complaints about CIL seem to be that very little of it has been spent on infrastructure. It has been reported in the press[3] that the 32 authorities which had adopted the levy by the end of 2013 (whereas the CRG says in its report dated October 2016 that, after a slow start, there were 130 authorities charging CIL – not including the Mayor of London and the London Legacy Development Corporation – with a further 88 authorities working towards adopting a CIL) had collected £166.3 million from the levy to date,[4] yet only £26.2 million (or 16%) had so far been spent on infrastructure, more than five years after the earliest adopters had started charging CIL.

10.5   In light of the above, CIL may not be delivering the infrastructure it was meant to, although others say that the retention of unspent levy is not in itself a sign of a problem. It is argued that the levy was designed to allow for the collection of CIL contributions from many developers over a number of years in order to fund infrastructure that was substantial enough to support large urban growth. In these circumstances, it is said that it should be no surprise that funds need to be accumulated before work on planned projects can be started. There is then a conflict between those who say that authorities should be using CIL as a mechanism to unlock development (perhaps by spending levy receipts within a deadline) and those who think that what is important is that, rather than being frittered away, CIL receipts should be safeguarded and utilised on the infrastructure that an independently audited process has confirmed is needed to support an authority's growth. A persistent complaint, however, is that whereas local authorities have to hand back unspent section 106 receipts within an agreed number of years, this does not apply to CIL, where the regulations do not deal with what is to happen if CIL receipts are not spent on infrastructure within a

---

[2]   In the edition of *Planning* published on 18/8/2017 (see editorial of Richard Garlick).

[3]   Again, see the edition of *Planning* published on 18/8/2017.

[4]   The report in 10.1 mentioned at 3.3.1 that, by the end of March 2015, CIL had raised approximately £170 million, whereas Mayoral CIL raised a further £140 million in 2015/2016. As against this, the original assessment suggested CIL might raise £4,700 million to £6,800 million over a 10-year period with the top end increasing to £1 billion in later assessments. Although collections will increase as CILs mature, receipts are still less than were initially predicted. It seems that the picture is a mixed one, with some charging authorities collecting around the level expected, but others receiving as little as 50% of what they had anticipated, which they attribute largely to the number of subsequent exemptions.

given timescale. On the other hand, it is, of course, obvious that it takes time to build up funds for infrastructure (whether 'big ticket' or not).

PROPOSED CHANGES TO CIL IN THE AUTUMN BUDGET (NOVEMBER 2017)

10.6   Despite the CRG recommendation mentioned above, in its autumn Budget the Government merely proposed consultation on reform to CIL, including measures to accelerate the processes involved in introducing and revising CIL, as well as allowing authorities, where appropriate, to charge different (i.e. higher) rates which better reflect the uplift in land values arising from development (as opposed to a flat rate for all development of the same type) with a view to increasing receipts from CIL to help fill the infrastructure funding gap.

10.7   Other mooted changes to CIL involve:

(a)   the removal of restrictions on pooling section 106 obligations (under which local planning authorities (LPAs) can pool no more than five section 106 contributions towards any one project) in certain circumstances, such as in the case of strategic development planned on several large strategic sites;

(b)   speeding up the implementation of CIL;

(c)   index-linking CIL rates to house price inflation with a view to reducing the need to revise charging schedules, rather than tying them to the Building Cost Information Service's construction costs index;

(d)   giving combined authorities and joint committees with statutory plan-making functions the option to impose a strategic infrastructure tariff, along the lines of the London Mayoral CIL for Crossrail.

10.8   In the circumstances, this section of the book will deal with the law on CIL as it stands at the moment, notwithstanding the likelihood of reform in the medium to long term and the view of the CRG that it would not be sensible to leave matters as they are.[5] This begs the question as to how far future reform will go.

---

[5]   The CRG reports states at 4.2.1 of:

'The failure to achieve the original aims of CIL, the complexities of the current system, including the inconsistent patchwork approach to developer contributions on a national basis, the creation of a costly bureaucracy and the potential to achieve significant improvements with some measure of change all point to a need for reform.'

PURPOSE OF CIL

10.9   Other than section 106 agreements or in the case of highway agreements under section 278 of the Highways Act 1980 (HA 1980), developers may be asked to make contributions for infrastructure by way of CIL in the case of those authorities which do not seek to recover for infrastructure by way of planning obligations.[6] The purpose of the CIL is to ensure that the costs incurred in supporting the development of an area can be funded (wholly or partly) by owners or developers of land in a way that does not make the development of the area economically unviable.[7]

10.10   CIL is not intended to overlap with section 106 contributions towards infrastructure, with developers paying twice for the same item of infrastructure. It achieves this by ensuring that when a charging authority introduces the CIL, it sets out a list of those projects or types of infrastructure that it intends to fund, or may fund, through the CIL. For transparency, charging authorities should have set out at examination how their section 106 policies will be varied, and the extent to which they have met their section 106 targets. Relevant local policy changes should be implemented at the same time that their charging schedule is introduced and integrated as soon as practicable into the relevant local plan.[8]

---

[6]   Planning Act 2008, Pt II makes provision for the levy, and the detail is to be found in the Community Infrastructure Levy Regulations 2010 (as amended by the 2014 Regulations) (CILR). See also the NPPG for the CIL.

[7]   Planning Act 2008, s 205 (as amended by LA 2011, s 115(1)).

[8]   CILR, reg 123, which limits the use of planning obligations. Where a reg 123 list includes a generic type of infrastructure (such as education or transport), s 106 contributions should not be sought on any specific projects in that category. Site-specific contributions, through the CIL, should only be sought where this can be justified with reference to the underpinning evidence on infrastructure planning which was made publicly available at the charging schedule examination. The charging authority's proposed approach to s 106 contributions should be set out, and the public examination should be based on evidence. Where a reg 123 list includes single-project infrastructure, the charging authority should not seek any planning obligations in relation to that infrastructure. Regulations restrict the use of pooled contributions towards items that may be funded via the CIL. At that point, no more may be collected in respect of a specific infrastructure project or a type of infrastructure through a s 106 agreement, if five or more obligations for that project or type of infrastructure have already been entered into since 6/4/2010, and it is a type of infrastructure that is capable of being funded by the CIL. Where a s 106 agreement makes provision for a number of stage payments as part of a planning obligation, these payments will collectively count as a single obligation in relation to the pooling restriction. What all this means is that an infrastructure project on the charging authority's list of infrastructure which it proposes to fund with the CIL (commonly known as the 'Regulation 123 list') cannot be funded by s 106 contributions. In effect, CIL restricts the use of generic s 106 tariffs for items that are capable of being funded by the CIL, and authorities which refer to specific types of infrastructure (e.g. education), rather than specific projects, in their s 106 agreements, will be unable to collect more than five contributions towards those generic funding pots once the pooling restriction is in force (contributions for highway works that are secured through HA 1980, s 278 are not subject to the pooling restriction).

10.11 CIL may be payable on development which creates net additional floor space, where the gross internal area of new build exceeds 100 square metres. That limit does not apply to new houses or flats, but a charge can be levied on a single house or flat of any size, unless it is built by a 'self builder'.[9] However, certain developments will not pay CIL:

(a) development of less than 100 square metres;[10]
(b) houses, flats, residential annexes and residential extensions which are built by 'self builders';[11]
(c) social housing that meets the relief criteria;[12]
(d) charitable development that meets the relief criteria;[13]
(e) buildings into which people do not normally go;[14]
(f) buildings into which people go only intermittently for the purpose of inspecting or maintaining fixed plant or machinery;[15]
(g) structures which are not buildings, such as pylons and wind turbines;
(h) specified types of development which local authorities have decided should be subject to a 'zero' rate and specified as such in their charging schedules;
(i) vacant buildings brought back into the same use;[16]
(j) where the CIL liability is calculated to be less than £50 (the chargeable amount is deemed to be zero so no CIL will be due);
(k) mezzanine floors, inserted into existing buildings, unless they form part of a wider planning permission that seeks to provide other works as well.

10.12 Charging authorities[17] have power to charge the CIL in respect of the development of land in their area. The amount of the charge must be set out in a charging schedule issued by the charging authority,[18] which must set out rates or

9 See CILR, regs 54A and 54B, and the guidance issued on 12/6/2014 in the NPPG, in the section 'Community Infrastructure Levy', under the heading 'Relief: Self build exemption', starting at Paragraph: 135 Reference ID: 25-135-20140612.
10 See CILR, reg 42 on minor development exemptions, unless this is a whole house, in which case the levy is payable.
11 See CILR, regs 42A, 42B, 54A and 54B.
12 As set out in CILR, reg 49 or reg 49A.
13 As set out in CILR, regs 43–48.
14 As set out in CILR, reg 6(2).
15 As set out in CILR, reg 6(2).
16 As set out in CILR, reg 40.
17 Which in England will be district and metropolitan district councils, London borough councils, unitary authorities, National Park authorities, the Broads Authority and the Mayor of London, and in Wales will be the county councils and National Park authorities.
18 In its draft form, the charging schedule is required to be subject to independent scrutiny and recommendation (including public consultation) by an examiner (and it is for the charging authority as to how it responds to any recommended modifications) to ensure due compliance with Planning Act 2008, Pt II and the CILR. See Planning Act 2008, s 212 (examination), s 212A

other criteria by reference to which the amount of CIL chargeable in respect of development in its area is to be determined.[19] In setting rates or other criteria, a charging authority is required to have regard to actual or expected costs of infrastructure and to matters specified in the CILR, such as the economic viability of a development and other actual or expected sources of funding for infrastructure.[20] The amount of the CIL chargeable at any given rate is calculated by applying the formula set out in regulation 40(5) of the CILR.

10.13 The charging authority is required to apply the collected CIL to supporting development by funding the provision, improvement, replacement, operation or maintenance of infrastructure[21] which, for these purposes, includes roads and other transport facilities, flood defences, schools and other educational facilities, medical facilities, sporting and recreational facilities, and open spaces.[22] However, provision is made enabling regulations to be made which add, remove or vary items within the scope of permitted infrastructure for these purposes, along with regulations dealing with a host of other matters that are referable to, or otherwise incidental to, funding on infrastructure, including the imposition of a duty which requires the charging authority to pass on the collected CIL to third parties.[23]

10.14 In terms of payment of the CIL,[24] a liability to pay arises once the chargeable development is commenced.[25] On the grant of a planning permission which permits development, the collecting authority issues a 'liability notice' on the relevant person[26] or on the person who has assumed liability to pay the charge[27] and on each person known to the authority as owner of the land[28] setting out particulars of the CIL, the date and procedure for payment and the consequences of non-payment.[29] A commencement notice must thereafter be

---

(examiner's recommendations) and s 213 (approval), as amended (respectively) by LA 2011, s 114(3), (4) and (5)–(7). The machinery for dealing with charging schedules can be found in CILR, Pt 3, regs 11–30.

[19] Planning Act 2008, s 211(1).

[20] Planning Act 2008, s 211(2).

[21] Planning Act 2008, s 216(1) (as amended by LA 2011, s 115(5)).

[22] Planning Act 2008, s 216(2) (as amended).

[23] Planning Act 2008, ss 216A and 216B.

[24] And the chargeable amount payable in respect of a chargeable development is a local land charge (CILR, reg 66(1)).

[25] Planning Act 2008, ss 206(1), 208 and 209(1).

[26] Which expression is defined in CILR, reg 65(12).

[27] And a person who has assumed liability for CIL before the commencement of the development becomes liable when development is commenced in reliance on planning permission.

[28] CILR, reg 65(3).

[29] CILR, reg 65(2). Reference should be made to the Community Infrastructure Levy (Amendment) Regulations 2018 (SI 2018/172) which amend reg 128A of the CILR which concerns

submitted to the collecting authority no later than the day before the day on which the chargeable development is to be commenced.[30] Unless a collecting authority has received a commencement notice or has reason to believe that development was commenced earlier than the intended commencement date, the collecting authority must determine the day on which a chargeable development was commenced.[31] There follows a demand notice served on each person liable to pay the CIL in respect of the chargeable development,[32] and unless an agreed regime for payment by instalments is in place, payment in full is required to be made at the end of the period of 60 days beginning with the intended commencement date.[33] On the other hand, the CIL is due in full on the intended commencement date if no one has assumed liability to pay or the where the collecting authority has received a commencement notice and has determined a deemed commencement date, unless the collecting authority has determined a deemed commencement date, in which case payment will be due in full on that date. Where the collecting authority transfers liability to pay an amount to the owners of the relevant land, payment of that amount is due in full immediately.[34] The collecting authority also has power to accept what is described as a land payment in satisfaction of the whole or any part of the CIL due in respect of the chargeable development.[35]

ENFORCEMENT

10.15 In terms of enforcement, the collecting authority may, in certain circumstances, impose a surcharge,[36] and is also entitled to claim late payment interest.[37] Where the CIL is unpaid and the collecting authority considers it expedient that development should stop until it has been paid, it may issue a notice warning of its intention to issue a CIL stop notice,[38] and if this fails to work, a

---

development that is initially granted planning permission before CIL was implemented, and is then subsequently amended after CIL is introduced. The amendment provides additional clarity to ensure that charging authorities calculate CIL liabilities in line with policy intent (see Explanatory Memorandum to regs).

[30] CILR, reg 67(1).

[31] CILR, reg 68.

[32] CILR, reg 69 (and a charging authority may accept payment by instalments (see regs 69(2)(f), 69B and 70)).

[33] CILR, reg 70(7).

[34] CILR, reg 71.

[35] CILR, reg 73, albeit subject to the conditions mentioned in reg 73(6), including where an agreement to make the land payment is entered into before the chargeable development is commenced (such an agreement may not form part of a s 106 agreement: reg 73(7)(b)).

[36] CILR, regs 80 and 85.

[37] CILR, reg 87.

[38] CILR, reg 89.

CIL stop notice may be issued.[39] It will be an offence to contravene such notice.[40] The collecting authority also has other powers: it can apply for an injunction[41] or a charging order.[42] It can also enforce the local land charge[43] or apply for a liability order leading to enforcement and distress and sale of the debtor's assets.[44] Exceptionally, it can also seek commitment to prison[45] or pursue insolvency.[46]

APPEALS, RELATION WITH OTHER DEVELOPER CONTRIBUTIONS AND RELIEF

10.16 Appeals can be lodged against some aspects of CIL.[47] Guidance also exists dealing with the relation of CIL to other developer contributions (planning obligations and highway agreements)[48] and the forms of relief available from CIL.[49]

---

[39] CILR, reg 90.

[40] CILR, reg 93.

[41] CILR, reg 94.

[42] CILR, reg 103.

[43] CILR, reg 107.

[44] CILR, reg 98.

[45] CILR, reg 100.

[46] CILR, reg 105.

[47] NPPG at Paragraph: 089 Reference ID: 25-089-20140612 to 25-092-20140612.

[48] NPPG at Paragraph: 093 Reference ID: 25-093-20140612 to 25-107-20140612.

[49] NPPG at Paragraph: 108 Reference ID: 25-108-20140612 to 25-170-20140612. A collecting authority must satisfy itself that by granting relief or an exemption, it is not breaching state aid rules, which is an obligation owed by public authorities under EU law (see NPPG at Paragraph: 155 Reference ID: 25-155-20140612 to 25-170-20140612), although state aid is permissible in certain limited circumstances (NPPG at Paragraph: 158 Reference ID: 25-158-20140612).

Chapter 11

Purchase Notices and Blight Notices

PURCHASE NOTICES

11.1   Where: (a) planning permission has been refused or granted subject to conditions; (b) it has been revoked or modified by the imposition of conditions;[1] or (c) a discontinuance order has been made,[2] the owner may serve[3] a purchase notice on the relevant authority if, in cases (a) and (b):

(a)   the land has become incapable of reasonably beneficial use in its existing state; and

(b)   in a case where planning permission was granted subject to conditions or was modified by the imposition of conditions, the land cannot be rendered capable of reasonably beneficial use by the carrying out of the permitted development in accordance with those conditions; and

(c)   in any case, the land cannot be rendered capable of reasonably beneficial use by the carrying out of any other development for which planning permission has been granted or for which the local planning authority (LPA) or the Secretary of State has undertaken to grant permission;[4]

or if, in the case of (c), as a result of the making of a discontinuance order, the following conditions are met:

(d)   that by reason of the order the land is incapable of reasonably beneficial use in its existing state; and

---

[1]   TCPA 1990, s 97.

[2]   TCPA 1990, s 102 or Sch 9, para 1 (discontinuance of mineral working).

[3]   Within 12 months of the decision of the LPA or the Secretary of State (Town and Country Planning General Regulations 1992 (SI 1992/1492), reg 12), although these Regulations confer power on the Secretary of State to extend that period where service is delayed for good reasons.

[4]   TCPA 1990, s 137(1)–(3).

(e)   that it cannot be rendered capable of reasonably beneficial use by the carrying out of any other development for which planning permission has been granted, whether by that order or otherwise.

11.2   The notice requires the authority to purchase the land from the owner and to be paid compensation as if the land was being compulsorily purchased from him. Once a notice has been served, the authority[5] is required to serve a response notice within three months. The authority either accepts the purchase notice and buys the land, or it may reject it, in which case it must refer the notice to the Secretary of State who may, if he is not satisfied that the land is incapable of reasonably beneficial use, refuse to confirm it or, if he is so satisfied, then he may confirm it (in whole or part – in which event, it confirms the normal compulsory acquisition procedure) or grant planning permission, the refusal of which gave rise to the notice, or he may direct that planning permission for some other development may be granted if applied for.[6]

REASONABLY BENEFICIAL USE

11.3   This expression is not expressly defined in the TCPA 1990, but it is provided that in determining whether land is incapable of reasonably beneficial use, no account shall be taken of any prospective use involving new development other than development within paragraph 1 or 2 of Schedule 3, or where the purchase notice follows a refusal or conditional grant of planning permission if it would contravene the condition set out in Schedule 10.[7]

11.4   Cases under this head turn on their own particular facts, but the test is a rigorous one. The true test, however, is not whether the land is less valuable to the owner than if developed in accordance with the owner's wishes, but whether the existing use is reasonably beneficial to the owner or a prospective owner in all the relevant circumstances of the particular site. The decision of the Secretary of State to confirm or not to confirm a purchase notice may be challenged by any person aggrieved by his decision.[8] This will be on conventional public law grounds for questioning decisions, such as where the decision was wrong in law

---

5   Which can be a district council, London borough, metropolitan or shire district council, including a unitary council, Welsh county or county borough or National Park authority. As is indicated by TCPA 1990, s 137A, only in limited circumstances may a purchase notice be served in relation to Crown land.

6   See TCPA 1990, ss 139–143.

7   TCPA 1990, s 138(1), although regard may be had to any planning permission for other development which had been granted or which the LPA had undertaken to grant (*Gavaghan v Secretary of State for the Environment* [1989] 1 PLR 88).

8   Under TCPA 1990, s 288.

or was *Wednesbury* unreasonable or otherwise resulted from the failure of the Secretary of State to have regard to a relevant and material consideration. In other words, the assessment of whether there was 'reasonably beneficial use' is a matter for the judgment of the decision-maker such that a court would have to consider whether a decision that the land was capable of reasonably beneficial use in its existing state (and so not to confirm the decision-notice) was (in effect) so surprising that it could be regarded as irrational.

BLIGHT NOTICES

11.5   We are dealing here with blighted land, i.e. land affected by planning proposals of public authorities which is under threat of compulsory purchase and, as a result, becomes virtually unsaleable. In such a case, a notice may be served by the owner which requires the authority to purchase his land, which will mean that the owner will not have to wait until the relevant authority is ready to proceed with the relevant scheme and compulsorily purchase the land.[9]

11.6   The categories of land in respect of which a blight notice may be served typically involve land allocated for the functions of a government department, local authority or statutory undertaker.[10] Other than having a qualifying interest in the land or agricultural unit, it is a pre-condition for service of a blight notice that the owner has made reasonable efforts to sell his interest in the land, and because of the blight he has been unable to sell except at a price substantially lower than that for which it might reasonably have been expected to sell if it were not blighted land.[11]

11.7   A blight notice may only be served on the relevant authority or body authorised to acquire the land compulsorily (such as a highway authority) by an owner-occupier of domestic or non-domestic property whose net annual value for

---

[9]   TCPA 1990, Pt VI, Chapter II, ss 149–171.

[10]   Blighted land is identified in TCPA 1990, Sch 13. Blighted land comprises: (a) land identified in a development plan document or otherwise earmarked by resolutions of the local authority or by a direction of the Secretary of State for public functions; (b) land authorised to be acquired compulsorily or in respect of which a compulsory purchase order is in force; (c) land within an area described as the site for a new town or within an area intended to be designated as a general improvement area; (d) slum clearance and renewal areas; (e) land identified in a development plan or indicated in an order (including a new street order) or scheme or which is subject to a compulsory purchase order which is required for highway purposes; and (f) land identified in a national policy statement as suitable (or potentially suitable) for that description of development as, for instance, where the compulsory acquisition of land is authorised in an order granting consent for a nationally significant infrastructure project.

[11]   TCPA 1990, s 150(1); the exception to this pre-condition is where land is authorised by a special enactment to be compulsorily acquired or where a compulsory purchase order is in force or where land is authorised to be acquired by an order granting development consent.

rating is less than (currently) £34,800.[12] A notice may also be served by a personal representative of a person who at his death would have been entitled to serve a blight notice or a mortgagee.[13] The notice must also require the recipient of the notice to buy all of the land even if only part of it is blighted.[14] The recipient's counter-notice (to be served within two months of the service of the blight notice unless, that is, the authority is willing to purchase the land) may state that the recipient proposes to acquire only part of the land but not the remainder,[15] and the notice will only be upheld on this ground if the acquiring authority can show that it can acquire part without compromising the amenity of the remaining land.[16] In the case of an agricultural unit, the notice may require the recipient to purchase part or even the whole of the farm, provided, in the case of the latter, it can be shown that the unaffected area is not reasonably capable of being separately farmed, either by itself or in conjunction with other land.[17] In such a case, the recipient of the notice must, if it objects to a claim involving the purchase of the whole of the farm, claim in its counter-notice that this claim is not justified, which will have to be determined by the Upper Tribunal.[18] On the other hand, if the tribunal finds that the loss of the blighted land will not mean that the rest of the farm is incapable of being separately farmed then it shall declare that the blight notice is a valid notice in relation to the affected area, but not in relation to the unaffected area.[19]

11.8   A further significant ground of objection arises in certain cases where the authority does not propose to acquire the land during the period of 15 years from the date of its counter-notice.[20]

---

[12]   TCPA 1990, s 168, where the terms 'owner-occupier' and 'resident occupier' are defined. See also Town and Country Planning (Blight Provisions) (England) Order 2010 (SI 2010/498) (the same provision has also been made for Wales). The effect of this is that owners of investment property cannot serve a blight notice.

[13]   TCPA 1990, ss 161 and 162. The claimant may also be the owner-occupier of an agricultural unit, which term is defined in s 171.

[14]   TCPA 1990, s 150(1)–(3).

[15]   TCPA 1990, s 151(4)(c).

[16]   *Hurley v Cheshire County Council* (1976) 31 P & CR 433. In this case, proposals for a dual carriageway involved taking 300 square yards from the garden of the claimant's house. He was unable to sell the house at a reasonable price because of the proposals. It was held by the Lands Tribunal that the blight notice requiring the council to purchase the house and land was valid since the onus lay on the council to satisfy the tribunal that the proposed acquisition would not necessarily seriously affect the amenity or convenience of the house. The tribunal found that the amenity of the house would unavoidably be seriously affected.

[17]   TCPA 1990, s 158.

[18]   TCPA 1990, s 159(1) and (3).

[19]   TCPA 1990, s 159(5).

[20]   This applies in relation to TCPA 1990, Sch 13, paras 1, 3 or 13, i.e. where the blight arises from the provisions of the development plan or highways.

11.9   It is for the claimant to refer a counter-notice to the tribunal within two months of its service upon him.[21] Unless it is shown to the satisfaction of the tribunal that the objection is not well founded, the tribunal shall uphold the objection.[22] An objection on the grounds that the authority: (a) does not intend to acquire the blighted land; or (b) proposes to acquire only part of the blighted land; or (c) does not propose to exercise its powers of acquisition in relation to any part of the land within a period of 15 years, will not be upheld unless it is shown to the satisfaction of the tribunal to be well founded.[23] Nor will the tribunal uphold an objection in the case of an agricultural unit on the ground that the authority wishes to acquire only part of the claimant's land unless it is satisfied that the claimant's assertion that the rest of the land is incapable of being farmed is justified.[24] If the tribunal decides not to uphold the objection, the tribunal shall declare the blight notice to be a valid notice.[25] If the tribunal upholds the objection but only on the ground that the authority wishes to acquire only part of the affected land, the tribunal will declare the notice to be valid only in relation to that part of the claimant's land.[26] If the blight notice is declared to be valid (either because the authority has not served a counter-notice or because its objections have not been upheld) the tribunal will also give directions specifying the date on which the notice to treat is deemed to have been served, and the blight notice will, as a consequence, become subject to the usual compulsory purchase procedure.[27] In a case where the authority has acknowledged its liability to acquire only part of the claimant's land,[28] but objects to acquiring any further land, the claimant may either refer the counter-notice to the tribunal or else he may accept the authority's claim and withdraw his claim in relation to the rest of his land, in which event the compulsory purchase procedure applies only in relation to that part of the claimant's land which the authority has agreed to purchase.[29]

---

[21]   TCPA 1990, s 153(1).

[22]   TCPA 1990, s 153(3).

[23]   TCPA 1990, s 153(4).

[24]   TCPA 1990, s 158.

[25]   TCPA 1990, s 153(5).

[26]   TCPA 1990, s 153(6).

[27]   TCPA 1990, ss 153(7) and 154.

[28]   TCPA 1990, s 151(4)(c).

[29]   TCPA 1990, s 154(5).

Chapter 12

Viability

INTRODUCTION

12.1   Viability assessment is a process of assessing whether a site is financially viable, by looking at whether the value generated by a development is more than the cost of developing it. This includes looking at the key elements of gross development value, costs, land value, landowner premium, and developer return.

12.2   The National Planning Policy Framework 2012 (NPPF) states that local plans should be deliverable and that the sites and scale of development identified in the plan should not be subject to such a scale of obligations and policy burdens that their ability to be developed viably is threatened. NPPF policy on viability applies also to decision-taking. Viability is clearly very important where planning obligations or other costs are being introduced. In such cases decisions must be underpinned by an understanding of viability in order that realistic decisions are made to support development. Where the viability of a development is in question, local planning authorities (LPAs) should look, wherever possible, to be flexible in applying policy requirements.

12.3   The National Planning Practice Guidance (NPPG) sets out the Government's recommended approach to viability assessment for planning. The approach supports accountability for communities by enabling them to understand the key inputs to and outcomes of viability assessment.

NATIONAL PLANNING PRACTICE GUIDANCE

12.4   The following are extracts from the revised NPPG under this head which was published on 24/7/2018 at the same time as revisions to the NPPF. The NPPG deals with viability under four heads: (a) viability and plan-making; (b) viability and decision taking; (c) standardised inputs to viability assessment; and (d) accountability:

Viability and plan making

How should plan makers set policy requirements for contributions from development?[1]

Plans should set out the contributions expected from development. This should include setting out the levels and types of affordable housing provision required, along with other infrastructure (such as that needed for education, health, transport, flood and water management, green and digital infrastructure).

These policy requirements should be informed by evidence of infrastructure and affordable housing need, and a proportionate assessment of viability that takes into account all relevant policies, and local and national standards, including the cost implications of the Community Infrastructure Levy (CIL) and section 106. Policy requirements should be clear so that they can be accurately accounted for in the price paid for land. To provide this certainty, affordable housing requirements should be expressed as a single figure rather than a range. Different requirements may be set for different types of site or types of development.

How should plan makers and site promoters ensure that policy requirements for contributions from development are deliverable?[2]

The role for viability assessment is primarily at the plan making stage. Viability assessment should not compromise sustainable development but should be used to ensure that policies are realistic, and that the total cumulative cost of all relevant policies will not undermine deliverability of the plan.

It is the responsibility of plan makers in collaboration with the local community, developers and other stakeholders, to create realistic, deliverable policies. Drafting of plan policies should be iterative and informed by engagement with developers, landowners, and infrastructure and affordable housing providers.

Policy requirements, particularly for affordable housing, should be set at a level that takes account of affordable housing and infrastructure needs and allows for the planned types of sites and development to be deliverable, without the need for further viability assessment at the decision making stage.

It is the responsibility of site promoters to engage in plan making, take into account any costs including their own profit expectations and risks, and ensure that proposals for development are policy compliant. The price paid for land is not a relevant justification for failing to accord with relevant policies in the plan.

Should every site be assessed for viability in plan making?[3]

Assessing the viability of plans does not require individual testing of every site or assurance that individual sites are viable. Plan makers can use site typologies to

---

[1]   NPPG at Paragraph: 001 Reference ID: 10-001-20180724.

[2]   NPPG at Paragraph: 002 Reference ID: 10-002-20180724.

[3]   NPPG at Paragraph: 003 Reference ID: 10-003-20180724.

determine viability at the plan making stage. Assessment of samples of sites may be helpful to support evidence. In some circumstances more detailed assessment may be necessary for particular areas or key sites on which the delivery of the plan relies.

What is meant by a typology approach to viability?[4]
A typology approach is where sites are grouped by shared characteristics such as location, whether brownfield or greenfield, size of site and current and proposed use or type of development. The characteristics used to group sites should reflect the nature of sites and type of development proposed for allocation in the plan.

Average costs and values can be used to make assumptions about how the viability of each type of site would be affected by all relevant policies. Comparing data from existing case study sites will help ensure assumptions of costs and values are realistic and broadly accurate. In using market evidence it is important to disregard outliers. Information from other evidence informing the plan (such as Strategic Housing Land Availability Assessments) can help inform viability assessment.

Why should strategic sites be assessed for viability in plan making?[5]
It is important to consider the specific circumstances of strategic sites. Plan makers can undertake site specific viability assessment for sites that are critical to delivering the strategic priorities of the plan. This could include, for example, large sites, sites that provide a significant proportion of planned supply, sites that enable or unlock other development sites or sites within priority regeneration areas. Information from other evidence informing the plan (such as Strategic Housing Land Availability Assessments) can help inform viability assessment for strategic sites.

How should site promoters engage in viability assessment in plan making?[6]
Plan makers should engage with landowners, developers, and infrastructure and affordable housing providers to secure evidence on costs and values to inform viability assessment at the plan making stage.

It is the responsibility of site promoters to engage in plan making, take into account any costs including their own profit expectations and risks, and ensure that proposals for development are policy compliant. It is important for developers and other parties buying (or interested in buying) land to have regard to the total cumulative cost of all relevant policies when agreeing a price for the land. Under no circumstances will the price paid for land be a relevant justification for failing to accord with relevant policies in the plan.

Where up-to-date policies have set out the contributions expected from development, planning applications that comply with them should be assumed to be viable. It is up to the applicant to demonstrate whether particular circumstances justify the need for

---

[4]   NPPG at Paragraph: 004 Reference ID: 10-004-20180724.
[5]   NPPG at Paragraph: 005 Reference ID: 10-005-20180724.
[6]   NPPG at Paragraph: 006 Reference ID: 10-006-20180724.

a viability assessment at the application stage. An illustrative list of circumstances where viability should be assessed in decision making is set out below.

Viability and decision taking

Should viability be assessed in decision-taking?[7]
Where up-to-date policies have set out the contributions expected from development, planning applications that comply with them should be assumed to be viable. It is up to the applicant to demonstrate whether particular circumstances justify the need for a viability assessment at the application stage.

Such circumstances could include, for example where development is proposed on unallocated sites of a wholly different type to those used in viability assessment that informed the plan; where further information on infrastructure or site costs is required; where particular types of development are proposed which may significantly vary from standard models of development for sale (for example build to rent or housing for older people); or where a recession or similar significant economic changes have occurred since the plan was brought into force.

How should a viability assessment be treated in decision making?[8]
Where a viability assessment is submitted to accompany a planning application this should be based upon and refer back to the viability assessment that informed the plan; and the applicant should provide evidence of what has changed since then.

The weight to be given to a viability assessment is a matter for the decision maker, having regard to all the circumstances in the case, including whether the plan and viability evidence underpinning the plan is up to date, any change in site circumstances since the plan was brought into force, and the transparency of assumptions behind evidence submitted as part of the viability assessment.

Any viability assessment should reflect the government's recommended approach to defining key inputs as set out in National Planning Guidance.

How should viability be reviewed during the lifetime of a project?[9]
Plans should set out circumstances where review mechanisms may be appropriate, as well as clear process and terms of engagement regarding how and when viability will be reassessed over the lifetime of the development to ensure policy compliance and optimal public benefits through economic cycles.

Where contributions are reduced below the requirements set out in policies to provide flexibility in the early stages of a development, there should be a clear agreement of how policy compliance can be achieved over time. As the potential risk to developers is already accounted for in the assumptions for developer return in

---

[7]   NPPG at Paragraph: 007 Reference ID: 10-007-20180724.
[8]   NPPG at Paragraph: 008 Reference ID: 10-008-20180724.
[9]   NPPG at Paragraph: 009 Reference ID: 10-009-20180724.

viability assessment, realisation of risk does not in itself necessitate further viability assessment or trigger a review mechanism. Review mechanisms are not a tool to protect a return to the developer, but to strengthen local authorities' ability to seek compliance with relevant policies over the lifetime of the project.

Standardised inputs to viability assessment

What are the principles for carrying out a viability assessment?[10]
Viability assessment is a process of assessing whether a site is financially viable, by looking at whether the value generated by a development is more than the cost of developing it. This includes looking at the key elements of gross development value, costs, land value, landowner premium, and developer return.

This National Planning Guidance sets out the government's recommended approach to viability assessment for planning. The approach supports accountability for communities by enabling them to understand the key inputs to and outcomes of viability assessment.

Any viability assessment should be supported by appropriate available evidence informed by engagement with developers, landowners, and infrastructure and affordable housing providers. Any viability assessment should follow the government's recommended approach to assessing viability as set out in this National Planning Guidance and be proportionate, simple, transparent and publicly available. Improving transparency of data associated with viability assessment will, over time, improve the data available for future assessment as well as provide more accountability regarding how viability informs decision making.

In plan making and decision making viability helps to strike a balance between the aspirations of developers and landowners, in terms of returns against risk, and the aims of the planning system to secure maximum benefits in the public interest through the granting of planning permission.

How should gross development value be defined for the purpose of viability assessment?[11]
Gross development value is an assessment of the value of development. For residential development, this may be total sales and/or capitalised net rental income from developments. Grant and other external sources of funding should be considered. For commercial development broad assessment of value in line with industry practice may be necessary.

For broad area-wide or site typology assessment at the plan making stage, average figures can be used, with adjustment to take into account land use, form, scale, location, rents and yields, disregarding outliers in the data. For housing, historic information about delivery rates can be informative.

[10] NPPG at Paragraph: 010 Reference ID: 10-010-20180724.
[11] NPPG at Paragraph: 011 Reference ID: 10-011-20180724.

For viability assessment of a specific site or development, market evidence (rather than average figures) from the actual site or from existing developments can be used. Any market evidence used should be adjusted to take into account variations in use, form, scale, location, rents and yields, disregarding outliers. Under no circumstances will the price paid for land be a relevant justification for failing to accord with relevant policies in the plan.

How should costs be defined for the purpose of viability assessment?[12]
Assessment of costs should be based on evidence which is reflective of local market conditions. As far as possible, costs should be identified at the plan making stage. Plan makers should identify where costs are unknown and identify where further viability assessment may support a planning application.
Costs include:

- build costs based on appropriate data, for example that of the Building Cost Information Service
- abnormal costs, including those associated with treatment for contaminated sites or listed buildings, or costs associated with brownfield, phased or complex sites. These costs should be taken into account when defining benchmark land value
- site-specific infrastructure costs, which might include access roads, sustainable drainage systems, green infrastructure, connection to utilities and decentralised energy. These costs should be taken into account when defining benchmark land value
- the total cost of all relevant policy requirements including contributions towards affordable housing and infrastructure, Community Infrastructure Levy charges, and any other relevant policies or standards. These costs should be taken into account when defining benchmark land value
- general finance costs including those incurred through loans
- professional, project management, sales, marketing and legal costs incorporating organisational overheads associated with the site. Any professional site fees should also be taken into account when defining benchmark land value
- explicit reference to project contingency costs should be included in circumstances where scheme specific assessment is deemed necessary, with a justification for contingency relative to project risk and developers return

How should land value be defined for the purpose of viability assessment?[13]
To define land value for any viability assessment, a benchmark land value should be established on the basis of the existing use value (EUV) of the land, plus a premium for the landowner. The premium for the landowner should reflect the minimum return at which it is considered a reasonable landowner would be willing to sell their land. The premium should provide a reasonable incentive, in comparison with other options available, for the landowner to sell land for development while allowing a sufficient contribution to comply with policy requirements. This approach is often called 'existing use value plus' (EUV+).

---

[12] NPPG at Paragraph: 012 Reference ID: 10-012-20180724.
[13] NPPG at Paragraph: 013 Reference ID: 10-013-20180724.

In order to establish benchmark land value, plan makers, landowners, developers, infrastructure and affordable housing providers should engage and provide evidence to inform this iterative and collaborative process.

What factors should be considered to establish benchmark land value?[14]
Benchmark land value should:

- be based upon existing use value
- allow for a premium to landowners (including equity resulting from those building their own homes)
- reflect the implications of abnormal costs; site-specific infrastructure costs; and professional site fees and
- be informed by market evidence including current uses, costs and values wherever possible. Where recent market evidence is used to inform assessment of benchmark land value this evidence should be based on developments which are compliant with policies, including for affordable housing. Where this evidence is not available plan makers and applicants should identify and evidence any adjustments to reflect the cost of policy compliance. This is so that historic benchmark land values of non-policy compliant developments are not used to inflate values over time.

In plan making, the landowner premium should be tested and balanced against emerging policies. In decision making, the cost implications of all relevant policy requirements, including planning obligations and, where relevant, any Community Infrastructure Levy (CIL) charge should be taken into account.

Where viability assessment is used to inform decision making under no circumstances will the price paid for land be a relevant justification for failing to accord with relevant policies in the plan. Local authorities can request data on the price paid for land (or the price expected to be paid through an option agreement).

What is meant by existing use value in viability assessment?[15]
Existing use value (EUV) is the first component of calculating benchmark land value. EUV is the value of the land in its existing use together with the right to implement any development for which there are policy compliant extant planning consents, including realistic deemed consents, but without regard to alternative uses. Existing use value is not the price paid and should disregard hope value. Existing use values will vary depending on the type of site and development types. EUV can be established in collaboration between plan makers, developers and landowners by assessing the value of the specific site or type of site using published sources of information such as agricultural or industrial land values, or if appropriate capitalised rental levels at an appropriate yield. Sources of data can include (but are not limited to): land registry records of transactions; real estate licensed software packages; real estate market reports; real estate research; estate agent websites; property auction

---

[14] NPPG at Paragraph: 014 Reference ID: 10-014-20180724.
[15] NPPG at Paragraph: 015 Reference ID: 10-015-20180724.

results; valuation office agency data; public sector estate/property teams' locally held evidence.

How should the premium to the landowner be defined for viability assessment?[16]

The premium (or the 'plus' in EUV+) is the second component of benchmark land value. It is the amount above existing use value (EUV) that goes to the landowner. The premium should provide a reasonable incentive for a land owner to bring forward land for development while allowing a sufficient contribution to comply with policy requirements.

Plan makers should establish a reasonable premium to the landowner for the purpose of assessing the viability of their plan. This will be an iterative process informed by professional judgement and must be based upon the best available evidence informed by cross sector collaboration. For any viability assessment data sources to inform the establishment the landowner premium should include market evidence and can include benchmark land values from other viability assessments. Any data used should reasonably identify any adjustments necessary to reflect the cost of policy compliance (including for affordable housing), or differences in the quality of land, site scale, market performance of different building use types and reasonable expectations of local landowners. Local authorities can request data on the price paid for land (or the price expected to be paid through an option agreement).

Can alternative uses be used in establishing benchmark land value?[17]

For the purpose of viability assessment alternative use value (AUV) refers to the value of land for uses other than its current permitted use, and other than other potential development that requires planning consent, technical consent or unrealistic permitted development with different associated values. AUV of the land may be informative in establishing benchmark land value. If applying alternative uses when establishing benchmark land value these should be limited to those uses which have an existing implementable permission for that use. Where there is no existing implementable permission, plan makers can set out in which circumstances alternative uses can be used. This might include if there is evidence that the alternative use would fully comply with development plan policies, if it can be demonstrated that the alternative use could be implemented on the site in question, if it can be demonstrated there is market demand for that use, and if there is an explanation as to why the alternative use has not been pursued. Where AUV is used this should be supported by evidence of the costs and values of the alternative use to justify the land value. Valuation based on AUV includes the premium to the landowner. If evidence of AUV is being considered the premium to the landowner must not be double counted.

---

[16]   NPPG at Paragraph: 016 Reference ID: 10-016-20180724.

[17]   NPPG at Paragraph: 017 Reference ID: 10-017-20180724.

How should a return to developers be defined for the purpose of viability assessment?[18]
Potential risk is accounted for in the assumed return for developers at the plan making stage. It is the role of developers, not plan makers or decision makers, to mitigate these risks. The cost of complying with policy requirements should be accounted for in benchmark land value. Under no circumstances will the price paid for land be relevant justification for failing to accord with relevant policies in the plan.

For the purpose of plan making an assumption of 15–20% of gross development value (GDV) may be considered a suitable return to developers in order to establish the viability of plan policies. Plan makers may choose to apply alternative figures where there is evidence to support this according to the type, scale and risk profile of planned development. A lower figure may be more appropriate in consideration of delivery of affordable housing in circumstances where this guarantees an end sale at a known value and reduces risk. Alternative figures may also be appropriate for different development types.

How does viability assessment apply to the build to rent sector?[19]
The economics of build to rent schemes differ from build for sale as they depend on a long term income stream. For build to rent it is expected that the normal form of affordable housing provision will be affordable private rent. Where plan makers wish to set affordable private rent proportions or discount levels at a level differing from national planning policy and guidance, this can be justified through a viability assessment at the plan making stage. Developers will be expected to comply with build to rent policy requirements.

However, for individual schemes, developers may propose alternatives to the policy, such as variations to the discount and proportions of affordable private rent units across a development, and the ability to review the value of a scheme (rent levels) over the duration of its life. Plan makers can set out in plans where review mechanisms will be used for build to rent schemes.

Scheme level viability assessment may be improved through the inclusion of two sets of figures, one based on a build to rent scheme and another for an alternative build for sale scheme. This would enable authorities to compare and understand the differences, and agree any necessary adjustments to the affordable private rent contribution.

Accountability

How should a viability assessment be presented and published to ensure accountability?[20]
Complexity and variance is inherent in viability assessment. In order to improve clarity and accountability it is an expectation that any viability assessment is prepared with professional integrity by a suitably qualified practitioner and presented

[18] NPPG at Paragraph: 018 Reference ID: 10-018-20180724.
[19] NPPG at Paragraph: 019 Reference ID: 10-019-20180724.
[20] NPPG at Paragraph: 020 Reference ID: 10-020-20180724.

in accordance with this National Planning Guidance. Practitioners should ensure that the findings of a viability assessment are presented clearly. An executive summary should be used to set out key findings of a viability assessment in a clear way.

The inputs and findings of any viability assessment should be set out in a way that aids clear interpretation and interrogation by decision makers. Reports and findings should clearly state what assumptions have been made about costs and values (including gross development value, benchmark land value including the landowner premium, developer's return and costs). At the decision making stage, any deviation from the figures used in the viability assessment of the plan should be explained and supported by evidence.

Should a viability assessment be publicly available?[21]
Any viability assessment should be prepared on the basis that it will be made publicly available other than in exceptional circumstances. Even in those circumstances an executive summary should be made publicly available. Information used in viability assessment is not usually specific to that developer and thereby need not contain commercially sensitive data. In circumstances where it is deemed that specific details of an assessment are commercially sensitive, the information should be aggregated in published viability assessments and executive summaries, and included as part of total costs figures. Where an exemption from publication is sought, the planning authority must be satisfied that the information to be excluded is commercially sensitive. This might include information relating to negotiations, such as ongoing negotiations over land purchase, and information relating to compensation that may be due to individuals, such as right to light compensation. The aggregated information should be clearly set out to the satisfaction of the decision maker. Any sensitive personal information should not be made public.

An executive summary prepared in accordance with data standards published by government and in line with the template (template to be published in autumn 2018) will present the data and findings of a viability assessment more clearly so that the process and findings are accessible to affected communities. As a minimum, the government recommends that the executive summary sets out the gross development value, benchmark land value including landowner premium, costs, as set out in this guidance where applicable, and return to developer. Where a viability assessment is submitted to accompany a planning application, the executive summary should refer back to the viability assessment that informed the plan and summarise what has changed since then. It should also set out the proposed developer contributions and how this compares with policy requirements.

Why should local authorities monitor and report on developer contributions?[22]
It is important that developers are accountable to communities and that communities are able to easily see where contributions towards infrastructure and affordable housing have been secured and spent.

---

21 NPPG at Paragraph: 021 Reference ID: 10-021-20180724.

22 NPPG at Paragraph: 022 Reference ID: 10-022-20180724.

How should section 106 agreements be published?[23]

Local authorities are required to keep a copy of any planning obligation together with details of any modification or discharge of the planning obligation and make these publicly available on their planning register.

Government recommends that each section 106 agreement includes an executive summary prepared using the standard template (to be published in autumn 2018). The government recommends that the executive summary sets out details of the development and site, and what is to be provided by each planning obligation, including information on any affordable housing that is to be provided, and any trigger points or deadlines for contributions.

Local authorities are expected to use all of the funding they receive through planning obligations in accordance with the terms of the individual planning obligation agreement. This will ensure that new developments are acceptable in planning terms; benefit local communities and support the provision of local infrastructure.

How should developer contributions be monitored?[24]

Using the executive summary of each section 106 agreement, government recommends that local authorities record the details of each planning obligation using the standard open data monitoring tool (template to be published in autumn 2018).

How should developer contributions be reported?[25]

Local authorities charging the Community Infrastructure Levy (CIL) must report on the levy as prescribed under regulation 62 of the Community Infrastructure Regulations 2010 (as amended). Parish and town councils must also report on CIL receipts passed to them from the charging authority through the neighbourhood portion of the levy, as prescribed in regulation 62A. Charging authorities must publish a report on their website by 31 December each year.

Using data on CIL and planning obligations, the government recommends that local authorities prepare an infrastructure funding statement using the standard template in an open data format (template to be published in autumn 2018) that sets out infrastructure requirements, and for both CIL and section 106 planning obligations, anticipated funding from developer contributions, and the choices local authorities have made about how these contributions will be used. Infrastructure funding statements should include information on, but not limited to, contributions made towards and delivery of affordable housing, education, health, transport, green, flood and water management, and digital infrastructure.

Infrastructure funding statements should be reviewed annually to report on the amount of funding received via developer contributions and how this funding has

---

[23] NPPG at Paragraph: 023 Reference ID: 10-023-20180724.

[24] NPPG at Paragraph: 024 Reference ID: 10-024-20180724.

[25] NPPG at Paragraph: 025 Reference ID: 10-025-20180724.

been used. Local authorities should use the monitoring tool (tool under development) to help prepare the infrastructure funding statement in a standard format. Infrastructure funding statements should be published annually online. Local authorities can also report this data in authority monitoring reports.

How can local authorities fund monitoring of developer contributions?[26]
Local authorities can use their existing administrative systems to monitor developer contributions. Government recommends that local authorities use the open data monitoring and reporting templates (templates to be published in autumn 2018).

How should monitoring and reporting inform plan reviews?[27]
The information in the infrastructure funding statement should feed back into reviews of plans to ensure that policy requirements for developer contributions remain realistic and do not undermine deliverability of the plan.

How should local authorities and applicants promote the benefits of development to communities?[28]
Local authorities and applicants are encouraged to work together to better promote and publicise the infrastructure that has been delivered through developer contributions. This could be through the use of on-site signage, local authority websites, or development-specific websites, for example.

DISCUSSION

12.5   Viability assessments place weight on 'competitive returns … to enable the development to be deliverable' which generally means within the industry a profit margin of at least 20%.[29] It is argued that developers exploit viability concerns to reduce the amount of affordable housing which they are required in order to attain a 20% margin of profit and inflate their bids for land. Industry sources argue, however, that the appraisal of viability assessments is done through due process and that decisions are not taken by LPAs on a whim. Indeed, review mechanisms within planning obligations enable LPAs to secure higher levels of affordable housing from developers if market conditions improve over the life of a development.

---

[26] NPPG at Paragraph: 026 Reference ID: 10-026-20180724.

[27] NPPG at Paragraph: 027 Reference ID: 10-027-20180724.

[28] NPPG at Paragraph: 028 Reference ID: 10-028-20180724.

[29] Report published by housing charity Shelter in October 2017. See article by Jamie Carpenter: 'Do viability rules favour developer returns over affordable housing?' in *Planning*, published on 17/11/2017.

12.6   It is said[30] that the factor which has the largest impact is land value, namely what is paid for the land by the developer. NPPG says that land or site value should reflect policy requirements and planning obligations and, where appropriate, CIL but this does not always happen in practice. There is evidence that developers are paying over the odds for land as they are reasonably confident that the NPPF's competitive returns policy will protect their profit level.[31]

12.7   It is also open to question[32] whether 20% is even the generally accepted margin of profit that developers can work with (or what they will necessarily get as an assumption in a viability assessment) as their profit margins will vary according to the size and risk profile associated with the proposed development and a minimum threshold on profit can be a lending criteria for banks. Moreover, although an assumed profit figure of 20% has become a starting position for a number of developers, before the last recession the figure was 15% or even lower.[33] Indeed, some recent appeal decisions show that inspectors are not always relying on a 20% level of profit.[34]

12.8   It seems to be the case that the present system is over-burdened with viability assessment because in practice many local plans present affordable housing quotas as targets rather than as expectations and state that these requirements are 'subject to viability'.[35]

12.9   Some LPAs are looking to introduce what has been described as an open book approach to viability involving the submission by developers (which will go on the LPA's online planning register) of unredacted viability assessments (as a validation requirement) alongside their planning applications in cases where proposals do not comply with the necessary policy requirements. Only in

---

[30]   See fn 29 (*Planning* article).

[31]   Citing from the *Planning* article in fn 29 what was said by Mike Kiely, Chair of the Planning Officers Society.

[32]   As is claimed by Shelter in fn 29.

[33]   Citing again from the *Planning* article in fn 29 what was said by Mike Kiely, Chair of the Planning Officers Society.

[34]   The *Planning* article in fn 29 cites an appeal involving 14 flats in NW London (DCS Number: 200-006-828), where the inspector considered that a developer profit of 20% was 'not unreasonable or excessive', whereas in a 93 home scheme in North Yorkshire, another inspector considered a profit level of between 18% and 19% sustainable (DCS Number: 200-006-895).

[35]   Gillian Macinnes Associates is reported to have said as much in the same *Planning* article in fn 29, adding that 'Everything is being subject to a viability assessment ... It's creating a whole industry'. The same article notes that in the week 17/11/2017 consultation closed on proposals to limit the use of viability assessment at the application stage. The consultation proposed to make clear in the NPPF that 'where policy requirements have been tested for their viability, the issue should not usually need to be tested again at the planning application stage'.

exceptional circumstances would some redaction be allowed.[36] This begs the question as to whether, if the public (and not just members or officers) are enabled to scrutinise viability assessments lodged by developers, there will be an increase in the number of objections (whether ill-informed or not) to proposals for development which will only operate to delay the process still further.

12.10   When preparing viability assessments, planners are required to calculate a benchmark land value on the basis of the land's existing use value (EUV) plus a premium for the landowner. The premium should reflect the minimum return at which it is considered a reasonable landowner would be willing to sell their land for development. This approach is often called 'existing use value plus' (EUV+). To arrive at an appropriate minimum premium an assessment should consider the market evidence in the case of comparable sites which have recently been granted planning permission and can include benchmark land values from other viability assessments. The prices paid for such land, suitably adjusted, can then be compared to EUVs for those sites to ascertain an appropriate premium or uplift additional to EUV for the landowner of the site being considered. Any data used should identify any adjustments necessary to reflect the cost of policy compliance (including for affordable housing), or differences in the quality of land, site scale, market performance of different building use types and reasonable expectations of local landowners. Data can also be requested on the price paid for the land or the price expected to be paid through an option agreement. By using standardised inputs in viability assessments the chances are that developers will find it much harder in the future to negotiate lower levels of affordable housing provision on the basis of the price paid for the site.

Parkhurst Road Limited v Secretary of State for Communities and Local Government and the Council of the London Borough of Islington[37]

12.11   This recent case provides important guidance on valuation evidence for the purposes of viability assessments in planning applications and appeals. The case involved viability in connection with the provision of affordable housing (the proposal involved a 96-home scheme on a 0.6 hectare former Territorial Army

---

36   In August 2017, the Mayor of London published viability supplementary planning guidance that adopted a full publication approach. A growing number of LPAs, mostly in London, have taken such a stance. On 5/1/2018, Brighton and Hove Council was reported to be poised to publish unredacted viability reports on schemes. The requirement in their local plan was that developments of five or more homes must include affordable housing, with 40% required in schemes involving more than 15 homes. If schemes met these requirements, then applicants for permission would only need to provide an affordable housing statement at the same validation stage.

37   [2018] EWHC 991 (Admin).

site in Holloway). The court rejected a challenge where the claimant was offering to provide only 10% affordable housing whereas the LPA was contending that 34% would be a reasonable level for the site (against a borough-wide target of 50%). The court concluded that it was clear that the appeal proposal would not provide the maximum reasonable level of affordable housing in accordance with local plan policies.[38] The following are the main extracts from the judgment of Holgate J to which those concerned with viability in the context of affordable housing might well care to give close scrutiny:

> 6. The proposal before the 2015 inquiry was that 16 of the units should be affordable housing (14% of the total number of units). LBI contended that the proportion proposed was inadequate, relying on local policies that required each scheme to provide the "maximum reasonable amount of affordable housing" in the context of an overall affordable housing target of 50% of all new housing across the Borough.
>
> 7. It appears from paragraphs 62 and 63 of the 2015 decision letter that a number of inputs to the viability appraisals carried out by the two parties were agreed at that stage, notably the sales values achievable on the residential units and development costs, including £2.67m for the costs of complying with *other* planning obligations and the payment of the Community Infrastructure Levy ("CIL"). However, the parties disagreed upon an important input, namely the Benchmark Land Value ("BLV"), that is the price at which a reasonable landowner would be sufficiently incentivised so as to be willing to sell the site for alternative development, having regard to the requirements of relevant planning policies and obligations.
>
> 8. PRL used a figure updated from the purchase price it had paid for the site as an input into its viability analysis, representing "a fixed acquisition cost." On this assumption, the resultant profit levels for the developer were below normal target values, and so PRL contended that residential development restricted to the scale proposed in the application would not be deliverable if a greater proportion of affordable housing were to be required.
>
> 9. LBI disagreed with that approach. Using the same values as those adopted by PRL save for the site acquisition cost, the Council carried out a series of residual valuations inputting alternative affordable housing proportions of 50%, 40% and 32% which produced residual land valuations for the site of £4.98m, £7.32m and £9.35m respectively. They contended that the price which PRL had paid for the site was excessive since it did not properly reflect the policy requirement to maximise

---

[38] The appellants had sought to justify 10% affordable housing provision on a purchase price of £13.25 million and comparable transactions on other schemes in the area, arguing that a higher level would make their scheme unviable. Citing the site's established use value, plus a premium to reflect the developer's profit aspirations, the LPA argued that the appropriate 'benchmark value' was £6.75 million which justified 34% affordable provision. The judge found it 'clear' that the appeal proposal would not provide the maximum reasonable level of affordable homes sought by the council.

the affordable housing component on each scheme, in the context of the 50% "target".

10. It was confirmed during the hearing before me that PRL has never made available in the planning process the viability appraisal in 2013 upon which it based its successful bid of £13.25m. Given the substantial reliance placed by PRL upon that bid, that document was plainly of direct relevance to the weight that could be placed upon the actual purchase price for the appeal site. It would have revealed the assumptions made about the costs of planning obligations (including affordable housing) and CIL. It is also possible, if not likely, that that bid was influenced by the prospect of achieving a significantly larger scheme than the reduced scheme for 112 units proposed in 2015.

11. The Inspector who conducted the 2015 inquiry acknowledged that if viability appraisals are conducted using market prices which are inflated by bidders ignoring or diminishing requirements in development plan policies to provide affordable housing, that may undermine compliance with those policies. He said this at DL 72.

> "In this context I can understand the wider concern of the Council about the possible effect of inputting purchase prices which are based on a downgrading of the policy expectation for affordable housing on the eventual outcome of a scheme viability appraisal. If such prices are used to justify a lower level of provision, developers could then in effect be recovering the excess paid for a site through a reduced level of affordable housing provision. Such a circularity has been recognised in research for the RICS, and the Council in its SPD and the GLA (in its Development Appraisal Toolkit Guidance Notes of 2014) are alive to this potential outcome of using purchase price as an input in viability assessment. The Council postulates an undesirable scenario of diminishing returns of affordable housing and eradication of the potential to achieve its delivery. It argues that the current appeal is an opportunity to return to a proper approach."

This "circularity," or self-fulfilling prophecy, became a central issue at the inquiry in 2017 which led to the decision now being challenged. The issue may also arise where an actual purchase price is inflated because of overly optimistic expectations about the amount of development for which planning permission might be granted in due course.

12. The Inspector also recognised that a residual land valuation may be unduly influenced by one party's view about the development which the site can accommodate and thus be too orientated towards a "scheme value," rather than the underlying land value of the site reflecting its attractions to all potential bidders in the market (DL 73).

13. The Inspector did not accept LBI's case on affordable housing provision because it was not supported by any market based evidence (DL64). There remained the market evidence advanced by PRL. They relied upon the price they had paid to the

MoD for the site and the closeness of competing bids to that price (DL65), a subsequent unsolicited *offer* from one of the unsuccessful bidders (DL 66), an independent valuation strongly influenced by evidence from the sale of the site (DL67), and an analysis of 21 land sales in Islington since 2010 (DL68). The Inspector recognised that the "comparables" varied in terms of location, nature, size, constraints, scheme content and affordable housing provision and also that the assumptions made by purchasers were unknown (DL68 to 71).

14. The Inspector accepted that each of the methods used by PRL had limitations, but nonetheless, in his judgment, they gave a consistent indication that the price paid by PRL "was not of a level significantly above a market norm" and there was no evidence to the contrary (DL69). Indeed, he considered that the comparable market evidence, which was said to indicate a value for the appeal site of between £12.98m and £16.44m, "supports a higher valuation for the site than that used by the appellant" (DL74). Accordingly, he concluded that PRL's land value figure of £13.26m "can be regarded as adequately reflecting policy requirements on affordable housing" (i.e. should be treated as the BLV) and PRL's proposal would achieve the "maximum reasonable amount of housing" for the site (DL75).

15. Although PRL's appeal was dismissed on other grounds, LBI were very concerned about the approach taken by the Inspector to viability assessment in order to determine whether "the maximum reasonable amount of affordable housing" was being provided. They contemplated making an application for judicial review. Pre-action protocol correspondence was exchanged. However, proceedings were not commenced and the issues were left to be revisited at the 2017 inquiry.

16. The Council's concern about the 2015 decision is perfectly understandable. For example, the Inspector's reasoning did not suggest that he had considered the crucial questions he had identified in DL72, "the circularity issue," in relation to any of the pieces of evidence relied upon by PRL. In addition, it could be said that the consistency which he believed was shown by this evidence, when considered as a whole, also begged the very same question. It does not follow that, merely because an analysis is based upon a substantial amount of market evidence, the conclusions drawn will be untainted by the circularity problem. That will depend upon whether the transactions in the data base adequately reflected, for example, the requirements of relevant planning policies and, if not, the adequacy of the steps taken, if any, to adjust that information to overcome that problem.

The 2017 public inquiry
17. PRL made a further application for full planning permission on 22 January 2016. The scheme was further reduced in scale to 96 units so as to address the design criticisms made in the 2015 decision letter. When LBI refused planning permission on 13 May 2016 they did not object to the scale or design of the proposal. Instead only two reasons for refusal were given. The first stated that PRL had "failed to demonstrate that the proposed development will provide the maximum reasonable amount of affordable housing taking account of the borough wide strategic target of 50% and the financial viability of the proposal". The second refusal related to the

lack of adequate section 106 obligations to mitigate the effects of the development. Those objections reappeared as the two main issues defined by the Inspector in paragraph 4 of his decision letter. This challenge is solely concerned with the way in which the Inspector dealt with the first issue.

18. When the parties exchanged their evidence in advance of the inquiry, PRL contended that the scheme could no longer provide any affordable housing, whereas LBI argued that 50% of the proposed units should be affordable. By the time the inquiry closed this gap has narrowed somewhat. Using a revised BLV of £11.9m for the acquisition of the site (a reduction of 10% from the figure previously used of £13.26m), PRL proposed that 10% of the units be provided as affordable housing. Using a BLV of £6.75m, LBI contended that the appropriate proportion should be 34% (DL8).

19. As Mr Harris observed, it was no longer contended by LBI that this was a case in which the 50% target should be input as a policy requirement into the viability appraisal in order to determine the appropriate value of the site as a residual. It appears that during the course of the inquiry the figures used to estimate development costs had been increased. This resulted in LBI's residual land valuation (assuming a 50% affordable housing provision) to decrease from £7.15m to £2.4m. The Inspector recorded the Council's acceptance that it was unlikely that a site value of £2.4m would have been sufficient to incentivise a "willing landowner" to sell the land. Instead, LBI maintained that the appropriate figure for the BLV was £6.75m (DL19). The Inspector agreed with that opinion (DL50).

20. PRL submits that the Inspector's acceptance of £6.75m as the BLV was vitiated by legal error in his assessment of LBI's evidence and that this tainted his rejection of PRL's viability appraisal. The Defendants submit firstly that the Inspector's decision that the BLV for the site was £6.75m cannot be impugned. Secondly, they submit that even if the Court should take a different view, none of the points made by PRL affects the basis upon which the Inspector concluded that PRL's viability appraisal failed to demonstrate that the proposal for 10% affordable housing represented the "maximum reasonable amount" that the site should provide. Accordingly, any error was wholly immaterial when the decision letter is read fairly and as a whole and in the light of the way in which the parties' cases were presented to the Inspector.

21. It is helpful at this stage to point out the widely differing approaches which were taken by the parties at the 2017 inquiry.

22. LBI submitted that the site was exactly the type of site that should be making a substantial contribution towards affordable housing. It was common ground that the existing use was redundant and so the existing use value ("EUV") was "negligible" (DL16 and 18). There was no alternative form of development which could generate a higher value for an alternative use ("AUV") than the development proposed by PRL (DL16 to 18). The site did not suffer from abnormal constraints or costs (DL18). As Mr Daniel Kolinsky QC put it on behalf of LBI, there was considerable

"headroom" in the valuation of such a site enabling it to provide a substantial amount of affordable housing in accordance with policy requirements. LBI contended that the achievement of that objective was being frustrated by PRL's use of a greatly inflated BLV for the site which failed properly to reflect those requirements. The circularity problem had not been addressed by PRL's case (see eg. paragraphs 3 to 13 of LBI's opening submissions and paragraph 3 of their closing submissions).

23. PRL's case was that an approach based on EUV with some uplift was inappropriate where the EUV of the site was negligible. Accordingly, an alternative approach was needed to establish BLV using market value or "market signals". Circularity could be avoided by disregarding any transactions which "are significantly above the market norm". PRL relied upon evidence as to:

(i)   The bid process in 2013 and the purchase price paid;
(ii)   A "Red Book" valuation of market value for the site;
(iii)   An unsolicited, unconditional offer for the site;
(iv)   Analysis of comparable transactions.

This was substantially the same approach as PRL had relied upon in the 2015 inquiry (paragraphs 41 to 64 of PRL's opening submission).

24. Ultimately, the Inspector took the view that PRL's approach had failed to give adequate effect to policy requirements for affordable housing. For example, in DL 48 and 49, he said:

> "48. Whilst I attach limited weight to the Red Book exercise, which is required to be in accordance with professional standards, it is a market valuation which does not, in my view, adequately demonstrate proper consideration of, or give adequate effect to, the guidance in PPG or the requirements of the development plan. I do not accept the appellant's position that the level of affordable housing provision is not relevant to determining land value, as any notional willing land owner is required to have regard to the requirements of planning policy and obligations in their expectations of land value. It is unknown what the expectations of the MoD were in this case, but it would obviously not refuse bids above that expectation.
>
> 49. The appellant's case relies to a large extent on the fact that the development plan does not require 50% affordable housing provision on individual sites. However, reliance on policy compliance at any level of provision underplays the strong policy imperative to ensure the 'maximum reasonable' provision with the strategic target in mind. The clear and unambiguous policy position, clarified by the guidance contained in the Council's Development Viability SPD is that 50% affordable housing provision is the starting point and that any provision below that level, whilst capable of being policy compliant, will require robust justification."

...

Planning policies and related documents
National Planning Policy Framework
29. The NPPF contains policies intended "to boost significantly the supply of housing." Thus, local planning authorities are required to ensure that their local plan meets "the full objectively assessed needs for market and affordable housing" in so far as that is consistent with other policies in the framework (paragraph 47). Paragraph 50 states that where an authority has identified that affordable housing is needed, it should set policies for meeting that need on site, unless off-site provision or a financial contribution of broadly equivalent value can be "robustly justified".

30. Paragraph 173 of the NPPF requires that "careful attention" be given to viability and costs in both "plan-making and decision-taking". The "scale of obligations and policy burdens" should not threaten the ability to carry out development viably:

> "To ensure viability, the costs of any requirements likely to be applied to development, such as requirements for affordable housing, standards, infrastructure contributions or other requirements should, when taking account of the normal cost of development and mitigation, provide competitive returns to a willing land owner and willing developer to enable the development to be deliverable."

31. There are three points to be noted about paragraph 173. First, it is recognised that affordable housing imposes an economic cost on the carrying out of development. But as a matter of principle that is no different from the costs of other planning requirements, such as highway or other infrastructure necessary for the development to take place. A transparent, properly prepared viability appraisal which demonstrates that the overall cost of planning obligations is too great for development to be viable can enable the planning authority to exercise a judgment about the relative importance of each of the obligations *in that particular case*. It also assists the decision-maker to balance the desirability of securing those obligations against planning disbenefits which are said to constrain the amount or type of value-generating development which can be carried out on the site.

32. Second, it is recognised that a "competitive return" must be allowed not only for the developer but also the owner of the land upon which the development is to be sited.

33. Third, a viability appraisal is required to assess an appropriate return for a land owner who is said to be "willing". The concept of a "willing seller" commonly features in legal principles applied to a wide range of open market valuations. The "willing seller" is a hypothetical character with no special characteristics or attributes, but who is assumed to be willing to sell at the best price he can *reasonably* obtain in the open market (*Trocette Property Co Ltd v Greater London Council* (1974) 28 P & CR 408, 416). Likewise, in the classic statement in *Inland Revenue Commissioners v Gray* [1994] STC 360 Hoffmann LJ (as he then was) explained that the hypothetical seller is an anonymous but reasonable vendor, who goes about the sale as a prudent man of business. The hypothetical purchaser is also assumed to

behave reasonably and to make proper enquiries about the property. He reflects reality in that he embodies whatever actually was the demand for the property at the relevant time. The concept of the open market involves the assumption that the whole world was free to bid for the property, and then forming a view about what in real life would have been the best price reasonably obtainable. The term "willing" indicates that it must be assumed that the vendor and purchaser behaved as would reasonably be expected of prudent parties.

National Planning Practice Guidance
34. Part of the NPPG deals with viability assessment. Following on from paragraph 173 of the NPPF, paragraph 001 of the Guidance states that where the effect of planning obligations on development viability needs to be assessed, decision-making should be underpinned by an understanding of viability to ensure "realistic decisions are made to support development and promote economic growth." Where the viability of a development is in question, planning authorities "should look to be flexible in applying policy requirements wherever possible". I take that statement to refer to situations in which the overall burden of the obligations is such as to render a development non-viable. Even so, the NPPG recognises that it may not be proper for the authority to compromise on policy requirements.

35. In the context of decision-taking, paragraph 016 states that a site is viable if the value generated by its development exceeds the costs of developing it (including planning obligation costs) and "also provides sufficient incentive for the land to come forward and the development to be undertaken".

36. Paragraph 019 of the NPPG states:

> *"How should the viability of planning obligations be considered in decision-taking?*
> In making decisions, the local planning authority will need to understand the impact of planning obligations on the proposal. Where an applicant is *able to demonstrate to the satisfaction of the local planning authority* that the planning obligation would cause the *development to be unviable*, the local planning authority *should be flexible in seeking planning obligations.*
>
> This is *particularly relevant for affordable housing contributions* which are often the largest single item sought on housing developments. These contributions should not be sought without regard to individual scheme viability. The financial viability of the individual scheme should be carefully considered in line with the principles in this guidance." (emphasis added)

The NPPG is similar in effect to provisions in local policies which place the responsibility on the developer to demonstrate non-viability (see paragraph 41 et seq below). No doubt this reflects the point that in cases where viability is in issue, the developer is effectively asking to be allowed to depart from normal policy requirements and, in any event, is normally well placed to provide information on viability which can then be tested.

37. Paragraph 023 of the NPPG was regarded by both PRL and LBI as being of central importance. It states:

> *"Land value*
> Central to the consideration of viability is the assessment of land or site value. Land or site value will be an important input into the assessment. The most appropriate way to assess land or site value will vary from case to case but there are common principles which should be reflected.
>
> In all cases, land or site value should:
>
> - *reflect policy requirements* and *planning obligations* and, where applicable, any Community Infrastructure Levy charge;
> - *provide a competitive return to willing developers and land owners* (including equity resulting from those wanting to build their own homes); and
> - *be informed by comparable, market-based evidence wherever possible.* Where transacted bids are significantly above the market norm, they should not be used as part of this exercise." (emphasis added)

38. Paragraph 024 of the NPPG states:

> *"Competitive return to developers and land owners*
> The National Planning Policy Framework states that viability should consider "competitive returns to a willing landowner and willing developer to enable the development to be deliverable." This return will vary significantly between projects to reflect the size and risk profile of the development and the risks to the project. A rigid approach to assumed profit levels should be avoided and comparable schemes or data sources reflected wherever possible.
>
> A competitive return for the land owner is the price at which a reasonable land owner would be willing to sell their land for the development. The price will need to provide an incentive for the land owner to sell in comparison with the other options available. Those options may include the current use value of the land or its value for a realistic alternative use that complies with planning policy." (emphasis added)

39. Paragraphs 023 and 024 of the NPPG contain the essential ingredients which define the Benchmark Land Value to be used in a viability appraisal. I agree with LBI's submission that paragraph 023 of the NPPG requires that site value to respect *all three* of the stated requirements. Thus, what is to be regarded as comparable market evidence, or a "market norm", should "reflect policy requirements" in order to avoid the "circularity" problem identified in DL72 of the 2015 decision letter. That may require the comparable evidence to be adjusted so as to be on the correct basis. If there are substantial difficulties in making these adjustments to a particular piece of market evidence, the decision-maker may give it correspondingly reduced weight, or even little or no weight. That would be a matter of judgment for the decision-maker after examining the specific evidence put forward on a case by case basis.

40. Furthermore, in some cases a competitive return in terms of the site value payable to the landowner may need to give him an incentive to sell which exceeds a relatively high existing use value or the value of a "realistic alternative use [to that proposed] that complies with planning policy" (see paragraph 024). That was not an issue affecting PRL's appeal site as such (DL 16–17). But market evidence of "comparable" transactions which had been influenced by high EUV's or AUV's might need to be adjusted by the valuer (see eg. DL18 and DL22).

The London Plan (March 2016)
41. Policy 3.3 of the Spatial Development Strategy for Greater London places strategic importance on increasing the supply of housing in order to meet needs. Policy 3.11 requires London boroughs to set overall targets in their local plans for the amount of affordable housing needed in their area to reflect the strategic priority given to this land use and to maximising affordable housing, as well as taking into account the viability of future developments.

42. Policy 3.12A requires that when determining proposals on individual sites "the maximum reasonable amount of affordable housing" should be sought having regard to eight matters which include "(b) The affordable housing targets adopted" in the local plan, "(c) The need to encourage rather than restrain residential development" and "(f) The specific circumstances of individual sites". Paragraph 3.71 of the "reasoned justification" for the policy states that the planning authority should take into account economic viability and continues:

"Developers should provide development appraisals to demonstrate that each scheme provides the maximum reasonable amount of affordable housing output."

Islington Core Strategy and Development Viability SPD
43. Policy CS12 G requires that 50% of additional housing to be built in Islington over the plan period should be affordable. It is common ground that this is a borough-wide, rather than a site-specific, requirement. For individual sites the policy seeks "the maximum reasonable amount of affordable housing" from private residential and mixed-use schemes involving 10 or more units. "It is expected that many sites will deliver at least 50% of units as affordable, subject to a financial viability assessment, the availability of public subsidy and individual circumstances on the site."

44. These policy requirements are elaborated in LBI's Development Viability Supplementary Planning Document ("SPD") (January 2016). For a proposal of the present kind, page 11 of the SPD requires an applicant to submit a viability appraisal providing certain information with the application. LBI will then consider whether the approach adopted by the applicant and inputs used are appropriate and whether the levels of planning obligations proposed are the maximum that can viably be supported (paragraph 3.18).

45. Referring to policy CS12 of the Core Strategy, the SPD requires the viability testing supplied by the applicant to start with the policy target of 50% affordable

housing and, depending on the circumstances of the site, test higher or lower levels of affordable housing incrementally until "the maximum reasonable level" is determined. "Lower levels should only be considered where warranted by genuine viability constraints under the terms of the guidance in this SPD" (paragraphs 6.71 to 6.73). Where the issue is said to be land value, lower levels of affordable housing should only be considered where "an acceptable benchmark land value" (informed by comparable market evidence which is compliant with planning policy) could not be achieved. Paragraph 6.74 of the SPD continues:

> "It is therefore not the case that any level of affordable housing provision between 0 and 100% can be assumed to potentially be acceptable from the outset, without reference to viability testing the application site under the terms of this guidance including an acceptable benchmark. The use of such an assumption as a basis for determining land value, which is then applied as a fixed input within a viability assessment, is not evidence of a genuine viability constraint but, as noted above, is the result of a circular approach which has the potential to pre-determine and distort the outcome of the viability assessment process."

46. Subject to recognising the need for a degree of flexibility in the application of policy requirements (see NPPG paragraphs 001 and 019), the policy approach in the Core Strategy and SPD accords with the approach in the NPPG as summarised above.

The Developer's responsibility
47. I agree with Mr Buley (who appeared for the Secretary of State) and Mr Kolinsky QC that the effect of the policies in the London Plan and Islington Core Strategy (together with the NPPG) is that where an applicant seeking planning permission for residential development in Islington proposes that the "maximum reasonable amount of affordable housing" is lower than the borough-wide 50% target on viability grounds, it is his responsibility to demonstrate that that is so.

48. The relevant policy framework here is not materially distinguishable from that considered by HHJ Gilbart QC (as he then was) in *Vicarage Gate Limited v First Secretary of State* [2007] EWHC 768 (Admin) at paragraphs 44 to 54. He held that where, in the context of determining a planning application, a policy requires a party (eg. an applicant) to demonstrate a state of affairs, then although it is correct to say that he is not under a *legal* burden of proof, the effect in forensic terms is nevertheless similar. "The decision-maker will still be looking for the party identified by the policy to adduce evidence of the kind prescribed by the policy to the standard set by the policy" (paragraph 48). In such a case, it is permissible for an Inspector to reject that party's case as lacking sufficient cogency to satisfy the policy (paragraph 54). Thus, a policy requirement can give rise to an *evidential* burden. In *Harris v First Secretary of State* [2007] EWHC 1847 (Admin), Lloyd-Jones J (as he then was) took the same approach (paragraphs 43 to 44).

49. Mr Harris QC placed emphasis upon the reference in paragraph (c) of Policy 3.12A of the London Plan to "the need to encourage rather than restrain residential

development". But this is only one of eight matters in paragraphs (a) to (h) to which decision-makers should have regard and Policy 3.12A does not give paragraph (c) any additional, let alone overriding, weight as against the seven other criteria. Accordingly, paragraph (c) provides no basis for distinguishing in this case the approach set out in *Vicarage Gate* and *Harris*.

RICS Professional Guidance: Financial Viability in Planning
50. Although this is not a planning policy document, it is helpful to refer to it next because it has been relied upon in certain planning policy documents and in the 2017 decision letter. It explains some of the valuation concepts to which they refer. The document was published in August 2012. Page 1 explains its status so far as members of the Royal Institution of Chartered Surveyors are concerned. It is not a "practice statement" laying down mandatory requirements to which members must adhere. Instead, it is a "guidance note" which "provides users with recommendations for accepted good practice as followed by competent and conscientious practitioners." The note points out that it is for each surveyor to decide on the appropriate procedure to follow in any particular case. But where members do not follow the practice recommended in the document, "they should do so only for a good reason."

51. The RICS note states that the residual valuation method is an accepted method for the valuation of development schemes and land. It is used, for example, where direct comparison with other transactions is not possible because of "the individuality of development projects" (paragraph 2.2.1). It can be used to establish a residual site value for *the landowner,* by assuming an appropriate level of return for *the developer* (paragraph 2.2.2). The majority of financial viability assessments use the residual approach, but it is important both to benchmark and to have regard to comparable market evidence in so far as that is available (paragraph 2.2.3).

52. Paragraph 2.3.1 defines "site value" as a benchmark in the following terms:

"Site Value should equate to the market value subject to the following assumption: that the value has regard to development plan policies and all other material planning considerations and disregards that which is contrary to the development plan."

"Market value" is defined as:

"The estimated amount for which an asset should exchange on the date of valuation between a willing buyer and a willing seller in an arm's length transaction after proper marketing wherein the parties had each acted knowledgably, prudently and without compulsion."

This is essentially the same explanation as that given by Hoffmann LJ in *IRC v Gray.* The RICS's definition of site value is consistent with paragraph 023 of the NPPG (see paragraphs 38 to 40 above).

53. Paragraphs 3.6.1.1 to 3.6.1.2 state that the price actually paid for the site may or may not be relevant to assessing financial viability according to how closely the price

paid conforms to the definition of "site value" (including compliance with planning policy). As the Guidance Note says:

> "A viability appraisal is taken at a point in time, taking account of costs and values at that date. A site may be purchased some time before a viability assessment takes place and circumstances might change. This is part of the developer's risk. Land values can go up or down between the date of purchase and a viability assessment taking place; in a rising market developers benefit, in a falling market they may lose out.
>
> A developer may make unreasonable/over-optimistic assumptions regarding the type and density of development or the extent of planning obligations, which means that it has overpaid for the site."

54. At DL25 the Inspector referred to paragraph 4.2.1 of the Guidance note which identifies the importance of viability assessment being "supported by *adequate* comparable evidence" (emphasis added).

55. Paragraph 3.4.7 of the Guidance Note also identifies difficulties in using comparable evidence:

> "Sale prices of comparable development sites may provide an indication of the land value that a landowner might expect, but it is important to note that, depending on the planning status of the land, the market price will include risk-adjusted expectations of the nature of the permission and associated planning obligations. If these market prices are used in the negotiation of planning obligations then account should be taken of any expectation of planning obligations that are embedded in the market price, or valuation in the absence of a price. In many cases, relevant and up-to-date comparable evidence may not be available, or the diversity of development sites requires an approach not based on direct comparison."

Box 13 summarises the position by stating that even limited comparable evidence is important for establishing site value, provided that it is "appropriate".

56. In a similar vein the Inspector noted in DL 23 that:

> "Para 4.4 of the RICS Valuation Information Paper 12 states "Generally, high density or complex developments, urban sites and existing buildings with development potential, do not easily lend themselves to valuation by comparison. The differences from site to site (for example in terms of development potential or construction cost) may be sufficient to make the analysis of transactions problematical. The higher the number of variables and adjustments for assumptions, the less useful the comparison."

57. Paragraph 3.4.1 of the Guidance Note describes the estimation of site value using EUV. The approach involves the addition of a premium, often between 10 and 40% to EUV (see the Glossary in Appendix F) to arrive at a value at which it is supposed

that a reasonable land owner would sell. This method is referred to as "EUV Plus". The Guidance Note discourages reliance upon EUV Plus as the sole basis for arriving at site value, because the uplift is an arbitrary number and the method does not reflect the workings of the market. Furthermore, the EUV Plus method is not based upon the value of the land if the redevelopment involves a different land use (eg. an office building redeveloped for a residential scheme).

58. On the other hand, the Guidance Note recognises (paragraph 3.4.1) that once the land value of a site has been established (an "outcome"), that figure can be disaggregated or re-expressed as an EUV plus a premium, which may be of assistance in judging, or cross-checking, the reasonableness of the site value which has been found by other means.

Housing Supplementary Planning Guidance
59. This policy document was adopted by the Mayor of London in March 2016. Notwithstanding the views expressed in the RICS's 2012 Guidance Note on the EUV Plus method, paragraph 4.1.4 of the SPG states:

> "On balance, the Mayor has found that the 'Existing Use Value plus' approach is generally most appropriate for planning purposes, not least because of the way it can be used to address the need to ensure that development is sustainable in terms of the NPPF and Local Plan requirements, he therefore supports this approach. The 'plus' elements will vary on a case by case basis based on the circumstances of the site and owner and policy requirements. "

60. Paragraph 4.1.5 of the SPG states:

> "4.1.5 A 'Market Value' approach is only acceptable where, in line with the NPPG the value reflects all policy requirements and planning obligations and any CIL charges. Recent research carried out by RICS found that the 'Market Value' approach is not being applied correctly and "if market value is based on comparable evidence without proper adjustment to reflect policy compliant planning obligations, this introduces a circularity, which encourages developers to overpay for sites and try to recover some or all of this overpayment via reductions in planning obligations" (RICS 2015 p 26). Thus, a market value approach should only be accepted where it can be demonstrated to properly reflect policy requirements and take account of site specific circumstances. In many cases this will require an adjustment of market comparables to take account of policy compliant planning obligations."

61. In November 2016 the Mayor issued a draft SPG "Homes for Londoners" for consultation. This document reinforces his preference for the EUV Plus method and suggests that other methods would only be considered in exceptional circumstances and if robustly justified (see paragraphs 3.36 and 3.42 to 3.47).

Islington LBC — Development Viability SPD
62. This Supplementary Planning Document was adopted in January 2016. Paragraph 6.48 explains that the "EUV plus" approach is commonly used to assess

whether a residual land value from a development scheme provides a competitive return for the landowner. LBI takes the view that the EUV Plus approach should form the primary basis for determining BLV in most cases (paragraph 6.52).

63. The Council also accepts that comparable, market-based evidence can be used to inform the BLV (paragraphs 6.58 to 6.59). But in paragraph 6.60 the SPG points out that there are a number of potential difficulties in the transparent analysis of market transactions for land:

- "The full facts of past transactions are rarely available and bids for land may have overestimated actual value.
- There is potential for transactions to not fully reflect current planning policy requirements such as those relating to affordable housing and density, as required by PPG *in all cases.*
- Sites may have a differing 'inherent' value depending on the presence or absence and nature of income generating existing uses.
- Land transactions are typically based on assumptions of growth in values (whereas viability assessments are normally based on current values).
- Transactions may relate to sites of different sizes, densities, mix of uses and costs to facilitate development.
- Reliance on transactions that are not comparable, that do not reflect the Development Plan policies as they relate to the application site, or that are based on assumptions of growth may lead to inflated site values. This would restrict the ability to secure development that is sustainable and consistent with the Development Plan."

Consequently, paragraph 6.61 states that it is vital that transactions are "genuinely comparable and that they reflect planning policy."

A summary of the issues between the parties in these proceedings
64. Mr Harris QC reordered the Claimant's grounds of challenge. Beginning with ground 2 he submitted that the Inspector's decision to accept LBI's BLV of £6.75m was based upon his acceptance of a method advanced by its expert Mr Andrew Jones ("the Jones method"), a comparative method of valuation which claimed to analyse market data in a manner which addressed the circularity issue and avoided the need to make large numbers of adjustments to reflect differences between sites (see eg. paragraphs 4.55 to 4.57 of Mr Jones's proof). Mr Harris submitted that it was shown at the inquiry that this method was logically flawed and did not achieve what it claimed to do. The Inspector did not address those important points in his decision, and he applied the Jones method in a manner which was inconsistent with his understanding of it. Lastly, under ground 2 it was submitted that the Inspector failed to recognise in his decision letter substantial changes in LBI's valuation case by the time the end of the inquiry was reached.

65. Under ground 3 the Claimant advances criticisms of the way in which the Inspector treated certain comparable transactions when arriving at his decision to accept LBI's BLV figure of £6.75m.

66. Under ground 1 it is said that the Inspector erred in concluding that LBI's case was based on the EUV Plus approach, and that this was supported by recent policy statements. It is plain that LBI did not use an EUV Plus method in order to arrive at a BLV of £6.75m.

67. The Defendants resist each of these contentions. But they also submit that, in any event, the Claimant's criticisms do not vitiate the essential conclusions in the decision letter upon which the Inspector decided that PRL's proposal failed to provide "the maximum reasonable amount of affordable housing." Between DL 42 and 49 the Inspector explained why he thought PRL's valuation exercise was flawed and accordingly it had failed to show that no more than 10% affordable housing could reasonably be provided on the site. Thus, the proposal conflicted with important planning policies (DL 70 and DL 96). The Claimant has not made any legal challenge to the findings in DL 42 to 49, which remain unaffected by the criticisms advanced against other parts of the decision letter. Although the Inspector accepted the LBI's BLV of £6.75m, he did not go so far as to accept their case that 34% affordable housing should be provided. It was sufficient for the Inspector to dismiss the appeal that he did not accept that 10% was adequate, given the policy framework and the principle set out in the *Vicarage Gate*_decision.

68. In order to address these rival contentions, it is necessary examine how LBI put its case at the 2017 inquiry.

LBI's case at the 2017 Inquiry
69. The inquiry sat in January 2017 and then adjourned to two different weeks in March before finally concluding on 27 April 2017. During that time additional evidence was adduced by both of the principal parties and the valuation evidence was altered. Both sides made closing submissions in writing. PRL sought to address LBI's case as it stood by the end of the inquiry. Accordingly, in this hearing both parties looked to LBI's closing submissions to identify the contentions it was advancing at that stage, by way of both evidence and submission.

70. Between paragraphs 91 and 204 of their closing submissions LBI examined the evidence before the inquiry and how it related to the relevant policy requirements topic by topic. The LBI's submissions then drew the threads together (paragraphs 205 to 206), made submissions as to why PRL's approach did not address the "circularity problem" (paragraphs 207 to 213), dealt with sense-checking (paragraphs 214 to 219), explained why the 2015 decision letter had failed to address the circularity problem (paragraphs 220 to 225) and concluded by submitting (paragraphs 225 to 230) that: -

i)   PRL's use of market evidence to appraise site value did not make necessary adjustments for differences between comparables and the assumptions required to be made for the appeal site applying paragraph 023 of the PPG and RICS guidance;
ii)   PRL's revised site value of £11.9m should be rejected;
iii) PRL's proposal of 10% affordable housing was inadequate because its estimate of BLV was unsound.

In their conclusions (paragraph 302 to 306), LBI submitted that PRL had not shown that the proposal provided the maximum reasonable amount of affordable housing and so the appeal should be dismissed.

71. LBI referred to the common ground that the EUV of the appeal site was nominal and submitted that, for the delivery of affordable housing, the site benefited from not having to overcome the "constraint" of a high EUV. LBI's case was that this negligible EUV was a relevant factor in determining BLV. Because a reasonable landowner would have no other use for the land, he would be incentivised to release it for residential development so as to be able to gain a return. It was therefore pointless to debate the difference between a BLV of £6.75m or £11.9m in terms of a percentage or absolute uplift in value for the landowner from EUV. Even the lower number represented "a very large premium indeed over the existing use value" (paragraphs 91 to 99).

72. LBI noted that PRL had not sought to rely upon any AUV in order to derive the BLV. The appeal site was not constrained by a high AUV for some different use from the residential scheme proposed which the latter would have to overcome. Furthermore, the residential capacity of the appeal site had become "ascertainable and reasonably firmly settled". The proposed scheme for 96 units represented the optimum use of the land (paragraphs 100 to 109).

73. LBI dealt with residual land valuations at paragraphs 110 to 124 of its closing submissions. In summary, LBI submitted: -

i)   Although sensitive to small changes in inputs, a residual valuation has the potential to provide a "helpful signpost" for what the BLV should be, particularly in the valuation of complex sites for which comparable evidence is hard to come by;

ii)   The range of residual land values is a relevant part of the evidence base for testing the BLV's adopted by each side at the inquiry;

iii)   During the inquiry, Mr Jones, LBI's valuer, had substantially revised his residual valuation downwards to £2.4m, with the consequence that it no longer "actively support[ed]" his BLV of £6.75m, but that did not mean that residual land values had ceased to be a material part of the overall evidence base;

iv)   When CBRE's residual valuation relied upon by PRL was adjusted to provide 50% affordable housing instead of an assumed 16%, the residual land value was £7.32m, very much closer to Mr Jones's BLV of £6.75m;

v)   But care must be taken to avoid misusing residual appraisals. Because PRL's expert valuer, Mr Fourt, had inappropriately continued to use a BLV of £13.26m as a *fixed* input in those appraisals, as the development capacity of the site had been progressively reduced, so the affordable housing proportion had been artificially diminished. Instead, the proper approach was to reassess site value by taking proper account of both development capacity and policy requirements as inputs.

74. LBI's primary submissions on market evidence were contained in paragraphs 125 to 193 of their closing. In summary, LBI submitted: -

i)   It is necessary to look for comparable evidence as close as possible to that which is being valued, to ascertain the circumstances of those transactions, and make appropriate and transparent adjustments to reflect (a) differences from the appeal site and (b) the assumptions required by paragraph 023 of the PPG and the RICS Guidance Note. Whether evidence can properly be regarded as comparable can be affected by difficulties in making such adjustments, including the extent to which a market bid has disregarded or diminished the effect of planning policy requirements (paragraphs 125 to 130);

ii)   No weight could be placed upon the price paid for the site in 2013 in different market conditions and with inflated expectations as to the development capacity of the site. The development appraisal which would have been prepared by PRL to inform its bid for the site had not been produced to the inquiry (paragraphs 133 to 143);

iii)   There was insufficient information on the factors which had informed competing bids for the site in 2013 (eg. site capacity or level of affordable housing) and so no sensible conclusions could be drawn from this material (paragraphs 144 to 151);

iv)   No weight could be placed on the unsolicited offer in May 2015 by an unsuccessful bidder in the 2013 sale because of the absence of any information on the assumptions which had informed that offer (paragraph 152);

v)   CBRE's residual valuation approach undermined PRL's case and supported LBI's position for reasons summarised in paragraph 73(iv) above (paragraphs 153 to 155);

vi)   Mr Fourt's attempt to identify "market norms" for deriving land value from 27 transactions was of no use. A good many of the sites were not remotely comparable. Some did not involve the application of relevant planning policies. The range of factors affecting the sites prevented the making of meaningful comparisons with the appeal site (paragraphs 156 to 162). Mr Kolinsky showed the court paragraphs 6.4 to 6.8 of Mr Fourt's proof which stated that his analysis of the 27 transactions in Islington between 2010 and 2016 had been "deliberately high level". It made no adjustments for planning permission, location, planning obligations or site specific development costs. The exercise simply involved averaging all this high level data and stating that the level of affordable housing provided had been 16% on average. A second exercise which adjusted for land price inflation but which otherwise averaged the data set produced similar answers;

vii)   Mr Fourt's five "key comparables" did not, as a set, provide a reliable foundation for drawing conclusions on the value of the appeal site, given the differences between them although the Coppetts Wood Hospital site was "more promising" (paragraphs 163 to 170). Mr Kolinsky showed the court those parts of Mr Fourt's evidence which dealt with this material so as to confirm that he made no adjustments to deal with, for example, differences between the sites. However, LBI submitted to the Inspector that analysis of three of the sites more closely comparable to the appeal site produced figures for land value much nearer to LBI's assessment than PRL's, even before making any other necessary adjustments (eg. for high EUVs) which might well have reduced the analysed land value further (paragraphs 171 to 175);

viii) LBI relied upon 351 Caledonian Road because of its comparability to the appeal site in terms of location and size and submitted that it indicated a land value for the appeal site of £6.432m (paragraphs 176 to 192);

ix) A pattern of evidence supported Mr Jones's opinion that the BLV was £6.75m, namely the winning bid for the site even if adjusted solely for development capacity (£8.32m), 351 Caledonian Road (£6.432m) and a per unit analysis of Mr Fourt's 3 best comparables (using figures accepted by Mr Fourt), subject to the need for further adjustments (paragraph 193).

75. It is important to note that in paragraph 194 of its closing submissions, LBI submitted that the analysis could and should stop there. In other words, it was submitted that the evidence before the Inspector, particularly that relied upon by PRL was inadequate to show that the proposed scheme included "the maximum reasonable amount of affordable housing". However, paragraphs 195 to 200 of LBI's closing submissions dealt with an additional issue which had arisen at the inquiry, namely what *unit* should be used in order to express data on other transactions in terms which could be *compared* with the appeal site. I will return to this subject when dealing with ground 2 of the challenge.

76. In paragraphs 201 to 204 of its closing, LBI submitted that distortions introduced by the use of indexation to adjust for differences in the dates of transactions should be addressed by confining the exercise to "sufficiently recent" comparables.

77. In "drawing the threads together" LBI submitted that a proper approach to site value should take account of the negligible EUV, the very substantial premium over EUV available as an opportunity to incentivise a reasonable landowner to sell whilst at the same time meeting reasonable planning requirements, the absence of any AUV or realistic opportunity to realise an alternative to the development proposed and the fact that the development capacity of the appeal site had become fairly well-established. BLV should also be informed by market value, having regard to the extent to which it is possible to achieve sufficient comparability and the need for proper and transparent adjustments to render any comparisons valid and to accord with paragraph 023 of the PPG and RICS guidance. Without relying upon differences of approach to "per unit analysis," LBI explained why Mr Jones's approach to BLV gave effect to these considerations and Mr Fourt's did not (paragraph 205 to 206). LBI explained why it considered that PRL's evidence, including its generalised evidence asserting "market norms" failed to address the "circularity" problem (paragraphs 207 to 213).

78. At paragraph 214 to 219 of its closing LBI set out its submissions on why PRL's BLV of £11.9m failed tests for sense-checking. For example, LBI referred to "relatively unconstrained" sites which had yielded affordable housing between 38% and 50% of total units and submitted that site-specific circumstances explained why lower contributions had been made on other sites (see paragraph 215). LBI also suggested that an approach which used uncontroversial inputs, but allowed for affordable housing requirements to be taken into account as a further input, would produce much lower residual land values for the appeal site than £11.9m (paragraphs 217 to 218).

79. At paragraphs 220 to 227 of its closing, LBI explained why DL 73 to 75 of the 2015 decision letter should be treated as having failed to address the "circularity" problem identified in DL 72.

80. LBI asked the Inspector to reject PRL's approach to BLV and its value of £11.9m and as a consequence, the proposal to provide only 10% of the units as affordable housing.

A summary of the 2017 decision letter

...

87. There then followed an important conclusion by the Inspector: -

"In this case, the appellant has not provided as evidence the assumptions made in its viability appraisal supporting its winning bid for the site and this information is also unavailable for the other bidders, or any other 'comparable' site identified. Therefore, I treat the market evidence provided with some caution. That is not to diminish the importance of market evidence as a key consideration in determining land value, but it must be truly comparable and meet the other aspects of PPG guidance at paragraph 023 on viability."

That conclusion underlay the remainder of the Inspector's reasoning on the BLV issue. It should be noted that Mr Harris QC did not seek to challenge it. Indeed, it could not be challenged.

...

Ground 1
94. It is convenient to deal with the Claimant's grounds in the order set out in the claim. PRL submits that the Inspector erred in law because in DL 14 and DL 15 he incorrectly stated that LBI was promoting an EUV Plus method of valuation when that was not the case, he relied upon recent policy as endorsing the use of that approach and he relied upon his erroneous misunderstanding of the Council's position as one reason for not accepting PRL's contention that a market value approach was "the only reasonable means by which to establish the land value". The Claimant adds that the Inspector's error was all the more significant because in reality LBI had advanced a purely market-based approach and so DL 14 was flawed by an internal inconsistency.

95. Mr Kolinsky referred to paragraph 4.16 and 4.19 of Mr Jones's proof of evidence. At that stage his residual valuation of the site was £7.15m. He relied upon the percentage and absolute size of the uplift that represented over an "optimistic" EUV of £700,000 as providing "a more than adequate incentive" to the landowner to release the site for development. Similarly Mr Wacher, LBI's Development Viability Manager, stated that although the BLV in this case could not be *derived* by adding a percentage of up to 30% to EUV, nonetheless comparison of the value generated by the development for the landowner with the EUV still remained "highly relevant". An estimated BLV of £6.75m was said to represent a return of about

9 times the EUV, which was competitive and sufficient to incentivise a reasonable landowner to sell the site (paragraph 6.30 of rebuttal proof). This approach was relied upon by LBI in its closing submissions (see paragraph 71 above). The uplift was said to represent the sufficient "plus" or premium for the landowner.

96. The approach taken by LBI was entirely consistent with paragraph 3.4.1 of the RICS Guidance Note (see paragraph 58 above). The figure which Mr Jones had arrived at by £6.75m was re-expressed as an EUV plus a premium, in order to judge the reasonableness of the BLV figure which had been arrived at.

97. At DL 19 the Inspector said: -

"Having engaged with market evidence, something that it failed to do in the previous appeal, the Council consider that a value of £6.75m is the appropriate BLV, including a significant uplift above the EUV, and representing the Plus element of the EUV Plus approach."

This confirms that the Inspector correctly understood the way in which LBI had used the EUV Plus method in accordance with paragraph 3.4.1 of the RICS Guidance Note. DL 40 does not suggest any inconsistency in the Inspector's reasoning. He considered that the EUV Plus method, in the manner applied here, was an appropriate method in this case and preferable "to a *purely* market value approach, allowing for value to have regard to the market as a *consideration, rather than the determining factor*" (emphasis added). In that paragraph the Inspector was referring to his criticisms of PRL's purely market based approach, which he had already rejected in DL 31 to 36.

98. For these reasons I reject ground 1 of the challenge.

Ground 2

The Inspector's comments on using units of accommodation to compare land prices
99. In order to make a comparison between land prices on one site and another, valuers generally express the data they are analysing by reference to a common unit of comparison. So Mr Fourt analysed information in terms of, for example, price per acre, price per sq ft and price per habitable room (DL 31). Ground 2 relates to DL 26 to 30 where the Inspector considered three other comparative techniques using value *per unit of accommodation* which the parties had suggested.

100. In relation to a suggestion from LBI that land value be divided by the total number of units (both market and affordable housing) the Inspector said (DL 26): -

"this attributes value to the affordable housing units (where provided) and it is agreed between the parties that the commercial value of these is limited. It can, therefore, have the effect of artificially reducing land or site values when comparing sites that provided affordable housing against those that did not."

101. He then dealt with an approach suggested by PRL (DL 27): -

"The appellant seeks to discount the affordable housing units and divide the land value by the number of market units but this has the result of inflating the unit prices on schemes that have provided larger proportions of affordable housing, incorrectly giving an impression of higher land value. As the full circumstances that led to the various levels of affordable housing on other sites is unknown, neither of these methodologies is of particular value"

102. Mr Kolinsky QC explained that DL 27 related to a paradox pointed out at the inquiry by LBI (for example in paragraph 200 of their closing submissions). If a high price paid for a site was influenced by a low provision of affordable housing and that price is divided by a correspondingly high number of market units, that figure will be expressed as a relatively low land value per unit. But if a lower price paid for a site was influenced by a high provision of affordable housing, and is then divided by a relatively low number of market units, that figure will be expressed as a relatively high land value per unit. These relationships "turn things on their head".

103. PRL does not seek to challenge the Inspector's comments in DL 26 and DL 27 on those two approaches.

104. The challenge relates to an approach put forward by Mr Jones (DL 28): -

"A more reliable comparison is the Council's methodology, which assumes a 50% affordable housing contribution for all transactions analysed (as the starting point in policy) and to divide the land purchase price by the remaining 50% market dwellings. Whilst actual affordable housing provision on various sites differs, this can be assumed to account for downward revisions from 50% affordable housing provision in light of site specific circumstances evidenced in those individual planning applications. *Therefore*, this method allows a comparison across sites without being affected by differing levels of affordable housing provision and avoids importing assumptions and circumstances from other sites that do not apply to the appeal site." (emphasis added).

105. At paragraphs 4.56 to 4.57 of his proof Mr Jones contended that by using a divisor based on a number of market units which assumed that 50% affordable housing had been provided on each site, whether or not that was the case, he was adjusting land value so as to (i) reflect LBI's policy, (ii) avoid the issue of "circularity" and (iii) comply with paragraph 023 of the PPG.

106. Plainly, a challenge to an Inspector's judgment on valuation matters which is no more than a disagreement with his or her assessment of the merits, cannot be advanced under the guise of a complaint of Wednesbury unreasonableness (*Newsmith Stainless Limited v Secretary of State for the Environment, Transport and the Regions* [2017] PTSR 1126 paragraphs 6 to 7). But an irrationality challenge may succeed where it is shown, for example, that the decision proceeds from flawed logic or "an error of reasoning which robs the decision of logic" (*R v Parliamentary Commissioner for Administration ex parte Balchin* [1996] EWHC Admin 152 at paragraph 27; *R v North and East Devon Health Authority ex parte Coughlan* [2001]

QB 213, 244 at paragraph 65). That was how Mr Harris QC presented his main challenge under ground 2.

107. PRL's case before the Inspector on this subject was set out in their closing submissions at paragraphs 299 to 324. In summary, PRL demonstrated that Mr Jones's method did not produce a land value which reflected the policy target of 50% affordable housing at all. Whatever level of affordable housing was assumed in Mr Jones's method (whether 50% or some other percentage), it would always generate the same BLV. In his approach the level of affordable housing, rather than being a factor which in part defined the BLV, was treated in effect as being irrelevant to it. Arithmetically this was so because the 50% assumption used to determine the unit of comparison, the divisor applied to the land price, was also used to determine BLV for the appeal site when the per unit figure was applied to 50% of the 96 units to be constructed on that site. The choice of the 50% affordable housing parameter turned out to be self-cancelling and of no consequence to the exercise. The same would apply to any alternative affordable housing percentage used in Mr Jones's method.

108. This should not have come as any surprise to the parties at the inquiry because the exercises carried out in Tables 4 and 5 of Mr Jones's proof, the latter expressing land price per *total* number of units and the former per *market* unit (assuming 50% affordable housing), both produced a land value for the appeal site of £5.29m as an average across the transactions analysed. Not only is this apparent from a simple inspection of the two tables, it was explicitly stated in paragraph 4.77 of Mr Jones's proof. Not surprisingly therefore, neither Defendant sought to refute Mr Harris's submission on this particular point.

109. However, it is necessary for the court to articulate the flawed logic in Mr Jones's method, and not simply rely upon Mr Harris's arithmetical exercise. There are at least two points. First, if an actual land price was inflated by an over-optimistic expectation about the overall development capacity of the site, that price may nonetheless have assumed a correct proportion of affordable housing, planning obligations and other development costs. An erroneous judgment about the site's capacity is not corrected by applying a 50% affordable housing assumption to the number of units on the site. Halving the per unit divisor has nothing to do with removing that flaw in the land price. That should be addressed by adjusting the land price to a proper basis.

110. This first point is but one example of a second, more fundamental flaw in Mr Jones's method. It assumes that any differences between comparables and the appeal site can be properly allowed for simply by applying the 50% affordable housing assumption to the divisor and that no adjustment needs to be made to the land price itself before it is expressed in a comparative form, whether that be per unit of accommodation or per unit of area. The appeal site suffered from no unusual physical or economic constraints. The price paid for another site might have been high relative to the appeal site because of a high EUV and/or AUV. Alternatively, the price may have been influenced by abnormal development and planning costs, which in turn may explain why a lower contribution of affordable housing had been properly justified. Mr Jones's method illogically assumes that there is no need to adjust the

land price because the approach taken to the divisor addresses all such differences between sites. Plainly it cannot. Whatever *number of units* the land price is divided by, the effect of these differences on land price remains in the numerator and therefore in the per unit figure derived from that price.

111. For these reasons, I am unable to accept Mr Buley's submission that the second sentence of DL 28 explains the third sentence of that paragraph or anything in DL 29. The logic in DL 28 was flawed in so far as the Inspector was led by LBI to accept that Mr Jones's approach overcame the problem of comparison between land prices being affected by differences in the levels of affordable housing provided or by assumptions and circumstances affecting other sites which were inapplicable to the appeal site (last sentence of DL 28).

112. The next and essential question is whether the legal error in DL 28 vitiated the basis upon which the Inspector rejected PRL's case that a 10% affordable housing provision represented the maximum reasonable level. It is a well-established principle that, if it can be seen from reasoning in the decision letter untainted by the legal error identified that the Inspector would necessarily have reached the same decision, namely to dismiss the appeal, if his decision has not contained that error, then the Court will exercise its discretion against the quashing of the decision. In such circumstances the error is treated as being of no materiality or significance to the legal validity of the decision (*Simplex GE (Holdings) Limited v Secretary of State for the Environment* [2017] PTSR 1041; *R (Smith) v NE Derbyshire PCT* [2006] 1 WLR 3315; *R (Smech Properties) v Runnymede BC* [2016] JPL 677 at paras 25 to 39; *Secretary of State for Communities and Local Government v South Gloucestershire Council* [2016] JPL 798 at paras. 24 to 29). Because a decision on a planning appeal must be expressed through a formal document setting out the Inspector's reasons in accordance with a statutory obligation, the court may more readily be able to see whether the error *might* have made a difference to the outcome arrived at by the Inspector, or whether the court can be satisfied from untainted reasoning that his decision would inevitably have been the same. The *Simplex* exercise does not involve the court second-guessing what might happen on any future redetermination if the decision were to be quashed. That would beg the question which the court is to decide (*Goodman Logistics Developments (UK) Ltd v Secretary of State for Communities and Local Government* [2017] JPL 1115 at paras. 95–98).

113. As I have already explained, PRL's case that it had discharged the policy requirement to provide the reasonable maximum level of affordable housing was in any event rejected by the Inspector for the reasons given in DL 31 to 36 and DL 38 to 48. In this context it is also important to note that the Inspector's wholesale and robust rejection of the Claimant's valuation case was supplemented by his rejection at DL 49 of its incorrect approach to the application of development plan policy. None of the Inspector's reasoning in these paragraphs was affected by his earlier comments in DL 28 on the approach of Mr Jones to *per unit comparison*, or by his comments in DL 26 to 27 on the use of other forms of *per unit comparison*. The Inspector's rejection of PRL's viability case was based upon entirely different and very much more fundamental criticisms. No legal challenge has been made to any part of DL31 to 36 and DL 38 to 48.

114. I appreciate that in DL 37 the Inspector stated that he preferred Mr Jones's method of comparing market data to others, but I cannot accept the submission that this tainted his rejection of PRL's viability case. Plainly, the rejection at DL 40 to 48 of PRL's valuation exercises relating to *the appeal site itself* had nothing to do with that method. The Inspector's earlier rejection at DL 31 to 36 of PRL's comparative analysis of market evidence did not rely upon Mr Jones's method (or the criticism in DL 27 of Mr Fourt's approach). The criticisms made of PRL's viability case were free-standing points largely drawn from LBI's case in its closing submissions preceding paragraph 195. They were not therefore related to the technique described in DL 28 (or indeed in DL 26 to 27). For example, the Inspector criticised PRL's evidence because the variables between sites were unknown and/or adjustments had not been made. There has been no challenge to that reasoning. The fact that the Inspector did not appreciate that the particular method identified in DL 28 also suffered from these problems does not vitiate his positive reasons for rejecting the Claimant's valuation case, especially in the context where it was for the Claimant to justify its proposal that 10% affordable housing represented the maximum reasonable amount that could be provided (see paragraphs 47 to 49 above).

115. Mr Harris QC sought to demonstrate that the Inspector's criticisms of PRL's evidence were tainted by his acceptance of LBI's BLV figure of £6.75m. He contended that that figure was derived, indeed solely derived from Mr Jones's method described in DL 28. I reject that submission for a number of reasons.

116. Ironically, the first reason involves PRL's own arithmetical demonstration of the flawed logic of Mr Jones's alternative basis of comparison (see paragraph 107 above). Whether the divisor used by Mr Jones assumed 50% affordable housing (i.e. his table 4) or the total number of units provided (his table 5), or assumed any other percentage of affordable housing, the land value he derived for the appeal site would still be £5.29m (see paragraph 108 above and paragraph 4.77 of Mr Jones's proof). Mr Harris QC was therefore wrong to insist that the BLV shown in Mr Jones's table 1 was based solely on the exercise in his table 4 using the method described in DL 28. For completeness, I should mention that during the hearing there was a dispute as to whether Mr Jones had conceded this point. The court cannot resolve such a dispute in proceedings of this nature. But, in any event, there is no need to do so because, as I have explained, the point is academic. It is therefore right to say that Mr Jones's table 1 relied in part upon the figure of £5.29m derived from his table 5.

117. Plainly, Mr Jones's BLV figure of £6.75m was significantly greater than £5.29m. According to DL 29, that was explained by a weighting exercise which Mr Jones had carried out, although the Inspector did not find it necessary to rely upon that further analysis.

118. Second, it is plain from table 1 and from LBI's closing submissions that the Council also relied upon residual valuation to support the figure of £6.75m. In table 1 Mr Jones had also relied upon his residual valuation of £7.15m as part of a basket of material. That assumed 50% affordable housing provision. By the end of the inquiry that valuation had fallen to £2.4m and did not "actively support" Mr Jones's judgment that the BLV was £6.75m (see also DL 19). But paragraph 116 of LBI's

closing submissions nevertheless relied upon a residual valuation approach to support the figure of £6.75m (paragraph 73(iv) above). In my judgment there was no legal requirement for the Inspector to refer explicitly to that particular point in his decision letter. That document was addressed to the parties on the basis that they would be familiar with the cases which had been advanced and the way in which they had evolved by the end of the inquiry.

119. Third, the Inspector found that the evidence on the Coppetts Wood Hospital transaction supported LBI's BLV of £6.75m. That was a matter of judgment for the Inspector and is not open to legal challenge.

120. Fourth, the Inspector was aware of limitations in Mr Jones's comparative technique (see DL 30). But, in any event, in DL 49 to 50 he decided that the majority of the evidence before him was "not adequately comparable" to provide a robust justification by PRL for the level of affordable housing it had proposed. On the other hand, other evidence which he considered to be of value showed that LBI's BLV of £6.75m was "not out of kilter with the market" (see DL 34 and 35). Plainly this was so very much lower than PRL's figures of £13.26m revised downwards to £11.9m, which were closely related to the price paid in May 2013, that in DL 50 the Inspector said that "an inflated land value [should not] be subsidised by a reduction in affordable housing".

121. Accordingly, I am satisfied from reasoning in the decision letter that is untainted by the legal error I have identified, that the Inspector's decision to reject the adequacy of the proportion of affordable housing proposed would inevitably have been the same if he had not made that error. It follows that the decision should not be quashed because of that error.

122. I should add that in DL 73 to 82, 92 and 96 the Inspector dismissed the appeal for a further reason, namely the inadequacy of the review mechanism contained in PRL's unilateral undertaking under section 106 dated 27 April 2017. This formed part of his consideration of the second main issue defined in DL 4. No legal challenge has been made to that part of the decision letter. Furthermore, PRL has not suggested that the legal error arising from DL 28 influenced in any way the Inspector's reasons for deciding that the review mechanism in the undertaking was unacceptable and conflicted with relevant planning policies. The Inspector explicitly stated in DL 78 that:

> "These matters alone render the submitted [unilateral undertaking] incapable of securing an appropriate review mechanism, were the appeal to succeed."

This freestanding basis for the dismissal of the appeal constitutes a separate reason as to why the decision should not be quashed because of the legal error identified above.

Whether there was an internal inconsistency in the decision letter
123. Next, Mr Harris QC criticised the Inspector for applying Mr Jones's method as described in DL 28 in an inconsistent manner. In DL 29 the Inspector stated that this method could only be applied to sites purchased without planning permission, but in DL 30 he referred to evidence on 12 sites, 5 of which had the benefit of planning

permission. Although this was a point made by Mr Fourt, PRL complains that the Inspector did not address it.

124. In view of my rejection of the main points raised by PRL under ground 2, this complaint raises no additional point of any significance. The Inspector's rejection of PRL's affordable housing proposal was based upon its own intrinsic lack of merit. It did not depend upon the application of the method described in DL 28, nor therefore could it have been affected by any defective application of that method.

125. Although it is unnecessary to go further, I also accept the argument in paragraph 57 of LBI's skeleton. As the Inspector recognised, sites with planning permission would have a relatively higher value than sites without permission (all other things being equal). The appeal site did not have planning permission. Accordingly, the removal of sites with planning permission, and therefore relatively more valuable than those without, would have the effect of reducing the average value of the remaining sites. That works against the Claimant's argument that the BLV should have been greater. It would increase the "headroom," thus enabling a greater level of affordable housing to be provided.

Adequacy of reasons
126. Finally under ground 2, PRL criticises the Inspector for failing to address part of LBI's case (and PRL's response) as it had evolved by the close of the inquiry. Mr Harris referred to the three aspects summarised in paragraph 193 of LBI's closing submissions (see paragraph 74(ix) above). The complaint is that the Inspector made no mention of (a) the adjustment of the 2013 purchase price of the appeal site for its reduced development capacity and (b) the evidence on 351 Caledonian Road as a comparable. It is suggested that he had not appreciated how far LBI's case had altered by the end of the inquiry. Essentially, this was a reasons challenge.

127. It is well-established that an Inspector does not have to rehearse every point or argument raised by a party (see *Bloor* at paragraph 19). The Inspector is not writing an examination paper. To require him to refer to every material consideration would impose an unjustifiable burden. Consequently, an argument that an Inspector has not understood the materiality of a point to the decision, must necessarily be limited to the main issues and "then only when all other known facts and circumstances appear to point overwhelmingly to a different decision". In order to establish a reasons challenge a claimant must show that the decision letter gives rise to "a substantial doubt" as to whether the decision-maker made an error of law. Even then, a claimant must show that he has been substantially prejudiced by the legally inadequate reasoning, for example, by a developer being unable to assess the prospects of obtaining an alternative planning permission (*South Bucks DC v Porter (No 2)* [2004] 1 WLR 1953, 1961–4).

128. In my judgment, there was no legal requirement for the Inspector to refer expressly to the outcome of the exercise in which the purchase price paid in May 2013 was adjusted for a reduction in the development capacity of the site. In DL 42 to DL 45 the Inspector explained why he gave only "limited weight" to PRL's reliance on that purchase price. In DL 17, 24, 42 and 43, the Inspector was plainly

aware of the reduction in the capacity of the site and of the lack of evidence about the development assumptions underlying the various bids in the sale. The Inspector rejected PRL's case. There was no legal requirement for him to refer to a piece of evidence which only served to further undermine that case.

129. It is common ground that the Inspector did not refer to evidence on the transaction at 351 Caledonian Road. As I have already explained, that evidence was relied upon by LBI in order to support its assessment of the BLV (see paragraph 74(viii) above). Mr Harris QC sought to criticise LBI's analysis by reference to paragraph 192 of the Council's closing submissions because it involved the total number of unit method of comparison criticised in DL 26. In fact, PRL's Closing Submissions criticised LBI's reliance upon this material because of the use of Mr Jones's method of comparison referred to in DL 28. As we have seen there is no arithmetical difference between the two. Either way, this was simply a criticism of the figure of £6.432m derived by LBI from the evidence on 351 Caledonian Road. Mr Harris QC did not identify any further issue on this comparable, nor did he suggest that the PRL had sought to rely upon it in order to provide positive support for its case.

130. Given that the Inspector rejected PRL's affordable housing case for reasons which did not depend upon resolving any issue about the analysis of the comparable at 351 Caledonian Road, he was not legally obliged to deal with the issue identified by Mr Harris QC. Furthermore, the Inspector rejected PRL's case for reasons which did not depend upon his acceptance of LBI's BLV of £6.75m or the precise basis upon which that figure had been estimated.

131. In any event, PRL cannot show that it has been substantially prejudiced by the absence of any explicit reasoning on the two points which have been raised. The Claimant knows in legally sufficient detail why its affordable housing case was rejected. It knows that if it is to pursue a further proposal with only 10% affordable housing (or some other proportion less than 50%) it must put forward a "robust justification" for that case, which would include a viability assessment overcoming the defects in its evidence identified by the Inspector in the 2017 decision letter.

132 For all these reasons I reject the various challenges advanced under ground 2.

Ground 3

…

140. For these reasons I reject ground 3.

Conclusions
Outcome of the claim
141. I accept that grounds 1 and 2 could not be rejected without full argument and so I accept that they did cross the threshold for arguability. However, ground 3 was hopelessly unarguable. Consequently, I grant permission to apply for statutory review limited to grounds 1 and 2. However, for the reasons set out above the application for statutory review is dismissed.

12.12 In a lengthy postscript to his judgment Holgate J made some important observations about viability assessment and the application of paragraph 023 of the NPPG ('Land Value'). In it he urged professional bodies and ministers to rethink existing guidance on development viability in a bid to clear up 'misunderstandings' over market valuation concepts and techniques. The aim, Holgate J said, should be to avoid protracted land value disputes, streamline decision-making and keep the judiciary out of arguments over 'detailed valuation material':

Postscript
142. One of the key objectives in our planning system is efficiency in decision-making, in order to avoid delay in bringing about necessary or beneficial development. In this context the present case strikingly illustrates the importance of seeking to overcome uncertainty on how viability assessment should properly be carried out. Similar schemes on the same site have been approached by two different Inspectors in very different ways. That is not in itself unlawful, but from a practical perspective it does make it more difficult for practitioners and participants in the planning process to predict the likely outcome and to plan accordingly. It also leads to a proliferation of litigation. The second inquiry in the present case lasted nine days and, even then, a further two day hearing in the High Court followed. It appears that similar issues are being argued on sites all over London and, no doubt, in other parts of the country as well. Appeal decisions which are said to support rival positions are seized upon as part of an increasingly adversarial process. Decisions of the High Court are also subjected to intense scrutiny and added to the forensic palette, whilst overlooking the point that the court's role is limited to review on public law principles, and not to determine whether a decision was right or wrong on its merits.

143. The present case illustrates the tension that has arisen in the application of paragraph 023 of the PPG. But the plain intention of that paragraph is to promote harmonisation between the three specified requirements when they are applied in decision-making. Thus, when estimating a BLV for a site, the application of the second and third requirements should "reflect", and not "buck," relevant planning policies (including those for the delivery of affordable housing). On the other hand, the proper application of those policies should be "informed by," and not "buck," an analysis of market evidence which reflects those policies (or where appropriate is adjusted to do so). As the PPG recognises, "realism" is needed when these matters are taken into account in decision-making. So, to take one example, a judgment may need to be made on relaxing one or more planning requirements or objectives where that would render a development on the site in question non-viable according to a viability case which uses (inter alia) land values which have adequately taken planning policies into account.

144. According to the basic principles set out in the NPPF and the NPPG, it is understandable why a decision-maker may, as a matter of judgment, attach little or no weight to a developer's analysis which claims to show a "market norm" for BLV by doing little more than averaging land values obtained from a large number of transactions within a district. If those values are inflated by, for example, a

misjudgment about a site's development capacity and/or by a failure to factor in appropriate planning requirements, such an exercise does not establish a relevant "norm" for the purposes of paragraph 023 of the PPG. Such data should be adjusted (subject to any issues about reliability and cross-checking). A failure to obtain adequate information about comparables relied upon (including the planning context and circumstances influencing bids and the transacted price) would not be acceptable where development appraisal or viability is dealt with in the Lands Chamber or in an arbitration, and it is difficult to see why the position should be different where the same type of issue arises in the present type of case.

145. On the other hand, it is understandable why developers and landowners may argue against local policy statements that BLV should simply conform to an "EUV plus a percentage" basis of valuation, especially where the document has not been subjected to independent statutory examination prior to adoption. Some adherents appear to be promoting a formulaic application of "EUV plus." But as the RICS advised its members in its 2012 Guidance Note, an uplift of between 10 and 40% on existing use value is an arbitrary number and the method does not reflect the workings of the market (see paragraph 57 above). It has not been suggested that this valuation approach takes into account the value of the new land use for which the site is to be sold, whereas it might be said that a reasonable landowner would treat that as a primary consideration in valuing his property. In this context a document issued by a professional institution setting out "accepted good practice" for chartered surveyors ought to command great respect in the planning process unless there is a sound reason to the contrary. If, for example, a site value were to be negotiated so as to respect planning policy requirements properly but that price substantially exceeded an uplift of say 40% (or any other policy-specified percentage) on the existing use value of the site, the question would be posed why should that evidence not be treated as relevant to BLV? Otherwise, might it not be suggested that there is a risk of policy attempting to "buck" the market (see paragraph 143 above)? There is a difference between a policy which may have the effect of influencing market value, as compared with one which disregards levels of market value arrived at quite properly in arm's length transactions and consistent with the correct application of planning policies and sound valuation principles.

146. Mr Buley briefly referred to consultation proposals for the NPPG published in March 2018. They suggest using "standardised inputs" in viability assessments. To arrive at an appropriate minimum premium to be added to EUV it is suggested that an assessment should look at comparable sites that have recently been granted planning permission in accordance with relevant policies. The prices paid for such land, suitably adjusted, can then be compared to EUVs for those sites to ascertain an appropriate premium or uplift additional to EUV for the landowner of the site being considered.

147. It might be thought that an opportune moment has arrived for the RICS to consider revisiting the 2012 Guidance Note, perhaps in conjunction with MHCLG and the RTPI, in order to address any misunderstandings about market valuation concepts and techniques, the "circularity" issue and any other problems encountered

in practice over the last 6 years, so as to help avoid protracted disputes of the kind we have seen in the present case and achieve more efficient decision-making. The High Court is not the appropriate forum for resolving issues of the kind which the Inspectors dealing with the Parkhurst Road site had to consider. It is very much to be hoped that the court is not asked in future to look at detailed valuation material as happened in these proceedings.

Chapter 13

Appeals and Review of Planning Decisions[1]

RIGHT OF APPEAL AGAINST LOCAL AUTHORITY DECISIONS ON PLANNING MATTERS

13.1   If an application for planning permission is refused by the local planning authority (LPA), or if it is granted with conditions which the applicant considers unacceptable (including where planning permission has been applied for to develop land without compliance with conditions previously imposed),[2] an appeal can be made[3] to the Secretary of State against the decision or the conditions. An appeal also lies to the Secretary of State in the case of a refusal or conditional grant of any consent, agreement or approval required by a planning condition or in relation to any approval of the LPA required under a development order.[4] It may be, of course, that re-engagement with the LPA with a view to making the proposal more acceptable, so that a revised application could then be submitted, would be a more pragmatic way of dealing with matters.

13.2   An appeal may also be made if the LPA fails to issue a decision within the prescribed period: the deadline is eight weeks for non-major applications, 13 weeks for major applications and 16 weeks in the case of applications subject

---

1   Note the guidance to be found in the revised versions of the four procedural guides on: (a) planning appeals; (b) called-in planning applications; (c) enforcement notice appeals; and (d) lawful development certificate appeals, published by the Planning Inspectorate (PINS) on 23/3/2016.

2   TCPA 1990, s 73.

3   The appellant must be the applicant for permission (or his successor in title) who may not even be the owner of the land who has no independent right of appeal if he was not the applicant. The right of appeal under TCPA 1990, s 78 is disapplied in the case of determinations by an LPA where it proposes to develop the land itself or jointly with a third party in the case of land in which it has an interest (Town and Country Planning General Regulations 1992 (SI 1992/1492), regs 3 and 5(1)(a)).

4   TCPA 1990, s 78(1) and (2).

to an environmental impact assessment (EIA) (albeit subject to written agreement to extend the decision-making period).

TIME LIMIT FOR SUBMITTING AN APPEAL

13.3   Most planning appeals must be received within six months of the date of the decision notice or, in the case of a non-determination appeal, on the expiry of the prescribed or agreed period.[5] Where an appeal relates to an application for householder planning consent, and is to be determined via the fast-track Householder Appeals Service, there are only 12 weeks to make the appeal.[6] There are different deadlines within which to submit an appeal under the Commercial Appeals Service.[7]

POWERS OF THE SECRETARY OF STATE ON APPEAL

13.4   The Secretary of State may allow or dismiss the appeal, or reverse or vary any part of the decision of the LPA, whether or not the appeal relates to that part, and he may deal with the application as if it had been made to him in the first instance.[8] In other words, appeals are determined on the same basis as the original application. The decision will be made taking into account national and local policies, and the broader circumstances in place at the time of the decision. Where any change between the original planning decision and the appeal has the potential to affect the outcome, all parties will have an opportunity to comment on the new material.

13.5   In terms of appeal procedure and guidance, reference should be made to the Planning Inspectorate Procedural Guide in relation to planning appeals issued on 26/1/2018. The guide applies to the process involved in the case of planning appeals, householder development appeals, minor commercial appeals, listed building appeals, advertisement appeals and discontinuance notice appeals.

---

5   DMPO, art 37, and the Town and Country Planning (Development Management Procedure) (Wales) Order 2012 (SI 2012/801). The notice of appeal is on the prescribed form obtained from the Secretary of State and is effective once served on the Secretary of State (along with copies of the necessary documentation mentioned in DMPO, art 37) and should be lodged with the First Secretary of State at Temple Quay House, 2 The Square, Temple Quay, Bristol BS1 6PN (or in Wales at The National Assembly for Wales, Cathays Park, Cardiff CF1 3NQ). Copies of the notice and accompanying documents should also be served on the LPA.

6   See Planning Inspectorate Procedural Guide, Annex C.

7   Appeals related to shop fronts must be submitted within 12 weeks. Advertisement consent appeals must be submitted within eight weeks.

8   TCPA 1990, s 79(1).

Reference should also be made to the Planning Policy Guidance Note (PPG) in the section 'Appeals'.[9]

WHO DECIDES THE APPEAL AND BY WHAT PROCEDURE?

13.6   Nearly all appeals are decided by inspectors of the Planning Inspectorate (which will be referred to as PINS where the context permits).[10] Only a very small percentage are decided by the Secretary of State, and these tend to be the very large or contentious proposed schemes (these are known as 'recovered appeals').[11] Recovered appeals can occur at any stage of the appeal, even after the site visit, a hearing or an inquiry has taken place. In recovered cases, the inspector will not make the decision but instead will write a report and include a recommendation to the Secretary of State who will make the decision.[12]

13.7   The Secretary of State will consider recovery in line with the criteria set out in a Parliamentary Statement on 30/6/2008. Guidance on propriety in ministerial decisions on planning matters is also available.[13] There may be other cases which merit recovery because of particular circumstances.[14] A recovered appeal will be determined via written representations, a hearing or an inquiry in the same way as other planning appeals.

13.8   The vast majority of planning appeals are determined by way of written representations,[15] although this may be inappropriate where the case involves

---

[9]   NPPG at Paragraph: 001 Reference ID: 16-001-20140306 to 16-064-20140306.

[10]   Note the existence of the process of ex gratia payments when PINS has made an error on a planning appeal. There is no legal right to such compensation, but it is the policy of PINS to make payments in certain circumstances where justified. See *D2M Solutions Ltd v Secretary of State for Communities and Local Government* [2017] EWHC 3409 (Admin). A new policy has been in place for claims made after 1/4/2016 ('Claims for Repayment of Additional Costs (Ex Gratia Scheme)'). Section 4 of this document describes matters which are not covered by the scheme and would include payments referable to the 'negative impacts on property prices or profits, as they are not direct additional costs'.

[11]   See *Encyclopedia of Planning* at P79.40-54 for Secretary of State's cases (post-inquiry procedures).

[12]   See NPPG at Paragraph: 005 Reference ID: 16-005-20150917.

[13]   Guidance on Planning Propriety Issues, published by the Department of Communities and Local Government in February 2012.

[14]   See list of examples set out in NPPG at Paragraph: 005 Reference ID: 16-005-20160713.

[15]   See Town and Country Planning (Appeals) (Written Representations Procedure) (England) Regulations 2009 (SI 2009/452), Pt 2, as amended by the Town and Country Planning (Appeals) (Written Representations Procedure and Advertisements) (England) (Amendment) Regulations 2013 (SI 2013/2114).

disputed questions of fact which called for cross-examination in order for the dispute to be resolved.[16] The criteria for a determination by written representations are:[17]

(a) the planning issues raised or, in an enforcement appeal, the grounds of appeal, can be clearly understood from the appeal documents and, if required (and a small number of appeals do not require a site visit and can be dealt with on the basis of the appeal documents), a site inspection; or

(b) the issues are not complex and the inspector is not likely to need to test the evidence by questioning or to clarify any other matters; or

(c) in an enforcement appeal, the alleged breach, and the requirements of the notice, are clear.

13.9 Fairness does not demand that there should be a general obligation upon an appellant in every case conducted by the written representations procedure, to disclose documents which contained facts which were adverse to his appeal. However, a duty to disclose material facts which were adverse to the appellant's case would probably arise where the appellant had chosen to give voluntary disclosure of a document containing factual material or voluntary disclosure of information in non-documentary form, and his failure to disclose other documents or information would have the effect of misleading or even potentially misleading an inspector about the true nature of the undisclosed material.[18]

---

16 *Shaw v Secretary of State for the Environment and Wirral Metropolitan Borough Council* [1998] JPL 962. See also *Mahajan v Secretary of State for Transport, Local Government and the Regions* [2002] EWHC 33 (Admin), where a decision by a planning inspector, dealing with an appeal by way of written representations, to accord written statements from the appellant limited weight on the basis that they were untested was flawed in view of his failure to provide reasons and his apparent disregard of the source, content, consistency and reliability of the written material. The court held that although a written representation procedure was not unfair in principle, in the circumstances of this case, fairness necessitated that there should have been a careful examination of the untested written material and a consideration of its relative merit rather than according it limited undifferentiated weight just because it was untested. The inspector should have given reasons for the conclusions reached in the light of the written material. There was uncertainty in the absence of proper reasons as to whether the inspector had carried out such an exercise but, if he had, the appellant had not been given adequate reasons as to why the written material was rejected. Planning Inspectorate Procedural Guide, Annex C contains the written representations procedure for an appeal against a refusal of a householder application, an application for advertisement consent and a 'minor commercial' (shop front) application, and Annex D contains the procedure for other written representations appeals.

17 See Planning Inspectorate Procedural Guide, Annex K.

18 *Eley v Secretary of State for Communities and Local Government* [2009] EWHC 660 (Admin); *Birds Eye Walls Ltd v Harrison* [1985] ICR 278.

13.10 In some cases, something less than a full-blown public inquiry may be warranted. In these cases, the appeal may be determined by way of an informal hearing,[19] the criteria for which will be as follows:

(a)   the inspector is likely to need to test the evidence by questioning or to clarify matters (as for instance where detailed evidence on housing land supply needs to be tested by questioning); or

(b)   the status or personal circumstances of the appellant are at issue (as, for instance, whether in traveller appeals the definition in Annex 1 of the Department for Communities and Local Government (DCLG)'s planning policy for traveller sites is met, or in agricultural dwelling appeals); or

(c)   there is no need for evidence to be tested through formal questioning by an advocate or given on oath; or

(d)   the case has generated a level of local interest such as to warrant a hearing; or

(e)   it can reasonably be expected that the parties will be able to present their own cases (supported by professional witnesses if required) without the need for an advocate to represent them; or

(f)   in an enforcement appeal, the grounds of appeal, the alleged breach, and the requirements of the notice, are relatively straightforward.[20]

13.11 Lastly, appeals may be determined by way of a public inquiry.[21] The criteria for a public inquiry as are follows:[22]

---

[19]   Planning Inspectorate Procedural Guide, Annex E contains the procedure for hearings (effectively a round-table discussion led by the inspector).

[20]   See criteria for the appropriateness of hearings at Annex K of the Planning Inspectorate Procedural Guide. Procedure is governed by Town and Country Planning (Appeals) (Written Representations Procedure) (England) Regulations 2009 (SI 2009/452), Pt 2, as amended by the Town and Country Planning (Appeals) (Written Representations Procedure and Advertisements) (England) (Amendment) Regulations 2013 (SI 2013/2114).

[21]   Planning Inspectorate Procedural Guide, Annex F contains the procedure for inquiries, and Annex G contains the procedure for an appeal which has been 'recovered' and is proceeding by an inquiry.

[22]   See Planning Inspectorate Procedural Guide, Annex K at p 70, which notes that the prospect of legal submissions being made is not, on its own, a reason why a case would need to be conducted by way of a public inquiry. In such a case, the matters on which complex legal submissions will be required will need to be explained to PINS at the outset of the appeal or otherwise at the earliest opportunity, including why they may warrant an inquiry. Procedure is governed by the Town and Country Planning Appeals (Determination by Inspectors) (Inquiries Procedure) (England) Rules 2000 (SI 2000/1625), as amended by the Town and Country Planning (Hearings and Inquiries Procedures) (England) (Amendment) Rules 2009 (SI 2009/455) and by the Town and Country Planning (Hearings and Inquiries Procedure) (England) (Amendment) Rules 2013 (SI 2013/2137) (Inquiries Procedure Rules).

(a)   there is a clearly explained need for the evidence to be tested through formal questioning by an advocate (although this does not preclude an appellant representing themselves as an advocate); or

(b)   the issues are complex (such as evidence involving large amounts of highly technical data); or

(c)   the appeal has generated substantial local interest to warrant a local inquiry as opposed to dealing with the case by way of an informal hearing;[23] or

(d)   in an enforcement appeal, evidence needs to be given on oath (such as where witnesses are giving factual evidence about how long the alleged unauthorised use has been taking place); or

(e)   in an enforcement appeal, the alleged breach, or the requirements of the notice, are unusual and particularly contentious.

PARTIES INVOLVED AT AN INQUIRY AND THE BURDEN OF PROOF

13.12   The main parties will be the appellant and the LPA, and although the LPA will call its evidence first, the appellant will have the right of final reply.[24] Statutory parties (i.e. any owner or agricultural tenant of the affected land) and Rule 6 parties (i.e. any person required by the Secretary of State to serve a statement of case)[25] are also entitled to appear and give evidence.

---

[23]   In such a case, the LPA should indicate which procedure it considers would be most appropriate, taking account of the number of people likely to attend and participate at the event. PINS will take that advice into account in reaching its decision as to the appropriate appeals procedure.

[24]   See the Planning Inspectorate Guide to taking part in planning and listed building consent appeals proceeding by an inquiry – England; (issued in April 2016) at para 13 in the section, 'What happens at the inquiry', where at para 13.10 it is stated that the inspector has a discretion to decide the order of appearances at the inquiry. However, paras 13.11–13.14 give an order of appearances which an inspector will normally follow, namely, that the appellant will be asked to make a brief opening statement first. The LPA will then make its opening statement and its witnesses will then give their evidence in turn. The appellant will then present its case. As for closing statements, the LPA will go first.

[25]   See the Planning Inspectorate Guide to Rule 6 for interested parties involved in an inquiry – planning appeals and called-in applications – England (issued in April 2016). Rule 6 status refers to Inquiries Procedure Rules, rule 6(6), which provides that:

   'The Secretary of State may in writing require any other person who has notified him of an intention or wish to appear at an inquiry, to send within four weeks of being so required: (a) three copies of their statement of case to him; and (b) a copy of their statement of case to any statutory party, and the Secretary of State shall, as soon as practicable after receipt, send a copy of each such statement of case to the LPA and to the applicant/appellant.'

   In the Guide at para 2.1, it is stated that if a party wished 'to take a very active part in the inquiry', they should request:

13.13 In terms of the burden of proof, it has been said that the term 'burden of proof' was not appropriate in the context of planning appeals. The task of the inspector is to consider the facts and contentions put before him at the inquiry and, in light of what he ascertained at the inquiry and his view of the site, to decide whether there were any sound and clear-cut reasons for allowing the appeal and granting planning permission or for refusing planning permission.[26]

COSTS[27]

13.14 Unless a party has behaved unreasonably and the unreasonable behaviour has directly caused another party to incur unnecessary or wasted expense in the appeal process, parties will normally be expected to bear their own appeal costs. If an order for costs is made by the Secretary of State it may be either for the whole of the expense incurred (on the ground that it should not have been necessary for the matter to be determined by the Secretary of State or the inspector), or for only a part of such expense (depending on the manner in which a party has behaved in the appeal process).

13.15 Unreasonable behaviour in connection with an award of costs may be either procedural (i.e. relating to the process) or substantive (i.e. relating to the issues arising from the merits of the appeal). The inspector has a discretion when deciding an award, enabling extenuating circumstances to be taken into account. Reference should be made to the National Planning Practice Guidance (NPPG) in the section 'Appeals', which contains a very helpful (non-exhaustive) list of examples of unreasonable behaviour which may result in an award of costs

---

'Rule 6 status ... However, to avoid making the inquiry too repetitious, we encourage participants with similar views to group together and elect a spokesperson to appear at the inquiry on the group's behalf. You should state who you are representing (for example, a parish council or local community group), why you want "Rule 6 status" and briefly explain what you can bring to the inquiry that another party may not. It is unusual for 'Rule 6 status' to be granted to individuals.'

Paragraph 2.2 goes on to say, 'Rule 6 parties can offer significant value to the inquiry process. However this is only the case where Rule 6 parties add substantively to the case being made by the LPA or the appellant (for an appeal) or the applicant (for an application which has been 'called-in')'.

[26] *J.A. Pye (Oxford) Estates Ltd v West Oxfordshire District Council* (1984) 47 P & CR 125; *Christchurch Borough Council v Secretary of State for the Environment* (1994) 68 P & CR 116.

[27] LGA 1972, s 250(5); TCPA 1990, ss 320(2), 322 and 322A, and Sch 6, para 6(4).

against: (a) an LPA;[28] (b) an appellant;[29] (c) statutory consultees;[30] and (d) interested parties who choose to be recognised as Rule 6 parties under the Inquiries Procedure Rules.[31]

13.16 Applications for costs should be made as soon as possible and no later than the following deadlines:[32]

(a) In the case of appeals determined by the Householder Appeals Service, Commercial Appeals Service, and appeals against Tree Preservation Orders (TPOs), the application for costs must be made when the appeal is submitted, if the application is made by the appellant, or within 14 days of the date of the 'Start date' letter for the appeal if the application is made by the local authority.

(b) In the case of appeals determined by written representations, the application for costs must be made no later than the final comments stage, although the Planning Inspectorate may set an alternative deadline.

(c) In the case of hearings and inquiries:

   (i) all costs applications must be formally made to the inspector before the hearing or inquiry is closed, but it is good practice to make such an application before the hearing or inquiry as it can be amended or added to as necessary in oral submissions;

   (ii) if the application relates to the behaviour at a hearing or inquiry, the applicant should tell the inspector before the hearing closes that they are going to make a costs application and the inspector will then hear the application and the response by the other party, and the applicant

---

28 See NPPG at Paragraph: 047 Reference ID: 16-047-20140306 and 16-048-20140306 (behaviour giving rise to a *procedural* award such as lack of co-operation and delay in providing information), and 16-049-20140306 (behaviour giving rise to a *substantive* award such as preventing or delaying development which should clearly be permitted; or where the LPA had failed to substantiate its reasons for refusal; had unreasonably asserted a five-year supply of housing land; had provided only vague and generalised assertions about the proposal's impact; or had ignored its officers' advice and its own local plan policies).

29 See NPPG at Paragraph: 052 Reference ID: 16-052-20140306 (behaviour giving rise to a *procedural* award against an appellant such as a failure to co-operate in providing information) and 16-053-20140306 (to a *substantive* award such as where the appeal or a ground of appeal had no reasonable prospect of succeeding as, for instance, where an appeal proposal concerned the same development, on the same site, assessed against the same development plan policies and national policy, as one dismissed previously), and 16-054-20140306 (where an appeal is withdrawn without good reason).

30 See NPPG at Paragraph: 055: Reference ID: 16-055-20140306.

31 See NPPG at Paragraph: 056: Reference ID: 16-056-20140306.

32 See NPPG at Paragraph: 035: Reference ID: 16-035-20140306. Anyone making a late application for an award of costs outside these timings will need to show good reason for having made the application late, if it is to be accepted by the Secretary of State for consideration.

will have the final word. The decision on the award of costs will be made after the hearing or inquiry.

(d) For all procedures, no later than four weeks after receiving notification of the withdrawal of the appeal or enforcement notice or other planning matter which is the subject of the proceedings, irrespective of procedure.

JUDICIAL CHALLENGE OF DECISIONS OF THE SECRETARY OF STATE

13.17 The decision of the Secretary of State or of an inspector is final and may not be questioned in any legal proceedings whatsoever[33] except on a point of law, although it is possible for an 'aggrieved party' to question the validity of any decision of the Secretary of State in the High Court.[34]

---

[33] TCPA 1990, s 79(5); see also s 284(1)(e) and 3(b) (which specifically refers to s 78, which confers a right of appeal against planning decisions and a failure to take such decisions).

[34] Under TCPA 1990, s 287 (challenges to the validity of a statutory development plan or Simplified Planning Zone scheme and certain other orders), and s 288(1) and (4) (in the case of other orders mentioned in s 284, specifically s 284(1)(f) and (3)(b) which includes planning decisions under s 78). The grounds of appeal under s 288(1) are that the order under appeal was not within the powers of the 1990 Act or that any of the relevant requirements have not been complied with in relation to the order. Since 26/10/2015, there is now a requirement for leave to be obtained in the case of s 288 challenges (for which application must be made within six weeks beginning with the date when the order is confirmed, or the date on which action is taken (s 288(4B)), which in practice will be the date of the Secretary of State's decision letter or, in the case of an order for costs, the date on which the order was made) – see s 288(4A) (requirement for leave) (see Criminal Justice and Courts Act 2015 (Commencement No 3 and Transitional Provisions) Order 2015 (SI 2015/1778), which brought into force Criminal Justice and Courts Act 2015 (subject to transitional provisions), s 91 and Sch 16. Such cases are heard by the Planning Court. In *Croke v Secretary of State for Communities and Local Government* [2016] EWHC 2484 (Admin), the appellant wished to challenge the decision of an inspector to refuse permission for certain operational development. The deadline for bringing a challenge was known by the claimant to be 23/3, and he had arranged for the papers to be hand-delivered before the court office closed at 4.30pm. However, security staff refused entry at 4.25pm on the ground that the counters were closed. The claimant attended the court ofice in person the next day at 3.30pm but was not seen until 5pm, when he was informed that he had the wrong form. He was not permitted to complete the correct form at that time, but was told to return the next day, which was Good Friday. The date of issue was the first working day after Good Friday, which was on 29/3. The appellant argued that due to the court's inaccessibility, the court was not functioning on 23/3, which meant that the deadline for his s 288 claim should be extended to the next working day (following *Kaur v Russell & Sons Ltd* [1973] QB 336, where the Court of Appeal held that the last day for doing an act in the Court Office is a day on which the office is not open, the act is done in time if it is done on the next day when the office is open). The court held that the principle in *Kaur* did not apply where a litigant had been physically prevented from accessing the court office on the last day before expiry of the time limit. Litigants had to anticipate that a court might be busy or that there might be security procedures preventing them from accessing the court office before it closed for the day.

13.18 For these purposes, a person would normally be regarded as 'aggrieved'[35] if he had made objections or representations during the appeal procedure and if his complaint was that the decision was not properly made. In other words, it would suffice if a person had taken part in the inquiry but merely being resident in a property adjoining the proposed development site would not be enough.[36]

JURISDICTION OF THE PLANNING COURT

13.19 The jurisdiction of the Planning Court includes claims involving judicial review[37] or statutory challenges involving planning permission, enforcement of planning control, highways and other rights of way and village greens.[38] Claims for judicial review (founded on illegality, irrationality and procedural impropriety, for which the court's permission to proceed is required)[39] must be filed promptly and in any event, where the claim relates to a decision made by the Secretary of State or LPA under the Planning Acts, the claim form must be filed no later than six weeks from the date of the decision challenged.[40]

Bloor Homes East Midlands Ltd v Secretary of State for Communities and Local Government and Hinckley and Bosworth Borough Council

13.20 In an ordinary case involving a challenge to a decision of the Secretary of State or one of his inspectors,[41] one can do no better than cite from the decision of Lindblom J (as he then was) in *Bloor Homes East Midlands Ltd v Secretary of*

---

[35] And so have the necessary standing to bring a challenge under TCPA 1990, ss 287–288.

[36] See *Walton v Scottish Minsters* [2013] PTSR 51 at [86]–[87] per Lord Hope (followed in *Crawford-Brunt v Secretary of State for Communities and Local Government* [2015] EWHC 3580 (Admin), where the claim to standing failed as neither applicant had made objections or representations during the appeal procedure and merely lived in neighbouring properties).

[37] Claims for judicial review are brought under both CPR, Pt 54 and Senior Courts Act 1981, s 31(6).

[38] See CPR, rule 54.21(2)(a) and PD 54E (Planning Court Claims).

[39] CPR, rule 54.4.

[40] CPR, rule 54.5(5). See *Gerber v Wiltshire Council* [2016] EWCA Civ 84, where (amongst other reasons) the court considered that it was inappropriate to extend time (CPR, rule 3.10: good reason for extension of time) for bringing a legal challenge simply because an objector did not notice what was happening, or because of reliance on incorrect legal advice, applying *Finn-Kelcey v Milton Keynes Borough Council* [2008] EWCA Civ 1067.

[41] Involving statutory challenges under TCPA 1990, s 288 in the case of decisions on appeals under s 78.

State for Communities and Local Government and Hinckley and Bosworth Borough Council:[42]

19. The relevant law is not controversial. It comprises seven familiar principles:

(1)   Decisions of the Secretary of State and his inspectors in appeals against the refusal of planning permission are to be construed in a reasonably flexible way. Decision letters are written principally for parties who know what the issues between them are and what evidence and argument has been deployed on those issues. An inspector does not need to 'rehearse every argument relating to each matter in every paragraph' (see judgment of Forbes J. in *Seddon Properties v Secretary of State for the Environment* (1981) 42 P&CR 26 at p.28).

(2)   The reasons for an appeal decision must be intelligible and adequate, enabling one to understand why the appeal was decided as it was and what conclusions were reached on the 'principal important controversial issues'. An inspector's reasoning must not give rise to a substantial doubt as to whether he went wrong in law, for example by misunderstanding a relevant policy or by failing to reach a rational decision on relevant grounds.[43] But the reasons need refer only to the main issues in dispute, not to every material consideration (see the speech of Lord Brown of Eaton-under-Heywood in *South Bucks District Council and another v Porter (No.2)* [2004] 1 WLR 1953, at p.196B–G).

(3)   The weight to be attached to any material consideration and all matters of planning judgment are within the exclusive jurisdiction of the decision-maker. They are not for the court. A local planning authority determining an application for planning permission is free, 'provided that it does not lapse into *Wednesbury* irrationality' to give material considerations 'whatever weight [it]

---

[42]   [2014] EWHC 754 (Admin) at [19] (and applied in *Cheshire East Borough Council v Secretary of State for Communities and Local Government* [2016] EWHC 694 (Admin)). See also *Secretary of State for Communities and Local Government v Hopkins Homes Ltd* [2017] 1 WLR 1865, where it was said that the NPPF was no more than 'guidance' and therefore 'a material consideration' in the determination of a planning application. It did not provide a statutory test and did not displace or distort the primacy given by statute to the development plan. The NPPF was to be interpreted in its overall context and, where the guidance related to decision-making in planning applications, it had to be interpreted in all cases in the context of TCPA 1990, s 70(2) and PCPA 2004, s 38(4), to which the NPPF was subordinate. While recourse to the court was necessary for the resolution of distinct issues of law or for consistency of interpretation in relation to specific policies, the court's role was not to be overstated and courts should respect the expertise of specialist planning inspectors and start with the presumption that they would have correctly understood the policy framework. Inspectors had primary responsibility for resolving disputes between LPAs and developers in individual cases over the practical application of policies, at national or local level, and their position was in part analogous with that of expert tribunals. Accordingly, courts were to exercise caution against intervening unduly in policy judgments falling within the inspectors' area of special competence (see [21]–[25] and [72]–[75]).

[43]   *Baroness Cumberlege of Newick v Secretary of State for Communities and Local Government* [2017] EWHC 2057 (Admin), where the Secretary of State had granted planning permission for residential development on the basis that a relevant local development plan policy was out of date. His decision was quashed because he had failed to take account of a previous finding that the policy was up to date.

thinks fit or no weight at all' (see the speech of Lord Hoffmann in *Tesco Stores Limited v Secretary of State for the Environment* [1995] 1 WLR 759, at p.780F–H). And, essentially for that reason, an application under section 288 of the 1990 Act does not afford an opportunity for a review of the planning merits of an inspector's decision (see the judgment of Sullivan J, as he then was, in *Newsmith v Secretary of State for the Environment* [2001] EWHC Admin 74, at paragraph 6).

(4)   Planning policies are not statutory or contractual provisions and should not be construed as if they were. The proper interpretation of planning policy is ultimately a matter of law for the court. The application of relevant policy is for the decision-maker. But statements of policy are to be interpreted objectively by the court in accordance with the language used and in its proper context. A failure properly to understand and apply relevant policy will constitute a failure to have regard to a material consideration, or will amount to having regard to an immaterial consideration (see judgment of Lord Reed in *Tesco Stores v Dundee City Council* [2012] P.T.S.R. 983, at paragraphs 17–22).

(5)   When it is suggested that an inspector has failed to grasp a relevant policy one must look at what he thought the important planning issues were and decide whether it appears from the way he dealt with them that he must have misunderstood the policy in question (see the judgment of Hoffmann L.J., as he then was, in *South Somerset District Council v The Secretary of State for the Environment* (1993) 66 P&CR 80, at p.83E–H).

(6)   Because it is reasonable to assume that national planning policy is familiar to the Secretary of State and his inspectors, the fact that a particular policy is not mentioned in the decision letter does not necessarily mean that it has been ignored (see, for example, the judgment of Lang J. in *Sea & Land Power & Energy Limited v Secretary of State for Communities and Local Government* [2012] EWHC 1419 (QB), at paragraph 58).

(7)   Consistency in decision-making is important both to developers and local planning authorities, because it serves to maintain public confidence in the operation of the development control system. But it is not a principle of law that like cases must always be decided alike. An inspector must exercise his own judgment on this question, if it arises (see, for example, the judgment of Pill L.J. in *Fox Strategic Land and Property Limited v Secretary of State for Communities and Local Government* [2013] 1 P&CR 6, at paragraphs 12 to 14, citing the judgment of Mann L.J. in *North Wiltshire District Council v Secretary of State for the Environment* [1992] 65 P&CR 137, at p.145).

Cawrey Ltd v Secretary of State for Communities and Local Government

13.21   In *Cawrey Ltd v Secretary of State for Communities and Local Government*,[44] Gilbart J relied on the foregoing analysis of Lindblom J in *Bloor*

---

44   [2016] EWHC 1198 (Admin).

Homes East Midlands Ltd. Cawrey Ltd involved a developer's challenge against a refusal of planning permission by the LPA (which had been upheld by an inspector) for the erection of 158 dwellings because of harm to the landscape contrary to local policy and the National Planning Policy Framework 2012 (NPPF). The developer applied for judicial review on the grounds that the inspector had misinterpreted the development plan and the NPPF, and gave inadequate reasoning in his conclusions concerning the impact on the landscape and on recreational use. The application was refused by Gilbart J. The case is a clear example of just how difficult it is nowadays to challenge decisions of inspectors when it comes to matters of planning judgment. *Cawrey Ltd* is also useful as it contains a very helpful analysis (which is set out below) of the interplay between policies in the development plan and the NPPF and the true status of the latter in the decision-making process.

13.22   In his judgment, Gilbart J set out the list of seven principles mentioned by Lindblom L.J in paragraph 13.20 and at [42] stated as follows:

> 42. I would add the following, given the issues in this case: an Inspector appointed to conduct a planning appeal must:
>
> (8)   have regard to the statutory Development Plan (see s 70(1) TCPA 1990);
> (9)   have regard to material considerations (s 70(1) TCPA 1990);
> (10) determine the proposal in accordance with the Development Plan unless material considerations indicate otherwise (s 38(6) PCPA 2004);
> (11) consider the nature and extent of any conflict with the Development Plan; *Tesco Stores Ltd v Dundee City Council* [2012] UKSC 13 at [22] per Lord Reed;
> (12) consider whether the development accords with the Development Plan, looking at it as a whole – see *R(Milne) v Rochdale MBC (No 2)* [2000] EWHC 650 (Admin), [2001] JPL 470, [2001] Env LR 22, (2001) 81 P&CR 27, [2000] EG 103 per Sullivan J at [46]–[48]. There may be some points in the plan which support the proposal but there may be some considerations pointing in the opposite direction. He will require to assess all of these and then decide whether in light of the whole plan the proposal does or does not accord with it; per Lord Clyde in *City of Edinburgh Council v Secretary of State for Scotland* [1997] UKHL 38, [1997] WLR 1447, 1998 SC (HL) 33 cited by Sullivan J in *R(Milne) v Rochdale MBC (No 2)* at [48];
> (13) apply national policy unless s/he gives reasons for not doing so – see Nolan LJ in *Horsham District Council v Secretary of State for the Environment and Margram Plc* [1993] 1 PLR 81 following Woolf J in *E.C. Gransden & Co Ltd v Secretary of State for the Environment* [1987] 54 P & CR 86 and see Lindblom J in *Cala Homes (South) Ltd v Secretary of State for Communities & Local Government* [2011] EWHC 97 (Admin), [2011] JPL 887 at [50].
>
> I would add one other matter of principle:

(14) If it is shown that the decision maker had regard to an immaterial consideration, or failed to have regard to a material one, the decision will be quashed unless the Court is satisfied that the decision would necessarily have been the same: see *Simplex GE (Holdings) Ltd v Secretary of State for the Environment* (1989) 57 P & CR 306.

43. It follows from the above that NPPF was very relevant to the determination of the appeal. But it was so because, as a statement of Government policy, it was a material consideration; no more and no less. While the arguments were directed towards paragraph 49 of NPPF, it is important to note what Lindblom L.J said in *Suffolk Coastal* at [42] and [43] about NPPF generally:

'42. The NPPF is a policy document. It ought not to be treated as if it had the force of statute. It does not, and could not, displace the statutory "presumption in favour of the development plan", as Lord Hope described it in *City of Edinburgh Council v Secretary of State for Scotland* [1997] 1 WLR 1447 at 1450B–G. Under section 70(2) of the 1990 Act and section 38(6) of the 2004 Act, government policy in the NPPF is a material consideration external to the development plan. Policies in the NPPF, including those relating to the "presumption in favour of sustainable development", do not modify the statutory framework for the making of decisions on applications for planning permission. They operate within that framework – as the NPPF itself acknowledges, for example, in paragraph 12 ... It is for the decision-maker to decide what weight should be given to NPPF policies in so far as they are relevant to the proposal. Because this is government policy, it is likely always to merit significant weight. But the court will not intervene unless the weight given to it by the decision-maker can be said to be unreasonable in the *Wednesbury* sense.

43. When determining an application for planning permission for housing development the decision-maker will have to consider, in the usual way, whether or not the proposal accords with the relevant provisions of the development plan. If it does, the question will be whether other material considerations, including relevant policies in the NPPF, indicate that planning permission should not be granted. If the proposal does not accord with the relevant provisions of the plan, it will be necessary to consider whether other material considerations, including relevant policies in the NPPF, nevertheless indicate that planning permission should be granted.'

44. I refer also to paragraphs [46]–[47] which deal with what must now be seen as the inappropriate application and consideration of NPPF, including to some extent judicially:

'46. We must emphasise here that the policies in paragraphs 14 and 49 of the NPPF do not make "out-of-date" policies for the supply of housing irrelevant in the determination of a planning application or appeal. Nor do they prescribe how much weight should be given to such policies in the decision. Weight is, as ever, a matter for the decision-maker (see the speech of Lord Hoffmann in *Tesco Stores Ltd v Secretary of State for the Environment* [1995] 1 WLR 759, at p.780F–H). Neither of those paragraphs of the NPPF says that a development plan policy for the supply of housing that is "out-of-date" should be given no weight, or minimal weight, or, indeed, any specific amount of weight. They do not say that such a policy should simply be ignored or disapplied. That idea appears to have found favour in some of the first instance judgments where this question has arisen. It is incorrect.

47.   One may, of course, infer from paragraph 49 of the NPPF that in the Government's view the weight to be given to out-of-date policies for the supply of housing will normally be less than the weight due to policies that provide fully for the requisite supply. The weight to be given to such policies is not dictated by government policy in the NPPF. Nor is it, nor could it be, fixed by the court. It will vary according to the circumstances, including, for example, the extent to which relevant policies fall short of providing for the five-year supply of housing land, the action being taken by the local planning authority to address it, or the particular purpose of a restrictive policy – such as the protection of a "green wedge" or of a gap between settlements. There will be many cases no doubt, in which restrictive policies, whether general or specific in nature, are given sufficient weight to justify the refusal of planning permission despite their not being up-to-date under the policy in paragraph 49 in the absence of a five-year supply of housing land. Such an outcome is clearly contemplated by government policy in the NPPF. It will always be for the decision-maker to judge, in the particular circumstances of the case in hand, how much weight should be given to conflict with policies for the supply of housing that are out-of-date. This is not a matter of law; it is a matter of planning judgment (see paragraphs 70 to 75 of Lindblom J's judgment in *Crane*, paragraphs 71 and 74 of Lindblom J's judgment in *Phides*, and paragraphs 87, 105, 108 and 115 of Holgate J's judgment in *Woodcock Holdings Ltd v Secretary of State for Communities and Local Government and Mid-Sussex District Council* [2015] EWHC 1173 (Admin)).'

45. I respectfully suggested in *Dartford Borough Council v Secretary of State for Communities and Local Government & Anor* [2016] EWHC 649 (Admin) that *Suffolk Coastal* had laid to rest several disputes about the interpretation of NPPF, both as to the particular paragraphs it addressed, but also generally. Before *Suffolk Coastal* it had been striking that NPPF, a policy document, could sometimes have been approached as if it were a statute, and as importantly, as if it did away with the importance of the decision maker taking a properly nuanced decision in the round, having regard to the development plan (and its statutory significance) and to all material considerations. In particular, I would emphasise the passage in Lindblom L.J's judgment at [42]–[43], which restates the role of a policy document, and just as importantly how it is to be interpreted and applied. NPPF is not to be used to obstruct sensible decision making. It is there as policy guidance to be had regard to in that process, not to supplant it. Given Point 6 in the list of principles set out by Lindblom J, an Inspector is not, as a general rule, required to spell out the provisions

of NPPF. However if s/he were minded to depart from it, then the authorities cited above are clear that reasons must be given for doing so.

...

47. In that context, I turn to the issues before me. The first observation I must make is that however disappointing it must be to the Claimant that the Inspector has not endorsed a proposal which had been supported by HBBC's professional officers, he was the decision maker, and the earlier endorsement cannot affect the analysis of the Decision Letter. I should stress however that at no time did Ms Ogley try and argue that the recommendation for approval should be taken into account in the analysis which this Court had to conduct. To have done so would have been inappropriate.

48. I accept the proposition advanced by Mr Buley that in this case one must start with the Development Plan. It was for the Inspector to determine as a matter of planning judgment whether or not there was a breach of it, looking at it as a whole. Given the Inspector's thorough and reasoned critique of the effect of the development on the character and appearance of the area, there can be no doubt that the proposal was found to be in conflict with Policy NE5. He was entitled to find that the objective of that policy remained relevant and up to date. Given his finding on the 5 year supply, it cannot be argued that paragraph [49] of NPPF applied so as to affect the weight to be given to that conflict. The breach of RES5 goes along with it, as the effect of NE5 at this point is to maintain the urban boundary. But on any view, the Inspector had given powerful reasons why the extension of the urban area at this point would cause significant harm. It is impossible to argue that he did not address the nature and extent of the conflict with these policies.

49. The argument of the Claimant that the matters to which the Inspector referred are not relevant in terms of landscape assessment is misconceived. He had given reasons which identified why harm would flow from the extension of the built up area at this point. NPPF undoubtedly recognises the intrinsic character of the countryside as a core principle. The fact that paragraph [109] may recognise that some has a value worthy of designation for the quality of its landscape does not thereby imply that the loss of undesignated countryside is not of itself capable of being harmful in the planning balance, and there is nothing in *Stroud DC v SSCLG* [2015] EWHC 488 per Ouseley J or in *Cheshire East BC v SSCLG* [2016] EWHC 694 per Patterson J which suggests otherwise. Insofar as Kenneth Parker J in *Colman v SSCLG* may be interpreted as suggesting that such protection was no longer given by NPPF, I respectfully disagree with him. For it would be very odd indeed if the core principle at paragraph [17] of NPPF of 'recognising the intrinsic beauty and character of the countryside' was to be taken as only applying to those areas with a designation. Undesignated areas – 'ordinary countryside' as per Ouseley J in *Stroud DC* – may not justify the same level of protection, but NPPF, properly read, cannot be interpreted as removing it altogether. Of course if paragraph [49] applies (which it did not here) then the situation may be very different in NPPF terms.

50. Whether that loss of countryside is important in any particular case is a matter of planning judgment for the decision maker. In any event, extant policies in a

Development Plan which are protective of countryside must be had regard to, and in a case such as this a conflict with them could properly determine the s 38(6) PCPA 2004 issue. If the conclusion has been reached that the proposal does conflict with the development plan as a whole, then a conclusion that a development should then be permitted will require a judgment that material considerations justify the grant of permission. If reliance is then placed on NPPF, one must remember always what Lindblom LJ has said in *Suffolk Coastal* about its status. It is not suggested in this case that this is one where the NPPF paragraph [14] test applies, which given the Inspector's findings on the effect on the landscape, and the fact that HBBC is the Borough, and Ratby the settlement, where the policies considered in Bloor applied, is unsurprising. Nor is it suggested that he should have applied NPPF [49] given his findings on housing land. There is in my judgment nothing at all in NPPF which requires an Inspector to give little or no weight to extant policies in the Development Plan. Were it to do so, it would be incompatible with the statutory basis of development control in s 38(6) PCPA 2004 and s 70 TCPA 1990.

13.23   It is then plain, following *Cawrey Ltd v Secretary of State for Communities and Local Government*, that there is nothing in the NPPF which requires a planning inspector to give little or no weight to policies in a development plan. Were it to do so, it would be incompatible with the statutory basis of development control which, as previously indicated, requires an inspector:

(a)   to have regard to the statutory development plan;[45]
(b)   to have regard to material considerations;[46] and
(c)   to determine the proposal in accordance with the development plan unless material considerations indicate otherwise.[47] In the exercise of his planning judgment in *Cawrey Ltd*, the inspector had looked at the development plan as a whole and made a clear finding that the proposal did not accord with it because of the breaches of other local policies. Whilst it was his finding that there was a strong case for affordable housing and local housing, those benefits were, in his view, outweighed by the landscape harm. Accordingly, it was the view of Gilbart J that the inspector's decision was one that he had been entitled to make and the application for a quashing order was refused.

Mansell v Tonbridge and Malling BC and Croudace Portland and East Malling Trust

13.24   Mention should also be made of what was said by Lindblom L.J in *Mansell v Tonbridge and Malling BC and Croudace Portland and East Malling Trust*:[48]

---

[45]   TCPA 1990, s 70(1).
[46]   TCPA 1990, s 70(1).
[47]   PCPA 2004, s 38(6).
[48]   [2017] EWCA Civ 1314 at [41].

[41] The Planning Court – and this court too – must always be vigilant against
excessive legalism infecting the planning system. A planning decision is not
akin to an adjudication made by the court (see [50] of my judgment in *Barwood
v East Staffordshire BC*). The courts must keep in mind that the function of
planning decision-making has been assigned by Parliament, not to judges, but
– at local level – to elected councillors with the benefit of advice given to them
by planning officers, most of whom are professional planners, and – on appeal
– to the Secretary of State and his inspectors. They should remember too that
the making of planning policy is not an end in itself, but a means of achieving
reasonably predictable decision-making, consistent with the aims of the
decision-maker. Though the interpretation of planning policy is, ultimately, a
matter for the court, planning policies do not normally require intricate
discussion of their meaning. A particular policy, or even a particular phrase or
words, will sometimes provide planning lawyers with a "doctrinal
controversy". But even when the higher courts disagree as to the meaning of
the words in dispute, and even when the policy-maker's own understanding of
the policy has not been accepted, the debate in which the lawyers have engaged
may turn out to have been in vain – because, when a planning decision has to
be made, the effect of the relevant policies, taken together, may be exactly the
same whichever construction is right (see at [22] of my judgment in *Barwood
v East Staffordshire BC*). That of course may not always be so. One thing,
however, is certain, and ought to be stressed. Planning officers and inspectors
are entitled to expect that both national and local planning policy is as simply
and clearly stated as it can be, and also – however well or badly a policy is
expressed – that the court's interpretation of it will be straightforward, without
undue or elaborate exposition. Equally, they are entitled to expect – in every
case – good sense and fairness in the court's review of a planning decision, not
the hypothetical approach the court is often urged to adopt.

13.25 It seems plain, therefore, that it will only be in cases involving obvious
error[49] that the court is likely to intervene against decisions of the LPA or an

---

[49] *In R (Thornton Hall Estates Hotel Ltd) v Wirral MBC* [2018] EWHC 560 (Admin), unconditional
and permanent planning permission for the erection of three marquees on a Green Belt site was
quashed where it had been granted on an erroneous basis, namely, the omission of conditions
including a five-year time limit which had clearly been envisaged by the LPA in approving
permission. To have allowed the marquees to remain in place would subvert the public interest in
the integrity of the planning process and be contrary to the public interest. The officer's report to
the planning committee (in 2010) had noted that the marquees constituted inappropriate
development within the Green Belt, but that the income generated from the marquees' use would
enable the restoration of historic gardens which were in decline and at risk, and that that
constituted the very special circumstances necessary to overcome the presumption against
inappropriate development. The report to the planning committee had recommended allowing the
application subject to a number of conditions, including that planning permission should be for a
limited period of five years. The purpose of that condition was to enable the financial situation to
be reviewed, thereby minimising the impact on the Green Belt from the marquees' erection. The
planning committee resolved to accept the report's recommendation and to grant permission
subject to the suggested conditions, including the five-year time limit. In 2011 the LPA purported
to grant conditional planning permission but no conditions were set out in the decision document.

inspector on appeal. In most cases where the findings of the decision-maker turn on matters of planning judgment, the court can usually be expected to defer to the views of the decision-maker.[50]

REPORTS OF PLANNING OFFICERS

13.26 The principles on which the court will act when criticism is made of a planning officer's report to committee are summarised by Lindblom LJ at [42] in *Mansell v Tonbridge and Malling BC and Croudace Portland and East Malling Trust*, where he said this:[51]

> 42. ... To summarise the law as it stands:
>
> ▪ The essential principles are as stated by the Court of Appeal in *R. v Selby DC Ex p. Oxton Farms* [1997] E.G.C.S. 60 (see, in particular, the judgment of Judge L.J, as he then was). They have since been confirmed several times by this court, notably by Sullivan L.J in *R. (on the application of Siraj) v Kirklees MBC* [2010]

The marquees remained in place after the intended five-year period expired in December 2016. The claimant (which operated a nearby hotel and was a competitor of the interested party on whose property the marquees were sited) contended that the planning permission should be quashed as it had been granted on an erroneous basis, namely, the mistake in omitting the planning conditions. It asserted that the interested party had received a windfall benefit to which it was not entitled and that there should be a strong presumption in granting relief despite the long delay. The LPA did not contest the claim. The court found against the interested party despite its argument that the presence of the marquees on its land was lawful and would remain so in the future, without any time limit, by virtue of the unconditional planning permission, and that it had accepted over 180 bookings for dates up to 2020 affecting about 51,000 people. The court found that the interested party had been aware of the inconsistency between the permission as issued and the permission as envisaged by the LPA and had chosen to remain silent about it. Its decision to accept bookings for a time when the marquees' presence was legally precarious was made at its own risk.

50 *Jelson Ltd v Secretary of State for Communities and Local Government and Hinckley and Bosworth BC* [2018] EWCA Civ 24 is another recent example where the court failed to intervene in the exercise of a decision-maker's planning judgment. It was a case where a planning inspector had dismissed an appeal against an LPA's refusal of outline planning permission for housing development. The court held that the inspector did not err on clear and demonstrable public law grounds in identifying the full, objectively assessed needs for housing of the area.

51 See also *Travis Perkins (Properties) Ltd v Westminster CC* [2017] EWHC 2738 (Admin) where, in refusing an application for judicial review, the court held that an officer's report should not be laboriously dissected in order to find fault. The case, following *St Modwen Developments Ltd v Secretary of State for Communities and Local Government* [2017] EWCA Civ 1643, makes it plain that those attempting to bring challenges which rely on the dissection of committee reports are rarely likely to be successful. In practice, the courts will usually adopt a broad-brush approach in considering whether the report has sufficiently engaged with the issues. In *St Modwen Developments Ltd* at [7], Lindblom LJ had cautioned against 'hypercritical scrutiny' of, *inter alia*, planning officer reports which should not be 'laboriously dissected in an effort to find fault'.

EWCA Civ 1286 at [19], and applied in many cases at first instance (see, for example, the judgment of Hickinbottom J, as he then was, in *R. (on the application of Zurich Assurance Ltd, t/a Threadneedles Property Investments) v North Lincolnshire Council* [2012] EWHC 3708 (Admin) at [15]).

■ The principles are not complicated. Planning officers' reports to committee are not to be read with undue rigour, but with reasonable benevolence, and bearing in mind that they are written for councillors with local knowledge (see judgment of Baroness Hale of Richmond in *R. (on the application of Morge) v Hampshire CC* [2011] UKSC 2 at [36], and the judgment of Sullivan J, as he then was, in *R. v Mendip DC Ex p. Fabre* [2017] P.T.S.R. 1112; (2000) 80 P.& C.R. 500 at 509). Unless there is evidence to suggest otherwise, it may reasonably be assumed that, if the members followed the officer's recommendation, they did so on the basis of the advice that he or she gave (see the judgment of Lewison L.J in *R. (on the application of Palmer) v Herefordshire Council* [2016] EWCA Civ 1061 at [7]). The question for the court will always be whether, on a fair reading of the report as a whole, the officer has materially misled the members on a matter bearing upon their decision, and the error has gone uncorrected before the decision was made. Minor or inconsequential errors may be excused. It is only if the advice in the officer's report is such as to misdirect the members in a material way – so that, but for the flawed advice it was given, the committee's decision would or might have been different – that the court will be able to conclude that the decision itself was rendered unlawful by that advice.

■ Where the line is drawn between an officer's advice that is significantly or seriously misleading – misleading in a material way – and advice that is misleading but not significantly so will always depend on the context and circumstances in which the advice was given, and on the possible consequences of it. There will be cases in which a planning officer has inadvertently led a committee astray by making some significant error of fact (see, for example, *R. (on the application of Watermead Parish Council) v Aylesbury Vale DC* [2017] EWCA Civ 152). There will be others where the officer has simply failed to deal with a matter on which the committee ought to receive explicit advice if the local planning authority is to be seen to have performed its decision-making duties in accordance with the law (see, for example, *R. (on the application of Williams) v Powys CC* [2017] EWCA Civ 427; [2017] J.P.L. 1236 – in this case the planning officer's report said nothing about the application of the duty in relation to the proposed development in the Planning (Listed Buildings and Conservation Areas) Act 1990, s.66(1) (and the need to have special regard to the desirability of preserving the setting of a listed building), nor had the matter been discussed when the committee was considering the proposal. The committee's members had not been advised how, or even whether, the s.66(1) duty should be discharged, and were given no guidance on the conclusion they should reach in the performance of that duty. It was held that the lack of relevant advice from the officer and of any relevant discussion before the committee amounted to an error of law. The possible impact of the proposed wind turbine on the church's setting engaged the s.66(1) duty, and the LPA had failed to discharge it. The grant of planning permission was accordingly quashed so that the LPA could take the decision again properly directing itself on the s.66(1) duty). But unless there is some distinct and material defect in the officer's advice, the court will not interfere.'[52]

---

[52] In the same case, the Chancellor of the High Court said at [62] that ' … planning decisions are to be made by members of the Planning Committee advised by planning officers. In making their decisions, they must exercise their own planning judgment and the courts must give them space to make that judgment'. At [63], he said:

'Appeals should not, in future, be mounted on the basis of a legalistic analysis of the different formulations adopted in a planning officer's report. An appeal will only succeed, as Lindblom LJ has said, if there is some distinct and material defect in the report. Such reports are not, and should not be, written for lawyers, but for councillors who are well-versed in local knowledge and local factors. Planning committees approach such reports utilising that local knowledge and much common-sense. They should be allowed to make their judgments freely and fairly without undue interference by courts or judges who have picked apart the planning officer's advice on which they relied.'

At [64], he also said:

'It is also appropriate to reiterate what Lindblom LJ said at [35] of the *East Staffordshire* case to the effect that planning decision-makers have to exercise planning judgment as much when the presumption in favour of sustainable development is applicable as they do when it is not. The presumption may be rebutted when it is applicable, and planning permission may be granted where it is not. In each case, the decision-makers must use their judgment to decide where the planning balance lies based on material considerations. It is not for the court to second guess that planning judgment once it is exercised, unless as I have said it is based on a distinct and material defect in the report.'

See also *R (Crematoria Management Ltd) v Welwyn Hatfield BC* [2018] EWHC 382 (Admin), where a challenge by a neighbouring crematorium operator was allowed in a case where an LPA had granted itself planning permission for new crematoria facilities at a cemetery situated in the Green Belt. The court held that given the Green Belt location, the LPA had to demonstrate that there was a need for new crematoria facilities, in which the capacity of other crematoria in the area had to be taken into account. The 'need assessment' submitted by the LPA indicated that Broxbourne crematorium was close to its maximum capacity and that had been factored into the analysis. However, the capacity of the Broxbourne crematorium had not been factored in, meaning that the planning committee was wrongly advised that existing crematorium facilities were inadequate. The committee had therefore been misled about a material consideration and its decision to grant planning permission had been vitiated by legal error (*R v Selby DC ex parte Oxton Farms* [2017] PTSR 1103 applied). Senior Courts Act 1981, s 31(2A) did not assist the LPA as it was held that it was not 'highly likely' that the outcome would have been the same had the error not occurred. The prospect that the Broxbourne crematorium had spare capacity was a factor of some significance, and it was held that it could not be said that the decision would have been the same had the committee been told about it.

Chapter 14

Enforcement of Planning Control

INTRODUCTION

14.1   It should be understood that being in breach of planning control[1] is not a criminal offence. It is only when enforcement action[2] is taken by a local planning authority (LPA) to combat development which has taken place without the required planning permission or in breach of any condition or limitation subject to which planning permission has been granted[3] that criminal proceedings may be instituted against the offender. This chapter deals with the various steps which may be taken to prevent actual or threatened breaches of planning control, including enforcement action, and the periods within which enforcement action must be taken.

14.2   It is thought that in most cases people will cease acting in breach of planning control when they are threatened with enforcement action by the local authority which has a statutory duty to investigate breaches. Whether steps are taken to enforce any breach is a matter for the discretion of the authority, which is bound to have to prioritise its resources. However, there does appear to have been change since authorities started using the Proceeds of Crime Act 2002 to claw back benefits accrued from breaches of planning control such as arise in the case of unauthorised sub-division of residential property.

---

[1]   TCPA 1990, s 171A, for the meaning of what constitutes: (a) a breach of planning control; and (b) taking enforcement action.

[2]   Meaning (principally) the issue of an enforcement notice (defined in TCPA 1990, s 172) or an enforcement warning notice (defined in s 173ZA) or the service of a breach of condition notice (defined in s 187A).

[3]   In the case of permitted development, under a development order.

WHEN MIGHT FORMAL ENFORCEMENT ACTION NOT BE APPROPRIATE?

14.3   This issue is addressed in the National Planning Practice Guidance (NPPG) in the section 'Ensuring Effective Enforcement'.[4] Although the guidance does not condone a wilful breach of planning control, it is suggested that enforcement action should be proportionate to the breach of planning control to which it relates, and taken when it is expedient to do so. It is suggested that in deciding what is the most appropriate response to a breach of planning control, an LPA should usually avoid taking enforcement action where: (a) there is only a trivial or technical breach of control which causes no material harm or adverse impact on the amenity of the site or the surrounding area; (b) where the development is acceptable on its planning merits and formal enforcement action would solely be to regularise the development; and (c) where, in its assessment, the LPA considers that an application for retrospective planning permission is the appropriate way forward to regularise the situation as, for example, where planning conditions may need to be imposed.

TIME LIMITS FOR ENFORCEMENT ACTION[5]

14.4   Where there has been a breach of planning control consisting in the carrying out without planning permission of building, engineering, mining or other operations in, on, over or under land (i.e. unauthorised operational development), no enforcement action may be taken after the end of the period of four years beginning on the date on which those operations were substantially completed.[6]

14.5   Where there has been a breach of planning control consisting in the change of use of any building to use as a dwelling-house, no enforcement action may be taken after the end of the period of four years beginning with the date of breach.[7]

---

4   NPPG at Paragraph 011: Reference ID: 17b-011-20140306.

5   In default of taking enforcement action within the prescribed periods (subject to the rules on concealment), the right to take such action in relation to the breach of planning control lapses and the development or existing use will be lawful provided it does not infringe any breach of condition notice or enforcement notice then in force. See TCPA 1990, s 174(2)(d), where it is a defence to an enforcement notice that at the time when the notice was issued, no enforcement action could be taken in respect of the breach of planning control.

6   TCPA 1990, s 171B(1). See *Sage v Secretary of State for the Environment, Transport and the Regions* [2003] UKHL 22, [2003] 1 WLR 983.

7   TCPA 1990, s 171B(2). This provision applies to the unauthorised sub-division of a single dwelling-house into two or more separate dwelling-houses (which will be a question of fact and degree) (see *Doncaster Metropolitan Borough Council v Secretary of State for the Environment* [2002] EWHC

14.6   There is no restriction on when enforcement action may be taken in relation to a failure to obtain planning permission for the demolition of certain buildings in conservation areas in England.[8]

14.7   In the case of any other breaches of planning control,[9] no enforcement action may be taken after the end of the period of ten years beginning with the date of breach.[10]

14.8   The foregoing time limits do not prevent: (a) the service of a breach of condition notice if an enforcement notice in respect of the breach is already in force; or (b) taking further enforcement action if, during the period of four years ending with that action being taken, the LPA has taken enforcement action in relation to that breach.[11]

TIME LIMITS IN CASES OF CONCEALMENT – PLANNING ENFORCEMENT ORDERS

14.9   Because of the risk that persons may take advantage of their own actions in concealing breaches of planning control, with effect from 6/4/2012 a new procedure enables LPAs to take enforcement action once the ordinary periods for doing this have elapsed.[12] The position now is that where it appears to the LPA that there may have been a breach of planning control, it may apply to a

---

808 (Admin); *Van Dyck v Secretary of State for the Environment* (1993) 66 P & CR 61; *Arun District Council v First Secretary of State* [2006] EWCA Civ 1172, [2007] 1 WLR 524.

[8]   Involving relevant demolition within the meaning of TCPA 1990, s 196D.

[9]   In other words, all breaches of planning control, other than in cases involving unauthorised operational development or the unauthorised change of use of any building to use as a dwelling-house, must be brought within ten years of the date of breach. This will include breaches of planning control involving unauthorised changes of use or a breach of any condition subject to which planning permission was granted.

[10]   TCPA 1990, s 171B(3). In *Thurrock Borough Council v Secretary of State for the Environment, Transport and Regions* [2001] JPL 1388, it was held that a material change of use of land amounting to a breach of planning control lasted for a period of ten years if the use was continuous throughout that period. Whilst a short period of inactivity could not amount to a cessation of the unlawful activity, longer periods could, and cessation of the unlawful use merely constituted compliance with the law. In other words, significant periods of disuse will not count towards the rolling period of ten years in order to give rise to immunity.

[11]   TCPA 1990, s 171B(4). As where an LPA has withdrawn an earlier enforcement notice in relation to the same breach of planning control (see *Jarmain v Secretary of State for the Environment, Transport and Regions (No 1)* [2000] JPL 1063, where the court held that the words 'that breach' in s 171B(4)(b) referred to the physical situation on the land and that whilst the section could not be used to cover two different developments, it could be used to cover the same actual breach, which had been described in two different ways).

[12]   TCPA 1990, ss 171BA–171BC.

magistrates' court for a 'planning enforcement order'.[13] If an order is made,[14] enforcement action may be taken in respect of the apparent breach in the period of one year commencing at the end of 22 days beginning with the date of the order (or later date if there is a legal challenge),[15] and it is immaterial that the ordinary time limits for taking enforcement action may have expired, nor will it prevent the taking of enforcement action after the end of the year within which such enforcement action may be taken.

14.10   This procedure requires the LPA to apply for a planning enforcement order within a period of six months beginning with the date on which evidence of the apparent breach of planning control sufficient in the opinion of the LPA to justify the application came to the authority's knowledge.[16] In making a planning enforcement order (which must identify the apparent breach of planning control to which it relates and the date on which the court's decision was given),[17] the court must be satisfied, on the balance of probabilities: (a) that the apparent breach has (to any extent) been deliberately concealed; and (b) that the court considers it just to make the order, having regard to all the circumstances.[18]

POWERS AVAILABLE TO A LOCAL PLANNING AUTHORITY TO DEAL WITH ENFORCEMENT

Planning contravention notice

14.11   This is a useful investigative power whereby an LPA may gather any information they want for enforcement purposes from the owner or occupier of the land or whoever is carrying out operations on the land or who is using it for any purpose, where it appears to it that there may have been a breach of planning control, and can be a step which may lead to enforcement action.[19] It is a criminal offence for any person on whom a planning contravention notice has been served to fail, after the end of the period of 21 days beginning with the day of service, to

---

[13]   TCPA 1990, s 171BA(1).

[14]   TCPA 1990, s 171BA(2).

[15]   TCPA 1990, s 171BA(4).

[16]   TCPA 1990, s 171BB(1). For these purposes, a certificate signed on behalf of the LPA and stating the date on which evidence sufficient in the authority's opinion to justify the application came to the authority's knowledge will be conclusive evidence of that fact (see s 177BB(2)). See also s 171BB(4) for the provisions dealing with service of an application for a planning enforcement order and particulars as to the persons entitled to appear before, and be heard by, the court hearing the application.

[17]   TCPA 1990, s 171BC(2).

[18]   TCPA 1990, s 171BC(1).

[19]   TCPA 1990, s 171C.

comply with any requirement of the notice.[20] It is also an offence to give false or misleading statements.[21] It is a defence for a person to prove that he had a reasonable excuse for failing to comply with any requirement of the planning contravention notice.[22] Reference should also be made to the NPPG in the section 'Ensuring Effective Enforcement'.[23]

14.12 A planning contravention notice can be used to invite its recipient to respond constructively to the LPA about how any suspected breach of planning control may be satisfactorily remedied.

POWER OF ENTRY

14.13 Whereas a planning contravention notice operates to provide an LPA with information about suspected breaches of planning control, the authority may require access onto the land or into buildings to enable it to investigate matters more thoroughly. For these purposes, the LPA has a right of entry, with or without a warrant, to ascertain whether there is or has been any breach of planning control.[24] There must, of course, be reasonable grounds for the exercise of these powers and in the case of a dwelling-house, 24 hours' notice must be given.[25] Where entry is refused, a warrant may be obtained.[26] It will be an offence to wilfully obstruct a person acting in pursuance of a right of entry.[27]

TEMPORARY STOP NOTICE

14.14 An LPA may also issue a temporary stop notice enabling it to halt for 28 days activities on land which it thinks constitute a breach of planning control and where it considers it expedient that the activity (or any part of the activity)

---

[20] TCPA 1990, s 171D(1). A person guilty of an offence under s 171D(1) shall be liable on summary conviction to a fine not exceeding level 3 on the standard scale (s 171D(4)).

[21] TCPA 1990, s 171D(5). A person convicted of an offence under s 171D(5) will be liable on summary conviction to a fine not exceeding level 5 on the standard scale (£1,000) (s 171D(6)).

[22] TCPA 1990, s 171D(3).

[23] NPPG at Paragraph: 015 Reference ID: 17b-015-20140306 to 17b-016-20140306

[24] TCPA 1990, ss 196A–196C.

[25] TCPA 1990, s 196A(4).

[26] TCPA 1990, s 196B(1).

[27] TCPA 1990, s 196C(2) (liability to a fine not exceeding level 3 on the standard scale – £1,000).

should be stopped immediately.[28] The notice may be served on the person whom the authority thinks is carrying on the activity, a person whom the authority thinks is an occupier of the land, and any person whom the authority thinks has an interest in the land.[29] The authority must display on the land a copy of the notice and a statement of the effect of the notice and of section 171G of the Town and Country Planning Act 1990 (TCPA 1990).[30]

14.15 A temporary stop notice ceases to have effect after 28 days (or at the end of such shorter period starting on that day as is specified in the notice) or if it is withdrawn by the LPA.[31] However, the notice cannot prohibit the use of a building as a dwelling-house,[32] nor will it prohibit the carrying out of an activity which has been carried out (whether or not continuously) for a period of four years ending with the day on which the copy of the notice is first displayed.[33] For these purposes, any period during which the activity is authorised by planning permission must be ignored.[34] Any further notices will only be permissible if the LPA has already taken some other enforcement action in relation to the breach.[35] A person commits an offence if he contravenes (including by causing or permitting such contravention) a temporary stop notice.[36] It will be a defence to show that the notice had not been served or properly displayed on the land,[37] or that the accused did not know, and could not reasonably be expected

---

[28] *Carespec Ltd v Wolverhampton City Council* [2016] EWHC 521 (Admin). A temporary stop notice is intended for urgent situations only and was not designed to be susceptible to judicial review.

[29] TCPA 1990, s 171E(4).

[30] TCPA 1990, s 171E(5).

[31] TCPA 1990, s 171E(7).

[32] TCPA 1990, s 171F(1)(a).

[33] TCPA 1990, ss 171F(2) and 171E(6).

[34] TCPA 1990, s 171F(4).

[35] TCPA 1990, s 171F(5).

[36] TCPA 1990, s 171G(1) and (2). A party convicted of an offence under this section shall be liable to a fine, and there is no maximum fine even for a summary conviction (s 171G(6)). It was formerly the case that on summary conviction a party guilty of an offence was liable to a fine not exceeding £20,000 or to an unlimited fine on conviction on indictment. However, s 171G(6) was amended by Sch 4(1), para 18(2) of the Legal Aid, Sentencing and Punishment of Offenders Act 2012 (Fines on Summary Conviction) Regulations 2015 (SI 2015/664), with effect from 12/3/2015, subject to transitional provisions. In determining the amount of any fine, the court must have regard in particular to any financial benefit which has accrued, or has appeared to accrue, to the person convicted in consequence of the offence (s 171G(7)). It should be noted that an offence under the section may be charged by reference to a day or a longer period of time (s 171G(3)) and that a person may be convicted of more than one offence in relation to the same temporary stop notice by reference to different days or periods of time (s 171G(4)).

[37] In accordance with TCPA 1990; and s 171E(5)(a).

to know, of its existence.[38] There are also provisions as to compensation in relation to loss arising from the prohibition caused by a temporary stop notice.[39] Reference should also be made to the NPPG in the section 'Ensuring Effective Enforcement'.[40]

BREACH OF CONDITION NOTICE – ENFORCEMENT OF CONDITIONS

14.16 Provision is made for the service by the LPA of a breach of condition notice on any person who is carrying out or has carried out the development or any other person in control of the land, requiring him to secure compliance with such of the conditions specified in the notice which are not being complied with.[41] It shall then be the obligation of the person served with the notice to take those steps which the authority considers necessary to remedy the breach complained of.[42] The period allowed for compliance is not less than 28 days from service of the notice, which may be extended by a further notice.[43] A breach of condition notice may be withdrawn, but a withdrawal of the notice does not affect the power of the authority to serve a further breach of condition notice in relation to the conditions specified in the earlier notice or any other conditions.[44] If at the end of the time allowed for compliance with the breach of condition notice, any of the conditions specified in the notice are still not complied with and the steps specified in the notice have not been taken, or as the case may be, the activities specified in the notice have not ceased, the person who is in breach of the notice will be guilty of an offence.[45] It shall be a defence for a person charged with an offence to prove that he took all reasonable measures to secure compliance with the conditions (or limitations) specified in the notice, or that he no longer had

---

[38] TCPA 1990, s 171G(5)(b).

[39] TCPA 1990, s 171H, which is only partially in force.

[40] NPPG at Paragraph 036: Reference ID: 17b-036-20140306 to 17b-045-20140306.

[41] TCPA 1990, s 187A.

[42] TCPA 1990, s 187A(5).

[43] TCPA 1990, s 187A(7).

[44] TCPA 1990, s 187A(6).

[45] TCPA 1990, s 187A(8) and (9). The offence is summary with the maximum fine not exceeding level 4 in England (£2,500) or level 3 in Wales (£1,000).

control of the land.[46] There is no right of appeal to the Secretary of State against a breach of condition notice whose validity may be challenged by way of an application to the High Court for judicial review. Reference should also be made to the NPPG in the section 'Ensuring Effective Enforcement'.[47]

INJUNCTIONS RESTRAINING BREACHES OF PLANNING CONTROL

14.17 An LPA may also apply to the High Court or county court for an injunction to restrain any actual or apprehended breach of planning control whether or not it has exercised, or is proposing to exercise, any of its other enforcement powers.[48] Such injunctions are particularly common in cases involving the parking of caravans and/or encampments and/or works within Green Belts or on green

---

[46] TCPA 1990, s 187(11).

[47] NPPG at Paragraph: 046 Reference ID: 17b-046-20140306 to 17b-049-20140306.

[48] TCPA 1990, s 187B. The procedure is set out at CPR, Pt 8. See PD 8A at paras 9 and 20. In cases of urgency, application should be made for an interim injunction (see *American Cyanamid v Ethicon Ltd* [1975] AC 396 for the principles underlying the grant of an interim injunction), although applications should usually be made with notice. In the case of a permanent injunction, the position is as stated by Lord Bingham in *South Bucks District Council v Porter (No 1)* [2003] UKHL 26, [2003] 2 AC 558, at [20] (citing with approval from Simon Brown LJ, in the Court of Appeal) and [27]–[38]. This case involved gypsies living on land in breach of planning control. The court held: (a) that the jurisdiction under s 187B was an original and not supervisory jurisdiction, and a defendant seeking to resist the grant of an injunction was not restricted to reliance on those grounds which would found an application for judicial review; (b) that the court had a discretion under s 187B which had to be exercised judicially; the courts would be strongly disposed to grant an injunction where it appeared that a breach or apprehended breach would continue or occur unless and until effectively restrained by law and that nothing short of an injunction would provide effective restraint; (c) issues of planning policy and judgment were matters for the LPA and the Secretary of State, but the court was not precluded from entertaining issues not directly related to planning policy or judgment; nor need the court refuse to consider the possibility that a pending or prospective application for planning permission might succeed; (d) LPAs were entitled to consider the personal circumstances of the gypsies; if it appeared that the LPA had fully considered the issues of hardship and had nonetheless resolved that it was necessary or expedient to seek an injunction, that would ordinarily weigh heavily in favour of granting relief, since the court must accord respect to the balance which the planning authority had struck between public and private interests; and (e) it was for the court to decide whether the remedy sought was just and proportionate in all the circumstances. In the event, the appeals of the local authorities in three conjoined cases were dismissed.

spaces.[49] In such cases it is open to the court to make an order against persons unknown for limited periods prohibiting the stationing of caravans and/or preventing development without planning permission.[50] The breach of an

---

[49] *Runnymede Borough Council v Doig* [2017] EWHC 2013 (Admin), where a group of travellers who had remained at a site despite a local authority obtaining an injunction against them were ordered to vacate the site within ten days. Although the travellers had an outstanding planning application for the site, they were not overwhelmingly likely to succeed, which meant that it did not tip the balance in their favour. It was a case where the site had been transformed into a building site with the intention of creating a caravan camp for travellers. No planning permission had been sought, and the defendants had simply moved their caravans onto the site. A planning application had been made online, but it was treated as invalid until certain procedural requirements had been met. Despite the local authority obtaining injunctive relief forbidding the carrying out of further works on the site and preventing the defendants from residing on the land, they did not leave the site. The judge dismissed applications for an appeal and a stay in respect of their obligation to leave the land, considering that doing so would not cause significant disruption to the health and welfare of the defendants' children. The defendants remained on site and were in contempt of court. The defendants sought a variation in the terms of the order which would allow them to remain at the site until the determination of their planning application. The application was refused. The court held that unless there was new material before the court which altered the balance in favour of the defendants, permitting a variation in the terms of the order would undermine the order that had already been made. The evidence of the defendants' personal circumstances was not materially different than that already put before the court. Although the prospect of success on the planning application could have tipped the balance in favour of the defendants, the best that could be said for their prospects was that they existed; they were nowhere near being overwhelmingly likely to succeed. There was no reason to vary the order, and the witness statement evidence did not persuade the court that any variation to the original order, which was still reasonable and proportionate, would be justified, and the defendants accordingly had to vacate the site within ten days of the hearing.

[50] *Waltham Forest LBC v Persons Unknown* [2018] EWHC 240 (QB); Lang J found that it was just and proportionate to grant a three-year, final, borough-wide injunction preventing travellers from encamping on any Green Spaces and an interim injunction preventing the same from happening on industrial sites. The travellers' activities, which were in breach of planning control, were causing a nuisance and health risks, and the local authority had already incurred considerable expense in cleaning up the sites. The local authority owned the Green Spaces in the borough, including 129 parks and woodland areas. Travellers had been camping on them in large groups, using mobile homes and caravans, in breach of planning control. Their activities were interfering with the safe use of the Green Spaces and were causing a nuisance. They were also creating health risks due to the deposits of excrement, fire hazards and the fly tipping of industrial waste, such as asbestos. It sought and obtained a borough-wide injunction, as previous injunctions against specific sites had meant that the travellers had simply moved on to other Green Spaces in the borough. The travellers' activities had gone on for a number of years. The terms of the interim injunction had been posted at the sites and had successfully reduced the planning control breaches. After the interim injunction had been granted, the travellers moved on to the industrial estates, targeting unprotected sites. The local authority therefore successfully sought a borough-wide injunction to restrain encampments on industrial sites, including eight car parks and five industrial estates. In granting the application, Lang J held that any interference with an individual's right to respect for his or her home, even if in accordance with national law and directed to a legitimate aim, had to be proportionate (following *South Buckinghamshire DC v Porter (No 1)* [2003] 2 AC 558).The court was satisfied that unless the injunction was continued, the unauthorised use of the Green Spaces would resume and that a borough-wide approach had been successful in other areas

injunction may lead to committal, although the court has a discretion to deal with matters such as by imposing a suspended prison term.

14.18 Reference should also be made to the NPPG in the section 'Ensuring Effective Enforcement'.[51]

(*Harlow DC v McGinley* [2017] EWHC 1851 (QB) applied). The Green Spaces were for the local residents to enjoy, and it was not a case where the travellers would be made homeless as a direct result of the order. Continuing the injunction was both just and proportionate. It was appropriate to grant the injunction for three years to protect the residents and to act as a deterrence. In the case of the industrial sites, the court was satisfied that the travellers were causing disruption and that the industrial sites were not being used for their intended purposes, creating health risks. The local authority would incur considerable expense cleaning the sites up. There was a serious issue to be tried, and damages were not an adequate remedy. It was just and convenient in the circumstances to grant an interim injunction. It was not appropriate to grant a final injunction with regard to the industrial sites without giving the travellers an opportunity to respond at a return date. *Enfield LBC v Persons Unknown*, unreported, 4/10/2017, QBD, is another case where the court granted a three-year prohibitory injunction against persons unknown who had been setting up encampments on public Green Spaces which had disrupted residents' use of the areas and had created hazardous waste, among other anti-social consequences. The local authority had applied for possession orders in respect of plots of land, but they had had a limited effect. It had successfully sought an interim injunction three months earlier, and incursions had reduced since that time. Enforcement officers had posted 346 notices of the order across 130 sites, and it had also been published in local newspapers and on the local authority's website, along with the return date. On such evidence, the court was satisfied that there had been proper service of the interim injunction and that the return date had been made known so that anyone who had wanted to attend the final hearing had had notice. It was also satisfied that applications for possession of land had not been ineffective in resolving the problem and that the interim injunction had been effective and that an injunction against persons unknown for three years was overwhelmingly the appropriate course for the future protection of Green Spaces and to restrain criminal activity which disrupted use of the land, caused loss of amenity, produced hazardous waste and created costs. See also *Ali v Newham LBC*, 26/1/2018, unreported, QBD, HH Judge Walden-Smith, where the trustees of a mosque and religious centre were held to their undertaking given almost seven years previously to submit a planning application for development that would comply with the local plan, failing which they would remove the unauthorised development. See also *Basingstoke and Deane BC v Eastwood* [2018] EWHC 179 (QB), an injunction would not be varied to enable the applicant and his family to continue their occupation of the land in circumstances where the applicant's prospects of success with his planning application were remote and where his rights under European Convention for the Protection of Human Rights and Fundamental Freedoms 1950, Art 8 and those of his family were engaged, but the extent of the interference was limited (*Mid-Bedfordshire DC v Brown* [2004] EWCA Civ 1709 and *Broxbourne BC v Robb* [2011] EWCA Civ 1355 applied).

51 NPPG at Paragraph: 050 Reference ID: 17b-050-20140306 and 17b-051-20140306 (the latter of which concerns the important issue of seeking an injunction against an unknown person where the LPA will have to provide affidavit evidence of its ability to ascertain the identity of the proposed defendant(s), within the time reasonably available, and the steps taken in attempting to do so).

ENFORCEMENT NOTICE

14.19 The LPA may issue an enforcement notice where it appears to it that:

(a) there has been a breach of planning control; and
(b) it is expedient to issue the notice, having regard to the provisions of the development plan and to any other material considerations.[52]

14.20 The notice must be served[53] on the owner and on the occupier of the land to which it relates and on any other person having an interest in the land who, in the opinion of the authority, is materially affected by the notice.[54] The notice must be served not more than 28 days after its date of issue and not less than 28 days before the date specified in it as the date on which it is to take effect.[55] There is no restriction on the number of enforcement notices which may be served in relation to the same breach.[56]

14.21 There are provisions dealing with: (a) the giving of an assurance as regards prosecution;[57] (b) the contents and effect of the notice;[58] (c) variation and

---

[52] TCPA 1990, s 172(1).

[53] TCPA 1990, s 329, which deals with the service of notices or other documents under the Act. In *Newham LBC v Ahmed* [2016] EWHC 679 (Admin), the court held that a local authority had been entitled to serve an enforcement notice on property owners at their address as it appeared on the Land Registry proprietorship register if, as was found, it was the respondents' last known address, and to have done so by ordinary post, pursuant to the Local Government Act 1972 (LGA 1972), s 233(2). It was unnecessary for it to send the notice by recorded delivery or registered post as required by TCPA 1990, s 329(1)(c). It was held that the methods of service in LGA 1972, s 233 are in addition to the methods permitted in the 1990 Act (applying *Gloucestershire CC v Keyway (Gloucester) Ltd* [2003] EWHC 3012 (Admin)).

[54] TCPA 1990, s 172(2).

[55] TCPA 1990, s 172(3). See *R (Stern) v Horsham District Council* [2013] PTSR 1502.

[56] *Biddle v Secretary of State for the Environment, Transport and Regions* [1999] JPL 835.

[57] TCPA 1990, s 172A (which may be withdrawn under s 172A(2)).

[58] TCPA 1990, s 173. In *Miller-Mead v Minister of Housing and Local Government* [1963] 2 QB 196, Upjohn LJ posed this simple test at p 232, namely, 'Does the notice tell [the person on whom it is served] fairly what he has done wrong and what he must do to remedy it?'. In *Saraodia v Redbridge LBC* [2017] EWHC 2347 (Admin), an enforcement notice that had required the owner of a house to remove a two-storey side extension and a single-storey rear extension, when in fact the house had a single-storey side extension and both a single and two-storey rear extension, was found to be hopelessly unclear and was a nullity. The notice could not have been saved by TCPA 1990, s 176 (which allows the Secretary of State, on an appeal under s 174, to correct defects, errors or any misdescription in the enforcement notice or to vary its terms, thereby correcting flaws in the notice, provided it will not cause injustice to the appellant or the LPA), as the amendments it required were too extensive and could not have been made without injustice to the owner. It follows that where a notice cannot be remedied under s 176 because the Secretary of State cannot be satisfied that it will not cause injustice as above, he will allow the appeal and may quash the notice. Enforcement notices that are incapable of being remedied under s 176 (because

withdrawal;[59] (d) appeals;[60] (e) execution and cost of works required by the notice;[61] (f) offence where the notice is not complied with;[62] (g) effect of planning permission, etc. on enforcement or breach of condition notices;[63] (h) effect of enforcement notice against subsequent development;[64] and (i) enforcement by the Secretary of State.[65] The intention within this section is to deal only with the main issues surrounding the issue and effect of enforcement notices.

14.22 The object of an enforcement notice is to notify recipients: (a) exactly what, in the view of the LPA, constitutes a breach of planning control;[66] and (b) what steps need to be taken, or what activities are required to cease in order to remedy the breach of which complaint is made.[67]

---

none of the statutory grounds of appeal arise) can also be challenged by way of judicial review as, for instance, where an enforcement notice is issued without authority. See also *Beg, Beg, Beg and Baig Nasser v Luton BC* [2017] EWHC 3435 (Admin), where the notice was not found to have been a nullity (in the sense that there was something obviously wrong with it on its face) and where arguments as to invalidity should have been pursued on an appeal to the Secretary of State.

59   TCPA 1990, s 173A.

60   TCPA 1990, ss 174–177.

61   TCPA 1990, s 178. The section is one which gives an LPA power to enter land and take the necessary steps required by an enforcement notice which have not been taken within the compliance period and to recover from the owner of the land any expenses reasonably incurred by them in doing so. The power is exercisable summarily, although it is good practice to give notice of the intended exercise of this power to an owner or occupier of the land, not least in potentially sensitive situations. A decision to exercise this power would be subject to judicial review. See *R (Eastwood) v Windsor and Maidenhead RLBC* [2016] EWCA Civ 437, where the Court of Appeal rejected a challenge to the decision of the LPA to exercise its powers under s 178 to enter and clear land which was being occupied as an unauthorised caravan site. The LPA had already waited for a considerable period of time before implementing its enforcement notice, and during that time serious harm to the public interest had continued by reason of the caravan encampment on Green Belt land.

62   TCPA 1990, s 179.

63   TCPA 1990, s 180.

64   TCPA 1990, s 181.

65   TCPA 1990, s 182.

66   TCPA 1990, s 173(1)(a) (and the notice should also specify the paragraph in s 171A(1) within which, in the opinion of the authority, the breach of planning control falls, namely whether it is: (a) a breach arising from the carrying out of development without the required planning permission; or (b) the failure to comply with any condition or limitation subject to which planning permission has been granted (s 173(2)).

67   TCPA 1990, s 173(3) and (4). It is vital that the enforcement notice should clearly specify the steps that should be taken to achieve compliance, otherwise the notice would be defective and any conviction for breaching its terms is liable to be quashed. The steps required by an enforcement notice could only be for the purposes of remedying the breach. They could not act against works that were not part of the breach (*Kestrel Hydro v Secretary of State for Communities and Local Government* [2016] EWCA Civ 784).

14.23 An enforcement notice may, for instance, require: (a) the alteration or removal of any buildings or works and the reinstatement of the land to its former condition;[68] (b) the carrying out of any building or other operations; (c) any activity on the land not to be carried on (except to the extent specified in the notice);[69] (d) the contour of a deposit of refuse or waste materials on land to be modified by altering the gradient or gradients of its sides; or (e) in the case of a notice issued in respect of a breach of planning control consisting of the demolition of a building, the construction of a replacement building which is as similar as possible to the demolished building.[70] The notice must also specify the date on which it is to take effect,[71] the period for compliance[72] and the reasons why the LPA considers it expedient to issue the notice. It must also specify those policies and proposals in the development plan which are considered relevant to the decision to issue the notice and the boundaries of the land to which it relates. The notice must also be accompanied by an explanatory note which must inform

---

[68] It was reported in *Planning* on 22/2/2017 that Wandsworth LBC had issued an enforcement notice requiring a developer to demolish a 12-flat development. In that case, planning permission had been given in 2008 to build 12 flats. The consent permitted the construction of nine one-bedroom flats and a further three with two bedrooms. As built, there were eight two-bedroom flats and four with just one bedroom by virtue of the use of a basement to provide two of the flats, which would not have been permitted as the area was prone to flooding and previous tenants in the basement had been affected by flooding. Further, the basement had little or no natural light; most of the flats were also too small and had sub-standard amenity space and the completed building was not in accordance with the approved drawings. The breaches led to enforcement action which required the developer to undo all the elements of the development for which he did not have permission, which meant in practice that he would be forced to demolish the entire building and start again. The Chair of the Planning Committee is reported to have said that it was 'difficult to recall a more outrageous flouting of the planning laws and for doing so I'm afraid he must remove what is there and replace it with a new building that conforms to design standards and provides the people living there with proper facilities and appropriate living space'.

[69] *Kestrel Hydro v Secretary of State for Communities and Local Government* [2016] EWCA Civ 784; when an LPA took enforcement action in respect of an unauthorised change of use of land, the notice could require the cessation of the unauthorised use and the removal of any building works that facilitated, and were integral to, that use (approving the principle in *Murfitt v Secretary of State for the Environment and East Cambridgeshire DC* (1980) 40 P & CR 254 and *Somak Travel Ltd v Secretary of State for the Environment* (1988) 55 P & CR 250). In the circumstances, an enforcement notice directed at an unauthorised change of use could lawfully require the land to be restored to its pre-change condition by the cessation of the unauthorised use and the removal of the associated works, provided the works were integral to, or part and parcel of, the unauthorised use. The principle did not apply to works that had previously been undertaken for some lawful use and were capable of being employed for some lawful use once the unlawful use had ceased. However, it could apply to unauthorised changes of use where the associated works, viewed on their own, would have become immune from enforcement under s 171B(1); whether the principle applied was a question of fact and degree.

[70] TCPA 1990, s 173(5)–(7).

[71] TCPA 1990, s 173(8).

[72] TCPA 1990, s 173(9).

the recipient of the notice of his rights of appeal and the names and addresses of the persons served.[73] Where an enforcement notice could have required any buildings or works to be removed, or any activity to stop, but has stipulated some lesser requirements (i.e. where there is under-enforcement), and all the requirements of the notice have been complied with, planning permission is deemed to be granted for those remaining operations or use where the enforcement notice could have required such activities to cease but did not do so.[74] Similarly, where an enforcement notice requires the construction of a replacement building and all the requirements of the notice with respect to that construction have been complied with, planning permission is deemed to be granted in respect of the development consisting of that construction.[75]

14.24 An enforcement notice may be varied (such as by extending the compliance period) or withdrawn, whether or not the notice has taken effect.[76]

ENFORCEMENT BY THE SECRETARY OF STATE

14.25 The Secretary of State also has power to issue an enforcement notice should he consider it expedient to do so.[77] However, before doing so he must first consult the LPA.[78]

APPEAL AGAINST ENFORCEMENT NOTICE

14.26 Appeal lies to the Secretary of State on the following grounds:[79]

---

[73] Town and Country Planning (Enforcement Notices and Appeals) (England) Regulations 2002 (SI 2002/2682), regs 4–5 (and in Wales, Town and Country Planning (Enforcement Notices and Appeals) (Wales) Regulations 2003 (SI 2003/394), regs 3–4).

[74] TCPA 1990, s 173(11). An LPA must consider carefully the ramifications of under-enforcement, as a poorly drafted enforcement notice could give rise to the unintended consequence that planning permission would be granted across the remainder of the planning unit after the requirements of the notice had been complied with. LPAs must also take care not to attempt to fashion a conditional permission by under-enforcing breaches. The requirements of an enforcement notice are not planning conditions and do not have the same effect.

[75] TCPA 1990, s 173(12).

[76] TCPA 1990, s 173A.

[77] TCPA 1990, s 182.

[78] TCPA 1990, s 182(2).

[79] TCPA 1990, s 174 (although a decision as to the 'expediency' of issuing a notice or in not taking enforcement action or, exceptionally, if the notice is a nullity, then, in such cases, the steps taken by the LPA may also be challenged by judicial review (*R (Gazelle Properties Ltd) v Bath and*

(a) that in respect of any breach of planning control which may be constituted by the matters stated in the notice, planning permission ought to be granted, or the condition or limitation concerned ought to be discharged;[80]

(b) that in respect of any breach of planning control identified in the notice, those matters have not occurred;[81]

(c) that those matters (if they have occurred) do not constitute a breach of planning control;[82]

(d) that, at the date when the notice was issued, no enforcement action could be taken in respect of any breach of planning control which may be constituted by those matters;[83]

(e) that copies of the enforcement notice were not served as required;[84]

North West Somerset Council [2011] JPL 702; *R v Sevenoaks District Council ex parte Palley* [1995] JPL 915; *Rhymney Valley District Council v Secretary of State for Wales* [1985] JPL 27).

[80] TCPA 1990, s 174(2)(a). This ground is not available where the land is in England and the enforcement notice was issued at a time: (a) after the making of a related application for planning permission; but (b) before the end of the period applicable under s 78(2) in the case of that application (see s 174(2A)–(2B)).

[81] TCPA 1990, s 174(2)(b). See *Benson v Secretary of State* [2018] EWHC 700 (Admin) where, under TCPA 1990, s 289, the court ordered the inspector to attend the hearing and for the issue of cross-examination to be considered first at the substantive hearing. The context involved the inspector's refusal to admit in evidence: (a) bank statements showing rental receipts; and (b) a letter from an apparent tenant confirming his residence between 2010 and 2013, in order to justify the claimant's assertion that an annexe to residential property that had been in use as a self-contained dwelling for four consecutive years since it was built in 2007 was immune from enforcement action. It was claimed that the inspector had failed to exercise his discretion correctly to admit the documents and in any event failed to give reasons. The court held that a power to permit cross-examination of a planning inspector should be exercised extremely sparingly and only where the interests of justice required it. The view taken was that the bank statements were potentially relevant and that a consideration of the bank statements (and to a lesser extent the tenant's letter) might have led to a different conclusion to that reached by the inspector.

[82] TCPA 1990, s 174(2)(c).

[83] TCPA 1990, s 174(2)(d), namely, where the time limits for taking enforcement action in s 171B have expired (i.e. in the case of operational development, no enforcement action may be taken after the end of the period of four years, beginning with the date on which the operations were substantially completed; in the case of the change of use of a building to use as a single dwelling-house, no action may be taken after the end of the period of four years beginning with the date of breach; and in the case of any other breach of planning control (viz: material changes of use), no enforcement action may be taken after the end of the period of ten years beginning with the date of breach). There is no restriction on when enforcement action may be taken in relation to a breach of planning control in respect of relevant demolition within the meaning of s 196D (i.e. demolition of unlisted buildings in conservation areas).

[84] TCPA 1990, s 174(2)(e) (as required by s 172). Although by s 176(5), it is open to the Secretary of State to disregard the failure to serve a person who ought to have been served with the notice if neither the appellant nor that person have been substantially prejudiced by the failure to serve him.

(f)   that the steps required by the notice to be taken, or the activities required by the notice to stop, exceed what is necessary to remedy any breach of planning control which may be constituted by those matters or, as the case may be, to remedy any injury to amenity which has been caused by any such breach;[85]

(g)   that the period for compliance falls short of what should reasonably be allowed;[86]

(h)   where the breach of planning control relates to relevant demolition,[87] an appeal may also be brought on the grounds that: (i) the demolition was urgently necessary in the interests of health or safety; (ii) it was not practicable to secure safety or health by works of repair or works affording temporary support or shelter; and (iii) the demolition was the minimum measure necessary.[88]

14.27   Any appeal to the Secretary of State must be made *before* the date specified in the enforcement notice as the date on which it is to take effect.[89] There is no power to extend time. An appellant must submit a statement in writing specifying the grounds on which he is appealing, along with such further information as may be prescribed, either when giving notice of the appeal to the Secretary of State or within the prescribed time.[90] Where an appeal is brought the enforcement notice shall be of no effect pending the final determination or withdrawal of the appeal.[91]

---

[85]   TCPA 1990, s 174(2)(f).

[86]   TCPA 1990, s 174(2)(g) (see also s 173(9)).

[87]   Within the meaning of TCPA 1990, s 196D (i.e. demolition of certain buildings in a conservation area).

[88]   TCPA 1990, s 174(2C).

[89]   TCPA 1990, s 174(3) (where the ways in which notice of the appeal should be given to the Secretary of State before the date on which the enforcement notice is to take effect are set out).

[90]   TCPA 1990, s 174(4). The contents of the written statement of appeal (which must specify the grounds and facts relied on) and the prescribed time for submitting it if it does not accompany the notice of appeal (to be no later than 14 days from the date on which the Secretary of State sends the appellant a notice requiring him to provide him with his written statement) is governed by Town and Country Planning (Enforcement Notices and Appeals) (England) Regulations 2002 (SI 2002/2682), reg 6 (and in Wales, Wales, Town and Country Planning (Enforcement Notices and Appeals) (Wales) Regulations 2003 (SI 2003/394), reg 5).

[91]   TCPA 1990, s 175(4).

TWO RECENT CASES WHERE INSPECTORS WERE FOUND TO HAVE MADE NO ERRORS OF LAW WHEN UPHOLDING ENFORCEMENT NOTICES

Alderson v Secretary of State for Communities and Local Government[92]

14.28 *Alderson* involved the stationing of a caravan for residential purposes and the construction of decking. It concerned a farm where the owner began planting fruit and nut trees and, in 2012, brought a static caravan onto the land. The owner claimed that it was only used for accommodation for those involved in the harvesting of the fruit. The first enforcement notice alleged that the owner had changed the use of the land from agriculture to a mixed use for agriculture and the stationing of a caravan for residential purposes. The second notice alleged that the owner had erected decking around the caravan without planning permission. The notices required the removal of the caravan and decking. In dismissing the first appeal, the inspector found that there was little or no evidence of any use of the caravan other than simply as residential accommodation and that planning permission for its retention could not be granted as the care and nurture of the fruit or nuts did not require an on-site presence. In relation to the decking, the inspector found that the requirement to remove it was not excessive in order to remedy the breach of planning control. The owner appealed alleging, in relation to the first notice, that the caravan was ancillary to the agricultural use of the land and it was not necessary to require its removal as it was fulfilling an agricultural function. In relation to the second notice, the owner alleged that the inspector had erred in finding that the requirement to remove the decking was not excessive. The owner's appeal was dismissed. Although the inspector could have granted planning permission for a mixed use of the land for agricultural and for the stationing of a caravan, she did not do so. The conclusions she reached were found to have been reasonably open to her and did not show any error of law. In terms of the ancillary use of the caravan, the inspector had contemplated some ancillary agricultural use, but not enough to change her conclusion that the alleged breach of planning control had occurred. In any event, planning permission on appeal could only be granted in relation to all or any of the matters said to constitute a breach of planning control. The inspector could not therefore grant planning permission for the retention of the caravan for agricultural purposes as that was not a part of the breach of planning control alleged and would not involve development for which permission was needed. It was also not open to the inspector to find that the steps required by the notice exceeded what was necessary to remedy the breach of planning control as the owner had not raised that issue on appeal to the inspector. In any event, it would have been inconsistent with the

---

[92]   [2017] EWHC 1415 (Admin).

inspector's findings as to the use of the caravan and its effects to have decided that it was not necessary to cease that use. In relation to the second notice (and the decking), the inspector had decided that suggestions made by the owner that the size of the decking could be reduced were not clear or precise and so it was not feasible to alter the requirements of the notice. This was a matter for the planning judgment of the inspector. Once the caravan had been removed, no purpose would be served by the decking whether it was reduced in size or not. It was found that the inspector had addressed the right questions and had determined that it was necessary to remedy the breach of planning control by removing the decking. The inspector was not required to consider whether any lesser steps would remedy any injury to amenity as that was not the basis of the notice.

Arnold v Secretary of State for Communities and Local Government[93]

14.29 In *Arnold* the Court of Appeal dismissed an appeal against the dismissal of an appeal against an enforcement notice. The appellants' Arts and Crafts home was in the Green Belt and in an Area of Outstanding Natural Beauty (AONB). They had built two large extensions, erroneously believing that they were permitted development. An enforcement notice was issued requiring demolition. The appellants appealed and submitted three alternative development schemes (the central question was whether the inspector had failed lawfully on a section 174 appeal to consider alternatives to the development against which the enforcement notice was directed). The inspector had held that the scale of the development amounted to a new dwelling. He directed that planning permission could only be granted in respect of matters stated in the notice as constituting a breach of planning control, and that he should not consider alternative proposals that fell outside the scope of the notice. The inspector held that it was questionable whether he could substitute any of the alternative schemes but that, in any event, they all fell outside the scope of the enforcement notice. He found that parts of the building were not functionally and physically severable so as to enable permission to be granted in part and that the alternatives were not acceptable to overcome the planning harm caused to the openness of the Green Belt. The judge on appeal said that the inspector had considered the alternative schemes and he had been entitled to reach his conclusions. The issues on appeal were whether the inspector had: (a) misdirected himself as to his power to grant planning permission for an alternative scheme; and (b) undertaken a sufficient assessment of the alternatives. The Court of Appeal dismissed the appeal, holding that it was necessary to read the inspector's conclusions fully, in their proper context, and bearing in mind that the decision letter had been written principally for the parties to the appeals who were familiar with the evidence and submissions. Particular

---

93   [2017] EWCA Civ 231.

passages in the inspector's conclusions should not be isolated from others that were also relevant to the specific point being considered. When that was done, no error could be found in the inspector's approach. He had not made the mistake of ignoring any alternative proposal on the basis that it was materially different from the subject matter of the enforcement notice. He had considered whether it was possible to exercise his statutory power to grant planning permission for a part of the matters constituting the alleged breach of planning control in the enforcement notice. His findings that the alternative proposals were materially different forms of development to what constituted the deemed application for planning permission, and about severability and acceptability, could not be challenged. The court found that, having directed himself properly to his powers, the inspector was not obliged to spell out for each alternative scheme the same basic conclusions as he expressed in respect of all of them. He had been well aware of the differences between the alternative schemes, and if those differences had been significant in his assessment he would have said so.

SECRETARY OF STATE'S POWERS IN THE CASE OF ENFORCEMENT NOTICE APPEALS

14.30 The Secretary of State has the power to correct any defect, error or misdescription in the enforcement notice or may vary the terms of the enforcement notice, provided he is satisfied that the correction or variation will not cause injustice to the appellant or the LPA.[94] Where the Secretary of State

---

[94]   TCPA 1990, s 176(1). *Wealden District Council v Secretary of State for the Environment* [1983] JPL 234; *Harrogate Borough Council v Secretary of State for the Environment* [1987] JPL 288; *R v Secretary of State for the Environment ex parte P.F. Ahern (London) Ltd* [1989] 2 PLR 96; *Duguid v Secretary of State for the Environment, Transport and the Regions* (2001) 82 P & CR 6 (applying *Mansi v Elstree Rural District Council* (1965) 16 P & CR 153); *Moore v Secretary of State for Communities and Local Government* [2012] EWCA Civ 1202 (where it was said that if there was an obvious alternative that would overcome the planning difficulties at less cost and disruption than total cessation, the inspector should have considered it, applying *Tapecrown Ltd v First Secretary of State* [2006] EWCA Civ 1744); *Secretary of State for Communities and Local Government v Ahmed* [2014] 2 EGLR 197 (where the Court of Appeal upheld the decision of the judge saying that he had been correct to find that a planning inspector had erred in law by overlooking the possibility of a grant of planning permission and a variation of an enforcement notice as an alternative to the demolition of a new building and reinstatement of the old one – the court held that an inspector had wide powers to determine whether there was any acceptable solution short of a complete remedy of the breach and should be prepared to modify the requirements of the enforcement notice and grant permission subject to conditions. Although the appellant had made his fall-back position of converting the new building to conform to the original planning permission (i.e. in his reliance on ground (f)), the first instance judge had been correct to find that the principle in *Moore* and *Tapecrown* could be extended to a consideration under ground (a) of a point raised under ground (f). In other words, in order to make development acceptable in planning terms, the Secretary of State may need to consider whether it would be appropriate to grant planning permission under ground (a) in combination with a suitable variation

allows the appeal he *may* quash the enforcement notice (and in a case brought under ground (a), he may, as a consequence, also grant planning permission for the unauthorised development or discharge the condition or limitation in question).[95] The appeal may, though, be dismissed if the appellant fails to provide his written grounds of appeal within the prescribed period.[96] He may also allow an appeal and quash the notice if the LPA fails to comply with various procedural requirements.[97] An appeal lies to the High Court, with the permission of that court, on any point of law against decisions of the Secretary of State on enforcement appeals. The Secretary of State may also state a case for the opinion of the High Court.[98] Because a notice will be suspended until the appeal against the enforcement appeal has finally been determined (including by way of an appeal to the Court of Appeal),[99] a power is introduced[100] whereby the High Court may on such terms as it thinks fit (which may include terms requiring the LPA to give an undertaking as to damages or any other matter) order that the notice shall have effect, or have effect to such extent as specified in the order, pending the final determination of the proceedings.

GRANT OR MODIFICATION OF PLANNING PERMISSION ON ENFORCEMENT NOTICE APPEALS

14.31   The Secretary of State is given power to grant planning permission on the determination of an enforcement appeal. This is linked to the ground of appeal that the matters of which complaint is made (or any part of those matters) would justify the grant of planning permission.[101] Power also exists to discharge any

---

of the steps required by the enforcement notice to be taken to remedy the breach of planning control under ground (f). Although it is not the function of the Secretary of State to formulate the appellant's case, it may be prudent for him to invite comment from the parties as to the appropriateness of proposed alterations to the unauthorised development if he considered that they may make it acceptable in planning terms).

95   TCPA 1990, s 176(2); s 174(2)(a).

96   TCPA 1990, s 174(4).

97   i.e. those identified in s 175(1)(a), (b) and (d).

98   TCPA 1990, s 289(1), (3) and (6).

99   TCPA 1990, s 175(4); *R v Kuxhaus* [1988] QB 631.

100 TCPA 1990, s 289(4A).

101 TCPA 1990, ss 177(1)(a) and 174(2)(a). For these purposes, the Secretary of State is required to have regard to the provisions of the development plan, so far as material to the subject matter of the enforcement notice, and to any other material considerations. In such a case (i.e. where the appellant's statement under s 174(4) specifies the ground mentioned in s 174(2)(a)), the applicant is deemed to have made an application for planning permission in respect of the matters stated in the enforcement notice as constituting a breach of planning control (s 177(5)).

condition or limitation subject to which planning permission was granted[102] and to issue a certificate of lawfulness.[103]

VARIATION AND WITHDRAWAL OF ENFORCEMENT NOTICES AND EFFECT OF PLANNING PERMISSION ON ENFORCEMENT

14.32 As previously indicated, the LPA may, in its discretion, withdraw an enforcement notice or waive or relax any requirement of such notice and may in particular extend any period for compliance. These powers may be exercised whether or not the notice has taken effect and will not affect the power of the LPA to issue a further enforcement notice.[104] Further, where after the service of an enforcement notice or a breach of condition notice planning permission is granted for any development carried out before the grant of that permission, the notice will cease to have effect so far as inconsistent with that permission.[105] Where planning permission is granted after the service of a breach of condition notice, the notice will cease to have effect so far as it requires any person to secure compliance with the condition in question.[106] Both these provisions apply to override the requirements of an enforcement notice, otherwise it will remain in effect indefinitely.

NON-COMPLIANCE WITH AN ENFORCEMENT NOTICE

14.33 It is an offence not to comply with an enforcement notice (the liability is that of the person who is the owner of the land)[107] once the period for compliance has elapsed, and there is no outstanding appeal.[108] It is a defence for such person to show that he did everything he could be expected to do to secure compliance

---

[102] TCPA 1990, s 177(1)(b). Where the Secretary of State discharges a condition, he may substitute another condition or limitation for it, whether more or less onerous.

[103] TCPA 1990, s 177(1)(c) and s 191 (certificate of lawfulness).

[104] TCPA 1990, s 173A.

[105] TCPA 1990, s 180(1).

[106] TCPA 1990, s 180(2).

[107] *Oldham MBC v Tanna* [2017] 1 WLR 1970; the Court of Appeal held that when wishing to serve a notice relating to the property on the owner of a registered property, the obligation to make reasonable enquiries as to that person's 'last known address' or 'last known place of abode' would generally be satisfied by a search of the proprietorship register to ascertain the address of the registered proprietor.

[108] TCPA 1990, s 179(1) and (2).

with the notice.[109] It is also an offence for any person who has control of, or an interest in, the land (i.e. someone other than the owner of the land) to carry on

---

[109]   TCPA 1990, s 179(3). Where a person charged with an offence under s 179(2) or (5) has not been served with a copy of the enforcement notice and the notice is not contained in the register of enforcement notices kept under s 188, it shall be a defence for him to show that he was not aware of the existence of the notice (s 179(7)). Authorities on the defence under s 179(3) include *R v Beard* [1997] 1 PLR 64 per Hobhouse LJ at 71B (the words 'everything he could be expected to do' means 'everything he could reasonably be expected to do'); *Kent County Council v Brockman* [1996] 1 PLR 1; *R v Wood* [2002] JPL 219; *South Hams v Halsey* [1996] JPL 761; *Wycombe v Wells* [2005] JPL 1640; *Sevenoaks District Council v Harber* [2008] JPL 1343. See also *R v Wicks* [1998] AC 92, where the House of Lords found that it was not possible to raise a defence on the *vires* of the notice. In this instance, the defendant alleged that the planning authority had acted in bad faith and had taken immaterial matters into consideration. He alleged that he ought to have been entitled to raise those questions as a defence to a prosecution under s 179, but it was held that these arguments were irrelevant. In such a case (i.e. where the notice was not a nullity on its face), the defendant should have sought to quash the notice on appeal or by way of judicial review. In the circumstances, the availability of other defences to a prosecution under s 179 is greatly constrained by s 285(1), which provides that the validity of an enforcement notice shall not, except by way of an appeal under s 174(2), be questioned in any proceedings whatsoever (including criminal and judicial review proceedings) on any of the grounds on which such an appeal may be sought. *R v Wicks* left open the possibility of whether there were in fact residual grounds of challenge to an enforcement notice (i.e. *mala fides*, bias or some other procedural impropriety which vitiated the decision to issue the notice) outside s 174(2). In other words, the issue of whether it was expedient for the LPA to issue the enforcement notice under s 172(1)(b) had to be challenged by way of judicial review and could not be raised under s 174 (enforcement appeals), or as a defence to criminal proceedings under s 179(2), or as a defence to a planning injunction under s 187B (*Northwest Estates Plc v Buckinghamshire County Council* [2003] 3 PLR 46). See also *R (Gazelle Properties Ltd) v Bath and NE Somerset Council* [2011] JPL 702; *R (Matthews) v Secretary of State for Communities and Local Government* [2014] EWHC 129 (Admin). See also *Wychavon District Council v Rodenhurst* [2016] EWHC 2917 (Admin), where the Divisional Court ruled that a district judge had erred in finding that a retrospective planning application offered a defence against enforcement notices. The authority had argued that the findings of the district judge had subverted the statutory planning regime. Section 174(2)(a) offers recipients of enforcement notices a process for arguing that permission should be granted for unauthorised development and it was an abuse of process for the appellants to raise the same issue under s 179(3). Burnett LJ agreed holding that an enforcement notice can only be challenged under s 174. He said that under the district judge's reading of s 179(3), the retrospective application would effectively suspend the enforcement process until all appeal routes had been exhausted and would subvert the statutory regime. He noted that the sole focus of s 179(3) is whether practical impediments render compliance unfeasible. In *Mirza v Newham LBC* [2017] 2 CrAppR 29, a s 179(3) defence failed in circumstances where an owner wife claimed that she had entrusted the management of her property to her husband and could herself do nothing about the breach as she had not known about it. The Court of Appeal approved the trial judge's direction to the jury that they should focus on what the appellant did or did not do. The duty to comply rested on the wife as owner of the property and 'all she could rely upon to show that she had done all that could reasonably be expected of her to secure compliance with the notice was the reasonableness of her decision to entrust everything to her husband because that was all she had done and she knew nothing further'. Reference should be made to a recent case stated appeal by an LPA, namely, *Camden LBC v Galway-Cooper*, 22/5/2018, unreported, QBD (Admin), where, having found that, due to ground settlement, it was not feasible for homeowners to restore their home to the condition it had been in before they built a three-storey extension without planning

(after the end of the compliance period) any activity which is required by the notice to cease or to cause or permit such an activity to be carried on.[110] A person guilty of these offences[111] shall be liable to an unlimited fine even for summary conviction.[112] In determining the amount of any fine, the court is likely to have regard to any financial benefit which has been accrued or appears likely to accrue in consequence of the offence.[113] Prosecuting authorities are also able to apply for a confiscation order under the Proceeds of Crime Act 2002 with a view to the recovery of any financial benefit accruing to the defendant in consequence of the offence.[114]

---

permission, it was found that a district judge had been entitled to find that they had taken all possible steps to comply with the enforcement notice and had made out a defence under s 179(3) (the authority was ordered to pay the homeowners' costs notwithstanding the fact that the unauthorised extension was allowed to remain in place).

[110] TCPA 1990, s 179(4) and (5). The s 179(7) defence (i.e. where the accused can show that he was not aware of the existence of the notice in circumstances where he has not been served with the notice and where the notice is not contained in the appropriate register kept under s 188) also applies to the control or interest offence under s 179(5).

[111] Which may be charged by reference to any day or longer period of time and a person may be convicted of a second or subsequent offence under the relevant subsection by reference to any period of time following the preceding conviction for such an offence (s 179(6)).

[112] It was formerly the case under TCPA 1990, s 179(8) that on summary conviction, a party guilty of an offence was liable to a fine not exceeding £20,000 or to an unlimited fine on conviction on indictment. However, s 179(8) was amended by Legal Aid, Sentencing and Punishment of Offenders Act 2012 (Fines on Summary Conviction) Regulations 2015, Sch 4(1), para 18(3), with effect from 12/3/2015, subject to transitional provisions. There is now no maximum fine even for summary conviction.

[113] TCPA 1990, s 179(9).

[114] Irrespective of fines and costs, the amount of any confiscation payment can also be substantial in cases involving, for instance, the unauthorised conversion of a house into flats or the erection of outbuildings without permission. Confiscation orders in excess of £100,000 in London arising from the recovery of rental income are not uncommon. It was reported in *Planning* in May 2018 that a case involving the LB of Islington resulted in a company being fined and ordered to pay costs and compensation in excess of £300,000 (representing the proceeds of the unauthorised use) following the conversion of a single house into five flats without planning permission. In such cases, it can pay those in breach to appeal enforcement notices where the time for compliance is extended. In 2014, the Court of Appeal dismissed appeals in a case involving enforcement action brought by Runnymede BC, 22/1/2014, unreported, against landowners arising from their failure to remove a two-storey building, 48 parked caravans and waste on their Surrey farm. The overall confiscatory payments, as between the two owners, amounted to £248,246. It was said in the report on the case that the court heard that despite numerous attempts by the authority to force the removal or demolition of illegally placed items and buildings on the farm, the breaches of the enforcement notice continued.

ENDURING EFFECT OF AN ENFORCEMENT NOTICE

14.34 The enforcement notice remains effective even after it has been complied with.[115] Any provision of an enforcement notice requiring the use of the land to be discontinued shall operate as a requirement that it shall be discontinued permanently, from which it follows that any resumption of that use will be in contravention of the enforcement notice.[116] If any development is carried out on land by way of reinstating or restoring buildings or works which have been removed or altered in compliance with an enforcement notice, the notice shall be deemed to apply in relation to the buildings or works as reinstated or restored as it applied before in relation to the buildings or works before they were removed or altered.[117]

14.35 It is a criminal offence to carry out development (without planning permission) by way of reinstating or restoring buildings or works which have been removed or altered in compliance with an enforcement notice. The fine on summary conviction shall not exceed level 5 on the standard scale.[118] However, no person shall be guilty of an offence under section 179(2) of the TCPA 1990 (under which an owner of land in breach of an enforcement notice shall be guilty of an offence) for failing to take any steps required to be taken by an enforcement notice by way of the removal or alteration of what has been so reinstated or restored.[119]

14.36 Where, at any time after an enforcement notice has taken effect: (a) any development is carried out on the land by way of reinstating or restoring buildings or works which have been altered or removed in compliance with the notice; and (b) the LPA proposes, in the exercise of its powers,[120] to take steps to enter the land and take the steps required by the notice in default of the owner or occupier doing so, it shall give the owner and occupier not less than 28 days' notice of its intention to do so before taking such action.[121]

---

[115] TCPA 1990, s 181(1). And will, of course, be enforceable against any successor in title, provided it has been registered as a local land charge.

[116] TCPA 1990, s 181(2).

[117] TCPA 1990, s 181(3).

[118] TCPA 1990, s 181(5)(a).

[119] TCPA 1990, s 181(5)(b).

[120] TCPA 1990, s 178(1); s 178(1)(b) entitles the authority to recover from the owner any expenses reasonably incurred by it in entering the land and taking the steps required by the enforcement notice.

[121] TCPA 1990, s 181(4).

ISSUE ESTOPPEL

14.37 A determination by the Secretary of State on any of the grounds mentioned in section 174(2)(b)–(e) of the TCPA 1990 gives rise to an issue estoppel but not in relation to any decision involving the grant or refusal of planning permission under section 174(2)(a). This will clearly be material in relation to a second enforcement notice directed towards the same breach of planning control.[122]

GUIDANCE

14.38 Government guidance on enforcement notices can found in the NPPG in the section 'Ensuring Effective Enforcement',[123] and in paragraph 207 of the NPPF in the section 'Decision-taking' ('Enforcement action is discretionary, and local planning authorities should act proportionately in responding to suspected breaches of planning control').

REGISTRATION

14.39 LPAs must keep a register of enforcement and stop notices and other enforcement action.[124]

STOP NOTICE

14.40 A stop notice[125] can prohibit any or all of the activities which comprise the alleged breaches of planning control specified in a related enforcement notice,

---

[122] *Thrasyvoulou v Secretary of State for the Environment* [1990] 2 AC 273.

[123] NPPG, reference 17b-018-20140306 to 17b-023-20140306. The policy for Wales is set out in *Planning Policy Wales* (Welsh Government, Edition 7, July 2014) at Chapter 3. It should also be noted that TCPA 1990, s 188 requires every LPA to keep a register containing such information as may be prescribed with respect to planning enforcement orders, enforcement notices, enforcement warning notices (Wales – s 173ZA), stop notices and breach of condition notices which relate to land in their area (DMPO, art 43 and in Wales (as set out in Town and Country Planning (Development Management Procedure) (Wales) Order 2012 (SI 2012/801), art 30).

[124] TCPA 1990, s 188; the prescribed information which the register must contain will be found in DPMO, art 43.

[125] Which may be served by the LPA (TCPA 1990, s 183) or by the Secretary of State (s 185), although the latter must not serve a stop notice without consulting the LPA.

ahead of the deadline for compliance in that enforcement notice.[126] A stop notice cannot be served independently of an enforcement notice.

14.41 An LPA must specify in the stop notice when it is to take effect. It must normally be no less than three days (or later than 28 days) after the date when the notice is served.[127] When there are special reasons for specifying an earlier date, a stop notice may take effect before three days, in which case, a statement of reasons must be served with it. There are restrictions on what a stop notice can prohibit.[128] For instance, a stop notice may not prohibit the use of any building as a dwelling-house, although it may be used to prohibit the use of land as a site for a caravan occupied by a person as his or her own main residence.

14.42 If the linked enforcement notice is quashed, varied or withdrawn, or the stop notice is withdrawn, compensation may be payable in certain circumstances[129] and subject to certain limitations.[130] The power to serve a stop notice is discretionary, although the LPA must be satisfied that it is expedient that any relevant activity should cease before the expiry of the period of compliance specified in an enforcement notice. The stop notice should prohibit only what is essential to safeguard amenity or public safety in the neighbourhood, or to prevent serious or irreversible harm to the environment or surrounding area. There are provisions for compensation for loss due to a stop notice.[131] There is also guidance on stop notices.[132]

14.43 A person who contravenes a stop notice after a site notice has been displayed, or the stop notice has been served on him, is guilty of an offence.[133] A

---

[126] TCPA 1990, s 183(1). A stop notice must be served by the LPA either when it serves the enforcement notice or afterwards. A stop notice applies where the LPA wishes to prohibit the carrying out of the relevant activity on land which is the subject of an enforcement notice: hence the two remedies will be taken together.

[127] TCPA 1990, s 184(3).

[128] TCPA 1990, s 183(4) and (5).

[129] *Sample v Alnwick District Council* [1984] JPL 670.

[130] TCPA 1990, s 186(5). For the claims procedure, see Town and Country Planning Regulations 1992 (SI 1992/1492), reg 12. The time within which any claim for compensation is to be made is 12 months from the decision in respect of which the claim is made or such longer time as the Secretary of State may allow. Disputed claims for compensation are determined by the Upper Tribunal. No compensation is, however, payable: (a) in respect of a stop notice in the case of any activity which, at any time when the notice is in force, constitutes or contributes to a breach of planning control; or (b) in the case of a claimant who was required to provide information under s 171C or under Local Government (Miscellaneous Provisions) Act 1976, s 16, in respect of any loss which could have been avoided if he had provided the information or had otherwise co-operated with the LPA when responding to the notice.

[131] TCPA 1990, s 186.

[132] NPPG at Paragraph: 028 Reference ID: 17b-028-20140306 to 17b-036-20140306.

[133] TCPA 1990, s 187(1).

person guilty of this offence is liable on summary conviction to a fine and there is no maximum fine even for summary conviction.[134] In determining the amount of fine imposed, the court is to have regard to any financial benefit which has accrued, or appears likely to accrue, in consequence of the offence.[135] There is no right of appeal to the Secretary of State against the prohibitions contained in a stop notice. The validity of a stop notice, and the propriety of the decision of the LPA to issue it, may, however, be challenged by way of judicial review.

---

[134] TCPA 1990, s 187(2). It was formerly the case that on summary conviction, a party guilty of an offence was liable to a fine not exceeding £20,000 or to an unlimited fine on conviction on indictment. However, s 187(2) was amended by Legal Aid, Sentencing and Punishment of Offenders Act 2012 (Fines on Summary Conviction) Regulations 2015, Sch 4(1), para 18(4), with effect from 12/3/2015, subject to transitional provisions.

[135] By s 187(3) in proceedings for an offence under this section, it is a defence for the accused to prove: (a) that the stop notice was not served on him; and (b) that he did not know, and could not reasonably have been expected to know, of its existence.

Chapter 15

Lawful Development Certificates

CERTIFICATES OF LAWFULNESS OF EXISTING USE OR DEVELOPMENT

15.1   If any person wishes to seek clarification as to whether: (a) his use of land; or (b) any operations[1] which have been carried out in, on, over or under his land; or (c) any other matter constituting a failure to comply with any condition or limitation subject to which planning permission has been granted, is lawful (and the relevant date for these purposes is the date on which the application is made),[2] he may apply[3] to the local planning authority (LPA) for a certificate of lawfulness

---

[1]   There is a clear alignment between 'use' and 'operations' and the definition of development in TCPA 1990, s 55, and the requirement to obtain planning permission for 'development' (*Government of the Republic of France v Royal Borough of Kensington and Chelsea* [2016] JPL 387 at [35]: this was a case where the court held that on a proper construction of Planning (Listed Buildings and Conservation Areas) Act 1990 (LBA 1990), s 26H, and TCPA 1990, Pt VII, s 192 (involving a certificate of lawfulness of proposed use or development) a landowner could apply for certificates of lawful development in respect of listed building consent and planning permission, respectively, so long as the time limit for the works' implementation had not yet expired: the provisions were not restricted to certifying the lawfulness of proposed works).

[2]   TCPA 1990, s 191(4) and (5)(d).

[3]   TCPA 1990, s 191(1). Article 39 of the Town and Country Planning (Development Management Procedure) (England) Order 2015 (DMPO) (or in Wales Town and Country Planning (Development Management Procedure) (Wales) Order 2012 (SI 2012/801), art 28), specifies the contents of an application and how it must be submitted along with other prescribed information about the application and its management through to the form of any issued certificate (for instance, art 39 covers valid and invalid applications, acknowledgment of applications, entitlement to require the applicant to provide further information, the timescale for determining the application (generally eight weeks beginning with the receipt of a valid application), the duty to give full reasons in the notice of decision for any refusal (together with information as to appeal rights) and the form of any issued certificate). There is a different application form for each type of certificate, but either type must be accompanied by sufficient factual information/evidence for an LPA to decide the application, along with the relevant fee. An application needs to describe precisely what is being applied for and the land to which the application relates. Without sufficient or precise information, an LPA may be justified in refusing a certificate. This does not preclude another application being submitted if more information can be produced. Although the applicant

of existing use or development (CLEUD),[4] specifying the land and describing the use, operations and other matters. It should be noted that the grant of a certificate applies only to the lawfulness of the development and does not remove the need to comply with any other legal requirements.[5]

15.2   For these purposes, uses and operations are lawful (and the lawfulness of any use, operations or other matter for which a certificate is in force shall be conclusively presumed)[6] if: (a) no enforcement action may then be taken in respect of them (i.e. either because they did not involve development or require planning permission or because the time for enforcement action has expired[7] or for any other reason); or (b) they do not contravene any of the requirements of an enforcement notice then in force.[8] Similarly, any matter constituting a failure to

---

is responsible for providing sufficient information to support an application, the LPA may canvass evidence before determining the application which it must obviously share with the applicant who may, of course, wish to produce rebuttal evidence of his own. In the case of applications for existing use, if an LPA has no evidence itself, nor any from others, to contradict or otherwise make the applicant's version of events less than probable, there is no good reason to refuse the application, provided the applicant's evidence alone is sufficiently precise and unambiguous to justify the grant of a certificate on the balance of probability. An LPA is under no statutory duty to consult third parties, but it may, as indicated, be reasonable for it to seek evidence from third parties, such as parish councils or neighbours, although views on the planning merits of the application or whether the applicant has any private rights to be able to carry out the operation, use or activity in question are irrelevant when determining the application which will depend on whether, on the facts of the case and relevant planning law, the specific matter is or would be lawful (see NPPG at Paragraph: 005 Reference ID: 17c-005-20140306 to 17c-014-20140306).

4   Lawful development certificates replaced 'established use' certificates in 1992. An application to convert an established use certificate to a lawful development certificate needs to be made like any other application for a certificate. The effect and value of any existing established use certificates remains unchanged, but they are not considered to have been made under s 191. The key difference is that the old style certificates could certify an established use and provide immunity from enforcement action, but not that the development was lawful (see NPPG at Paragraph: 014 Reference ID: 17c-014-20140306). It is possible, by application, to convert an established use certificate to a lawful development certificate.

5   Such as the Building Regulations 2010, or the LBA 1990, as amended, or other licensing or permitting schemes.

6   TCPA 1990, s 191(6).

7   TCPA 1990, s 191(3A) draws in the new time limits in cases involving concealment (s 171BA) by providing that time will be taken not to have expired if: (a) the time for applying for a planning enforcement order has not expired; (b) an application has been made for such an order which has not yet been determined; or (c) a planning enforcement order has been made in relation to the matter and the enforcement year for the order has not yet expired.

8   TCPA 1990, s 191(2). This subsection clearly defines what is or is not lawful for the limited purposes of the Act. In *R v Epping Forest District Council ex parte Philcox* [2002] PLCR 3, it was held that it does not matter that the activity may be unlawful for other reasons (as being in contravention of Environmental Protection Act 1990, s 33), yet still justifies the grant of a certificate. It may be added that an enforcement notice is not in force where an enforcement appeal is outstanding or an appeal has been upheld and the decision has been remitted to the Secretary of State for redetermination, but that redetermination is still outstanding.

comply with any condition or limitation subject to which planning permission has been granted will also be lawful on the same grounds.[9]

15.3   It should be noted that: (a) an LPA only needs to consider whether, on the facts of the case and relevant planning law, the specific activity is or would be lawful; (b) planning merits are not relevant at any stage either on the application or on the appeal process;[10] (c) an LPA would be wrong to reject the unchallenged evidence of an applicant without good reason;[11] and (d) where the applicant is relying on no enforcement action having been taken in the ten-year period, in assessing whether a material change of use had been immune from enforcement, the LPA should consider whether enforcement action could have been taken at any time within the ten-year period (and the burden is on the LPA to show that such action could have been taken).[12]

15.4   An LPA is not bound by the description of the use or operation described in the application. It may, for instance, modify that description or substitute another if justified by the evidence available to it.[13] The LPA may also issue a certificate in relation to the whole or any part of the land claimed in the application or, where the application specifies two or more uses, operations or other matters, for all of them or some one or more of them.[14]

15.5   The certificate, once issued, must: (a) specify the land to which it relates; (b) describe the use, operations or other matter in question (in the case of any use falling within one of the classes specified in the Use Classes Order 1987, identifying it by reference to that class); (c) give reasons for determining the use, operations or other matters to be lawful; and (d) specify the date of the application

---

[9]   TCPA 1990, s 191(3).

[10]   Views expressed by third parties on the planning merits of the case, or on whether the applicant has any private rights to carry out the operation, use or activity in question, are irrelevant when determining the application.

[11]   *Gabbitas v Secretary of State for the Environment & Newham LBC* [1985] JPL 630.

[12]   *Thurrock BC v Secretary of State for the Environment, Transport and the Regions* [2002] EWCA Civ 226.

[13]   TCPA 1990, s 191(4).

[14]   TCPA 1990, s 193(4).

for the certificate.[15] A certificate must also be in the prescribed form.[16] Precision in the terms of the certificate is vital.[17]

CERTIFICATES OF LAWFULNESS OF PROPOSED USE OR DEVELOPMENT

15.6   Any person wishing to ascertain whether: (a) any *proposed* use of buildings or other land; or (b) any operations *proposed* to be carried out in, on, over or under land would be lawful, may make an application to the LPA specifying the land and describing the use or operations in question. A certificate in this instance (which is not a planning permission) is called a certificate of lawfulness of *proposed* use or development.[18] In this case the LPA needs to be satisfied that the use or operations described in the application would be lawful if instituted or begun at the time of the application.[19] As with applications for a CLEUD, neither the applicant nor the LPA is required to notify anyone of the application or afford anyone with an opportunity of making representations on the application. Such applications should also be registered. LPAs have no power to modify or substitute a new description of the *proposed* use or operation given in the application,[20] although they do have power to issue a certificate for the

---

[15]   TCPA 1990, s 191(5).

[16]   As set out in the form in DMPO, Sch 8 (or in Wales, the form in Town and Country Planning (Development Management and Procedure) (Wales) Order 2012 (SI 2012/801), Sch 7), or in a form substantially to the same effect. The description contained in a certificate should be drawn with care and precision and be limited to the exact use in question (see *Main v Secretary of State for the Environment, Transport and Regions* (1999) 77 P & CR 300; *Broxbourne Borough Council v Secretary of State for the Environment* [1980] QB 1).

[17]   Details of what must be included in each type of lawful development certificate can be found in TCPA 1990, s 191(5) or s 192(3). The prescribed form can be found in DMPO, Sch 8. A CLEUD must include a description of the use, operations or other matter for which it is granted regardless of whether the matters fall within a use class. But where it is within a use class, a certificate must also specify the relevant class. In all cases, the description needs to be more than simply a title or label in order to avoid future problems over interpretation. This is important for uses which do not fall within any use class (i.e. a *sui generis* use). Where a certificate is granted for one use in the case of a planning unit where there is mixed or composite use, then that situation will need to be carefully reflected in the certificate. Failure to do so may result in a loss of control over any subsequent intensification of the certified use.

[18]   TCPA 1990, s 192(1). Application procedure in the case of s 192 applications is contained in DMPO, art 39 (or in Wales, in accordance with Town and Country Planning (Development Management and Procedure) (Wales) Order 2012 (SI 2012/801), art 28). It is customary for s 192 applications to be supported by statutory declarations rather than by witness statements or affidavits. Applicants are informed of the authority to whom such an application may be made in DMPO, art 11 (combined with art 39(6)). DMPO, art 39.

[19]   TCPA 1990, s 192(2).

[20]   As they have in the case of applications under TCPA 1990, s 191 (see s 191(4)).

whole or part of the application land, and where an application specifies two or more uses, operations or other matters, they may issue a certificate for all of them or some one or more of them.[21] Moreover, a certificate[22] shall not affect any matter constituting a failure to comply with any condition or limitation subject to which planning permission has been granted unless that matter is described in the certificate.[23]

REVOCATION AND OFFENCES

15.7   An LPA may revoke a certificate[24] if, on the application for the certificate: (a) a statement was made or document used which was materially false; or (b) any material information was withheld.[25] Criminal liability also exists for false or misleading statements, or withholding material information for the purpose of procuring a particular decision on an application for the issue of a certificate of lawfulness.[26]

CHALLENGING A DECISION NOT TO GRANT A CERTIFICATE OR FAILING TO DETERMINE AN APPLICATION WITHIN THE PRESCRIBED PERIOD

15.8   Where an application for a certificate is refused in whole or part, or where it is not determined within the prescribed period of eight weeks from the making of the application (or within such extended period as may be agreed in writing by

---

[21]   TCPA 1990, s 193(4).

[22]   Under either TCPA 1990, s 191 or s 192.

[23]   TCPA 1990, s 193(5).

[24]   Under either TCPA 1990, s 191 or s 192. The LPA is required to give prior notice to the owner and occupier of the land and to any other person who, in the opinion of the authority, is liable to be affected by the revocation (see DMPO, art 39 (or in Wales, Town and Country Planning (Development Management and Procedure) (Wales) Order 2012 (SI 2012/801), art 28)). See *R v Surrey County Council ex parte Bridge Court Holdings Ltd* [2000] 4 PLR 30.

[25]   TCPA 1990, s 193(7). The process which an LPA must follow in these circumstances is set out in DMPO, art 39. If the LPA proposes to revoke a certificate, it must give notice of its proposal as set out in art 39, and the recipient of the notice is then afforded an opportunity to make representations.

[26]   TCPA 1990, s 194(1). A person guilty of an offence under this section shall be liable, on summary conviction, to a fine not exceeding the statutory maximum or, on conviction on indictment, to imprisonment for a term not exceeding two years, or a fine, or both.

the applicant and the LPA), the applicant[27] may appeal to the Secretary of State.[28] The basis for appealing a refusal or non-determination falls within narrow grounds. If the Secretary of State considers that the LPA's refusal to grant a certificate is not well founded then he should grant the applicant a certificate, but if he is satisfied that the LPA's refusal was well founded (or would have been if it had issued a decision), he shall dismiss the appeal.[29] Before determining an appeal to him, the Secretary of State shall, if either the appellant or the LPA so wish, give each of them an opportunity of appearing before, and being heard by, a person appointed by the Secretary of State for the purpose.[30] The decision of the Secretary of State on such appeal shall be final[31] although it can be challenged by way of judicial review on the usual grounds (i.e. error of law, procedural error or irrationality).[32]

---

[27]   There is no third party right of appeal from a decision of the LPA on a s 191 or s 192 application, which means that a third party wishing to challenge a decision must do so by way of judicial review.

[28]   TCPA 1990, s 195(1). By s 195(6), Sch 6 applies to appeals under this section (such appeals are transferred to inspectors subject to the Secretary of State's power to recover jurisdiction in any particular case). There is no time limit for appeals, and the decision of the Secretary of State on such an appeal shall be final (s 196(3)). As to the scope of the powers of the Secretary of State, in *Cottrell v Secretary of State for the Environment* [1982] JPL 443, an applicant sought an established use certificate for use of a caravan in a field. The Secretary of State dismissed the appeal on a ground different from that of the LPA. The applicant's appeal was dismissed as it was held that the Secretary of State was only required to grant a certificate upon being satisfied that the local authority was wrong in law. He was entitled to uphold the authority's decision on different grounds. For guidance on s 195 appeals, see PINS Guidance *Procedural Guide: Certificate of lawful use or development appeals – England* (July 2015). As there is no third party right of appeal, any third party wishing to challenge an LPA's decision to grant a certificate on a s 191 or 192 application must do so by way of judicial review. The validity of a decision on an appeal may be challenged in the High Court under s 288.

[29]   TCPA 1990, s 195(2) and (3). The inference from the wording of these sub-sections suggests that appeals are limited to a review of the LPA's decision, although they are invariably treated as de novo appeals, which means that the parties and interested person may submit fresh evidence to the Secretary of State which was not before the LPA.

[30]   TCPA 1990, s 196(1).

[31]   TCPA 1990, s 196(3).

[32]   On an application under TCPA 1990, s 288. In *KP JR Management Co Ltd v Richmond-upon-Thames* [2018] EWHC 84 (Admin), it was held that a local authority had been entitled to grant a CLEUD certifying that the mooring of a specified number of boats for residential and private leisure purposes at a site on the Thames was lawful. The claimant had challenged the defendant local authority's refusal to issue an enforcement notice relating to the increased residential use of a pontoon and moorings on the Thames, and also its grant of a CLEUD certifying that the mooring of boats for residential and private leisure purposes was lawful. The first interested party let the mooring to boats, causing disquiet amongst local residents arising from the increased use of the site. The claimant company was formed by local residents to take action against the local authority in relation to the site. The second interested party was a rowing club who supported the claim. In its application for a CLEUD (which was granted and allowed the mooring to be used: (a) by four boats permanently for residential purposes; (b) by two boats for residential and/or private leisure

REGISTRATION

15.9 LPAs must keep a register of applications for certificates of lawfulness and of decisions made on such applications.[33]

---

purposes; and (c) by four boats for private leisure purposes), the first interested party claimed that two movable boats in residential use had subsisted at the site for at least ten years, together with movable leisure craft and ancillary vessels, and that the mooring of the specified boats for mixed residential and leisure purposes was therefore lawful within the meaning of TCPA 1990, s 191. The claimant claimed that the decision to issue a CLEUD was unlawful as (i) the local authority had wrongly made its decision on the basis that the planning unit comprised the mooring and pontoon area as a whole; and (ii) there was insufficient evidence to establish that residential use had subsisted for at least ten years prior to the date of the CLEUD application. The challenge to the CLEUD was rejected. Lang J held that the local authority had to make a planning judgment as to the appropriate planning unit which was a matter of fact and degree. Where there was more than one relevant unit of occupation, the decision-maker had to make a judgment accordingly. The court would not interfere with an exercise of planning judgment and would only intervene if an error of law was established (*Burdle v Secretary of State for the Environment* [1972] 1 WLR 1207; *Johnston v Secretary of State for the Environment* 73 LGR 22; *Church Commissioners for England v Secretary of State for the Environment* (1996) 71 P & CR 73; and *Gregory v Secretary of State for the Environment* (1990) 60 P & CR 413 applied). The court also held that in the exercise of its planning judgment, the local authority had been entitled to conclude that the mooring and pontoon area as a whole was the appropriate planning unit. It was found that there was ample evidence on which the local authority could conclude that there had been continuous residential use of at least two vessels moored at the site for more than ten years prior to the application for the CLEUD. Further, the content and degree of particularisation in a CLEUD was a matter of judgment for the local authority, based on the evidence (*R (Flint) v South Gloucestershire Council* [2016] EWHC 2180 (Admin) applied – *Flint* was a case where it was held that an LPA had been entitled to grant a lawful development certificate under TCPA 1990, s 191, for an existing use of land and buildings as a shooting school in breach of planning conditions limiting the hours of operation and the number of persons being instructed at any one time).

[33] TCPA 1990, s 193(6) taken with s 69(1)(a), and DMPO, art 40(7); see also TCPA 1990, s 196(4), which provides that the prescribed information required to be contained in a register of planning applications kept under s 69 shall include information in respect of certificates under s 191 or s 192 granted by the Secretary of State.

Chapter 16

Environmental Impact Assessment

INTRODUCTION

16.1   This chapter deals with the legislation covering environmental impact assessment (EIA).

16.2   The process of EIA in the context of town and country planning is governed by the Town and Country Planning (Environmental Impact Assessment) Regulations 2017[1] (EIA Regulations 2017).[2] These regulations apply to development which is given planning permission under Part III of the Town and Country Planning Act 1990.[3] The EIA Regulations 2017 consolidate, with amendments, the provisions of the EIA Regulations 2011.

16.3   The EIA Regulations 2017 apply the amended Directive 2014/52/EU[4] 'on the effects of certain public and private projects on the environment'. They apply

---

[1]   SI 2017/571, which came into force on 16/5/2017. The Town and Country Planning (Environmental Impact Assessment) (Wales) Regulations 2017 came into force on the same date. The new regs are based on a revised Directive 2014/52/EU.

[2]   The EIA Regulations 2017 revoke the Town and Country Planning (Environmental Impact Assessment) Regulations 2011 (EIA Regulations 2011) where appropriate, subject to certain transitional arrangements contained in the EIA Regulations 2017, reg 76, which provide that the EIA Regulations 2011 continue to apply where, before 16/5/2017, a person or body has submitted an Environmental Statement (ES) or has requested a scoping opinion, or in respect of a local development order an LPA has prepared an ES or a scoping opinion, or requested a scoping direction. The screening provisions set out in the EIA Regulations 2011, Pts 1 and 2 will also continue to apply to requests for a screening opinion or direction made or initiated before 16/5/2017.

[3]   See NPPG at Paragraphs: 004 Reference ID: 4-004-20170728 to 016 Reference ID: 4-016-20170728, where the types of development covered by the EIA Regulations 2017 are set out in detail.

[4]   Usually referred to as the 'Environmental Impact Assessment Directive' to the planning system in England. The main changes from the EIA Regulations 2011 are: (a) to the circumstances in which a project may be exempt from EIA regulation; (b) to the introduction of co-ordinated procedures for projects which are also subject to assessment under European Directive 92/43/EEC on the conservation of natural habitats and of wild fauna and flora or European Directive

only to certain types of development and can even apply to permitted development. The local planning authority (LPA), the Secretary of State or an inspector must not grant consent for EIA development unless an EIA has been carried out.[5]

16.4   The screening thresholds for industrial estate development and urban development projects were raised in April 2015 as set out in the Annex to the guidance on the EIA Regulations 2011. Projects which are wholly outside sensitive areas and do not exceed the revised screening thresholds are not Schedule 2 development and should not be screened by the LPA. Where the LPA has, prior to 6/4/2015, screened a project which does not exceed the relevant revised threshold and has determined that it is EIA development, it will continue as such. It remains, as usual, open to the applicant to request that the Secretary of State issues a screening direction to determine whether a development is likely to have significant effects on the environment. Subsequent applications in relation to development which was determined to be EIA development prior to 6/4/2015, but which is below the thresholds introduced in 2015, should continue to be treated as EIA development.

PURPOSE OF EIA

16.5   The aim of EIA is to protect the environment by ensuring that an LPA, when deciding whether to grant planning permission for a project which is likely to have significant effects on the environment, does so in the full knowledge of the likely significant effects and takes this into account in the decision-making process.[6] The EIA Regulations 2017 set out a procedure for identifying those projects which should be subject to an EIA and for assessing, consulting and coming to a decision on those projects which are likely to have significant effects on the environment.

2009/147/EC of the European Parliament and of the Council on the conservation of Wild Birds (the Birds or Habitats Directives); (c) to the list of environmental factors to be considered as part of the EIA process; (d) to the information to be provided to inform a screening decision and the criteria to be applied when making a screening decision; (e) to the way in which an ES is to be prepared, including an amendment to the information to be included in it, the introduction of a requirement that it should be based upon a scoping opinion (where one has been obtained) and a requirement that it is to be prepared by a competent expert; (f) to the means by which the public is to be informed of projects which are subject to the EIA process, and (g) the introduction of a requirement for decision-makers to avoid conflicts of interest.

[5]   Regulation 3.

[6]   Regulation 4, which sets out the EIA process, namely, the preparation of an ES and the carrying out of any consultation, publication and notification required by the EIA Regulations 2017 or any other enactment in respect of EIA development.

16.6   EIA will only apply to a small proportion of projects. LPAs already have a well-established general responsibility to consider the environmental implications of developments which are subject to planning control. The EIA Regulations 2017 integrate EIA procedures into this framework and should only apply to projects which are likely to have significant effects on the environment. Pre-application engagement is also clearly important in identifying when, and in what respects, a proposal should be subject to an EIA.

OVERVIEW OF EIA

16.7   The EIA process has five broad stages: screening; scoping; preparing an Environmental Statement (ES); making a planning application and consultation; and decision-making.

Screening[7]

16.8   This is determining whether a project falls within the remit of the EIA Regulations 2017 (i.e. whether it is likely to have a significant effect on the environment and therefore requires an EIA). A 'screening opinion' is a written statement of the opinion of the LPA as to whether development is EIA development. A 'screening direction' is a direction made by the Secretary of State as to whether development is EIA development. Screening should normally take place at an early stage in the design of the project. However, it can occur after a planning application has been made or even after an appeal has been made.

Scoping

16.9   This is determining the extent of the issues to be considered in the assessment and reported on in the ES. An applicant can ask the LPA for its opinion on what information needs to be included. This is called a 'scoping opinion'. Scoping directions may also be made by the Secretary of State.[8]

Preparing an Environmental Statement

16.10   The ES must include at least the information reasonably required to assess the likely significant environmental effects of the development listed in regulation 18(3) and comply with regulation 18(4).[9] An applicant must ensure that

---

[7]   EIA Regulations 2017, Pt 2 (regs 5–7), which deals with screening.

[8]   Pt 4, regs 15–16.

[9]   *Berkeley v Secretary of State for the Environment, Transport and Regions* [2001] 2 AC 603); the ES may consist of one or more documents, but it must constitute a single, accessible and easily

the ES is prepared by competent experts. The ES must be accompanied by a statement from the developer outlining the relevant expertise or qualifications of such experts.[10] The LPA must also make available any relevant environmental information in their possession.[11]

Making a planning application and consultation

16.11 The ES must be publicised electronically and by public notice. The statutory consultation bodies and the public must be given an opportunity to give their views about the proposed development and the ES.

Decision-making

16.12 The ES must be taken into account by the LPA and/or the Secretary of State in deciding whether or not to grant consent for the development.

---

comprehensible compilation of the relevant environmental information. It was also essential that the ES should be made available to the public and the public should be given an opportunity to comment on it. The case involved an appeal against a refusal to quash a planning permission relating to the redevelopment of a football stadium located on the bank of a river. The appellant argued that the permission had been granted without consideration of the need for an EIA. It was held that the court was not empowered to retrospectively dispense with the requirement to carry out an EIA on the ground that the outcome would have been the same or that the LPA or the Secretary of State had all the information required to reach a decision on environmental issues. The Secretary of State had granted planning permission for the redevelopment of the stadium. At first instance, an attempt to quash the decision failed (on the grounds that the Secretary of State had failed to consider the need to carry out an EIA in accordance with Council Directive 85/337/EEC). The decision at first instance was upheld by the Court of Appeal, but an appeal was allowed in the HL, where it was held that in cases where the Directive applied, a planning permission would only be upheld if substantial compliance had been shown.

10   See NPPG at Paragraph: 043 Reference ID: 4-043-20170728 to Paragraph: 045 Reference ID: 4-045-20170728 (dealing with submission of documents and publicity requirements).

11   See NPPG at Paragraph: 034 Reference ID: 4-034-20170728 to Paragraph: 045 Reference ID: 4-045-20170728, under the main heading: 'Preparing an Environmental statement'. The sub-headings deal with the following matters: (a) Who is responsible for preparing the ES? (b) What information should the ES contain? (c) Does an applicant have to obtain a formal opinion from the LPA on the scope of an ES? (d) Can an applicant request a scoping direction from the Secretary of State? (e) Does the applicant need to comply with a scoping opinion or direction? (f) What information should the consultation bodies provide? (g) What aspects of the environment need to be considered? (h) Does an applicant need to consider alternatives? (i) Consultation bodies (viz: Natural England, Environment Agency, the Marine Management Organisation and any other bodies designated by statutory provision as having specific environmental responsibilities and which the LPA or Secretary of Sate considers are likely to have an interest in the application); and (j) What steps should LPAs take to avoid conflicts of interest when bringing forward their own development?

WHEN IS AN EIA REQUIRED?

16.13 The LPA (or the Secretary of State as the case may be) should determine whether the project is of a type listed in Schedule 1 to the EIA Regulations 2017 or Schedule 2. If it is listed in Schedule 1, an EIA is required in every case (Schedule 1 involves major development whereas Schedule 2 involves lesser development). Schedule 2 is broken down into types of development and the applicable thresholds and criteria. If a project is listed in Schedule 2, the LPA should consider whether it is likely to have significant effects on the environment.[12]

16.14 If a proposed project is listed in the first column in Schedule 2 and exceeds the relevant thresholds or criteria set out in the second column (sometimes referred to as 'exclusion thresholds and criteria') the proposal needs to be screened by the LPA to determine whether significant effects on the environment are likely and hence whether an EIA is required. Projects listed in Schedule 2 which are located in, or partly in, a sensitive area also need to be screened, even if they are below the thresholds or do not meet the criteria.[13] Projects which are described in the first column of Schedule 2 but which do not exceed the relevant thresholds, or meet the criteria in the second column of the schedule, or are not at least partly in a sensitive area, are not Schedule 2 development.

PROCEDURE FOR DECIDING WHETHER A SCHEDULE 2 PROJECT IS LIKELY TO HAVE SIGNIFICANT EFFECTS ON THE ENVIRONMENT

16.15 When screening, the LPA must take account of the selection criteria in Schedule 3.[14] Every case should be considered on its own merits in a balanced way. When an LPA or the Secretary of State issues their opinion, they must state the main reasons for their conclusion with reference to the relevant criteria in Schedule 3. Where it is determined that the proposed development is not EIA development, the LPA must state any features of the proposed development and

---

[12] In determining whether a particular proposal is included within one of the categories of development listed in Sch 1 or Sch 2, see NPPG at Paragraph: 030 Reference ID: 4-030-20170728 and Paragraph: 031 Reference ID:4-031-20170728.

[13] Sensitive areas are described in the EIA Regulations 2017 at reg 2 and include, as one might expect, SSSIs, National Parks, the Broads, properties appearing on the World Heritage List, scheduled monuments within the meaning of the Ancient Monuments and Archeological Areas Act 1979, AONBs and European sites designated under the Birds or Habitats Directives (see further details at NPPG at Paragraph: 032 Reference ID: 4-032-20170728).

[14] Which refer to the characteristics of the development, its location and the types and characteristics of the potential impact, although not all the criteria will be relevant in every case.

any measures envisaged to avoid, or prevent what might otherwise have been, significant adverse effects on the environment.[15] LPAs will also need to consider carefully how such measures are secured. This will usually be through planning conditions or planning obligations.

16.16 Only a very small proportion of Schedule 2 development will require EIA. To aid LPAs in determining whether a project is likely to have significant environmental effects, a set of indicative thresholds and criteria have been produced. The table gives an indication of the types of impact that are most likely to be significant for particular types of development. Where there is no requirement to use a screening checklist, LPAs can nonetheless ensure that the relevant issues are considered and to provide a clear audit trail.[16]

16.17 Having completed a screening exercise, the LPA must provide a screening opinion indicating either that an EIA is required (a 'positive screening opinion') or is not required (a 'negative screening opinion'). The Secretary of State can also direct that an EIA is required in circumstances where, although the development of a type listed in Schedule 2 does not meet the relevant criteria or exceed the relevant thresholds, it is still likely to have significant environmental effects.[17]

---

[15] Regulation 5.

[16] For indicative screening thresholds, see www.government/uploads/system/uploads/ attachmentdata/file/630689/eia-thresholds-table.pdf, which contains four columns. Column 2 represents the 'exclusion thresholds' in Sch 2, below which the EIA does not need to be considered (subject to the proposal not being in a sensitive area). The figures in column 3 are indicative only and are intended to determine whether significant effects are likely. However, when considering the thresholds, it is important to also consider the location of the proposed development. In general, the more environmentally sensitive the location, the lower the threshold at which significant effects are likely. It follows, therefore, that the thresholds should only be used in conjunction with the general guidance in determining whether an EIA is required and, in particular, the guidance on environmentally sensitive areas. Column 4 illustrates the issues that are most likely to be needed to be considered for different development types. However, there will be other issues which will be specific to the nature of the environment receptor. For example, ecological impacts are likely to be an issue for all development which is proposed to be located in an SSSI designated for its wildlife value. For the EIA screening checklist, see www.gov.uk/ government/publications/environmental-impact-assessmenmt-screening-checklist; see also NPPG at Paragraph: 057 Reference ID: 4-057-2070720.

[17] Regulation 5(7).

OBTAINING A SCREENING OPINION FROM THE LPA

16.18 If anyone considering carrying out development of a kind listed in Schedule 2 is unsure whether their proposed development requires an EIA, they may request the LPA to provide a screening opinion on the need for an EIA.[18]

16.19 Generally, it will fall to LPAs in the first instance to consider whether a proposed development requires an EIA. However, the Secretary of State is empowered to make directions in relation to the need for an EIA. Such screening directions can be made of the Secretary of State's own volition, or following a request from any person. Directions of the Secretary of State will normally be made in response to a request from a developer. Where the LPA's opinion is that EIA is required, or where an LPA fails to provide a screening opinion within three weeks (or within an extended period agreed in writing with the person making the request), the person who requested the screening opinion of the LPA may request that the Secretary of State make a screening direction. However, any person, where they consider a proposed development requires an EIA, may write to the Secretary of State requesting a screening direction, even though neither the relevant LPA nor the applicant takes that view.[19]

TREATMENT OF MULTIPLE APPLICATIONS

16.20 An application should not be considered if, in reality, it is an integral part of a more substantial development.[20] In such cases, the need for EIA must be considered in the context of the whole development. In other cases it is

---

[18] The request should include the information set out at reg 6(1). When compiling the information, the developer must take into account the criteria of Sch 3 and, where relevant, the results of any relevant EIAs required under other EU legislation. In most cases, the environmental assessment that is most likely to be relevant is the strategic environmental assessment undertaken during the preparation of the local plan for the area. Requirements for making any such submitted documents available to the public are set out in reg 28. Developers are encouraged to identify any features of their proposed development and any mitigation measures envisaged to avoid or prevent what might otherwise have been significant adverse effects on the environment and to include these within the information required to inform the screening decision. See also NPPG at Paragraph: 023 Reference ID: 4-023-20170728. LPAs should also have regard to the possible cumulative effects arising from any existing or approved development (Paragraph: 024 Reference ID: 4-024-20170728).

[19] NPPG at Paragraph: 020 Reference ID: 4-020-20170728.

[20] *R v Swale BC ex parte RSPB* [1991] 1 PLR 6.

appropriate to establish whether each of the proposed developments could proceed independently.[21]

CAN AN ES BE SUBMITTED WITHOUT A SCREENING OPINION?

16.21 This is acceptable but the applicant must make it clear that the information submitted is intended to constitute an ES. In cases of doubt, the LPA should issue a screening opinion and should ask for further information if they need it.[22] Clearly if an EIA is not required, the information, if material, will still be taken into account on the LPA's decision to grant planning permission.

WHAT IF A PLANNING APPLICATION FOR A SCHEDULE 2 DEVELOPMENT IS NOT ACCOMPANIED BY AN ES?

16.22 When an LPA receives an application which appears to be an application for Schedule 2 development, and the application has not been the subject of a screening opinion or direction and there is no accompanying ES, the LPA must provide an opinion on the need for an EIA as if the applicant had requested such a screening opinion under regulation 6.[23] If the screening opinion is that an EIA is required, the LPA must notify the applicant in writing in accordance with regulation 11 that an ES is necessary. The developer has, within 21 days of receipt of such notification, to reply to the LPA stating their intention to provide an ES or to request a screening direction from the Secretary of State. If the developer has not replied within 21 days the planning application will be deemed to have been refused. If the developer responds indicating that an ES will be provided, the LPA should suspend consideration of the application unless they are already minded to refuse permission because of other material considerations, in which case they should so as quickly as possible and, in any event, before the end of the 21-day period when the application is deemed to have been refused.[24]

---

21 *R (Candlish) v Hastings BC* [2006] Env LR 13; *Baker v Bath & NE Somerset Council* [2009] All ER (D) 169 (Jul).

22 See further information requirements in reg 6(2) and (3).

23 Regulation 8.

24 NPPG at Paragraph: 027 Reference ID: 4-027-20170728.

CALLED-IN APPLICATIONS WHERE THERE IS NO ES

16.23 The Secretary of State will consider whether the development is EIA development and will make a screening direction and will, if necessary, seek further information from the applicant. If an EIA is found to be required, the LPA and the applicant will be informed. There is no right of appeal against such a notification. An applicant must reply within three weeks stating that an ES will be provided. Otherwise, at the end of such period, the Secretary of State will inform the applicant that no further action will be taken on the application. Where the Secretary of State decides that no screening opinion is required, and there has been no previous screening opinion to that effect, the Secretary of State will make a screening direction to that effect which the LPA must ensure is placed on the planning register.

PROCEDURE FOR PLANNING APPEALS

16.24 The matter is dealt with in a similar way to a called-in application and the same procedures and time limits apply.[25] However, where an inspector dealing with an appeal considers that an EIA might be required, that question will be referred to the Secretary of State in which case the inspector will be precluded from determining the appeal (except by refusing permission) until he receives a screening direction from the Secretary of State. If the latter directs that an EIA is required the inspector may not determine the appeal (except by refusing permission) until the applicant has submitted an ES. The Secretary of State may direct than an EIA is required at any time before the appeal is determined.[26]

DETERMINING PLANNING APPLICATIONS THAT HAVE BEEN SUBJECT TO AN EIA

16.25 There are specific arrangements for considering and determining planning applications that have been subject to an EIA. These arrangements include consideration of the adequacy of the information provided, consultation, reaching a reasoned conclusion on the significant environmental effects of the proposed development, publicity, and informing consultation bodies and the public of both the decision and the main reasons for it. The LPA must take into account the information in the ES, the responses to consultation and any other relevant information when determining a planning application.

---

[25] Regulation 14.

[26] NPPG at Paragraph: 029 Reference ID: 4-029-20170728.

16.26 The LPA can always ask an applicant to provide further information.[27] Additional information of a substantive nature submitted voluntarily by an applicant must be treated in the same way as information required by the LPA. The 16-week time limit (albeit subject to extension by written agreement) for the determination of an EIA application continues to run while any correspondence about the adequacy of the information in an ES is taking place.[28] The Secretary of State can also request additional information when determining a planning appeal.[29] Such further information will be regulated by the Inquiries Procedure Rules relating to the submission of evidence to local planning inquiries.[30]

16.27 If planning permission or subsequent consent is to be granted, the LPA must consider whether it is appropriate to require steps to be taken to monitor any mitigating measures identified through the EIA process. LPAs should also consider whether to include, where appropriate, provisions for any potential remedial action.[31]

16.28 Mitigation measures proposed in an ES are designed to limit or remove any significant adverse environmental effects of the development. LPAs will need to consider how these mitigation measures may be secured, as for instance, by way of planning conditions and planning obligations (either unilaterally or between the LPA and the developer). However, a condition requiring the development to be 'in accordance with the Environmental Statement' lacks clarity in the measures which need to be taken.

16.29 In cases where a consent procedure involves more than one stage (a multi-stage consent), for example, a first stage involving an outline planning permission and a second stage dealing with reserved matters, the effects of a project on the

---

27 Does the ES contain all the information specified in regs 18(3) or (4) and any additional information specified in Sch 4? If further information is required, the LPA must ask for it under regs 25 and 26. All information provided must be publicised and consulted on. All information provided should be limited to the 'main' or 'significant' environmental effects to which a development is likely to give rise and must be on relevant matters and directly relevant to reaching a reasoned conclusion on the significant effects of the proposed development on the environment. The LPA, the Secretary of State or an inspector may also require an applicant or appellant to produce evidence to verify any information in the ES.

28 Where an ES has not been submitted with a planning application, but the applicant indicates that they propose to provide one, consideration of the application should be suspended until the ES has been received (reg 20(8)).

29 NPPG at Paragraph: 048 Reference ID: 4-048-20170728.

30 Town and Country Planning (Inquiries Procedure) (England) Rules 2000 (SI 2000/1624); Town and Country Planning Appeals (Determination by Inspectors) (Inquiries Procedure) (England) Rules 2000.

31 Regulation 26. Such measures must be proportionate. See NPPG at Paragraph: 063 Reference ID: 4-063-20170728.

environment should normally be identified and assessed when determining the outline permission.[32]

---

[32] NPPG at Paragraph: 056 Reference ID: 4-056-20170728, regarding multi-stage consents.

Chapter 17

Habitats and Species Regulations 2017

INTRODUCTION

17.1   The Conservation of Habitats and Species Regulations 2017 (Habitats Regulations 2017) incorporate into the law in England and Wales the requirements of the EU Directives on:

(a)   the conservation of natural habitats and of wild fauna and flora;[1] and
(b)   wild birds.[2]

17.2   The following is no more than a brief overview of the provisions of the Habitats Regulations 2017 which came into force on 30/11/2017. The Habitats Regulations 2010 were amended ten times since they were last consolidated in 2010 and the legislation has been consolidated yet again, making only minor changes reflecting changes to related legislation.[3]

17.3   A more detailed analysis of the provisions of the Habitats Regulations 2017 is beyond the scope of this book.

---

[1]   Council Directive 92/43/EEC of 21/5/1992 on the conservation of natural habitats and of wild fauna and flora (Habitats Directive), as last amended by Council Directive 2013/17/EU of 10/6/2013.

[2]   Council Directive 79/409/EEC of 2/4/1979 on the conservation of wild birds, replaced by the Council Directive 2009/147/EC of 30/11/2009 on the conservation of wild birds (Birds Directive), as last amended by Council Directive 2013/17/EU of 10/6/2013.

[3]   In summary, the Habitats Regulations 2017 provide for the designation and protection of 'European sites', the protection of 'European protected species' and the adaptation of planning and other controls for the protection of European sites. By reg 42, those species identified in Sch 2 and their breeding sites/resting places are protected. It is in relation to these species that a European Protected Species Licence is required. The extent of the revocations affecting the 2010 Regulations is very limited (see Sch 7 and Explanatory Note).

OVERVIEW OF HABITATS REGULATIONS 2017

17.4   They impose duties on public bodies (including planning authorities) to exercise their nature conservation powers so as to comply with the Habitats Directive on the conservation of natural habitats and of wild fauna and flora and the new Wild Birds Directive on the conservation of wild birds.[4]

17.5   They make provision for the selection, designation, registration and notification of sites to be protected under the Habitats Directive ('European sites').[5] Special Areas of Conservation (SACs) are strictly protected sites designated under the Habitats Directive. Special Protection Areas (SPAs) are similarly strictly protected sites classified in accordance with the Birds Directive, Article 4. They are classified for rare and vulnerable birds and for regularly occurring migratory species.

17.6   They make provision for management agreements in relation to European sites.[6]

17.7   They make provision in respect of European sites for:

(a)   the control of damaging operations;
(b)   the control of potentially damaging operations including the power to make special nature conservation orders, stop notices and restoration orders;
(c)   the provision of byelaws (including the creation of a criminal offence for breach of a stop notice); and
(d)   compulsory purchase.[7]

---

[4]   Regulation 9 requires public bodies to exercise their nature conservation functions so as to comply with the Habitats Directive and the new Wild Birds Directive; reg 10 imposes duties on public bodies in relation to wild bird habitats; and reg 11 requires nature conservation bodies to review and report on whether the obligations under reg 10 have been met.

[5]   Habitats Regulations 2017, regs 10–19 make provision for the selection, designation (or, in the case of special protection areas, classification), registration and notification of sites to be protected under the Habitats Directive ('European sites'). Regulations 23–36 make provision in respect of European sites for: (i) control of damaging operations; (ii) special nature conservation orders and restoration orders (see Sch 1 which has effect with respect to the making, confirmation and coming into operation of special nature conservation orders and amending and revoking orders); (iii) byelaws; and (iv) compulsory purchase. Regulations 37–40 make provision for the protection of European marine sites.

[6]   Habitats Regulations 2017, regs 20–22.

[7]   Habitats Regulations 2017, regs 23–36.

17.8   They make provision for the protection of European marine sites and the making of management schemes in relation to such sites.[8]

17.9   They make provision for the protection of wild animals and plant species and habitats, including the surveillance of the conservation status of natural habitats and species protected under the Habitats Directive and the creation of a criminal offence to kill, capture or disturb those animals or to trade in them, along with the licensing of certain activities relating to animals and plants.[9]

17.10   They also require the effect on a European site to be considered before the granting of various consents or authorisations, including the grant of planning permission.[10]

---

[8]   Habitats Regulations 2017, regs 37–40.

[9]   Habitats Regulations 2017, Pt 3, provides for the protection of certain wild animals and plants (see reg 42 and Sch 2, which list those species of protected animals listed in Annex IV(a) to the Habitats Directive, which have a natural range which includes any area in Great Britain and are referred to in reg 42 as 'European protected species of animals' and comprises (Sch 2) all Bats, Large Blue Butterfly, Wild Cat, Dolphins, Porpoises and Whales, Dormouse, Pool Frog, Sand Lizard, Fisher's Estuarine Moth, Great Crested Newt, Common Otter, Lesser Whirlpool Ram's-horn Snail, Smooth Snake, Sturgeon, Natterjack Toad and Marine Turtles). Regulation 43 makes it an offence, subject to exceptions, deliberately to capture, kill or disturb those animals or to trade in them. Regulation 45 prohibits the use of certain methods of capturing or killing wild animals. Regulation 47 makes it an offence, subject to exceptions, deliberately to pick, collect, cut or destroy those plants or to trade in them. Part 4 provides additional protection of habitats and wild animals and plants. Regulation 50 imposes a duty on the Secretary of State and Welsh Ministers to make arrangements for the surveillance of the conservation status of natural habitats and species protected under the Habitats Directive. Regulation 52 requires them to make arrangements to establish a system to monitor the incidental capture and killing of animals listed in Annex IV(a) to the Habitats Directive. Regulation 54 makes it an offence deliberately to introduce from a ship into the sea new species that are not native to Great Britain. Part 5 provides for the licensing of certain activities relating to animals and plants. The offences under Part 3 do not apply to anything done in accordance with a licence. Regulation 59 makes it an offence to make a false statement or representation for the purpose of obtaining a licence. Regulation 60 makes it an offence to contravene or fail to comply with a licence condition.

[10]   Part 6 deals with the assessment of plans and projects. Regulations 63–69 require the effect on a European site to be considered before the granting of consents or authorisations of a kind specified in regs 70–104; reg 70 is concerned with the grant of planning permission; reg 75 is concerned with general development orders; reg 79 is concerned with special development orders; reg 81 is concerned with neighbourhood development orders; reg 82 is concerned with Simplified Planning Zones; reg 83 is concerned with Enterprise Zones; reg 84 is concerned with the grant of development consent under the Planning Act 2008; reg 87 is concerned with the construction or improvemnent of highways or roads; reg 89 is concerned with consents under the Electricity Act 1989; reg 93 is concerned with authorisations under the Pipe-Lines Act 1962; reg 97 is concerned with orders under the Transport and Works Act 1992; reg 101 is concerned with environmental permits under the Environmental Permitting (England and Wales) Regulations 2016 (SI 2016/1154); reg 102 is concerned with abstraction and works under water legislation; reg 103 is concerned with marine works and reg 104 is concerned with the grant of derogations under Nitrate

17.11 A competent authority (which includes the Secretary of State, a government department, statutory undertaker, public body of any description or person holding a public office, the Welsh Ministers or any person exercising any of the functions of these parties)[11] may not give any consent or permission or other authorisation for a plan or project which is likely to have a significant effect on a European site and is not directly connected with or necessary to the management of that site, without making an appropriate assessment of the implications for that site in view of its conservation objectives.[12] However, if the competent authority is satisfied that, there being no alternative solutions, the plan or project must be carried out for imperative reasons of overriding public interest (which may be of a social or economic nature), it may agree to the plan or project notwithstanding a negative assessment of the implications for the European site or the European offshore marine site.[13]

17.12 Provision is also made for enforcement, including powers of entry, powers of search, powers in relation to specimens and samples and for offences.[14]

17.13 Provision is also made for the advisory role of the Joint Nature Conservation Committee, Natural England, the Natural Resources Body for Wales and Scottish Natural Heritage.[15]

Pollution Prevention Regulations 2015 (SI 2015/668), Pt 8, or Nitrate Pollution Prevention (Wales) Regulations 2013 (SI 2013/2506), Pt 3A.

[11] Regulation 7.

[12] Regulation 63. LPAs are required to carry out these assessments to make sure plans or projects affecting sites in and around EU designated SACs or SPAs have no harmful effects on them. An assessment has two stages: a screening stage and then a full 'appropriate assessment' (see fn 47 in Chapter 2 on plan-making).

[13] Regulation 64.

[14] Habitats Regulations 2017, Pt 7, regs 123–125 sets out the enforcement powers of wildlife inspectors and constables, including powers of entry, search and taking of samples.

[15] Habitats Regulations 2017, regs 134 and 135.

Chapter 18

Development in the Green Belt

INTRODUCTION

18.1   The importance of restricting development in Green Belts (by allowing Green Belt boundaries to be altered or by restricting inappropriate development in the Green Belt except in very special circumstances) is given prominent treatment in the National Planning Policy Framework 2012 (NPPF) at paragraphs 79 to 92. For the purposes of decision-taking, these policies are material considerations which local planning authorities (LPAs) should take into account.[1] Reference should also be made to the decision of the Court of Appeal in *Turner v Secretary of State for Communities and Local Government*[2] and the correct approach to 'openness'. On the other hand, in order to meet five-year housing supply targets some LPAs are looking at ways of removing Green Belt constraints in order to accommodate development.[3] In other words, because current Strategic Housing Market Assessments are showing higher housing requirements than are disclosed in current local plans, LPAs are having to consult on options to accommodate additional development involving the release of greenfield sites, including within the Green Belt. As against this, opponents argue in favour of options involving the intensification of existing settlements (through use of brownfield land), the expansion of urban areas, the creation of larger settlements through the merger of existing settlements, and the creation of entirely new settlements.[4]

---

[1]   NPPF, para 212.

[2]   [2016] EWCA Civ 466. See para 18.10.

[3]   It was, for instance, reported in *Planning* on 28/6/2018 that North Hertfordshire DC's emerging local plan (which is currently undergoing examination) proposes to remove a 37 hectare site from the Green Belt with a view to making a strategic housing allocation for approximately 700 homes.

[4]   Clearly, the weight to be given to housing shortfall and whether it constitutes 'very special circumstances' within the meaning of NPPF, para 87 is a matter of planning judgment (*R (Khan) v LB Sutton* [2014] EWHC 3663 (Admin)). In *Hunston Properties Ltd v Secretary of State for Communities and Local Government* [2013] EWCA Civ 1610, (a case where the issue had been whether any very special circumstances had been demonstrated to outweigh the Green Belt

POLICIES AFFECTING GREEN BELTS IN NPPF (PLAN-MAKING AND DECISION-TAKING)

18.2   The relevant policies are set out below in full:

9. Protecting Green Belt land

79. The Government attaches great importance to Green Belts. The fundamental aim of Green Belt policy is to prevent urban sprawl by keeping land permanently open; the essential characteristics of Green Belts are their openness and their permanence.

80. Green Belt serves five purposes:

- to check the unrestricted sprawl of large built-up areas;
- to prevent neighbouring towns merging into one another;
- to assist in safeguarding the countryside from encroachment;
- to preserve the setting and special character of historic towns; and
- to assist in urban regeneration, by encouraging the recycling of derelict and other urban land.

81. Once Green Belts have been defined, local planning authorities should plan positively to enhance the beneficial use of the Green Belt, such as looking for opportunities to provide access; to provide opportunities for outdoor sport and recreation; to retain and enhance landscapes, visual amenity and biodiversity; or to improve damaged and derelict land.

82. The general extent of Green Belts across the country is already established. New Green Belts should only be established in exceptional circumstances, for example when planning for larger scale development such as new settlements or major urban extensions. If proposing a new Green Belt, local planning authorities should:

- demonstrate why normal planning and development management policies would not be adequate;
- set out whether any major changes in circumstances have made the adoption of this exceptional measure necessary;

---

objection), the court held that one of the considerations was likely to be the scale of the shortfall. Other factors included the planning context within which that shortfall was to be seen. Where the district was subject on a considerable scale to policies protecting much or most of the undeveloped land from development except in exceptional or very special circumstances, then it might be wholly unsurprising that there was not a five-year supply of housing land. A decision-maker may then be entitled to conclude that some degree of shortfall in housing land supply was inevitable, which might affect the weight to be attached to the shortfall. The Green Belt might come into play both in that broader context and in the site specific context where it was the trigger for the requirement that very special circumstances be shown. That was an approach which took account of the need to read the NPPF as a whole. It would be irrational to say that one took account of the constraints embodied in the policies of the NPPF, such as the Green Belt, and yet to require a decision-maker to close his eyes to the existence of those restraints when making a development control decision. They were clearly relevant planning considerations in both exercises.

- show what the consequences of the proposal would be for sustainable development;
- demonstrate the necessity for the Green Belt and its consistency with Local Plans for adjoining areas;
- show how the Green Belt would meet the other objectives of the Framework.

83. Local planning authorities with Green Belts in their area should establish Green Belt boundaries in their local plans which set the framework for Green Belt and settlement policy. Once established, Green Belt boundaries should only be altered in exceptional circumstances, through the preparation or review of the Local Plan.[5] At that time, authorities should consider the Green Belt boundaries having regard to their intended permanence in the long term, so that they should be capable of enduring beyond the plan period.

84. When drawing up or reviewing Green Belt boundaries local planning authorities should take account of the need to promote sustainable patterns of development. They should consider the consequences for sustainable development of channelling development towards urban areas inside the Green Belt boundary, towards towns and villages inset within the Green Belt or towards locations beyond the outer Green Belt boundary.

85. When defining boundaries, local planning authorities should:

- ensure consistency with the Local Plan strategy for meeting identified requirements for sustainable development;
- not include land which it is unnecessary to keep permanently open;
- where necessary, identify in their plans areas of 'safeguarded land' between the urban area and the Green Belt, in order to meet longer-term development needs stretching well beyond the plan period;
- make clear that the safeguarded land is not allocated for development at the present time. Planning permission for the permanent development of safeguarded land should only be granted following a Local Plan review which proposes the development;
- satisfy themselves that Green Belt boundaries will not need to be altered at the end of the development plan period; and
- define boundaries clearly, using physical features that are readily recognisable and likely to be permanent.

---

5   Simply preparing a new local plan or having a suitable site available for housing is not an exceptional circumstance which justifies the exclusion of land from the Green Belt. Something more must have occurred which justifies a change apart from a different view on planning grounds of where the Green Belt boundary should lie. It will, however, assist if a planning inspector has approved a joint strategy adopted by three LPAs for housing development where it was clear from her report that she had in mind the broad content of NPPF, para 83 relating to 'exceptional circumstances' justifying alteration to Green Belt boundaries and had reached an evidence-based conclusion that such circumstances existed (*Claverton Parish Council v Nottingham City Council* [2015] EWHC 1078 (Admin)). There is no test that Green Belt land should only be released as a last resort (*IM Properties Development Ltd v Lichfield DC* [2014] PTSR 1484).

86. If it is necessary to prevent development in a village primarily because of the important contribution which the open character of the village makes to the openness of the Green Belt, the village should be included in the Green Belt. If, however, the character of the village needs to be protected for other reasons, other means should be used, such as conservation area or normal development management policies, and the village should be excluded from the Green Belt.

87. As with previous Green Belt policy, inappropriate development is, by definition, harmful to the Green Belt and should not be allowed except in very special circumstances.[6]

88. When considering any planning application, local planning authorities should ensure that substantial weight is given to any harm to the Green Belt. 'Very special circumstances'[7] will not exist unless the potential harm to the Green Belt by reason of inappropriateness, and any other harm,[8] is clearly outweighed by other considerations.

---

[6]   Whether housing shortfall constitutes 'very special circumstances' is a matter of planning judgment for the decision-maker. The crucial question for an inspector in such a case is not if there is a shortfall in housing land supply, but rather, have very special circumstances been demonstrated to outweigh the Green Belt objection? Such circumstances are not automatically demonstrated simply because there is less than a five-year supply of housing land. One of the considerations to be reflected in the decision on 'very special circumstances' is likely to be the scale of the shortfall. But there are other factors, as well, such as the planning context in which that shortfall is to be seen. The context could be that the district in question is subject on a considerable scale to policies protecting much or most of the undeveloped land from development except in exceptional or special circumstances. If that was the case, then it might be wholly unsurprising that there is not a five-year supply of housing land when measured against the figures of household projections. A decision-maker would then be entitled to conclude (if such was the planning judgment) that some degree of shortfall in housing land supply, as measured simply by household formation rates, is inevitable (*Hunston Properties Ltd v Secretary of State for Communities and Local Government* [2014] JPL 599). See also *R (Khan) v Sutton LBC* [2014] EWHC 3663 (Admin), where the court emphasised that whether 'very special circumstances' existed was a matter of planning judgment by the decision-maker.

[7]   It is permissible to treat a shortfall in housing land supply as one of a number of very special circumstances (*R (Lee Valley Regional Park Authority) v Broxbourne BC* [2016] Env LR 30). The classes of 'very special circumstances' are not closed. In *Davis v Secretary of State for Communities and Local Government* [2016] EWHC 274 (Admin), the court held (following *Timmins v Gedling BC* [2015] EWCA Civ 10, in a case involving enforcement proceedings affecting a field shelter and hardstandings neither of which had any effect on openness but were nonetheless found by the inspector to have a detrimental impact on the visual amenity of the area) that under the NPPF any development in the Green Belt was to be treated as *prima facie* 'inappropriate' and could only be justified by special circumstances save in the defined circumstances set out in paras 89 and 90. The court also found that there was no general principle that the inspector should have applied a lower test simply because the hardstandings did not affect openness.

[8]   The phrase 'any other harm' extended to non-green-belt harm. There is no doubt that the policy exists to protect the essential characteristics of the Green Belt, but there is nothing illogical in requiring all non-green-belt factors to be taken into account in deciding whether planning permission should be granted on what would be non-green-belt grounds (i.e. 'very special circumstances') for development that was, by definition, harmful to the Green Belt (*Redhill*

89. A local planning authority should regard the construction of new buildings[9] as inappropriate in Green Belt. Exceptions to this are:

- buildings for agriculture and forestry;
- provision of appropriate facilities for outdoor sport, outdoor recreation and for cemeteries, as long as it preserves the openness of the Green Belt and does not conflict with the purposes of including land within it;
- the extension or alteration of a building provided that it does not result in disproportionate additions over and above the size of the original building;
- the replacement of a building,[10] provided the new building is in the same use and not materially larger than the one it replaces;
- limited infilling in villages,[11] and limited affordable housing for local community needs under policies set out in the Local Plan;[12] or

---

Aerodrome Ltd v Secretary of State for Communities and Local Government [2014] EWCA Civ 1386).

[9] *Lloyd v Secretary of State for Communities and Local Government* [2014] EWCA Civ 839; the term 'building' did not include a mobile home (or a movable structure stationed on a site), with the result that the replacement of a mobile home with a building on a Green Belt site amounted to inappropriate development. Even where, as in *Lloyd*, a mobile home had a certificate of lawful use, it remained a structure stationed on land of an inherently temporary nature. Unlike new buildings, they were constructed of short-term materials and had to be capable of being moved off site. To allow para 89 to refer to mobile homes as 'buildings' would seriously undermine the protection of the Green Belt, as it would allow the replacement of mobile structures with buildings as appropriate development. Based on the statutory context, the term 'building' did not include a mobile home.

[10] *Tandridge DC v Secretary of State for Communities and Local Government* [2015] EWHC 2503 (Admin); the term 'building' could extend to new 'buildings' provided they were in the same use and not materially larger than the single building they were replacing. The decision of the inspector was upheld. The inspector was found to have considered the relative sizes of the existing buildings and the two proposals and had reached a conclusion by comparing their physical dimensions, their bulk, height, mass and prominence. He had also considered that such issues were part of the materiality of the comparative scale in accordance with *Surrey Homes Ltd v Secretary of State for the Environment, Transport and the Regions* [2001] JPL 379 (Note). The court also found that it was correct to adopt the same approach in respect of the 'not materially larger' test in NPPF, para 89, as had been applied to its predecessor in para 3.6 of PPG2 (Planning Policy Guidance 2: Green belts, January 1995, amended March 2001).

[11] *R (Tate) v Northumberland CC* [2018] EWCA Civ 1519; the Court of Appeal held that the question of 'limited infilling' in a village for the purpose of NPPF, para 89 (fifth bullet) would always be essentially a question of fact and planning judgment for the decision-maker. There was no definition of 'infilling' or 'limited infilling' in the NPPF, nor any guidance there, to assist that exercise of planning judgment. It was not the kind of question to which the court should put forward an answer of its own and neither would it readily interfere with the decision-maker's own view (*Wood v Secretary of State for Communities and Local Government* [2015] EWCA Civ 195 followed). See fn 5.

[12] *R (Robb) v South Cambridgeshire DC* [2017] EWHC 594 (Admin); an LPA was found to have erred in granting permission for the erection of ten affordable dwellings on a greenfield site on the edge of a village in the Green Belt. The local plan policy was clear that permission for affordable housing should be granted only when all its stated criteria were met. It was the intention of NPPF, para 89 (fifth bullet) that relevant local plan policy had been complied with.

- limited infilling or the partial or complete redevelopment of previously developed sites (brownfield land), whether redundant or in continuing use (excluding temporary buildings), which would not have a greater impact on the openness of the Green Belt and the purpose of including land within it than the existing development.

90. Certain other forms of development are also not inappropriate in Green Belt provided they preserve the openness of the Green Belt and do not conflict with the purposes of including land in Green Belt. These are:

- mineral extraction;[13]
- engineering operations;
- local transport infrastructure which can demonstrate a requirement for a Green Belt location;
- the re-use of buildings provided that the buildings are of permanent and substantial construction; and
- development brought forward under a Community Right to Build Order.

91. When located in the Green Belt, elements of many renewable energy projects will comprise inappropriate development. In such cases developers will need to demonstrate very special circumstances if projects are to proceed. Such very special circumstances may include the wider environmental benefits associated with increased production of energy from renewable sources.

92. Community Forests offer valuable opportunities for improving the environment around towns, by upgrading the landscape and providing for recreation and wildlife. An approved Community Forest plan may be a material consideration in preparing development plans and in deciding planning applications. Any development proposals within Community Forests in the Green Belt should be subject to the normal policies controlling development in Green Belts.

---

13   'Mineral extraction' can include mineral exploration and appraisal (*Europa Oil and Gas v Secretary of State for Communities and Local Government* [2014] JPL 1259). The Court of Appeal held that a proposed development which involved exploratory drilling for hydrocarbons in the Green Belt was 'mineral extraction' for the purposes of NPPF, para 90 (first bullet) and a local development plan policy. It was held that a policy statement should be interpreted objectively in accordance with the language used, read always in its proper context. Onshore oil and gas development had three phases, namely exploration, appraisal and production, and it was held that these were essentially components of one process: the one process they naturally made up was the overall process of extraction. Looking at the specific context of the NPPF as a whole, it was found that there was a strong case for interpreting 'mineral extraction' broadly.

COMMENT ON THE TYPICAL DEVELOPMENT CONTEXT

18.3   Questions of development commonly arise in pockets of the Green Belt where development has previously occurred, perhaps a redundant nursery site (with the remnants of past uses often strewn across the site or amongst the trees which, more often than not, will eventually be assimilated into the surrounding landscape if they are not carted away as rubbish), or where other mixed uses have taken place over a prolonged period. A development proposal in such circumstances is more than likely to be associated with the restoration of what has become an untidy (and perhaps even contaminated) site in the countryside for which there is limited demand in its existing state with, as its object, residential development coupled with an abundance of associated landscaping. There will almost invariably be local opposition to what will be perceived to be urbanisation of the countryside. The fact that these are usually smaller sites in the countryside makes it more than likely that developers will be seeking permission for high cost market housing (with affordable provision off-site) for which there is bound to be limited local need. LPAs must grapple with such applications all the time and it is never easy.

18.4   Such sites commonly also fall within an area subject to a range of countryside designations such as Green Belt, Area of Outstanding Natural Beauty (AONB), Area of Great Landscape Value (AGLV) or Site of Special Scientific Interest (SSSI). The proposed development site may well also lie within a Special Protection Area (SPA)/Special Area of Conservation where development is greatly constrained. Also, nearby, there may even be a Local Nature Reserve (LNR), scheduled monuments (and there are over 200 categories of monument on the schedule, ranging from prehistoric standing stones to the sites of old collieries) or occasional areas of ancient woodland within the surrounding heaths and plantations. In such cases, local plan policies are bound to harmonise with national policies. How, then, should such applications for planning permission be approached in the context of policies (local and national) which limit the prospect of development and which aim to conserve and enhance the distinctiveness of the landscape character of such areas within the district? On any footing, the prospect of redevelopment is going to be greatly enhanced in the case of previously developed sites, and developers will obviously select such sites with care.

WHEN IS NEW DEVELOPMENT LIKELY TO BE FEASIBLE IN THE GREEN BELT?

18.5   In the case of Green Belt policy within the NPPF (whose drafting could have been clearer), the position is that the construction of new buildings in the

Green Belt is inappropriate development and should not be approved except in very special circumstances.[14]

18.6   There are six exceptions to this, one of which[15] is where new buildings are to be constructed on a previously developed site (brownfield land) which will not be considered as inappropriate development provided the new development would not have greater impact on the openness of the Green Belt than the existing development. If it would, then, in order to justify a grant of planning permission, the developer would have to show *very special circumstances* which arise when the harm to openness *is clearly outweighed by other considerations.*[16]

18.7   On the other hand, if the site is not brownfield land, the developer will have to show either that one of the other exceptions arise under paragraph 89 of the NPPF (such as buildings for agriculture and forestry) or that there are *very special circumstances* which will not exist *unless the potential harm to the Green Belt by reason of inappropriateness, and any other harm, is clearly outweighed by other considerations.* The threshold for approval is admittedly a high one.

---

[14]   *Brown v Ealing LBC* [2018] EWCA Civ 556; where the court found that a planning officer had not erred in law in concluding that 'very special circumstances' existed to justify the grant of planning permission for otherwise inappropriate development on metropolitan open land (MOL). Furthermore, she had not misinterpreted or misapplied a policy within the London Plan which required the 'loss of protected open spaces' to be 'resisted'. The case involved a long-running dispute over the proposed new training ground for Queen's Park Rangers FC, which was located on land within MOL (effectively Green Belt within London), which was also designated as Community Open Space, although between the mid-1960s and 2013, it had been used for formal sports and recreation since when the site had been vacant (although used by some members of the public for informal recreation and access). The land was required by the football club for a new training ground and academy facility comprising numerous football pitches and other facilities. The present claim challenged the officer's report to committee and raised the issue as to whether the LPA had erred in its approach to 'very special circumstances' and to Policy 7.18 of the London Plan. The challenge was rejected by the Court of Appeal, which found that the LPA, with the benefit of the officer's advice, had not neglected to consider any relevant planning issue or failed to have regard to any material consideration or that, on any relevant issue, its exercise of planning judgement was unreasonable in the *Wednesbury* sense. The officer's report was found to be comprehensive and thorough, its conclusions were clearly reasoned and well within the ambit of a lawful planning judgment on the issue of whether there were 'very special circumstances'. The officer had given that factor due weight in two different respects: first, outweighing a 'loss' that would be caused by the development itself, and secondly, meeting an existing need that would not be satisfied without the development.

[15]   NPPF, para 89, sixth bullet point.

[16]   NPPF, para 88.

R (Lee Valley Regional Park Authority) v Epping Forest District Council

18.8   Reference should be made to *R (Lee Valley Regional Park Authority) v Epping Forest District Council*,[17] where the Court of Appeal considered the

---

[17]   [2016] EWCA Civ 404. The development in this case included the construction of a large glasshouse in the metropolitan Green Belt within Lee Valley Regional Park. This was less than a kilometre from the Lee Valley SPA and Ramsar site (note: Ramsar sites are wetlands considered to be of international importance). Epping Forest District Council granted planning permission for a development which included the glasshouse, an application for judicial review failed and an appeal was also dismissed. In the Court of Appeal, Lindblom LJ agreed with the analysis of Dove J that the true position was that development that was not in principle 'inappropriate' in the Green Belt was 'appropriate to the Green Belt' and was the reason why it did not have to be justified by 'very special circumstances'. Lindblom LJ said at [25] and [26]:

'That was the basic analysis underlying the judge's conclusion, with which I agree, "that appropriate development is deemed not harmful to the Green Belt and its [principal] characteristic of openness in particular ...". Dove J saw support for this conclusion in the judgment of Ouseley J at first instance in *Europa Oil and Gas v Secretary of State for Communities and Local Government* [2013] EWHC 2643 (Admin) (at paragraphs 64 to 78). I think he was right to do so. Ouseley J captured the point well when he said (in paragraph 66 of his judgment) that under the policies in paragraphs 89 and 90 of the NPPF "considerations of appropriateness, preservation of openness and conflict with Green Belt purposes are not exclusively dependent on the size of buildings or structures but include their purpose", and that "... two materially similar buildings [,] one a house and one a sports pavilion, are treated differently in terms of actual or potential appropriateness". Thus, as Ouseley J said: "The Green Belt may not be harmed by one but is harmed necessarily by another. The one it is harmed by because of its effect on openness, and the other it is not harmed by because of its effect on openness. These concepts are to be applied ... in the light of a particular type of development". That reasoning was adopted and applied by HHJ Pelling QC, sitting as a deputy judge of the High Court, in *Fordent Holdings Ltd v Secretary of State for Communities and Local Government* [2013] EWHC 2844 (Admin) (at paragraphs 33 to 35 of his judgment). An appeal against Ouseley J's decision was later dismissed by this court ([2014] EWCA Civ 825). In that appeal Richards LJ (at paragraphs 35 to 41 of his judgment, with which Moore-Bick and Kitchin LJJ agreed) expressly endorsed the "general thrust" of Ouseley J's reasoning in the passage of his judgment referred to by Dove J, including the observations I have quoted from paragraph 66 (see, in particular, paragraph 37 of Richards LJ's judgment).

[26] That is not to say, of course, that proposals for the erection of agricultural buildings in the Green Belt will escape other policies in the NPPF, and in the development plan, including policies directed to the visual effects of development and the protection of the countryside or the character of the landscape. Policies of this kind will bear not only on proposals for development that is inappropriate in the Green Belt but also on proposals for development that is appropriate. When such policies are applied, the size and bulk of the building, and its "siting, materials [and] design" (the factors referred to in paragraph 3.15 of PPG2), are likely to be important considerations. Establishing the status of a proposed development – inappropriate in the Green Belt or appropriate – remains only the first step for the decision-maker (see, for example, the judgment of Stuart-Smith LJ in *Pehrsson v Secretary of State for the Environment* [1990] 3 PLR 66 at p. 72; and Sullivan J's judgment in *Heath and Hampstead Society*, at paragraph 33, where he described this as a "threshold question"). As paragraph 88 of the NPPF makes plain, inappropriate development can prove to be acceptable if "very special circumstances" are shown to exist, because "the potential harm to the Green Belt by reason of

meaning and effect of the NPPF in the case of the construction of agricultural buildings in the Green Belt which, in its decision, should not be approached as being harmful either to the openness of the Green Belt or to the purposes of including land in the Green Belt. It was said that the true position in respect of national policy for the Green Belt was that development which was not, in principle, 'inappropriate' in the Green Belt was development 'appropriate to the Green Belt'. It was considered that, on a sensible contextual reading of the relevant policies in paragraphs 79 to 92 of the NPPF, development appropriate in – and to – the Green Belt was not inimical to the fundamental aim of Green Belt policy '*to prevent urban sprawl by keeping land permanently open*', or to '*the essential characteristics of Green Belts*' (emphasis added), namely '*their openness and permanence*' (emphasis added),[18] or to the five purposes served by the Green Belt.[19] It was said that was the real significance of a development being appropriate in the Green Belt, and the reason why it did not have to be justified by '*very special circumstances*' (emphasis added).[20]

18.9   The approach to the grant of planning permission in the case of *brownfield land* within the Green Belt is suggested to be as set out below:

(a)   Is the site governed by Green Belt policy?
(b)   Is the site previously developed land?
(c)   Will the proposed development have a greater impact on the openness of the Green Belt than the existing development (such as the example of the derelict nursery site) which it will replace?
(d)   Considerations of appropriateness, the preservation of openness and conflict with Green Belt purposes are not exclusively dependent on the appearance, volume and scale of the existing and proposed developments but may include their purpose. It is also open to a decision-taker to take into account the visual impact of the proposed development on the openness of the Green Belt. The evaluation of the existing and proposed development was a matter of planning judgment. Accordingly, the approach to openness, for the purpose of NPPF, paragraph 89 (bullet point 6) is not concerned solely with a mathematical comparison of the relevant dimensions of the existing lawful use and the proposed development. (It would be absurd if any additional

---

inappropriateness, and any other harm, is clearly outweighed by other considerations" (see generally the decisions of this court in *Doncaster Metropolitan Borough Council v Secretary of State for the Environment, Transport and the Regions* [2002] JPL 1509, and *R (Basildon District Council) v First Secretary of State* [2005] JPL 942). And development that is not inappropriate, because it is within one of the exceptional categories in paragraphs 89 and 90 and thus not potentially harmful to the Green Belt "by reason of inappropriateness", may still be unacceptable for other planning reasons. In this case, however, that was not so.'

18   These are references taken from NPPF, para 79.
19   NPPF, para 80.
20   NPPF, para 87.

development would be harmful to openness as it would render unworkable the provisions dealing with allowable development in the Green Belt in the NPPF.)

(e) If the proposed development is going to have a negative impact on openness by comparison with the existing development, is the developer still in a position to show that a grant of planning permission would be justified by very special circumstances? This requires the developer to show that the potential harm to the Green Belt would be clearly outweighed by other considerations. On the other hand, planning permission would be relatively easier to obtain if the developer could show that the proposed development was: (i) not in principle inappropriate in the Green Belt (and accordingly did not have to be justified by very special circumstances); and/or (ii) would not, in fact, have a greater impact on the openness of the Green Belt which takes into account the visual impact upon openness of the new development (such as where the development is liable to cause only minor harm to the appearance of the area) and is not limited to measuring the volume of the existing and proposed structures on the site.

(f) Will the proposed development escape other policies in the NPPF or in the local plan, including policies directed towards the visual effects of development and the protection of the countryside or the character of the landscape? Such policies will have a bearing on the appropriateness of the proposals for development. Such policies might very well be affected by the size and bulk of the proposed buildings. This is just as important to the decision-maker. In other words, development which may be within one of the exceptional categories within NPPF, paragraphs 89 and 90, and thus deemed not to be potentially harmful to the Green Belt by reason of inappropriateness, may still be unacceptable for other planning reasons.

HOW IS THE LPA (OR AN INSPECTOR) TO JUDGE IMPACT ON OPENNESS?

Turner v Secretary of State for Communities and Local Government

18.10 The term 'openness' is not defined in the NPPF. However, in *Turner v Secretary of State for Communities and Local Government*,[21] the Court of Appeal gave important guidance on the interpretation of 'openness' as used in paragraph 89 of the NPPF in the section 'Protecting Green Belt land'. The case involved an appeal by a landowner against a decision upholding a determination of a planning inspector that a planning permission should not be granted for residential

---

21   [2016] EWCA Civ 466.

development in the Green Belt. The landowner owned a site in the Green Belt on which was sited a static caravan and a yard from which he ran a business storing, repairing and selling commercial vehicles. Certificates of lawful use existed for the caravan and the storage of 11 lorries in the yard. The landowner sought permission to replace the caravan and storage yard with a three-bedroom bungalow, and to use land adjacent to the site to continue his business. Permission was refused on the ground that the proposal constituted inappropriate development in the Green Belt. The landowner appealed on the ground that his proposal was not inappropriate because it would have no greater impact on openness of the Green Belt than the existing development, and so fell within the exception in the sixth bullet point of paragraph 89 of the NPPF. The inspector upheld the local authority's refusal of permission. He found that although the volume of the bungalow might be the same as that of the caravan and lorries, the impact of the two developments could not be judged simply by measured volume. He found that the bungalow would have a greater visual impact on the openness of the Green Belt than did the existing development. The landowner contended that when considering the sixth bullet point, the inspector had failed to carry out a proper volumetric comparison of the existing and proposed developments, and had wrongly conflated the concepts of openness and visual impact.

18.11 Reference should be made at the outset to earlier authority on 'openness' before reverting to the recent guidance in *Turner*, which is now of considerable importance when it comes to development on brownfield land in the Green Belt. In *Timmins v Gedling Borough Council*,[22] Green J stated as follows:[23]

> Any construction harms openness quite irrespective of its impact in terms of its obtrusiveness or its aesthetic attractions or qualities. A beautiful building is still an affront to openness, simply because it exists. The same applies to a building which is camouflaged or rendered unobtrusive by felicitous landscaping.

18.12 Appeals were dismissed in *Timmins*,[24] but the holding of Green J on what is meant by openness was not questioned. Green J had cited from *R (Heath & Hampstead Society) v London Borough of Camden*,[25] where Sullivan J explained the difference between openness and visual impact in the context of paragraph 3.6 of Planning Policy Guidance Note 2 (PPG2).[26] Sullivan J said this:[27] 'The extent to which openness is, or is not, visible from public vantage points and the extent

---

22   [2014] EWHC 654 (Admin).

23   [2014] EWHC 654 (Admin) at [74].

24   [2015] EWCA Civ 10.

25   [2007] EWHC 977 (Admin).

26   PPG2 (Planning Policy Guidance 2: Green belts, January 1995, amended March 2001) was replaced by the NPPF on 27/3/2012.

27   [2007] EWHC 977 (Admin) at [21].

to which a new building in the Green Belt would be visually intrusive are a separate issue'. He continued:[28]

> The loss of openness (i.e. unbuilt on land) within the Green Belt or Metropolitan Open Land is of itself harmful to the underlying policy objective. If the replacement dwelling is more visually intrusive there will be further harm in addition to the harm by reason of inappropriateness, which will have to be outweighed by those special circumstances if planning permission is to be granted (paragraph 3.15 of PPG2, above). If the materially larger replacement dwelling is less visually intrusive than the existing dwelling then that would be a factor which could be taken into consideration when deciding whether the harm by reason of inappropriateness was outweighed by very special circumstances.

18.13 And as Green J put it in *Timmins*:[29]

> [72] … openness was a concept which related to the absence of building; it is land that is not built upon. Openness is hence epitomised by the lack of buildings but not by buildings that are unobtrusive or camouflaged or screened in some way: …

> [73] It is clear … that measures taken to limit the intrusiveness of a development whilst not affecting the assessment of openness may nonetheless be relevant to the 'very special circumstance' weighing exercise. Hence openness and visual impact are different concepts; yet they can nonetheless relate to each other. The distinction is subtle but important.

18.14 The judgment of the Court of Appeal in *Turner v Secretary of State for Communities and Local Government*[30] was delivered by Sales LJ, who dismissed the landowner's appeal. The following are those parts of his judgment which are material to the finding of the court that visual impact may be taken into account in assessing, for the purpose of the sixth bullet point of paragraph 89 of the NPPF, the extent to which a proposed development had an impact on the openness of the Green Belt:

> [11] In his oral submissions, Mr Rudd developed the first ground somewhat. His submission was that the Inspector was wrong to say that no valid comparison could be made between the volume of moveable chattels (mobile home and lorries) on the site and a permanent structure in the form of the proposed bungalow; on the proper construction of the concept of 'openness of the Green Belt' as used in the sixth bullet point in para. 89 of the NPPF the sole criterion of openness for the purpose of the comparison required by that bullet point was the volume of structures comprising the existing lawful use of a site compared

---

28   [2007] EWHC 977 (Admin) at [22].

29   [2015] EWCA Civ 10 at [72]–[73].

30   [2016] EWCA Civ 466.

with that of the structure proposed by way of redevelopment of that site ('the volumetric approach'); a comparison between the volume of existing development on the site in this case in the form of the mobile home and 11 lorries as against the volume of the proposed bungalow showed that there would be a lesser impact on the openness of the Green Belt if the existing development were replaced by the bungalow and the Inspector should so have concluded; and the Inspector erred by having regard to a wider range of considerations apart from the volume of development on the site (including the factor of visual impact) in para. 14 of the decision on the way to reaching his conclusion at para. 15. This last point overlaps with the second ground of challenge and it is appropriate to address both grounds together, as the judge did.

[12] I do not accept these submissions by Mr Rudd. First, in so far as it is suggested that the Inspector did not address himself to the comparative exercise called for under the sixth bullet point in para. 89, the suggestion is incorrect. The Inspector set out that bullet point and then proceeded to make an evaluative comparative assessment of the existing lawful use and the proposed redevelopment in paras. 10 to 15 of the decision.

[13] The principal matter in issue is whether the Inspector adopted an improper approach to the question of openness of the Green Belt when he made that comparison. The question of the true interpretation of the NPPF is a matter for the court. In my judgment, the approach the Inspector adopted was correct and the judge was right to so hold.

[14] The concept of 'openness of the Green Belt' is not narrowly limited to the volumetric approach suggested by Mr Rudd. The word 'openness' is open-textured and a number of factors are capable of being relevant when it comes to the particular facts of a specific case. Prominent amongst these will be factors relevant to how built up the Green Belt is now and how built up it would be if redevelopment occurs (in the context of which, volumetric matters may be a material concern, but are by no means the only one) and factors relevant to the visual impact on the aspect of openness which the Green Belt presents.

[15] The question of visual impact is implicitly part of the concept of 'openness of the Green Belt' as a matter of the natural meaning of the language used in para. 89 of the NPPF. I consider that this interpretation is also reinforced by the general guidance in paras. 79–81 of the NPPF, which introduce section 9 on the protection of Green Belt Land. There is an important visual dimension to checking 'the unrestricted sprawl of large built-up areas' and the merging of neighbouring towns, as indeed the name 'Green Belt' itself implies. Greenness is a visual quality: part of the idea of the Green Belt is that the eye and the spirit should be relieved from the prospect of unrelenting urban sprawl. Openness of aspect is a characteristic quality of the countryside, and 'safeguarding the countryside from encroachment' includes preservation of that quality of openness. The preservation of 'the setting ... of historic towns'

obviously refers in a material way to their visual setting, for instance when seen from the distance across open fields. Again, the reference in para. 81 to planning positively 'to retain and enhance landscapes, visual amenity and biodiversity' in the Green Belt makes it clear that the visual dimension of the Green Belt is an important part of the point of designating land as Green Belt.

[16] The visual dimension of the openness of the Green Belt does not exhaust all relevant planning factors relating to visual impact when a proposal for development in the Green Belt comes up for consideration. For example, there may be harm to visual amenity for neighbouring properties arising from the proposed development which needs to be taken into account as well. But it does not follow from the fact that there may be other harms with a visual dimension apart from harm to the openness of the Green Belt that the concept of openness of the Green Belt has no visual dimension itself.

[17] Mr Rudd relied upon a section of the judgment of Green J in *R (Timmins) v Gedling Borough Council* [2014] EWHC 654 (Admin) at [67]–[78], in which the learned judge addressed the question of the relationship between openness of the Green Belt and visual impact. Green J referred to the judgment of Sullivan J in *R (Heath and Hampstead Society) v Camden LBC* [2007] EWHC 977 (Admin); [2007] 2 P&CR 19, which related to previous policy in relation to the Green Belt as set out in Planning Policy Guidance 2 ('PPG 2'), and drew from it the propositions that 'there is a clear conceptual distinction between openness and visual impact' and 'It is therefore wrong *in principle* to arrive at a specific conclusion as to openness by reference to visual impact': para. [78] (Green J's emphasis). The case went on appeal, but this part of Green J's judgment was not in issue on the appeal: [2015] EWCA Civ 10; [2016] 1 All ER 895.

[18] In my view, Green J went too far and erred in stating the propositions set out above. This section of his judgment should not be followed. There are three problems with it. First, with respect to Green J, I do not think that he focused sufficiently on the language of section 9 of the NPPF, read as part of the coherent and self-contained statement of national planning policy which the NPPF is intended to be. The learned judge does not consider the points made above. Secondly, through his reliance on the *Heath and Hampstead Society* case Green J has given excessive weight to the statement of planning policy in PPG 2 for the purposes of interpretation of the NPPF. He has not made proper allowance for the fact that PPG 2 is expressed in materially different terms from section 9 of the NPPF. Thirdly, I consider that the conclusion he has drawn is not in fact supported by the judgment of Sullivan J in the *Heath and Hampstead Society* case.

[19] The general objective of PPG 2 was to make provision for the protection of Green Belts. Paragraph 3.2 stated that inappropriate development was, by definition, harmful to the Green Belt. Paragraph 3.6 stated:

'Provided that it does not result in disproportionate additions over and above the size of the original building, the extension or alteration of dwellings is not inappropriate in Green Belts. The replacement of existing dwellings need not be inappropriate, providing the new dwelling is not materially larger than the dwelling it replaces …'.

[20] It was the application of this provision which was in issue in the *Heath and Hampstead Society* case. It can be seen that this provision broadly corresponds with the fourth bullet point in para. 89 of the NPPF and that it has a specific focus on the relative size of an existing building and of the proposed addition or replacement.

[21] The NPPF was introduced in 2012 as a new, self-contained statement of national planning policy to replace the various policy guidance documents that had proliferated previously. The NPPF did not simply repeat what was in those documents. It set out national planning policy afresh in terms which are at various points materially different from what went before. This court gave guidance regarding the proper approach to the interpretation of the NPPF in the *Timmins* case at para. [24]. The NPPF should be interpreted objectively in accordance with the language used, read in its proper context. But the previous guidance – specifically *Timmins*, as in this case and in *Redhill Aerodrome Ltd v Secretary of State for Communities and Local Government* [2014] EWCA Civ 1386; [2015] 1 P&CR 36 to which the court in *Timmins* referred, the guidance on Green Belt policy in PPG 2 – remains relevant. In particular since in promulgating the NPPF the Government made it clear that it strongly supported the Green Belt and did not intend to change the central policy that inappropriate development in the Green Belt should not be allowed, section 9 of the NPPF should not be read in such a way as to weaken protection for the Green Belt: see *Redhill Aerodrome* case at [16] per Sullivan LJ, quoted in *Timmins* at [24].

[22] The *Heath and Hampstead Society* case concerned a proposal to demolish an existing residential building on Metropolitan Open Land (which was subject to a policy giving it the same level of protection as the Green Belt) and replace it with a new dwelling. Sullivan J rejected the submission that the test in para. 3.6 was solely concerned with a mathematical comparison of relevant dimensions: [19]. However, he accepted the alternative submission that the exercise under para. 3.6 was primarily an objective one by reference to size, where which particular physical dimension was most relevant would depend on the circumstances of a particular case, albeit with floor space being an important criterion: [20]. It was not appropriate to substitute a test such as 'providing the new dwelling is not more visually intrusive than the dwelling it replaces' for the test actually stated in para. 3.6, namely whether the new dwelling was materially larger or not: [20]. As Sullivan J said, 'Paragraph 3.6 is concerned with the size of the replacement dwelling, not with its visual impact': [21]. In that regard, also at para. [21], he relied in addition on para. 3.15 of PPG 2 which made specific provision in relation to visual amenities in

the Green Belt. Neither para. 3.6 of PPG 2 (with its specific focus on comparative size of the existing and replacement buildings) nor para. 3.15 of PPG 2 refer to the concept of the 'openness of the Green Belt'. They do not correspond with the text of the sixth bullet in para. 89 of the NPPF, and section 9 of the NPPF contains no provision equivalent to para. 3.15 of PPG 2. It is therefore not appropriate to treat this part of the judgment in *Heath and Hampstead Society* as providing authorative guidance on the interpretation of the sixth bullet point in para. 89 of the NPPF. At paras. [22] and [36]–[38] Sullivan J emphasised that the relevant issue in the case concerned the application of para. 3.6 of PPG 2 and whether the proposed replacement house was materially larger than the existing house.

[23] At para. [22] Sullivan J said, 'The loss of openness (i.e. unbuilt on land) within the Green Belt or Metropolitan Open Land is of itself harmful to the underlying policy objective'. Since the concept of the openness of the Green Belt has a spatial or physical aspect as well as a visual aspect, that statement is true in the context of the NPPF as well, provided it is not taken to mean that openness is only concerned with the spatial issue. Such an interpretation accords with the guidance on interpretation of the NPPF given by this court in the *Timmins* and *Redhill Aerodrome* cases, to the effect that the NPPF is to be interpreted as providing no less protection for the Green Belt than PPG 2. The case before Sullivan J was concerned with a proposed new, larger building which represented a spatial intrusion upon the openness of the Green Belt but which did not intrude visually on that openness, so he was not concerned to explain what might be the position under PPG 2 generally if there had been visually intrusion instead or as well.

[24] Sullivan J gives a general reason for the importance of spatial intrusion at para. [37] of his judgment:

'The planning officer's approach can be paraphrased as follows:

"The footprint of the replacement dwelling will be twice as large as that of the existing dwelling, but the public will not be able to see very much of the increase."

It was the difficulty of establishing in many cases that a particular proposed development within the Green Belt would of itself cause "demonstrable harm" that led to the clear statement of policy in para. 3.2 of PPG 2 that inappropriate development is, by definition, harmful to the Green Belt. The approach adopted in the officer's report runs the risk that Green Belt or Metropolitan Open Land will suffer the death of a thousand cuts. While it may not be possible to demonstrate harm by reason of visual intrusion as a result of an individual – possibly very modest – proposal, the cumulative effect of a number of such proposals, each very modest in itself, could be damaging to the essential quality of openness of the Green Belt and Metropolitan Open Land.'

[25]   This remains relevant guidance in relation to the concept of openness in the Green Belt in the NPPF. The same strict approach to protection of the Green Belt appears from para. 87 of the NPPF. The openness of the Green Belt has a spatial aspect as well as a visible aspect, and the absence of visual intrusion does not of itself mean that there is no impact on the openness of the Green Belt as a result of the location of a new or materially larger building there. But, as observed above, it does not follow that openness of the Green Belt has no visual dimension.

[26]   What is also significant in this paragraph of Sullivan J's judgment for present purposes is the last sentence, from which it appears that Sullivan J considered that a series of modest visual intrusions from new developments would be a way in which the essential quality of the openness of the Green Belt could be damaged, even if it could not be said of each intrusion that it represented demonstrable harm to the openness of the Green Belt in itself. At any rate, Sullivan J does not say that openness of the Green Belt has no visual dimension. Hence I think that Green J erred in *Timmins* in taking the *Heath and Hampstead Society* case to provide authority for the two propositions he sets out at para. [78] of his judgment, to which I have referred above.

[27]   Turning back to the Inspector's decision in the present case, there is no error of approach by the Inspector in his assessment of the issue of impact on the openness of the Green Belt. In paras. 11 to 13 the Inspector made a legitimate comparison of the existing position regarding use of the site with the proposed redevelopment. This was a matter of evaluative assessment for the Inspector in the context of making a planning judgment about relative impact on the openness of the Green Belt. His assessment cannot be said to be irrational. It was rational and legitimate for him to assess on the facts of this case that there is a difference between a permanent physical structure in the form of the proposed bungalow and a shifting body of lorries, which would come and go; even following the narrow volumetric approach urged by the appellant the Inspector was entitled to make the assessment that the two types of use and their impact on the Green Belt could not in the context of this site be 'directly compared as proposed by the appellant' (para.13). The Inspector was also entitled to take into account the difference in the visual intrusion on the openness of the Green Belt as he did in para. 14.

CASES ON 'OPENNESS' SINCE *TURNER*

R (Boot) v Elmbridge Borough Council[31]

18.15   The case involved a judicial review of a decision to grant planning permission for a new sports facility (comprising a football and athletics stadium

---

[31]   [2017] EWHC 12 (Admin).

with associated buildings, training pitches and car parking) in the Green Belt.[32] It was to be located on a former landfill site on which there was already a football pitch, informal open space and scrub land. The officer's report noted that the provision of facilities for outdoor sport and recreation were exceptions to the rule that an LPA should regard the construction of new buildings as being inappropriate in the Green Belt provided such development preserved the openness of the Green Belt and did not conflict with the purposes of including land within it. The officer's report concluded that the proposed sports facility was appropriate development. Although the report noted that there would be some limited adverse impact on the landscape, visual amenity and openness, there would be significant benefits in terms of facilitating the beneficial use of land within the Green Belt. The LPA accepted that conclusion and granted planning permission.

18.16 The court held that the LPA had erred in its interpretation of NPPF, paragraph 89 (second bullet), and the planning permission was quashed. It was found that paragraph 89 (second bullet) did not permit any harm at all to the openness of the Green Belt.[33] If it was established that a proposed sports facility would harm the openness of the Green Belt then, regardless of the extent of that harm, it would not be appropriate development and there would have to be very special circumstances justifying the grant of planning permission. A development that would have any adverse effect on openness would not comply with a policy that required openness to be maintained or preserved. The decision-maker had no latitude to find otherwise on the basis that the adverse impact was not significant.[34] In *Boot* the LPA had concluded that the sports facility would have an adverse impact on openness but nevertheless granted permission without considering whether there were very special circumstances justifying it.[35]

Smith v Secretary of State for Communities and Local Government[36]

18.17 This was a case where an inspector had found that a proposed scheme for the conversion of a commercial building which was in the Green Belt to provide two residential dwellings amounted to inappropriate development and would harm openness. A challenge to the inspector's decision to uphold the LPA's refusal of permission failed. The court held that openness was an open concept and various factors would bear on it (applying *Turner*). The court could not accept

---

[32] Sports facilities, etc. within the meaning of NPPF, para 89 (second bullet).

[33] Following *South Lakeland DC v Secretary of State for the Environment* [1992] 2 AC 141 and *R (Lee Valley Regional Park Authority) v Epping Forest DC* [2016] EWCA Civ 404.

[34] Applying *West Lancashire BC v Secretary of State for Communities and Local Government* [2009] EWHC 3631 (Admin).

[35] In other words, whether the harm would be outweighed by other considerations (NPPF, para 88).

[36] [2017] EWHC 2562 (Admin).

that openness was confined to visual impact arising from buildings. The inspector had raised the fact that the garden areas associated with the two dwellings would be enclosed by fences, bin storage, parking and domestic paraphernalia accompanying domestic use and that those matters would have an impact on openness

R (Samuel Smith Old Brewery (Tadcaster)) v North Yorkshire[37]

18.18 The appellants appealed against the refusal of their claim for judicial review of planning permission granted by a mineral planning authority (MPA) for an extension to the operational face of a quarry which lay within a Green Belt. The claimants owned farmland in the area and the first claimant drew water from a major aquifer running beneath the quarry for use in its brewing business. They had objected to the quarry's extension.

18.19 The planning officer considered that the proposed development would preserve the openness of the Green Belt within NPPF, paragraph 90 (viz: mineral extraction) and the MPA accepted the officer's recommendation and granted permission. The officer had advised that the term 'openness' was commonly taken to mean the absence of built development. She considered that, because the application site immediately abutted the existing operational quarry, it would not introduce development into that area on a scale that would conflict with the aim of preserving openness. The officer concluded that the proposal would not materially harm the character and openness of the Green Belt and recommended that permission be granted. The appellants complained that the planning officer had misdirected the committee on the policy for minerals extraction in the Green Belt at paragraph 90 in that she had not referred specifically to the visual impact of the proposed development on the openness of the Green Belt. Accordingly, it was argued that the committee had approached its decision on the erroneous basis that the proposal was not for 'inappropriate development' in the Green Belt and did not have to be justified by 'very special circumstances' in accordance with NPPF, paragraph 87. The judge hearing the claim for judicial review rejected the challenge, holding that the officer was not required to take visual impact into account.

18.20 The appeal was allowed. The court explained (following *Turner v Secretary of State for Communities and Local Government*) that visual impact was one of the relevant factors in interpreting the concept of the 'openness of the Green Belt'. To exclude visual impact, as a matter of principle, from a consideration of the likely effects of development on the openness of the Green Belt, would be artificial and unrealistic. It was found to be inherent in the policy

---

[37]   [2018] EWCA Civ 489.

of NPPF, paragraph 90, that a realistic assessment had to include any likely perceived effects on openness as well as spatial effects. When a development was likely to have visual effects within the Green Belt, the decision-maker was required to consider how those effects bore on the question of whether the development would preserve the openness of the Green Belt. Where that planning judgment was not exercised, effect would not be given to the paragraph 90 policy, which amounted to a misunderstanding and misapplication of that policy and thus an error of law. The officer's report demonstrated that she had fallen into such error, since she had not made it clear that visual impact was potentially relevant to its approach to the effect of the development on the openness of the Green Belt, and hence whether the proposed development was inappropriate and required 'very special circumstances' for its approval. The advice she gave was therefore defective and the grant of planning permission was unlawful. It is also plain that the 'openness' of the Green Belt in paragraph 90 is not synonymous with the concept of no physical change, otherwise the policy would be unworkable.[38]

---

[38] *Europa Oil and Gas Ltd v Secretary of State for Communities and Local Government* [2013] EWHC 2643 (Admin).

Chapter 19

Areas of Outstanding Natural Beauty, Sites of Special Scientific Interest, National Parks and Other Areas of Conservation or Protection

AREAS OF OUTSTANDING NATURAL BEAUTY

19.1   Natural England[1] may designate areas which are not in National Parks as Areas of Outstanding Natural Beauty (AONBs) for the purposes of conserving and enhancing the natural beauty of those areas.[2]

19.2   Local planning authorities (LPAs) have the power to take such action as appears to them expedient for the accomplishment of the purpose of conserving and enhancing the natural beauty of the AONB.[3] The Secretary of State may also set up conservation boards to manage AONBs, in which event functions will be transferred to it, but this will not include responsibility for the development plan, development control or planning enforcement.[4]

19.3   The next issue concerns the impact of an AONB designation (where great weight is required to be given to conserving landscape and scenic beauty) in the context of national planning policy.

19.4   Paragraph 115 of the National Planning Policy Framework 2012 (NPPF) provides that:

---

[1]   Or The Natural Resources Body for Wales (see the Natural Resources Body for Wales (Functions) Order 2013 (SI 2013/755)).

[2]   Countryside and Rights of Way Act 2000, s 82. The procedure for designation orders can be found in s 83 (local consultation, publicity, and confirmation by the Secretary of State or in Wales by the National Assembly for Wales). AONBs include such well-known areas of scenic beauty as the Northumberland Coast, the Cotswolds, the Isles of Scilly, the Isle of Wight, the Surrey Hills and the Gower Peninsula.

[3]   Countryside and Rights of Way Act 2000, s 84(4).

[4]   Countryside and Rights of Way Act 2000, s 86. See also s 89 and the duty of conservation boards and local authorities to prepare (and periodically review) management plans for the AONB and the discharge of their functions in relation to that section.

Great weight should be given to conserving landscape and scenic beauty in National Parks, the Broads and Areas of Outstanding Natural Beauty, which have the highest status of protection in relation to landscape and scenic beauty ...

19.5   The NPPF, paragraph 116 provides that:

planning permission should be refused for major developments in these designated areas except in exceptional circumstances and where it can be demonstrated they are in the public interest. Consideration of such applications include an assessment of:

- the need for the development, including in terms of any national considerations, and the impact of permitting it, or refusing it, upon the local economy;
- the cost of, and scope for, developing elsewhere outside the designated area, or meeting the need for it in some other way; and
- any detrimental effect on the environment, the landscape and recreational opportunities, and the extent to which that could be moderated.

19.6   If only a small part of the proposed site for development lies within an AONB it will not trigger paragraph 116.[5]

19.7   In *R (Aston) v Secretary of State for Communities and Local Government,*[6] Wyn Williams J determined that the meaning of the phrase 'major developments' in paragraph 116 of the NPPF:[7]

---

[5]   *R (Cherkley Campaign Ltd) v Mole Valley DC* [2014] EWCA Civ 567; where only one fairway and one tee would have been within the AONB in a development comprising a hotel and spa complex and golf facilities. It was found that the actual development within the AONB could not reasonably be regarded as major development 'in' the AONB, even when account was taken of the fact that it formed part of a larger golf course development, the rest of which was immediately adjacent to the AONB.

[6]   [2013] EWHC 1936 (Admin). Followed in *R (The Forge Field Society) v Sevenoaks DC* [2015] JPL 22. In DCS Number: 400-013-431, plans for 20 homes in the Cornwall AONB were refused as major development, despite a need for local homes. In DCS Number 200-005-666, an inspector accepted that plans to redevelop a derelict factory site in a National Park village with 26 homes fell within the definition of major development in the Town and Country Planning (Development Management Procedure) (England) Order 2010 (SI 2010/2184). However, he held that the resulting improvement in the village's appearance meant that the scheme passed the exceptional circumstances test allowed for in national policy. In DCS Number 200-006-471 (2017), 32 dwellings, retaining walls and associated infrastructure were allowed on a sloping site in an AONB adjoining a settlement in Devon, despite harm to the AONB. It was a case where the LPA could only show a two-year supply of housing land. The inspector considered that as the site adjoined a settlement, was enclosed on all sides and its topography severely restricted views into and out of the site, as did high banks and mature vegetation, the proposal would have limited visual impact, confined to just the site itself, which would not intrude into the rural landscape or setting of the settlement. The inspector also held that the development did not constitute major development in an AONB, and so para 116 was not engaged. Irrespective of the presumption against major development in AONB's development, the 'tilted balance' may yet favour development where housing land supply is less than five years and where the development is liable to cause only minor harm to the character and appearance of the area.

[7]   [2013] EWHC 1936 (Admin) at [94].

... was that which would be understood from the normal usage of those words. Given the normal meaning to be given to the phrase the Inspector was entitled to conclude that the Third Defendant's application to erect 14 dwelling-houses on the appeal site did not constitute an application for major development.

19.8   It is, then, a matter of planning judgment in any particular case whether development falls within paragraph 116 of the NPPF.[8]

19.9   Where a proposal involved housing development, paragraph 116 had to be read together with the policies for housing need and supply in paragraph 47 and paragraph 48. The decision-maker had to consider whether there were exceptional circumstances justifying planning permission. While that might involve considering the availability of alternative sites, paragraph 116 did not prescribe an assessment process and did not direct a decision-maker to consider sites across the whole of an LPA's area.[9]

SITES OF SPECIAL SCIENTIFIC INTEREST

19.10 A designation under this head arises when Natural England notifies the site as a Site of Special Scientific Interest (SSSI),[10] the criterion for which is that the land is of special interest by reason of its flora, fauna, or geological or

---

[8]   *R (Mevagissey Parish Council) v Cornwall Council* [2013] EWHC 3684 (Admin); the grant of planning permission for the development of 21 affordable homes at a coastal site within an AONB was quashed where the LPA had rejected the planning officer's recommendation for refusal of permission without making clear in its summary of reasons how and why it had departed from her interpretation of the relevant policies. The court summarised the principles governing the provisions of summary reasons as required by Town and Country Planning (Development Management Procedure) (England) (Amendment) Order 2013 (SI 2013/1238), arts 2 and 7(a). It was a case where the court held that notwithstanding the fact that the conservation of landscape and scenic beauty in an AONB was given enhanced status in the NPPF, the planning committee had given no reason for deliberately departing from the guidance. A pressing need for affordable housing might be a significant factor in the assessment of whether the circumstances were exceptional, but it was not, on its own, determinative, because there might be alternative sites that were more suitable. This was exactly the planning officer's conclusion. The committee had to exercise its own judgment and was entitled to reach a different conclusion, but it had not indicated that it had correctly identified, understood and applied the relevant policies. Its conclusion that the provision of affordable housing outweighed any impact on the AONB presupposed that it had identified exceptional circumstances, but there was no suggestion in the summary grounds that it had. Also, it appeared that it had performed a simple balancing exercise rather than giving the conservancy of the AONB greater weight, and it had not considered any alternative sites. The inadequacy of reasons was a clear reflection of the committee's failure to grapple with the issues that the policy required it to deal with, and, as a result, the grant of planning permission was quashed.

[9]   *Wealden DC v Secretary of State for Communities and Local Government* [2017] EWCA Civ 39.

[10]   Most SSSIs are privately owned or managed; others are owned or managed by public bodies or non-governmental organisations.

physiographical features.[11] There are also provisions enabling Natural England: (a) to vary a notification;[12] and (b) to de-notify all or part of an SSSI if it is no longer of special interest, in which event it will cease to be an SSSI.[13]

19.11   Once a site has been notified, the owners and occupiers are not permitted to carry out any of the operations specified in the notification unless Natural England has consented in writing (and there is a right of appeal to the Secretary of State) or the operation is carried out in accordance with a management agreement or management notice.[14] An owner or occupier of land who, without reasonable excuse,[15] contravenes the terms of a notification is guilty of an offence with a maximum fine on summary conviction of £20,000 and an unlimited fine in the Crown Court. The court also has power to order restoration of the damaged land where this is practicable. An offence is also committed where an owner or

---

[11]   Wildlife and Countryside Act 1981 (as amended) (WCA 1981), s 28. Natural England makes its notification to the LPA, to every owner or occupier of the land and to the Secretary of State. A notification shall specify the time (not being less than three months) within which, and the manner in which, representations or objections with respect to it may be made. The notification shall not only specify the flora, fauna, or geological or physiographical features by reason of which the land is of special interest, but also any operations (such as agricultural activities) appearing to Natural England to be likely to damage that flora, fauna or those features. The notification shall also contain a statement of Natural England's views about the management of the land, including any views Natural England may have about the conservation and enhancement of flora, fauna or geological or physiographical features. Within nine months of making the notification to the Secretary of State, Natural England may either withdraw the notification or confirm it, with or without modifications (there are special provisions in relation to land above mean low-water mark and any land covered by estuarial waters (and qualifying adjoining land)). Natural England's power to confirm a notification with modifications shall not be exercised so as to add to the operations specified in the notification or extend the area to which it applies. Once the owner or occupier has been notified by Natural England confirming the notification with modifications, the notification shall have effect in its modified form in relation to so much of that land (if any) as remains subject to it. A notification under s 28(1)(b) to every owner or occupier of the land shall be a local land charge. In discharging their functions under s 28, the Secretary of State, Natural England and the Countryside Council for Wales are required to exercise their functions so as to secure compliance with the requirements of the Habitats Directive (see Conservation (Natural Habitats, & etc.) Regulations 1994 (SI 1994/2716), reg 3(2) and (4)).

[12]   WCA 1981, s 28A (a special procedure exists in s 28B–C if Natural England wishes to enlarge a notified area).

[13]   WCA 1981, s 28D.

[14]   WCA 1981, ss 28E, 28J and 28K.

[15]   It is a reasonable excuse for a person to carry out an operation (or to fail to comply with a requirement to notify Natural England about proposed work under WCA 1981, s 28E) if the operation in question was authorised by planning permission (and of course: (a) development plans are bound to contain policies affecting SSSIs; and (b) Natural England must also be consulted on applications for planning permission affecting SSSIs) (unless the operation required both planning permission and the permission of a s 28G authority, in which case the defence will not be available unless both have been obtained) or the operation was an emergency operation particulars of which were notified to Natural England as soon as practicable after the commencement of the operation (s 28P(4)).

occupier of the land fails to comply with a requirement of a management notice (i.e. where the owner or occupier has failed to give effect to the provisions of an agreed management scheme).[16] Various public bodies (including statutory undertakers and local authorities) (referred to as 'section 28G authorities') are under a duty to take reasonable steps to further the conservation and enhancement of the flora, fauna or geological or physiographical features of the SSSI.[17] SSSIs are also likely to be protected under the Habitats Regulations 2017[18] which incorporate into the law in England and Wales the requirements of the Special Areas of Conservation (SACs) under the Habitats Directive and the Special Protection Areas (SPAs) under the Birds Directive.

NATIONAL PARKS

19.12 The legislative process, which began in 1949,[19] culminated in the Natural Environment and Rural Communities Act 2006, which transferred the operations of the Countryside Agency to Natural England, which is authorised[20] by order submitted to and confirmed by the Secretary of State, to designate land as a National Park.[21] It was only in 1995[22] that National Parks were run as independent authorities which included the exercise of planning functions within the Park

---

[16] WCA 1981, s 28P(8).

[17] WCA 1981, s 28G. Such bodies are also required to give notice to Natural England of proposed operations likely to damage the SSSI (s 28I – this section applies where the permission of a s 28G authority is required before operations may be carried out). The s 28G authority must wait until the expiry of 28 days beginning with the date of its notice to Natural England before deciding whether to give its permission, unless Natural England has notified the authority that it need not wait until then.

[18] See Chapter 17.

[19] The National Parks and Access to the Countryside Act 1949 established a National Parks Commission which, in 1968, was renamed as the Countryside Commission, and in 1999 became the Countryside Agency.

[20] National Parks and Access to the Countryside Act 1949, s 5(2). This provision provides that in relation to 'those extensive tracts of country in England and Wales as to which it appears to Natural England that by reason of – (a) their natural beauty, and (b) the opportunities they afford for open-air recreation, having regard both to their character and to their position in relation to centres of population, it is especially desirable that the necessary measures shall be taken for the purposes mentioned in the last foregoing subsection'. Section 5(2A) provides that Natural England 'may (a) when applying subsection (2)(a) in relation to an area, take into account its wildlife and cultural heritage, and (b) when applying subsection (2)(b) in relation to that area, take into account the extent to which it is possible to promote opportunities for the understanding and enjoyment of its special qualities by the public. (3) The said areas, as for the time being designated by order made by Natural England and submitted to and confirmed by the Minister, shall be known as, and are hereinafter referred to as, National Parks'.

[21] Special Acts of Parliament may be used to establish statutory authorities for their management (e.g. the Broads Authority was set up through the Norfolk and Suffolk Broads Act 1988).

[22] Environment Act 1995, s 63, under which the Secretary of State was empowered to establish independent National Park authorities.

where development and permitted development rights are strictly controlled, if not removed altogether by the use of article 4 directions.

19.13 The following is a list of current National Parks in the United Kingdom:

> Brecon Beacons
> Broads
> Cairngorms
> Dartmoor
> Exmoor
> Lake District
> Loch Lomond and the Trossachs
> New Forest
> North Yorkshire Moors
> Northumberland
> Peak District
> Pembrokeshire Coast
> Snowdonia
> South Downs
> Yorkshire Dales

19.14 It will be recalled that NPPF, paragraph 115, provides that great weight should be given to conserving landscape and scenic beauty in National Parks. Paragraph 116 also provides that planning permission should be refused for major developments in National Parks except in exceptional circumstances. In other words, the purpose of National Parks is to conserve and enhance landscapes within the countryside whilst promoting public enjoyment of them and having regard for the social and economic wellbeing of those living within them. Development is thus strictly controlled in National Parks and development which is visually intrusive and which will detract from the often remote and tranquil character and appearance of the landscape is unlikely to be permitted.

OTHER DESIGNATED AREAS OF CONSERVATION OR PROTECTION[23]

Ancient woodlands

19.15 In the United Kingom an ancient woodland is a woodland that has existed continuously since 1600 (or 1750 in Scotland). Before those dates, planting of new woodland was uncommon, so a wood present in 1600 was likely to have developed naturally. In most ancient woods, the trees and shrubs have been cut

---

[23] Listed in alphabetical order and comprising a mix of international, national and local designations.

down periodically as part of the management cycle. Provided that the area has remained as woodland, it is considered ancient woodland. Since it may have been cut over many times in the past, ancient woodland does not necessarily contain very old trees. For many species of animal and plant, ancient woodland sites provide the sole habitat, and conditions on these sites are much more suitable than in other sites. Ancient woodland in the United Kingdom, rather like in the case of rainforest in the tropics, is home to rare and threatened species. For these reasons, ancient woodland is often described as an irreplaceable resource. Ancient woodland is formally defined on maps by Natural England and equivalent bodies.

19.16 Many ancient woodlands have legal protection of various types but it is not automatically the case that any ancient woodland is protected. Some examples of ancient woodland are nationally or locally designated such as SSSIs. Others have no designations at all. However, ancient woodlands require special consideration when they are affected by planning applications.[24]

Areas of Great Landscape Value

19.17 An Area of Great Landscape Value (AGLV) (which is a local designation) is land which is considered to have particular scenic value and is therefore protected and enhanced through the planning process. If an area is designated as an AGLV in the development plan, development is restricted, especially if it will affect the distinctive character or quality of the landscape.

Areas of Special Protection

19.18 Sanctuary Areas, originally designated under the Protection of Birds Act 1954, were amended to Areas of Special Protection under the Wildlife and Countryside Act 1981 (WCA 1981). Designation aims to prevent the disturbance and destruction of the birds for which the area was identified, by making it unlawful to damage or destroy either the birds or their nests and in some cases by prohibiting or restricting access to the site.

Country Parks

19.19 Country Parks are statutorily declared and managed by local authorities in England and Wales under the Countryside Act 1968. They are primarily intended for recreation and leisure opportunities close to population centres and do not necessarily have any nature conservation importance.

---

[24] NPPF, para 118 (bullet 5).

Heritage Coasts

19.20 A Heritage Coast is a section of coast exceeding one mile in length that is of exceptionally fine scenic quality, substantially undeveloped and containing features of special significance and interest. The designation is agreed between local authorities and Natural England as an aid to LPAs in planning and managing their coastlines.

Local Green Space designation

19.21 Local Green Space designation in the development plan provides special protection against development for green areas of particular importance to local communities.

Local Nature Reserves

19.22 Under the National Parks and Access to Countryside Act 1949, Local Nature Reserves (LNRs) may be declared by local authorities after consultation with Natural England or Natural Resources Wales. LNRs are declared and managed for nature conservation, and to provide opportunities for research and education, or simply enjoying and having contact with nature.

Marine Conservation Zones

19.23 Marine Conservation Zones (MCZs) can be established to protect nationally important marine wildlife, habitats, geology and geomorphology, and can be designated anywhere in English and Welsh inshore and UK offshore waters. They are established under the Marine and Coastal Access Act 2009.

Marine Nature Reserves

19.24 The purpose of Marine Nature Reserves (MNRs) (which are established under the Wildlife and Countryside Act 1981 for England and Wales) is to conserve marine flora and fauna and geological features of special interest, while providing opportunities for study of marine systems. They are a mechanism for the protection of nationally important marine (including subtidal) areas. Their designation requires the agreement of statutory and voluntary bodies and interest groups. Designated MNRs include Lundy Island (in England), Skomer Island (in Wales) and Strangford Lough (in Northern Ireland). The introduction of the Marine and Coastal Access Act 2009 has meant that in England and Wales MNRs are to be replaced by MCZs. Elsewhere, a number of voluntary MNRs have been established by agreement between non-governmental organisations (NGOs), stakeholders and user groups. These have no statutory basis.

National Nature Reserves

19.25 National Nature Reserves (NNRs) are declared by Natural England under the National Parks and Access to Countryside Act 1949 and the Wildlife and Countryside Act 1981. NNRs contain examples of some of the most important natural and semi-natural terrestrial and coastal ecosystems in the United Kingdom. They are managed to conserve their habitats or to provide special opportunities for scientific study of the habitats, communities and species represented within them. In addition, they may be managed to provide public recreation that is compatible with their natural heritage interests.

National Trust

19.26 The National Trust (for England, Wales and Northern Ireland) and the National Trust for Scotland are independent charities which conserve the cultural, built and natural heritage of the United Kingdom. Both National Trusts own or have protective covenants over land of historic interest or natural beauty. Under the National Trust Act 1907 and the National Trust for Scotland Order Confirmation Acts 1935 and 1938 their holdings are inalienable and cannot be sold or mortgaged. The Trusts have powers to create byelaws relating to access and management of the land.

Natura 2000

19.27 Natura 2000 is the name of the European Union-wide network of nature conservation sites established under the EC Habitats and Birds Directives. This network will comprise SACs and SPAs.

Nature Improvement Areas

19.28 Nature Improvement Areas (NIAs) were established to create joined-up and resilient ecological networks at a landscape scale.[25] They are run by partnerships of local authorities, local communities and landowners, the private sector and conservation organisations with funding provided by the Department of the Environment, Food and Rural Affairs (Defra) and Natural England. The 12 winning NIA projects were chosen after a competitive process announced in the Natural Environment White Paper. The 12 NIA projects started on 1/4/2012 and the funding ended on 31/3/2015. In addition to the 12 national NIAs, local

---

[25] Landscape-scale conservation is a holistic approach to conservation, concerned with biodiversity and local economies, agriculture, eco-tourism, geodiversity and the health and social benefits of the environment.

partnerships and local planning authorities can identify and agree where locally determined NIAs can be set up.[26]

NGO properties

19.29 A variety of NGOs, such as the John Muir Trust, Plantlife, the Royal Society for the Protection of Birds, Wildlife Trusts and the Woodland Trust, own or manage nature reserves or other areas of land that are important for biodiversity. These sites may be intended primarily for nature conservation, and/or for other purposes such as the protection of landscape features or the provision of public access to the countryside. These areas of themselves have no statutory basis but a large number will be designated SSSIs/NNRs/SPAs/SACs/ Ramsar sites, etc.

Ramsar sites

19.30 A Ramsar site[27] is a wetland site designated of international importance under the Convention on Wetlands which is known as the Ramsar Convention which is an intergovernmental environmental treaty established in 1971 by UNESCO which came into force in 1975. It provides for national action and international co-operation regarding conservation of wetlands. Originally intended to protect sites of importance, particularly water fowl habitats, the Convention has broadened to cover all aspects of wetland conservation and wise use, recognising wetlands as eco-systems that are extremely important for biodiversity conservation in general and for the well-being of human communities. The Convention adopts a broad definition of 'wetland', namely 'areas of marsh, fen, peatland or water, whether natural or artificial, permanent or temporary, with water that is static or flowing, fresh, brackish or salt, including areas of marine water the depth of which at low tide does not exceed six metres'. Wetlands 'may incorporate riparian and coastal zones adjacent to the wetlands, and islands or bodies of marine water deeper than six metres at low tide lying within the wetlands'.

Regionally Important Geological and Geomorphological Sites

19.31 Regionally Important Geological and Geomorphological Sites (RIGS) are the most important places for geology and geomorphology outside statutorily protected land such as SSSIs. Sites are selected under locally developed criteria, according to their value for education, scientific study, historical significance or

---

26 Locally determined NIAs are encouraged to apply the criteria, the monitoring and evaluation framework and lessons learned from the 12 initial NIAs to assist their development and process.

27 There are currently 157 sites designated as Ramsar sites in the UK.

aesthetic qualities. Whilst not benefiting from statutory protection, RIGS are equivalent to local wildlife sites and will be protected and enhanced through the planning process.

Sensitive Marine Areas

19.32 Sensitive Marine Areas (SMAs) are non-statutory marine areas notable for their marine, animal and plant communities or which provide ecological support to adjacent statutory sites. A further aim is to raise awareness and disseminate information to be taken into account in estuarine and coastal management planning. These areas rely on the co-operation of users and local communities for sustainable management.

Special Areas of Conservation

19.33 Special Areas of Conservation (SACs) (including coastal SACs) are designated under the EC Habitats Directive. The Directive applies to the United Kingdom and to Gibraltar. SACs are areas that have been identified as best representing the range and variety within the EU of habitats and (non-bird) species listed on Annexes 1 and II to the Directive. SACs in terrestrial areas and territorial marine waters out to 12 nautical miles are designated as indicated in Chapter 17 herein ('Habitats and Species Regulations 2017'). Where the United Kingdom has jurisdiction beyond its territorial waters such sites are designated under the (currently) Offshore Marine Habitats and Species Regulations 2017. Sites which have been adopted by the EC, but not yet formally designated by governments of members states, are known as Sites of Community Importance.

Special Landscape Areas

19.34 Special Landscape Area (SLA) designation in the development plan provides protection for locally significant and attractive landscapes that are of comparable quality to AONBs and which should be protected and enhanced through the planning process.

Special Protection Areas

19.35 Special Protection Areas (SPAs) are classified by the Government under the EC Birds Directive (see Chapter 17 herein: 'Habitats and Species Regulations 2017'). SPAs are areas of the most important habitat for rare (listed on Annex 1 to the Directive) and migratory birds within the EU. SPAs in terrestrial areas and territorial marine waters out to 12 nautical miles are classified under the WCA 1981, and, where the United Kingdom has jurisdiction beyond its territorial waters, are designated (currently) under the Offshore Marine Habitats and Species Regulations 2017.

Woodland Parks/Forest Parks

19.36   Woodland Parks are similar to Forest Parks but are smaller in scale and located near to centres of population. Forest Parks, Forest Nature Reserves or Woodland Parks are identified and managed by the Forestry Commission England, Forestry Commission Scotland and Natural Resources Wales primarily for recreation purposes.

World Heritage Sites

19.37   World Heritage Sites are designated to meet the United Kingdom's commitments under the World Heritage Convention. These sites are designated for their globally important cultural or natural interest and require appropriate management and protection measures.

Chapter 20

The Contribution of National Policy in Protecting the Natural Environment

INTRODUCTION

20.1   National and local policies strive to enhance the natural environment. Dealing with development proposals which cause significant harm to nature conservation and to the character, appearance and intrinsic beauty of unspoilt countryside areas are typical problems encountered in decision-making. Poor quality design, increased flood risk, adverse impact on the setting of a nearby Area of Outstanding Natural Beauty (AONB) or heritage site, the loss of best and most versatile farmland, and poor access to everyday services and facilities (which conflict with the aims of achieving sustainable development) are all factors which exacerbate these problems and which will, more often than not, either individually or cumulatively, result in a refusal of planning permission even where the site is one without designation or valued status.

20.2   Local planning authorities (LPAs) and inspectors typically encounter proposals where developers claim that there is only minor landscape impact or where the need for homes outweighs any harm to the landscape, particularly where there is an absence of any formal designation of landscape value and/or where it is even accepted by the LPA that local housing needs cannot be met on brownfield land alone. Development is also problematic where local plan policy defines a settlement boundary and restricts development in the open countryside beyond. The risk also exists that to allow development would set a precedent and make it more difficult for similar proposals to be resisted in the future and thus lead to the harmful cumulative erosion of the countryside around the edge of a settlement.

20.3   To mitigate these adverse impacts, developers invariably offer schemes for mitigation, including land remediation, ecological improvements or provision for landscaping, in order that the scheme might not appear incongruous or be perceived to have an urbanising effect on the landscape. That said, however well designed, new buildings, estate roads, street lighting and domestic paraphernalia will invariably erode the unspoilt open nature of sites in the countryside. In such cases, even where a five-year supply of housing land does not exist, decision-takers, in the exercise of their planning judgment, are more than likely to support National Planning Policy Framework 2012 (NPPF) objectives of protecting the scenic beauty and character of the countryside (and the distinctiveness of settlements) by refusing planning permission.

Secretary of State for Communities and Local Government v Hopkins Homes revisited

20.4   This introduction would be incomplete without a reference (albeit by way of a reminder) to *Secretary of State for Communities and Local Government v Hopkins Homes Ltd*,[1] where the Supreme Court examined the relationship between paragraphs 14 and 49 of the NPPF.

20.5   In *Hopkins Homes* the Supreme Court clarified that the absence of a five-year housing land supply triggered the presumption in paragraph 14 of the NPPF, although it was a matter of planning judgment as to whether or not policies for the supply of housing were in fact out of date under NPPF paragraph 49, which has a narrow meaning. What it now means is that other groups of policies, such as policies for the protection of the countryside, whilst they might affect the operation of housing policies, are not to be treated as if they are policies for the supply of housing within the meaning of paragraph 49. See also *Crane v Secretary of State for Communities and Local Government*,[2] where Lindblom J said that neither paragraph 49 nor paragraph 14 prescribes the weight to be given to policies in an out-of-date plan, although one may infer from paragraph 49 that the weight to be given to out-of-date policies 'for the supply of housing' will normally be less, often considerably less, than the weight due to policies which provide fully for the requisite supply. In other words, the weight to be given to out-of-date policies will vary according to the circumstances, including the extent to which the policies actually fall short of providing for the required five-year supply, and the prospect of development soon coming forward to make up the shortfall.

20.6   In short, paragraph 49 of the NPPF acts as a trigger to the operation of the 'tilted balance' under paragraph 14. In the absence of relevant or up-to-date development plan policies, the balance would be tilted in favour of granting permission unless the impacts of doing so would significantly and demonstrably outweigh the benefits, or where specific policies in the development plan indicate that development should be restricted. Examples of such policies mentioned in

[1]   [2017] UKSC 37.

[2]   [2015] EWHC 425 (Admin) at [71].

the NPPF include polices relating to sites protected under the Birds and Habitats Directives and/or designated as Sites of Special Scientific Interest (SSSI); land designated as Green Belt, Local Green Space, an AONB, Heritage Coast or within a National Park (or the Broads Authority); designated heritage assets; and locations at risk of flooding or coastal erosion.

20.7   The aim of this chapter is to identify some of the material national policies affecting development in rural areas (in relation to guidance on both planning policies and decision-making) and some significant recent case law. The chapter will also touch upon policies within the NPPF which deal with proposals which will increase the supply of renewable and low carbon energy.

NPPF – SECTION 6: 'DELIVERING A WIDE CHOICE OF HIGH QUALITY HOMES'

New dwellings in the countryside

20.8   Section 6 of NPPF includes the following:

> 52. The supply of new homes can sometimes be best achieved through planning for larger scale development, such as new settlements or extensions to existing villages and towns that follow the principles of Garden Cities. Working with the support of their communities, local planning authorities should consider whether such opportunities provide the best way of achieving sustainable development. In doing so, they should consider whether it is appropriate to establish Green Belt around or adjoining any such new development.
>
> ...
>
> 54. In rural areas, exercising the duty to cooperate with neighbouring authorities, local planning authorities should be responsive to local circumstances and plan housing development to reflect local needs, particularly for affordable housing, including through *rural exception sites where appropriate* [emphasis added].[3] Local planning authorities should in particular consider whether allowing some market housing would facilitate the provision of significant additional affordable housing to meet local needs.

---

[3]   Rural exception sites are sites for affordable housing development in rural locations where market housing would not normally be acceptable because of planning policy constraints. Homes can be brought forward on these sites only if there is a proven unmet local need for affordable housing and a planning obligation is in place to ensure that the homes will always remain affordable. Such homes will be for people in housing need and prioritised for those with a strong local connection to the parish.

55. To promote sustainable development in rural areas, housing should be located where it will enhance or maintain the vitality of rural communities. For example, where there are a group of smaller settlements, development in one village may support services in a village nearby. *Local planning authorities should avoid new isolated homes in the countryside unless there are special circumstances* [emphasis added][4] such as:

- the essential need for a rural worker to live permanently at or near their place of work in the countryside; or
- where such development would represent the optimal viable use of a heritage asset or would be appropriate enabling development to secure the future of heritage assets; or
- where the development would re-use redundant or disused buildings and lead to an enhancement to the immediate setting; or
- the exceptional quality or innovative nature of the design of the dwelling. Such a design should:

  - be truly outstanding or innovative, helping to raise standards of design more generally in rural areas;
  - reflect the highest standards in architecture;
  - significantly enhance its immediate setting; and
  - be sensitive to the defining characteristics of the local area.

20.9   Although well-designed new dwellings may be permitted in circumstances involving a visual improvement to the site arising from, say, the removal of an unsightly existing building and outbuildings, new isolated development in the countryside which is remote from a local settlement and its services and facilities can also be harmful to a highly valued landscape unless they are of exceptional quality and significantly enhance their immediate setting. It is plain that under paragraph 55 (and the policy is undoubtedly a rigorous one with a high quality standard) the aim of promoting sustainable development in rural areas is to be achieved by locating new dwellings within settlements and by avoiding 'new isolated homes in the countryside' except where there are special circumstances. For many rural sites the obstacles to be overcome are exacerbated by protective designations such as Green Belts, AONBs or other constraints which set the bar even higher. In the result, existing settlements are the preferred location for new housing developments in rural areas.

---

4   *Braintree District Council v Secretary of State for Communities and Local Government* [2018] EWCA Civ 610, where it was held that para 55 and the reference to the avoidance of 'new isolated homes in the countryside' in the absence of special circumstances, meant physically isolated in the sense of being isolated from a settlement, rather than being isolated from services and facilities. The court supported the dictionary definition of 'isolated' as meaning 'far away from other places, buildings or people' rather than isolation from services. It means that LPAs cannot rely on settlement boundaries on maps as a means of differentiating between locations where development is acceptable and isolated locations where it is not.

NPPF – SECTION 11: 'CONSERVING AND ENHANCING THE NATURAL ENVIRONMENT'[5]

20.10 Section 11 of NPPF includes the following:

109. The planning system should contribute to and enhance the natural and local environment by:

- *protecting and enhancing valued landscapes* [emphasis added],[6] geological conservation interests and soils;

---

[5] Note reference to 'valued landscapes' in paragraph 109 (first bullet) and footnote.

[6] Although the term 'valued landscapes' is not defined in the NPPF, it has been held in *Ceg Land Promotions II Ltd v Secretary of State for Housing and Communities* [2018] EWHC 1799 (Admin) that in determining whether a proposed development site was a 'valued landscape' within the meaning of para 109, it was necessary to consider the site as part of the wider landscape, rather than limit the consideration to the site's particular circumstances. Even though a site lacks a formal designation of landscape value (which is not the same as valued landscape) its visibility in the wider landscape might well mean that any development would appear as a significant incursion into open countryside. Such a site might well have local value and even well-used footpaths crossing the site which afford panoramic views. On the other hand, if it is a less sensitive site and is no more than general countryside it might not override a housing deficit. Such a site might well have limited landscape quality with no heritage, wildlife or ecological assets and no recreational or leisure function. There clearly has to be some demonstrable physical attribute to make the land valued and thus give it enhanced protection (see *Stroud DC v Secretary of State for Communities and Local Government* [2015] EWHC 488 (Admin) at [13]–[16], [18]). A question posed by the inspector in DCS Number: 200-005-667 was whether, on the landscape evidence, the site's landscape and scenic quality, representativeness and recreational value showed that it was 'more than mere countryside'. On that appeal he was satisfied that the site met the criteria for a valued landscape outlined in *Stroud* and concluded that harm to the area's character and appearance significantly and demonstrably outweighed the benefits of the proposal. It is clear that in deciding whether or not a site comprises a 'valued landscape', evidence that a landscape is valued by a community is not enough in itself to give it valued landscape status (see decisions on schemes in County Durham (DCS Number: 200-005-628) and Norfolk (DCS Number: 200-005-550)). However, as indicated in *Stroud*, the site must display something more to elevate it above general countryside. The inspector in the appeal in DCS Number: 200-005-667 said that he was assisted in making his assessment by the range of useful factors set out in the Landscape Institute's *Guidelines for Landscape and Visual Impact Assessment*. In DCS Number: 200-006-015 the inspector also said that he, too, was assisted by the published guidance on landscape and visual impact assessments. He had considered more helpful the LPA's analysis which looked at the relationship between people and place in the wider context rather than the appellants' narrower approach which focused on whether key features of landscape character areas were present in and around the site. In DCS Number 200-006-923 the inspector, referring to *Stroud*, found that the site's landscape value should be assessed as an integral part of its surroundings, rather than on its own merits. She noted that the site was seen in the context of an adjoining AONB and SSSI. While finding that the development would result in the loss of an important part of a valued landscape, she accepted that this did not amount to a specific policy requirement for development to be restricted. In her view, para 109's exhortation for the planning system to contribute to and enhance the natural and local environment by 'protecting and enhancing 'valued landscapes' comprises an aspiration rather than a restriction. In the event,

- recognising the wider benefits of ecosystem services;
- minimising impacts on biodiversity and providing net gains in biodiversity where possible, contributing to the Government's commitment to halt the overall decline in biodiversity, including by establishing coherent ecological networks that are more resilient to current and future pressures;
- preventing both new and existing development from contributing to or being put at unacceptable risk from, or being adversely affected by unacceptable levels of soil, air, water or noise pollution or land instability; and
- remediating and mitigating despoiled, degraded, derelict, contaminated and unstable land, where appropriate.

110. In preparing plans to meet development needs, the aim should be to minimise pollution and other adverse effects on the local and natural environment. Plans should allocate land with the least environmental or amenity value, where consistent with other policies in this Framework.

111. Planning policies and decisions should encourage the effective use of land by re-using land that has been previously developed (brownfield land), provided that it is not of high environmental value. Local planning authorities may continue to consider the case for setting a locally appropriate target for the use of brownfield land.

112. Local planning authorities should take into account the economic and other benefits of the best and most versatile agricultural land. Where significant development of agricultural land is demonstrated to be necessary, local planning authorities should seek to use areas of poorer quality land in preference to that of a higher quality.

113. Local planning authorities should set criteria based policies against which proposals for any development on or affecting protected wildlife or geodiversity sites or landscape areas will be judged. Distinctions should be made between the hierarchy of international, national and locally designated sites,[7] so that protection is

---

applying the 'tilted balance' in para 14, the inspector concluded that moderate to substantial harm to the area's landscape character and the town's rural setting, along with some limited harm to the setting of the AONB, cumulatively outweighed the scheme's benefits, despite the acknowledged need for more homes in the area. Lastly, reference should also be made to DCS Number: 400-018-015 in which, despite a significant local housing land shortfall, plans for 123 homes on the edge of Exeter were rejected because of their effect on valued parkland and the urban setting. In this case the authority only had a two-year supply of housing land. The inspector considered that the site had a distinctly rural character, with alluring views towards an estuary and hills, and contributed significantly to the city's landscape setting. In assessing whether it formed part of a valued landscape under para 115, he placed great weight on references to the site in the adopted development plan and a recent management plan, its distinctive landscape qualities and numerous objectors' perceptions. He concluded that the proposal would dramatically change the parkland's character and appearance, contrasting awkwardly with its natural greenspace and resulting in a serious adverse effect.

7   Circular 06/2005 provides further guidance in respect of statutory obligations for biodiversity and geological conservation and their impact within the planning system.

commensurate with their status and gives appropriate weight to their importance and the contribution that they make to wider ecological networks.

114. Local planning authorities should:

- set out a strategic approach in their Local Plans, planning positively for the creation, protection, enhancement and management of networks of biodiversity and green infrastructure; and
- maintain the character of the undeveloped coast, protecting and enhancing its distinctive landscapes, particularly in areas defined as Heritage Coast, and improve public access to and enjoyment of the coast.

115. Great weight should be given to *conserving landscape and scenic beauty in National Parks, the Broads and Areas of Outstanding Natural Beauty* [emphasis added],[8] which have the highest status of protection in relation to landscape and scenic beauty. The conservation of wildlife and cultural heritage are important considerations in all these areas, and should be given great weight in National Parks and the Broads.[9]

116. Planning permission should be refused for major developments in these designated areas except in exceptional circumstances and where it can be demonstrated they are in the public interest. Consideration of such applications should include an assessment of:

- the need for the development, including in terms of any national considerations, and the impact of permitting it, or refusing it, upon the local economy;
- the cost of, and scope for, developing elsewhere outside the designated area, or meeting the need for it in some other way; and
- any detrimental effect on the environment, the landscape and recreational opportunities, and the extent to which that could be moderated.

117. To minimise impacts on biodiversity and geodiversity, planning policies should:

- plan for biodiversity at a landscape-scale across local authority boundaries;
- identify and map components of the local ecological networks, including the hierarchy of international, national and locally designated sites of importance for biodiversity, wildlife corridors and stepping stones that connect them and areas identified by local partnerships for habitat restoration or creation;
- promote the preservation, restoration and re-creation of priority habitats, ecological networks and the protection and recovery of priority species

---

[8] In *Stroud DC v Secretary of State* [2015] EWHC 488 (Admin), the court held that views into an AONB from the outside were not subject to para 115, although views into the surrounding landscape out of the AONB and the effect of development upon them were relevant considerations. In other words, the beauty in the AONB might be harmed if looking out of it into the surrounding landscape one saw ugliness.

[9] *English National Parks and the Broads: UK Government Vision and Circular 2010* provides further guidance and information about their statutory purposes, management and other matters.

populations, linked to national and local targets, and identify suitable indicators for monitoring biodiversity in the plan;
- aim to prevent harm to geological conservation interests; and
- where Nature Improvement Areas are identified in Local Plans, consider specifying the types of development that may be appropriate in these Areas.

118. When determining planning applications, local planning authorities should aim to conserve and enhance biodiversity by applying the following principles:

- if significant harm resulting from a development cannot be avoided (through locating on an alternative site with less harmful impacts), adequately mitigated, or, as a last resort, compensated for, then planning permission should be refused;
- proposed development on land within or outside a Site of Special Scientific Interest likely to have an adverse effect on a Site of Special Scientific Interest (either individually or in combination with other developments) should not normally be permitted. Where an adverse effect on the site's notified special interest features is likely, an exception should only be made where the benefits of the development, at this site, clearly outweigh both the impacts that it is likely to have on the features of the site that make it of special scientific interest and any broader impacts on the national network of Sites of Special Scientific Interest;
- development proposals where the primary objective is to conserve or enhance biodiversity should be permitted;
- opportunities to incorporate biodiversity in and around developments should be encouraged;
- planning permission should be refused for development resulting in loss or deterioration of irreplaceable habitats, including ancient woodland and the loss of aged or veteran trees found outside ancient woodland, unless the need for, and benefits of, the development in that location clearly outweigh the loss; and
- the following wildlife sites should be given the same protection as European sites:

  - potential Special Protection Areas and possible Special Areas of Conservation;
  - listed or proposed Ramsar sites;[10] and
  - sites identified, or required, as compensatory measures for adverse effects on European sites, potential Special Protection Areas, possible Special Areas of Conservation, and listed or proposed Ramsar sites.

119. The presumption in favour of sustainable development (paragraph 14) does not apply where development requiring appropriate assessment under the Birds or Habitats Directives is being considered, planned or determined.

120. To prevent unacceptable risks from pollution and land instability, planning policies and decisions should ensure that new development is appropriate for its location. The effects (including cumulative effects) of pollution on health, the natural

---

[10]   Potential Special Protection Areas (SPAs), possible Special Areas of Conservation (SACs) and proposed Ramsar sites are sites on which Government has initiated public consultation on the scientific case for designation as an SPA, candidate SAC or Ramsar site.

environment or general amenity, and the potential sensitivity of the area or proposed development to adverse effects from pollution, should be taken into account. Where a site is affected by contamination or land stability issues, responsibility for securing a safe development rests with the developer and/or landowner.

121. Planning policies and decisions should also ensure that:

■ the site is suitable for its new use taking account of ground conditions and land instability, including from natural hazards or former activities such as mining, pollution arising from previous uses and any proposals for mitigation including land remediation or impacts on the natural environment arising from that remediation;

■ after remediation, as a minimum, land should not be capable of being determined as contaminated land under Part IIA of the Environmental Protection Act 1990; and

■ adequate site investigation information, prepared by a competent person is presented.

122. In doing so, local planning authorities should focus on whether the development itself is an acceptable use of the land, and the impact of the use, rather than the control of processes or emissions themselves where these are subject to approval under pollution control regimes. Local planning authorities should assume that these regimes will operate effectively. Equally, where a planning decision has been made on a particular development, the planning issues should not be revisited through the permitting regimes operated by pollution control authorities.

123. Planning policies and decisions should aim to:

■ avoid noise from giving rise to significant adverse impacts[11] on health and quality of life as a result of new development;

■ mitigate and reduce to a minimum other adverse impacts on health and quality of life arising from noise from new development, including through use of conditions;

■ recognise that development will often create some noise and existing businesses wanting to develop in continuance of their business should not have unreasonable restrictions put on them because of changes in nearby land uses since they were established;[12] and

■ identify and protect areas of tranquillity which have remained relatively undisturbed by noise and are prized for their recreational and amenity value for this reason.

■ Planning policies should sustain compliance with and contribute towards EU limit values or national objectives for pollutants, taking into account the presence of Air Quality Management Areas and the cumulative impacts on air quality from

---

[11] See Explanatory Note to the Noise Policy Statement for England (Department of the Environment, Food and Rural Affairs).

[12] Subject to the provisions of the Environmental Protection Act 1990 and other relevant law.

individual sites in local areas. Planning decisions should ensure that any new development in Air Quality Management Areas is consistent with the local air quality action plan.

- By encouraging good design, planning policies and decisions should limit the impact of light pollution from artificial light on the local amenity, intrinsically dark landscapes and nature conservation.

POLICIES WITHIN THE NPPF WHICH CONTRIBUTE TO ENERGY GENERATION FROM RENEWABLE AND LOW CARBON SOURCES

20.11 The relevant policies are those at paragraphs 97 to 98:

97. To help increase the use and supply of renewable and low carbon energy, local planning authorities should recognise the responsibility on all communities to contribute to energy generation from renewable or low carbon sources. They should:

- have a positive strategy to promote energy from renewable and low carbon sources;
- design their polices to maximise renewable and low carbon energy development while ensuring that adverse impacts are addressed satisfactorily, including cumulative landscape and visual impacts;
- consider identifying suitable areas for renewable and low carbon energy sources, and supporting infrastructure, where this would help secure the development of such sources;[13]
- support community-led initiatives for renewable and low carbon energy, including developments outside such areas being taken forward through neighbourhood planning; and
- identify opportunities where development can draw its energy supply from decentralised, renewable or low carbon energy supply systems and for co-locating potential heat customers and suppliers.

98. When determining planning applications, local planning authorities should:

---

[13] (The following is fn 17 in the NPPF – to be read with para 97 (third bullet)):

'In assessing the likely impacts of potential wind energy development when identifying suitable areas, and in determining planning applications for such development, planning authorities should follow the approach set out in National Policy Statement for Renewable Energy Infrastructure (read with relevant sections of the Overarching National Policy Statement for Energy Infrastructure, including that on aviation impacts). Where plans identify areas as suitable for renewable and low-carbon energy development, they should make clear what criteria have determined their selection, including for what size of development the areas are considered suitable.'

- not require applicants for energy development to demonstrate the overall need for renewable or low carbon energy and also recognise that even small-scale projects provide a valuable contribution to cutting greenhouse emissions;
- approve the application[14] if its impacts are (or can be made) acceptable. Once suitable areas for renewable and low carbon energy have been identified in plans, local planning authorities should also expect subsequent applications for commercial scale projects outside these areas to demonstrate that the proposed location meets the criteria used in identifying suitable sites.

20.12 On-shore wind turbine approvals received a set back in 2015 in consequence of a Written Ministerial Statement made by the then Secretary of State for Communities and Local Government, Greg Clark, on 18/6/2015, setting out new considerations to be applied to proposed wind energy development.[15] The focus of the statement was that local people should have the final say on wind farm applications. The statement provided (albeit subject to a transitional provision) that when determining planning applications for wind energy development involving one or more wind turbines, LPAs should only grant planning permission if: (a) the development site is in an area identified as suitable for wind energy development in a local or neighbourhood plan; and (b) following consultation, it can be demonstrated that the planning impacts identified by affected local communities have been fully addressed and that the proposal has their backing. The statement went on to provide that, applying these new considerations, suitable areas for wind energy development will need to have been allocated clearly in a local or neighbourhood plan. Maps showing the wind resource as favourable to wind turbines, or similar, will not be sufficient. Whether a proposal has the backing of the affected local community is a planning judgment for the LPA. Where a valid planning application for a wind energy development had already been submitted to a local planning authority and the development plan does not identify suitable sites, the following transitional provision applied, namely that LPAs can find the proposal acceptable if, following consultation, they are satisfied it has *addressed* the planning impacts identified by affected local communities and therefore has their backing. The statement means that applications for wind turbines are unlikely to meet with approval where local policies are unhelpful or even non-existent.

---

[14] The following is fn 18 in the NPPF – to be read with para 98 (second bullet): 'Unless material considerations indicate otherwise.'

[15] The WMS came shortly before the reduction in government subsidies through Feed-in tariff cuts after February 2016 (particularly in the case of solar) in the case of small-scale generation of electricity using eligible renewable technologies (namely wind, hydropower, energy from biomass and anaerobic digestion) the effect of which has been to make smaller projects less attractive.

20.13 In *R (Holder) v Gedling Borough Council*[16] the Court of Appeal had to consider the transitional provision whereby the LPA could find the wind energy development acceptable if 'they are satisfied that it has addressed the planning impacts identified by local communities and therefore has their backing'. It was a case where several objections had been made to the development. The officer concluded that all negative planning impacts had been addressed but were outweighed by the public benefits of the development and had therefore been acceptable. The appellant argued that the transitional provision should be read as meaning that the LPA had to be satisfied that the proposal had eliminated *all* the negative impacts identified by the local community. He contended that the negative impacts on visual amenity and cultural heritage had not been resolved and that the LPA could not be satisfied that the proposal had the local community's backing and find that acceptable for the purposes of the ministerial statement.

20.14 The appellant's contentions were rejected. The court held that the natural meaning of the statement was that an LPA could find a proposal to be acceptable if it sufficiently addressed the planning impacts identified through consultation with the local community to the extent that it could properly conclude, in the exercise of its planning judgment, that the balance of opinion in the community was likely to be in favour of the proposal. In the planning context the natural meaning of the expression *addressed* was *sufficiently addressed*, taking into account mitigating factors and countervailing benefits. If the draftsman had intended a stronger meaning, appropriate stronger language would have been used. Clearly not all members of the local community would have responded to the consultation exercise. Accordingly the LPA had to make a judgment, taking account of the representations received and assessing the weight and significance of any objections raised, as to where the balance of opinion was likely to lie within the local community as a whole, including those who had not made representations. Such a judgment would require the LPA to consider whether the proposal had sufficiently addressed planning impacts mentioned by the community. It would consider measures and decide whether it could be satisfied that the balance of view within the community as a whole was positive. That balance could be positive even though some planning impacts had not been wholly eliminated, but had been sufficiently dealt with, and even though some members of the community might never be persuaded to view the proposed development in a favourable light. The statement did not elevate those members of the community whose views were opposed to the proposal into arbiters of the view of the local community as a whole. The court stated that the ministerial statement was intended to be additional policy guidance and the main provisions of the NPPF within section 10 were left unaltered. The court held that the statement was plainly not intended to be at odds with national policy in relation

---

16   [2018] EWCA Civ 214.

to renewable energy, nor with policies in local plans made in conformity with NPPF provisions promoting renewable energy.

20.15 Nonetheless on-shore wind turbine approvals still encounter great difficulty. Applications give rise to objections on a number of compelling grounds, such as those involving harm to the visual impact to the surrounding countryside or on air traffic safety grounds or in relation to adverse impacts on birdlife, particularly in designated areas of sensitive ecology for wild fowl or where there are heritage assets in the vicinity whose setting is liable to be harmed by the presence of wind turbines. Clearly wind turbines (along with their connecting power lines to the National Grid) can appear as an alien intrusive feature on the landscape and finding suitable sites and overcoming local objections will never be easy, no matter that the NPPF contains policies which promote renewable energy. At the end of the day, and particularly where large numbers of wind turbines are involved, inspectors are more than likely to find that the negatives of such a proposal outweigh the positives.[17]

20.16 Solar farms are the large-scale application of solar photovoltaic panels to generate electricity usually to feed into the grid. The position is in stark contrast to wind farms as solar is at ground level, makes virtually no noise or waste and has no moving parts. Many solar farms are even grazed by sheep or combined with other farming. Solar arrays are usually installed in the countryside and can be visually contained by hedges and trees. Planning difficulties arise where the proposals involves the loss of best and most versatile land or land of sufficient quality as to tip the balance against the proposal. The scale of the development may be such as to give rise to adverse impact on the character and appearance of the area. On the other hand, local impact may be more limited and the benefits of the scheme may outweigh the negatives. Alternatively, in Green Belts such developments might very well impact negatively on openness and in AONB the test of exceptional circumstances will very probably be difficult to satisfy.

---

[17] See *R (Williams) v Powys CC* [2017] EWCA Civ 427, where the Court of Appeal allowed an appeal quashing the grant of planning permission for the erection of a single wind turbine as the LPA had failed to address its duty under Planning (Listed Buildings and Conservation Areas) Act 1990, s 66(1), where the setting of a listed building was concerned. The fact that the possible effect of the proposed development on the setting of a listed building (a Grade II listed church 1.5 kilometres away on the other side of the hill) had not been identified as an issue in responses to local consultation, or in representations made by third parties, did not of itself relieve the LPA of its s 66(1) duty. The application for permission was remitted to the LPA so that it could take the decision again, properly directing itself on the s 66(1) duty. See also *R (Mynnydd y Gwynt Ltd) v Secretary of State for Business, Energy and Industrial Strategy* [2018] EWCA Civ 231, where the court found that the Secretary of State had made no error of law in refusing permission for a wind farm in mid Wales due to its potential impact on red kites coming from an adjoining special protection area (SPA).

Chapter 21

Powers of the Local Planning Authority to Require Land to be Cleaned Up

POWER TO REQUIRE PROPER MAINTENANCE OF LAND

21.1   Where it appears to the local planning authority (LPA) that the *amenity* of a part of its area, or of an adjoining area, is adversely affected by the condition of land in its area, it may serve on the owner and occupier of the land[1] a notice requiring steps for remedying the condition of the land to be taken within such period as may be specified.[2]

21.2   Any person on whom a notice has been served may appeal to a magistrates' court (with a further appeal to the Crown Court)[3] (or in Wales to the Welsh Ministers) on various grounds:[4]

(a)   that the condition of the land does not adversely affect the amenity of any part of the LPA's area, or of any adjoining area;

(b)   that the condition of the land is attributable to, and as such results in the ordinary course of events from, the carrying on of operations or a use of land which is not in contravention of Part III of the Town and Country Planning Act 1990 (TCPA 1990) (control over development);

(c)   that the requirements of the notice exceed what is necessary for preventing the condition of the land from adversely affecting the amenity of part of the LPA's area, or of any adjoining area; and

---

[1]   There are several options to help in tracing the owner or occupier of a potential s 215 site, for example by: (a) Land Registry search; (b) Companies House search; (c) internet search; (d) private investigators; and (e) information-gathering notices.

[2]   TCPA 1990, s 215.

[3]   TCPA 1990, s 218.

[4]   The grounds are relatively limited and a carefully thought out, reasonable and skilfully composed notice should reduce the chances of an appeal being successful.

(d)   that the period specified in the notice as the period within which any steps required by the notice are to be taken falls short of what should reasonably be allowed.[5]

21.3   Where an appeal is brought, the notice to which it relates shall be of no effect pending the final determination or withdrawal of the appeal.[6]

21.4   This procedure is probably of limited effect in practice in view of the defence that the activities in respect of which complaint is made do not constitute a breach of planning control.[7] In other words, action should not be taken against land, the poor condition of which is attributable in some way to the carrying out of operations or a use of land in accordance with Part III of the TCPA 1990.

21.5   Provision is made for penalties for non-compliance by an owner or occupier of land with a notice served under this part.[8] Where the notice has come into effect and the required steps have not been taken, the LPA has a power to go onto the land in order to clean it up itself and it can recover its reasonable expenses from the owner of the land.[9] Where direct action is to be taken, prior warning should be given by letter that the LPA and its appointed contractors intend to carry out the steps required by the notice. It is recommended that this is backed up by the display of a suitable notice of intent on the site carrying the same information. Prior warning of intended prosecution should also be given by letter.[10]

SCOPE OF POWER

21.6   Section 215 of the TCPA 1990 has been effectively used on large vacant industrial sites, town centre street frontages, rural sites, derelict buildings and semi-complete development, as well as the more typical rundown residential properties and overgrown gardens. In certain circumstances, early consideration of the use of section 215 could prevent a need for use of section 54 of the Planning (Listed Buildings & Conservation Areas) Act 1990 (Urgent Works Notice). Another context in which section 215 notices may be used successfully is in relation to listed buildings and their setting, and in the enhancement of conservation areas.

---

5   TCPA 1990, s 217(1)(a)–(d).
6   TCPA 1990, s 217(3).
7   TCPA s 217(1)(b).
8   TCPA 1990, s 216. A maximum fine of £1,000 with a fine of up to £100 per day in the event of continuing default.
9   TCPA 1990, s 219 (such expenses are a charge on the land).
10   See examples of both letters at Annex E to the January 2005 Best Practice Guidance on s 215.

21.7   The scope of works that can be required in section 215 notices is wide and includes planting, clearance, tidying, enclosure, demolition, re-building, external repairs and repainting. Potential sites can sometimes go beyond the remit of a section 215 notice so there may be other more appropriate powers that an LPA can rely upon in order to effect a remedy, for example:

(a)   sections 76 to 79 of the Building Act 1984 for defective premises, dangerous buildings, ruinous and dilapidated buildings and neglected sites;
(b)   section 29 of the Local Government (Miscellaneous Provisions) Act 1982 for works on unoccupied buildings;
(c)   sections 79 to 82 of the Environmental Protection Act 1990 for abatement or prohibition of a nuisance;
(d)   under the listed building legislation, such as Repairs and Urgent Works Notices;
(e)   completion notices in the case of partially completed development under sections 94 and 95 of the TCPA 1990;
(f)   compulsory purchase orders.

DEFINITION OF 'AMENITY'

21.8   'Amenity' is a broad concept and is not formally defined in the legislation or procedural guidance, i.e. it is a matter of fact and degree and, certainly, common sense. Each case will be different, and what would not be considered amenity in one part of an LPA's area might well be considered so in another. LPAs will therefore need to consider the condition of the site, the impact on the surrounding area and the scope of their powers in tackling the problem before they decide to issue a notice.[11] A case that stresses the adverse impact of the site on the local street scene will undoubtedly carry weight before the magistrates if the notice is challenged.

R (Lisle-Mainwaring) v Kensington and Chelsea RLBC – limits of TCPA 1990, section 215

21.9   In this well-known case,[12] the claimant owned a building which had been in use as offices in a conservation area. She changed its use to storage and painted its façade in red and white stripes, which was lawful under Schedule 2, Part 2, paragraph C2 to the Town and Country Planning (General Permitted Development) (England) Order 2015 (GPDO). The local authority served a

---

[11]   This definition comes from the January 2005 Best Practice Guidance for s 215 and was approved by Supperstone J in *Berg v Salford City Council* [2013] EWHC 2599 (Admin) at [33]–[34].

[12]   [2017] EWHC 904 (Admin).

section 215 notice on her stating that the amenity of its area was adversely affected by the condition of the land and that she should paint the building white. The magistrates' court and the Crown Court upheld that requirement and found that the painting in stripes affected the condition of the land and adversely affected amenity. It also found that although the condition of the land had resulted from the carrying on of operations which were not in contravention of Part III of the TCPA 1990, because painting was lawful development, the appeal under section 217(1)(b) had to be rejected, because otherwise any appeal would always be successful where the condition of the land was the consequence of lawful operations, making the words '[resulting from] the ordinary course of events [of lawful development]' in section 217(1)(b) otiose.

21.10　There were two issues on the judicial review of the decision of the Crown Court upholding a notice served under section 215 of the TCPA 1990. The first issue was whether section 215 applied in relation to the aesthetics of a building or land; the second was whether painting fell outside the 'ordinary course of events' of lawful operation or use of the land under section 217(1)(b) so as to remove the right of appeal.

21.11　The court allowed the judicial review. Gilbart J held that in considering what was meant by the 'condition of the land' in section 215, one had to be careful to avoid a catch-all definition that exceeded the proper bounds of the power. The context of section 215 was to deal with land or buildings whose condition, in the usual sense of the word, was such as to cause an adverse effect on amenity, not with questions of aesthetics or taste. It was also not intended to exercise a control over development which affected the choice of the exterior finish in a way which should instead have been dealt with by way of a direction under article 4 of the GPDO, or for the modification of the existing permission with the corresponding right to compensation. The term 'condition' did include appearance, but the question was whether it was proper to use a section 215 notice where the complaint was not one of lack of maintenance or repair, but one of aesthetics.[13]

21.12　The heading in section 215 'power to require proper maintenance of land' was found to be directed to the maintenance of the land or the fabric of a building, and it was hard to see how one could criticise a building owner for a want of maintenance on the basis that they had chosen a colour scheme which was thought unattractive. Parliament had not sought to prevent landowners from painting their houses in any colours they wished, unless an article 4 direction had been made. To allow an authority to use section 215 to deal with issues which related to aesthetics, as opposed to disrepair or dilapidation, fell outside the planning code. The court held that the authority had ample steps available to it under the code to protect amenity and which would expose it to minimal cost. It could have issued

---

[13]　Following *Britt v Buckinghamshire CC* [1964] 1 QB 77.

a notice requiring repainting of a building under TCPA 1990, section 102,[14] where, if upheld, compensation for the loss of the rights removed is likely to have been the cost of repainting.[15] The effect of upholding the notice would be to give an authority the power to cause buildings to be removed, altered or repainted because it disliked the appearance created, on grounds that related only to aesthetics. The court held that it was an improper use of section 215 to use it to alter a lawful painting scheme when there was no suggestion that there was any want of maintenance or repair in the land. Furthermore, section 215 does not entitle the authority either to address the motive of a landowner, such as whether the painting scheme came about because of an owner's eccentricity or pique.

21.13 In relation to section 217(1)(b), the relevant question was not whether amenity harm arose in the ordinary course of events from lawful operations or use, but whether the condition of the land did so. Given that class C2 permitted painting in any colour, the court found it hard to see how a choice of colour other than white, or multiple colours, could fall outside the ordinary course of events. In the result, the finding of the court was that the section 215 notice should be quashed.

---

14 Orders requiring discontinuance of use or removal of buildings or works.
15 Applying *Allsop v Derbyshire Dales DC* [2012] EWHC 3562 (Admin).

Chapter 22

Tree Preservation Orders, Trees in Conservation Areas and Hedgerows

TREE PRESERVATION ORDERS AND TREES IN CONSERVATION AREAS

Relevant law

22.1   Special controls over trees can be found in Part VIII (sections 197 to 214D) of the Town and Country Planning Act 1990 (TCPA 1990) (as amended) and in the Town and Country Planning (Tree Preservation) (England) Regulations 2012 (2012 Regulations).[1] Section 192 of the Planning Act 2008 made further amendments to the TCPA 1990 which allowed for the transfer of provisions from within existing Tree Preservation Orders (TPOs) to regulations. Part 6 of the Localism Act 2011 (LA 2011) also amended section 210 of the TCPA 1990 concerning time limits for proceedings in regard to non-compliance with TPO regulations.

22.2   For policy guidance (updated on 6/3/2014), see the National Planning Practice Guidance (NPPG) in the section 'Tree Preservation Orders and trees in conservation areas'.[2]

Local planning authority's duty

22.3   Local planning authorities (LPAs) are under a general duty to ensure (whenever necessary) that when granting planning permission they make adequate provision, by the imposition of conditions, for preserving and protecting

---

[1]   SI 2012/605. For Wales, see the Town and Country Planning (Trees) Regulations 1999 (SI 1999/ 1892). TPOs made before 6/4/2012 continue to protect the trees and woodlands they cover. The legal provisions listed in TPOs made before 2012 have, however, been cancelled and replaced by the provisions contained in the 2012 Regulations. There is no need for pre-2012 orders to be remade, amended or reissued.

[2]   NPPG at Paragraph: 001 Reference ID: 36-001-20140306 to 36-172-20140306.

trees.[3] They also have power to make TPOs in the case of specific trees or woodlands.[4] A TPO may be made and confirmed by a TPO in the form prescribed in the Schedule to the 2012 Regulations or in a form substantially to the same effect.[5]

What is a TPO?

22.4   A TPO is an order made by an LPA[6] in England (and authorities can initiate this process themselves or in response to a request made by any other party) to protect specific trees, groups of trees or woodlands if it appears to them to be 'expedient in the interests of amenity'.[7] An order prohibits the:

> cutting down,
> topping,

---

3   TCPA 1990, s 197.

4   TCPA 1990, s 198. The power arises where 'it is expedient in the interests of amenity to make provision for the preservation of trees or woodlands in their area'. 2012 Regulations, reg 3 and Sch 1 provide for a TPO to be made in respect of: (a) single trees; (b) a group of trees; (c) an area on a map; and (d) a woodland, which will also require careful designation on a map.

5   2012 Regulations, reg 3. The TPO will take effect provisionally on the day it is made until: (a) the expiry of six months; (b) the date when the order is confirmed; or (c) the date on which the authority decides not to confirm the order, whichever first occurs (reg 4). The procedure after making an order and the process involving objections and representations can be found in reg 6. The procedure for confirmation of a TPO (which may occur with or without modifications) can be found in reg 5. The process of publicising the confirmation of the TPO, together with the action which must be taken where the TPO is not confirmed and with the variation and revocation of such orders, can be found at regs 8–11. By reg 12, every LPA shall keep a register containing details of every application for a TPO and the authority's decision in relation to each such application, of appeals and their determination by the Secretary of State, and details of any conditions with respect to replanting attaching to any consent granted under reg 17(1).

6   County councils can make TPOs but there are restrictions in areas where there is both a district planning authority and a county planning authority. In these areas the county council may only make an order: (a) where necessary in connection with the grant of planning permission; (b) on land which is not wholly lying within the area of a single district council; and (c) on land in which the county council holds an interest.

7   The term 'amenity' is not defined in law, so authorities need to exercise judgment when deciding whether it is within their powers to make an order. Orders should be used to protect selected trees and woodlands if their removal would have a significant negative impact on the local environment and its enjoyment by the public. Before authorities make or confirm an order they should be able to show that protection would bring a reasonable degree of public benefit in the present or future (see NPPG at Paragraph: 007 Reference ID: 36-007-20140306). When considering whether trees should be protected by an order, authorities are advised to develop ways of assessing amenity value of trees in a structured and consistent way, taking into account the criteria mentioned in NPPG at Paragraph: 008 Reference ID: 36-008-20140306 under the headings: (i) Visibility; (ii) Individual, collective and wider impact; and (iii) Other factors relevant to an assessment of amenity value such as the importance to nature conservation or response to climate change which factors alone would not warrant the making of a TPO.

lopping,
uprooting,
wilful damage, and
wilful destruction,

of trees without the LPA's written consent. If consent is given, it can be subject to conditions which must be followed.[8] The Secretary of State's view is that cutting roots is also a prohibited activity and requires the authority's consent.

What are the tree owner's responsibilities?

22.5   Owners of protected trees must not carry out, or cause or permit the carrying out, of any of the prohibited activities without the written consent of the local authority. As with owners of unprotected trees, they are responsible for maintaining their trees, with no statutory rules setting out how often or to what standard. The LPA cannot require maintenance work to be done to a tree just because it is protected. However, the authority can encourage good tree management, particularly when determining applications for consent under a TPO. This will help to maintain and enhance the amenity provided by protected trees. It is clearly important that trees are inspected regularly and that necessary maintenance is carried out to make sure that they remain safe and healthy.

Challenging a TPO

22.6   A TPO is subject to challenge in the High Court.[9] In response to an application for consent to cutting down, topping, lopping or uprooting of any tree in respect of which a TPO is in force,[10] the authority may, as indicated, grant consent conditionally or unconditionally (which consent shall be valid for a period of two years and will run with the land, and the works for which such consent is granted may only be carried out once), or it may refuse consent.[11] Where consent is refused or is granted conditionally or, in the case of the non-determination of an application to fell, etc. within a period of eight weeks beginning with the date on which the application was received by the authority, there is a right of appeal to the Secretary of State.[12] Any appeal should be made

---

[8]   2012 Regulations, reg 13.

[9]   Under TCPA 1990, s 288, within six weeks from the date when the order is confirmed (s 284(1)(e) and (2)(c)).

[10]   Made in accordance with 2012 Regulations, reg 16.

[11]   See 2012 Regulations, reg 17.

[12]   See 2012 Regulations, reg 19(1).

within 28 days from the date of receipt of the authority's decision or such longer period as the Secretary of State may allow.[13]

Compensation for refusal of consent to fell

22.7   If a person establishes that loss or damage has been caused or incurred as a consequence of the refusal of any consent required by the 2012 Regulations,[14] or the grant of any consent subject to conditions, or the refusal of any consent, agreement or approval required under such a condition, that person shall be entitled to compensation from the authority.[15] However, no claim may be made: (a) if more than 12 months have elapsed since the date of the authority's decision or, where the decision is the subject of an appeal to the Secretary of State, the date of the final determination of the appeal; or (b) if the amount in respect of which the claim would otherwise have been made is less than £500;[16] nor will any compensation be payable (c) for loss of development value[17] or other diminution in the value of the land; or (d) for loss or damage which was not reasonably foreseeable when consent was refused or was granted subject to conditions; or (e) for loss or damage reasonably foreseeable by that person and attributable to that person's failure to take reasonable steps to avert the loss or damage or to mitigate its extent; or (f) for costs incurred in appealing to the Secretary of State against the refusal of consent required under the Regulations or the grant of any such consent subject to conditions.[18] Questions of disputed compensation are determined by the Upper Tribunal.[19]

---

[13]   See 2012 Regulations, reg 19(2) (which also deals with the time for appealing in cases of non-determination). TCPA 1990, Sch 6 (determination of certain appeals by persons appointed by the Secretary of State) shall apply to appeals under reg 19. A copy of the notice of appeal should also be sent to the LPA at the same time as the appellant gives written notice to the Secretary of State who will thereafter supply an information questionnaire to the authority (reg 21) and may also seek other information from the parties as necessary (reg 22). Determination by the Secretary of State is to be in accordance with reg 23, in that the appeal may be allowed or dismissed, or any part of the authority's decision reversed or varied. The Secretary of State may deal with the appeal as if the application had been made to him in the first instance. The decision of the Secretary of State on the appeal shall be final (reg 23(5)) although it may be subject to challenge by judicial review on the usual basis.

[14]   2012 Regulations, Pt 4.

[15]   See 2012 Regulations, reg 24(1).

[16]   See 2012 Regulations, reg 24(2). There are special conditions in relation to the refusal of consent for felling in the course of forestry operations of any part of a woodland area (reg 24(3)).

[17]   Meaning an increase in value attributable to the prospect of development; and in relation to any land, the development of it shall include the clearing of it (2012 Regulations, reg 24(11)).

[18]   See 2012 Regulations, reg 24(4).

[19]   See 2012 Regulations, reg 24(8).

22.8   It is not uncommon for felling requests to be made in circumstances where the proximity of protected trees near buildings has given rise to subsidence, or at least to a risk of settlement, unless the protected trees are removed. The fact that the tree or trees is/are causing damage to buildings will clearly be a relevant factor in the decision of the authority (or Secretary of State) as to whether to grant or refuse consent to fell. However, the authority (and the Secretary of State on appeal) may nonetheless decide (because of the overriding importance of the trees to the amenity of the area) to refuse consent to fell, in which case they may well be liable for substantial compensation. It may be, of course, that the buildings were already damaged and in need of work on their foundations before consent for felling was refused, in which case there would be no liability for compensation for what would have been pre-existing loss (and it is clearly a question of fact as to whether any loss claimed was such as might reasonably be considered as arising naturally from the refusal of consent). In such a case, the correct quantum calculation is the difference between the cost of the works necessary to prevent future damage following the refusal of consent to fell and the cost of those works which would have been necessary if consent had been given.[20]

Duty to replant

22.9   If any tree in respect of which a TPO is in force is: (a) removed, uprooted or destroyed in contravention of the 2012 Regulations;[21] or (b) where the removal was authorised only on the grounds that the tree was dead or dangerous,[22] it shall be the duty of the owner of the land to plant another tree of an appropriate size and species at the same place as soon as he reasonably can.[23] The replacement tree will continue to be subject to the TPO, and the duty to replant will attach to the person who is from time to time the owner of the land. The duty[24] is, however,

---

[20]   *Duncan v Epping Forest District Council* [2004] RVR 275. See also *Deane v Bromley Borough Council* [1992] JPL 279; *Factorset Ltd v Selby District Council* [1995] 40 EG 133; *Buckle v Holderness Borough Council* (1996) 71 P & CR 428.

[21]   See 2012 Regulations, reg 13 – prohibited activities.

[22]   See 2012 Regulations, reg 14(1)(a)(i) and (c), and reg 25.

[23]   TCPA 1990, s 206(1), although the LPA may dispense with this requirement (s 206(2)).

[24]   Arising under TCPA 1990, s 206(1). See *Distinctive Properties (Ascot) Ltd v Secretary of State for Communities and Local Government* [2015] EWCA Civ 1250, where the court considered the correct approach to quantifying how many trees had been removed and how many needed replacing for the purposes of the landowner's duty under s 206. The court also approved and expanded upon the legal definition of 'tree' in *Palm Developments Ltd v Secretary of State for Communities and Local Government* [2009] EWHC 220 (Admin). In *Distinctive Properties*, a landowner appealed against a tree replacement notice. The landowner had cleared an area of woodland in breach of a TPO and the notice obliged the landowner to replant 1,280 saplings. The landowner appealed on the basis that only 25 trees had in fact been removed. The landowner's appeal was dismissed on the ground that the presence of stumps was insufficient evidence as the clearance had also involved the removal of saplings and other potential trees which might have germinated from the seeds. The landowner's appeal to the High Court was dismissed. The judge

only enforceable where the LPA serves on the owner a tree replanting notice, which must be served within four years from the date of the alleged non-compliance of the duty to replant. Such a notice shall specify a period at the end of which it is to take effect, and the specified period shall be a period of not less than 28 days beginning with the date of service of the notice.[25] There is a right of appeal to the Secretary of State against a replanting notice,[26] and a further right of appeal on a point of law to the High Court.[27] If the owner fails to replant, the LPA may enter the land and replant any trees which are required to be replanted, and it may recover the expenses of doing so from the owner of the land.[28] It is not an offence to fail to comply with a tree replanting notice. Enforcement is through the mechanism of the LPA entering on the land and replanting the trees which have been felled and recovering the costs of so doing from the owner of the land.

---

recorded the parties' agreement that the term 'tree' included 'saplings', but not 'seeds' or 'seedlings', and that the planning inspector had been entitled to rely on that uncontroversial position. He found that he did not need to decide whether the s 206 obligation meant replacing the same number of trees that had been destroyed because, under s 208, the landowner had the burden of proving that the number of trees lost was less than the specified replacement number. He concluded that it would be impossible for the landowner to discharge that burden where young trees and saplings were concerned, and he accepted the planning authority's evidence that standard planting densities provided a reasonable estimate of the number of new trees required. The Court of Appeal dismissed the landowner's appeal. It was held that ss 206 and 207 had to be read together. Under s 206(3) it was sufficient to replace the trees removed 'by planting the same number of trees'. The same restriction applied to the power in s 207 to enforce the s 206 duty, but it did not make it any easier to reach a figure for the number of trees lost in the case of a protected woodland. Any estimate would have to be a crude one rather than an accurate count. Furthermore, a woodland TPO protected woodland rather than individual trees, and would vary from year to year. The High Court had been right to emphasise that the burden of proof was on the landowner. If a landowner cleared protected woodland without taking other action to establish the number of trees, the LPA could treat the burden of proof as not having been discharged. In the context of a woodland, TPOs were designed for the 'preservation ... of woodlands' in accordance with s 198(1). They could only do that by requiring the replacement of lost trees, but an inspector's reference to 'reinstating the woodland' rather than to a number of trees would not be wrong in law. The inspector had also been right to accept the standard planting density as an estimate for the number of trees lost. Lastly, the court found that a tree was to be regarded as a tree at all stages of its life and would include a seedling of a tree species, but not a mere seed. In the result, neither the LPA nor the inspector had erred in law by relying upon the inclusion of 'seedlings/saplings' when arriving at an estimate of the number of trees on site before the clearance.

25   TCPA 1990, s 207.
26   TCPA 1990, s 208(1).
27   TCPA 1990, s 289(2).
28   TCPA 1990, s 209(1).

Enforcement

22.10 It is an offence[29] for any person: (a) to cut down, uproot or wilfully destroy a tree in contravention of a TPO;[30] or (b) to wilfully damage, top or lop a tree in such a manner as to be likely to destroy it;[31] or (c) to cause or permit the carrying out of any of these activities. The penalty on summary conviction is a fine not exceeding £20,000, or on conviction on indictment to an unlimited fine. In determining the amount of fine, the court is to have regard to any financial benefit which has accrued or appears likely to accrue to the defendant in consequence of the offence.[32] It is also an offence to commit any other contravention of the 2012 Regulations.[33]

22.11 The LPA has other powers in cases where it considers it necessary to prevent actual or apprehended offences under the TCPA 1990. It may apply for an injunction[34] or exercise a right of entry without a warrant or with a warrant (where admission to the land has been refused).[35]

---

[29] TCPA 1990, s 210.

[30] It is an offence to cut down a tree the subject of a TPO with or without knowledge of the existence of the order (*Maidstone Borough Council v Mortimer* [1980] 3 All ER 552; *R v Alath Construction Ltd* [1990] 1 WLR 1255; *Forestry Commission v Grace* [1992] 1 EGLR 28).

[31] The 'wilful destruction' of a tree protected by a TPO is the inflicting on it of so radical an injury that the tree is rendered useless and ought to be felled. Location is also relevant. See *Barnet London Borough Council v Eastern Electricity Board* [1973] 2 All ER 319.

[32] See *R v Davey* [2013] EWCA Crim 1662, where the Court of Appeal upheld a fine of £75,000 plus an undisputed confiscation order of £50,000 (representing the increase in value of the defendant's property as a result of the removal of the tree) in a case where the defendant had arranged for the removal of his neighbour's tree as the tree was evidently spoiling his view of Poole Harbour.

[33] TCPA 1990, s 210(4) (contained in 2012 Regulations, Pt 3). See reg 13 where there is substantial overlapping with s 210(1) although there are exceptions to the reg 13 prohibited activities to be found in reg 14 (which does not prevent the cutting down, topping, lopping or uprooting of a tree: (a) which is dead; (b) in compliance with an Act of Parliament or so far as may be necessary for the prevention or abatement of a nuisance; (c) by or at the request of a statutory undertaker where the land is operational land and the work is necessary; (d) various works under the HA 1980; (e) national security; (f) where the tree is cultivated for the production of fruit in the course of a business; (g) in order to implement a planning permission (but not an outline permission or permitted development); (h) at the request of the Environment Agency to enable the agency to carry out permitted development; (i) at the request of a drainage body in specified circumstances; (j) the removal of dead branches from a living tree; (k) works necessary to remove an immediate risk of serious harm; (l) pruning in accordance with good horticultural practice of any tree cultivated for the production of fruit; (m) works in accordance with a request or notice served by a licence holder under Electricity Act 1989, Sch 4, para 9.

[34] TCPA 1990, s 214A.

[35] TCPA 1990, ss 214B–214D. It is an offence to wilfully obstruct a person in the exercise of a right of entry.

Trees in conservation areas

22.12 There are special provisions in relation to all trees in a conservation area in respect of which there is no TPO in force.[36] In such cases, any person who does any act which might be prohibited by the 2012 Regulations shall be guilty of an offence. This provision will not apply so far as the act in question is authorised by an order granting development consent.[37] It shall be a defence for any person charged with an offence under this provision to prove that he served notice of his intention to do the act in question on the LPA, and that he did the act in question with the consent of the authority or after the expiry of the period of six weeks from the date of the notice, but before the expiry of the period of two years from that date.[38] The financial penalties under this section are the same as those mentioned in para 23.10. A duty to replant also arises, although it may be dispensed with by the LPA.[39]

HEDGEROWS

22.13 Controls over hedgerows can be found in the Hedgerows Regulations 1997.[40] They protect most countryside hedgerows from being removed (including being uprooted or otherwise destroyed).[41] The regulations are administered by the LPA, whose consent is required for the removal of a hedgerow (or part of a

---

[36] TCPA 1990, s 211(1) and (2), with the detailed exceptions mentioned in 2012 Regulations, reg 15, along with the replanting controls mentioned in s 213, which are similar to the controls in s 206.

[37] TCPA 1990, s 211(1A).

[38] TCPA 1990, s 211(3).

[39] TCPA 1990, s 213.

[40] SI 1997/1160. See guidance from Natural England 'Countryside hedgerows: protection and management' (last updated 16/8/2017) at www.gov.uk/government/organisations/natural-england.

[41] See Hedgerows Regulations 1997, regs 3(1) and (2). The regulations apply to any hedgerow growing in, or adjacent to, any common land, protected land (meaning land managed as a nature reserve in pursuance of National Parks and Access to Countryside Act 1949, s 21 or land in relation to which a notification under WCA 1981, s 28 is in force, namely Sites of Special Scientific Interest), or land used for agriculture, forestry or the breeding or keeping of horses, ponies or donkeys, if: (a) it has a continuous length of, or exceeding, 20 metres; or (b) it has a continuous length of less than 20 metres and, at each end, meets (whether by intersection or junction) another hedgerow. A hedgerow is also one to which the regulations apply if it is a stretch of hedgerow forming part of a hedgerow. However (see reg 3(3)), the regulations do not apply to any hedgerow within the curtilage of, or marking a boundary of the curtilage of, a dwelling-house. A hedgerow which meets (whether by intersection or junction) another hedgerow is to be treated as ending at the point of intersection or junction (see reg 3(4)). For the purposes of ascertaining the length of any hedgerow: (a) any gap resulting from a contravention of the regulations; and (b) any gap not exceeding 20 metres, shall be treated as part of the hedgerow.

hedgerow). The LPA has 42 days to respond to a written request for the removal of a hedgerow.[42] It may issue:

(a) a hedgerow retention notice[43] if the hedge is 'important'[44] and must be kept;[45] or

(b) a written notice giving permission for the removal of the hedgerow in the manner proposed.[46]

22.14 If the LPA has not responded to the applicant's written notice[47] to remove the hedgerow within 42 days, the applicant may proceed with the removal as proposed.[48] A written permission for the removal of the hedgerow subsists for two years from the date the written notice was issued to remove the hedgerow.[49]

Where removal may be permissible without consent

22.15 Removal of a hedgerow may, in certain circumstances, be permitted under the regulations,[50] but in cases where removal is required for making a new

---

[42] See Hedgerows Regulations 1997, reg 5(6) (i.e. a hedgerow removal notice in the Form contained in Sch 4).

[43] See Hedgerows Regulations 1997, reg 5(2).

[44] See Hedgerows Regulations 1997, reg 4. An LPA shall not give a hedgerow retention notice in respect of a hedgerow which is not an 'important' hedgerow (see reg 5(5)(a)). The criteria for determining 'important' hedgerows is contained in reg 4, which provides that a hedgerow is 'important' (for the purposes of both the regulations and Environment Act 1995, s 97 (hedgerows)), if it, or the hedgerow of which it is a stretch: (a) has existed for 30 years or more; and (b) satisfies at least one of the criteria listed in Sch 1, Pt 2, which lists a number of important archaeological, historical, wildlife and landscape factors which the LPA is required to take into account.

[45] See Hedgerows Regulations 1997, reg 5(5)(b). An LPA shall give a hedgerow retention notice within the specified period of 42 days in respect of an 'important' hedgerow unless satisfied, having regard in particular to the reasons given for its proposed removal in the hedgerow removal notice, that there are circumstances which justify the hedgerow's removal.

[46] See Hedgerows Regulations 1997, reg 5(1)(b)(i).

[47] I.e. the hedgerow removal notice served by the owner on the LPA under Hedgerows Regulations 1997, reg 5(1)(a).

[48] See Hedgerows Regulations 1997, reg 5(1)(b)(ii) and (c), and reg 5(6).

[49] See Hedgerows Regulations 1997, reg 5(1)(d).

[50] See Hedgerow Regulations 1997, reg 6(1), where removal of a hedgerow is permitted if it is required: (a) for making a new opening in substitution for an existing opening; (b) for obtaining temporary access to any land in order to give assistance in an emergency; (c) for obtaining access to land where another means of access is not available or is available only at disproportionate cost; (d) for purposes of national defence; (e) for carrying out development for which planning permission has been granted or is deemed to have been granted (with specified exceptions); (f) for carrying out work under statutory powers for the purpose of flood defence or land drainage; (g) for preventing the spread of any plant pest or tree pest in the exercise of statutory powers; (h) in the discharge of highway functions by the Secretary of State; (i) in the case of any felling,

opening in substitution for an existing opening which gives access to land,[51] the person removing it shall fill the existing opening by planting a hedge within eight months of the making of the new opening. A person who contravenes or fails to comply with this requirement is guilty of an offence.[52] In determining the amount of any fine, the court shall, in particular, have regard to any financial benefit which has accrued or appears likely to accrue to the offender (which may be a corporate body) in consequence of the offence.[53]

Enforcement

22.16 It is an offence[54] for a person to intentionally or recklessly remove, or to cause or permit another person to remove, a hedgerow in contravention of the regulations,[55] unless the LPA has consented to the removal of the hedgerow (and the work is carried out in accordance with the proposal specified in the hedgerow removal notice) or a period of 42 days has elapsed without the authority having given to that person a hedgerow retention notice stating that the work may not be carried out.

22.17 There are provisions enabling an LPA to require an owner (or where the hedgerow has been removed by or on behalf of a relevant utility operator,[56] to give such notice to that operator) to plant another hedgerow.[57] A person to whom a hedgerow retention notice is given may, within 28 days (or such longer period as the Secretary of State may allow), appeal to the Secretary of State.[58] Where it is considered necessary, the LPA may also apply to the court for an injunction[59]

---

lopping or cutting back required or permitted as a consequence of any notice given or order made under Electricity Act 1989, Sch 4, para 9; or (j) for the proper management of the hedgerow.

[51] See Hedgerows Regulations 1997, reg 6(1)(a).

[52] See Hedgerow Regulations 1997, reg 7(2). The punishment on summary conviction is a fine not exceeding level 3 on the standard scale (currently £1,000).

[53] See Hedgerow Regulations 1997, reg 7(6) and (7).

[54] Hedgerows Regulations 1997, reg 7(1). A person guilty of an offence under reg 7(1) shall be liable on summary conviction to a fine not exceeding £5,000, or on conviction on indictment, to an unlimited fine.

[55] Namely contrary to: (a) Hedgerows Regulations 1997, reg 5(1) (i.e. where a hedgerow has been removed but not in compliance with a proposal contained in an approved hedgerow removal notice); or (b) reg 5(9) (i.e. where a hedgerow has been removed notwithstanding the fact that the LPA issued a hedgerow retention notice stating that work relating to the hedgerow may not be carried out and that notice had not been withdrawn).

[56] As defined in Hedgerow Regulations 1997, reg 2(1).

[57] See Hedgerows Regulations 1997, reg 8 (whether or not proceedings are instituted against the owner under reg 7).

[58] See Hedgerows Regulations 1997, reg 9.

[59] See Hedgerows Regulations 1997, reg 11.

and may also enter land without a warrant[60] or with a warrant,[61] and it is an offence for anyone to wilfully obstruct a person acting in the exercise of a right of entry.[62]

Public records

22.18 Each LPA shall compile and keep available for public inspection a record[63] of: (a) every hedgerow removal notice received by it;[64] (b) every hedgerow retention notice issued by it; (c) every notice given by it to the person who gave the hedgerow removal notice stating that the hedgerow may be removed;[65] and (d) every determination notified to it by the Secretary of State[66] arising from an appeal against a hedgerow retention notice[67] or a notice requiring a person to plant another hedgerow.[68]

---

[60] See Hedgerows Regulations 1997, reg 12.

[61] See Hedgerows Regulations 1997, reg 13.

[62] See Hedgerows Regulations 1997, reg 14(3) (on summary conviction the liability is a fine not exceeding £5,000).

[63] See Hedgerows Regulations 1997, reg 10.

[64] See Form of hedgerow removal notice served under Hedgerows Regulations 1997, reg 5(1)(a) in Sch 4.

[65] I.e. under Hedgerow Regulations 1997, reg 5(1)(b)(i).

[66] See Hedgerows Regulations 1997, reg 9(3).

[67] See Hedgerows Regulations 1997, reg 5(2).

[68] See Hedgerows Regulations 1997, reg 8.

Chapter 23

Listed Buildings and Conservation Areas

INTRODUCTION

23.1   This chapter covers the preservation of listed buildings and conservation areas (both of which are governed by the Planning (Listed Buildings and Conservation Areas) Act 1990 (better known as the Listed Buildings Act 1990 (LBA 1990)).[1] This Act provides specific protection for buildings and areas of special architectural or historic interest. The Ancient Monuments and Archaeological Areas Act 1979 provides specific protection for scheduled monuments, and the Protection of Wrecks Act 1973 provides specific protection for protected wreck sites. Any decisions relating to listed buildings and their settings and conservation areas must address the statutory considerations of the LBA 1990.[2]

23.2   The conservation of heritage assets is a core planning principle. In the case of buildings, generally the risks of neglect and decay of heritage assets are best addressed through ensuring that they remain in active use that is consistent with their conservation. Such assets are therefore likely to require changes to be made from time to time in contrast to archaeological sites where periodic changes may not be necessary. Where changes are proposed, the National Planning Policy Framework 2012 (NPPF) sets out a clear framework for both plan-making and decision-making to ensure that heritage assets are conserved and, where appropriate, enhanced, in a manner that is consistent with their significance.[3]

---

[1]   For national policy and guidance see: (a) NPPF paras 126–141 (within the section 'Conserving and enhancing the historic environment'); and (b) in the corresponding section within the NPPG starting at Paragraph: 001 Reference ID: 18a-001-20140306.

[2]   See in particular ss 16, 66 and 72, as well as satisfying the relevant policies within the NPPF and local development plan.

[3]   The policy in addressing substantial and less than substantial harm to designated heritage assets is set out in the NPPF, paras 132–134.

CORE POLICIES IN ADDRESSING SUBSTANTIAL AND LESS THAN SUBSTANTIAL HARM IN THE NPPF

23.3   The policy in addressing substantial and less than substantial harm to designated heritage assets is set out in the NPPF, paragraphs 131 to 134:

> 131. In determining planning applications, LPAs should take account of:
>
> - the desirability of sustaining and enhancing the significance of heritage assets and putting them to viable uses consistent with their conservation;
> - the positive contribution that conservation of heritage assets can make to sustainable communities including their economic vitality;
> - the desirability of new development making a positive contribution to local character and distinctiveness.
>
> 132. When considering the impact of a proposed development on the significance of a designated heritage asset, great weight should be given to the asset's conservation. The more important the asset, the greater the weight should be. Significance can be harmed or lost through alteration or destruction of the heritage asset or development within its setting. As heritage assets are irreplaceable, any harm or loss should require clear and convincing justification. Substantial harm to or loss of a grade II listed building, park or garden should be exceptional. Substantial harm to or loss of designated heritage assets of the highest significance, notably scheduled monuments, protected wreck sites, battlefields, grade I and II listed buildings, grade I and II registered parks and gardens, and World Heritage Sites, should be wholly exceptional.
>
> 133. Where a proposed development will lead to substantial harm to or total loss of significance of a designated heritage asset, LPAs should refuse consent, unless it can be demonstrated that the substantial harm or loss is necessary to achieve substantial public benefits that outweigh that harm or loss, or all of the following apply:
>
> - the nature of the heritage asset prevents all reasonable uses of the site; and
> - no viable use of the heritage asset itself can be found in the medium term through appropriate marketing that will enable its conservation;
> - conservation by grant-funding or some form of charitable or public ownership is demonstrably not possible; and
> - the harm or loss is outweighed by the benefit of bringing the site back into use.
>
> 134. Where a development proposal will lead to less than substantial harm to the significance of a designated heritage asset, this harm should be weighed against the public benefits of the proposal, including securing its optimum viable use.

PRESERVATION OF LISTED BUILDINGS

23.4   Ministerial powers and duties in relation to listed building control vests in the Department for Digital, Culture, Media & Sport (DCMS) (and in Wales by the Welsh Government). The DCMS is responsible for identifying and compiling lists[4] of buildings of special architectural or historic interest or approving, with or without modifications, such lists as are compiled by Historic England (officially, the Historic Buildings and Monuments Commission for England),[5] or by other persons or bodies, and may amend any list so compiled or approved.[6] The purpose of listing is with a view to the guidance of local planning authorities (LPAs) in the performance of their functions[7] and to prohibit unauthorised works to listed buildings.[8] It should be noted that LPAs also identify (and locally list) non-designated heritage assets. These are buildings, monuments, sites, places, areas or landscapes identified as having a degree of significance meriting consideration in planning decisions, but which are not formally designated as heritage assets.[9]

---

[4] Listed buildings are in practice classified as Grade I or Grade II. There is no statutory requirement for this. Grade I buildings are buildings of exceptional interest, whereas Grade II buildings are particularly important buildings of more than special interest which warrant every effort being made to preserve them (see Circular 1/07, para 6.6). The procedure by which buildings are added to the list is informal and reference should be made to the DCMS guidance 'Principles of Selection for Listed Buildings' (March 2010).

[5] Historic England identifies and designates registered parks, gardens and battlefields. World Heritage Sites are inscribed by the United Nations Educational, Scientific and Cultural Organisation (UNESCO). In most cases conservation areas are designated by LPAs. Historic England administers all the national designation regimes.

[6] LBA 1990, ss 1(1)–(3). The Secretary of State is not required to consult the owner of a building that it is intended to be listed (although it is open to any person to contend on appeal from a refusal of listed building consent that the building is not of special architectural or historic interest and ought to be removed from any list compiled or approved by the Secretary of State under s 1 (see s 21(3)). If, however, the Secretary of State decides that a building should be listed then he must notify the LPA who must notify the owner and occupier (s 2(3)). To introduce an element of certainty about listing, it is possible to apply to the Secretary of State for the issue of a certificate that he does not intend to list the building. The issue of such a certificate will preclude the Secretary of State from listing the land for a period of five years (LBA 1990, s 6).

[7] Under the TCPA 1990, and the LBA 1990 (see s 1(1)).

[8] The term 'listed building' may include, in addition to the building itself (unless the list entry indicates otherwise): (a) any object or structure fixed to a building; and (b) any object or structure within the curtilage of the building which, although not fixed to the building, forms part of the land and has done so since before 1/7/1948 (s 1(5)). There are a number of authorities on what will constitute a structure within the curtilage of a listed building: *Debenhams plc v Westminster City Council* [1987] AC 396; *Skerritts of Nottingham Ltd v Secretary of State for the Environment, Transport and the Regions* [1999] JPL 932; *Lowe v First Secretary of State* [2003] 08 EG 129 (CS); *Sumption v Greenwich London Borough Council* [2007] EWHC 2776 (Admin). The prohibition on works to listed buildings may involve works to the interior of the building if they affect the special character of the building (see s 1(5)) or works which do not even fall within the definition of development or which are permitted developments.

[9] NPPF, para 135, provides as follows:

   'The effect of an application on the significance of a non-designated asset should be taken into account in determining the application. In weighing applications that affect directly or

Sanctions

23.5   The result of listing is that it becomes an offence[10] to carry out any works for the demolition of the building or for its alteration or extension in any manner which would affect its character as a building of special architectural or historic interest without listed building consent.[11] The LPA may (in addition to prosecution) also issue a listed building enforcement notice with a view to the

---

indirectly non designated heritage assets, a balanced judgment will be required having regard to the scale of any harm or loss and the significance of the heritage asset.'

See also: (i) NPPG at Paragraph: 039 Reference ID: 18a-039-20140306; (ii) NPPG at Paragraph: 040 Reference ID: 18a-040-20140306, which deals with non-designated assets of archeological interest (see NPPF, para 139); (iii) NPPG at Paragraph: 041 Reference ID: 18a-041-20140306, which deals with the identification of non-designated heritage assets (local lists incorporated into local plans identify non-designated heritage assets which are judged against published criteria generated as part of the process of producing a local list); and (iv) NPPG at Paragraph: 042 Reference ID: 18a-042-20140306, which deals with how Neighbourhood Development Orders and Community Right to Build Orders take account of heritage conservation.

10   Under LBA 1990, s 9. Section 7 contains a prohibition on works for the demolition of a listed building or for its alteration or extension in any manner which would affect its character as a building of special architectural or historic interest, unless the works are authorised by the LPA or the Secretary of State on an application for listed building consent made under s 10 *and* they are executed in accordance with the terms of the consent and of any conditions attached to it (s 8). In the case of demolition (involving demolition of the whole or substantially the whole of the building, see *Shimizu (UK) Ltd v Westminster City Council* [1997] JPL 523), there is an additional requirement that notice of the proposal to execute such works has been given to Historic England (formerly English Heritage)/the Royal Commission on the Ancient and Historical Monuments of Wales, which is to be afforded the opportunity (of at least one month following the grant of consent to demolish the building) to access the building for the purpose of recording it. The offence is one of strict liability from which it follows that evidence of the defendant's intent or state of mind is irrelevant (*R v Wells Street Metropolitan Stipendiary Magistrate ex parte Westminster City Council* [1986] 3 All ER 4).

11   LBA 1990, s 7 sets out the basis of the system of listed building control (i.e. no unauthorised works to listed buildings); s 8 deals with the pre-conditions for the authorisation of works in the case of listed buildings; and s 9 makes it an offence to contravene s 7 (i.e. no listed building consent and a failure to comply with a condition attached to a consent). There are defences under s 7(3): (a) that the works were urgently necessary in the interests of health and safety or the preservation of the building; (b) that it was not practicable to secure health or safety or, as the case may be, the preservation of the building by works of repair or works for affording temporary support or shelter; (c) that the works carried out were limited to the minimum measures immediately necessary; and (d) that notice in writing justifying in detail the carrying out of the works was given to the LPA as soon as reasonably practicable. Section 9(4) provides that a person guilty of an offence under s 9 shall be liable: (a) on summary conviction to imprisonment for a term not exceeding six months or a fine not exceeding £20,000, or both; or (b) on conviction on indictment to imprisonment for a term not exceeding two years or an unlimited fine, or both. In determining the amount of any fine, the court shall in particular have regard to any financial benefit which has accrued or appears likely to accrue to the offender in consequence of the offence (s 9(5)). It is also an offence to demolish a listed building, or to cause such work to be done, without giving notice to Historic England (s 8(2)).

restoration of the building.[12] Failure to comply with an enforcement notice is also

---

[12] LBA 1990, s 38. Such notice may be appealed (on any of the grounds listed in s 39(1)) to the Secretary of State (who, *inter alia*, may quash or vary the listed building enforcement notice or may grant listed building consent for all or part of the works to which it relates or may even remove the building from the statutory list), and thereafter to the High Court on a question of law (s 65). See *Dill v Secretary of State for Communities and Local Government* [2017] EWHC 2378 (Admin); where a property owner applied: (i) to quash the decision of the Secretary of State, by his inspector, to uphold a listed building enforcement notice; and (ii) against the inspector's decision upholding the LPA's refusal of his retrospective application for listed building consent. The listing concerned two early 18th-century urns made of lead and the limestone piers/pedestals they rested on. The owner had inherited them, together with the house in which they were situated, in 1993. The house had been designated a Grade II listed building in 1966, and the urns and piers had been added to the listing in 1986. The owner, then unaware of the listing, had sold the items in 2009 and they were exported. In 2014, the LPA realised that the items had been removed and began correspondence with the owner. His retrospective application for listed building consent to remove the urns and piers was refused by the LPA, which issued a listed building enforcement notice requiring their reinstatement. The owner appealed against those decisions. The inspector found that when the piers and urns were listed in 1986, they had become 'listed buildings' in their own right, subject to all the protective provisions of the Act, and that he was unable to 'go behind' the listing. He rejected the owner's contentions that they had been listed by mistake or were not of special architectural or historic interest, having considered expert advice from Historic England and the Society for the Preservation of Ancient Buildings. He stated that it was inconceivable that listed building consent could be countenanced for the total removal of the piers and urns to an unknown and unspecified location, and accepted the LPA's submission that to grant consent for such works would create an extremely dangerous precedent, potentially endangering the preservation of innumerable other designated heritage assets. He therefore upheld the enforcement notice and refusal of listed building consent. On the application for judicial review, there were three questions, namely had the inspector erred in: (a) considering that he could not go behind the fact of listing; (b) finding that the urns and piers were 'buildings' within the meaning of the Act; and (c) concluding that the items were of special architectural or historical significance. In dismissing the appeal, Singh J held: (a) An inspector had no power to quash an entry on the statutory list on the grounds of unlawfulness. A landowner affected by the listing could challenge it by way of judicial review, or apply to the Secretary of State to remove a building from the list. The fundamental purpose of having a statutory list was to enable members of the public to inspect it and regulate their affairs accordingly. A listing decision might, as in the present case, have been made decades before an appeal; in the meantime, many third parties, as well as the LPA, would have relied on the fact of listing. If an inspector could go behind the fact of listing, that would lead to unacceptable uncertainty in a context where Parliament had clearly thought it right that there should be clarity and certainty. The most a planning inspector could do was to decide that something was incapable unreasonably of being considered to be a building at all. Since statuary was capable as a matter of law of falling within the wide definition of a building, which included a structure or erection, the inspector had correctly fulfilled his role. (b) There were three different ways in which something might qualify as a 'listed building': (i) by being included on the statutory list maintained by the Secretary of State; (ii) by being an object or structure fixed to a building which was on the list; (iii) by being an object or structure which lay within the curtilage of a building which was on the list. Those were not alternative methods of qualifying as a listed building and were not cumulative. The urns and piers were not regarded as listed buildings by reason of the fact that they were fixed to a building on the list, nor because they lay within the curtilage of such a building: rather, they were 'buildings' within the extended statutory definition of that term which had been listed in their own right in 1986. (c) It was

an offence.[13] Where the LPA (or Historic England) considers it expedient, it may apply to the court for an injunction to restrain any actual or threatened contravention of the LBA 1990.[14]

Exceptions

23.6   There are exceptions to the scheme of control for certain ecclesiastical buildings and redundant churches[15] or to any building which is a scheduled monument.[16]

PLANNING PRACTICE GUIDANCE

Plan-making: the historic environment

23.7   LPAs should set out in their local plan a positive strategy for the conservation and enjoyment of the historic environment. In developing their strategy, LPAs should identify specific opportunities within their areas for the conservation and enhancement of heritage assets. This could include, where appropriate, the delivery of development within their settings that will make a positive contribution to, or better reveal the significance of, the heritage asset. The delivery of the strategy may require the development of specific policies, for

---

reasonably likely that, when listing the items in 1986, the then Secretary of State would have acted on professional advice, and no evidence had been adduced that he had not. In any event, the inspector had taken account of current professional advice that the items were worthy of being on the statutory list and should remain there. Those were essentially matters of planning judgment for the opinion of the Secretary of State rather than for the court, subject to review on the ground of irrationality. The inspector had accordingly been entitled to find as he had.

13   LBA 1990, s 43(2). See defences in s 43(4). The LPA may also carry out the work and recoup the expenses reasonably incurred by it in doing so under s 42.

14   LBA 1990, s 44A (see also under TCPA 1990, s 187A). The Commission may in its own name bring proceedings for an injunction to restrain any contravention of the Act (s 44A(4)).

15   See LBA 1990, s 60(1), in the case of buildings mentioned in Ecclesiastical Exemption (Listed Buildings and Conservation Areas) (England) Order 2010 (SI 2010/1176), arts 5–8. Sections 7–9 do not apply to the demolition of redundant churches in pursuance of a pastoral or redundancy scheme (within the meaning of the Pastoral Measure Act 1983) (see s 60(7)).

16   Under Ancient Monuments and Archaeological Areas Act 1979, s 1 (see LBA 1990, s 61). Scheduling takes precedence over listing. Section 2 of the 1979 Act makes it an offence (in the absence of a scheduled monument consent) to demolish, damage, destroy, remove or repair a scheduled monument or any part of it or to make any alterations or additions thereto, or to carry out any flooding or tipping operations on land in, on or under which there is a scheduled monument. It is a defence for an accused to prove that he took all reasonable precautions and exercised all due diligence to avoid or prevent damage to the monument. In the case of removal, repairs, alterations or additions, it is a defence for the defendant to prove that he did not know and had no reason to believe that the monument was within the area affected by the works or (as the case may be) that it was a scheduled monument.

example, in relation to the use of buildings and design of new development and infrastructure. LPAs should consider the relationship and impact of other policies on the delivery of the strategy for conservation.[17]

23.8   LPAs are encouraged to consider making clear and up-to-date information on their identified non-designated heritage assets accessible to the public, both in terms of the criteria used to identify assets and information about the location of existing assets. In this context, the inclusion of information about non-designated assets in local plans can be helpful, as can the identification of areas of potential for the discovery of non-designated heritage assets with archaeological interest.[18] Neighbourhood plans should also include enough information about local heritage to guide decisions and put broader strategic heritage policies from the local plan into action at a neighbourhood scale. Where relevant, designated heritage assets within the plan areas should be clearly identified at the start of the plan-making process so that they can be appropriately taken into account. In addition, and where relevant, neighbourhood plans need to include enough information about non-designated heritage assets including sites of archaeological interest to guide decisions. LPA heritage advisers should be able to advise on local heritage issues that should be considered when preparing a neighbourhood plan. The local historical environment record and any local list[19] will be important sources of information on non-designated heritage assets.[20]

DECISION-TAKING: THE HISTORIC ENVIRONMENT

23.9   In considering whether to grant planning permission for development which affects a listed building or its setting, the LPA (or the Secretary of State) is to have 'special regard' to the desirability of preserving the building or its setting or any features of special architectural or historic interest which it possesses.[21]

---

[17] NPPG at Paragraph: 004 Reference ID: 18a-004-20140306.

[18] NPPG at Paragraph: 006 Reference ID: 18a-006-20140306.

[19] Local heritage listing is a means for a community and LPA to jointly identify heritage assets that are valued as distinctive elements of the local historic environment. The Local Heritage List identifies those heritage assets that are not protected by statutory designations. A Local Heritage List provides clarity on the location of these assets and what it is about them that is significant. They are NOT listed buildings. The Local Heritage List is not restricted to buildings. It may comprise sites, places or areas such as village greens or ponds. It may include structures such as bridges or sluices, and the historic street furniture such as letter-boxes, signposts and telephone boxes. Local Heritage Assets are not given any protection through law although LPAs do encourage the use of appropriate materials and design and that repairs should be conducted on a like-for-like basis.

[20] NPPG at Paragraph: 007 Reference ID: 18a-007-20140306.

[21] LBA 1990, s 66(1). See *Barnwell Manor Wind Energy Ltd v East Northamptonshire District Council* [2014] EWCA Civ 137, in which the Court of Appeal clarified the duty of LPAs under

This is the key protection for listed buildings when it comes to the grant of planning permission in the case of unlisted buildings in close proximity to listed buildings, where harm to the listed building or its setting may prove to be a substantial obstacle to development. Accordingly, it is a question of planning judgment as to whether, for instance, the harm to the setting of the listed heritage asset is such that it cannot be saved by conditions despite a shortfall in housing land supply in the district. In the case of proposals for development in rural areas, it is common for inspectors to cite the loss of agricultural character to be detrimental to the setting of listed buildings (and conservation areas), typically with significant harm also being caused to non-designated heritage assets. On the other hand, if the harm is found to be less than substantial, it is open to the decision-maker to weigh the harm against the public benefits accruing from the development.[22]

23.10 In legislation and designation criteria, the terms 'special architectural or historic interest' of a listed building and the 'national importance' of a scheduled monument are used to describe all or part of the identified heritage asset's significance.[23] Heritage assets may be affected by direct physical change or by change in their setting. Being able to properly assess the nature, extent and importance of the significance of a heritage asset, and the contribution of its setting, is very important to an understanding of the potential impact and acceptability of development proposals.[24] In most cases, the assessment of the significance of the heritage asset by the LPA is likely to require expert evidence in addition to information provided by the historic environment record, similar sources of information and inspection of the asset itself. Advice may be sought from appropriately qualified staff and experienced in-house experts or professional consultants, complemented as appropriate by consultation with National Amenity Societies and other statutory consultees.[25]

23.11 A Design and Access Statement is required to accompany certain applications for planning permission and applications for listed building consent. These statements provide a flexible framework for an applicant to explain and justify their proposal with reference to its context. In cases where both a Design

---

s 66(1) (or, as the case may be, the Secretary of State) in considering whether to grant planning permission for development affecting listed buildings or their setting, to have special regard to the desirability of preserving such buildings (or any features of special architectural or historic interest which they possess) or their setting. See also *Steer v Secretary of State for Communities and Local Government* [2017] EWHC 1456 (Admin). *Barnwell Manor* and *Steer* are dealt with in detail below.

22   NPPF, para 134.

23   NPPG at Paragraph: 008 Reference ID: 18a-008-20140306.

24   NPPG at Paragraph: 009 Reference ID: 18a-009-20140306.

25   NPPG at Paragraph: 010 Reference ID: 18a-010-20140306.

and Access Statement and an assessment of the impact of the proposal on a heritage asset are required, applicants can avoid unnecessary duplication and demonstrate how the proposed design has responded to the historic environment through including the necessary heritage assessment as part of the Design and Access Statement.[26]

SOME RECENT HERITAGE AUTHORITIES

23.12 Reference should be made to *Barnwell Manor Wind Energy Ltd v East Northamptonshire District Council*,[27] in which the Court of Appeal clarified the duty of LPAs under section 66(1), in considering whether to grant planning permission for development affecting listed buildings or their setting, to have special regard to the desirability of preserving such buildings (or any features of special architectural or historic interest which they possess) or their setting (a duty reinforced by section 67 which requires the LPA to give publicity to any planning application which would, in their opinion, affect the setting of a listed building). *Barnwell Manor* involved a developer's appeal against a decision quashing a planning inspector's grant of planning permission for the construction of a four-turbine wind farm development near a site owned by the National Trust at Sudborough in Northamptonshire which was covered by a range of heritage designations and included a Grade 1 listed building. The developer's appeal was dismissed by the Court of Appeal. Section 66(1) provides as follows:

> In considering whether to grant planning permission for development which affects a listed building or its setting, the local planning authority or, as the case may be, the Secretary of State shall have special regard to the desirability of preserving the building or its setting or any features of special architectural or historic interest which it possesses.

23.13 At first instance,[28] Lang J held that 'special weight' should be given to the desirability of preserving the setting of listed buildings and that it would be wrong to treat harm as simply another factor in the planning balance. In other words, it was necessary to qualify Lord Hoffmann's statement in *Tesco Stores Ltd v Secretary of State for the Environment*[29] that the weight to be given to a material consideration was a question of planning judgment for the LPA. Lang J's view was that the inspector did not in the balancing exercise accord 'special weight' or considerable importance to 'the desirability of preserving the setting'. He had treated the harm to the setting and the wider benefit of the wind farm proposal as

---

[26] NPPG at Paragraph: 012 Reference ID: 18a-012-20140306.

[27] [2014] EWCA Civ 137.

[28] [2013] EWHC 473 (Admin).

[29] [1995] 1 WLR 759 at 780.

if those two factors were of equal importance. In *Bedford BC v Secretary of State for the Communities and Local Government,*[30] Jay J declined to follow the approach of Lang J in *Barnwell Manor.* His view was that the term 'special regard' in section 66 meant only that the weight to be given to the harm to the setting of the listed building on the one hand, and the advantages of the proposal on the other, was entirely a matter of planning judgment for the LPA. In the Court of Appeal in *Barnwell Manor,* the approach of Lang J was endorsed. Sullivan LJ rejected the argument that this interpretation was contrary to the well-established proposition that questions of weight are generally for the decision-maker, subject only to a rationality overview. He said that the principle in *Tesco Stores* was not in doubt, but that it concerned an ordinary determination under section 72(2) (in which the LPA has to consider the development plan and any other material considerations) and not section 66(1) or section 72(1) of the LBA 1990 (which requires special attention to be given in planning determinations to the desirability of preserving or enhancing the character or appearance of a conservation area). Sullivan LJ took the view that the inspector was wrong to attach greater weight to a Planning Policy Statement (PPS22 Renewable Energy), which said that the wider environmental and economic benefits of all proposals for renewable energy, whatever their scale, are material considerations which should be given significant weight. Sullivan LJ said that Parliament had made the power to grant permission having regard to material considerations expressly subject to the section 66(1) duty. In the circumstances, where, for instance, in a case involving the installation of wind turbines, the harm to the setting of a listed building was less than substantial, this would lessen the strength of the presumption against the grant of planning permission.

23.14   *Barnwell Manor* was applied by Lindblom J in *R (Forge Field Society) v Sevenoaks DC,*[31] in which he quashed a decision granting permission for affordable housing because of the failure to give effect to the section 66(1) duty. In *R (JH and FW Green Ltd) v South Downs National Park Authority,*[32] Stuart-Smith J held 'that the LPA's task is to weigh any harm to the significance of a designated heritage asset against the public benefits of the proposal and that securing viable optimum use is only one part of that balancing exercise'.

23.15   In *Jones v Mordue,*[33] the Court of Appeal held that the inspector, in granting permission for the erection of a single wind turbine, had given appropriate weight to preserving the setting of listed buildings and provided sufficient reasons for his decision, consistently with *Save Britain's Heritage v*

---

[30]   [2013] EWHC 2847 (Admin).

[31]   [2015] JPL 22.

[32]   [2018] EWHC 604 (Admin) at [66].

[33]   [2015] EWCA Civ 1243, [2016] 1 WLR 2682.

Number 1 Poultry Ltd[34] and *South Bucks DC v Porter (No 2)*,[35] under which the court had to ask itself, whenever a planning decision was challenged on the ground of a failure to give reasons, whether the applicant's interests had been substantially prejudiced by the deficiency of reasons given (*Save Britain's Heritage*), which guidance was followed by a summary of the relevant principles in *South Bucks* that the reasons had to be intelligible and adequate so as to enable the reader to understand why the matter was decided as it was and what conclusions were reached on the important issues, disclosing how any issue of fact was resolved; reasons could be briefly stated, the degree of particularity depending entirely on the nature of the issues falling for decision.

23.16 In *R (Williams) v Powys County Council*,[36] the Court of Appeal again considered the section 66(1) duty where the setting of a listed building was concerned. Lindblom LJ explained at [53] that:

> the circumstances in which the s.66(1) duty has to be performed where the setting of a listed building is concerned will vary considerably, and with a number of factors. What are those factors? Typically, I think, they will include the nature, scale and siting of the development proposed, its proximity and likely visual relationship to the listed building, the architectural and historic characteristics of the listed building itself, local topography, and the presence of other features – both natural and man-made – in the surrounding landscape or townscape. There may be other considerations too. Ultimately, the question of whether the section 66(1) duty is engaged will always depend on the particular facts and circumstances of the case in hand.

23.17 See also [56], where Lindblom LJ expressed his reluctance to lay down some universal principle for ascertaining the extent of the setting of a listed building. He did though say that:

> if a proposed development is to affect the setting of a listed building there must be a distinct visual relationship of some kind between the two – a visual relationship which is more than remote or ephemeral, and which in some way bears on one's experience of the listed building in its surrounding landscape or townscape ...[37]

23.18 In *R (Perry) v London Borough of Hackney*,[38] Patterson J held that the question to be addressed under sections 66(1) (listed buildings) and 72(1) (conservation areas) was not a simple balancing exercise, but was one which needed to have a 'special regard' or 'special attention' to the heritage assets

34   [1991] 1 WLR 153.
35   [2004] 1 WLR 1953.
36   [2017] EWCA Civ 427.
37   See also NPPF, paras 131–135.
38   [2015] JPL 454.

([120]). Historic England should be consulted where the LPA thinks that the proposed development would affect the setting of a listed building.[39] See also *Gerber v Wiltshire Council*[40] and *R (Goring-on-Thames Parish Council) v South Oxfordshire DC*,[41] where it was held that the LPA had not erred in granting permission for a hydropower scheme at a weir located within a conservation area and an AONB. An issue involved the impact of the scheme on listed buildings within a conservation area. The claim for judicial review failed. The court found that knowledgeable groups like the claimant had not previously raised listed buildings and their setting as a concern. This had never been an issue in the planning application, and it was accordingly unnecessary for the planning officer to identify each building to confirm that there would be no material impact upon it. Since there was no harm to any listed building which the LPA was required to take into account, the section 66(1) duty, namely, to investigate whether there was any harm to listed buildings within the conservation area, did not arise. Nothing in the officer's report suggested that special priority was given to the issue of harm to the conservation area in accordance with section 72. Instead, the planning permission had simply concluded that the impact on the historic merits of the conservation area and visual effect on amenity constituted less than substantial harm, which was outweighed by the public benefit of renewable energy generation through use of the river. It was found to be highly likely that the outcome would not have been substantially different if the LPA had applied the correct test. There was simply no prospect that the issue would have made any difference to the overall planning balance if the decision had been taken in accordance with section 72.

23.19 *Secretary of State for Communities and Local Government v Steer*[42] involved conjoined appeals against a High Court decision upholding an LPA's refusal to grant a developer planning permission for a housing development involving 400 houses on farmland which had once formed part of the estate of a Grade 1 listed building (Kedleston Hall) in Derbyshire which was acknowledged to be of exceptional historic and architectural interest. The whole site was close

---

[39]   As required by Planning (Listed Buildings and Conservation Areas) Regulations 1990 (SI 1990/1519), reg 5A (which makes provision for the publicity of applications for planning permission affecting the setting of listed buildings).

[40]   [2015] EWHC 524 (Admin) at [52] and [2016] EWCA Civ 84.

[41]   [2016] EWHC 2898 (Admin). The *Goring-on-Thames* case is also relevant on a procedural point (the application for permission to appeal having been dismissed by a single judge of the Court of Appeal), in that the Court of Appeal ([2018] EWCA Civ 860) considered CPR, rule 52.30 (and the reopening of a final determination of any appeal), holding that to be successful under CPR, rule 52.30 an applicant would need to show that: (a) the grounds of appeal had not been sufficiently confronted and dealt with, to the extent that the appeal process had been critically undermined; and (b) there is a powerful probability that permission to appeal would have been granted if the judge had adequately dealt with the grounds of appeal.

[42]   [2018] EWCA Civ 1697 (also known as *Catesby Estates v Steer*).

to two conservation areas. Section 66(1) required special regard to be given to the desirability of preserving the affected listed asset or its setting. NPPF, paragraph 132 indicated that the significance of an asset could be harmed by development within its setting, which it defined as the surroundings in which the asset was experienced. The National Planning Practice Guidance (NPPG) explained that setting might be more extensive than curtilage and that although the views of or from an asset were important, the way in which it was experienced was influenced by a range of environmental factors. The LPA refused permission on the basis that it would harm the setting and significance of the hall and parkland. At a subsequent inquiry, a planning inspector directed that permission should be granted. Objectors had argued that even though the development site would not intrude upon the views to and from the listed building, it lay within the setting of both. They relied on the fact that the site had originally formed part of the estate, remained in its historic agricultural use and was important in preserving a sense of a parkland landscape at the centre of a managed rural estate. However, the inspector had found that something more visual or physical was necessary. He concluded that the development site lay within the setting of the parkland but that, with appropriate landscaping, it would not lie within the setting of the listed building. Moreover, he found that the development would cause 'less than substantial' harm to that of the parkland. The judge at first instance overturned the inspector's decision, holding that, by treating visual connections between the asset and the development as essential and determinative, he had taken too narrow an approach to the meaning of 'setting' in section 66(1). The Court of Appeal allowed the appeal and reinstated the decision of the inspector to allow planning permission. The court found that although the setting of a heritage asset was not statutorily defined, implicit in section 66(1) was the idea that setting could be affected by development, whether within or outside it. Thus, the decision-maker was required to understand what the asset's setting was and whether the development site either lay within it or was in some way related to it. Identifying the extent of an asset's setting and whether the development would affect it was a matter of applying planning judgment to the circumstances of the case, and unless there was a clear error of law in the decision-maker's approach, the court should not intervene. The decision-maker had to have regard to relevant policy and guidance and to the principle that considerable importance and weight had to be given to the desirability of preserving that setting (*R (Friends of Hethel Ltd) v South Norfolk DC* followed).[43] The court held that for a proposed development to affect the setting, there had to be a distinct visual relationship between the two. That relationship had to be more than remote or ephemeral, and it had to bear on how the asset was experienced in its surrounding landscape (*R (Williams) v Powys CC* followed).[44] However, that did not mean that other factors were to be ignored;

---

[43] [2010] EWCA Civ 894, [2011] 1 WLR 1216.
[44] [2017] EWCA Civ 427, [2018] 1 WLR 439.

economic, social and historical considerations were also relevant.[45] The court found that the inspector had not adopted too narrow an interpretation of 'setting' and had correctly applied the relevant policies and guidance. It was found that he had been entitled to look for visual effects to ascertain the extent of the setting, and his indication that there needed to be something more physical or visual than the historical considerations relied on by the objectors was a planning judgment on the facts, not a statement of general principle. He was saying simply that the historical connection between the listed building and the farmland was, by itself, insufficient.[46]

PLANNING PRACTICE GUIDANCE

The setting of a heritage asset and how it should be taken into account[47]

23.20 A thorough assessment of the impact on setting needs to take into account, and be proportionate to, the significance of the heritage asset under consideration and the degree to which proposed changes enhance or detract from that significance and the ability to appreciate it.

23.21 Setting is the surroundings in which an asset is experienced and may therefore be more extensive than its curtilage. All heritage assets have a setting, irrespective of the form in which they survive and whether they are designated. The extent and importance of setting is often expressed by reference to visual considerations. Although views of, or from, an asset will play an important part, the way in which an asset in its setting is experienced is also influenced by other environmental factors such as noise, dust and vibration from other land uses in the vicinity, and by an understanding of the historic relationship between places. For instance, buildings that are in close proximity but are not visible from each other may have an historic or aesthetic connection that amplifies the experience of the significance of each. The contribution that setting makes to the significance of the heritage asset does not depend on there being public rights or an ability to access or experience that setting.

23.22 When assessing any application for development which may affect the setting of a heritage asset, LPAs may need to consider the implications of cumulative change. They may also need to consider the fact that developments

---

[45] See [24]–[30] of the judgment.

[46] In *Planning* on 26/7/2018, Richard Kimblin QC is reported to have said this: 'This decision makes clear that the battleground for these debates should be planning inquiries, not the courts. Courts should only be involved where there are clear or hard-edged legal errors'.

[47] NPPG at Paragraph: 013 Reference ID: 18a-013-20140306.

which materially detract from the asset's significance may also damage its economic viability now or in the future, thereby threatening its ongoing conservation.

SHOULD THE DETERIORATED STATE OF A HERITAGE ASSET BE TAKEN INTO ACCOUNT?

23.23 Disrepair and damage and their impact on viability can be a material consideration in deciding an application. However, where there is evidence of deliberate damage to or neglect of a heritage asset in the hope of making consent or permission easier to gain, the LPA should disregard the deteriorated state of the asset.[48] In such cases, LPAs may need to consider exercising their repair and compulsory purchase powers to remedy deliberate neglect or damage.[49]

WHAT IS A VIABLE USE FOR A HERITAGE ASSET AND HOW IS IT TAKEN INTO ACCOUNT?[50]

23.24 As the vast majority of heritage assets are in private hands, sustaining heritage assets in the long term often requires an incentive for their active conservation. Accordingly, putting heritage assets to a viable use is likely to lead to the investment in their maintenance necessary for their long-term conservation.

23.25 Some heritage assets have limited or even no economic end use. A scheduled monument in a rural area may preclude any use of the land other than as a pasture, whereas a listed building may potentially have a variety of alternative uses such as residential, commercial and leisure. In a small number of cases, a heritage asset may be capable of active use in theory, but be so important and sensitive to change that alterations to accommodate a viable use would lead to an unacceptable loss of significance.

23.26 It is important that any use is viable, not just for the owner, but also for the future conservation of the asset. It is obviously desirable to avoid successive

---

[48] NPPF, para 130.

[49] NPPG at Paragraph: 014 Reference ID: 18a-014-20140306.

[50] NPPG at Paragraph: 015 Reference ID: 18a-015-20140306. NPPF, para 131, provides that in determining planning applications LPAs should take account of: (first bullet) the desirability of sustaining and enhancing the significance of the heritage assets and putting them to viable uses consistent with their conservation; (second bullet) the positive contribution that conservation of heritage assets can make to sustainable local communities including their economic viability; (third bullet) the desirability of new development making a positive contribution to local character and distinctiveness.

harmful changes carried out in the interests of repeated speculative and failed uses. If, however, there is only one viable use, that use is the optimum viable use. If there is a range of alternative viable uses, the optimum use is the one likely to cause the least harm to the significance of the asset, not just through necessary initial changes, also but as a result of subsequent wear and tear and likely future changes.

23.27 The optimum viable use may not necessarily be the most profitable one.[51] It might be the original use, but that may no longer be economically viable or

---

[51] *R (Gibson) v Waverley Borough Council* [2015] EWHC 3784 (Admin); an earlier judgment regarding the optimum use of a heritage property as a single dwelling did not bind an LPA to regard the single dwelling option as the only optimum viable use for all time. The optimum use of the property was a matter of planning judgment for the LPA, based on current material circumstances. The property, which had been the former home of Sir Arthur Conan Doyle, had been used as an hotel since 2005. Thereafter the site, including the house, had lain dormant and the structural condition of the building had deteriorated. Planning permission granted to the property's former owner to convert the property into separate, residential units had been quashed following an earlier judicial review application, the court having ruled that the optimum viable use of the property was as a single dwelling-house. The first interested party, a charitable foundation, acquired the property with the intention of expanding its local educational establishment for children, teenagers and young adults with special needs. It sought permission for a change of use from hotel to educational use, with the erection of extensions and the carrying out of alterations following demolition of a modern extension and associated works, in order to provide additional premises for an upper school for children with mild learning difficulties. The LPA granted a conditional permission, having considered that the proposal would preserve the listed building's setting and satisfy the relevant statutory tests. The claimant contended that the grant of permission had effectively prevented the realisation of the property's optimum use. It was submitted that the earlier decision had established that the property's optimum use was as a single dwelling, and that since there had been inadequate marketing of the property as an hotel or single dwelling, there was no rational basis for suggesting that the optimum use was neither possible nor viable. Alternatively, it was argued that there was another optimum viable use for the property as a school without alterations or extensions. The application for judicial review was refused. (1) the earlier judgment did not, and was never intended to, bind the LPA to regard the single residential dwelling option as the only optimum viable use for all time. The judge had (previously) found that, because of an offer to purchase the property to implement its use as a single dwelling, that was the optimum viable use, albeit not the most profitable use. Whether single residential use of the building at any particular time was the optimum viable use was a matter on which the LPA had to form a judgment. It had considered all the relevant factors and had been justified in proceeding on the basis that single residential use was not a viable option, however optimum it might be in theory. The LPA's approach was not invalidated by a failure to identify single residential use as a viable option for preserving the heritage asset. (2) The LPA had been entitled to proceed on the basis that the proposal reflected in the new application was not merely the only viable educational use of the property, but, on the evidence available, that it was the only viable use of the property that would preserve it from further deterioration. There was a need to consider alternative, less harmful, uses of the same site when evaluating a proposal that would cause harm to a heritage asset (*R (Langley Park School for Girls Governors) v Bromley LBC* [2009] EWCA Civ 734 considered). However, the way in which that evaluation might be carried out would vary from case to case. The approval of extensions and alterations necessary for the provision of much-needed educational and training facilities for part of the disabled

even the most compatible with the long-term conservation of the asset. However, if from a conservation point of view there is no real difference between viable uses, then the choice of use is a decision of the owner. Harmful development may sometimes be justified in the interests of realising the optimum viable use of an asset, notwithstanding the loss of significance caused provided the harm is minimised.[52]

WHAT EVIDENCE IS NEEDED TO DEMONSTRATE THAT THERE IS NO VIABLE USE?[53]

23.28 Appropriate marketing is required to demonstrate the redundancy of a heritage asset.[54] The aim of such marketing is to reach all potential buyers who may be willing to find a use for the site that still provides for its conservation to some degree. If such a purchaser comes forward, there is no obligation to sell to them, but redundancy will not have been demonstrated.

HOW TO ASSESS IF THERE IS SUBSTANTIAL HARM[55]

23.29 What matters in assessing if a proposal causes substantial harm is the impact on the significance of the heritage asset. As the NPPF makes clear, significance derives not only from a heritage asset's physical presence, but also from its setting. Whether a proposal causes substantial harm will be a judgment for the decision-maker, having regard to the circumstances of the case and the policies in the NPPF. In general terms, substantial harm is a high test, so it may not arise in many cases. For example, in determining whether works to a listed building constitute substantial harm, an important consideration would be whether the adverse impact seriously affects a key element of its special architectural or historic interest. It is a degree of harm to the asset's significance rather than the scale of the development that is to be assessed. The harm may arise from works to the asset or from development within its setting.

23.30 While the impact of total destruction is obvious, partial destruction is likely to have a considerable impact, but, depending on the circumstances, it may

---

community which at the same time preserved and protected an important heritage asset from continuing dilapidation, and enabled public access to it, was pre-eminently a matter for the LPA's judgment.

[52] The policy in addressing substantial and less than substantial harm to heritage assets is set out in the NPPF, paras 132–134.

[53] NPPG at Paragraph: 016 Reference ID: 18a-016-20140306.

[54] In the circumstances set out in NPPF, para 133 (bullet 2).

[55] NPPG at Paragraph: 017 Reference ID: 18a-017-20140306.

still be less than substantial harm or conceivably not harmful at all, for example, when removing later inappropriate additions to historic buildings which harm their significance. Similarly, works that are moderate or minor in scale are likely to cause less than substantial harm or no harm at all. However, even minor works have the potential to cause substantial harm.

HARM IN RELATION TO CONSERVATION AREAS[56]

23.31 An unlisted building that makes a positive contribution to a conservation area is individually of lesser importance than a listed building.[57] If the building is important or integral to the character or appearance of the conservation area, then its demolition is more likely to amount to substantial harm to the conservation area.[58] However, the justification for its demolition will still be proportionate to the relative significance of the conservation area as a whole.

HOW CAN PROPOSALS AVOID OR MINIMISE HARM TO THE SIGNIFICANCE OF A HERITAGE ASSET?[59]

23.32 A clear understanding of the significance of the heritage asset and its setting is necessary to develop proposals which avoid or minimise harm. Early appraisals, a conservation plan or targeted specialist investigation can help to identify constraints and opportunities arising from the asset at an early stage. Such studies can reveal alternative development options, for example, more sensitive designs or different orientations, that will deliver public benefits[60] in a more sustainable and appropriate way.

---

[56] NPPG at Paragraph: 018 Reference ID: 18a-018-20140306.

[57] See NPPF, para 132.

[58] Engaging the tests in NPPF, para 133.

[59] NPPG at Paragraph: 019 Reference ID: 18a-019-20140306.

[60] NPPG at Paragraph: 020 Reference ID: 18a-020-20140306. The term 'public benefits' can be anything that delivers economic, social or environmental progress as described in NPPF, para 7. Public benefits should flow from the proposed development. They should be of a nature or scale to be of benefit to the public at large, and should not just be a private benefit. However, benefits do not always have to be visible or accessible to the public in order to be genuine public benefits and may include heritage benefits such as sustaining or enhancing the significance of the heritage asset and the contribution of its setting; reducing or removing risks to a heritage asset; or securing the optimum viable use of a heritage asset in support of its long-term conservation.

PROCEDURE FOR OBTAINING LISTED CONSENT

23.33 The procedures for obtaining listed consent are set out in the LBA 1990[61] and in the Planning (Listed Buildings and Conservation Areas) Regulations 1990,[62] or in Wales in the Planning (Listed Buildings and Conservation Areas) (Wales) Regulations 2012.[63] The provisions are modelled on applications for planning permission, although, as one might expect, there are additional requirements as to publicity and consultation[64] involving the Secretary of State[65] and/or Historic England and/or the National Amenity Societies. The LPA has power to grant or refuse applications for listed building consent and to impose conditions, provided the requirements as to notification have been met and the 28-day suspension period has been observed in cases of demolition.[66] The Secretary of State may also give directions calling in the application.[67] An LPA is required to notify the Secretary of State if it intends to grant listed building consent, in which case the Secretary of State has a period of 28 days to decide whether to call in the application.[68]

---

[61] LBA 1990, ss 10–16. Where development involves the demolition or alteration of a listed building, separate applications must be made for planning permission and listed building consent.

[62] SI 1990/1519.

[63] SI 2012/793.

[64] See NPPG at Paragraph: 050 Reference ID: 18a-050-20140306, through to Paragraph: 062 Reference ID: 18a-062-20140306 under '7. Consultation and notification requirements for heritage related applications'. Of particular importance are Tables 1–7 which set out the broad and detailed consultation requirements in the case of applications for planning permission and listed building consent (and involving Historic England, the National Amenity Societies, the Gardens Trust and the Secretary of State).

[65] The Secretary of State also has power to make directions under LBA 1990, s 15 with a view to: (a) relaxing the notification requirements of ss 13–14 (see Arrangements for Handling Heritage Applications – Notification to Historic England and National Amenity Societies and the Secretary of State (England) Direction 2015, paras 5 and 6); and (b) allowing the Secretary of State to direct LPAs to notify him or such other persons as may be specified of any applications for listed building consent and of any decisions taken thereon (see para 4 of the same Direction).

[66] LBA 1990, s 16(1). The consent also runs with the land 'except in so far as it otherwise provides' which implies that a consent may only be personal (s 16(3)).

[67] LBA 1990, s 12.

[68] LBA 1990, s 13.

HERITAGE CONSENT PROCESS

Is listed building consent the same as planning permission?[69]

23.34 Listed building consent and planning permission are two separate regimes. So for some proposed works, both planning permission and listed building consent will be needed, and sometimes only one, or neither, is required.

When is an application for planning permission required to carry out works to a listed building?[70]

23.35 This will depend on the particular works involved, but in general terms:

- an application for planning permission is required if the works would usually require a planning application if the building was not listed;
- an application for planning permission is not required if the works would normally be permitted development, there are no restrictions on the permitted development rights in respect of listed buildings and the permitted development rights have not been removed locally;
- an application for planning permission is not required if the works would not constitute 'development', e.g. internal works to listed buildings.

23.36 The requirement for listed building consent is not the same as for planning permission. So for some proposed works, both planning permission and listed building consent will be needed and sometimes only one, or neither, is required.

When is listed building consent required?[71]

23.37 Any works to demolish any part of a listed building or to alter or extend it in a way that affects its character as a building of special architectural or historic interest require listed building consent, irrespective of whether planning permission is also required. It is important to note that it may be a criminal offence to fail to apply for consent when it is required. For all grades of listed building, unless the list entry indicates otherwise, the listing status covers the entire building, internal and external, objects fixed to it and sometimes also attached and curtilage buildings or other structures.

23.38 Undertaking works, or causing works to be undertaken, to a listed building which would affect its character as a building of special historic or architectural

---

[69] NPPG at Paragraph: 043 Reference ID: 18a-043-20140306.
[70] NPPG at Paragraph: 044 Reference ID: 18a-044-20140306.
[71] NPPG at Paragraph: 045 Reference ID: 18a-045-20140306.

interest, without first obtaining listed building consent, is an offence under section 9 of the LBA 1990.

What is a listed building heritage partnership agreement?[72]

23.39 A listed building heritage partnership agreement is an agreement between an LPA and the owner(s) of a listed building or group of listed buildings which grants listed building consent. It allows the LPA to grant listed building consent for the duration of the agreement for specified works of alteration or extension (but not demolition) of those listed buildings covered by the agreement (see sections 26A and 26B of the LBA 1990).

23.40 Listed building heritage partnership agreements remove the need for the owner(s) concerned to submit repetitive applications for listed building consent for works covered by the agreement.

23.41 When considering whether to grant listed building consent in a listed building heritage partnership agreement, LPAs are required to have special regard to the desirability of preserving the building or its setting or any features of special architectural or historic interest possessed by the listed building(s) to be included in the agreement and should take account of the relevant policies in the NPPF.[73]

What is a local listed building consent order?[74]

23.42 Local listed building consent orders are made by LPAs and grant listed building consent for works of any description for the alteration or extension (but not demolition) of listed buildings in their area (see sections 26D–26G and 28A of, and Schedule 2A to, the LBA 1990). This means that owners and developers do not need to submit repetitive applications for listed building consent for works covered by an order.

23.43 When considering making a local listed building consent order, LPAs are required to have special regard to the desirability of preserving the listed building(s) to which the order applies, their setting or any features of special

---

[72] NPPG at Paragraph: 046 Reference ID: 18a-046-20140306.

[73] See also NPPG at Paragraph: 064 Reference ID: 18a-064-20140306, and at Paragraph: 065 Reference ID: 18a-065-20140306 which deal, respectively, with the length of such agreements and the procedures which an LPA needs to follow.

[74] NPPG at Paragraph: 066 Reference ID: 18a-066-20140306.

architectural or historic interest they possess and should take account of the relevant policies in the NPPF.[75]

What is a certificate of lawfulness of proposed works?[76]

23.44 A certificate of lawfulness of proposed works provides formal confirmation that proposed works of alteration or extension (but not demolition) of a listed building do not require listed building consent because they do not affect the character of the listed building as a building of special architectural or historic interest (section 26H of the LBA 1990).

23.45 Certificates of lawfulness of proposed works are only available in respect of works which have not yet been carried out – they cannot be obtained retrospectively.

23.46 Works for which a certificate of lawfulness of proposed works is issued must be undertaken within ten years from the date of the issue of the certificate.

23.47 Any person wishing to obtain a certificate must submit an application to their LPA. The procedures for applications, and appeals against refusal or non-determination of an application, are set out in the Planning (Listed Buildings) (Certificates of Lawfulness of Proposed Works) Regulations 2014.[77]

Is an application for planning permission required to carry out works to an unlisted building in a conservation area?[78]

23.48 Planning permission is required for the demolition of certain unlisted buildings in conservation areas (known as 'relevant demolition').

23.49 Generally, the requirement for planning permission for other works to unlisted buildings in a conservation area is the same as it is for any buildings

[75] See also NPPG at: (a) Paragraph: 067 Reference ID: 18a-067-20140306; (b) Paragraph: 068 Reference ID: 18a-068-20140306; (c) Paragraph: 069 Reference ID: 18a-069-20140306; and (d) Paragraph: 070 Reference ID: 18a-070-20140306 which deal with, respectively, the duration of such orders, procedures to be followed by an LPA when making such orders, differences between a listed building heritage partnership agreement and a local listed building consent order, and the nature of a listed building consent order made by the Secretary of State.

[76] NPPG at Paragraph: 071 Reference ID: 18a-071-20140306.

[77] There is no obligation on anyone to apply for such a certificate and if a person is satisfied that any minor works they want to carry out to a listed building do not require listed building consent they can, if they wish, proceed with those works without obtaining any confirmation from the LPA. On the other hand, owners are encouraged to discuss the matter with their LPA in case of doubt as to whether listed building consent is required before submitting any application.

[78] NPPG at Paragraph: 047 Reference ID: 18a-047-20140306.

outside a conservation area, although some permitted development rights are more restricted in conservation areas.

23.50 Demolishing an unlisted building in a conservation area, without first obtaining planning permission where it is needed, is an offence under section 196D of the LBA 1990.

Granting listed building consent

23.51 In granting listed building consent, the LPA may (without prejudice of the power of the LPA to grant consent subject to conditions)[79] impose conditions which, in particular, require: (a) the preservation of particular features of the building; (b) making good any damage after the works are completed; (c) reconstruction following execution of the works; (d) subsequent approval of design and other details; (e) postponement of demolition until redevelopment is imminent; and (f) personal consents.[80] The duration of a listed building consent is comparable to the period applicable to planning permissions (i.e. works to be begun within three years beginning with the date of the grant or such other period as may be determined by the LPA).[81]

Appeals

23.52 There is a right of appeal to the Secretary of State[82] (jurisdiction is now transferred to inspectors) against the refusal of the LPA to grant listed building consent or against any condition imposed on a grant of such consent, or where the LPA fails to determine the application within the prescribed period (eight weeks or longer if agreed), or refuses an application for the variation or discharge of conditions subject to which such consent had been granted, or grants it and adds new conditions, or where an application for approval of details is refused or granted subject to conditions.[83] An appeal must be made within six months of the

---

[79] LBA 1990, s 16(1). A procedure exists allowing conditions to be varied or discharged on application under s 19, although a variation or discharge under this section must not: (a) vary a condition subject to which a consent was granted by extending the time within which the works must be started; and (b) discharge such a condition.

[80] LBA 1990, s 17.

[81] LBA 1990, s 18.

[82] LBA 1990, s 20(1). The Secretary of State may allow or dismiss the appeal or may reverse or vary any part of the authority's decision and may deal with it as if it had been made to him in the first instance. The decision of the Secretary of State on an appeal under s 20 is final (s 22(3)) subject to challenge (made within six weeks of the date of the decision) in the High Court under s 63(1), namely that the decision is not within the powers of the Act or that any of the relevant requirements have not been complied with in relation to it.

[83] LBA 1990, s 20(1).

notice of decision or the expiry of the prescribed or agreed period for appealing, or such longer time as the Secretary of State may allow.[84]

Revoking or modifying a listed building consent

23.53   A listed building consent may be revoked or modified by the LPA to such extent as it considers expedient.[85] The power may be exercised before the works have been completed, but is ineffective in the case of works which have already been carried out.[86] In exercising its powers, the LPA shall have regard to the development plan and to any other material considerations.[87] Opposed orders do not take effect unless they have been confirmed by the Secretary of State, who may hold a public local inquiry before deciding how to deal with the matter.[88] Where the listed building consent is revoked or modified (other than in unopposed cases), the LPA is liable to pay compensation for abortive expenditure and any other loss or damage which is directly attributable to such order.[89]

Listed building purchase notices

23.54   The owner of land may serve a listed building purchase notice on the LPA if the refusal of listed building consent[90] has left the land without any reasonably beneficial use.[91]

Building preservation notices

23.55   The LPA may also serve a building preservation notice on an owner or occupier of an unlisted building in its area which: (a) is of special architectural or historic interest; and (b) is in danger of demolition or of alteration in such a way

---

[84]   Planning (Listed Buildings and Conservation Areas) Regulations 1990 (SI 1990/1519), reg 8(1).

[85]   LBA 1990, s 23(1).

[86]   LBA 1990, s 23(3).

[87]   LBA 1990, s 23(2).

[88]   LBA 1990, s 24. The alternative procedure for unopposed orders is set out in s 25, and s 26 deals with the process before the Secretary of State.

[89]   LBA 1990, ss 28 and 30(1)(b); although no compensation is payable for any work carried out before the grant of listed building consent is revoked or for any other loss or damage (not being loss or damage consisting of depreciation of the value of an interest in land) arising out of anything done or omitted to be done before the grant of listed building consent. See also s 31 for general provisions as to compensation for depreciation. In cases of dispute, compensation is determined by the Upper Tribunal.

[90]   Or has been granted subject to conditions, or where such consent granted on an application is revoked or modified.

[91]   LBA 1990, s 32. If the LPA serves a counter-notice rejecting the owner's purchase notice, it is referred to the Secretary of State who may confirm the purchase notice and, if confirmed, the ordinary compulsory purchase procedures apply.

as to affect its character as a building of such interest. A building preservation notice comes into force as soon as it has been served and continues in force (as if the building were a listed building) for six months or earlier if the Secretary of State includes the building in a list compiled or approved under section 1 of the LBA 1990. If the Secretary of State notifies the LPA that he does not intend to list the building, the authority shall notify the owner and occupier of that decision. Following such notification by the Secretary of State, no further building preservation notice may be served by the LPA for a period of 12 months.[92] A liability for compensation arises in circumstances where the building is not listed and where the building preservation notice lapses.[93]

Right of entry to carry out repairs to a listed building

23.56 If a listed building is in urgent need of repair and is wholly or partly unoccupied, the LPA may enter the building, on giving the owner not less than seven days' notice, and carry out the necessary work, but, if the building is occupied, only to those parts of the building which are not in use.[94] If the building is in England, the Secretary of State may authorise Historic England to carry out any urgent works which appear to him to be urgently necessary for its preservation, or if the building is in Wales, he may himself execute any such works.[95]

Compulsory purchase

23.57 The Secretary of State or LPA may consider the option of the compulsory purchase (failing an acquisition by agreement)[96] of a listed building in need of repair.[97] Compensation in relation to the compulsory acquisition of a listed

---

[92] LBA 1990, s 3. Before serving such notice, the LPA must request the Secretary of State to consider listing the building (s 3(2)(a)).

[93] LBA 1990, s 29. See *Sample (Warkworth) Ltd v Alnwick District Council* [1984] JPL 670.

[94] LBA 1990, s 54. See *R v Secretary of State for Wales ex parte Swansea City Council* [1999] JPL 524.

[95] Recoupment of expenses from the owner of the building by the LPA or by the Secretary of State or the Commission in the discharge of their responsibilities under LBA 1990, s 54 is provided for under s 55.

[96] LBA 1990, s 52, which need not be confined to a listed building, provided the building in question is of special architectural or historic interest.

[97] LBA 1990, s 47, the pre-condition for whose exercise is the service of a repairs notice on the owner under s 48 (at least two months previously) specifying the works which the authority or the Secretary of State considers to be reasonably necessary for the proper preservation of the building. The owner is not obliged to carry out such repairs, nor, it seems, are the owner's means likely to be relevant in specifying what works are reasonably necessary. See *Robbins v Secretary of State for the Environment* [1989] 1 All ER 878; *Rolf v North Shropshire District Council* [1988] JPL 103.

building will be assessed on the basis of an assumption (the effect of which will be to enhance value) that listed building consent would be granted for any works for the alteration or extension of the building or for its demolition for the purpose of development of any class specified in Schedule 3 to the TCPA 1990 (i.e. development not constituting new development).[98]

Other provisions intended to preserve or enhance heritage assets

23.58 Other provisions of interest involve dangerous structure orders,[99] grants for repair and maintenance,[100] the offence of intentionally causing or permitting the doing of damage to a listed building (which will extend to the owner of the building)[101] and special considerations affecting planning functions.[102]

---

[98] LBA 1990, s 49; i.e. compensation is not assessed on the basis of the site's full redevelopment value on the assumption that it has been cleared. However, where the building has deliberately been allowed to fall into disrepair for the purpose of justifying its demolition (which implies that something more is required than mere dereliction) and the development or redevelopment of the site or any adjoining site, the authority may include in the compulsory purchase order as submitted to the Secretary of State for confirmation a direction for minimum compensation (s 50) (and the Secretary of State may do likewise where he acquires compulsorily under s 47, provided he is satisfied that such a direction is justified). There is a right of appeal to the magistrates (with a further right of appeal to the Crown Court) which may quash the direction for minimum compensation in the compulsory purchase order as confirmed or made by the Secretary of State. A direction for minimum compensation, if confirmed, means a direction that, for the purpose of assessing compensation, it is to be assumed that: (a) planning permission would not be granted for any development or redevelopment of the site of the building; and (b) that listed building consent would not be granted for any works for the demolition, alteration or extension of the building other than development or works necessary for restoring it to and maintaining it in a proper state of repair. This punitive basis for the assessment of compensation on a compulsory purchase of land only arises in this context.

[99] LBA 1990, s 56, whereby the LPA is required to consider using its powers under ss 47 and 48 (compulsory purchase and repairs notices), or s 54 (power to carry out urgent repairs for the preservation of a listed building) before proceeding with its powers under Building Act 1984, s 77 (under which, in the case of a building or structure which is in a dangerous condition, a local authority may apply to a magistrates' court for an order requiring the owner to execute such work as may be necessary to obviate the danger or, if he so elects, to demolish the building or structure); or s 78 (where the local authority make take emergency measures itself in the case of dangerous buildings or structures and may also recover the reasonable expenses of so doing from the owner); or under London Building Acts (Amendment) Act 1939, s 62 (in the case of dangerous and ruinous buildings and of works, such as shoring up, required to be carried out, if necessary, by way of court order on the complaint of the local authority under s 65, in remedying the dangerous condition of the building).

[100] LBA 1990, ss 57–58.

[101] LBA 1990, s 59, which is a separate offence to that involving unauthorised works under s 9.

[102] LBA 1990, s 66(1) and s 67 (publicity for applications affecting setting of listed buildings; see Planning (Listed Buildings and Conservation Area) Regulations 1990 (SI 1990/1519), reg 5A (as

Conservation areas

23.59 Part II of the LBA 1990 contains the statutory code for conservation areas, the concept of which was introduced by the Civic Amenities Act 1967. The provisions governing conservation areas are to be contrasted with those governing listed buildings. For instance, a conservation area is not a form of inferior protection to be bestowed on a single building with a curtilage which simply fails to make the listing grade. There is, however, no rule that land and buildings enclosed as a single entity could not be an 'area' for the purposes of the designation of such area as a conservation area.[103]

---

inserted by the Planning (Listed Buildings and Conservation Areas) (Amendment) (England) Regulations 2004) makes provision for publicity in the case of applications for planning permission affecting the setting of listed buildings.

[103] See *R (GRA Acquisition Ltd) v Oxford City Council* [2015] EWHC 76 (Admin), where it was found that Oxford Stadium could be an 'area' for the purposes of LBA 1990, s 69. See also *R v Canterbury City Council ex parte Halford* [1992] 2 PLR 137 (the section refers to an area and it is unnecessary that every part of that area should have on it something of interest). See also *R v Swansea City Council ex parte Elitestone Ltd* [1992] EGCS 72 and *R v Surrey County Council ex parte Oakimber Ltd* (1995) 70 P & CR 649, where, in light of both cases, it seems plain that the Act confers a broad discretion on authorities to designate land in their area as areas of special architectural or historic interest, the character or appearance of which it is desirable to preserve or enhance. In *Oakimber Ltd*, a claim for judicial review failed in a case where the authority had designated an area of over 350 acres at Brooklands near Weybridge as a conservation area. The area encompassed the former racing track and airfield as a site of historic interest. This was despite the presence of a large-scale commercial and residential development on the site extending to over 2 million square feet. It was alleged that the authority had failed to have regard to the area which should be properly designated as being of historic interest. It was also claimed to be irrational on the basis that there were few features of interest beyond the Brooklands museum, and that there had already been extensive commercial development of the site. The claim was dismissed. It was held that if there was to be a conservation area, it would be appropriate that the area should be broadly contained by the racing track. The line that had been drawn was not irrational. The whole of the area was of historic interest despite the fact that it was largely covered by a modern development. The presence of large-scale commercial and residential development did not remove the site's historic interest. It was held that the court would be slow to interfere with a decision made after proper consultation in circumstances where there had been no allegation of procedural impropriety and where the authority had considerable local knowledge, especially where one of the grounds of the application was irrationality. As against this, a challenge was successful in *R (Arndale Properties Ltd) v Worcester City Council* [2008] EWHC 678 (Admin) (followed by Collins J in *R (Metro Construction Ltd) v Barnet London Borough Council* [2009] EWHC 2956 (Admin)), where it was claimed that the real reason for the designation had been to prevent the demolition of a particular building on land owned by the claimant for judicial review. It was held that the planning committee had failed to consider fully the criteria for designation (the officer's report was criticised as inadequate regarding the proposed designation). In *Trillium (Prime) Property GP Ltd v Tower Hamlets London Borough Council* [2011] EWHC 146 (Admin), a designation was also quashed as it had been vitiated by an officer's report which was misleading in a significant way. For example, members were not told that the area (a former labour exchange building together with four adjacent Victorian warehouses) had previously been rejected for designation or that the labour exchange building

Duty of LPA to consider designation and to review past designations

23.60 Every LPA:[104] (a) shall, from time to time, determine which parts of its area are areas of special architectural or historic interest, the character or appearance of which it is desirable to preserve or enhance; and (b) shall designate those areas as conservation areas.[105] The duty is one which also requires the authority to review the past exercise of its functions and to determine whether any parts or further parts of its area should be designated as conservation areas.[106]

Designation procedure

23.61 The designation procedure is relatively simple and does not require the approval of the Secretary of State.[107] Once made, a designation (and it can be made by ordinary resolution of the authority) must be notified to the Secretary of State[108] and to Historic England.[109] In the case of designations made by the Secretary of State, the latter must notify the relevant LPA and Historic England

---

had been refused local listing because of its lack of architectural merit; members had been given the wrong impression that the proposal had the support of English Heritage; further, reliance had been placed on the protection of the natural environment and on the ecological value and biodiversity of the area, which was not a lawful consideration in the decision to designate. The report should have dealt with the case in a balanced way, especially in the absence of any reference to or analysis of the possible case against it, which those not consulted might have put. However, the court did recognise that the threat to a specific building could be a legitimate reason for designation, where the existence of the building was an important factor in determining the preservation or enhancement of the character or appearance of the area. See also NPPF, para 127, which provides: 'When considering the designation of conservation areas, local planning authorities should ensure that an area justifies such status because of its special architectural or historic interest, and that the concept of conservation is not devalued through the designation of areas that lack special interest.'

[104] In non-metropolitan areas, this will be the district council or unitary council, but outside a National Park a county planning authority may also designate conservation areas. In Greater London, the Historic Buildings and Monuments Commission and the London borough councils have power to designate conservation areas. The Secretary of State may also designate (LBA 1990, s 69(3)).

[105] LBA 1990, s 69(1).

[106] LBA 1990, s 69(2). The designation of any area as a conservation area shall be a local land charge (s 69(4)).

[107] Before making its determination under LBA 1990, s 69, a county planning authority (or National Park authority) must consult the district council of which any part of the land is included in the area to which the proposed determination relates (Sch 4, para 4(2)). Similarly, in Greater London, the Commission must consult with the relevant London borough council and any designation by them must only be with the prior approval of the Secretary of State (s 70(2) and (4)).

[108] LBA 1990, s 70(5)(a).

[109] LBA 1990, s 70(5)(b) (in the case of an area in England).

(if it affects an area in England).[110] Notice of such designations (and it also applies in the case of variations or cancellations of any such designation) must be published in the *London Gazette* and in at least one local newspaper.[111] Notice should also be entered in the local land charges register.[112] There is no provision dealing with objections or representations, and the scheme for designating conservation areas operates outside the ordinary local plan preparation process, even though the local plan will undoubtedly contain policies dealing with the protection to be afforded to conservation areas.

Consequences of designation

23.62 The LPA is under a duty to formulate and publish proposals for the preservation and enhancement of conservation areas (i.e. a conservation area plan) within its area. Proposals must be submitted for consideration to a public meeting in the area to which they relate and the LPA shall have regard to any views concerning the proposals expressed by persons attending the meeting.[113]

23.63 In the exercise, with respect to any buildings or other land in a conservation area, of any of their functions under (*inter alia*) the Planning Acts, the LPA (and the Secretary of State) are under a positive duty to pay special attention to the desirability of preserving or enhancing the character or appearance of that area.[114]

---

[110] LBA 1990, s 70(6).

[111] LBA 1990, s 70(8). There is no procedure which requires an LPA to individually notify owners or occupiers of properties within the affected area.

[112] LBA 1990, s 69(4).

[113] LBA 1990, s 71.

[114] LBA 1990, s 72(1). Accordingly, there is a much higher standard of control over development in a conservation area and the position under this section mirrors that under s 66(1) in the case of listed buildings and its setting. See *Bath Society v Secretary of State for the Environment* [1991] 1 WLR 1303; *South Lakeland District Council v Secretary of State for the Environment* [1991] JPL 654; *R (Maxwell) v Wiltshire County Council* [2011] EWHC 1840 (Admin); *East Northamptonshire District Council & Barnwell Manor Wind Energy Ltd v Secretary of State for Communities and Local Government* [2014] EWCA Civ 137, [2014] 1 WLR 45; *R (Forge Field Society) v Sevenoaks District Council* [2014] EWHC 1895 (Admin). It is now plain that in considering whether to grant planning permission, the LPA is required: (a) by s 66(1) to have special regard to the desirability of preserving the nearby listed buildings or their setting; and (b) in the case of s 72(1), is also obliged to pay special attention to the desirability of preserving or enhancing the character or appearance of a conservation area. Having 'special regard' or paying 'special attention' involves more than merely giving weight to those matters in the planning balance, 'preserving' in the context of ss 66(1) and 72(1) meant doing no harm (see *Forge Field Society*, following *South Lakeland*). There is a strong statutory presumption against granting planning permission for any development which would fail to preserve a listed building's setting or a conservation area's character or appearance. A local authority is not allowed to treat the desirability of preserving those elements as mere material considerations to which it could simply

23.64 Planning applications in cases where the LPA thinks that the proposed development would affect either the setting of a listed building or the character or appearance of a conservation area must be publicised (in the form of a notice in the local press, along with the display of a notice on or near the application site), and due regard had to any representations received in consequence of that publicity.[115]

23.65 Permitted development rights are restricted in conservation areas.[116]

23.66 The demolition of certain buildings in conservation areas (and elsewhere) may require consent.[117]

23.67 Conservation areas may be affected by regulations made for the control of certain types of illuminated advertisements in those areas which justify a degree of special protection on the grounds of amenity. In such cases, an area of special control order for advertisements may be approved. Before formally proposing an

---

attach such weight as it saw fit; when a local authority finds that a proposed development would harm a listed building's setting or a conservation area's character and appearance, it is required to give that harm considerable importance and weight (see *Forge Field Society*, following *Barnwell Manor Wind Energy Ltd*). In *Field Forge Society*, Lindblom J determined that the LPA had balanced the harm to heritage assets against the benefit of providing affordable housing, and had granted planning permission on the basis that the harm was not overriding. Lindblom J ruled that that was a false approach: its effect had been to reverse the statutory presumption against approval. That basic error was fatal to the planning permission. In the circumstances, the LPA should have considered alternative sites (or less harmful uses of the same site in the evaluation of a proposal that could cause harm to a heritage asset – see *R (Gibson) v Waverley Borough Council* [2015] EWHC 3784 (Admin)) because there were clear objections to the proposed development. See also *Jones v Mordue* [2015] EWCA Civ 1243.

[115] LBA 1990, ss 67 and 73, and see Planning (Listed Buildings and Conservation Areas) Regulations 1990 (SI 1990/1519) reg 5A, (inserted by the Planning (Listed Buildings and Conservation Areas) (Amendment) (England) Regulations 2004 (SI 2004/2210)). For Wales, see Planning (Listed Buildings and Conservation Areas) (Wales) Regulations 2012 (SI 2012/793), reg 10, which was revoked and replaced by the 1990 Regulations. In England, the LPA must also send a copy of the (publicity) notice to Historic England.

[116] And permitted development rights may, of course, also be withdrawn by the LPA by way of art 4 directions which apply within specified conservation areas. NPPF, para 200 provides that 'The use of art 4 directions should be limited to situations where this is necessary to protect legal amenity or the wellbeing of the area'. See the helpful comment under this head in the *Encyclopedia of Planning*, Vol 1, at 2-5200–2-5202/1.

[117] See LBA 1990, s 74 (and the need in Wales for conservation area consent in the case of the demolition of buildings in a conservation area); the TCPA 1990 already provides that demolition of buildings requires planning permission (see ss 55(1A)(a) and 57(1)), but reference should be made to GPDO, Sch 2, Pt 1, which is concerned with permitted development rights in the case of heritage and demolition. Demolition of a scheduled ancient monument will require consent under the Ancient Monuments and Archaeological Areas Act 1979, and the demolition of a listed building will usually require consent under the LBA 1990. See *Encyclopedia of Planning* at L74.03 for helpful details on this complex topic.

area of special control, the LPA is expected to consult local trade and amenity organisations about the proposal. Before a direction to remove deemed planning consent is made for specific advertisements, LPAs will be expected to demonstrate that the direction would improve visual amenity and that there is no other way of effectively controlling the display of that particular class of advertisement.[118]

23.68 There are grants and loans available for the preservation or enhancement of conservation areas.[119]

23.69 All trees in conservation areas enjoy special protection.[120]

---

[118] See Town and Country Planning (Control of Advertisements) (England) Regulations 2007 (SI 2007/ 783), regs 7 and 20, and NPPF, para 68.

[119] LPA 1990, ss 77–80 (for Wales, see town scheme agreements in ss 79–80).

[120] TCPA 1990, ss 211–214 and 214A–D. There are exceptions to this protection listed in Town and Country Planning (Tree Preservation) (England) Regulations 2012, reg 15.

Chapter 24

Revisions to the National Planning Policy Framework (July 2018)

INTRODUCTION

24.1   On 24/7/2018 (following the closure of the consultation on 10/5/2018), the Government published revisions to the National Planning Policy Framework 2012 (NPPF) issued in 2012. Planning practice guidance will, where necessary, be updated in due course to reflect these revisions. Under the transitional arrangements set out in Annex 1 to the revised NPPF, plans submitted[1] prior to 24/1/2019 will be examined against the original NPPF, whereas examination in the case of plans submitted after this date will take place under the revised NPPF.

24.2   The revised NPPF has been updated and amended to accommodate judicial decisions on issues of interpretation (such as arose in the conjoined appeals of *Suffolk Coastal District Council v Hopkins Homes Ltd; Richborough Estates Partnership LLP v Cheshire East Borough Council*,[2] which considered the former paragraph 49 and its relation with paragraph 14), the need to simplify housing requirements both in the context of plan-making and appeals and to accelerate the delivery of residential development. To illustrate the scope of the revisions, the new NPPF runs to 73 pages, 211 paragraphs and two annexes, in contrast to 59 pages, 207 paragraphs and three annexes in the case of the original version published in 2012.

24.3   Those routinely involved in planning matters will doubtless wish to download their own copy of the revised NPPF. Unfortunately, the Department of

---

[1]   For spatial development strategies, 'submission' in this context means the point at which the Mayor sends to the Panel copies of all representations made in accordance with Town and Country Planning (London Spatial Development Strategy) Regulations 2000 (SI 2000/1491), reg 8(1), or equivalent. For neighbourhood plans, 'submission' in this context means where a qualifying body submits a plan proposal to the LPA in accordance with Neighbourhood Planning (General) Regulations 2012, reg 15.

[2]   [2017] UKSC 37, [2017] 1 WLR 1865.

Housing, Communities and Local Government (DHCLG) has not produced an updated version of the NPPF which can be read alongside the former version in order that the various changes can be seen at a glance. This is beyond the scope of this book and what is proposed instead is that the main changes will be addressed herein in the approximate order in which they appear in the revised NPPF.

PRESUMPTION IN FAVOUR OF SUSTAINABLE DEVELOPMENT[3]

24.4   The following is taken from the new paragraph 11 of the NPPF:

> For **plan-making** this means that:
>
> (a)   plans should positively seek opportunities to meet the development needs of their area, and be sufficiently flexible to adapt to rapid change;
>
> (b)   strategic policies should, as a minimum, provide for objectively assessed needs for housing and other uses, as well as any needs that cannot be met within neighbouring areas,[4] unless:
>
>> (i)   the application of policies in this Framework that protect areas or assets of particular importance provides a strong reason for restricting the overall scale, type or distribution of development in the plan area;[5] or
>>
>> (ii)   any adverse impacts of doing so would significantly and demonstrably outweigh the benefits, when assessed against the policies in this Framework taken as a whole.

24.5   It should therefore be noted, in the case of plan-making, that there is a requirement to provide for objectively assessed needs, unless specific policies in the NPPF provide 'a strong reason' not to do so.

24.6   The remainder of paragraph 11 provides:

---

[3] Now in NPPF, para 11.

[4] As established through statements of common ground (see para 27 [of the revised NPPF]).

[5] The policies referred to are those in this Framework (rather than those in development plans) relating to: habitats sites (and those listed in para 176) and/or designated as Sites of Special Scientific Interest; land designated as Green Belt, Local Green Space, an Area of Outstanding Natural Beauty (AONB), a National Park (or within the Broads Authority) or defined as Heritage Coast; irreplaceable habitats; designated heritage assets (and other heritage assets of archaeological interest ...); and areas at risk of flooding or coastal change.

For **decision-taking** this means:

(c) approving development proposals that accord with an up-to-date development plan without delay; or

(d) where there are no relevant development plan policies, or the policies which are most important for determining the application are out-of-date,[6] granting planning permission unless:

  (i) the application of policies in this Framework that protect areas or assets of particular importance provides a clear reason for refusing the development proposed;[7]

  (ii) any adverse impacts of doing so would significantly and demonstrably outweigh the benefits, when assessed against the policies in this Framework taken as a whole.

24.7 It should further be noted that, in the case of decision-taking, the former reference to where 'the development plan is absent or silent, or relevant policies are out-of-date' is replaced by 'no relevant development plan policies, or the policies which are most important for determining the application are out-of-date'.

24.8 The presumption in favour of granting permission (which arises, for instance, in cases where relevant policies are out of date) now applies unless (with reference to policies which protect the environment) there is 'a clear reason for refusing the development proposed' (the wording of the former paragraph 14 was that development should be allowed unless specific policies in the NPPF 'indicate that development should be restricted').

ADOPTION OF THE APPROACH ADVOCATED IN THE WRITTEN MINISTERIAL STATEMENT OF DECEMBER 2016 IN THE CASE OF NEIGHBOURHOOD PLANS[8]

24.9 Paragraph 14 provides:

14. In situations where the presumption (at paragraph 11(d) – *see 24.6 above*) applies to applications involving the provision of housing, the adverse impact of allowing

---

[6] This includes, for applications involving the provision of housing, situations where the local planning authority cannot demonstrate a five-year supply of deliverable housing sites (with the appropriate buffer, as set out in para 73); or where the Housing Delivery Test indicates that the delivery of housing was substantially below (less than 75% of) the housing requirement over the previous three years. Transitional arrangements for the Housing Delivery Test are set out in Annex 1.

[7] See fn 5. It should be noted that this is a closed list which notably excludes valued landscapes and severe traffic impact which the Secretary of State has considered to be such policies under the former NPPF.

[8] See para 3.34.

development that conflicts with the neighbourhood plan is likely to significantly and demonstrably outweigh the benefits, provided all of the following apply:[9]

(a)   the neighbourhood plan became part of the development plan two years or less before the date on which the decision is made;

(b)   the neighbourhood plan contains policies and allocations to meet its identified housing requirement;

(c)   the local plan authority has at least a three year supply of deliverable housing sites (against its five year housing supply requirement, including the appropriate buffer as set out in paragraph 73); and

(d)   the local planning authority's housing delivery was at least 45% of that required[10] over the previous three years.

24.10 In short, where the paragraph 11 presumption in favour of sustainable development otherwise applies in the absence of relevant or up-to-date plan policies, the adverse impact of allowing housing schemes which conflict with neighbourhood plans will be presumed to 'significantly and demonstrably outweigh the benefits' where the paragraph 14 proviso applies.

CROSS-BOUNDARY CO-OPERATION

24.11 New cross-boundary working requirements are introduced which require strategic policy-making authorities to provide and maintain statements of common ground with neighbouring authorities (paragraph 27).

PLAN REVIEWS

24.12 Paragraph 33 provides that policies in local plans and spatial development strategies should be reviewed to assess whether there is a need for updating every five years and should then be updated as necessary.[11]

24.13 Paragraph 33 continues:

Relevant strategic policies will need updating at least once every five years if their applicable local housing need figure has changed significantly; and they are likely to require earlier review if local housing need is expected to change significantly in the near future.

---

9   Transitional arrangements are set out in Annex 1.

10   Assessed against the Housing Delivery Test, from November 2018 onwards.

11   In fact reviews at least every five years are a legal requirement for all local plans: see Town and Country Planning (Local Planning) (England) Regulations 2012, reg 10A.

This might appear to be a less stringent review requirement than that proposed in the March 2018 draft, which referred only to actual or anticipated 'increases' in housing need figures.

PLANNING PERFORMANCE AGREEMENTS

24.14 The NPPF and the guidance encourage pre-application engagement. Where the application is going to be large and/or complex, applicants and local planning authorities (LPAs) may sometimes enter into planning performance agreements with a view to agreeing timescales, actions and resources for handling the application. Paragraph 46, in its final form, states that such agreements, '… might achieve a faster and more effective application process … (and) are likely to be needed for applications that are particularly large or complex to determine'.

VIABILITY

24.15 There is more clarity now on the need for viability assessments along with an expectation that they will be publicly available. The new policy should be read together with the new Planning Policy Guidance Note (PPG) on viability.

24.16 The new policy on viability is to be found at paragraph 57:

> Where up-to-date policies have set out the contributions expected from development, planning applications that comply with them should be assumed to be viable. It is up to the applicant to demonstrate whether particular circumstances justify the need for a viability assessment at the application stage. The weight to be given to a viability assessment is a matter for the decision-maker, having regard to all the circumstances of the case, including whether the plan and the viability evidence underpinning it is up-to-date, and any change in site circumstances since the plan was brought into force. All viability assessments, including any undertaken at the plan-making stage, should reflect the recommended approach in national planning guidance, including standardised inputs, and should be made publicly available.

NEW MEANING OF 'DELIVERABLE'

24.17 The new glossary adopts a new definition to the term 'deliverable', replacing the previous definition contained in paragraph 47 (second bullet at footnote 11) which provided that:

> To be considered deliverable, sites should be available now, and be achievable with a realistic prospect that housing will be delivered on the site within five years and in particular that the development of the site is viable.

It will be recalled that the former paragraph 49 provided:

> Relevant policies for the supply of housing should not be considered up-to-date if the local planning authority cannot demonstrate a five-year supply of deliverable housing sites.

The position is now covered under the new paragraph 73 which provides that LPAs

> Should identify and update annually a supply of specific deliverable sites sufficient to provide a minimum of five years' worth of housing against their housing requirement ...

24.18 The new meaning of the term 'deliverable' is set out below and is stricter than the interpretation favoured by the Court of Appeal in *St Modwen v Secretary of State for Communities and Local Government and East Riding of Yorkshire Council:*[12]

> **Deliverable:** To be considered deliverable, sites for housing should be available now, offer a suitable location for development now, and be achievable with a realistic prospect that housing will be delivered on the site within five years. Sites that are not major development, and sites with detailed planning permission, should be considered deliverable until permission expires, unless there is clear evidence that homes will not be delivered within five years (e.g. they are no longer viable, there is no longer a demand for the type of units or sites have long term phasing plans). Sites with outline planning permission, permission in principle, allocated in the development plan or identified on a brownfield register should only be considered deliverable where there is clear evidence that housing completions will begin on site within five years.[13]

---

[12] [2018] JPL 398, where the Court of Appeal held that to be considered deliverable and included within the five-year supply, a site did not necessarily have to have planning permission already granted for housing development on it. Sites might be included in the five-year supply if the likelihood of housing being delivered on them within the five-year period was no greater than a 'realistic prospect'. That did not mean that for a site properly to be regarded as 'deliverable' it had necessarily to be certain or probable that housing would in fact be delivered upon it, or delivered to the fullest extent possible, within five years.

[13] Critics argue that the new definition effectively means that only sites with detailed planning permission will make up the five-year requirement. What of those cases where delivery is beyond an LPA's control? For instance, in many cases one cannot be certain when development will begin on site, such as arises in the case of outline permissions which will often be subject to ownership transactions and revised options for delivery before a final construction programme can be drawn up. What of supervening downturns in the housing market which would mean a reduction in the number of completions coming forward but would not necessarily mean that there was a need for more permissions? The point being made is that LPAs are only responsible for granting permissions and not completions which, paradoxically, might mean that LPAs will be incentivised to set lower figures in their plans which they might find it easier to deliver. The new test might also lead to unintended consequences, such as where developers delay development on brownfield sites to force a release of other more desirable greenfield sites.

INTRODUCTION OF A NEW STANDARDISED METHOD OF CALCULATING HOUSING NEED

24.19 The calculation of housing need is now dealt with under main heading 5, 'Delivering a sufficient supply of homes' (at paragraphs 59 to 79). The new standardised methodology for calculating housing needs (which is aimed at simplifying the setting of a figure for housing need in the context of plan-making and appeals) is introduced at paragraph 60, which states:

> To determine the minimum number of homes needed, strategic policies should be informed by a local housing need assessment, conducted using the standard method in national planning guidance – unless exceptional circumstances justify an alternative approach which also reflects current and future demographic trends and market signals. In addition to the local housing need figure, any needs that cannot be met within neighbouring areas should also be taken into account in establishing the amount of housing to be planned for.

24.20 The new standardised method of calculating housing need takes the Government's household growth projections and applies an affordability ratio, comparing local house prices with workplace earnings, to produce a need figure (with a cut-off point to prevent the authorities' need figures exceeding a certain fixed limit). The Government hopes that the new standardised method of calculating housing need will end protracted disputes on this issue during local plan examinations. In its consultation response, the DHCLG said that it will consider adjusting the methodology in order to meet its 300,000-homes-per-year target by the mid-2020s in view of household growth projections which are expected to be less than previous estimates (in fact, the deficiency is likely to result in some 80,000 too few homes a year).[14]

24.21 Reference should be made to the updated National Planning Practice Guidance (NPPG) issued on 24/7/2018, under the heading: 'Housing and economic development needs assessments' which explains (and contains worked examples of) how the minimum annual local housing need figure is to be calculated using the standard method (using three steps: step 1 – setting the baseline; step 2 – adjusting to take account of affordability; and step 3 – capping the level of any increase).

---

[14] In his article in *Planning* on 26/7/2018 Christopher Young QC said:

'The government has been right to issue a health warning alongside the new NPPF, because otherwise it will mean less houses overall – which would be a complete own goal for a government keen to talk the language of a housing crisis. What needs to happen is a rapid return to the Local Plans Expert Group's version of the standard methodology.'

24.22 It seems plain that authorities facing a big increase in assessed need will have to review how they can meet the increase which might well have a number of unintended consequences, such as: (a) a slow down in the preparation of plans to meet the increase; (b) a divergence between the amount of land allocated for housing and the actual take-up which might mean that developers will cherry-pick sites, not just within a single LPA area but between one area and another; (c) undermining economic growth strategies in certain areas (principally in the north of England) where the LPAs plan only for a minimum number of additional dwellings using the standard method, which focuses future housing growth in areas of highest need and so fails to take account of future economic aspirations elsewhere; (d) distorting actual housing need by linking it to workplace-based earnings which may not recognise the nuances of the different ways in which people live and work in different areas across the country; and (e) risking setting development targets which exceed what the construction industry is able to deliver in any particular area for which deficit the LPA will be responsible.

AFFORDABLE HOUSING

24.23 Provision is made for this in new paragraphs 62 to 64:

62. Where a need for affordable housing is identified, planning policies should specify the type of affordable housing required,[15] and expect it to be met on-site unless:

(a)   off-site provision or an appropriate financial contribution in lieu can be robustly justified; and

(b)   the agreed approach contributes to the objective of creating mixed and balanced communities.

---

[15]   Applying the definition in Annex 2 to the NPPF, viz: (a) Affordable housing for rent meeting the following conditions: (i) the rent is set in accordance with the Government's rent policy for Social Rent (which had been omitted in the draft version) or Affordable Rent, or is at least 20% below local market rents (including service charges where applicable); (ii) the landlord is a registered provider except where it is included as part of a Build to Rent scheme; (iii) it includes provisions to remain at an affordable price for future eligible households, or for the subsidy to be recycled for alternative affordable housing provision; (b) starter homes (as per Housing and Planning Act 2016, ss 2 and 3); (c) discounted market sales housing (housing which is sold at a discount of at least 20% below local market value (eligibility is to be determined with regard to local incomes and local house prices)); and (d) other affordable routes to home ownership which is housing provided for sale which could not be achieved through the market (such as shared ownership, relevant equity loans, other low cost homes for sale (at a price equivalent to at least 20% below market value) and rent to buy). Where public grant funding is provided there should be provisions for homes to remain at an affordable price for future eligible households, or for any receipts to be recycled for alternative affordable housing provision, or refunded to the Government or the relevant authority specified in the funding agreement.

[The above gives rise to a presumption in favour of affordable housing.]

63. Provision for affordable housing should not be sought for residential developments that are not major developments, other than in designated rural areas (where policies may set a lower threshold of 5 units or fewer). To support the re-use of brownfield land, where vacant buildings are being reused or redeveloped, any affordable housing contribution due should be reduced by a proportionate amount.[16]

64. Where major development involving the provision of housing is proposed,[17] planning policies and decisions should expect at least 10% of the homes to be available for affordable home ownership,[18] unless this would exceed the level of affordable housing required in the area, or significantly prejudice the ability to meet the identified affordable housing needs of specific groups. Exemptions to this 10% requirement should also be made where the site or proposed development:

(a)   provides solely for Build to Rent homes;
(b)   provides specialist accommodation for a group of people with specific needs (such as purpose-built accommodation for the elderly or students);
(c)   is proposed to be developed by people who wish to build or commission their own homes; or
(d)   is exclusively for affordable housing, an entry-level exception site or rural exception site.

SMALL SITES REQUIREMENT

24.24 Paragraph 68(a) provides that in the provision of land for new homes, LPAs should identify a sufficient supply and mix of sites. LPAs should:

identify, through the development and brownfield registers, land to accommodate at least 10% of their housing requirement on sites no larger than one hectare, unless it can be shown, through the preparation of relevant plan policies, that there are strong reasons why this 10% target cannot be achieved.

24.25 Under the draft version, the small sites requirement had been 20%, which was considered too high and inflexible to use in practice. Such a policy is intended to promote a good mix of sites as well as give a boost to small- and medium-sized builders on sites which are often built-out relatively quickly.

---

[16]   Equivalent to the existing gross floor space of the existing buildings. This does not apply to vacant buildings which have been abandoned.

[17]   In the new glossary the expression 'major development' means: 'For housing, development where ten or more homes will be provided, or the site has an area of 0.5 hectares or more.'

[18]   As part of the overall affordable housing contribution from the site.

LARGE SCALE DEVELOPMENT

24.26 Paragraph 72 contains a proviso which is supportive of larger scale development. The first part of this paragraph (with emphasis added) is set out below:

> The supply of large numbers of new homes can often be best achieved through planning for larger scale development, such as new settlements or significant extensions to villages and towns, *provided they are well located and designed, and supported by the necessary infrastructure and facilities ...*

24.27 New guidance says that before proposing such development, strategic policy-makers should consider the opportunities presented by existing or planned investment in infrastructure, the area's economic potential and the scope for net environmental gains. The paragraph also requires LPAs: (a) to ensure that the size and location of such developments will support a sustainable community (72(b)); (b) to make a realistic assessment of likely delivery rates (72(d)); and (c) to identify opportunities for supporting rapid implementation (such as through joint ventures or locally-led development corporations) (72(d)).[19]

NEW HOUSING DELIVERY TEST

24.28 Provision for this (and other matters in relation to housing delivery) will be found at paragraphs 73 to 76, which are set out in full in view of their importance. The new test should be read with the draft measurement rule book published alongside the draft NPPF. It is plain that LPAs will now have to meet a tougher test to prove that their supply of housing sites are deliverable (see paragraph 24.17 where the new test for deliverability is set out):

> 73. Strategic policies should include a trajectory illustrating the expected rate of housing delivery over the plan period, and all plans should consider whether it is appropriate to set out the anticipated rate of development for specific sites. Local planning authorities should identify and update annually a supply of specific deliverable sites sufficient to provide a minimum of five years' worth of housing against their housing requirement set out in adopted strategic policies,[20] or against

---

[19] The delivery of large-scale developments may need to extend beyond an individual plan period, and the associated infrastructure requirements may not be capable of being identified fully at the outset. Anticipated rates of delivery and infrastructure requirements should therefore be kept under review and reflected as policies are updated.

[20] For the avoidance of doubt, a five-year supply of deliverable sites for travellers – as defined in Annex 1 to Planning Policy for Traveller Sites – should be assessed separately, in line with the policy in that document.

their local housing need where the strategic policies are more than five years old.[21] The supply of specific deliverable sites should in addition include a buffer (moved forward from later in the plan period) of:

(a)   5% to ensure choice and competition in the market for land; or

(b)   10% where the local planning authority wishes to demonstrate a five year supply of deliverable sites through an annual position statement or recently adopted plan,[22] to account for any fluctuations in the market during that year; or

(c)   20% where there has been significant under delivery of housing over the previous three years, to improve the prospect of achieving the planned supply.[23]

74. A five year supply of deliverable housing sites, with the appropriate buffer, can be demonstrated where it has been established in a recently adopted plan, or in a subsequent annual position statement which:

(a)   has been produced through engagement with developers and others who have an impact on delivery, and been considered by the Secretary of State; and

(b)   incorporates the recommendations of the Secretary of State, where the position on specific sites could not be agreed during the engagement process.

75. To maintain the supply of housing, local planning authorities should monitor progress in building out sites which have permission. Where the Housing Delivery Test[24] indicates that delivery has fallen below 95% of the local planning authority's housing requirement over the previous three years, the authority should prepare an action plan in line with national planning guidance, to assess the causes of under-delivery and identify actions to increase delivery in future years.

76. To help ensure that proposals for housing development are implemented in a timely manner, local planning authorities should consider imposing a planning condition providing that development must begin within a timescale shorter than the

---

[21]   Unless these strategic policies have been reviewed and found not to require updating.

[22]   For the purposes of paras 73b and 74 a plan adopted between 1 May and 31 October will be considered 'recently adopted' until 31 October of the following year; and a plan adopted between 1 November and 30 April will be considered recently adopted until 31 October in the same year.

[23]   From November 2018, this will be measured against the Housing Delivery Test, where this indicates that delivery was below 85% of the housing requirement.

[24]   The new glossary defines this expression as follows: 'Housing Delivery Test: Measures net additional dwellings provided in a local authority area against the homes required, using national statistics and local authority data. The Secretary of State will publish the Housing Delivery Test results for each local authority in England every November'. In terms of implementation, Annex 1 provides as follows: 'The Housing Delivery Test will apply from the day following the publication of the Housing Delivery Test results in November 2018'. Accordingly, the Housing Delivery Test (HDT) is an annual measurement of housing delivery in the area of the relevant plan-making authorities although it does not apply to National Park Authorities, the Broads Authority or to development corporations without full plan-making and decision-making powers. In short, the HDT is a percentage measurement of the number of net homes delivered against the number of homes required as set out in the relevant strategic policies for the areas covered by the HDT.

relevant default period, where this would expedite the development without threatening its deliverability or viability. For major development[25] involving the provision of housing, local planning authorities should also assess why any earlier grant of planning permission for a similar development on the same site did not start.

24.29 It is noteworthy under this head that clarity is given to neighbourhood plans in delivering housing and to the part which LPAs are expected to play in assisting them prior to the adoption of a strategic plan (see paragraph 66).

24.30 The new Housing Delivery Test (HDT) for LPAs comes into force in November 2018. Put shortly, the test will measure the number of homes created against local housing need and will penalise LPAs that under-deliver against various thresholds over a three-year period (see also paras 2.47–2.53 where the new HDT is also addressed). This includes applying the presumption in favour of sustainable development where delivery is found to be below the percentages set out below. It is thought that the new HDT will make a real difference to delivery. Updated guidance is promised.

24.31 At paragraph 215, it is provided that for the purpose of footnote 7 (to be read with paragraph 11(d) – which is concerned with the consequences of out-of-date development plan policies):

delivery of housing which was substantially below the housing requirement means where the Housing Delivery Test results published in:

(a)   November 2018 indicate that delivery was below 25% of the housing required over the previous three years;
(b)   November 2019 indicate that delivery was below 45% of the housing required over the previous three years;
(c)   November 2020 indicate that delivery was below 75% of the housing required over the previous three years.

LOCATIONAL REQUIREMENTS OF STORAGE AND DISTRIBUTION OPERATIONS

24.32 Paragraph 82 states:

Planning policies and decisions should recognise and address the specific locational requirements of different sectors. This includes making provision for clusters or networks of knowledge and data-driven, creative or high technology industries; and

---

[25]   The glossary defines 'major development' in the case of housing as development where ten or more homes will be provided, or the site has an area of 0.5 hectares or more.

for storage and distribution operations at a variety of scales and in suitably accessible locations.

This requirement was absent from the draft revisions, which made no mention of this sector.

TOWN CENTRE USES

24.33 There are changes to the sequential approach to town centre uses. Paragraph 86 provides:

> Local planning authorities should apply a sequential test to planning applications for main town centre uses which are neither in an existing centre nor in accordance with an up-to-date plan. Main town centre uses should be located in town centres, then in edge of centre locations; and only if suitable sites are not available (or expected to become available within a reasonable period) should out of centre sites be considered.

In short, suitable sites in the town centre or edge-of-centre locations include not only those that are 'available', but also those 'expected to become available within a reasonable period'.

MAKING EFFECTIVE USE OF LAND

24.34 The revised NPPF has a new main section on 'Making effective use of land', which states that planning policies and decisions should promote an effective use of land in meeting the need for homes and other uses, while safeguarding and improving the environment and ensuring safe and healthy living conditions.

COMPULSORY PURCHASE

24.35 Local authorities are encouraged to use their compulsory purchase powers to facilitate land assembly (paragraph 119).

24.36 The new section also has a sub-section entitled 'Achieving appropriate densities'. In the 2012 version of the NPPF, LPAs were required to set out their own approach to housing density to reflect local circumstances. The revised NPPF, at paragraph 122, states that:

> Planning policies and decisions should support development that makes efficient use of the land, taking into account:

(a)   the identified need for different types of housing and other forms of development, and the availability of land suitable for accommodating it;

(b)   local market conditions and viability;

(c)   the availability and capacity of infrastructure and services – both existing and proposed – as well as their potential for further improvement and the scope to promote sustainable travel modes that limit future car use;

(d)   the desirability of maintaining an area's prevailing character and setting (including residential gardens), or of promoting regeneration and change; and

(e)   the importance of securing well-designed, attractive ands healthy places.

24.37 Paragraph 123 deals specifically with existing or anticipated shortage of land for meeting identified housing needs. In such cases, it is stated:

> It is especially important that planning policies and decisions avoid homes being built at low densities, and ensure that developments make optimal use of the potential of each site. In these circumstances:
>
> (a)   plans should contain policies to optimise the use of land in their area and meet as much of the identified need for housing as possible. This will be tested robustly at examination, and should include the use of minimum density standards for city and town centres and other locations that are well served by public transport. These standards should seek a significant uplift in the average density of residential development within these areas, unless it can be shown that there are strong reasons why this would be inappropriate;
>
> (b)   the use of minimum density standards should also be considered for other parts of the plan area. It may be appropriate to set out a range of densities that reflect the accessibility and potential of different areas, rather than one broad density range; and
>
> (c)   local planning authorities should refuse applications which they consider fail to make efficient use of land, taking into account the policies in this Framework. In this context, when considering applications for housing, authorities should take a flexible approach in applying policies or guidance relating to daylight and sunlight, where they would otherwise inhibit making efficient use of a site (as long as the resulting scheme would provide acceptable living standards).

HEIGHTENED POLICY EMPHASIS ON QUALITY

24.38 The new NPPF places an emphasis on the creation of high quality buildings and places. It is clearly national policy that design should be taken very seriously during the design process and the revised framework embraces some detailed practical measures intended to drive up development quality. See section 12, 'Achieving well-designed places'. Paragraph 124 states:

> The creation of high quality buildings and places is fundamental to what the planning and development process should achieve. Good design is a key aspect of sustainable

development, creates better places in which to live and work and helps make development acceptable to communities. Being clear about design expectations, and how these will be tested, is essential for achieving this. So too is effective engagement between applicants, communities, local planning authorities and other interests throughout the process.

24.39 The new revisions reiterate that permission should be refused for poor design. Paragraph 130 states:

> Permission should be refused for development of poor design that fails to take the opportunities available for improving the character and quality of an area and the way it functions, taking into account any local design standards or style guides in plans or supplementary planning documents. Conversely, where the design of a development accords with clear expectations in plan policies, design should not be used by the decision-maker as a valid reason to object to the development. Local planning authorities should also seek to ensure that the quality of an approved development is not materially diminished between permission and completion, as a result of changes being made to the permitted scheme (for example through changes to approved details such as materials used).

24.40 A key challenge faced by LPAs is to properly resource the design function of their planning teams. It is also easy to imagine that LPAs under pressure to meet supply targets may be prepared to consider amended design of lower quality (unless that is, objections are raised by the public or councillors). The heightened policy on design will doubtless help LPAs to deal with developers looking to reduce costs (by reducing standards) on grounds of viability after obtaining planning permission.

GREEN BELT POLICY

24.41 Green Belt policy is now to be found in section 13 (whereas it had been in section 9 – policies relating to applications affecting the Green Belt are now to be found in paragraphs 143 to 147).

24.42 Amendments include, at paragraph 136, the necessity to provide a sound evidential basis for altering Green Belt boundaries, 'Once established, Green Belt boundaries should only be altered where exceptional circumstances are fully evidenced and justified, through the preparation and updating of plans …'.

24.43 The same policy also expands neighbourhood plan powers in relation to Green Belt boundary changes, 'Where a need for changes to Green Belt boundaries has been established through strategic policies, detailed amendments to those boundaries may be made through non-strategic policies, including neighbourhood plans'.

24.44 Paragraph 137 states:

> Before concluding that exceptional circumstances exist to justify changes to Green
> Belt boundaries, the strategic policy-making authority should be able to demonstrate
> that it has examined fully all other reasonable options for meeting its identified need
> for development. This will be assessed through the examination of its strategic
> policies, which will take into account the preceding paragraph, and whether the
> strategy:
>
> (a) makes as much use as possible of suitable brownfield sites and underutilised
>   land;
> (b) optimises the density of development in line with policies in chapter 11 of
>   this Framework, including whether policies promote a significant uplift in
>   minimum density standards in town and city centres and other locations well
>   served by public transport; and
> (c) has been informed by discussions with neighbouring authorities about whether
>   they could accommodate some of the identified need for development, as
>   demonstrated through the statement of common ground.

24.45 It is thought that the foregoing represents a tightening of Green Belt release
policy.

24.46 Paragraph 138 gives rise to an expectation that plans will set out ways in
which the impact of removing land from the Green Belt can be offset.

> … Where it has been concluded that it is necessary to release Green Belt land for
> development, plans should give first consideration to land which has been
> previously-developed and/or is well-served by public transport. They should also set
> out ways in which the impact of removing land from the Green Belt can be offset
> through compensatory improvements to the environmental quality and accessibility
> of remaining Green Belt land.

24.47 Paragraph 145(g) contains a new policy permitting the use of brownfield
land in the Green Belt for affordable housing, provided there is no substantial
harm to openness. The full sub-paragraph (formerly paragraph 89 (6th bullet))
provides:

> (g) limited infilling or the partial or complete redevelopment of previously
> developed land, whether redundant or in continuing use (excluding temporary
> buildings), which would:
>
> ▪ not have a greater impact on the openness of the Green Belt than the existing
>   development; or
> ▪ not cause substantial harm to the openness of the Green Belt, where the
>   development would re-use previously developed land and contribute to meeting an
>   identified affordable housing need within the area of the local planning authority.

PROTECTING THE NATURAL ENVIRONMENT

24.48 There is now a presumption that development which causes harm to irreplaceable habitats should be refused. Paragraph 175 provides that when determining applications, LPAs should apply the following principles:

> (c) development resulting in loss or deterioration of irreplaceable habitats (such as ancient woodland and ancient or veteran trees) should be refused, unless there are wholly exceptional reasons[26] and a suitable compensation strategy exists; ...

HERITAGE ASSETS

24.49 Paragraph 193 clarifies the position regarding the weight to be given to an asset's conservation, regardless of the amount of harm arising from the proposed development.

> When considering the impact of a proposed development on the significance of a designated heritage asset, great weight should be given to the asset's conservation (and the more important the asset, the greater the weight should be). This is irrespective of whether any potential harm amounts to substantial harm, total loss or less than substantial harm to its significance.

AGENT OF CHANGE PRINCIPLE

24.50 The revised NPPF confirms the 'agent of change' principle. To protect existing business from complaints from residents of newly-built schemes, paragraph 182 states:

> Where the operation of an existing business or community facility could have a significant adverse effect on new development (including changes of use) in its vicinity, the applicant (or 'agent of change') should be required to provide suitable mitigation before the development has been completed.

MINERALS

24.51 There is a new section dealing with oil, gas and coal exploration and extraction (paragraphs 209 to 211).

---

[26] Such as might arise in the case of infrastructure projects (including nationally significant infrastructure projects, order under the Transport and Works Act and hybrid bills), where the public benefit would clearly outweigh the loss or deterioration of habitat.

24.52 Specifically, paragraph 209(a) states that minerals planning authorities should:

> recognise the benefits of on-shore oil and gas development, including unconventional hydrocarbons,[27] for the security of energy supplies and supporting the transition to a low-carbon economy; and put in place policies to facilitate their exploration and extraction;

---

27   Which would involve proposals for hydraulic fracturing (or 'fracking').

Chapter 25

Assets of Community Value

INTRODUCTION

25.1   This chapter is concerned with assets of community value (ACVs) and the process by which such assets are to be included within a local authority's list of ACVs under the scheme[1] enacted in the Localism Act 2011 (LA 2011).[2] The statutory scheme (which is also known as the community right to bid) and the relevant Regulations[3] came into force in England on 21/9/2012.

25.2   The scheme gives local community groups a right to nominate a building or other land (from local pubs and shops to village halls, community centres and sports stadia) for listing by the local authority (the district or unitary council) as an ACV, the result of which is that when the asset is to be sold, local community groups will be in a position to make a bid to buy it in the open market at its open market value. Nominated assets may be owned by anybody, including the local authority and the Crown.

25.3   The community right to bid (and it should be stressed that there is no community right to buy the asset, merely to bid for it) only arises when the asset's owner decides to sell it. The scheme does not give a right of first refusal to the community group, unlike the equivalent scheme in Scotland, or a right to acquire the asset at a discount. This means that the local community bid to acquire the asset may be unsuccessful as the price or value of the asset is beyond the realistic reach of a community group, in which event the owners can, at the end of the moratorium period, sell to whomever they choose and at whatever price. The owners are also free to do what they want with their property while they own it and they can also negotiate terms with a third party during the moratorium period, although no sale can be concluded during that period unless it is with a local interest community group.

---

[1]   Which extends to England and Wales only (s 239(1)).

[2]   LA 2011, ss 88–108 (Pt 5, Ch 3).

[3]   The Assets of Community Value (England) Regulations 2012 (SI 2012/2421) (ACV Regulations).

25.4   That an asset is listed as an ACV may well be considered to be an important material consideration relating to the use and development of land to which an local planning authority (LPA) is to have regard in dealing with planning applications.[4]

WHAT LAND ASSETS ARE AFFECTED?

25.5   A local authority[5] is required to maintain a list of land[6] in its area that is 'land of community value'.[7] This list is known as its list of ACVs.[8] Where land

---

[4]   TCPA 1990, s 70(2); Planning and Compulsory Purchase Act 2004, s 38(6), 'If regard is to be had to the development plan for the purpose of any determination to be made under the planning Acts the determination must be made in accordance with the plan unless material considerations indicate otherwise'. The Government's guidance (Department for Communities and Local Government, *Community Right to Bid: Non-statutory advice note to local authorities* (DCLG, October 2012) at para 2.20) leaves it open to LPAs to decide whether the listing of an asset as an ACV is a material consideration and in practice this will often be the case. For instance, in two cases taken up by former DCLG ministers, pubs sold and then listed as ACVs have had planning permission refused, with their ACV status cited by both planning authorities in their decisions – this concerned: (a) an application to turn The Bittern pub in the Southampton, Itchen constituency of the Rt Hon John Denham MP (who is no longer the sitting MP for this constituency) into a drive-through McDonald's which was refused; and (b) an application to build on the site of The Porcupine pub (once demolished) in the Bromley and Chislehurst constituency of Robert Neill MP, which was also refused. It is arguable that greater clarity is required as to the status of an ACV listing when planning authorities are considering planning applications in order that investors and local community groups may know where they stand. For instance, to regard an ACV listing as a material consideration on planning applications would certainly be consistent with NPPF, para 70, which emphasises the need for planning and decisions to deal positively for the provision and use of community facilities in order to enhance the sustainability of communities and residential environments. Indeed, planning decisions should guard against the unnecessary loss of valued facilities and services. The Government is, however, unwilling to revise its non-statutory guidance as it takes the view that to do so would interfere with an LPA's discretion in its decision-making in individual cases. The concern is, of course, that if a listing is required to be treated as a material consideration then much-needed development in an area might be discouraged or even thwarted by listings in those cases where the price or value of the relevant land asset was well beyond the realistic reach of a community organisation and where the only reason for the listing was to hold up development.

[5]   LA 2011, s 106: a local authority in relation to England means: (a) a district council; (b) a county council for an area in England for which there are no district councils; (c) a London borough council; (d) the Common Council of the City of London; or (e) the Council of the Isles of Scilly. A local authority in relation to Wales means: (a) a county council in Wales; or (b) a county borough council.

[6]   LA 2011, s 108(1), 'land' for these purposes includes: (a) part of a building; (b) part of any other structure; and (c) mines or minerals, whether or not held with the surface.

[7]   LA 2011, s 87(1).

[8]   LA 2011, s 87(2).

is included in the list, the entry is to be removed from the list at the end of five years.[9]

25.6   A building or other land in a local authority's area is 'land of community value' if in the opinion of the authority:

(a)   an actual current use of the building or other land that is not an ancillary use[10] furthers the social wellbeing or social interests of the local community; and

(b)   it is realistic to think that there can continue to be non-ancillary use of the building or other land which will further (whether or not in the same way) the social wellbeing or social interests of the local community.[11]

25.7   The term 'social interests' includes each of the following: (a) cultural interests; (b) recreational interests; and (c) sporting interests.[12]

25.8   Land which may not currently be land of community value may still qualify for listing if, in the opinion of the authority, there was a time in the recent past when it did qualify and it is realistic to think that there would be a time in the next five years when it could qualify for listing as land of community value.[13] The

---

[9]   LA 2011, s 7(3).

[10]   The scheme accordingly focuses on the primary use of the land rather than on its ancillary uses, which is an important concept in planning control which concentrates on primary use as opposed to incidental or ancillary uses, which may be of a quite different character to a single primary use for the site with no distinction being drawn for planning purposes. Landowners can be expected to argue that the claimed community use may be ancillary to the use of other land and therefore non-qualifying. It is then important to identify the extent of the relevant land asset and to be certain that it has its own main use for the purposes of the LA 2011.

[11]   LA 2011, s 88(1).

[12]   LA 2011, s 88(6).

[13]   LA 2011, s 88(2). Specifically s 88(2) provides that land which may not currently be of community value may nonetheless still be deemed to be of community value:

'if in the opinion of the local authority – (a) there is a time in the recent past when an actual use of the building ... furthered the social wellbeing or interests of the local community, and (b) it is realistic to think that there is a time in the next five years when there could be non-ancillary use of the building or other land that would further (whether or not in the same way as before) the social wellbeing or social interests of the local community.'

In *BHL v St Albans City and District Council* [2016] UKUT 232 (ACC) (11/5/2016), the Upper Tribunal determined that the expressions 'actual current use' in s 88(1)(a) and 'an actual use' in s 88(2)(a) did not import an obligation that the use relied on had to be lawful, and that, in these circumstances, the use need not be lawful unless there is some other way in which the law provided that it should be. In this case, shortly before the land (which comprised a 12-acre parcel within the metropolitan Green Belt crossed by two public footpaths which had a 40-year history of use for walking and as recreational open space) was listed in September 2014, the appellant had lawfully erected fencing along the entire length of the footpaths interspersed with prohibitory signage. Although the fencing was damaged over the following months, any user would have

term 'realistic' in this context connotes a much lower test than the ordinary civil burden. It seems likely that the possibility of a revival in the future of qualifying community use will be 'realistic' provided it is not fanciful or unrealistic on the evidence. For instance, it might be shown that development was unlikely to occur within a commercially viable timescale, bringing with it the possibility that the owner might either sell the premises on the basis of its existing use or else be persuaded to agree to a resumption of relevant community use within the statutory period whilst he decided what to do with the land.[14] On the other hand, where

---

been trespassory. Following the erection of the fencing, the appellant applied for but failed to obtain planning permission to change the use of the field from agricultural use to the keeping of horses, yet the fencing remained in place and the appellant confirmed its intention to maintain exclusion of the land, other than in relation to the public footpaths. In the meantime, the decision to list was upheld by the First-tier Tribunal. The appellant appealed further to the Upper Tribunal which rejected the argument that (in effect) unlawful use (in the sense that it was trespassory) would not justify listing seeing as this was contrary to the clear words of the statute which, in s 88(2)(a), do not refer to an actual 'lawful' use of the building or other land. The landowner's remedy in such circumstances is to challenge the listing on the grounds of an absence of any social wellbeing or social interests of the local community. In other words, technical unlawfulness will not automatically block a listing under s 88 (not least where, as here, there had previously been no objections to the conduct subsequently). The Court of Appeal held (in dismissing the appeal) that the Upper Tribunal did not misdirect itself in law in its construction of the expression 'actual use' for the purposes of LA 2011, s 88, and that, as a result, the local authority had been entitled to list the land as an ACV despite the fact that it had recently been fenced against the public, from which it followed that any current use of it would be trespassory and unlawful (see *Banner Homes Ltd v St Albans City and District Council* [2018] EWCA Civ 1187). This case shows that recourse to the ACV process is yet another string to the bow of those who wish to resist development.

14 *Evenden Estates v Brighton and Hove City Council* [2015] UKFTT CR_2014_0015 (GRC) (24/3/2015). The case concerned a closed public house, and the issue was whether premises which had closed could have community use within the statutory period where an application for planning permission for conversion of the premises to residential use was pending. The First-tier Tribunal found that the premises qualified for listing despite the fact that there was an outstanding application for planning permission as it could still only be marketed on the basis of its existing use as a public house. The view was taken that as the application for planning permission had not been determined, the future of the premises was uncertain and a future qualifying community use was not unrealistic. On any footing, something would have to be done to the premises whilst the owner continued to press for a suitable planning permission, and it was unlikely that they would be left standing idle. They might even be sold on as a public house (even though this had been shown not to be a viable use) or otherwise used for another qualifying social interest, either of which were not unrealistic possibilities. A decision such as this can only but encourage local community groups to bring forward nominations for the listing of public houses with a view to preventing redevelopment with a view to facilitating the continued use of such premises for local community uses. See *BHL v St Albans City and District Council* [2016] UKUT 232 (ACC) (11/5/2016) where the future use point also arose. Section 88(2)(b) sets out as one condition for listing that 'it is realistic to think that there is a time in the next five years' when there could be a relevant use of the building or other land. The First-tier Tribunal had found that the requirements of s 88(2)(b) were satisfied. Reliance was placed on the fact that there had been a long history of peaceable use of the field and it did not consider it 'fanciful' to think that within the next five years there could be non-ancillary use of the land along the lines that pertained prior to the land being fenced. The First-tier Tribunal also said:

matters had moved on since the closure of the community asset, it may be entirely unrealistic to think that there would be a resumption of its former community use, particularly if developers were unlikely to give up their plans for the site.

25.9   The appropriate authority[15] also has wide powers to make regulations which preclude certain specified buildings or land from listing under the LA 2011.[16]

25.10   The term 'land of community value' is therefore extremely wide-ranging and will include almost any building or other land whose use is considered to be of value to the community, as will be the case where its use enhances cultural, recreational or sporting interests within the local authority's area.

25.11   The following types of land asset have been listed as ACVs (the list is not exhaustive): public houses;[17] community centres; shops and post offices; sports

---

'The timing of the decision to fence the footpaths – coming hard upon the listing under the 2011 Act – strikes me as material. Also of significance is the uncertain present planning position of the land, where a recent application for the grazing of horses has been refused. Whilst I note Banner Homes' current stated stance, it is not fanciful, given the history of the field, to think that Banner Homes may well conclude that their relations with the local community will best be served by restoring the status quo or by entering into some form of licence arrangement with the Residents' Association or similar grouping.'

Although the judge of the Upper Tribunal considered that it was always wiser to use the statutory language, in the present context he could not envisage 'any empty space between what is "not fanciful" and what is "realistic" and the First-tier Tribunal was not in error of law on this point'. It was also the view of the Upper Tribunal judge that the question of what is realistic 'is a matter of judgment for the local authority or, on appeal, for the First-tier Tribunal. It is not a matter of veto by the landowner'. The view was taken that the First-tier Tribunal had made a finding that was open to it on the particular facts of the case and the appeal was dismissed. Decisions like this again emphasise the importance of listing which, whilst not in itself sufficient to prevent land being developed, as a matter of planning policy may be sufficient to result in the refusal of planning permission while the land is listed. Indeed, there is anecdotal evidence that the status of land as an asset of community value is, in a number of instances, leading to the refusal of applications for planning permission. This means that an ACV listing could well be acting to cushion the decline in village green registrations (where recent reform and a number of decisions in the higher courts have limited the scope for registration) as a realistic basis for preventing or delaying development.

[15]   See fn 5.

[16]   LA 2011, s 88(3)–(5).

[17]   There are currently around 1,200 public houses listed although only a handful have been acquired by community groups. Public houses are the most popular type of asset to be listed as an ACV. The popularity of listing public houses before they have been put up for sale or sold (which has been vigorously promoted by the Campaign for Real Ale – CAMRA) has been accelerated by the closure (and subsequent redevelopment) of large numbers of such premises as a result of the smoking ban, cheap supermarket alcohol and (until recently) the ease with which permitted development rights could be utilised to convert pubs (a Class A4 planning use) to (for instance) shops or supermarkets selling alcohol (a Class A1 planning use) or to restaurants and cafés (a

stadia;[18] playing fields, parks and other public open space;[19] churches; libraries; car parks; and allotments. Other assets listed have included South Bank Undercroft, a pier, mills and museums, bus shelters and doctors' surgeries.

LAND WHICH IS NOT OF COMMUNITY VALUE AND WHICH CANNOT BE LISTED

Residential property[20]

25.12 The exclusion under this head includes land which is connected with the residence.[21] Land is connected with a residence if: (a) the land and the residence

---

Class A3 planning use) or even demolition. However, since 6/4/2015 (by virtue of an amendment made to the Town and Country Planning (General Permitted Development) (Amendment) (England) Order 2015 (SI 2015/659)), permitted development rights have been disapplied for specified periods in the case of the change of use or demolition of buildings used for a purpose falling within Class A4 (namely drinking establishments). The order provides that where a drinking establishment has been listed as an ACV, permitted development rights are disapplied (and for which, as a consequence, planning permission will be required) for five years unless the listing has been cancelled following a successful review or appeal, or because the local authority no longer considers the building to be of community value. Where the pub has only been nominated for listing, permitted development rights are disapplied for only 56 days, but if the asset is not listed then any change of use or demolition must still take place within one year of the request for listing. Before these changes, removing permitted development rights from specific buildings could only be secured by way of art 4 directions which local authorities were loath to use for fear of being liable for compensation (which is payable within 12 months of an art 4 direction being issued) which may occur where planning permission for development is refused which would otherwise have been permitted development or where permission is granted subject to more limiting conditions than the general permitted development order).

18 Included within this head are the football stadia of Anfield (home of Liverpool FC – on the nomination of a group calling itself the Spirit of Shankley), Old Trafford (home of Manchester United FC – on the nomination of the Manchester United Supporters' Trust), Portman Road (home of Ipswich Town FC – on the nomination of Ipswich Town Supporters' Trust), The Valley (home of Charlton Athletic FC – on the nomination of Charlton Athletic Supporters' Trust), St Andrews (home of Birmingham City FC – on the nomination of the Blues (Birmingham City) Trust), the Kassam stadium (home of Oxford United FC – on the nomination of OxVox, The Independent Oxford United Supporters' Trust) and Bloomfield Road (home of Blackpool FC).

19 Such as Myddleton Square in Islington. It is worthy of note that whereas land held by local authorities (in the exercise of their statutory powers) for the purposes of public recreation or on which recreation takes place by permission would not be registrable as a town or village green (*R (Barkas) v North Yorkshire County Council* [2014] UKSC 31) on the ground that such use was 'by right' and not 'as of right', such land, even if held on this basis, would not be precluded from listing as an ACV. Publicly owned land used for local sports or other community purposes (perhaps even for circuses and funfairs in the summer months) would probably have little difficulty in qualifying for listing.

20 ACV Regulations, reg 3 and Sch 1, paras 1–2.

21 ACV Regulations, Sch 1, para 2. The term 'residence' means a building used or partly used as a residence and a building is a residence if: (a) it is normally used or partly used as a residence, but

are owned by a single owner; and (b) every part of the land can be reached from the residence without having to cross land which is not owned by that single owner.[22] This exclusion includes gardens, outbuildings and other associated land, including land which cannot be reached from the residence by reason only of intervening land in other ownership on which there is a road, railway line, river or canal, provided that it is reasonable to think that the requirement in point (b) above would be satisfied if the intervening land were to be removed leaving no gap.[23] Land may still be listed, even if it comprises a residence together with land connected with that residence, if: (a) the residence is a building that is only partly used as a residence; and (b) but for that residential use of the building, the land would be eligible for listing.[24] This exception to the general exclusion in the case of residential land applies where an asset which could otherwise be listed contains integral residential quarters, such as might apply to accommodation as part of a public house or a caretaker's flat.

Land licensed for use as a residential caravan site[25]

25.13 Under this head, we are concerned with land in respect of which a site licence is required under Part 1 of the Caravan Sites and Control of Development Act 1960, or would be so required if paragraphs 1, 4, 5 and 10 to 11A of Schedule 1 to that Act were omitted (i.e. some types of residential caravan site which do not need a licence).

Operational land of statutory undertakers[26]

25.14 This exclusion concerns land as defined in TCPA 1990, section 263, namely, land used for the purposes of the undertaking concerned, or if an interest is held in it for that purpose. Thus it includes land which the undertaker owns for

---

for any reason so much of it as is normally used as a residence is temporarily unoccupied; (b) it is let or partly let for use as a holiday letting; (c) it, or part of it, is an hotel or is otherwise principally used for letting or licensing accommodation to paying occupants; or (d) it is a house in multiple occupation as defined in Housing Act 2004, s 77. However, a building or other land is *not* a residence if: (a) it is land on which currently there are no residences but for which planning permission or development consent has been granted for the construction of residences; (b) it is a building undergoing construction where there is planning permission or development consent for the completed building to be used as a residence, but construction is not yet complete; or (c) it was previously used as a residence but is in the future to be used for a different purpose and planning permission or development consent for a change of use to that purpose has been granted.

22   ACV Regulations, Sch 1, para 1(2).
23   ACV Regulations, Sch 1, para 1(3) and (4).
24   ACV Regulations, Sch 1, para 1(5).
25   ACV Regulations, Sch 1, para 3.
26   ACV Regulations, Sch 1, para 4.

future operational use, but will not include land which is held purely for investment.

WHO MAY NOMINATE AN ASSET FOR INCLUSION IN THE LIST OF ACVs?

25.15 Local authorities can only list land in response to a nomination by a community body.[27] For a local group to be able to nominate land (known as a 'community nomination') it will have to demonstrate that its activities are wholly or partly concerned with the local authority area where the asset sits or with a neighbouring authority (an authority which shares a boundary with the authority in which the asset is located).

25.16 A 'community nomination' may be made:[28] (a) by a parish council in respect of land in England in the parish council's area;[29] (b) by a community council in respect of land in Wales in the community council's area;[30] or (c) by a person that is 'a voluntary or community body' (being an unincorporated group) with 'a local connection'.[31]

25.17 The ACV Regulations provide that 'a voluntary or community body' means:

(a)   a body designated as a neighbourhood forum pursuant to section 61F of the TCPA 1990;[32]
(b)   a parish council;[33]
(c)   an unincorporated body: (i) whose members include at least 21 individuals; and (ii) which does not distribute any surplus it makes to its members;[34]
(d)   a charity;[35]
(e)   a company limited by guarantee which does not distribute any surplus it makes to its members;[36]

---

27   LA 2011, s 89(1).
28   LA 2011, s 89(2)(b).
29   LA 2011, s 89(2)(b)(i).
30   LA 2011, s 89(2)(b)(ii).
31   LA 2011, s 89(2)(b)(iii).
32   ACV Regulations, reg 5(1)(a).
33   ACV Regulations, reg 5(1)(b).
34   ACV Regulations, reg 5(1)(c).
35   ACV Regulations, reg 5(1)(d).
36   ACV Regulations, reg 5(1)(e).

(f)   a co-operative or community benefit society, i.e. a registered society within the meaning given by section 1(1) of the Co-operative and Community Benefit Societies Act 2014, other than a society registered as a credit union;[37]

(g)   a community interest company (which is a company which satisfies the requirements of Part 2 of the Companies (Audit, Investigations and Community Enterprise) Act 2004 (especially sections 26, 35 and 36(A)).[38]

25.18 The expression 'a local connection' is defined in the ACV Regulations,[39] which provide that a body (other than a parish council) has a local connection with land in a local authority's area if:

(a)   the body's activities (i.e. those bodies mentioned in 25.17 at (a), (c), (d), (e), (f) and (g) above) are wholly or partly concerned with the local authority's area or with a neighbouring authority's area;[40]

(b)   in the case of a bodies mentioned in 25.17 at (c), (e) and (f) above, they do not distribute any surplus they make to their members; instead, any surplus is wholly or partly applied for the benefit of the local authority's area or for the benefit of a neighbouring authority's area;[41] and

(c)   in the case of an unincorporated body, it has at least 21 local members.[42] For these purposes, the expression 'local member' means a member who is registered, at an address in the local authority's area or in a neighbouring authority's area, as a local government elector in the register of local government electors.[43]

25.19 Typically, a nomination will be made by an *ad hoc* body comprising a group of individuals, at least 21 of whom are local electors, which has been formed to try to save an asset, but which has not yet reached the stage of acquiring a formal charitable or corporate structure.

Contents of community nominations[44]

25.20 A community nomination must include: (a) a description of the nominated land including its proposed boundaries;[45] (b) a statement of all the information

---

[37]   ACV Regulations, reg 5(1)(f) and (3).

[38]   ACV Regulations, reg 5(1)(g).

[39]   ACV Regulations, reg 4.

[40]   ACV Regulations, reg 4(1)(a).

[41]   ACV Regulations, reg 4(1)(b).

[42]   ACV Regulations, reg 4(1)(c).

[43]   ACV Regulations, reg 4(3).

[44]   ACV Regulations, reg 6.

[45]   ACV Regulations, reg 6(a).

which the nominator has with regard to: (i) the names of the current occupants of the land; and (ii) the names and current last-known addresses of all those holding a freehold or leasehold estate in the land;[46] (c) the nominator's reasons for thinking that the authority should conclude that the land is of community value;[47] and (d) evidence that the nominator is eligible to make a community nomination.[48]

Procedure after a nomination has been made

25.21   The local authority must decide whether land nominated by a community nomination should be included in its list of ACVs within eight weeks of receiving the nomination.[49] The authority must take all practical steps to give the information that it is considering listing the land to: (a) a parish council if any of the land is in the council's area;[50] (b) the owner of the land;[51] (c) where the owner is not the freeholder of the land: (i) the holder of the freehold estate in the land;

---

[46]   ACV Regulations, reg 6(b).

[47]   ACV Regulations, reg 6(c).

[48]   ACV Regulations, reg 6(d).

[49]   ACV Regulations, reg 7. It should also be noted here that if different parts of any land are in different local authority areas, the local authorities concerned must co-operate with each other in carrying out their functions in relation to the nominated land or any part of it (LA 2011, s 102). This can arise, for instance, where nominations are made in relation to extensive tracts of undeveloped land in the countryside which straddle different local authority areas.

[50]   ACV Regulations, reg 8(a).

[51]   ACV Regulations, reg 8(b). The term 'owner' is defined in reg 19(3)(a) and LA 2011, s 107, and for these purposes is taken to mean the person in whom the freehold or leasehold estate is vested. The definition therefore ensures that only one level of legal proprietary rights will qualify as ownership for the purposes of the Act. If there are two or more qualifying leasehold estates in the same land, the owner of the land is the person in whom the qualifying leasehold estate is vested that is more or most distant from the freehold estate. In other words, if there are a number of leases, the leaseholder with a qualifying lease or sub-lease most distant from the freeholder will be the owner for the purposes of the Act. The term 'qualifying leasehold estate' means an estate by virtue of a lease of the land for a term which, when granted, had at least 25 years to run. Regulation 19(3)(a) provides that the term 'owner' will include a person who would be an owner as defined in s 107: (a) but for the effect of Land Registration Act 2002, s 7(1) and (2) (where a failure to comply with the obligation to register imposed by s 6 renders the transfer, grant or creation of a legal estate void, in which event (see s 7(2)(a)) the transferor holds the estate on a bare trust for the transferee; where a legal estate is granted or created in a case falling within s 4(1)(c)–(g) (certain leaseholds and the creation of a protected first legal mortgage), the grant or creation avoided operates as a contract for valuable consideration to grant or create the legal estate concerned (see s 7(2)(b)); or (b) in the case of dispositions which are required to be completed by registration (such as would apply, for instance, in the case of a lease for more than seven years or in pursuance of Housing Act 1985, Pt 5 (the right to buy)) within the meaning of Land Registration Act 2002, s 27(2)(b), as if the disposition to that person had in fact been completed by registration.

and (ii) the holder of any leasehold estate in the land other than the owner;[52] and (d) any lawful occupant of the land.[53]

25.22 The nomination must be considered by the local authority[54] and must be accepted if: (a) the land is in the authority's area; and (b) is of community value.[55] In such a case, the authority is required to include the land in its list of ACVs.[56] If the nomination is unsuccessful, the authority must give, to the person who made the nomination, the authority's written reasons for its decision that the land could not be included in its list of ACVs.[57]

25.23 Whenever land is included in, or removed from, a local authority's list of ACVs, the authority must give written notice of the inclusion or removal to the following persons: (a) the owner of the land;[58] (b) the occupier of the land if the occupier is not also the owner;[59] (c) if the land was included in the list in response to a community nomination, the person who made the nomination;[60] and (d) any person specified, or of a description specified, in regulations made by the Secretary of State in England and, in Wales, by the Welsh Ministers.[61]

25.24 However, where it appears to the authority that it is not reasonably practical to give such notice (i.e. where an authority is unable to give notice in the usual way due, for instance, to lack of names or addresses), the authority must instead take reasonable alternative steps for the purpose of bringing notice of these matters to the person's attention. This might well include a notice attached to a property. Any such notice should also provide details of the statutory provisions relating to community assets and bids under Chapter 3 of Part 5 of the LA 2011,[62] drawing particular attention to: (a) the consequences for the land and its owner of the land's inclusion in the list;[63] and (b) the right to ask for a review under section 92.[64]

---

[52] ACV Regulations, reg 8(c).

[53] ACV Regulations, reg 8(d).

[54] LA 2011, s 90(2).

[55] LA 2011, s 90(3).

[56] LA 2011, s 90(4).

[57] LA 2011, s 90(6).

[58] LA 2011, s 91(2)(a).

[59] LA 2011, s 91(2)(b).

[60] LA 2011, s 91(2)(c).

[61] LA 2011, s 91(2)(d). See ACV Regulations, reg 9, which also requires the authority to give written notice to any freeholders and leaseholders of the asset who are not the owners, together with the parish council if any of the land is within the council's area.

[62] LA 2011, s 91(3).

[63] LA 2011, s 91(3)(a).

[64] LA 2011, s 91(3)(b).

25.25 Lastly, a notice that the land is being removed from the list must state the reasons for the removal.[65]

RIGHT TO A REVIEW

25.26 The owner of land which has been included in a local authority's list of ACVs may ask the authority to review the authority's decision to include the land in the list.[66] The procedure for a listing review is set out in regulation 10 of, and Schedule 2 to, the ACV Regulations. The land will remain listed while the review is carried out. The AVC Regulations provide that a request for a listing review must be made in writing before the end of the period of eight weeks beginning with the day on which written notice of inclusion of the land in the list was given by the authority under section 91(2) of the LA 2011, or such longer period as the authority may in writing allow. Where the authority is forced to take alternative reasonable steps to bring the notice to the attention of the owner, a request for a listing review must be made before the end of a period of eight weeks beginning with the day on which the authority completes the taking of those steps.[67]

Procedure for reviews

25.27 An officer of the authority of appropriate seniority who did not take part in making the decision to be reviewed shall carry out the review and make the review decision.[68] The owner may appoint any representative to act on his or her behalf in connection with the review.[69] The local authority must provide any relevant documents to the owner or the owner's representative.[70] As soon as is practicable after the request for a review, the authority must notify the owner of the procedure to be followed in connection with the review.[71] An oral hearing must take place at the owner's written request,[72] but where no written request is made the authority may decide whether or not to include an oral hearing in the review process.[73] The owner and/or the owner's representative may make representations to the reviewer orally or in writing, or both orally and in writing.[74]

---

[65]   LA 2011, s 91(4).
[66]   LA 2011, s 92(1).
[67]   ACV Regulations, Sch 1, para 1.
[68]   ACV Regulations, Sch 1, para 4.
[69]   ACV Regulations, Sch 1, para 5(1).
[70]   ACV Regulations, Sch 1, para 5(2).
[71]   ACV Regulations, Sch 1, para 6.
[72]   ACV Regulations, Sch 1, para 7(1).
[73]   ACV Regulations, Sch 1, para 7(2).
[74]   ACV Regulations, Sch 1, para 8.

The authority must complete its review within eight weeks beginning with the date the authority receives the written request for the review, or such longer period as is agreed with the owner in writing.[75] It seems plain that an authority should usually be thinking in terms of an oral review hearing, and those representing owners should request this at an early stage in the process. The owner and the local authority must bear their own costs of the review.

25.28 Where an authority reviews its decision, it must notify the person who asked for the review: (a) of the decision on the review; and (b) of the reasons for the decision.[76] If the decision on the review is that the land should not have been listed as an AVC: (a) the authority must remove the entry for the land from the list;[77] and (b) where the land was included in the list in response to a community nomination: (i) the nomination becomes unsuccessful; and (ii) the authority must provide written reasons to the person who made the nomination.[78] The authority should also inform the owner of his right to an independent appeal if there is dissatisfaction with the outcome of the review.

APPEALS AGAINST LISTING REVIEW DECISIONS

25.29 An appeal may be made to the First-tier Tribunal (General Regulatory Chamber) against the decision on a listing review. An appeal may be made by either the owner or, if the land has been sold in the meantime, a subsequent owner of part or the whole of the land. It should be noted that a right of appeal does not extend to nominators if the local authority decide not to list the land. In such a case, the remedy is to seek a judicial review.

25.30 The time for appealing is 28 days from the date on which notice of the decision being appealed against was sent to the owner of the land. The land remains listed during the appeal process.[79]

25.31 If a local community group wishes to challenge a listing authority's decision not to list the asset in circumstances where the situation has materially changed, their best course of action is to re-nominate immediately. The legislation does not prevent re-nomination of the same land, although an authority will

---

[75] ACV Regulations, Sch 1, para 9.

[76] LA 2011, s 92(3).

[77] LA 2011, s 92(4)(a).

[78] LA 2011, s 92(4)(b).

[79] Appeals may be sent to: Tribunal Clerk, Community Right to Bid Appeals, HM Courts & Tribunals Service, First-tier Tribunals, PO Box 9300, Leicester LE1 8DJ, or emailed to: GRC.CommunityRights@hmcts.gsi.gov.uk.

always be looking for relevant new evidence or a change of circumstances if a fresh application for nomination is to stand any reasonable prospects of success.[80]

LIST OF LAND NOMINATED BUT UNLISTED

25.32 If the local authority does not agree that the asset nominated meets the required test for land of community value, or that the land falls within one of the excluded categories, it must place the land on a list of assets nominated but not listed, which it is also required to maintain.[81]

PUBLICATION AND INSPECTION OF LISTS

25.33 The local authority must publish its list of ACVs and its list of unsuccessful community nominations.[82] Both of these lists should be available for free inspection by any person, and the authority must provide a free copy of either list to anyone who asks for it.[83]

MORATORIUM REQUIREMENTS ON DISPOSALS OF LISTED LAND

25.34 This section deals with the moratorium requirements which apply only to 'a relevant disposal' of the land.[84] A disposal is a 'relevant disposal' in the case of freehold land if it is a disposal with vacant possession.[85] In the case of a qualifying leasehold estate,[86] the relevant disposal will be a grant or assignment

---

[80] Note, however, the possibility of a *res judicata* estoppel.

[81] LA 2011, s 93(1)–(4). Such list is known as the authority's 'list of land nominated by unsuccessful community nominations'. Where land is included in such list, the entry: (a) may (but need not) be removed from the list after five years (it is then for the local authority to decide how long it holds unsuccessful nominations on this list); and (b) while it is in the list, to include the reasons given to the person who made the nomination for the authority's decision not to include the land in the authority's list of ACVs, including any reasons given on any review of such decision. The purpose of such list is to ensure transparency and to avoid multiple nominations in the case of an asset which does not meet the relevant definition.

[82] LA 2011, s 94(1).

[83] LA 2011, s 94(2)–(5).

[84] LA 2011, s 95. In other words, the moratorium rules in s 95 apply only to disposals of listed land and would not, for instance, apply if a building was going to be demolished without being sold.

[85] LA 2011, s 96(2).

[86] LA 2011, ss 96(6) and 107(3)–(5): a 'qualifying leasehold estate' means an estate by virtue of a lease of the land for a term which, when granted, had at least 25 years to run. If there is only one leasehold estate the owner of the land is the person in whom that estate is vested. If there are a

of the leasehold estate with vacant possession.[87] If a 'relevant disposal' in the case of either freehold or leasehold land is made in pursuance of a binding agreement, the disposal is treated as being entered into when the agreement becomes binding.[88]

25.35 An owner of listed land must *not* enter into a relevant disposal *unless each* of what are described as conditions A–C is met.[89]

25.36 Condition A is that the owner has notified the local authority in writing of that person's wish to enter into a relevant disposal of the land.[90]

25.37 Condition B is that either:

(a) the interim moratorium period has ended[91] without the local authority having received during that period, from any community interest group,[92] a written request for the group to be treated as a potential bidder in relation to the land;[93] or

(b) the full moratorium period has ended.[94]

---

number of leases in the same land the owner, for these purposes, is the person whose lease is more distant (in terms of the number of intervening leasehold estates) from the freehold estate.

[87] LA 2011, s 96(3).

[88] LA 2011, s 96(4) (i.e. on exchange of contracts). Subject to this requirement, a relevant disposal is entered into when it takes place (s 96(5)).

[89] LA 2011, s 95(1).

[90] LA 2011, s 95(2). If a local authority receives notice under s 95(2) of an owner's wish to sell the listed land, it must cause to be entered in the list of ACVs particulars of such notice and the expiry dates of the initial moratorium period, the full moratorium period and the protected period that apply as a result of the notice (s 97(2)). If the land has been listed in response to a community nomination, the authority must also give written notice to the person who made the nomination of the matters to be listed following receipt of the owner's notice under s 95(2) (s 97(3)). The local authority is also required to publicise all of these matters in the area where the land is situated and it is for the local authority to determine how it does this (s 97(4)).

[91] LA 2011, s 95(6): the 'interim moratorium period' means the period of six weeks beginning with the date on which the local authority receives notification under Condition A (i.e. in accordance with s 95(2)).

[92] LA 2011, s 95(6): the term 'community interest group' is defined in ACV Regulations, reg 12(b).

[93] Once the authority receives from a community interest group a written request for the group to be treated as a potential bidder for the land, it must as soon as practicable either pass on the request to the owner or inform the owner of the details of the request (LA 2011, s 98(2)).

[94] LA 2011, s 95(3). The term 'the full moratorium period' means the period of six months beginning with the date on which the local authority receives notification under s 95(2) in relation to the disposal (s 95(6)).

25.38 Condition C is that the protected period has not ended.[95]

25.39 The moratorium provisions do not apply to those types of relevant disposals which are exempt. These exemptions are partly to be found in the LA 2011[96] and partly in the ACV Regulations,[97] and are set out at paragraphs 25.41–25.64.

MORATORIUM SUMMARY

25.40 A landowner may not dispose of listed land (except in those cases where the relevant disposals are exempt) until certain conditions are met:

(a) The landowner must first notify the authority that he intends to dispose of the land with vacant possession (i.e. by way of a sale of the freehold or the grant or assignment of a lease of at least 25 years), whereupon the local authority will duly publicise the proposed sale and will inform the community group who made the nomination.

(b) If, after a period of six weeks beginning with the date on which the local authority receives notification from the owner of the listed land that he intends to dispose of the land (i.e. the interim moratorium period), the authority has not received any request from any community interest group that they wish to be treated as a potential bidder for the land, the owner may sell or lease the land to any party.

(c) If, before the expiry of the six-week period, a community interest group notifies the local authority that it wishes to be treated as a potential bidder for the listed land (and it does not need to produce evidence that it will actually be in a position to make a bid for the land),[98] the full moratorium period of six months applies so that if, for instance, just before the end of the initial six-week period, the community group duly notifies the authority of its interest, there is then a further period of approximately four and a half months in which the community interest group can, if it wants, formulate a plan for its hoped-for purchase of the listed land. Until the full moratorium period of six months has elapsed, the owner may only sell the listed land to a community interest group.[99]

---

[95] LA 2011, s 95(4). The term 'the protected period' means the period of 18 months beginning with the date on which the local authority receives notification under s 95(2) in relation to the disposal (s 95(6)).

[96] LA 2011, s 95(5).

[97] ACV Regulations, reg 13(2) and Sch 3.

[98] The local authority must as soon as practicable let the owner know that this request has been received.

[99] ACV Regulations, reg 13(1).

(d)   Once the moratorium period of six months has ended, the owner may sell the listed land to any party within a period of 12 months (this is the expiry of the protected period). If the land is not sold before the protected period has expired (i.e. within 18 months beginning with the date on which the local authority received the owner's notification that he wished to sell the listed land), a further moratorium process must be followed before the owner can sell or grant a lease of the listed land.

EXEMPTIONS TO THE MORATORIUM PROVISIONS[100]

25.41   A disposal to a local community interest group which may be made during a moratorium period.[101]

25.42   A disposal which is a gift (including a gift to trustees of any trusts by way of settlement upon the trusts).[102]

25.43   A disposal by personal representatives of a deceased person in accordance with the provisions of a will or under the intestacy rules.[103]

25.44   A disposal by personal representatives in order to raise money to pay debts, liabilities or expenses in the course of the administration of a deceased's estate or to pay pecuniary legacies or satisfy some other entitlement under a will or under the intestacy rules.[104]

25.45   A disposal between family members – for these purposes a 'family member' is the owner's spouse or civil partner and descendants of the owner's grandparents, which includes the owner's parents but not the grandparents.[105]

25.46   A disposal of land which is only partly listed which satisfies the following conditions: (a) the land is owned by a single owner; and (b) every part of the land

---

[100]   In other words, where the disposal in question is not 'a relevant disposal' within the meaning of the LA 2011, s 95(1) with the result that the owner is not required to notify the authority of his intention to dispose of the land under s 95(2). If the owner is unsure as to whether or not he is going to succeed in making an exempt disposal, he may sensibly decide to notify the authority as a precaution for advice on whether the disposal is in fact exempt. The owner may feel it necessary to explain to the authority that the disposal is exempt, and the authority may find that this would be helpful to it if the owner did so.

[101]   ACV Regulations, reg 13(1).

[102]   LA 2011, s 95(5)(a).

[103]   LA 2011, s 95(5)(b).

[104]   LA 2011, s 95(5)(c).

[105]   LA 2011, s 95(5)(d).

can be reached from every other part without having to cross land belonging to a third party (and this condition will be taken to be satisfied if every part of the land cannot be reached from every other part of the land because the intervening land is a road, railway, river or canal, provided it was reasonable to think that this requirement would be made out if the intervening land were to be removed leaving no gap).[106]

25.47 A disposal of land on which a business is carried on, together with the sale of that business as a going concern.[107] The concern here is that whilst the rules permit land to be sold on which a business is carried on, the exemption is clearly open to abuse in circumstances where the purchaser (e.g. of a public house) has no intention of retaining the land in its present use.

25.48 A disposal occasioned by somebody becoming or ceasing to be a trustee.[108]

25.49 A disposal by trustees to donees in satisfaction of an entitlement under a trust or in the exercise of a power to re-settle trust property on other trusts.[109]

25.50 A disposal occasioned by a person ceasing to be a partner in a partnership.[110]

25.51 A disposal made in pursuance of a court order.[111]

25.52 A disposal made pursuant to a separation agreement made between spouses or civil partners including disposals made between former spouses or former civil partners relating to the care of dependent children.[112]

25.53 A transfer (not in pursuance of a court order) made in pursuance of a statutory provision relating to incapacity, with 'incapacity' widely defined to include physical and mental impairment and any interference with capacity to deal with financial and property matters.[113]

25.54 A disposal made in pursuance of a legally enforceable requirement that it should be made to a specific person, including: (a) disposals required under a planning obligation entered into in accordance with TCPA 1990, section 106; or

---

[106] LA 2011, s 95(5)(e) and ACV Regulations, Sch 3, para 11.

[107] LA 2011, s 95(5)(f).

[108] LA 2011, s 95(5)(g).

[109] LA 2011, s 95(5)(h).

[110] LA 2011, s 95(5)(i).

[111] ACV Regulations, Sch 3, para 1.

[112] ACV Regulations, Sch 3, para 2.

[113] ACV Regulations, Sch 3, para 3.

(b) made in pursuance of the exercise of a legally enforceable: (i) option to buy; (ii) nomination right; (iii) right of pre-emption; or (iv) right of first refusal, *provided* that, in the case of a disposal under (a), the land was *not* listed when the planning obligation was entered into, and in the case of a disposal under (b), the land was *not* listed when the option or other rights were granted.[114]

25.55 A disposal within the Crichel Down rules (i.e. where the land was acquired by way of compulsory purchase, but is no longer required and the disposal is by way of return to the original owner or his successors and includes a person who has succeeded, otherwise than by purchase, to adjoining land from which the land was severed by the original purchase).[115]

25.56 A disposal by a lender under a power of sale (i.e. where the land was held as security for a loan).[116]

25.57 A disposal of land under bankruptcy or other insolvency proceedings – as defined by rule 13.7 of the Insolvency Rules 1986,[117] which extends to any proceedings under the Insolvency Act 1986 or the Rules.[118]

25.58 A disposal of land to a person whose acquisition is a statutory compulsory purchase.[119]

25.59 A grant of a tenancy of land pursuant to the provisions of Part 4 of the Agricultural Holdings Act 1986.[120]

25.60 A disposal by one body corporate to another where the second one is a 'group undertaking' in relation to the first.[121]

---

[114] ACV Regulations, Sch 3, para 4.

[115] ACV Regulations, Sch 3, para 5.

[116] ACV Regulations, Sch 3, para 6. The reference to a power of sale includes a power implied by virtue of Law of Property Act 1925, s 101(1)(i), which has been affected by the insertion of sub-section (1A) by Commonhold and Leasehold Reform Act 2002, Sch 5, para 2.

[117] SI 1986/1925.

[118] ACV Regulations, Sch 3, para 7.

[119] ACV Regulations, Sch 3, para 1(3) and 8.

[120] ACV Regulations, Sch 3, para 9. Agricultural Holdings Act 1986, Pt 4 makes provision for succession on the death or retirement of the current tenant of an agricultural holding.

[121] ACV Regulations, Sch 3, para 10. The term 'group undertaking' has the meaning given by Companies Act 2006, s 1161(5).

25.61   A disposal of a closed Church of England church, together with any land annexed or belonging to it, pursuant to a scheme under Part 6 of the Mission and Pastoral Measure 2011.[122]

25.62   A disposal by any person for the purpose of continuing health service provision on the land.[123]

25.63   A disposal of land to be held for the purpose of a school as defined in section 4 of the Education Act 1996, a 16 to 19 Academy or an institution within the further education sector as defined in section 91(3) of the Further and Higher Education Act 1992.[124]

25.64   A disposal of land which is subject to a statutory requirement regarding the making of the disposal, where that requirement could not be observed if the moratorium rules were complied with.

COMPENSATION AND ENFORCEMENT

25.65   A scheme exists to compensate owners, or former owners, of listed land who have incurred loss or expense which is unlikely to have arisen if the land had

---

[122]   Part 6 of the Measure, which came into force on 1/7/2012, concerns redundant churches and replaces Part 3 of Pastoral Measure 1983 No 1. Such churches may be sold, leased for an agreed purpose, demolished or transferred to the Churches Conservation Trust for preservation, following which outcomes it will be possible to list the building and land if appropriate.

[123]   The term 'health service provision' originally meant the services provided as part of the health service continued under National Health Service Act 2006, s 1(1), but which has since been substituted by Health and Social Care Act 2012, s 1, with effect from 1/10/2012. The new wording of 2006 Act, s 1(1), is not significantly different for the purposes of these regulations.

[124]   ACV Regulations, Sch 3, para 14. Education Act 1996, s 4, has been amended by Education Act 1997, s 51, Sch 7, para 10(b) and Sch 8, para 10(b); by Childcare Act 2006, s 95(1), (2) and (3); by Education Act 2002, Sch 22, Pt 3; by Education Act 2011, Sch 13, para 9(1), (2)(a) and (2)(b); and by the Apprenticeships, Skills, Children and Learning Act 2009 (Consequential Amendments) (England and Wales) Order 2010 (SI 2010/1080). A 16 to 19 Academy is an educational institution which meets the requirements of Academies Act 2010, s 1B, which was inserted into that Act by Education Act 2011, s 53(7), with effect from 1/4/2012. In relation to 1992 Act, s 91(3), amendments have been made to this section by Apprenticeships, Skills, Children and Learning Act 2009, Sch 8, para 1 and para 13(1) and (3). A 'school' does not include an independent school other than one in respect of which Academy arrangements have been entered into by the Secretary of State under Academies Act 2010, s 1. An 'independent school' has the meaning given in Education Act 1996, s 463, which was substituted by Education Act 2002, s 172, and has been amended by the Local Education Authorities and Children's Services Authorities (Integration of Functions) Order 2010 (SI 2010/1158).

not been listed.[125] Claims for compensation must be made to the local authority, which may award such amount as it may determine for such loss.[126]

25.66 Such claims may include a claim for the recovery of any loss which is wholly caused: (a) by the delay in entering into a binding agreement to sell the land because of the prohibition of relevant disposals[127] during any part of the period of six weeks (i.e. the interim moratorium period) after the date on which the authority received notification from the owner that he wishes to enter into a relevant disposal of the land (or if earlier, the earliest date on which it would have been reasonable for that notification to have been given to the authority);[128] or (b) in a case where the prohibition continues during the six months beginning with that date (or such earlier date) (i.e. the full moratorium period), by relevant disposals of the land being prohibited during any part of the relevant six months after that date (or such earlier date).[129]

25.67 Claims may also be made for the owner's reasonable legal expenses incurred in a successful appeal to the First-tier Tribunal against the authority's decision: (a) to list the land; (b) to refuse to pay compensation; or (c) with regard to the amount of compensation offered or paid.[130]

25.68 Claims for compensation must be in writing to the authority and be made before the end of 13 weeks after the loss or expense was incurred or finished being incurred. Claims for compensation must state the amount sought for each part of the claim and be accompanied by supporting evidence.[131] The authority must also give the claimant written reasons for its decisions with respect to a request for compensation.[132]

25.69 In the circumstances most claims for compensation will arise from the mere fact that the moratorium rules have been engaged. However, the Regulations are so framed that claims for loss may arise simply as a result of the land being listed.[133]

---

[125] ACV Regulations, reg 14.

[126] ACV Regulations, reg 14(1).

[127] LA 2011, s 95(1).

[128] LA 2011, s 95(2) and ACV Regulations, reg 14(3)(a)(i) and (4).

[129] ACV Regulations, reg 14(3)(a)(ii).

[130] ACV Regulations, reg 14(3)(b).

[131] ACV Regulations, reg 14(5).

[132] ACV Regulations, reg 14(6).

[133] ACV Regulations, reg 14(1)–(3).

25.70 Certain public bodies are not entitled to compensation.[134]

25.71 The Government agreed to meet the costs incurred by local authorities in making compensation payments in excess of £20,000 in a single financial year until March 2015. This is believed to be still the case. Local authorities can make a request for financial support, providing evidence of the compensation costs incurred, either in writing or by email to:

> The Community Assets Team
> 5/A4 Eland House
> Bressenden Place
> London SW1E 5DU
> Email: righttobid@communities.gsi.gov.uk

INTERNAL REVIEW OF COMPENSATION DECISIONS[135]

25.72 Any owner dissatisfied with the response of a local authority in relation to whether compensation should be paid or as to the amount payable to that person may request a review of its decision. A request for a review must be made before the end of the period of eight weeks, beginning with the date on which the authority provided the owner with written notification of its reasons or such longer period as the authority may allow.[136] The procedure for the review of a compensation decision is the same as that for listing reviews.[137] An appeal against a compensation review decision also lies to the First-tier Tribunal (General Regulatory Chamber).

ENFORCEMENT

25.73 A disposal of listed land is ineffective if it contravenes the prohibition contained in section 95(1) of the LA 2011. There is one saving and that is if the person making the disposal made all reasonable efforts to find out if the land is listed and did not know that this was the case at the time the disposal was entered

---

[134] Government departments, authorities and other bodies to which National Audit Act 1983, s 6, applies; bodies which receive the majority of their funding from public sources which may be examined by the Comptroller and Auditor General under National Audit Act 1983, s 7; and local authorities and other public authorities and bodies that are required to be audited under Audit Commission Act 1998, s 2.

[135] ACV Regulations, reg 16.

[136] ACV Regulations, Sch 2, para 2.

[137] ACV Regulations, Sch 2, paras 3–9.

into.[138] Because local authorities are required to enter the listed land in the local land charges register, prospective new owners will be aware that the land has been listed.[139]

25.74 The Land Registration Rules 2003 (LRR 2003) have been amended by the insertion of an additional form of standard restriction in Form QQ, which provides as follows:

> No transfer or lease is to be registered without a certificate signed by a conveyancer that the transfer or lease did not contravene section 95(1) of the Localism Act 2011.[140]

25.75 A listing authority is under a duty to apply for entry of the restriction in Form QQ where the land is registered (unless there is already a restriction in that form registered).[141] If the listed land is unregistered, then where the owner of the listed land (or a mortgagee under rule 21 of the LRR 2003, applying for first registration in the owner's name) applies for first registration, he must also apply for the entry of a restriction against his own title in Form QQ.[142] When a listed asset is disposed of and the new owner applies for first registration, he must provide with the application a certificate by a conveyancer that any conveyance or lease of the land while it was listed did not contravene section 95(1) of the LA 2011. A person must inform the local authority that the land has been entered on the Land Register as a result of an application for first registration and must also inform the authority if he has become the new owner of listed land and provide ownership details.[143]

25.76 The entry of a restriction in standard Form QQ will accordingly prevent unlawful disposals of listed land, in the case of registered land, in breach of section 95(1) of the LA 2011. It follows that these restrictions may only be overcome on a transfer or lease of listed land by the production of a conveyancer's certificate stating that there has been no contravention of section 95(1).[144] Following registration of the transfer or lease, the registrar will not generally cancel the restriction in the absence of an express application to that effect in

---

[138] ACV Regulations, reg 21.

[139] LA 2011, s 100, provides that if land is included in a local authority's list of ACVs, inclusion in the list will mean that it is protected as a local land charge.

[140] LRR 2003, Sch 4, as amended by ACV Regulations, reg 20 and Sch 4, para 6, with effect from 21/9/2012.

[141] LRR 2003, r 94(11)(a), as amended by ACV Regulations, Sch 4, para 4.

[142] LRR 2003, r 27A, as amended by ACV Regulations, Sch 4, para 2.

[143] ACV Regulations, reg 19.

[144] This will either be because Conditions A–C in LA 2011, s 95(2)–(4), have been met or because it is a relevant disposal to which s 95(5) and ACV Regulations, Sch 3 apply, and to which s 95(1) will accordingly not apply.

Form RX3. A listing authority is, however, under an obligation to remove the land from its list of ACVs after five years, or where the listing has been successfully challenged in the First-tier Tribunal, or where the authority for any reason no longer considers the land to be of community value.[145] Evidence of these matters should accompany the application to cancel the restriction, and, having caused the land to be listed, the authority is under an obligation, on removing the land from the list of ACVs, to apply to the registrar, as soon as practicable, for cancellation of the restriction, and the owner may require the authority to make the application where possible.[146]

---

[145] LA 2011, s 87(3), and ACV Regulations, reg 2(c).

[146] ACV Regulations, reg 18.

Chapter 26

Town and Village Greens

INTRODUCTION

26.1   The criteria for the registration of new town or village greens (TVGs) are to be found in section 15 of the Commons Act 2006 (CA 2006), which came into force in England on 6/4/2007 and in Wales on 6/9/2007. This provision has been the subject of reform in the Growth and Infrastructure Act 2013 which has made it much less easy to register land.

26.2   The village green process is quite unlike the planning process where an applicant for planning permission has no entitlement to permission and, in its decision whether to grant it, a local planning authority has to exercise an administrative discretion in accordance with the development plan and local and national policies. In the case of new greens, the registration authority is bound to register if the qualifying criteria for registration contained in section 15 of the CA 2006 are met, irrespective of whether it thinks it would be a good or bad thing to do so.

26.3   A landowner receives no compensation for the burden of owning land which is registered as a TVG which has no potential for development. Land subject to registration is usually worthless and even difficult to give away. For instance, it is difficult to insure such land and local authorities will be reluctant to accept transfers of such land from landowners looking to rid themselves of onerous maintenance responsibilities and constant superintendence.

26.4   The topic of village greens has an extensive jurisprudence. However, the focus of this chapter will be on the consequences of registration, the current regulatory framework and recent case law.

CONSEQUENCES OF REGISTRATION

26.5   Upon registration the land becomes subject to: (a) section 12 of the Inclosure Act 1857; and (b) section 29 of the Commons Act 1876. Under both enactments, the rights of local inhabitants are protected and development is prohibited by the imposition of criminal sanctions. These enactments (which for these purposes are known as the Victorian Statutes) apply to any land registered as a TVG.[1]

26.6   Under section 12 of the Inclosure Act 1857, it is an offence wilfully to lead, drive or draw any cattle or animal on the land without lawful authority,[2] lay any manure, soil, ashes, rubbish or other matter or thing thereon, or to do any other act whatsoever (whether wilfully or not) to cause damage to a green or to impede 'the use or enjoyment thereof as a place for exercise and recreation'. The purpose of this provision seems to have been to prevent nuisances such as bringing on animals and dumping rubbish.

26.7   Under section 29 of the Commons Act 1876, it is deemed to be a public nuisance (and an offence under the Inclosure Act 1857) to encroach or build upon or to enclose a green. This extends to causing any 'disturbance or interference with or occupation of the soil thereof which is made otherwise than with a view to the better enjoyment of such town or village green'. This provision seems primarily aimed at encroachments by fencing off or building on the land.

26.8   Although these sections appear, on their face, to give rise to very strict prohibitions (such as the prohibition against development), the conduct of which complaint is made is only likely to be considered to be an offence under section 12 of the Inclosure Act 1857, or deemed to be a public nuisance under section 29 of the Commons Act 1876, if the land has suffered harm which has materially interfered with the use of the land for informal recreation.

26.9   For both the Inclosure Act 1857 and the Commons Act 1876, the persons entitled to instigate criminal proceedings in a magistrates' court are the owners of the land, any inhabitant of the parish, the parish council or, where there is no parish council, the relevant district council.[3]

---

1   See *TW Logistics Ltd v Essex County Council* [2018] EWCA Civ 2172, where it was held that the Victorian statutes should not be construed so as to make illegal that which, under the statutory registration scheme, was legal if another reasonable construction was possible. It was held that the judge had correctly found that where a landowner was conducting his activities because of his lawful right to do so, those activities did not amount to a public nuisance under the statutes (*Oxfordshire County Council v Oxford City Council* [2006] UKHL 25, [2006] 2 AC 674 applied and *Massey v Boulden* [2002] EWCA Civ 1634, [2003] 1 WLR 1792 considered (see [63]–[80] of the judgment)).

2   Grazing cattle or livestock in the exercise of a registered right of common would not be unlawful, nor is it likely that a local inhabitant would be guilty of an offence under s 12 if he takes an animal onto the land in the exercise of his right to enjoy lawful sports and pastimes. This might include horse-riding if this activity had been a feature of qualifying use.

3   LGA 1972, s 189(3).

26.10   Section 34 of the Road Traffic Act 1988 makes it an offence to drive over, or park on, land not forming part of a road without lawful authority. It has been held that this section applies to greens.[4] Those driving on land with permission or by virtue of a right to do so will not be committing an offence under section 34, nor will it be an offence under section 34(1) to drive on a green within 15 yards of a public road solely for the purpose of parking.[5] Driving on a green may, however, also be an offence under the Victorian Statutes if it is frequent or gives rise to damage or if it involves regular parking on the land, thereby interrupting its use or enjoyment by others.[6]

REGULATORY FRAMEWORK UNDER CA 2006, SECTION 15

26.11   Initially, registration was provided for under the Commons Registration Act 1965 (CRA 1965). This enactment has been superseded by the CA 2006, Part 1 of which deals with the registration of common land and greens. Applications for registration are made under section 15. With the passage of time, it is no longer necessary to deal with applications made before the coming into force of the CA 2006 (and with it the repeal of section 13(b) of the CRA 1965).

26.12   An application for registration is made to a commons registration authority.[7] Registration is subject to the following regulations: (a) the Commons (Registration of Town and Village Greens) (Interim Arrangements) (England) Regulations 2007 (2007 Regulations);[8] (b) the Commons (Registration of Town

---

4   *Massey v Boulden* [2002] EWCA Civ 1634, [2003] 1 WLR 1792.

5   Road Traffic Act 1988, s 34(3).

6   See also *TW Logistics Ltd v Essex County Council* [2018] EWCA Civ 2172, which concerned the use by a landowner of working quays in the Port of Mistley in Essex over which an area of land had been registered as a TVG. The landowner had argued that the effect of registration would be to criminalise its continuing use of the TVG for the same commercial purposes as had taken place throughout the 20-year period, and for that reason the recreational use did not have the necessary quality to support the registration. The landowner's challenge was dismissed as the judge had found that the recreational uses of the quayside in the qualifying period were not displaced or excluded by, or incompatible with, the carrying on of commercial activity, and that there was sensible and sustained co-existence between the two groups of users. It was essentially a question of evaluating whether, as a matter of fact, the pre-existing use and recreational use were compatible. The judge had found that they were, and his careful evaluation should not be interfered with (*R (Lewis) v Redcar and Cleveland Borough Council* [2010] UKSC 11, [2010] 2 AC 70 followed (see [24]–[36] of the judgment)).

7   By CA 2006, s 4, a commons registration authority will be: (a) a county council in England; (b) a district council in England for an area without a county council; (c) a London borough council; and (d) a county or county borough council in Wales. The relevant registration authority will be the authority in whose area the land is situated.

8   SI 2007/457.

or Village Greens) (Interim Arrangements) (Wales) Regulations 2007;[9] and (c) the Commons Registration (England) Regulations 2014 (2014 Regulations)[10] (which replaced the Commons Registration (England) Regulations 2008 (2008 Regulations))[11] which apply only to the nine pioneer implementation areas as an extended pilot.[12] The 2007 Regulations apply to all other areas of England and Wales and will be superseded by the 2014 Regulations once the whole of Part 1 is in force in England and Wales (which is not yet in sight). Both sets of regulations deal mainly with the procedures for making applications and their determination, otherwise the law in this field is no different no matter where the land happens to be located.

WHO IS ENTITLED TO APPLY FOR REGISTRATION?

26.13 Any person or body (whether corporate[13] or unincorporated) may apply to register land as a TVG.[14] Applications are commonly made by representatives of *ad hoc* unincorporated associations of local inhabitants, which have been formed with the object of resisting development on the land. The landowner may also apply to register his land as a TVG,[15] in which case, the consent of any relevant leaseholder of, and the proprietor of any relevant charge over, the land will be required.[16] Where a landowner applies to register his own land, there is no requirement that the land should meet the ordinary tests for a TVG.

APPLICATION FORM

26.14 Outside the pioneer areas, the application to register is made on Form 44.[17] The form is relatively straightforward. In summary, the applicant is required to provide his name and address and those of his legal representatives (if any). He is also required to identify whether his application is based on qualifying use which is continuing at the date of the application or whether such use has already ceased (and if so, when) before the application was made. The land claimed as a TVG

---

9   SI 2007/2396.

10 SI 2014/3038.

11 SI 2008/1961.

12 Blackburn with Darwen, Cornwall, Devon (but not including unitary authorities), Hertfordshire, Herefordshire, Kent (but not including unitary authorities), Lancashire (but not Blackpool), Cumbria and North Yorkshire.

13 2007 Regulations, reg 3(2)(b).

14 CA 2006, s 15(1).

15 CA 2006, s 15(8).

16 CA 2006, s 15(9) and (10).

17 2007 Regulations, reg 3(2)(a); Sch, Form 44.

should be identified by its usual name, if it has one, and should also be shown on a map at a scale of at least 1:2500 with distinctive colouring to enable it to be clearly identified. The applicant is also required to identify the locality or neighbourhood within a locality in respect of which the application is made (and users of the claimed TVG must be inhabitants of the claimed locality or neighbourhood within a locality). This can be done by the inclusion of the relevant administrative area defined by name, but if this is not possible, then a map should be provided on which the locality or neighbourhood is clearly marked. The provision of a map of the relevant locality or neighbourhood is not essential, and an applicant will usually provide only the name of a claimed locality. It is by no means certain, however, that he will provide a map showing the geographical area of the putative neighbourhood, at least when making his application. A summary of the case for registration is required. The applicant is also required to name any person whom he believes to be the owner, tenant or occupier of the claimed green and should also provide a list of all supporting documents and maps accompanying the application. Indeed, applications are required to be accompanied by relevant documents in the possession of, or under the control of, the applicant, or to which he has a right of production.[18] In practice, applications are invariably accompanied by a number of completed evidence questionnaires and lengthy justificatory statements drafted by the applicant and/or by others who support the case for registration. Appropriate particulars are also required if the applicant is the owner of the land or if there has been a statutory interruption in its use (this is the so-called foot-and-mouth provision) which is to be disregarded.[19] Lastly, the application is required to be supported by a statutory declaration in the form accompanying Form 44. The statutory declaration must be signed by the applicant or by one of the applicants or by their solicitor. If the application is made by a body corporate or unincorporated body, it must be signed by the individual who signed the application on behalf of the applicant.

26.15 The 2014 Regulations[20] (in the case of TVGs claimed in the nine pioneer areas) substantively mirror the 2007 Regulations when it comes to making applications and their management.[21] The application is again required to be made

---

[18] 2007 Regulations, reg 3(2)(c).

[19] CA 2006, s 15(6).

[20] 2014 Regulations, Pt 3 (and it is worth mentioning that reg 17 makes provision for the payment of an application fee if required by the registration authority).

[21] See 2014 Regulations, Pt 3, reg 15 (making an application); reg 19 (land descriptions); reg 20 (management of application); reg 21 (registration authority's duty to publicise application); reg 23 (contents of notice of application – note that the period for making representations in relation to the application is to be at least 42 days after the date of the publishing, posting or service of the notice of the application on persons on whom the registration authority must serve the application (i.e. on owners, occupiers or tenants of the application land – Sch 7)); reg 23 (the contents of the notice which is required to be published, posted and served under reg 21); reg 24 (inspection of documents held by the registration authority); and reg 25 (the right of any person

on a standard form provided by the Secretary of State.[22] There are, however, differences when it comes to the mode of determining applications.

MANAGING THE APPLICATION

26.16 Under the 2007 Regulations (i.e. in the non-pioneer areas), on receipt of an application, the registration authority is required to give it a distinguishing number and should also stamp the application form indicating the date when it was received. The applicant must be sent a receipt[23] for his application containing a statement of the number allotted to it.[24] The registration authority is then required to send by post a notice[25] to every person whom it has reason to believe to be the owner, tenant or occupier of any part of the claimed green or to be likely to object to the application.[26] The registration authority must also publish the notice in one or more newspapers circulating in the area and must also send a copy of the notice and the application to every concerned authority.[27] The registration authority is also required, provided it is reasonably practical, to display the notice by affixing the same to some conspicuous object on any part of the land.[28]

26.17 The notice[29] should state that statements in objection to the application must be submitted to the registration authority within six weeks of receipt of such notice or the date on which the notice is published and displayed by the registration authority.[30] It is not unusual for extensions of time to be allowed to prospective objectors who may require further time to investigate the background, assemble their evidence and obtain legal advice with a view to the presentation of a comprehensive notice of objection in response to the application. Where an

---

    to make written representations to the registration authority about the application, copies of which must be served on the applicant).

[22]   2014 Regulations, reg 16; Form CA9.
[23]   Commons Registration (General) Regulations 1966 (SI 1966/1471), Form 6.
[24]   2007 Regulations, reg 4.
[25]   2007 Regulations, Sch, Form 45.
[26]   2007 Regulations, reg 5(1)(a).
[27]   2007 Regulations, reg 5(1)(b) and (3). A 'concerned authority' means a local authority (other than the registration authority) in whose area any of the land affected by the application lies, and includes a county council, a district council, a London borough council or a parish council. The concerned authority is required to display copies of the notice and must also make the application available for public inspection until informed by the registration authority of the disposal of the application.
[28]   2007 Regulations, reg 5(1)(c).
[29]   2007 Regulations, Sch, Form 45.
[30]   2007 Regulations, reg 5(2).

application appears not to be duly made (as, for instance, where the application has not been properly completed or where it is not accompanied by a plan (Form 44, Box 5) or statutory declaration), it is open to the registration authority to reject the application, but where it appears to the registration authority that the error might be corrected and the application put in order, it must not reject the application without first giving the applicant a reasonable opportunity of taking that action.[31] If, within the reasonable opportunity given, an applicant corrected errors in the application, the original application had full effect and was to be treated as having been made on the date on which the original defective application had been lodged. Determining what amounted to a 'reasonable opportunity' was a question of law for the court and is fact-specific.[32]

DETERMINING APPLICATIONS (NON-PIONEER AREAS)

26.18   The 2007 Regulations make no mention of the machinery for considering the application where there are objections.[33] In particular, no provision is made for an oral hearing. In the past, decisions have been delegated to a panel of members or, more normally, by the holding of a local hearing, usually before a specialist barrister, whose report would contain a recommendation as to the appropriate disposal of the application by the relevant regulatory committee or department of the relevant authority acting in its capacity as registration authority for the area in which the land was located. Termed 'non-statutory inquiries', these local hearings are quasi-judicial in character and derive from the exercise by the registration authority of its ancillary powers under section 111 of the LGA 1972 (i.e. to do acts which are calculated to facilitate, or are incidental or conducive to, the discharge of its functions, and such powers would cover the institution of an inquiry in an appropriate case).

---

[31]   2007 Regulations, reg 5(4).

[32]   *Church Commissioners for England v Hampshire County Council* [2014] EWCA Civ 634, where the Court of Appeal determined on the facts that a reasonable opportunity within 2007 Regulations, reg 5(4) had been exceeded and the court at first instance had been wrong to conclude otherwise.

[33]   See 2007 Regulations, regs 6–9; reg 6 merely requires the registration authority to consider the application once it has received objection statements and that it should not reject the application without giving the applicant an opportunity of dealing with the matters contained in any objection statement, and of any other matter which appears to the authority to afford possible grounds for rejecting the application; reg 7 deals with applications made by the owner of the land in respect of which the registration authority must satisfy itself that the applicant is the owner of the land and that any consents required by CA 2006, s 15(9) have been obtained; reg 8 deals with the method of registration; and reg 9 concerns the duty of the registration authority to notify those affected by the application of its determination, including every concerned authority.

26.19 In *R (Whitmey) v Commons Commissioners*,[34] Waller LJ suggested[35] that where there is a serious dispute, the procedure of 'conducting a non-statutory public inquiry through an independent expert' should be followed 'almost invariably'. However, the registration authority is not empowered by statute to hold a hearing and make findings that are binding on the parties, nor is there any power to take evidence on oath or to require the disclosure of documents or to make orders as to costs. However, the registration authority must act impartially, fairly and with an open mind, and its decision will not normally be open to challenge if it adheres to the recommendation of its inspector. It should be noted that in the non-pioneer areas, the registration authority, when it has disposed of the application, must give notice of that fact to the applicant and every person who has objected whose address is known. That notice must include, where it has granted the application, details of the registration (but no duty to state reasons for allowing the application) and, where it has rejected the application, the reasons for the rejection. This includes anyone who did object within time, or whose objection was considered.[36]

26.20 It was said in *R v Suffolk County Council ex parte Steed*[37] that an authority has an implied duty to take reasonable steps to acquaint itself with the relevant

---

[34] [2004] EWCA Civ 951. See also *Somerford PC v Cheshire East BC* [2016] EWHC 619 (Admin), where there were found to be sufficient disputes of factual issues raised to require a public inquiry. This was a case where an application to register was rejected by the registration authority following a decision by its independent expert not to hold an inquiry (who had concluded that the application land was part of the highway and therefore not registrable because user by local inhabitants was by right). The decision was set aside (relying on the guidance of Waller LJ in *Whitmey* that, in any case where there is a serious dispute, the registration authority should appoint an independent expert to hold a public inquiry and make findings in relation to the requisite facts) and the application to register was remitted for reconsideration after a public inquiry. One of the grounds of challenge was that the decision of the registration authority was procedurally erroneous in that the independent expert did not hold a public inquiry to find facts, which ground was accepted by Stewart J.

[35] [2004] EWCA Civ 951 at [62] and [66].

[36] 2007 Regulations (reg 9(2)). This is to be contrasted with the 2014 Regulations (reg 36(3)), which apply in the pioneer areas where the duty to give reasons applies whether the application has been granted or rejected. See, however, *R (NHS Property Services Ltd) v Surrey County Council* [2018] EWCA Civ 721 at [99] where, in the case of a decision to allow an application to register by a non-pioneer registration authority contrary to an inspector's recommendation, it was found: (a) that the registration authority had been under a duty at common law, in the context of the statutory regime for the registration of village greens, to give reasons for its decision to register the land (applying *Oakley v South Cambridgeshire DC* [2017] EWCA Civ 71, [2017] 1 WLR 3765, and *Dover DC v Campaign to Protect Rural England (Kent)* [2017] [2017] UKSC 79, [2018] 1 WLR 108); and (b) that Surrey CC's reasons for registering the land as a TVG were clear and sufficient and not unlawful. The court found that even if the reasons had been inadequate, the case had been one in which the court should nevertheless decline to quash the registration because there was no real possibility of its decision being different if it was compelled to state its reasons more fully.

[37] [1995] 75 P & CR 102 at 487; at 500–501 per Carnwath J.

information to enable it to correctly answer the correct question under what was then the CRA 1965. It was said by Carnwath J (as he then was), that 'Some oral procedure seems essential if a fair view is to be reached where conflicting recollections need to be reconciled'.

26.21 However, the registration authority does have discretion as to the procedure to be adopted, but that discretion is not unfettered, and it must be exercised in a manner that is not unfair to applicants or objectors. Although in a clear case where the application is bound to fail (because, for instance, the use of the land was with the owner's express permission), it could be dealt with summarily by way of rejection. As a general rule, however, in the case of disputed applications (and especially where the land is also owned by the registration authority), fairness will require that arrangements should be made by the registration authority to appoint an independent inspector (who will ordinarily make directions and be responsible for case management in advance of the inquiry), either to advise the registration authority on how the application should be proceeded with and/or in an appropriate case to hold a non-statutory public inquiry, following which the inspector would provide an advisory report containing a recommendation on whether the application to register should be allowed or rejected.

26.22 It should be noted that in *Oxfordshire County Council v Oxford City Council*,[38] it was held that the registration authority has no investigative duty which requires it to find evidence or to reformulate the applicant's case. It is required to deal only with the application and the evidence as presented by the parties.

DETERMINING APPLICATIONS (PIONEER AREAS)

26.23 A major difference between the 2007 Regulations (i.e. in the non-pioneer areas) and the 2008 and 2014 Regulations (i.e. in the pioneer areas) concerns the referral of certain applications for determination to the Planning Inspectorate (PINS).[39] This specifically applies in the pioneer areas where the registration authority has an interest in the outcome of the application, such that there is unlikely to be confidence in the authority's ability to determine the application impartially.[40] This will invariably arise, for instance, where the claimed TVG is owned by the registration authority, particularly where the land is required for development.

---

[38]   [2006] UKHL 25, [2006] 2 AC 674 at [61] per Lord Hoffmann.

[39]   2014 Regulations, reg 26.

[40]   2014 Regulations, reg 26(2) and (3).

26.24 The 2014 Regulations also make formal provision in relation to site inspections and the holding of public inquiries or informal hearings by the PINS.[41]

REPEAT APPLICATIONS (RES JUDICATA)

26.25 This arises where a further application is made which includes land which has been the subject of an earlier failed application to register. The issue is whether a cause of action estoppel arises which precludes the registration authority, as a matter of law, from proceeding to determine the later application on its merits. In all probability, a cause of action estoppel, which applies to public law determinations in a wide range of contexts, will preclude the re-opening of previous decisions made by registration authorities.[42]

---

[41] 2014 Regulations, reg 27(1)(f) and (2) (mode of determining applications); reg 28 (notice of public inquiry); reg 29 (public inquiries: general provisions); reg 30 (pre-inquiry meetings); reg 31 (procedure at inquiries); reg 32 (informal meetings before an inspector: procedure); reg 33 (site inspections by inspector: procedure); reg 34 (changes of procedure where a public inquiry or informal hearing is to be cancelled in circumstances where the registration authority or planning inspectorate determine that the application should be determined without holding an inquiry or, in the case of the PINS, where it wishes to hold an informal hearing instead of an inquiry (or vice versa)).

[42] See *Thrasyvoulou v Secretary of State for the Environment* [1990] 2 AC 273 at 289 (in a case where the House of Lords held that an issue estoppel arose out of a determination of a planning application), Lord Bridge stated:

'In relation to adjudications subject to a comprehensive self-contained statutory code, the presumption, in my opinion, must be that where the statute has created a specific jurisdiction for the determination of any issue which establishes the existence of a legal right, the principle of *res judicata* applies to give finality to that determination unless an intention to exclude the principle can properly be inferred as a matter of construction of the relevant statutory provisions.'

See also *R (Coke Wallis) v Institute of Chartered Accountants* [2011] UKSC 1, [2011] 2 WLR 103 (in which Lord Clarke at [27] said that *Thrasyvoulou* 'stressed the importance of the *res judicata* principle in terms which in my opinion apply equally to cause of action estoppel and to issue estoppels'). See also *Crown Estate Commissioners v Dorset County Council* [1990] 1 Ch 297, in which Millett J held that a decision of a Commons Commissioner acting under the CRA 1965 was capable of creating an issue estoppel. It is also clearly relevant that the limited mechanism for review under either CRA 1965, s 14, or the CA 2006, s 19, would be unnecessary if you could make repeated applications to register. This is arguably a strong indication of a statutory intention that decisions of commons registration authorities should be subject to a *res judicata* estoppel. Mention should also be made of the Defra Guidance Notes (last updated on 1/7/2014) for s 15 where, at para 61 (under the heading 'Repeated and withdrawn applications'), Defra states that an application may be resubmitted (and which a registration authority would be required to consider subject to any relevant time limits) where there was significant new evidence or where there had been a change in the law. However, beyond suggesting that registration authorities would be entitled to summarily reject repeated successive applications which did not raise any new issues for consideration, the implications of a *res judicata* were not specifically mentioned. It is suggested that such guidance may well be erroneous. In any case, the guidance

QUALIFYING CRITERIA FOR REGISTRATION IN OUTLINE

26.26 The application will be tested against the criteria in section 15(2) or (3) of the CA 2006. It must meet one of these tests:

(a) *Where the use is continuing* – section 15(2) applies where: (a) a significant number of the inhabitants of any locality, or of any neighbourhood within a locality, have indulged as of right in lawful sports and pastimes on the land for a period of at least 20 years; and (b) they continue to do so at the time of the application.

(b) *Where the use ended before the application was made* – section 15(3) applies where qualifying use for at least 20 years ended no more than one year before the date of the application.[43]

26.27 The necessary elements which have to be considered by the registration authority are thus as follows:

- a significant number;
- the inhabitants of any locality, or of any neighbourhood within a locality
- indulged ... in lawful sports and pastimes;
- as of right;

---

has no statutory force and even contains a disclaimer to this effect at para 17. Defra's position changes, however, in relation to its guidance on the implementation of Part 1 of the CA 2006 to registration authorities and the PINS (Part 1 concerns the maintenance of the registers of common land and village greens and how they can be amended to add new information or amend existing information). This guidance applies to the pioneer areas and should be considered in the context of the 2014 Regulations which came into force on 15/12/2014. At para 5.15 of its guidance, Defra states correctly that an identical, or near identical, application to one previously made and refused would entitle the registration authority to refuse to accept it, on common law grounds of *res judicata*. Defra also states that it would also be an abuse of process to raise in subsequent proceedings matters which could, and therefore should, have been raised in earlier non-judicial adjudications in public law. Now that it seems to be beyond doubt that the public interest in the finality and conclusiveness of judicial decisions should apply with equal force to adjudications under the CA 2006 (as they do to findings of a planning inspector), it is difficult to imagine that any court would uphold an applicant's right to make repeated, time consuming and costly applications in respect of the same land. However, that said, it must still be possible that were a repeat application to arise in circumstances where the earlier application had been rejected under the CRA 1965 (where it is arguable that the new statutory criteria would permit a different outcome) then, exceptionally, the registration authority may consider that it needs to look at any new evidence or material with a view to determining whether its earlier decision remains appropriate. Broadly speaking, this is Defra's view.

[43] The period of grace in CA 2006, s 15(3)(c), in relation to land in England (but not in Wales), was reduced from two years to one year with effect from 1/10/2013 (now s 15(3A)(a)). The reforms contained in Growth and Infrastructure Act 2013, ss 14–17 (and the amendments made to CA 2006, s 15) are considered separately.

- on the land;
- for a period of at least 20 years;
- where relevant, the date of cessation of use;
- where relevant, any interruption owing to statutory periods of closure (section 15(6));
- where relevant, the existence of an owner's statement (section 15A);
- where relevant, any planning permission affecting the land (section 15C/ Schedule 1A).

QUALIFYING CRITERIA FOR REGISTRATION IN DETAIL

26.28 It has been said that 'it is no trivial matter for a landowner to have land, whether in public or private ownership, registered as a town green'.[44] It is then important that all the elements necessary to justify registration should be strictly proved on the balance of probabilities to the satisfaction of the registration authority.

A significant number

26.29 The term 'significant number' has never been defined, but in *R v Staffordshire County Council ex parte Alfred McAlpine Homes Ltd*,[45] Sullivan J said that 'significant' did not mean a considerable or a substantial number. He said that the correct answer:

> ... is that the number of people using the land in question has to be sufficient to indicate that their use of the land signifies that it is in general use by the local community for informal recreation, rather than occasional use by individuals as trespassers.

26.30 In most cases, the fact that recreational user is more than trivial or sporadic will be sufficient to put a landowner on notice that a right is being asserted by local inhabitants over his land.[46]

26.31 It is then very much a matter of impression whether use is by a significant number of the inhabitants of any locality or of any neighbourhood within a locality. If, for instance, the neighbourhood is a small one, then only a handful of

---

[44] *R (Beresford) v Sunderland City Council* [2003] UKHL 60, [2004] 1 AC 889 at [2], where Lord Bingham agreed with Pill LJ's assertion in *R v Suffolk County Council ex parte Steed* [1996] P & CR 102 (CA).

[45] [2002] EWHC 76 (Admin) at [64].

[46] *Leeds Group Plc v Leeds City Council* [2010] EWCA Civ 1438, [2011] 2 WLR 1010 at [31].

users may suffice, provided they can give evidence of their own use and that observed by them in the case of others for the whole of the 20-year period.[47]

Spread

26.32 Connected to the issue of sufficiency of use there is the principle of 'spread'. At one time the argument was that unless the users were fairly spread across the claimed neighbourhood or locality, it could not be said that user was sufficient in law to indicate that the claimed green was in general use by local residents for informal recreation within the claimed neighbourhood or locality. Vos J dismissed a spread argument in *Paddico (267) Ltd v Kirklees Metropolitan Council and others*,[48] but the Court of Appeal did not address this issue. It was also held at first instance in *Lancashire County Council v Secretary of State for the Environment, Food and Rural Affairs*[49] that an absence of spread will not prevent registration, and this finding was approved in the Court of Appeal.[50] It now seems settled that there is no such requirement, and it cannot have been the

---

[47] *R v Staffordshire County Council ex parte Alfred McAlpine Homes Ltd* [2002] EWHC 76 (Admin). The importance of this case is that it appears that land can be registered on the basis of the evidence of a very few people (in *Staffordshire* only six witnesses were able to cover the whole 20-year period – see [73]–[77]). In *Powell v Secretary of State for the Environment, Food and Rural Affairs* [2014] EWHC 4009 (Admin) (a case involving a challenge against an order made under the Wildlife and Countryside Act 1981 (WCA 1981) for the recognition of a footpath in which the court had to consider the correct approach in determining whether there had been use as of right), it was held that the starting point must be an examination of the quality of the use which is relied upon. As Dove J put it, 'Was it of sufficient quantity to amount to the assertion of a right? Was it consonant in quality to the nature of the right being claimed?'. This *dictum* is clearly consistent with the decision in *R v Oxfordshire County Council ex parte Sunningwell Parish Council* [2000] 1 AC 335 at 357D, where it was said by Lord Hoffmann that the use must not be 'so trivial and sporadic as not to carry the outward appearance of user as of right'. It is then important to emphasise that when dealing with sufficiency of use, there not only has to be use by a significant number of local inhabitants in the relevant area, but also the use relied on must be of sufficient quantity and quality if it is to justify registration.

[48] [2011] EWHC 1606 (Ch).

[49] [2016] EWHC 1238 (Admin). Ouseley J considered this ground of objection to be untenable. As he said at [40]: 'The sometimes technical approach to statutory construction which one sees in commons cases cannot justify reading such a large criterion into the Act'. He also rejected the widespread recognition of spread in decisions of inspectors, 'Their decisions on law carry no authority here'.

[50] [2018] EWCA Civ 721 per Lindblom LJ at [74]–[80], who considered that the doctrine of spread would introduce a further, non-statutory, criterion for registration, which would be highly subjective, uncertain and liable to produce inconsistency. Other attempts to persuade the court that there was such a requirement failed in *R (Allaway) v Oxfordshire County Council* [2016] EWHC 2677 (Admin) at [69]–[73], and in *Leeds Group Plc v Leeds City Council* [2010] EWHC 810 (Ch) at [90], which was not doubted by the Court of Appeal in that case ([2010] EWCA Civ 1438).

intention of Parliament that both the locality and the neighbourhood had to be small enough to accommodate a proper spread of qualifying users.

The inhabitants of any locality

26.33 It is now settled law that if an application is advanced solely on the basis of a locality, it must be an area that can be identified as having legally significant boundaries.[51]

26.34 An area with legally significant boundaries is generally understood to mean a borough or a civil or ecclesiastical parish. Although there is no direct authority that a ward can be a locality, the weight of opinion is that it can be. For instance, in *R (Oxfordshire and Buckinghamshire Mental Health NHS Foundation Trust and Anor) v Oxfordshire County Council*[52] (also sometimes referred as the 'Warneford Meadow' case), HHJ Waksman QC noted (on a concession) that a locality 'had to be some form of administrative unit, like a town or parish or ward'.[53] It follows from all this that a plan showing merely an area within which people use the claimed TVG will simply not be good enough unless it embraces what can be identified as an administrative unit. If the words 'any locality' meant

---

[51] *Paddico (267) Ltd v Kirklees Metropolitan Council* [2012] EWCA Civ 262. For reference to authority on the issue of whether the claimed locality must have existed for the full period of 20 years, see *Lancashire County Council v Secretary of State for the Environment, Food and Rural Affairs* [2016] EWHC 1238 (Admin) per Ouseley J at [21]–[28], and *Paddico* at [2012] EWCA Civ 262 per Carnwath LJ at [62]. It is suggested that it is now tolerably clear that in the case of electoral wards, periodic boundary changes are unlikely to stop time running unless the identifiable community link has, as a matter of fact and degree, undergone significant change. As Ouseley J put it in *Lancashire*, it must still be essentially the same community. In *R (Lancashire CC) v Secretary of State for Environment, Food and Rural Affairs* [2018] EWCA Civ 721 at [72] Lindblom LJ found that small changes in the boundary of a locality would be insufficient to prevent it from being treated as a qualifying locality provided it had existed in some clearly identifiable form throughout. Mere adjustments in its boundaries would not be sufficient to prevent its existence as a coherent and continuous locality.

[52] [2010] EWHC 530 (Admin) at [69].

[53] See also *Paddico* in the Court of Appeal [2012] EWCA Civ 262 at [51] where Sullivan LJ cited with approval from *Halsbury's Laws of England* (4th edn, 2012, Vol 12, Part 1 'Custom and Usage') which states that:

'A custom must be certain in respect of the locality where it is alleged to exist ... This area must be defined by reference to the limits of some legally recognised administrative division, as for instance a county, a hundred, a forest, a region of marshland, a city, a town or borough, a parish, a township within a parish, a villa, a hamlet, a liberty, a barony, an honour, or a manor.'

However, Sullivan LJ did not agree with Vos J at first instance that a conservation area was capable of being a valid locality because, although it had legally significant boundaries, they were only significant for a particular statutory purpose: its 'boundaries would have been defined by reference to its characteristics as an area of special architectural or historic interest, the character or appearance of which it is desirable to preserve or enhance' (see s 69(1) of the Planning (Listed Buildings and Conservation Areas) Act 1990 (LBA 1990)) – rather than by reference to any community of interest on the part of its inhabitants.

any sufficiently identifiable area or areas, then Parliament is unlikely to have introduced the concept of a neighbourhood, as in such circumstances the expressions 'locality' and 'neighbourhood' would be synonymous.

Of any neighbourhood within a locality

26.35 In *R (Cheltenham Builders Ltd) v South Gloucestershire District Council*,[54] Sullivan J stated that whereas the term 'locality' in the context of TVGs meant a legally recognised administrative unit, a neighbourhood need not be an administrative unit and might include a housing estate. He also rejected the notion that a neighbourhood is any area of land that an applicant chooses to delineate on a plan. He said this:[55]

> The registration authority has to be satisfied that the area alleged to be a neighbourhood has a sufficient degree of cohesiveness, otherwise the word 'neighbourhood' would be stripped of any real meaning. If parliament had wished to enable the inhabitants of any area (as defined on a plan accompanying the application) to apply to register land as a village green, it would have said so.

26.36 *Cheltenham Builders Ltd v South Gloucestershire District Council*[56] was confirmed in *Oxfordshire County Council v Oxford City Council*,[57] where Lord Hoffmann spoke of a neighbourhood as not being an area of legal or technical significance. In *Paddico*, Vos J confirmed[58] the prior jurisprudence and said 'in section 22(1A), the term "neighbourhood" is to be understood as being a cohesive area and must be capable of meaningful description in some way'. The point was not directly for consideration by the Court of Appeal, but it is a necessary implication of the court's finding that whereas a locality must be an area known to the law, a neighbourhood will suffice if it is something less than this. It has been emphasised recently (at first instance) in *R (NHS Property Services Ltd) v Surrey County Council*[59] that the cohesion of a 'neighbourhood' is essentially a matter of impression and is not something which can be assessed by using some recognised technique. The Court of Appeal agreed,[60] holding that whether a claimed

---

54 [2003] EWHC 2803 (Admin).
55 [2003] EWHC 2803 (Admin) at [85].
56 [2003] EWHC 2803 (Admin).
57 [2006] UKHL 25, [2006] 2 AC 674 at [27].
58 [2011] EWHC 1606 (Ch) at [97].
59 [2016] EWHC 1715 (Admin) at [116].
60 [2018] EWCA Civ 721 at [103]–[109]. In this case it is noteworthy that the non-statutory inspector considered that the area claimed to be a neighbourhood fell well short of what was required to show that the area was a neighbourhood in law. The members of Surrey County Council's Planning and Regulatory Committee disagreed with the inspector's advice about this and the land was registered. The Court of Appeal held that the reasons given by the committee for differing with the view of their

neighbourhood had a sufficient degree of 'cohesiveness' was a matter of impression which allows ample scope for differences of opinion. In other words, the analysis was not one which involved the application of any specific statutory or non-statutory criteria or the application of any recognised method of assessment.

Reliance on one or more neighbourhoods straddling more than one locality

26.37 It is now settled law that reliance may be placed by an applicant on a neighbourhood or neighbourhoods within a locality or localities.[61]

Indulged ... in lawful sports and pastimes

26.38 Lawful sports and pastimes is a composite class[62] and, in practice, use of the land for dog-walking, children's play and general informal recreation will normally suffice to justify registration under section 15 of the CA 2006.

Right of way use – is it qualifying use?

26.39 Difficulties frequently arise where the predominant recreational user of the application land is that of user of paths such as would have appeared to a reasonable landowner to be referable to the exercise of existing, or the potential acquisition of new, public rights of way rather than rights sufficient to support a village green registration. In *Oxfordshire County Council v Oxford City Council,*[63] Lightman J said that the use of tracks will generally only establish public rights of way unless the use is wider in scope or the tracks are of such a character that use of them cannot give rise to a presumption of dedication at common law as a public highway. Lightman J also noted that where there was any doubt about the matter, the inference should be drawn of the exercise of the less onerous right rather than the more onerous right to use the land as green. The use of paths for recreational walking is capable of founding a case of deemed dedication of a

---

inspector and in forming a different impression on the relevant evidence were intelligible and adequate in the sense of explaining why the decision was what it was and there was no error of law.

61   *Leeds Group Plc v Leeds City Council* [2010] EWCA Civ 1438.

62   *R v Oxfordshire County Council ex parte Sunningwell Parish Council* [2000] 1 AC 335 at 356–357.

63   [2004] EWHC 12 (Ch), [2004] Ch 253 at [102]–[103]; assistance may be had from the village green report of Vivian Chapman QC in *Radley Lakes* (13/10/2007) at [304]–[305], who said that the main issue in such cases is whether the use would appear to a reasonable landowner as referable to the exercise of a right of way along a defined route or to a right to enjoy recreation over the whole of a wider area of land. If the appearance is ambiguous, then it shall be ascribed to a lesser right, i.e. a right of way.

highway unless it is merely ancillary to recreational activities such as sunbathing, fishing or swimming.[64]

26.40 The footpath issue was also addressed by Sullivan J in *R (Laing Homes Ltd) v Buckinghamshire County Council*.[65] Put shortly, where you have heavy use of footpaths around the perimeter of the application land, it becomes necessary to distinguish between use which would suggest to a reasonable landowner that the users believed they were exercising a public right of way and use which would suggest to such a landowner that the users believed they were exercising a right to indulge in lawful sports and pastimes across the whole of the land. A useful test is to discount walking, including dog-walking, on the footpaths in order to determine whether the other activities over the remainder of the land were of such a character and frequency as to indicate an assertion of a right over the whole of the application land. It was also usefully noted by Sullivan J that he did not consider that a dog's wanderings or the owner's attempts to retrieve his errant dog would suggest to the reasonable landowner that the dog-walker believed he was exercising a public right to use the land beyond the footpath for informal recreation. In the *Oxfordshire* case,[66] Lord Hoffmann approved of the guidance on this issue offered by Lightman J at first instance and by Sullivan J in *Laing Homes*.

As of right

26.41 The traditional formulation of the requirement that recreational use must be 'as of right' is that the use must be without force, secrecy or permission (these are the three so-called vitiating circumstances which will preclude use 'as of right').[67] There is now in practice a further vitiating factor and that is that recreational use must not be 'by right'.

---

[64] *Dyfed County Council v Secretary of State for Wales* (1989) 59 P & CR 275.

[65] [2003] EWHC 1578 (Admin), [2004] 1 P & CR 36 at [102]–[110].

[66] [2006] UKHL 25, [2006] 2 AC 674 at [68].

[67] *R v Oxfordshire County Council ex parte Sunningwell Parish Council* [2000] 1 AC 335 per Lord Hoffmann at 350H–351C. See also *R (Lewis) v Redcar and Cleveland Borough Council* [2010] UKSC 11, [2010] 2 AC 70, which concerned land belonging to a local authority which had been used as a golf course and by local inhabitants for informal recreation. The locals deferred to the golfers by keeping out of their way as they played on the fairways. The question for the Supreme Court was to determine whether use by local inhabitants could be as of right in circumstances where they overwhelmingly deferred to the activities of the golfers. The view of the Supreme Court was that deference did not preclude use as of right as the local inhabitants were merely behaving with courtesy and common sense towards members of the golf club who were out playing golf. The owner had contended that a reasonable owner would not have concluded that local inhabitants were asserting a village green right against him in circumstances where they deferred to the golfers. The court ruled that a reasonably alert owner could not have failed to recognise that the recreational use by local inhabitants was the assertion of a right and would

26.42 It has recently been established in the Supreme Court in *R (Barkas) v North Yorkshire County Council (Barkas)*[68] that where land is held by a local authority (either by acquisition or by virtue of an appropriation)[69] for statutory purposes

---

mature into an established right unless he took action to stop it. In *Lewis*, Lord Hope said at [67] that users must have been using the land as of right:

'that is to say, openly and in the manner that a person rightfully entitled would have used it. If the user for at least 20 years was of such amount and in such manner as would reasonably be regarded as being the assertion of a public right, ... the owner will be taken to have acquiesced in it – unless he can claim that one of the three vitiating circumstances applied in his case. If he does the second question is whether the claim can be made out. Once the second question is out of the way – either because it has not been asked or because it had been answered against the owner – that is the end of the matter.'

Lord Hope was also of the view that it was not a bar to registration that the two uses, that of the golfers and that of local inhabitants, co-existed, nor did he consider it necessary to superimpose upon the usual test for registration a further requirement that it would appear to a reasonable landowner that users were asserting a right to use the land for recreation. In concurring with the opinions of Lord Walker, Lord Brown and Lord Kerr, it was the view of Lord Hope ([106]–[107]) that, 'the focus must always be on the way the land has been used by the locals, and, above all, the quality of that user'. As Lord Kerr put it ([114]), 'Have they used them as if they had a right to use them? ... The question is whether they acted in a way that was comparable to the exercise of an existing right?'. *Powell v Secretary of State for the Environment, Food and Rural Affairs* [2014] EWHC 4009 (Admin) involved a challenge against an order made under the WCA 1981 for the inclusion of a public footpath on the definitive map and statement (DMS) where the court had to determine the correct approach to 'as of right' in the context of the test of presumed dedication of the footpath under HA 1980, s 31. The court held that the focus of the inquiry had to be on the use itself and how it would, assessed objectively, have appeared to the owner. The structure of the inquiry was first to examine the quality of the use relied upon and then, once the use had passed the threshold of being of sufficient quantity and suitable quality, to assess whether any of the vitiating elements from the tripartite test applied, judging the questions objectively from how the use would have appeared to the owner. Posing the tripartite test was the law's way of assessing whether or not it would be reasonable to expect that the use would be resisted by the owner.

[68]   [2014] UKSC 31. See Lord Neuberger at [24] and [46] and Lord Carnwath at [66].

[69]   A local authority's power of appropriation exists under LGA 1972, s 122(1). In *R (Goodman) v Secretary of State for Environment, Food and Rural Affairs* [2015] EWHC 2576 (Admin), Dove J ruled at [25]–[26] that an appropriation may not be inferred by conduct alone and that there is a need 'for identification – or recording in a resolution dealing with the land – that an appropriation had occurred'. He said that what is critical for these purposes is that before the power under s 122 of the LGA 1972 is exercised, the authority must be satisfied that the land 'is no longer required' for the purpose for which it is held which requires, he said, 'some conscious deliberative process so as to ensure that the statutory powers under which the land is held is clear and appropriation from one use to another cannot, in my view, be simply inferred from how the council manages or treats the land'. A conclusion that an appropriation of the land for public recreation could be inferred was rejected in *Goodman* where it was found to be wholly incompatible with the landowning authority's conduct as a planning authority which regarded the development of the land (for employment and as a link road) as an important factor in the forward planning process. There was, in the circumstances, no evidence that there had been 'some conscious deliberative process' on the part of the authority to make the land available for public recreational use the effect of which would be (at least on this ground) to preclude its registration as a village green. Dove J stated that there was nothing to detect in *Beresford* and *Barkas* 'any support for the

which allow it to be used by the public for recreation, the public's use of the land will be 'by right' and not 'as of right' (meaning 'as if by right') and thus non-qualifying. *Barkas* involved the use of recreational open space under the Housing Acts,[70] but the principle is applicable whenever land is held, for instance, for the purposes of the statutory right of public recreation under section 164 of the Public Health Act 1875 (PHA 1875)[71] (public walks or pleasure grounds) or section 10 of the Open Spaces Act 1906 (OSA 1906)[72] (open spaces – whether vested in the

---

proposition that appropriation pursuant to Section 122 of the 1972 Act from one power and purpose to another can be inferred from the authority's manner of dealing with or managing the land'. In the result, an appropriation may be express or implied from a decision of the authority which necessarily indicates an intention to hold the land for a purpose other than the purpose for which it was acquired or later appropriated.

[70] Comprising the Housing Acts of 1925, 1936, 1957 and 1985; the current position is that Housing Act 1985, s 12(1) (and the earlier Housing Acts contained similar provisions), empowers a local authority to provide and maintain (with the consent of the Minister) in connection with housing accommodation provided by them, recreation grounds which, in the opinion of the Minister, would serve a beneficial purpose in connection with the requirements of the persons for whom such housing accommodation is provided. Section 13(1) (and, as before, the earlier housing legislation contained a similarly worded provision) empowers a local authority to set out an open space on land acquired for housing purposes, but without having to obtain ministerial consent. The absence of ministerial consent for the setting out of recreation grounds under the Housing Acts is unlikely to be fatal to the lawful use of such land for recreation in view of the principle that administrative acts are valid unless and until quashed by a court and if the time has passed for them to be challenged then they stand notwithstanding that the reasoning on which they are based may have been flawed (see *R (Noble Organisation) v Thanet District Council* [2005] EWCA Civ 782 at [42] per Auld LJ). There is no authority holding that land held for the purposes of the Physical Training and Recreation Act 1937 and the Local Government (Miscellaneous Provisions) Act 1976 would not be registrable, but in light of *Barkas* it seems highly likely that local inhabitants would also have a legal right to recreate on land acquired or appropriated onto the purposes of 1937 Act, s 4(1). The 1937 Act authorised local authorities to:

> 'acquire, lay out, provide with suitable buildings and otherwise equip, and maintain lands … for the purpose of centres for the use of clubs … playing fields … or organisations having athletic, social or educational objects, and may manage those lands and buildings themselves … at a nominal or other rent to any person, club, society or organisation for use for any of the purposes aforesaid.'

By 1976 Act, s 19(5), land held for the purposes of 1937 Act, s 4, was to be held thereafter for the purposes of 1976 Act, s 19, which enables an authority to provide indoor and outdoor recreational facilities to such persons whom the authority thought fit, either with or without a charge.

[71] *Hall v Beckenham Corporation* [1949] 1 KB 716, where it was held that the corporation was bound to admit any member of the public who wanted to enter the park during the hours that it was open; *Blake v Hendon Corporation* [1962] 1 QB 283, where it was held that once land had been acquired under the PHA 1875 the public had a right of free and unrestricted use of the park.

[72] OSA 1906, s 9 permits local authorities to purchase and manage land for the purpose of it being used as public open space. Under s 10, open space under the Act is to be held and administered in trust to allow such land to be enjoyed by the public as an open space and for no other purpose. Land held for such purposes would not be registrable.

local authority or not).[73] This is to be contrasted with *Oxfordshire County Council v Oxford City Council*,[74] where, although the land was in public ownership, it had not been laid out or identified in any way for public recreational use and, indeed, was largely inaccessible.

26.43 The question arising from the decision of the Supreme Court in *Barkas* is whether land has been lawfully allocated or designated under statutory powers for public recreation. If it has, then user will not have been 'as of right', as the public will already have an entitlement to use the land for recreation. *Barkas* accordingly makes it clear that the public use of land pursuant to a statutory power to provide recreation land was sufficient to amount to the giving of a permission or a licence to local inhabitants so as to defeat a claim to that use being 'as of right'.

Highway land – is the use of such land 'as of right'?

26.44 There are two issues under this head: (a) whether the claimed green forms part of a publicly maintainable highway; and (b) if it does, how would it affect the application to register – would it preclude registration as a matter of law?

26.45 The highway issue can arise for decision in the case of substantial parcels of public open space at the side of roads. It is considered likely: (a) that highway land is not precluded by law from being registrable: and (b) that qualifying user on highway land is markedly constrained by the right of the public to use the land as a highway. If the land in issue is a highway, then the public's use of that land pursuant to their right to use it as highway must be discounted from the consideration as to whether it has become a TVG. This arises from *Director of Public Prosecution v Jones*,[75] which determined that the public can lawfully do anything reasonable on highway land which does not interfere with the public's right to pass and repass. In practice, most harmless activities on the land would therefore be qualifying activity, and what is left may either be too trivial to justify

---

73 In *Naylor v Essex County Council* [2014] EWHC 2560 (Admin), the authority did not own the land but had managed and maintained it as if it were public open space for all to use. The court upheld the decision of the inspector that the land should not be registered. The view taken was that the land was most likely to have been managed and controlled either under OSA 1906, s 9 or s 10, or under PHA 1875, s 164. The court determined that it made no difference to the rights which the public had to use the land that the use arose by virtue of an arrangement between the landowner and the authority where the authority had itself no legal interest in the land. The view was taken that local inhabitants had been using the land 'by right', in the sense of having permission to do so from the landowner pursuant to arrangements made between the landowner and the local authority securing the provision of land and its management as a piece of public open space.

74 [2006] UKHL 25, [2006] 2 AC 674.
75 [1999] 2 WLR 625.

registration or else may amount to an interference with the highway and be unlawful and thus non-qualifying in any event.

Use by force

26.46 Force does not just mean physical force as, for instance, where locked gates are broken open, where fencing is damaged or prohibitory signage is torn down and ignored. Use is by force (and thus non-peaceable) whenever it is contentious or allowed under protest. If, for instance, there is a state of perpetual warfare between the parties, there can obviously be no use 'as of right'.[76] If prohibitive signage is not seen because it has been torn down, then user is unlikely to have been as of right provided the steps taken by the landowner would otherwise have been sufficient to notify reasonable users that they should not be trespassing on the land (or that their user is permissive).[77] Village green rights cannot accrue as a consequence of the unlawful acts of others.[78]

Use by stealth or secrecy

26.47 Use that is secret or by stealth will not be use as of right because it would not come to the attention of the landowner. The owner must know or have the means of knowledge that the land is being used for lawful sports and pastimes.

Permissive use

26.48 Permission can be express, such as by erecting notices which in terms grant temporary permission to local people to use the land. An appropriate permissory notice would be in the following terms, 'The public have permission to enter this land on foot for recreation, but this permission may be withdrawn at any time'.[79] The best evidence of permission is where access is enjoyed under a contract or in return for a periodic payment.[80]

---

[76] *Megarry & Wade: The Law of Real Property* (8th edn, Sweet & Maxwell, London, 2012) 28-050.

[77] See *R (Oxfordshire and Buckinghamshire Mental Health Trust) v Oxfordshire County Council* [2010] EWHC 530 (Admin) at [22] and the eight principles identified by HHJ Waksman in determining whether the use of signage is sufficient to preclude either use as of right for TVG purposes or the presumption that the land has been dedicated as a highway. Where the owner of land has made its position about the use of its land clear through the erection of clearly visible prohibitory signage then unauthorised use of the land could not be 'as of right'. *Taylor v Betterment Properties (Weymouth) Ltd and Dorset County Council* [2012] EWCA Civ 250, followed in *R (Cotham School) v Bristol City Council* [2018] EWHC 1022 (Admin) and *Winterburn v Bennett* [2016] EWCA Civ 482, [2017] 1 WLR 646.

[78] *Taylor v Betterment Properties (Weymouth) Ltd and Dorset County Council* [2012] EWCA Civ 250 at [63].

[79] *R (Beresford) v Sunderland City Council* [2003] UKHL 60, [2004] 1 AC 889 at [72] and [79].

[80] *Gardner v Hodgson's Kingston Brewery Co Ltd* [1903] AC 229.

Permission implied from conduct

26.49 In *R (Beresford) v Sunderland City Council*,[81] the House of Lords concluded that a licence to use land must involve a 'positive act'[82] or amount to the communication of an 'overt act', which is intended to be understood as permission to do something which would otherwise be an act of trespass,[83] as opposed to a landowner's silent passive acquiescence in persons using his land which would not. The requirement for an 'overt act' does not mean that permission can only be communicated expressly. In *Beresford*, it was said by Lord Bingham that:[84]

> ... a landowner may so conduct himself as to make clear, even in the absence of an express statement, notice or record, that the inhabitants' use of the land is pursuant to his permission.

26.50 Lord Bingham suggested that an example of this would be where a landowner excluded locals on occasional days when he wished to use his land for his own purposes. By so doing, the landowner asserts his right to exclude, and so makes plain that the inhabitants' use on other occasions occurs because he does not choose on those occasions to exercise his right to exclude and so permits such use.[85] On the other hand, occasional challenges by a landowner to regulate use of the land (e.g. by asking dog-walkers to put their dogs on leads) would not preclude use as of right (i.e. by amounting to an implied permission) if they were in fact

---

81   [2003] UKHL 60, [2004] 1 AC 889.

82   [2003] UKHL 60, [2004] 1 AC 889 at [59] per Lord Rodger.

83   [2003] UKHL 60, [2004] 1 AC 889 at [75] and [83] per Lord Walker.

84   [2003] UKHL 60, [2004] 1 AC 889 at [5]. See also Lord Walker at [83].

85   See *R (Mann) v Somerset County Council* [2012] EWHC B14 (Admin), a decision of HHJ Owen QC, sitting as a judge of the High Court, which was handed down on 11/5/2012. *Mann* concerned privately owned land associated with a public house. Local inhabitants were excluded from parts of the land when ticketed beer festivals took place on three or four occasions along with the occasional holding of a funfair, again on part of the land, for which the public were charged an admission fee. The registration authority accepted the advice of its non-statutory inspector (whose decision was accepted by the court) and rejected the application to register. In *R (Goodman) v Secretary of State for the Environment, Food and Rural Affairs* [2015] EWHC 2576 (Admin), Dove J considered the decision in *Mann* in a case where publicly owned land had been the subject of ample licensed use for funfairs and other recreational activities throughout the relevant 20-year period. It was his view that for an implied permission to arise in such circumstances, there must be evidence that the landowner intended to grant permission to local inhabitants, whereas in this case they were consistent with recreational use on the whole of the land as of right. Dove J ruled that the inspector should not have found that use was permissive (following *Mann v Somerset County Council*) and that his decision (in what was an application in a pioneer authority) should be quashed in that he had failed to consider: (a) that the relevant land was in public ownership; and (b) that the nature and character of the events relied on (i.e. circuses and funfairs) were at least arguably consistent with a public entitlement to use the land.

attempts to accommodate conflicting uses, which is a question of fact on the evidence.[86]

26.51 In *Newhaven Port and Properties Ltd v East Sussex County Council*[87] the Supreme Court held that byelaws which permitted members of the public to use a beach for leisure purposes gave rise to an implied permission. The fact that the byelaws were not displayed did not mean that they did not operate as an effective licence rendering use of the beach by members of the public 'by right' rather than 'as of right'.

On the land

26.52 The expression 'on the land' in section 15 does not mean that the registration authority has to look for evidence that every square foot of the land has been used. Rather, the registration authority needs to be satisfied that for all practical purposes, it can sensibly be said that the whole of the land had been used for informal recreation during the relevant period, always bearing in mind that qualifying use will be heavier in some areas than in others. When areas of the claimed green have not been used or are inaccessible, the question for decision is whether the whole of the land is still registrable. The answer in truth is whether the unused areas are integral to the enjoyment of the whole of the land as might apply, for instance, in the case of borders and overgrown areas which can form part of the function and attractiveness of the area. The registration authority has power to sever from the application those parts of the land where qualifying use may not have taken place, either at all or not for the requisite period.[88]

26.53 There is a useful extract in *Oxfordshire County Council v Oxford City Council*[89] at first instance on this point, where Lightman J, under the heading 'Registrability as a green of land of which only part is accessible' said[90] (citing from what was said by Sullivan J in *R (Cheltenham Builders Ltd) v South Gloucestershire District Council*)[91] that:

> the onus is on the applicant to prove on the balance of probability that the land in question has become a green and thus that the whole, and not merely a part or parts, had been used for lawful sports and pastimes for not less than 20 years.

---

[86]   *R (Lancashire CC) v Secretary of State for Environment, Food and Rural Affairs* [2018] EWCA Civ 721 at [86].

[87]   [2015] UKSC 7, [2015] AC 1547.

[88]   *Oxfordshire County Council v Oxford City Council* [2006] UKHL 25, [2006] 2 AC 674.

[89]   [2004] EWHC 12 (Ch), [2004] Ch 253.

[90]   [2004] EWHC 12 (Ch), [2004] Ch 253 at [92]–[95].

[91]   [2003] EWHC 2803 (Admin) at [29].

26.54 Lightman J then went on to cite the following passage from *Cheltenham Builders*:[92]

> A common sense approach is required when considering whether the whole of the site was so used. A registration authority would not expect to see evidence of use of every square foot of a site, but it would have to be persuaded that for all practical purposes it could sensibly be said that the whole of the site had been so used for 20 years.

For a period of at least 20 years

26.55 Qualifying use has to be continuous throughout the 20-year period.[93] Temporary interruptions in use are not to be equated with a lack of continuity. It is essentially a matter of fact and degree for the decision-maker to determine whether the whole of the land has been available for lawful sports and pastimes continuously throughout the 20-year period. In *Taylor v Betterment Properties (Weymouth) Ltd and Dorset County Council*,[94] a material interruption took place on part of the land in circumstances where substantial drainage works had taken place on the land for upwards of two to three years involving partial fencing off (complete enclosure only continued for some four months), the presence of plant and equipment and spoil heaps on the land associated with substantial tunnelling operations, together with a footpath diversion order re-routing a public footpath around the perimeter of the works' site. Patten LJ said[95] that where competing uses can accommodate one another then time does not cease to run. However, he said that:

> the exclusion of the land on which the drainage works took place was complete and the use of the land for such purposes was not compatible with it remaining in use as a village green.

CONFLICTING STATUTORY REGIMES

The *Newhaven, Lancashire County Council* and *NHS Property Services Ltd* litigation

26.56 In *Newhaven Port and Properties Ltd v East Sussex County Council*, the Supreme Court held[96] that where Parliament had conferred on a statutory

---

92   [2004] EWHC 12 (Ch), [2004] Ch 253 at [93].
93   *Hollins v Verney* (1884) 13 QBD 304.
94   [2012] EWCA Civ 250.
95   [2012] EWCA Civ 250 at [70].
96   [2015] UKSC 7, [2015] AC 1547.

undertaker powers to acquire land compulsorily and to hold and use that land for defined statutory purposes, the CA 2006 did not enable the public to acquire user rights which were incompatible with the continuing use of the land for those statutory purposes. The court found that there was a clear incompatibility between the statutory functions of Newhaven Port and Properties Ltd in relation to the operational use of the harbour at Newhaven and the registration of the beach and the promenade as a village green. The fact that land may be owned by a public body which has statutory powers that it can apply in future to develop land is not, of itself, sufficient to create a *statutory incompatibility*. By contrast, in Newhaven, the statutory harbour authority held the harbour land for statutory harbour purposes which, in the event that works had to be executed in a way which affected the public's use of the beach were it registered as a green, would give rise to an obvious and irreconcilable clash as between the conflicting statutory regimes.[97]

26.57 By the time the *Newhaven* litigation reached the Supreme Court, there were three issues before the Court:

(a) Whether the fact that the beach was part of the foreshore precluded use 'as of right', on the basis that the public had an implied licence to use the foreshore which had not been revoked.
(b) Whether in the absence of such a licence, the public nonetheless had an implied licence to use the beach, as part of the harbour, in light of the byelaws which regulated the use of such land.
(c) Whether, in any event, section 15 of the CA 2006 could be construed so as to enable registration of land as a village green if such registration was incompatible with some other statutory function to which the land was to be put.

26.58 On the first issue, the Supreme Court elected not to decide the nature and extent of the public's right over the foreshore as it did not need to do so. Instead, the Court allowed the landowner's appeal on the second issue, namely, that because the byelaws permitted members of the public to use the beach for leisure purposes, permission could be implied. The fact that the byelaws were not displayed did not mean that they did not operate as an effective licence rendering use of the beach by members of the public 'by right' rather than 'as of right'. The Supreme Court found that it was unnecessary for a landowner to show that members of the public had to have it drawn to their attention that their use of the land was permitted in order for their use to be treated as being 'by right'. In so finding, the Supreme Court clearly applied the reasoning in *Barkas*.[98] There

---

[97] [2015] UKSC 7, [2015] AC 1547 at [93] and [101] per Lord Neuberger.
[98] [2014] UKSC 31.

follow two recent cases in which the principles of statutory incompatibility were examined in conjoined appeals in the Court of Appeal.

26.59 In *R (Lancashire County Council) v Secretary of State for Environment, Food and Rural Affairs*,[99] the interested party had appealed against the refusal of the registration authority to register land adjacent to a school as a TVG. The respondent Secretary of State's inspector allowed the appeal and granted the application to register. Lancashire applied for judicial review of that decision on the ground (*inter alia*) that the land was held for educational purposes and its registration as a TVG would be incompatible with that statutory purpose. The judge dismissed the claim and upheld the registration on the basis that even if the land had been used for educational purposes, which was not proved, there was no incompatibility between that use and the use of the land as a TVG. Lancashire appealed against the decision upholding the land's registration as a TVG.

26.60 In *R (NHS Property Services Ltd) v Jones*,[100] a non-statutory inspector had recommended refusal of an application, supported by the appellant interested party, to register a parcel of woodland adjoining a hospital as a TVG. The land was owned by the first respondent company. The second respondent local authority (Surrey County Council) rejected the inspector's recommendation and registered the land as a TVG. The company applied for judicial review of that decision on the grounds (*inter alia*) that the land's registration as a TVG was incompatible with its statutory purpose, since the land had always been held by one or another of several statutory bodies for purposes relating to healthcare. The judge allowed the claim on the basis of the statutory incompatibility objection. The appellant interested party appealed against the decision on statutory incompatibility.

26.61 Both appeals on statutory incompatibility were rejected by the Court of Appeal.[101] The court upheld the principles in the *Newhaven* case and saw no reason to refine or enlarge them in the two cases before the court. The court held that when another statutory regime was said to displace the registration provisions within the CA 2006, the issue would always be one of statutory construction. Section 15 did not enable rights to be acquired by the public where they were clearly incompatible with the continuing use of the land for its statutory purposes. In *Newhaven*, that clear incompatibility arose from the harbour company's statutory functions in relation to the harbour and the registration of the beach as a TVG. The circumstances in each of the two appeals were found to be different. Crucially, as a matter of statutory construction, there was no inconsistency of the

[99]   [2018] EWCA Civ 721.

[100]   [2018] EWCA Civ 721 (which was heard with the appeal in the *Lancashire County Council* case).

[101]   This litigation has not yet ended as on 31/10/2018 the Supreme Court granted permission to appeal on the statutory incompatibility ground.

kind that arose in *Newhaven* between the provisions of one statute and the provisions of the other. There were no 'specific' statutory purposes or provisions attaching to the particular land in either case. The statutory purpose for which Parliament had authorised the acquisition and use of the land and the operation of section 15 were not inherently inconsistent with each other.

26.62 In *Lancashire*, the statutory powers relied on were general in their character and content, comprising a local education authority's functions in securing educational provision in its area. There was no statutory obligation to maintain or use the relevant land in a particular way, or to carry out any particular activities on it. Lancashire would still be able to carry out its statutory educational functions if the public had a right to use the land as a TVG even though it might be or become more difficult or less convenient for them to do so. The same point applied in *NHS Property Services Ltd*'s appeal. There was no inherent inconsistency between the provisions in the statutory regime under which the land was held and the statutory provisions for registration as a TVG. The statutory functions on which the company relied and the statutory purposes underlying them were also general in character and content. There was, for example, no statutory duty to provide a hospital or any other healthcare service or facility on the relevant land, and the relevant statutory purposes on which the land was held were still capable of fulfilment through the landowner's ownership of other land comprised within the same title without recourse to the application land. There was, therefore, no statutory incompatibility in either case and both appeals failed on this ground. In the circumstances, an objection founded upon statutory incompatibility will fall within narrow limits.

De-registration and exchange

26.63 On 1/10/2007, sections 16 and 17 of the CA 2006 came into force. These sections deal with de-registration and exchange of common land and TVGs. The owner of such land may apply to the Secretary of State (upon payment of an application fee) for land ('the release land') to cease to be registered, in which event it will be removed from the register of TVGs. If the release land is more than 200 square metres in area, the application must include a proposal that further land ('the replacement land' – which must not already be registered as common land or as a village green) is to be registered as common land or as a village green in place of the release land.

26.64 The statutory tests are prescribed in section 16(6)–(8) of the CA 2006, which requires the decision-maker to have regard to the interests of those with rights in the land, the interests of the neighbourhood and the public interest. The public interest covers nature and landscape conservation, and the protection of public rights of access, archaeological remains and features of historic interest.

Defra's guidance[102] makes it clear that even if the release land is less than 200 square metres, an applicant would still be expected to offer replacement land, as it is the Government's policy objective not to allow the stock of common land and greens to diminish.

Amending the register to cancel a registration

26.65 With effect from 15/12/2014, section 19(2)(a) (correcting a mistake made by a registration authority in making or amending an entry in the register of TVGs) of, and paragraphs 8 and 9 of Schedule 2 (non-registration or mistaken registration under the CRA 1965) to, the CA 2006 came into force outside the pioneer areas.[103]

26.66 It is doubtful whether much will turn in practice on the national roll-out of paragraphs 8 and 9 of Schedule 2 in that the necessary criteria for the removal by the registration authority of mistakenly registered buildings or land under the CRA 1965 are limited in their effect, as we are dealing with the regime in place in the period 1965–1970.[104]

26.67 It seems likely that landowners will continue to adopt the remedy available under section 14(b) of the CRA 1965 (i.e. rectification ordered by the High Court in the case of erroneous entries made in the registers of town or village greens),[105] rather than leave matters for decision by the registration authority

---

[102] *Common Land consents policy* (November 2015, Defra).

[103] The Commons Act 2006 (Commencement No 7, Transitional and Savings Provisions) (England) Order 2014 (SI 2014/3026). The exercise or non-exercise of this power is presumably vulnerable to judicial review. The registration authority can either act on its own initiative or on the application of any person. It seems reasonable to assume that the re-hearing approach laid down in *Betterment* will apply by analogy in the case of disputed applications to the registration authority to correct mistakes under s 19(2)(a). Until s 14(b) is finally repealed outside the pioneer areas challenges will no doubt continue to be made under this section in the High Court rather than under the new procedures outlined in the 2014 Regulations in the case of applications to correct mistakes under s 19(2)(a) even though disputed applications have to be referred to the PINS (2014 Regulations, reg 26(3)).

[104] In the case of buildings registered as village greens, it has to be shown that at the time of provisional registration the land was covered by a building, or was within the curtilage of a building, and the provisional registration became final, since when the land has remained covered by a building. In the case of wrongly registered land, the registration authority has, in practice, to be satisfied: (a) that the land was provisionally registered; (b) that the provisional registration was not referred to a Commons Commissioner before it became final; and (c) that throughout the period of 20 years preceding the date of provisional registration, the land was, by reason of its physical nature, unusable by members of the public for the purpose of lawful sports and pastimes.

[105] The power of the High Court to rectify the register under CRA 1965, s 14(b) applies in those cases where the register has been amended in pursuance of s 13 where it appears that no amendment or a different amendment ought to have been made and that the error cannot be corrected in pursuance of regulations made under the Act (and none were) *and* where the court

under section 19(2)(a), which, by virtue of section 19(5), may still decide not to rectify the register if it considers that by reason of reliance reasonably placed on the register by any person or for any other reason, that it would, in all the circumstances, be unfair to rectify the register.

Challenging decisions of the registration authority

26.68 The options vary depending on whether the registration authority is a pioneer authority. Registrations made by non-pioneer authorities may be challenged by way of: (a) judicial review in cases of error of law, unreasonableness and unfairness; or (b) by way of section 14(b) of the CRA 1965[106] where rectification of the register and the removal of the offending registration may be sought in the High Court in consequence of an erroneous amendment of the register and where the court deems it just to rectify the register; and (c) since 15/12/2014, by way of application to the registration authority, under section 19(2)(a) of the CA 2006 (i.e. to correct mistakes made by the registration authority in making or amending any entry in the register).[107] Registrations made by pioneer authorities can be challenged by judicial review and by section 19 of the CA 2006, but not by way of application to the High Court under section 14(b) of the CRA 1965. There accordingly remains a heavy burden on registration authorities to correctly determine applications.

Judicial review

26.69 The usual challenge is based on error of law, but a determination of the registration authority would also be open to challenge if it had adopted an unfair procedure in determining the application or had failed to give reasons. The normal time limits and procedures apply for judicial review of a decision to register (three months). The decision that is to be reviewed is that of the relevant regulatory committee or, in pioneer areas, sometimes that of the PINS (by way of a claim made against the Secretary of State for the Environment, Food and Rural Affairs, with the landowning objector being joined as an interested party).

---

deems it just to rectify the register. This provision is considered below in the context of challenges to decisions of registration authorities. Section 14(b) continues in force except in the pioneer areas, although even in those areas the section will continue to apply in relation to amendments made to the register before CA 2006, Pt 1 was commenced, which was on 1/10/2008 in the case of the original seven pioneer areas, and on 15/12/2014 in the case of the two new pioneer areas of Cumbria County Council and North Yorkshire County Council.

[106] CRA 1965, s 14(a) involves rectification arising from fraudulent inducements encouraging the withdrawal of an objection to registration or to refrain from making an objection.

[107] Any such application should be made in accordance with the Commons Registration (England) Regulations 2014 (SI 2014/3038).

CRA 1965, section 14(b)

26.70 A number of challenges have been brought under section 14(b) of the CRA 1965 in the case of registrations made under section 22 or section 22(1A) of that Act. It should be noted, however, that until section 1 of the CA 2006 comes into force (and it is currently only in force in pioneer areas), section 14 of the CRA 1965 will continue in force outside the pioneer areas.[108] Where land was registered pursuant to section 13 of the CRA 1965, section 14(b) of that Act allowed the High Court to de-register when it appeared to the court: (a) that the original registration was in error; (b) that the error could not be corrected using the regulations made under the CRA 1965 (no such regulations were ever made); and (c) that the court deemed it 'just to rectify the register' ('the justice issue'). As indicated, this remedy continues to be available in the case of registrations made under section 15 of the CA 2006 outside the pioneer areas.

26.71 It was established in *Betterment Properties (Weymouth) Ltd v Dorset County Council*[109] that an application to de-register under section 14(b) of the CRA 1965 would be a re-hearing although it would be up to the judge to decide (pursuant to his case management powers) on the procedure and on what should be admitted as evidence at the trial. The court held that there is nothing to limit the width of the ensuing hearing. The court can, if necessary, look at the matter afresh even to the extent that local inhabitants would be free to seek to uphold the registration on some basis other than that which was advanced at the time of the application or non-statutory inquiry. The *Betterment* case proceeded to trial,[110] and after an eight-day hearing in which fresh evidence was called, Morgan J set aside the decision to register which had been made by a panel of three Dorset county councillors on the basis that their rejection of the landowner's case on: (a) non-peaceable user; and (b) interruption had been wrongly decided. The decision of Morgan J was confirmed on appeal[111] and in the Supreme Court on the justice issue.[112]

The justice issue

26.72 Merely proving that a registration authority made a mistake in registering land as a village green is not enough, as section 14(b) of the CRA 1965 provides

[108] This arises from Commons Act 2006 (Commencement No 2, Transitional Provisions and Savings) (England) Order 2007 (SI 2007/456), art 4, which provides that until CA 2006, s 1 comes into force in the non-pioneer areas, village green registers shall be maintained under the CRA 1965 and any registration will be treated as if it had in fact been made pursuant to CRA 1965, s 13(b) rather than under CA 2006, s 15.

[109] [2007] EWHC 365 (Ch) and upheld on appeal at [2008] EWCA Civ 22, [2009] 1 WLR 334.

[110] [2010] EWHC 3045 (Ch).

[111] [2012] EWCA Civ 250.

[112] [2014] UKSC 7.

that the register may only be amended if 'the court deems it just to rectify the register'. In *Betterment* at first instance, Morgan J was of the view that there is a *prima facie* presumption that land should be de-registered unless there is some other (usually very compelling reason) that makes it unjust to rectify the register. The unjust factors advanced by the appellant in *Betterment* included the gamble that the landowner had made in purchasing a registered green, the reliance local people had placed on the register when purchasing their homes, the landowner's delay in bringing their case under section 14(b) and the high value placed by the local community on the recreational space. No doubt, any factor could be potentially relevant depending on the circumstances of each case.

26.73 In *Paddico (267) Ltd v Kirklees Metropolitan Council*,[113] there was no evidence from local homeowners of potential loss of property values put before the court, merely a 'heartfelt plea' that the users of the land should be allowed to continue to enjoy the use of the land for recreation. Vos J placed most weight[114] on the registration having been challenged almost immediately by the owners and he further concluded, after hearing the evidence, that the owner would have challenged the use of his land for recreation if the original application (in 1996) had been rejected. Thus, although there was a 'reasonable expectation by the users that they would continue to be able to use the land', this was 'tempered somewhat by the fact that George Haigh Ltd (the owner at the time) had issued proceedings challenging the registration very shortly afterwards (in 1997)'. This attempt to de-register the land had effectively been abandoned (the original proceedings had been struck out following the imposition of an automatic stay arising from the introduction of the CPR) and it was almost 13 years before the new owner brought a new section 14 claim. Vos J concluded that apart from the delay in bringing proceedings, there was little other prejudice to the local inhabitants, and the view he took was that it was just to order rectification.

26.74 The reasoning in *Betterment* and *Paddico* at first instance seemed to be that the courts will seriously consider only economic justice (where the scales are invariably weighted in favour of the landowner), and that other extra-legal considerations would be disregarded or given less weight. However, the majority in the Court of Appeal in *Paddico*[115] disagreed with Vos J's approach. Sullivan LJ (with whom Carnwath LJ agreed) held that although the context was different, there was an analogy with the planning register and that members of the public were entitled to expect certainty and there was, therefore, a strong public interest in erroneous village green registrations being challenged at the earliest opportunity. The majority further held that whilst there was no prescribed time limit for making an application under section 14 of the CRA 1965, landowners

---

113 [2011] EWHC 1606 (Ch).

114 [2011] EWHC 1606 (Ch) at [117]–[119].

115 [2012] EWCA Civ 262 (Patten LJ dissenting).

could be expected to take reasonably prompt action. So that in *Paddico*, notwithstanding the fact that the registration was held by the court to be in error, the register was not rectified.[116] In *Betterment*, the same Court of Appeal came to the opposite conclusion as the delay had not been so lengthy, and the decision at first instance to cancel the registration was duly affirmed. Judicial review proceedings had been commenced by the owner soon after the decision to register (albeit that they were later discontinued), and there was then a period of over four years between the discontinuance of those proceedings and the bringing of the section 14 application by the landowner.

26.75 The decision of the Supreme Court on the issue of delay and factors relevant to delay in the case of challenges under section 14(b) of the CRA 1965 was handed down on 5/2/2014.[117] The Supreme Court ruled that the delay in neither case was sufficient to preclude the cancellation of the registrations. Although there is no time limit under section 14, the court may still consider prolonged delay accompanied by proof of actual detriment to be material when it comes to the 'justice' issue. Major points of significance which emerged from the judgment of Baroness Hale are these: (a) a claimant buying into section 14 proceedings (as happened in both *Betterment* and *Paddico*) will not be in a worse position than his predecessor; and (b) the prejudice to local inhabitants at being forced to give up a right which they should never have had is not very weighty. It surely follows from the decision of the Supreme Court that in making investment decisions, developers now have a real incentive to look behind village green registrations going back several years.

REFORMS TO CA 2006 IN THE GROWTH AND INFRASTRUCTURE ACT 2013, SECTIONS 14 TO 17

Section 15A – landowner statements in Form CA16

26.76 With effect from 1/10/2013, section 15A of the CA 2006[118] enables landowners to bring an end to qualifying user by the simple expedient of depositing with the registration authority a statement in the prescribed form.[119] A landowner statement stops the clock on the number of years of qualifying use. If the land has been used for less than 20 years, then the deposited statement

---

[116] Sullivan LJ concluded at [2012] EWCA Civ 262 at [39] that: 'While it must be desirable, in principle, that errors in a public register should be rectified, the delay of over 12 years was, by the standards of any reasonable legal process, so excessive as to make it not just to rectify the register'.

[117] [2014] UKSC 7.

[118] Added by Growth and Infrastructure Act 2013, s 15.

[119] Form CA16 must be accompanied by a map in the prescribed form identifying the land to which the statement relates. A fee will also have to be paid and registration authorities have the power to set their own fees.

prevents users obtaining the 20 years they need to apply for registration. If a landowner statement is deposited at a time when recreational use has already taken place over the land for 20 years or more, then the landowner statement triggers the one-year period of grace for making applications to register under section 15 now that the two-year period has been reduced.[120]

26.77 Section 15A of the CA 2006 mirrors section 31(6) of the HA 1980, which enables maps, statements and statutory declarations to be deposited by landowners with highway authorities, the effect of which will be to prevent their land being recorded as a highway on the definitive map on the basis of presumed dedication. This process will then have effect for 20 years in the case of highways statements deposited and highways declarations lodged after 1/10/2013, but for those statements and declarations lodged before this date, it will be ten years. As the effect of section 15A of the CA 2006 and section 31(6) of the HA 1980 is the same, landowners are now able to make a single application on Form CA16 to prevent their land from being either recorded as a highway on the definitive map or registered as a village green. Section 15B of the CA 2006[121] requires every registration authority to keep a register containing prescribed information about statements deposited with that authority (and any maps accompanying those statements) under section 15A. Landowners would be well advised to heed the advantages of a landowner statement in protecting their land from the risk of registration.

Section 15C – 'trigger' and 'terminating' events

26.78 The effect of section 15C of the CA 2006 (which came into force on 25/4/2013 – and the provision applies whether a trigger event occurs before or after this date)[122] is that the right to apply to register land as a TVG ceases to apply where a trigger event relating to the development of the land occurs, and becomes exercisable again only if a corresponding terminating event occurs. The trigger and terminating events are identified in the new Schedule 1A to the CA 2006. The CA 2006 also gives the Secretary of State power, subject to a resolution of each House of Parliament, to amend Schedule 1A including by adding new trigger and terminating events.[123] What we have here is a statutory pause in that the right to apply to register will revive on the occurrence of one of the terminating events specified in Schedule 1A.

---

[120] CA 2006, s 15(3A).

[121] Added by Growth and Infrastructure Act 2013, s 15: s 16(4) and (5) contains transitional provisions which provide (s 16(4)) that it does not matter whether a trigger event occurs before or after 25/4/2013, nor (s 16(5)) will s 15C apply in relation to an application made under s 15(1) which is sent to the registration authority (i.e. being the date of its submission) before 25/4/2013.

[122] Added by Growth and Infrastructure Act 2013, s 16(1).

[123] The so-called 'Henry VIII clause'.

26.79 Under section 15C of the CA 2006, applications to register will not be possible in the case of land which has planning permission (or a publicised planning application) or is identified for potential development in a local or neighbourhood plan (including draft development plans).[124] However, land would still be available for registration where no development is either proposed or the subject of ongoing community consultation. The statutory pause would, however, be lifted (for instance) in a case where an application for planning permission was withdrawn or refused and where the refusal was not challenged or where all means of challenging the refusal had been exhausted or in circumstances where, if permission had been granted, any period within which the development must be begun had expired without the development having been begun. If the trigger event has been ended by a terminating event, any period of interruption under section 15C is to be disregarded.[125]

26.80 The necessity to reform village green law was plain in that applications to register were having the effect of delaying or preventing permitted development altogether. The object of section 15C of the CA 2006 was to ensure that once land had become subject to the planning system (i.e. in circumstances where planning permission had already been granted or where a planning application had been publicised and a decision was yet to be made), it would not be registrable or otherwise become subject to village green law and in this way conflict is removed. The following points should, however, be noted:[126]

(a)   a publicised planning application (i.e. as a trigger event) does not have to be incompatible with recreational use;
(b)   there are no trigger events in relation to permitted development rights;
(c)   it is irrelevant that a planning application results only in a temporary permission (i.e. the expiry of a temporary permission is not a terminating event).

---

[124] *R (Cooper Estates Strategic Land Ltd) v Wiltshire Council* [2018] EWHC 1704 (Admin), where it was held that a local authority had erred in registering land as a new green where it had been identified, as part of a market town, as an area for potential development on a development plan, meaning that a trigger event under CA 2006, Sch 1A, para 4 had suspended the right to apply for registration. The fact that the land was part of the market town and not specifically identified was not a bar to the application of para 4. It was said that the statutory purpose of removing barriers to development would be significantly undermined if it only applied where the plan identified the area that was actually the subject of the application.

[125] CA 2006, s 15C(8).

[126] See article by Simon Adamyk, 'A Red Light for Village Greens? Lessons from the South Bank' [2015] JPEL 397–408, which very helpfully looked at the rationale of the 2013 amendment under CA 2006, s 15C and how this played out in the case of the application to register the Undercroft (a concrete area underneath the Queen Elizabeth Hall in the South Bank Centre), which was ultimately settled. The article helpfully summarises the arguments on each side after one and half days of submissions. It is the view of Simon Adamyk that the arguments of the registration authority (the London Borough of Lambeth) were to be preferred (see para 13.6, points (a)–(c)).

Chapter 27

Public Rights of Way

INTRODUCTION

27.1   This chapter is not intended to be an overview of the modern law of highways. Instead, the focus is on those aspects of the law which have a bearing on the development of land affected by ways over which the public enjoy a right to pass and repass along a defined route.

27.2   As far as development is concerned, there are two implications. First, at the planning stage, the effect of a proposed development on an existing right of way will be a material consideration in the grant of planning permission.[1] The local planning authority (LPA) will need to ensure that all rights of way affected by the proposed development are identified and the effect of development on such rights has been considered, as well as the need to protect and enhance such public rights.[2] Secondly, the grant of planning permission does not result in the automatic extinguishment or diversion of the public right of way, nor does it follow that such an order will automatically be made. Premature interference with a public right of way before such an order is made (whether or not planning permission has been granted) may result in the commission of a criminal offence.[3]

27.3   For those reasons, public rights of way are a key consideration in any proposed development and must be identified at an early stage. Identifying such rights has been made easier by way of the definitive map which is kept under continuous review by surveying authorities, but problems arise when public rights

---

[1]   See *Rights of Way Circular (1/09)* (Defra, October 2009) at para 7.2; see also para 7.4.

[2]   See National Planning Policy Framework (Department for Communities and Local Government, 27/3/2012) (NPPF), available at http://planningguidance.communities.gov.uk. See also *Rights of Way Circular (1/09)*. It will also need to take into account any modifications to the definitive map which the highway authority may be proposing to make.

[3]   Highways Act 1980 (HA 1980), s 137, which provides for an offence of 'wilful obstruction' of a public highway punishable by way of a financial penalty. Note that the grant of planning permission will not provide lawful authority for obstructing a highway.

of way may have arisen over time by implied dedication or statutory presumption and have yet to be entered onto the definitive map by the surveying authority. The problem is compounded by the aphorism 'once a highway, always a highway';[4] thus the mere fact that a right of way seems no longer to be in use by the public does not nullify such a right existing. The right cannot be abandoned nor can the right be diminished by disuse.[5] Nor can such a right be lost to the public by adverse possession.[6] The issues that are likely to arise therefore in relation to highways are not always as straightforward as they first appear.

27.4   The law is largely contained in the Highways Act 1980 (HA 1980), which consolidated previous legislation and the common law.

WHAT IS A PUBLIC RIGHT OF WAY?

27.5   The phrase 'public right of way' is used interchangeably with the word 'highway', of which there is no definition in the HA 1980.[7] That being the case, the common law provides the essential characteristics of what is, or is not, a public right of way.

27.6   It is said a highway is a '*dedication* to the *public* of the occupation of the surface of the land *for the purpose of passing and re-passing*' (emphasis added).[8] Such a dedication is made in perpetuity. The public's right to pass and re-pass along land which is so dedicated is thus not a time-limited or transitory right,[9] and a public right of way over private land will be binding on successors in title, hence the saying 'once a highway, always a highway'.[10] A dedication of land purporting to create a right of way which is time limited will not give rise to a highway at law. Where a highway has been created and it is a highway maintainable at public

---

4   *Dawes v Hawkins* (1860) 8 CB (NS) 848 at 857 and 858 per Byles J, which is the earliest case in which the maxim is used. See also *R (Smith) v Land Registry (Peterborough)* [2010] EWCA Civ 200; *Harvey v Truro RDC* [1903] 2 Ch 638 per Joyce J.

5   *Suffolk County Council v Mason* [1979] AC 705 at 710 per Lord Diplock; see the speech of Arden LJ in *R (Smith) v Land Registry (Peterborough)* [2010] EWCA Civ 200.

6   *R (Smith) v Land Registry (Peterborough)* [2010] EWCA Civ 200.

7   Other than within HA 1980, s 328, which simply provides that the word 'highway' within the Act refers to the whole or a part of any highway other than a ferry or waterway. The statute also makes it clear that a highway may pass over a bridge or tunnel.

8   *Oxfordshire County Council v Oxford City Council* [2004] EWHC 12 (Ch) at 293 per Lightman J.

9   *Dawes v Hawkins* (1860) 8 CB (NS) 848 at 857.

10   *Dawes v Hawkins* (1860) 8 CB (NS) 848 at 858 per Byles J; *R (Smith) v Land Registry (Peterborough)* [2010] EWCA Civ 200; *Harvey v Truro RDC* [1903] 2 Ch 638 per Joyce J.

expense, the highway authority responsible for maintaining the way will obtain an interest in the land over which the way runs.[11]

27.7 To be a highway, the land involved must be open to the public at large and not simply to a section of it.[12] A right of way which is provided pursuant to a contract, licence or otherwise, cannot be a highway at law, without more.[13] It has in the past been suggested that a public right of way was tantamount to an easement for the benefit of the public.[14] That is not correct and in reality the rights involved are very different.[15]

27.8 The right to 'pass and re-pass' must be over a defined route. There can be no public right of way to simply meander or wander over another's land,[16] but the right itself may be limited to a specific class of user (as set out below) and the way may be dedicated subject to other limitations, such as lawful obstructions.[17]

---

[11] HA 1980, s 263(1). The ownership of the subsoil will remain in the hands of the dedicating landowner, but the highway authority will obtain an interest in the 'top two spits'. See *Tunbridge Wells Corporation v Baird* [1896] AC 434. Where the public right of way is extinguished by a formal process the land will re-vest in the original landowner.

[12] *Poole v Huskinson* (1843) 11 M & W 827; *Bermondsey Vestry v Brown* (1865) LR 1 Eq 204.

[13] Or at least it cannot be a highway only because of the existence of such a licence. Private rights of way may exist alongside public rights. See *Austerberry v Oldham Corporation* (1885) 29 Ch D 750, 49 JP 532. *Austerberry* was a case concerning a road which was declared to be 'open to use of the public at large for all manner of purposes in all respects as a common turnpike road', but was to be subject to the payment of tolls. The court found this was not a dedication of the road to the public and was not a highway maintainable at public expense (although note that toll roads are now capable being highways).

[14] *Dovaston v Payne* (1795) 2 H Bl 527 at 531 per Heath J.

[15] *Rangeley v Midland Railway Company* (1868) 3 Ch App 305:

'in truth, a public road or highway is not an easement, it is a dedication to the public of the occupation of the surface of the land for the purpose of passing and repassing, the public generally taking upon themselves ... the obligation of repairing it. It is quite clear that this is a very different thing from an ordinary easement, where the occupation remains in the owner of the servient tenement subject to the easement.'

[16] *Oxfordshire County Council v Oxford City Council* [2004] EWHC 12 (Ch) at 293 per Lightman J, 'it is not possible to have a public right indefinitely to stray or meander over land or go where you like. If there is no made-up or definite enduring track, but merely a temporary or transitory track, that is evidence against a public right of way'. Note, however, the registration of land under Commons Act 2006 (CA 2006), s 15, as a town or village green which confers much greater rights on local inhabitants to use land for lawful sports and pastimes.

[17] An example being a footpath which is dedicated subject to the use of a stile or for that matter an object which projects onto the highway, such as a flap or flight of stairs: *Robbins v Jones* (1863) 15 CBNS 221. The way may also be dedicated subject to temporary obstructions such as the right to plough up the way, where the way crosses a field. See e.g. *Mercer v Woodgate* (1869) LR 5 QB 26.

Director of Public Prosecution v Jones[18] has made it clear, however, that in addition to the right of the public to 'pass and re- pass', the way may also be used for any other reasonable purpose, provided it does not cause a nuisance or an obstruction by unreasonably impeding 'the primary right of the public to pass and re-pass'.[19]

27.9   It is no longer the law that a highway must end in another public highway and, for the avoidance of doubt, a cul-de-sac is quite capable of being a public right of way.[20]

CLASSES OF HIGHWAY

27.10 Rights of way may be classified by the degree of restriction imposed on them. Broadly, these can be listed as follows:

(a)   *Footpaths* – a highway over which the public have a right of way on foot only, not being a footway.[21]

(b)   *Bridleways* – which include 'a right of way on foot and a right of way on horseback, or leading a horse, with or without a right to drive animals of any description along the highway'.[22]

(c)   *Restricted byways* – 'a highway over which the public have restricted byway rights, with or without a right to drive animals of any description along the highway'. This will include a right of way on foot or horseback (or leading a horse) and a right of way for vehicles other than mechanically propelled vehicles.[23]

---

18   [1999] 2 WLR 625. See also *Ineos Upstream Ltd v Persons Unknown* [2017] EWHC 2945 (Ch), where the court continued *quia timet* injunctions against protestors against fracking operations. It was said that if a final injunction were sought then, on the available evidence, the court was likely to restrain protestors from trespassing on the claimant's land and from causing a nuisance by substantially interfering with private rights of way. Although protests could be a reasonable use of the highway, it was likely that the trial judge would conclude that standing still, slow walking to block vehicles and lying in the road were not reasonable uses and therefore amounted to a public nuisance and a criminal offence under the HA 1980, s 137. A trial judge would also likely consider that the rights of the fracking operators would prevail over the protestors, ECHR, Art 10 and Art 11 rights.

19   [1999] 2 WLR 625 at 632 per Lord Irvine.

20   *Williams-Ellis v Cobb* [1935] 1 KB 310 at 320 per Lord Wright; *Rugby Charity Trustees v Merryweather* (1790) 11 East 375.

21   HA 1980, s 329. Note that a 'footway' is also defined in s 329 and includes 'a way comprised in a highway which also comprises a carriageway, being a way over which the public have a right of way on foot only'.

22   HA 1980, s 329.

23   Countryside and Rights of Way Act 2000, s 48.

(d) *Byway open to all traffic (BOAT)* – 'a highway over which the public have a right of way for vehicular and all other kinds of traffic, but which is used by the public mainly for the purpose for which footpaths and bridleways are so used'.[24]

27.11 In general, the superior right will incorporate the lesser.[25] Naturally, there are other classifications and the HA 1980 provides further definitions of classes of highway.[26] For the purposes of this chapter, it should be noted that in addition to footpaths, bridleways and restricted byways, certain 'special roads' exist which may be used only by a specific class of traffic as prescribed by the scheme creating them.[27] Such roads may also be created, however, by a development consent order under the provisions of the Planning Act 2008.[28] A motorway is an example of a special road over which only certain motor vehicles have a right to use the way.

27.12 Regard should also be had to 'carriageways', which simply refer to 'a way constituting or comprised in a highway, being a way other than a cycle track over which the public have a right of way for the passage of vehicles'.[29]

27.13 It is still possible to come across ways described formerly as 'roads used as public paths' or 'RUPPs'. As a result of sections 47 to 51 of the Countryside and Rights of Way Act 2000, all RUPPs still shown on the definitive map will automatically be converted to restricted byways. The term 'road used as a public path' is therefore no longer used to describe ways.

27.14 Special status is given to 'trunk roads'. A trunk road is effectively the name given for 'the principal roads in Great Britain, constituting [part of] the national system of routes for through traffic', which, by virtue of section 1(1) of the Trunk Roads Act 1936 (now repealed), became a trunk road. The highway authority for such a road is the relevant minister, as opposed to a local highway authority,[30] and

---

[24] Countryside and Rights of Way Act 1981, s 66(1). The definition has given rise to some confusion. See *Rights of Way Advice Note 8: Advice on the Definition of Byway Open to All Traffic* (Planning Inspectorate, February 2001). See also *Masters v Secretary of State for the Environment, Transport and the Regions* [2000] 2 All ER 788.

[25] An exception would be a 'special road', such as a motorway.

[26] See HA 1980, s 329.

[27] Highways Act 1959, s 11 as originally enacted. See now HA 1980, s 16. As for the conditions upon which such a highway may be created, see s 16(5). They may be created by: (a) the construction of a new way prescribed by the scheme; (b) appropriation; or (c) transfer of an existing highway.

[28] Planning Act 2008, s 235.

[29] HA 1980, s 329.

[30] Trunk Road Act 1936, s 1(1) as originally enacted. As to the current provisions, see HA 1980, ss 10 and 19.

the process by which such ways are stopped up or diverted and the relevant procedure can be slightly different.

CREATION OF HIGHWAYS

27.15   As far as possible, public rights of way should be identified at an early stage in the development process. In most cases, it will be obvious where such rights exist as they will be recorded on the definitive map (although not all classifications of highway will be so recorded),[31] but in some cases rights of way may have arisen by implied dedication at common law or by statutory presumption and have yet to be recorded. This part deals with the various ways in which such rights may arise.

AT COMMON LAW

Express dedication

27.16   At common law, a highway was created by dedication of the land as a way and acceptance of that dedication by the public. The reasons for this are largely historical in that, formerly, once a highway came into existence it was maintainable by the inhabitants of the local parish, thus acceptance as well as dedication in perpetuity were required.[32] Such a dedication, however, could be provided either expressly, or impliedly, in circumstances where there is evidence of use of the land 'as of right' by the public and acquiescence on the part of the landowner.

27.17   In the case of either express or implied dedication, it must be shown that the person dedicating the land had the necessary capacity,[33] and the relevant

---

[31]   Note the comments of Lord Diplock in *Suffolk County Council v Mason* [1979] AC 705:

    'the only classes of users of highways who are intended to be benefited by the recording of public rights of way are those who may conveniently be referred to as ramblers and riders; they go on foot and horseback ... the only kinds of highways with which the relevant provisions of the Act are concerned are those which are exclusively or mainly, used either by ramblers alone or both riders and ramblers.'

[32]   This was prior to the passing of the Highways Act 1835.

[33]   The person dedicating the way must have the capacity to grant rights over land for all time. A freehold owner is thus able to dedicate the land, but an individual with a leasehold interest will be unable to do so without the agreement of the lessor (and also by a mortgagee if the land is subject to mortgage). See *Dawes v Hawkins* (1860) 8 CB (NS) 848 at 857; *Attorney-General v Biphosphated Guano Co* (1879) 11 Ch D 327; and *Man O'War Station Ltd v Auckland City Council (No 2)* [2002] UKPC 32 at [49]. An express agreement in most cases will therefore take place between the freehold landowner and the relevant highway authority, save that such rights over a reversioner's land may in any event accrue by implied dedication or by statutory

intention, to dedicate. Express dedications now are more likely to take the form of a section 38 agreement or a public path creation agreement under the provisions of the HA 1980.

27.18 It is a characteristic of a highway that the way itself must be open to the public at large, thus any express dedication must declare a way to be open to the public as a whole, not simply to a particular class or group of persons.[34] An express dedication which purports to make a way open only to a class of persons is not a dedication which would give rise to a highway.[35]

27.19 A dedication, however, whether express or implied, may be subject to limitations such as those including the type of user (i.e. a right on foot, but no right by horseback) or make the way subject to obstructions such as a gate or stile. Thus actions which might normally constitute an offence, such as the installation of a gate or the ploughing up of the highway, might be lawful, as the dedication itself may be subject to such limitation.[36]

Implied dedication

27.20 Dedication may also be implied but, as with an express dedication, such an inference can only be drawn against a landowner with capacity. At common law implied dedication arises through the use of the land by the public *as of right*, that is to say without the use of force, stealth or by permission by the public and the acquiescence, without protest, in that use by the landowner.[37] The approach, in as far as it relates to use of a highway, seems to be (per Lord Blackburne in *Mann v Brodie*) that:[38]

> where there has been evidence of a user by the public so long and in such a manner that the owner of the fee, whoever he was, must have been aware that the public were

---

presumption. Land in the ownership of the Crown may be dedicated either expressly or impliedly, in the same way as private land. An express agreement in most cases will therefore take place between the freehold landowner and the relevant highway authority, although such rights over a reversioner's land may have already accrued by implied dedication or by statutory presumption.

[34] *Poole v Huskinson* (1843) 11 M & W 827.

[35] See *Austerberry v Oldham Corporation* (1885) 29 Ch D 750, 49 JP 532.

[36] In relation to gates, see *Davies v Stephens* (1836) 7 C & P 570. In relation to ploughing up of the highway, see *Mercer v Woodgate* (1869) LR 5 QB 26.

[37] See *Corsellis v London CC* [1907] 1 Ch 704; *Attorney General v Biphosphated Guano Company* (1879) 11 Ch D 327.

[38] (1885) 10 App Cas 378 at 386 per Lord Blackburne; see also *R (Lewis) v Redcar and Cleveland BC* [2010] UKSC 11 at [67] per Lord Hope (this was a village green case where qualifying use must also be *as of right*).

acting under the belief that the way had been dedicated and has taken no steps to disabuse them of that belief, it is not conclusive evidence, but evidence on which those who have to find the fact may find that there was a dedication by the owner.

27.21 The essence of *as of right* is one of presumed acquiescence on the part of the owner from which the law infers a fiction that dedication has taken place. Such user by the public must therefore be 'open and in the manner that a person rightfully entitled would have used it'.[39]

27.22 The key difference between implied dedication at common law and one of prescription, is that at common law there is no minimum or maximum period over which such dedication must take place.[40] Such a period could even be lower than the 20-year period created by section 31 of the HA 1980, which gives rise to a statutory presumption of dedication.[41] In either case, it should be noted that even where long use can be shown, the presumption can be rebutted and it is said that 'a single act of interruption by the owner is of much more weight, upon a question of intention, than many acts of enjoyment'.[42] As to the amount of use needed, this will depend on the circumstances.[43]

27.23 In the same way that a person expressly dedicating land must have the necessary capacity to do so, the use of land *as of right* must be use which the person with capacity to dedicate has acquiesced in. It is not, however, necessary for the person seeking to show a right of way has arisen, to prove the identity of the landowner. Nonetheless, such an application may be defeated by showing that there was nobody who could have dedicated the way.[44]

---

[39] *R (Lewis) v Redcar and Cleveland BC* [2010] UKSC 11 at [67] per Lord Hope.

[40] See e.g. *R v Hudson* (1732) 2 Stra 909; *North London Railway Co v St Mary, Islington* (1872) 27 LT 672; *Woodyer v Hadden* (1813) 5 Taunt 125 at 137. See also *Turner v Walsh* (1881) 6 App Cas 636 per Sir Montague ES Smith, 'the proper way of regarding these cases is to look at the whole of the evidence together, to see whether there has been such a continuous and connected user as is sufficient to raise the presumption of dedication'.

[41] See in particular *North London Railway Co v St Mary, Islington* (1872) 27 LT 672, where a period of 18 months was held to be sufficient.

[42] *Poole v Huskinson* (1843) 11 M & W 827 at 830. See also e.g. *Stoney v Eastbourne RDC* [1927] 1 Ch 367; *Mann v Brodie* (1885) 10 App Cas 378 at 386.

[43] See e.g. *R v South Eastern Railway Co* (1850) 16 LT (OS) 124; *Macpherson v Scottish Rights of Way and Recreation Society* (1888) 13 App Cas 744.

[44] But see *R v Petrie* (1855) 19 JP 483 per Coleridge J:

'I take the principle that, where there is satisfactory evidence of such user of the road, as to time, manner and circumstances, as would lead to the inference that there was a dedication by the owner of the fee, if it was shown who he was, it is not necessary to inquire who the individual was from whom the dedication, necessarily repealed from such a user, first proceeded.'

27.24 The situation becomes complicated where it involves land which has been the subject of a lease, and consequently the owner of the freehold has not been in possession of the land subject to the alleged dedication.[45] Where the relevant land has been the subject of a lease for the entire period of dedication, there may be real difficulties in establishing acquiescence on the part of the freeholder, although where user has been for a great length of time, it may be so presumed and would not prevent an argument that such rights had arisen prior to the relevant land being leased.[46]

27.25 Where the land involved has been leased to multiple tenants, the actions of the landowner during the intervening periods (when they go back into possession of the reversion and thereby regain the right to oust the public) will plainly be significant, as would evidence of actual knowledge on the part of the landowner of public use, coupled with a lack of steps to counter such use.[47]

27.26 There may additionally be difficulties in respect of implied dedication over land controlled by certain public bodies, such as railway undertakers. Such entities are creatures of statute and must act within the powers conferred upon them. Although it is possible for such a body to dedicate land expressly, it cannot do so where the existence of such a way would be incompatible with its objects.[48] The same is true in relation to implied dedication. Thus an implied dedication cannot be presumed where such a dedication is inconsistent with its objects. Note that it is possible, however, for implied dedication to take place over Crown land.[49]

27.27 As with express dedication, the creation of a right of way by implied dedication may create rights subject to limitation.[50] Similarly, use must be over a more or less defined route and not merely an indefinite passing over land:

> it is not possible to have a public right indefinitely to stray or meander over land or go where you like. If there is no made-up or definite enduring track but merely a temporary or transitory track, that is evidence against a public right of way.[51]

---

[45] Although note that under s 31(4) in relation to the statutory presumption, the owner of the reversion is expressly entitled to erect a sign to negative any suggestion that the presumption has arisen in circumstances where such a notice would not injure the business or occupation of the tenant.

[46] See *Davies v Stephens* (1836) 7 C & P 570.

[47] *R v Barr* (1814) 4 Camp 16; *Davies v Stephens* (1836) 7 C & P 570.

[48] See e.g. *South Eastern Railway Co v Cooper* [1924] 1 Ch 211.

[49] See e.g. the decision of the Privy Council in *Turner v Walsh* (1881) 6 App Cas 636.

[50] Such as a gate or stile.

[51] *Oxfordshire County Council v Oxford City Council* [2004] EWHC 12 (Ch) at 293 per Lightman J.

Acceptance

27.28   Acceptance of the dedication by the public in cases of implied use will be clear from the use of that land by the public as of right. In relation to express dedication, often these will take the form of agreements with the local highway authority.[52] The highway authority, to all intents and purposes, is the representative of the public and evidence that the authority has accepted the dedication, for example by showing that an appropriate committee of the highway authority has resolved to do so, may well be enough.[53]

User as of right

27.29   The concept of 'as of right' is considered in the context of village greens at Chapter 25 where the principles are just the same. As previously indicated, to be use as of right (meaning 'as if by right') user must be without force, stealth or by permission. A landowner seeking to grant permission over his land, but not intending to dedicate it as a highway, may grant a revocable or time limited permission. An unconditional or irrevocable permission may amount to acquiescence. Permission may be given expressly, such as in the case of erecting notices,[54] or by virtue of some other licence or contract of employment; alternatively, permission may be implied where such a finding is warranted on the evidence.[55] The subjective belief of those using the way, however, is entirely irrelevant.[56] Use by force is not confined only to physical force but may also arise

---

[52]   In the development context, these will often now be agreements under HA 1980, s 38, for which see paras 27.78–27.82.

[53]   *Secretary of State for the Environment, Transport and the Regions v Baylis (Gloucester) Ltd*, 14/4/2000, unreported, per Kim Lewison QC, sitting as a Deputy Judge of the High Court:

  'evidence of acceptance by the highway authority is, therefore, capable of amounting to proof of acceptance by the public. An acceptance could, in my judgment, be proved by showing that the highway authority had agreed in writing to accept the dedication or by showing that an appropriate committee of the highway authority resolved to do so. It is not invariably necessary to show actual exercise by members of the public of their rights of passage in the case of an express dedication.'

[54]   See in particular *R (Beresford) v Sunderland City Council* [2003] UKHL 60, [2004] 1 AC 889.

[55]   See *R (Beresford) v Sunderland City Council* [2003] UKHL 60, [2004] 1 AC 889 at [5] per Lord Bingham, 'a landowner may so conduct himself as to make clear, even in the absence of an express statement, notice or record, that the inhabitants' use of the land is pursuant to his permission. This may be done e.g. by excluding the inhabitants when the landowner wishes to use the land for his own purposes'. See also *R (Mann) v Somerset County Council* [2012] EWHC B14 (Admin), which was another village green case. The *Mann* case concerned local inhabitants who were excluded from parts of the land when ticketed beer festivals took place on land adjoining a public house. It was held that the land was not registrable.

[56]   This much is clear from the House of Lords' decision in *R v Oxfordshire County Council ex parte Sunningwell Parish Council* [1999] 3 WLR 160. See in particular the speech of Lord Hoffmann at 171. See also *Hue v Whiteley* [1929] 1 Ch 440 at 445 (although note that the decision must be

whenever use is contentious (or non-peaceable), as where gates, fencing or hedgerows are damaged or where prohibitory signage is ignored or torn down.[57]

Statutory presumption of dedication

27.30 In an attempt to simplify the process upon which inferences of dedication may be drawn, the Rights of Way Act 1932 introduced a statutory presumption of dedication after a period of 20 years' uninterrupted use 'as of right'. The relevant presumption is now contained in section 31(1) of the HA 1980, which provides that:

> (1)   Where a way over land, other than a way of such a character that use of it by the public could not give rise at common law to any presumption of dedication, has been actually enjoyed by the public as of right and without interruption for a full period of 20 years, the way is to be deemed to have been dedicated as a highway unless there is sufficient evidence that there was no intention during that period to dedicate it.

27.31 The effect of section 31(1) is that where the public have enjoyed *as of right* a way over land for a continuous period of 20 years, a rebuttable presumption arises that the way was dedicated as a highway. The presumption will not, however, apply in the case of the use of mechanically propelled vehicles.[58] Nor does it replace the common law rules.[59] Thus a way may arise in less than 20 years under common law, notwithstanding the statutory presumption. The presumption does not apply to Crown land.[60]

Without interruption

27.32 The 20-year period must be enjoyed 'without interruption'. Interruption means in this context an 'interruption in fact'. There must be some physical or actual interruption which prevents enjoyment. The mere absence of continuity of

---

read now in light of the *Sunningwell* decision). See also *Rights of Way Advice Note 6: The Sunningwell Judgment and the Meaning of 'as of right'* (Planning Inspectorate, October 2000).

57   *Taylor v Betterment Properties (Weymouth) Ltd and Dorset County Council* [2012] EWCA Civ 250; *R (Lewis) v Redcar and Cleveland Borough Council* [2009] 1 WLR 1461. See also *R (Oxfordshire and Buckinghamshire Mental Health NHS Foundation Trust) v Oxfordshire County Council* [2010] EWHC 530 (Admin) at [22], for the principles in relation to signage.

58   See Natural Environment and Rural Communities Act 2006 (NERC 2006), s 66. See also HA 1980, s 31(1A).

59   HA 1980, s 31(9) expressly provides that 'nothing in this section operates to prevent the dedication of a way as a highway being presumed on proof of user for any period less than 20 years, or being presumed or proved in any circumstances in which it might have been presumed or proved immediately before the commencement of this Act'.

60   Although note that dedication can take place against Crown land by implied dedication at common law. See e.g. *Turner v Walsh* (1881) 6 App Cas 636.

use will not necessarily constitute an 'interruption' for these purposes.[61] The blocking of a road by a broken down vehicle would not amount to an interruption[62] although an interruption of months or even years arising from enclosure of land (or other use by the owner of the land inimical to its continued use as a public right of way) almost certainly would.[63]

For a full period of 20 years

27.33 The period of usage must be for a continuous period of 20 years, calculated retrospectively from the date when the right of the public to use the way is brought into question.[64] The right may be brought into question by the erection of a notice in a visible place which is inconsistent with the dedication of the way as a highway, or 'by some other act'.[65] This will include the erection of a fence or installation of some other barrier across the way which is intended to prevent members of the public using the land, thereby making continued use of it contentious. The test in each case seems to be that stated by Denning LJ:[66]

> in order for the right of the public to have been 'brought into question', the landowner must challenge it by some means sufficient to bring it home to the public that he is

---

[61] *Jones v Bates* [1938] 2 All ER 237 per Scott LJ:

'The word "interruption" must be given its proper import in its grammatical context. A mere absence of continuity in the de facto user proved will not prevent the statute from running. If that were not so, the necessary proof in public right-of-way cases would often break down … simply because witnesses were not available to fill all the gaps in such proof.'

Temporary interruptions are unlikely to stop time running provided rights of a continuous nature (as opposed to occasional or only trivial use of the land) are being asserted (*Hollins v Verney* (1884) 13 QBD 304). The fact that nobody has been interrupted from using the way will not necessarily mean that the act failed to interrupt user. It is sufficient that the public could not have done so, had they chosen to use the way. See *Rowley v Secretary of State for Transport, Local Government and the Regions* [2002] EWHC 1040 (Admin) at [38] per Elias J; see also *Lewis v Thomas* [1950] 1 KB 438 at 444 per Lord Evershed: 'I agree that a barring, and particularly a deliberate barring, of a way for an appreciable period would not necessarily lose its effect merely because no one happened to try to use the way during that period'.

[62] *Fernlee Estates Ltd v City and County of Swansea and Another* [2001] EWHC 360 (Admin) at [16] (discussing *Lewis v Thomas* [1950] 1 KB 438).

[63] *Betterment Properties (Weymouth) Ltd v Dorset County Council* [2012] EWCA Civ 250 (a village green case), where an interruption was held to have taken place on part of the land in circumstances where substantial drainage works had taken place for upwards of two or three years involving a partial fencing off, the presence of plant and equipment and spoil heaps on the land associated with substantial tunnelling operations and a footpath diversion order re-routing a public footpath around the perimeter of the works' site.

[64] HA 1980, s 31(2).

[65] Where that notice has been maintained after 1/1/1934. HA 1980, s 31(3).

[66] *Fairey v Southampton County Council* [1956] 3 WLR 354 at 456 per Denning LJ. See also *R v Secretary of State for the Environment, Transport and the Regions ex parte Dorset County Council* [2000] JPL 396.

challenging their right to use the way, so that they may be apprised of the challenge and have a reasonable opportunity of meeting it. The landowner can challenge their right, for instance, by putting a barrier across the path or putting up a notice forbidding the public to use the path. When he does so, the public may meet the challenge.

27.34 The act which brings the right into question does not, however, have to be that of the landowner. Acts of third parties may be sufficient to bring the right into question.[67] In each case, it will not be necessary to make every user of the way aware of the challenge, but it has been said that:

> whatever means are employed, they must be sufficient at least to make it likely that some of the users are aware that the owner has challenged their right to use the way as a highway.[68]

No intention to dedicate the way

27.35 There has to be 'sufficient evidence that there was no intention' to dedicate the way.[69] Such evidence must be inconsistent with an intention to dedicate and it must be:

> existing and perceptible outside the landowner's consciousness, rather than simply being a proof of a state of mind.[70]

27.36 Such an intention must therefore be brought home to users of the way; thus, upon the true construction of section 31(1), 'intention' means what the relevant audience, namely the users of the way, would reasonably have understood the landowner's intention to be.[71] The test is therefore an objective one, focusing less on the subjective intent of the landowner and more on what the actions of the landowner would have said to users of the way said to be subject to the right. Those seeking to prevent such rights from arising would be well advised to employ one of the statutory means contained in section 31 of the HA 1980 to negative the presumption.

---

[67] *R (Godmanchester Town Council) v Secretary of State for the Environment, Food and Rural Affairs* [2007] UKHL 28.

[68] *R v Secretary of State for the Environment, Transport and the Regions ex parte Dorset County Council* [2000] JPL 396 at 403 per Dyson J.

[69] See *Fairey v Southampton County Council* [1956] 3 WLR 354 at 458 per Denning LJ.

[70] *R (Godmanchester Town Council) v Secretary of State for the Environment, Food and Rural Affairs* [2007] UKHL 28 at [33].

[71] *R (Godmanchester Town Council) v Secretary of State for the Environment, Food and Rural Affairs* [2007] UKHL 28 at [32].

Statutory means by which the presumption may be negatived

27.37 The statute expressly provides for ways in which the presumption will be negatived in the absence of proof of a contrary intention. These include the erection of a notice inconsistent with dedication of the land as a highway.[72] Where the land is let and in the possession of a tenant, the lessor is authorised by the statute to erect such a notice so as to prevent rights arising over the land, in circumstances where it does not injure the business or occupation of the tenant.[73] In cases of leased land, the mere fact that the land has been so leased will not give rise to a defence that the land cannot be subject to the statutory presumption. Clearly any notice must bring home to users of the land that the owner: (a) objected to trespass on his land to which he did not give his consent, or (b) that any use of his land is with his consent which may be withdrawn at any time, and, in any event, that (c) he does not intend to dedicate such land for use as a public highway.[74] Where such signage is torn down or defaced, the landowner may also give notice to the appropriate council[75] stating that the way has not been dedicated which will negative, without proof of a contrary intention, the presumption.[76] Where signs have been repeatedly torn down and there is a state of perpetual warfare between the landowner and the public, such use will, of course, not be *as of right* anyway so as to give rise to the presumption.[77]

---

[72] It is suggested that any sign making it clear that: (a) passage is enjoyed with the permission of the owner which may be withdrawn at any time; or (b) that no person is entitled to enter upon the land so as to make any entry thereafter non-peaceable and not as of right, would be sufficient for these purposes (see HA 1980, s 31(3)).

[73] HA 1980, s 31(4).

[74] See *R (Oxfordshire and Buckinghamshire Mental Health NHS Foundation Trust) v Oxfordshire County Council* [2010] EWHC 530 (Admin) at [22] for a useful guide of the principles in relation to signage.

[75] HA 1980, s 31(7) provides that the 'appropriate council' means the council of the county, metropolitan district or London borough in which the way or the land is situated or, where the way or land is situated in the City, the Common Council.

[76] HA 1980, s 31(5).

[77] Such use will be non-peaceable. See *Betterment Properties (Weymouth) Ltd v Dorset County Council* [2012] EWCA Civ 250, now the leading case on contentious use. It was a village green case where the landowner had tried, without success, to erect notices warning people of his land. Patten LJ stated at [48]–[49] that all the authorities in this area of the law were premised by the assumption that the landowner must take reasonable steps to bring his opposition to the actual notice of those using his land. For instance, any notices must be sufficient to make it clear that any use of the land was not consented to and would be regarded as a trespass. If the landowner keeps his opposition to himself and makes no outward attempt to prevent the unauthorised use of his land then he may be taken to have acquiesced. He also said that the landowner was not required to do the impossible. The response must be commensurate with the scale of the problem with which he is faced. Evidence from some users that they did not see the signs was not necessarily fatal to the landowner's case on whether user was as of right. It will, though, be highly relevant evidence as to whether the landowner has done enough to comply with what amounts to the giving

27.38 A landowner also has the option of protecting his rights by depositing with the appropriate council maps of his land and a statement indicating what ways he admits to have been dedicated as highways.[78] Declarations in the standard form may be made by the owner or by his successors in title and lodged by him or them with the appropriate council within 20 years from the original deposit or within the same number of years from the date on which any previous declaration was lodged to the effect that no additional ways over the land delineated on the map have been dedicated as a highway since the date of the deposit or the lodgement of the previous declaration, as the case may be, which will, in the absence of proof of a contrary intention, be sufficient evidence to negative the intention of the owner or his successors to dedicate any such additional land as a highway.[79] A similar situation now arises in the case of landowner statements under section 15A of the Commons Act 2006 (CA 2006). As the effect of section 15A of the CA 2006 and section 31(6) of the HA 1980 is the same, landowners are now able to make a single application on Form CA16 to prevent their land from being either recorded as a highway on the definitive map or registered as a village green. Plainly, if the declaration is going to be of effect, such a declaration would have to be made within every 20-year window thereafter as a minimum.

HA 1980 PROVISIONS

27.39 In addition to the creation of public rights of way by express or implied dedication and by virtue of the statutory presumption, the HA 1980 provides expressly for ways in which rights may be created by virtue of agreements, orders, declarations and construction.

---

of reasonable notice. In other words, if most peaceable users never saw any signs then the court has to ask whether this was because none were erected or because any that were erected were too badly positioned to give reasonable notice of the landowner's objection to the continued use of his land. Patten LJ also amplified the approach of Morgan J at first instance (namely whether a reasonable person knowing the relevant circumstances would conclude that the landowner was objecting to his use of the land) by stating that knowledge of the relevant circumstances should be confined to what was visible to any reasonable person using the land on a regular basis at the relevant time. Patten LJ also indicated that the applicant for registration in that case could not be heard to rely on the fact that users were unaware of the existence of signage when their ignorance of this was due only to the fact that they had been obliterated by the unlawful acts of some local residents. If the steps taken by the landowner would otherwise have been sufficient to notify local inhabitants that they should not trespass on the land then the landowner had done all that was required of him to make use of his land contentious.

[78] HA 1980, s 31(6).

[79] The relevant period is specified to be 20 years in England (s 31(6A)) and ten years in Wales (s 31(6B)).

Section 38 – creation by agreement

27.40 On large-scale developments, it is quite normal for estate roads to be made up to an adoptable standard and for agreements to be made in advance of completion as to the characteristics and location of such proposed roads. The key provision, section 38 of the HA 1980, is discussed later in the context of the adoption and making up of roads.

Public path creation agreements

27.41 Section 25 of the HA 1980 provides for the creation of a highway by way of an agreement between a local authority[80] and any person having the necessary power[81] to dedicate land as a footpath, bridleway or restricted byway.[82] Such an agreement may include provisions as to payment, and may additionally provide for the dedication of the way subject to conditions or limitations affecting the public right of way over it.[83] The same sort of restrictions as may affect a way created at common law, such as obstructions in the form of gates or stiles, may be incorporated. Notably, this section could be used to widen an existing right of way.

27.42 The local authority must consult any other local authority over which the land is situated.[84] This is presumably the case, as once the land is dedicated as a highway it shall be maintainable at public expense. It must have regard, pursuant to section 29, to the needs of agriculture and forestry and the desirability of conserving flora, fauna and geological and physiographical features.[85] Once the agreement has been made, it is the duty of the local authority to take all necessary steps for securing dedication in accordance with it.[86] After the dedication of the

---

80 A 'local authority' for the purposes of this section will be the London borough council or the common council as applicable within Greater London. Outside Greater London it will be a county or district council. See HA 1980, s 25(2). It will also include the National Park authorities and the Broads Authority, for which, see Norfolk and Suffolk Broads Act 1988, Sch 3.

81 A person dedicating at common law must have power to dedicate the land as a highway forever. It is suggested that those with a power to dedicate such land under this section will therefore be either the owner of the fee simple, or someone entitled to act as agent on his behalf. Those who have a mere life interest or term of years within the property will not therefore have sufficient interest to dedicate under this section, save where the tenant has the agreement of the owner of the fee simple. See in particular *Davies v Stephens* (1836) 7 Car & P 570; *Corsellis v London CC* [1907] 1 Ch 704; *Attorney General v Biphosphated Guano Company* (1879) 11 Ch D 327. In the case of a mortgage, the mortgagee must similarly consent.

82 HA 1980, s 25(1).

83 HA 1980, s 25(4).

84 HA 1980, s 25(3).

85 HA 1980, s 29.

86 HA 1980, s 25(5).

land in accordance with the agreement, the local authority which is party to the agreement shall give notice of the dedication by publication in a local newspaper circulating in the area.[87]

Other provisions

27.43 In addition to section 25 of the HA 1980, under section 30, a parish or community may enter into an agreement with a person with the necessary power to dedicate land where, in the opinion of the council, it would be beneficial to the inhabitants or 'any part thereof'.[88] Where it enters into such an agreement, it may contribute to the cost of carrying out works, or carrying out any works incidental to the agreement.[89] Notably, the power to enter into agreements under section 30 does not relate to any particular class of highway. The section is therefore presumed to relate to any form of highway, but highways created as a result of a section 30 agreement do not necessarily become maintainable at public expense.

27.44 Under section 35 of the HA 1980 there is also provision for the creation of walkways (i.e. ways which pass over, through or under parts of buildings or parts of any structure).[90]

Section 26 – creation by order

Public path creation orders

27.45 A local authority[91] or a strategic highways company may, by order, create a footpath, bridleway or restricted byway where it appears to it that there is a need for one (over land in its area) and that it is expedient to make the order.[92] Before making an order, it must have regard to the extent to which the way would add to the convenience or enjoyment of a substantial section of the public or residents in the area. It must also consider the effect the creation of the way would have on the rights of persons interested in the land, account being given as to the provision

---

[87] HA 1980, s 25(6).

[88] HA 1980, s 30(1), i.e. it need not be for the benefit of the community as a whole.

[89] HA 1980, s 30(2).

[90] See HA 1980, s 35, the Walkway Regulations 1973 (SI 1973/686) and the Walkways (Amendment) Regulations 1974 (SI 1974/735).

[91] 'Local authority' has the same meaning as in HA 1980, s 25, thus a 'local authority' for the purposes of this section will be the London borough council or the common council as applicable within Greater London. Outside Greater London it will be a county or district council. See s 25(2). It will also include the National Park authorities and the Broads Authority, for which, see Norfolk and Suffolk Broads Act 1988, Sch 3.

[92] HA 1980, s 26(1).

of compensation.[93] Naturally, the availability of compensation does not obviate the need to consider the adverse effect on neighbouring landowners.[94] When the local authority considers these questions, it must consider not just the need for the footpath, but also 'the detail of its alignment, length and width'.[95]

27.46 The Secretary of State also has powers to create a footpath, bridleway or restricted byway. The matters he must be satisfied with are identical to those in respect of a local authority or a strategic highways company, but before he makes an order he must consult with each local authority he must consult with each body which is a local authority in whose area the land concerned is situated.[96]

27.47 In either case, the making of an order has two stages: the making of the order; and the confirming of that order. An order made by the local authority can be confirmed by the authority where it is unopposed, but can only be confirmed by the Secretary of State in the case of opposed orders. Before it is confirmed, regard must be had to any rights of way improvement plan prepared by a local authority over which the land runs.[97] Any right of way so created may be subject to limitations or be unconditional.[98]

27.48 Where the way runs across land situated across more than one local authority area, the local authority intending to make the order must consult with the other local authority in which the highway subsists.[99] The relevant procedure is governed by Schedule 6 to the HA 1980.[100]

---

[93]   As to the provision of compensation see HA 1980, s 28. Compensation is payable in one of two circumstances under that section. The first is where it can be shown that the value of an interest in land is depreciated by the making of an order. The second is where a person has suffered damage by being disturbed as a consequence of the coming into effect of such an order (s 28(1)). Notably an 'interest' under that section is said to include 'any estate in land and any right over it, whether the right is exercisable by virtue of the ownership of an interest in land or by virtue of a licence or agreement'. Thus the persons entitled to compensation under the section are wider than simply the freehold landowner. Compensation may also be paid to owners of land not crossed by the highway, but a person seeking compensation under this section would not only need to prove loss, he would have to show that it would have been actionable at his suit if it had been effected otherwise than in the exercise of statutory powers (see s 28(5)).

[94]   *Jenkins v Welsh Assembly Government* [2010] EWCA Civ 1640.

[95]   See *MJI (Farming) Ltd v Secretary of State for the Environment, Food and Rural Affairs* [2009] EWHC 677 (Admin) at [25] *et seq*. The process should include examination of the land, together with the specified limitations and conditions. See in particular [25]–[28] and [33].

[96]   HA 1980, s 26(2). For the purposes of this section 'local authority' has the same meaning as in s 25(2) (and would include county and district councils and London borough councils).

[97]   HA 1980, s 26(3A).

[98]   HA 1980, s 26(4).

[99]   HA 1980, s 26(3).

[100] See also the Public Path Orders Regulations 1993 (SI 1993/11).

Section 34 – creation by declaration

27.49 A street which is not a highway and land to which section 232 of the HA 1980 applies, may become a highway by virtue of a declaration made by a county council, a metropolitan district council, a London borough council or the common council in accordance with Part XI of the HA 1980. The effect of the section is that roads constructed and so brought up to the requisite standard may, formally, be declared to be highways.

Section 24 – creation by construction

27.50 There are additional provisions in the HA 1980 in relation to the creation of highways by construction. Section 24 provides that the Minister for Transport (in England) or a strategic highways company may construct new highways.[101] Such a highway would automatically become maintainable at public expense. The power is not isolated to a particular class of highway, but where the Minister proposes to construct a new highway other than certain listed ways, which include a trunk road or special road, notice provisions will apply.[102]

REFORMS

27.51 Neither sections 53 to 55 of the Countryside and Rights of Way Act 2000 nor sections 20 to 26 of the Deregulation Act 2015 have yet come into force. Those practising in this area need to be aware of some of the proposed changes as they have implications for rights which have arisen historically by implied dedication or statutory presumption.

27.52 Sections 53 to 55 of the Countryside and Rights of Way Act 2000 prescribe a cut-off date (1/1/2026) for the recording on definitive maps of footpaths and bridleways created before 1949. Where old paths are not so recorded by that date they may be extinguished. Section 55 also provides that any unrecorded higher rights of way created before 1/1/1949 over a highway shown on a definitive map on the cut-off date as a footpath, bridleway or restricted byway (such as a vehicular right of way over a BOAT) and which is eligible for recording on a definitive map, will be extinguished immediately after the cut-off date.

27.53 The reasoning for the change seems to be that the investigation of applications based on evidence about the position before 1949 can be particularly

---

[101] HA 1980, s 24(1).

[102] HA 1980, s 24(1)(a)–(d).

difficult for authorities.[103] These sections will clearly have to be the subject of consultation before they are brought into effect.

27.54 The Deregulation Act 2015, when it comes into force, will insert supplementary provisions, some of which seem to be intended to bridge the gap where there are consequences to landowners as a result of an extinguishment pursuant to section 53 of the Countryside and Rights of Way Act 2000. In particular, section 22 will insert a section 56B into the Countryside and Rights of Way Act 2000 as to the creation of private rights of way, where the public right has been extinguished and, on the cut-off date, the exercise of a right of way is reasonably necessary to enable a person with an interest in land to obtain access to it.

THE HIGHWAY AUTHORITY AND ITS DUTIES

Introduction

27.55 The following sections are devoted to the issues surrounding ownership and maintenance of a publicly maintainable way.

27.56 A highway authority is the body largely responsible for the management, and, in many cases, the maintenance, of the country's highways. A local highway authority in most cases will be the body responsible for the highways in its geographical area, save where 'the Minister' or a strategic highways company (as set out below) is so responsible. In England, the local highway authority will be the county council, unitary authority or metropolitan district council for the area (where that area is outside London).[104] In London, Transport for London will be the highway authority for Greater London Authority (GLA) roads[105] and, in respect of all other roads, it will be the relevant London borough council or common council.[106] Where there are two tiers of authority, the county council will be the highway authority.[107]

27.57 'The Minister' will be the highway authority in certain circumstances. Broadly speaking, those circumstances will include cases where the highway is a trunk road, a special road provided by the Minister, or where some other

---

[103] See the Explanatory Notes to the Draft Bill, as introduced in the House of Commons on 5/6/2014.

[104] HA 1980, s 1(2).

[105] For GLA roads, see HA 1980, ss 14A–14D.

[106] HA 1980, s 1(2A) and (3). In Wales, it will be the council of a county or the county borough (s 1(3A)).

[107] See generally *Rights of Way Circular (01/09)* at para 1.10.

enactment or order expressly provides for the Minister to become the highway authority.[108] The Minister for these purposes is currently the Secretary of State for Transport in the case of England, and the Secretary of State for Wales, in respect of Wales.[109] The framework has slightly changed following the implementation of the Infrastructure Act 2015. The Highways Agency would formally have exercised many of the duties of the Minister. The Highways Agency has now been turned into a government-owned strategic highways company and will become the relevant highway authority, effectively instead of the Minister, in certain circumstances where, broadly speaking, it is appointed or directed to be.[110]

Ownership of the highway

27.58   Where the highway involved is not maintainable at the public expense, the highway simply stays in the ownership of the freehold landowner, save that the landowner's right will be subject to the public's right to pass and re-pass. Where the highway *is* maintainable at public expense, the highway authority itself may have purchased the land over which the way endures, either by compulsory purchase, or by some other agreement. Where it has not purchased the land, it will obtain an interest by virtue of section 263(1) of the HA 1980, which provides that:

> every highway maintainable at the public expense, together with the materials and scrapings of it, vests in the authority who are for the time being the highway authority for the highway.

27.59   The provision does not apply in the case of trunk or special roads.[111] There seems to be no express definition in the HA 1980 as to the extent of the interest. It has in the past been said the extent of that right is to obtain the top two spits,[112] with the freehold landowner of the land subject to the way retaining a right over the subsoil. It is now said that it:

> vests such property and such property only as is necessary for the control, protection, and maintenance of the street as a highway for public use.[113]

---

[108]   See HA 1980, s 1(1).

[109]   HA 1980, s 329 defines 'Minister' in England to be the Minister for Transport. Since the Act was passed, the position has changed and, as at the time of writing, such functions now fall to the Secretary of State for Transport.

[110]   See HA 1980, s 1(1A). See also Infrastructure Act 2015, s 1; *Transforming our Strategic Roads – A Summary* (Department for Transport, December 2014).

[111]   HA 1980, s 263(2). See ss 266 and 267.

[112]   Meaning the top two spade depths; see *Tithe Redemption Commissioners v Runcorn Urban District Council* [1954] Ch 383 at 407 per Lord Denning.

[113]   *Tunbridge Wells Corporation v Baird* [1896] AC 434 at 442.

27.60 This definition makes sense, given that it allows the authority to maintain and otherwise erect pillars, paving and fencing, etc. to ensure the safety of users of the way.[114] Actions which affect the subsoil may, however, require the consent of the landowner.[115] The highway authority itself is a creature of statute and must act within the powers given to it. It cannot create obstructions, other than those it is expressly authorised to license, and is under a positive duty to protect the rights of users of the highway.[116]

27.61 The dedication of land as a highway endures until it is extinguished through a formal process. When an order stopping up the highway takes effect, the highway authority's interest will determine and re-vest in the original landowner.[117]

27.62 Where the right of way is maintainable at public expense there are common law presumptions in relation to the ownership of the subsoil. Where the highway itself separates the properties of two adjoining landowners, it is presumed that the subsoil is owned by each owner up to the mid-point (*usque ad medium filum*). In most cases, there is unlikely to be much argument about ownership of the subsoil unless or until the highway itself is stopped up, whereupon the land would re-vest in each landowner and the presumption is likely to be of more significance. In those circumstances, the question arises as to whom the former highway land should re-vest (which would include any waste land between the former highway and the adjoining land).[118] Such a presumption is rebuttable and is seemingly based on the fiction that each landowner will have contributed equally to land upon which the highway endures. Evidence, therefore, of the real owner would rebut the presumption.

Private rights over highway land

27.63 There are two issues under this head. First, what activities and rights does the owner of land which is subject to a highway possess? Secondly, can private rights of way exist over highway land? In principle, there is no reason why a

---

[114] As to the power to erect such things, see HA 1980, s 66.

[115] There are exceptions, however, e.g. HA 1980, s 69, which empowers a highway authority to construct subways under carriageways for the purpose of protecting pedestrians and other road users from danger.

[116] HA 1980, s 130. The duty is one to 'assert and protect the rights of the public to the use and enjoyment of any highway for which they are the Highway Authority, including any roadside waste which forms part of it'.

[117] *Rolls v Vestry of St George the Martyr* (1880) 14 Ch D 785.

[118] *Steel v Prickett* (1819) 2 Stark 463.

private right of way cannot exist over the same land on which a highway endures.[119] It is said that:[120]

> the owner, who dedicates to public use as a highway a portion of his land, parts with no other right than a right of passage to the public over the land so dedicated, and may exercise all other rights of ownership, not inconsistent therewith; and the appropriation, made to and adopted by the public, of a part of the street to one kind of passage, and another part to another, does not deprive him of any rights as owner of the land, which are not inconsistent with the right of passage by the public.

27.64 In many cases, private rights over highway land will not be inconsistent with the public's right of passage and as such the two rights will simply co-exist. It is suggested the same principle applies as against both a neighbouring landowner's private right of way and those of a landowner to continue using his land. The dedication of land as a highway can, of course, take place (whether such dedication arises by express agreement, impliedly or by virtue of the statutory presumption) subject to limitations. A landowner who periodically ploughs a field crossed by a footpath that arises by implied dedication may continue to possess a right to plough up the field, notwithstanding it is an action which is very probably inconsistent with the primary right of the public to pass and re-pass.[121] The test seems to be in part whether the exercise of the private right is so inconsistent with the use of the land as a highway. Thus:

> the owner cannot derogate from the grant of a roadway made by him to the public, and cannot do anything which would really and substantially interfere with the right of passage by the public.[122]

27.65 In as far as some activities are concerned, there may be cases where the exercise of a private right over highway land will give rise to a criminal offence or civil wrong. In the context of an adjoining landowner, an example would be a person who has a private right of way to drive a vehicle over a footpath. This would be a *prima facie* offence under the Road Traffic Act 1988 in the absence of 'lawful authority'.[123] The question that arises in that context is what then

---

[119] Or for that matter that a landowner cannot continue to exercise such rights which are not inconsistent with the public's to pass and re-pass. See e.g. *Personal Representatives of Parker v Nottinghamshire County Council* [2009] EWHC 229 (Admin). That was a case concerning an application to confirm a modification order adding a restricted byway to a definitive map. The land over which the public right of way was said to subsist included the existence of a towpath over the route, which was provided for by the Trent Navigation Act 1783.

[120] *Vestry of St Mary, Newington v Jacobs* (1871–72) LR 7 QB 47 at 53 per Mellor J.

[121] See e.g. *Mercer v Woodgate* (1869) LR 5 QB 26.

[122] *Vestry of St Mary, Newington v Jacobs* (1871–72) LR 7 QB 47 at 53 per Mellor J.

[123] Road Traffic Act 1988, s 34, which creates an offence for a person to drive a mechanically propelled vehicle onto or upon a footpath, bridleway or restricted byway, in the absence of a lawful excuse.

happens to the private right of way? And for that matter, could an adjoining landowner acquire, by prescription, a right to do something which would constitute a civil or criminal wrong by virtue of the land's highway status?

27.66 A clearer picture has emerged since *Bakewell Management Ltd v Brandwood*,[124] where it was said there is no requirement of public policy that prevents the acquisition of an easement by prescription in breach of a statutory prohibition where it would have been lawful for the landowner to make such a grant and where such a grant would remove the criminality of the user. Thus even where, because of the highway's existence, an action in establishing an easement by prescription would amount to a tortious wrong or a criminal offence where there is 'no lawful authority', such rights may still so arise. The situation, of course, would be different where the actions required to establish an easement would simply amount to a criminal offence and could not be made lawful.[125]

MAINTENANCE OF THE HIGHWAY

Who is responsible for repair?

27.67 Historically, the inhabitants of the local parish were responsible for repair of highways in their area unless it could be shown that an individual or other body was responsible for its maintenance, which may have occurred as a result of statute,[126] prescription,[127] tenure or enclosure.[128]

---

[124] [2004] UKHL 14, [2004] All ER 305.

[125] The general rule is still that unlawful actions cannot give rise to the acquisition of legal rights, although prescription has always been an exception to this rule since the actions required to establish a prescriptive right will normally have resulted from a trespass. See *George Legge & Son Ltd v Wenlock Corp* [1938] AC 204, 'whilst there are statutes imposing duties or prohibitions which can be waived, there is no case in which repeated violation of the express terms of a modern statute passed in the public interest has been held to confer rights on the wrong doer'.

[126] Local or other Acts of Parliament may have provided expressly that a highway was not maintainable by the inhabitants of the local parish, but express words to that effect would be required.

[127] Liability could arise by way of prescription, but it was said the custom must have existed since time immemorial. Thus where the highway itself could be shown to post-date 1189, that would be enough to rebut such a claim.

[128] Where land over which a right of way subsisted became impassable, the courts had recognised that user of the highway might divert onto adjoining land. See *R v Oldreeve* (1868) 32 JP Jo 271 per Willes J:

'if there is a public way over a man's field, and he puts an obstruction upon it, then the public ... are entitled to go round a reasonable distance into his field by the side of the way, and use that as a temporary way until he removes the obstruction. But if the obstruction is caused by the actions of the elements, then no such right accrues to the public.'

33

27.68 Section 23 of the Highways Act 1835 effectively ended the automatic liability of the parish to repair all highways in their area. After that Act came into force, where highways were constructed or otherwise dedicated to the public, such ways would not become maintainable at public expense unless a certain procedure was followed.[129] The 1835 Act did not apply to footpaths and bridleways, but by virtue of the National Parks and Access to the Countryside Act 1949, the provisions of the 1835 Act were later applied to all public paths (unless created by a 'public path agreement') following implementation on 16/12/1949.[130]

27.69 Neither Act had retrospective effect and thus all highways which were maintainable before 1835 at public expense remain unaffected. After that date there will be some highways which, because the formalities of the Highways Act 1835 were not followed, will be repairable by nobody.[131]

27.70 By virtue of section 38 of the Highways Act 1959, the duty of the inhabitants to maintain highways in their area was effectively abolished. Highways maintainable at public expense will now largely be a matter for the relevant highway authority. Following the implementation of the HA 1980, a highway created after the implementation of the Act, will become automatically maintainable at public expense where:[132]

(a) the highway was constructed by the highway authority, otherwise than on behalf of some person who is not a highway authority;
(b) the highway was constructed by a council under Part II of the Housing Act 1985 (subject to certain conditions);[133]

Note that the right to deviate in respect of temporary obstruction has been held even for a period of 50 years. See *Dawes v Hawkins* (1860) 141 ER 1399. See also *R (Gloucester County Council) v Secretary of State for the Environment, Transport and the Regions* (2001) 82 P & CR 15 at [57] per Hallett J. Where the land had been enclosed, so as to prevent deviation, the landowner benefiting from the enclosure would be liable to maintain and keep the way in repair. Such a liability has now been abrogated by the HA 1980. Such liability would only in any event attract itself where the highway involved had existed from time immemorial: *Henn's Case* (1632) WJo 296.

[129] Note, however, that Highways Act 1835, s 23 as originally enacted did not apply to footpaths and bridleways. The position then changed with the implementation of the National Parks and Access to the Countryside Act 1949.

[130] National Parks and Access to the Countryside Act 1949, s 49.

[131] But see *Leigh Urban District Council v King* [1901] 1 QB 747.

[132] These are all outlined at HA 1980, s 36(2).

[133] The highway will be maintainable at public expense where a highway is constructed by a council within its area under Housing Act 1985, Pt II, other than one in respect of which the local highway authority is satisfied has not been properly constructed, and a highway constructed by a council outside its own area under Pt II, being in the latter case, a highway the liability to maintain which is vested in the council which is the local highway authority for the area in which the highway is situated. HA 1980, s 36(2)(b).

(c)   the highway is a trunk or special road;[134]
(d)   the highway is a footpath, bridleway or restricted byway which was created by virtue of a public path creation order, a public path diversion order or by virtue of an order under section 247 or section 257 of the TCPA 1990 or otherwise by a public path creation agreement;
(e)   the highway is a footpath, bridleway or restricted byway created by virtue of a rail crossing diversion order, or by an order under section 14 or section 16 of the Harbours Act 1964 or by virtue of section 1 or section 3 of the Transport and Works Act 1992;
(f)   the highway is a footpath, bridleway, restricted byway or a way over which the public have a right of way for vehicular and all other kinds of traffic created by virtue of a special diversion order or a Site of Special Scientific Interest (SSSI) order.

27.71   The list provided above is not exhaustive, but where a highway has been constructed after the coming into force of the HA 1980 and it does not fall in one of the above listed categories, the highway will generally not be maintainable at public expense, unless it has been formally adopted by one of the procedures discussed below.

27.72   Where a highway authority is of the view that a highway it is obliged to maintain is no longer necessary for public use, it can apply for an order to discharge its liability to so maintain the way.[135] A list of all publicly maintainable roads is kept by the relevant council (as above) for each area.[136] Broadly speaking, however, we can deduce that a highway will be publicly maintainable where:

(a)   the highway is a highway which existed before 31/8/1835 or a public path (bridleway or footpath) which existed before 16/12/1949;[137] or
(b)   the highway was created after 1835/1949 and the relevant procedure as applied at the time was followed so as to make the road maintainable at public expense;[138] or

---

[134]   Note that a trunk or special road will be maintainable at public expense, but not in respect of a bridge or some other part which another person is liable to maintain by virtue or a charter or special enactment, or by reason of tenure, enclosure or prescription. HA 1980, s 36(3).

[135]   See HA 1980, s 47.

[136]   HA 1980, s 36(6).

[137]   The dates provided relate to the implementation dates of the Highways Act 1835 and the National Parks and Access to the Countryside Act 1949, respectively.

[138]   The HA 1980 does not have retrospective effect and the Act makes it expressly clear that, where a highway was publicly maintainable for the purposes of the Highways Act 1959, it will continue to be so maintainable, HA 1980, s 36(1).

(c)   the highway has, as a result of some subsequent procedure, been formally
       adopted by the highway authority.[139]

ADOPTION OF ROADS

27.73 The HA 1980 provides for specific ways in which a highway may become
maintainable at public expense. Principally, these are contained in sections 37 and
38. The reader should also see the private street works code and the advanced
payments code, which are also dealt with below.

HA 1980, section 37

27.74 Section 37 of the HA 1980 allows for a person seeking to dedicate land as
a highway (i.e. where it has not yet been so dedicated) and who desires such a
way to become maintainable at public expense, to be able to give notice of his
proposal to the highway authority for the area in which the proposed way is
located. Such a notice must be served not less than three months before the date
of the proposed dedication. The notice must describe the location and width of
the proposed highway and the nature of the intended way.[140] Where a person seeks
to dedicate, as at common law, he must have the capacity to do so.

27.75 The council will then consider the notice and, if it decides that the
proposed highway will not be of 'sufficient utility' to the public to justify its being
maintained at the public expense, it may make a complaint to a magistrates' court
for an order to that effect. Alternatively, if the relevant highway authority decides
to issue a certificate that: (a) the way has been dedicated in accordance with the
terms of the applicant's original notice; and (b) that the way has been made up in
a satisfactory manner, and thereafter the way is maintained by the applicant, or
his successor in title, for a period of 12 months and the way is used during that
time 'as a highway', the highway will then become maintainable at public
expense.[141]

27.76 The council may decide to refuse such a certificate, but when it does so,
the applicant will have a right of appeal to the magistrates' court against the
refusal.[142] Where the court on hearing the application is satisfied that the

---

[139] See e.g. the provisions within HA 1980, s 38 as explained below where an existing highway (even
where it is currently maintainable by some other person as a result of any special enactment,
prescription or tenure) may become publicly maintainable by agreement.

[140] See also HA 1980, ss 320–322 in relation to the form of the notice.

[141] I.e. the way must be used by the public to pass and re-pass and for any other incidental activities
which do not substantially interfere with the public's primary right.

[142] A further appeal will lie to the Crown Court, HA 1980, s 317.

certificate ought to have been issued, it may make an order to that effect. In either case, the order from the court, or the certificate from the authority must be deposited with the proper officer of the council so as to allow for inspection of it by any member of the public.

27.77 The provisions of this section would seem to supply a developer with an alternative to the making of a section 38 agreement (as considered below). Unlike the provisions of section 38 of the HA 1980, there is no term which can provide for payment of a sum reflecting the costs of the continued maintenance of the way. Where the terms proposed by a highway authority for a section 38 agreement are not to the developer's commercial advantage, it may be that a section 37 application should be considered.[143]

HA 1980, section 38

27.78 Section 38(3) of the HA 1980 empowers the highway authority to make an agreement with a person specifying that it, the highway authority, will maintain either a highway already in existence or one which will be constructed. The person with whom the highway authority contracts must be willing, and have the necessary power, to dedicate land as a highway, or be a person proposing to dedicate land as a highway which has yet to be constructed, the construction being undertaken either by the highway authority or that person themselves. Such agreements may be made in advance of construction of the way to an adoptable standard by either the highway authority, or the person with whom it contracts. Maps may be used, but care must be taken to ensure that the proposed line of the dedication is accurate in reflecting the actual agreed development.[144] This is the provision which is generally used when a developer proposes to construct a road for subsequent adoption by the authority. If this course is followed, the developer need not make a deposit or give security under the advance payments code.[145] Where the way is yet to be built, the agreement can provide for a future date upon which the way will become publicly maintainable. The road will not become publicly maintainable until the date specified is met but there is no reason why dedication of the land as a highway could not take place before.

---

[143] See *R (Redrow Homes Ltd) v Knowsley Metropolitan Borough Council* [2014] EWCA Civ 1433, [2015] 1 WLR 386 at [20]–[22], where the court considered this expressly.

[144] See e.g. *Betterment Properties (Weymouth) Limited v James Carthy & Co Ltd* [2010] EWCA Civ 1401.

[145] HA 1980, s 219(4)(d).

27.79 The Minister is also empowered to make such agreements on a more or less identical basis as that summarised above, where he proposes that such a road will become a trunk road.[146]

27.80 Section 38(1) of the HA 1980 further empowers the local highway authority or the Minister (in case of trunk roads) to make an agreement to take over the liability to maintain a highway from a person who is responsible for the maintenance of an existing way, either by reason of any special enactment, tenure, enclosure or prescription.

27.81 An agreement made pursuant to section 38 of the HA 1980 for the dedication of a highway may incorporate conditions for the payment of expenses in relation to the construction, maintenance or improvement of the highway to which the agreement relates. The section 38 provisions are drafted widely, and a local authority may additionally include in the agreement 'any other relevant matters as the authority making the agreement thinks fit'.[147] A developer wishing to make an agreement under this section may be required by the highway authority to pay a commuted sum reflecting the future costs of maintaining the highway. Such a term is perfectly lawful.[148] It is presumed that such an agreement could also provide for the payment by the authority of any compensation that it may become liable to pay.[149] Where the agreement proposed by the highway authority is not commercially viable to the person seeking to obtain such an agreement, it may have recourse in the alternative to the provisions of section 37 above.[150]

27.82 Authorities will generally require a developer to support an agreement with a bond with a surety providing that the surety will pay to the authority the cost of making up the road in case of default by the developer. An authority would

---

[146] See HA 1980, s 38(3A).

[147] HA 1980, s 38(6).

[148] See *R (Redrow Homes Ltd) v Knowsley Metropolitan Borough Council* [2014] EWCA Civ 1433, [2015] 1 WLR 386. The case involved an agreement pursuant to HA 1980, s 38 in which both the developer (Redrow Homes) and Knowsley Metropolitan Borough Council, as the local highway authority, wished, in principle, that roads constructed to service a new estate of 525 homes would be dedicated pursuant to a s 38 agreement so that the roads would become maintainable at public expense. The council requested, as a term of the agreement, the payment of £39,000, said to be a commuted payment reflecting the future costs of maintaining street lights on the road. The developer challenged the legality of the term. The court found that there was nothing within the language of s 38(6) (which was expressed in wide and unqualified terms) to preclude the payment of such a sum reflecting the future cost of maintenance.

[149] See *Wiltshire CC v Crest Estates Ltd* [2005] EWCA Civ 1087.

[150] See *R (Redrow Homes Ltd) v Knowsley Metropolitan Borough Council* [2014] EWCA Civ 1433, [2015] 1 WLR 386 at [20]–[22], where the court considered this expressly.

be entitled to recover a sum from the surety, notwithstanding that new builders may have taken over the construction site as a whole.[151]

PRIVATE STREETS

27.83 In addition to sections 37 and 38 of the HA 1980, there are provisions which enable 'private streets' to become publicly maintainable. Part XI sets out two codes relating to the making up of such private streets to an adoptable standard. These are known as the private street works code (paragraph 27.88) and the advance payments code (paragraph 27.105).

What is a 'private street'?

27.84 For the purposes of the HA 1980, a 'private street' is defined negatively, to mean a 'street that is not a highway maintainable at public expense'. The definition, however, is expressly said to include: (a) land that is deemed to be a private street by virtue of a declaration under section 232 of the HA 1980;[152] and (b) (for the purposes of the application of the advance street works code) includes land which is shown as a proposed street on a deposited plan for the purposes of planning permissions under the TCPA 1990 or under building regulations.[153] The definition is relatively wide and the fact that part of the 'private street' in question is currently a highway maintainable at public expense will not preclude the rest of the way as being treated as a 'private street' for the purposes of the HA 1980.

27.85 The initial phrasing has two main components; it must be: (a) 'a street'; and (b) 'not a highway maintainable at public expense'. A 'street' for the purposes of the HA 1980 has the same meaning as it does in Part III of the New Roads and Street Works Act 1991. The definition is therefore the whole or any part of any of the following, irrespective of whether it is a thoroughfare:

(a)   any highway, road, lane, footway, alley or passage;
(b)   any square or court; and

---

[151] For a case where recovery from a surety took place after the signatories to the agreement went into liquidation, see e.g. *National Employers' Mutual Generation Insurance Association v Herne Bay UDC* (1972) 70 LGR 542.

[152] This section allows land which is defined by a development plan as the site of a proposed road, or as land required for the widening of an existing road which is less than byelaw width, to be declared, together with any land forming part of such existing road, to be a private street. Where a declaration is so made, the land will be deemed to have been dedicated to the use of the public as a highway and will be treated as a private street for the purposes of the private street works code.

[153] HA 1980, s 203(2).

(c) any land laid out as a way whether it is for the time being formed as a way or not.[154]

27.86 Where a street passes over a bridge or through a tunnel, references to the street will include the bridge or tunnel. The definition itself is relatively easy to understand and seems to encapsulate both land which has been dedicated as a highway, the definition for which is set out fully elsewhere, and other land. It does not appear that to be a 'street' for these purposes, that the public must have rights akin to a highway.[155] The wording 'irrespective of whether it is a thoroughfare' seems to carry this implication and on a basic level the word 'street' at common law had been given its ordinary meaning to include a thoroughfare which has a row of houses on one or both sides.[156]

27.87 Lists of highways maintainable at public expense are kept by the local highway authority.[157]

Private street works code

Street works

27.88 The private street works code is set out in sections 205 to 218 of the HA 1980. In short, section 205 allows a 'street works authority'[158] to resolve to execute street works where a private street is not, to its satisfaction 'sewered, levelled, paved, metalled, flagged, channelled, made good and lighted'. Such works may include 'any works which they think necessary for bringing the street, as regards [to] sewerage, drainage, level or other matters, into conformity with any other street'.[159] The consequent expenses incurred by the authority are recoverable as against the owners of the premises fronting the street. Where private street works are carried out in accordance with the procedure below, a declaration can eventually be made that the private street is maintainable at public expense.[160]

---

[154] See New Road and Street Works Act 1991, s 48(1). See also HA 1980, s 329.

[155] *West End Lawn Tennis Club (Pinner) Ltd v Harrow Corporation* (1965) 64 LGR 35.

[156] See e.g. *Galloway v London Corporation* (1866) LR 1 HL 34.

[157] HA 1980, s 36(6).

[158] The street works authority will vary depending on where the road is located. Street work authorities outside Greater London will comprise the county council or the council of the metropolitan district in which the street is located. Within Greater London, the street works authority will be the council of the borough, and as respects a street in the City, the Common Council. See HA 1980, s 203.

[159] HA 1980, s 206.

[160] See HA 1980, s 228, but note that this is subject to s 228(2) that where the owner of the private street, or, in the case of multiple owners, a majority of them, object within a certain period, the street will not become publicly maintainable although the authority may apply to a magistrates' court to overrule such objections.

Procedure

27.89 The process is started by a resolution from the council that it is dissatisfied with the sewering, levelling or paving, etc. of the private street in question. At that stage, the council's proper officer will then prepare a specification of the works referred to in the resolution with any necessary plans, providing an estimate of the probable expenses of carrying out the works, including a provisional apportionment of those expenses as against the premises liable to be charged.[161] These will then be submitted for approval by the authority, which will pass a further resolution approving the documents, either subject to amendment or otherwise. The specification of works and expenses should relate to the original resolution of dissatisfaction. In other words, it is precluded from including unrelated works.[162]

27.90 Once the resolution has been approved by the authority, a notice shall be published which must include certain specified particulars. Such a notice will be published once in two successive weeks in a local newspaper, be posted in a prominent position in a location near to the street for at least three successive weeks and, within seven days from the date of the first publication in the newspaper, be served on the owners of the premises shown in the provisional apportionment as liable to be charged with the expenses.[163] A statement of the likely apportioned sum will be included where notice is served on the owners of the frontage.[164] A copy of the resolution of approval must be made available at the relevant council offices for a period of one month at all reasonable hours.

27.91 The street works authority has power to amend the specification, plans, sections, estimate and/or the provisional apportionment, but where the estimate is increased, there are additional notice requirements.[165]

27.92 Once the street works have been executed and the expenses ascertained, a final apportionment is made by dividing the expenses in the same proportions as specified in the provisional apportionment and notice of the final apportionment served on the owners.

Objections

27.93 Objections can be taken at two stages: after the resolution of dissatisfaction and the relevant notices (and provisional apportionment) are served; and again

---

[161] HA 1980, s 502(3).

[162] See e.g. *Ware Urban District Council v Gaunt* [1960] 1 WLR 1364.

[163] HA 1980, s 205(5).

[164] HA 1980, s 205(6).

[165] See HA 1980, s 210(2).

after the final apportionment. In either case, objections can be raised by the 'owner'[166] of the premises said to be liable and should be brought within one month (i.e. one month from the date that the notice of provisional apportionment was served, or, as the case may be, the final apportionment). The time limit is not capable of extension.[167] In both cases, the grounds for objection are set out in the HA 1980. In the case of objections raised after the provisional apportionment, the grounds are:[168]

(a) that the alleged private street is not a private street;[169]
(b) that there has been some material informality, defect or error in relation to the resolution, notice plans sections or estimate;[170]
(c) that the proposed works are insufficient or unreasonable;[171]
(d) that the estimated expenses of the proposed works are excessive;
(e) that any premises ought to be excluded from or inserted in the provisional apportionment;[172]
(f) that the provisional apportionment is incorrect in respect of some matter of fact to be specified in the objection.

27.94 Objections, if not withdrawn, are heard in a magistrates' court. The court may quash in whole or in part or amend the resolution of approval, the specification, plans, sections, estimate and/or the provisional apportionment. The grounds listed are exhaustive. An appeal which does not list one of the above

---

[166] The word 'owner' is expressly defined within the HA 1980 as 'a person, other than a mortgagee not in possession, who, whether in his own right or as a trustee or agent for any other person, is entitled to receive the rack rent of the premises, or where the premises are not let on a rack rent, would be so entitled if the premises were so let': HA 1980, s 329. Note that where there is nobody that is able or would be able to receive a 'rack rent', the land will be *extra commercium*.

[167] HA 1980, s 209(1).

[168] HA 1980, s 217.

[169] The definition of 'private street' includes land which is 'not publicly maintainable'. The burden of proof will, at least initially, be on the highway authority to show that that land subject to the proceedings is a private street. See *Alsager UDC v Barratt* [1965] 1 All ER 889; *Attorney-General v Watford Rural District Council* [1912] Ch 417. The time that the alleged highway came into existence may be of relevance. Ancient highways, i.e. those created before the implementation of the Highways Act 1835, will be automatically maintainable by the public.

[170] The defect which is alleged, must be 'material'. *De minimis* departures will not provide a basis for objection. The utility of an objection under this section is seemingly only to delay the process. An authority will be entitled to simply start the procedure again from the beginning.

[171] As for the meaning of 'insufficient' and the word 'unreasonable', see *Mansfield v Butterworth* [1898] 2 QB 274. See also *Southgate Corporation v Park Estates (Southgate) Ltd* [1954] 1 All ER 520 – an application was found to be premature in light of the fact that Park Estates had secured planning permission for another development which would involve the proposed road subject to the works.

[172] This is covered, along with expenses, at paras 27.97–27.101. Arguments may arise that properties benefited but not directly 'fronting' the street subject to the works should be so charged.

grounds will fail,[173] although it could potentially be put forward as an appeal to the Minister.[174] There does not appear to be a provision to allow the amendment of the objection, and consequently such an objection may fail where the notice is incorrectly drafted.[175]

27.95   In respect of objections raised after the notice of final apportionment has been served, the grounds are slightly different. They are:

(a)   that there has been an unreasonable departure from the specification, plans and sections;

(b)   that the actual expenses have without sufficient reason exceeded the estimated expenses by more than 15%;

(c)   that the apportionment has not been made in accordance with section 211 of the HA 1980.

27.96   Much of the case law, unsurprisingly, has focused on the apportionment of expenses, which is dealt with in more detail below. Objections, if not withdrawn, are heard in a magistrates' court. The court may quash in whole or in part or amend the resolution of approval, the specification, plans, sections, estimate and/or the provisional apportionment. Costs are in the discretion of the court and, seemingly, those unsuccessfully objecting to the proposed works and/or the apportionment may be asked to pay the costs of the hearing.[176]

Expenses

27.97   As can be seen from the above, the expenses of works are provisionally apportioned after the resolution of dissatisfaction, but can be subsequently amended so as to be increased. Section 205 of the HA 1980 provides that the expenses incurred in undertaking works will be apportioned between the premises fronting the street subject to the works.[177] Where the works are completed on part of the street only, the expenses are apportioned between the premises fronting the length of the street subject to the works.[178] Premises which front part of the street which are not subject to the works will not be charged, even where they have access to the street.[179]

---

[173]   See e.g. *Wilson v Wrexham Corporation* [1960] 1 WLR 319.

[174]   See HA 1980, s 233. The time limit within which an appeal must be brought under this section is 21 days from the date on which a demand is made for the payment of expenses.

[175]   See e.g. *Brighton Borough Council v Peachy (Investments)* [1957] JPL 585.

[176]   HA 1980, s 209(3).

[177]   HA 1980, s 205(1).

[178]   HA 1980, s 205(2).

[179]   See *Chatterton v Glanford Rural District Council* [1915] 3 KB 707.

27.98 In settling the provisional apportionment, the council's proper officer will have regard to the benefit to be derived by any premises from the street works and the amount and value of any work already done by the owners or occupiers of the frontages.[180] The authority may also include in the apportionment premises which do not front the street, but have access to it through a court, passage or otherwise and which will, in the opinion of the authority, be benefited by the works 'if they think just' to do so.[181]

27.99 The case law has made it clear nonetheless that in most cases the 'overriding consideration' in assessing apportionment will be frontage.[182] The wording of the section that the expenses will be apportioned amongst the properties 'fronting the street', has been subject to litigation. According to the HA 1980, 'fronting' includes 'adjoining'.[183] It has been suggested that the words 'fronts', 'adjoins' and 'abuts' envisage actual contact between the premises and the street subject to the works.[184] Thus the owner/occupier of the top floor of a maisonette that is separated from the street by way of a small garden belonging to the ground floor, does not 'front' the street for the purposes of the code.[185] It is clear, however, that at the provisional apportionment stage, such an owner could be made to contribute towards the expenses on the basis that the property is receiving a benefit.

27.100 Subsequent case law has shown that it is not always necessary for there to be physical contact between the fronting property and the street. A property which is separated from the street by a small stream where there was a footbridge and carriageway over the stream was considered to 'adjoin' the street.[186] The court generally will adopt a purposive approach.[187] In *Lightbound v Higher Bebington Local Board* it was said:[188]

---

[180] HA 1980, s 207(2).

[181] This relates to the provisional apportionment of expenses stage, see HA 1980, s 207.

[182] See *Parkstone Primrose Laundry v Poole Corp* (1950) 114 JP 354.

[183] HA 1980, s 203(3).

[184] See e.g. *Buckinghamshire County Council v Trigg* [1963] 1 WLR 155 at 161 per Lord Parker.

[185] *Buckinghamshire County Council v Trigg* [1963] 1 WLR 155.

[186] *Wakefield Local Board v Lee* (1875) 1 Ex D 336, CA, note in particular at 342 where Cleasby B said, 'the most important word is "adjoining". Now it seems to me that, as the stream is very small, the premises are not really separated from the land and may be said to "adjoin"'.

[187] See e.g. *Lightbound v Higher Bebington Local Board* (1885) 16 QBD 577 at 584 per Bowen LJ, 'in construing the words you must look at the subject-matter of the section and see what is its scope and object. Here one has a section which presumably is intended to charge persons who are benefited by the work done and as soon as one finds that, one gets a kind of light shed on the words 'front, abut and adjoin'.

[188] (1885) 16 QBD 577 at 584–5.

in considering whether houses adjoin which are placed in close proximity to the part of the street which is to be paved, it is a most important fact, and, in many cases, a dominant fact, to see whether there is a substantial access and advantage which the houses enjoy from that portion of the street which is to be paved, and a substantial access and advantage of that kind, coupled with close proximity, may bring the case within the word 'adjoin,' though there is no actual touch.

27.101   Where the authority decides to apportion expenses against a property that does not front, but benefits from, the proposed works, it is preferable that the resolution states expressly that the authority 'think it just' to do so.[189]

Liability and recovery of expenses

27.102   The statute provides that it is the 'owners' of the relevant properties subject to the apportionment from which recovery is made. The word 'owner' is expressly defined in the HA 1980 to be:[190]

> ... a person, other than a mortgagee not in possession, who, whether in his own right or as a trustee or agent for any other person, is entitled to receive the rack rent of the premises, or where the premises are not let on a rack rent, would be so entitled if the premises were so let.

27.103   Where there is no person entitled to a rack rent, there is no 'owner' for the purposes of the statute. In those circumstances, the land in question is *extra commercium*. All land, including that which is *extra commercium*, should be considered in an apportionment on the basis of frontage.[191] The final sums due to the authority may be recovered in whole or by partial payments. Where partial payments are accepted, interest can be added at such a rate as the authority may determine.[192] Where the full sum has not been discharged, the sum is a charge (registrable under Part II of the local land charges register) on the premises providing the same powers and remedies as if the charge was a mortgage by deed, with powers of sale and lease and to appoint a receiver.[193] The authority can otherwise order payment by annual instalments, together with interest, over a period not exceeding 30 years.[194]

---

[189]   See *Oakley v Merthyr Tydfil Corporation* [1922] 1 KB 409 at 422. And see *Newquay Urban Council v Rickeard* [1911] 2 KB 846. It has been suggested that the term 'access' should be construed to exclude access obtained through a public street because there would be practically no end to the premises to which access may be obtained.

[190]   HA 1980, s 329.

[191]   *Herne Bay UC v Payne and Wood* [1907] 2 KB 130.

[192]   HA 1980, s 212(1).

[193]   HA 1980, s 212(3); see the Local Land Charges Act 1975.

[194]   HA 1980, s 212(4), and see Sch 13.

Exemptions

27.104   There are certain exceptions in the HA 1980 as to who can incur the expenses as set out above. Places of worship and burial grounds that are attached to such places are an example.[195] The minister or trustee of such a place will not be liable for apportioned expenses, which will instead be borne by the street works authority. There are, additionally, provisions in relation to railway or canal undertakers[196] and the Thames Water Authority/Port of London Authority.[197]

Advance payments code

27.105   The advance payments code is contained in sections 219 to 225 of the HA 1980. The code applies where the erection of a building is proposed, for which plans are required to be deposited with the local authority in accordance with building regulations, and the building will front onto a private street to which the 'street works authority'[198] would have power under the private streets works code to require works to be carried out.[199] Where those circumstances exist, the owner of the land on which the building is to be erected must supply or secure to the authority's satisfaction the payment of a sum reflective of that which, in the authority's opinion, would be payable under the street works code if it decided to carry out works (with regard to the frontage).[200] Where building works take place without that sum being so secured or paid, the owner of the land will have committed a criminal offence.[201]

27.106   The purpose of the code is therefore quite simple: it is to prevent a scenario in which a developer (as the most obvious example) fails to bring a road up to adoptable standard and thereby leaves the burden on the authority or the purchasers of the new buildings. In practice, most developers will seek to

---

[195]   HA 1980, s 215.

[196]   See HA 1980, s 216, and in particular s 216(1), which provides that such undertakers are not deemed to be owners or occupiers of land which wholly or partly fronts the street subject to the works, if the land has 'no direct communication with the street' and was used solely as 'part of their line of railway, canal or siding, station or towing path by the undertakers'. An undertaker should lodge an objection, where they have been served with notice that they will be liable to an apportioned sum in respect of the works, so as to avoid being bound by it. See *Watford Corporation v London Passenger Transport Board* [1945] KB 129.

[197]   For which, see HA 1980, s 218.

[198]   The identity of the street works authority will vary depending on where the street is located. Street works authorities outside Greater London will comprise the county council or the council of the metropolitan district in which the street is located. Within Greater London, the street works authority will be the council of the borough. See HA 1980, s 203.

[199]   HA 1980, s 219(1).

[200]   See HA 1980, s 220(3).

[201]   See HA 1980, s 219(2), but note the defence under s 219(3).

construct private streets to an adoptable standard and thereafter dedicate such streets.

27.107   It should be noted that the sections relating to the advance payment code are elaborate, and the following is merely a brief guide to the relevant law. The code itself is expressly excluded from applying in certain listed circumstances. The full section[202] should be consulted, but in brief the exclusions are:

(a)   where the owner of the land on which the building is to be constructed would be exempt from having to pay expenses under the street works code, as a result of a provision in that code;[203]
(b)   where the building to be constructed will be situated in the curtilage of, and be appurtenant to, an existing building;
(c)   where an agreement has been made by any person with the street works authority under section 38.

Procedure

27.108   Where a plan relating to the erection of a building is deposited with the relevant authority and the advance payments code applies, the street works authority will, within six weeks, serve a notice on the person depositing the plan, requiring the payment of a sum which, in the opinion of the street works authority, reflects the amount recoverable under the street works code (with regard to frontage), if it were to undertake such works.[204] Where a notice has been served and there is an objection, appeal lies to 'the Minister', who may substitute a smaller sum.[205]

27.109   Further notices may be sent either where it later appears that the sum specified in the original notice is greater than that which would be recoverable, or where the street works authority considers that no sum would be recoverable.[206] If the sum has been paid already, there is provision to refund the sum.[207]

27.110   Where the works are undertaken by a body other than the street works authority (i.e. in most cases, the developer) and the authority is satisfied of the

---

[202]   The relevant section is HA 1980, s 219(4)(a)–(i).

[203]   An example would be where the building is a place of worship.

[204]   HA 1980, s 220(1). Note that where the plans are not deposited with the street works authority, the relevant council has a duty (see s 220(2)) to inform the street works authority that the plans have been passed to it.

[205]   'The Minister' will be the Secretary of State for Transport for the purposes of the HA 1980. See HA 1980, s 220(6).

[206]   HA 1980, s 220(4).

[207]   See HA 1980, s 220(7)(a)–(c).

works, but payment has either been made or secured, the street works authority may refund the sum in whole or part.[208]

27.111 Similar provisions in relation to refunds are contained in section 222 of the HA 1980 where the amount paid is in excess of the cost of the works, or where the road is not adopted as a highway. In such circumstances, a refund and a release of the relevant security may take place.

27.112 Similarly, where the building works are not begun because either the owner discontinues the project, or the local authority declares the deposited plans of no effect, the sums already paid or secured will ordinarily be released in accordance with the provisions of section 223 of the HA 1980.

INTERFERENCES WITH PUBLIC HIGHWAYS

Introduction

27.113 Interferences with the public's right to pass and re-pass may take many different forms. They might be obstructions, the creation of dangers or indeed damage to the highway itself. Such interferences can carry both civil and criminal implications. The two principal forms of wrong discussed here are, first, offences and duties created expressly by the provisions of Part IX of the HA 1980, and, secondly, public nuisances.

HA 1980

Introduction

27.114 The policing of interferences falls largely to the local highway authority.[209] Section 130 of the HA 1980 places it under a statutory duty to assert and protect the rights of the public to use and enjoy public rights of way, thus the powers to prevent and police obstructions are largely funnelled into the hands of the highway authority. That being said, local councils which are not the local highway authority may also assert and protect the rights of the public,[210] and parish councils may notify the highway authority of obstructions, which will place

---

[208] HA 1980, s 221.

[209] As a generalisation this is correct, but note HA 1980, s 130(2) and (6). It also goes without saying that private individuals will be able to seek redress themselves in circumstances where the obstruction or interference has caused loss.

[210] HA 1980, s 130(2). Note the different wording of the sub-section, the council is not placed under a 'duty' as the highway authority is under s 130(1), the council is only empowered and 'may assert and protect the rights of the public'.

the highway authority under a duty to act, save in circumstances where it is satisfied that the representations are incorrect.[211]

27.115   Members of the public are also able to notify the highway authority of an obstruction and may serve a notice, requesting the removal of the interference (although subject to certain limitations).[212] The highway authority must then serve a notice within one month on every person whom it appears at that time is responsible for the obstruction.[213] Where the obstruction endures, the member of the public serving the original notice is empowered to take further steps to secure the removal of the obstruction by applying to a magistrates' court for an order requiring the highway authority to take specified actions in relation to the interference. Where such an application is made, there may be costs consequences which may be considerable, particularly in the case where there is an appeal from the decision of the magistrates.[214]

27.116   Notably, however, the duty under section 130 of the HA 1980 to assert and protect the public's right to use the highway does not give rise to an action for damages where the highway authority fails to remove obstructions and somebody thereby injures himself or suffers loss. Section 130 cannot be read so as to give rise to a general duty to remove obstructions or carry out precautionary inspections of the highway.[215]

---

[211]   See HA 1980, ss 130(6) and 130A(1), but note that such a request from a member of the public may not be sent if the obstruction complained of is a building or works for the construction of a building. For the procedure where a request is served by a member of the public, see s 130A(6) in respect of the steps the highway authority must take.

[212]   HA 1980, s 130A. Note the meaning of 'highway' within the section includes footpaths, bridleways, restricted byways and BOATs. Also note the limitations under s 130A(3) and (4).

[213]   Note the word 'responsible' will necessarily include the creator of the interference, but will include the person who has possession or control of the obstruction, which will include the owner. See HA 1980, s 130A(7).

[214]   As to the notices that it must serve, see HA 1980, s 130A(6). As to the procedure where the obstruction is not removed, see ss 130B and 130C. Those making an application to a magistrates' court must exercise particular care, given the costs implications under Magistrates' Court Act 1980, s 64 which may rebound onto the unsuccessful litigants. Also note, as to costs, the provisions of s 130D, which provides that before exercising powers in relation to costs, the Court shall have 'particular regard to any failure by the Highway Authority to give the applicant appropriate notice of, and information about, the grounds relied on by the authority'.

[215]   See *Ali v The City of Bradford Metropolitan District Council* [2010] EWCA Civ 1282. The claimant had tripped on what was said to be a stretch of footpath which had not been properly maintained. She claimed damages and based her action on a breach of statutory duty under HA 1980, s 130 and additionally brought a claim in nuisance. The court found that the pleadings contained no grounds for bringing the claim. It concluded that s 130 did not give rise to a civil action for damages. To require a local highway authority to regularly inspect all highways within its area would place excessive financial burden upon the authority, and there was no express provision placing such a duty upon them. Note, however, that there are provisions within the HA

27.117 It is noteworthy that there will in many cases be an overlap between offences created under the HA 1980 or some other Act of Parliament and the common law offence of public nuisance. Where the highway authority has available to it an offence under statute, it should ordinarily charge the matter under that Act, rather than as a public nuisance.[216] The availability of public nuisance is nonetheless of importance, particularly in cases where, for whatever reason, a highway authority fails to prosecute an interference with a highway and an adjoining landowner seeks compensation and can prove special damage.

Specific provisions of the HA 1980

27.118 It goes without saying that recourse to court action is ordinarily a last resort. Where structures have been erected on a highway, the highway authority will ordinarily serve a notice upon the person having control of the structure to remove it. Where the notice is not complied with, the authority itself may remove the obstruction and recover expenses from the party involved.[217] Similarly, where something is deposited on the highway so as to give rise to a nuisance, the highway authority is entitled to serve a notice requiring its removal on the person so depositing the item. Where that person fails to comply, enforcement will be by way of complaint to a magistrates' court, unless there are reasonable grounds for believing that the thing so deposited constitutes a danger to highway users and that the thing in question ought to be removed without delay.[218] There are other powers possessed by the highway authority to deal with actions likely to constitute a nuisance to highway users.[219]

27.119 Where the authority fails to secure compliance with a notice or where it otherwise decides that it wishes to prosecute, it may pursue an action for certain offences created by the HA 1980. This chapter does not seek to deal with all of the relevant offences created by the statute, but instead seeks to focus on the offences most likely to arise in a development context. Broadly, Part IX creates

---

1980 which do place a duty upon the highway authority to remove obstructions. See e.g. s 150 in relation to snow and soil.

[216] See *R v Rimmington; R v Goldstein* [2005] UKHL 63, [2006] 1 AC 459 at [31]–[40]. It may be appropriate to charge the matter as a public nuisance in some circumstances where a statutory offence is in existence, but generally the courts have said that good practice and respect for the primacy of statute will mean that the offence should be charged under the relevant Act of Parliament.

[217] HA 1980, s 143. Note that in the case of a highway which is maintained by a non-metropolitan district council, that council may exercise such a power.

[218] HA 1980, s 149. The notices which may be sent are directed at a differing class of persons to that under s 143. In the case of s 149 the notice is served on persons depositing the item on the highway, whereas s 143 is directed against persons in possession or control of the obstruction.

[219] See also HA 1980, s 163 (provisions as to the prevention of water falling onto a highway), s 164 (the removal of barbed wire), s 165 (dangerous land adjoining a street) and s 166.

offences which can be grouped into the following: (a) offences protecting the surface of the way from damage (sections 131 to 136); (b) offences preventing the creation of obstructions (sections 137 to 155); and (c) offences preventing the creation of dangers (sections 161 to 175).

Damage to the highway

27.120   In addition to obstructions, the HA 1980 provides for offences associated with damage to the highway itself. The relevant sections are sections 131 to 136, and they exemplify the importance of identifying rights of way at an early stage, as many of the offences provided by those sections are offences of strict liability. In each case, the offences are finable and prosecution will take place in a magistrates' court.

27.121   Under section 131 of the HA 1980 there are offences created in relation to: (a) excavation or the creation of a ditch in a carriageway;[220] (b) the removal of soil or turf without permission from any part of a highway; (c) depositing anything so as to cause damage to a highway; (d) lighting any fire, or discharging a firework or firearm within 50 feet from the centre of a carriageway; or (e) pulling down or obliterating a traffic sign placed on or over a highway.[221] In each case, the offence is only committed where there is an absence of lawful authority or excuse, but the offences are otherwise of strict liability. Ignorance of the need to seek legal authority before excavating the highway will be no defence.[222]

27.122   There are further offences in relation to the disturbance of the surface of a footpath, bridleway or highway consisting of a carriageway so as to render it inconvenient for the public to pass and re-pass, where the person causing the disturbance has no lawful authority for doing so, or excuse.[223] Some disturbances can, however, be authorised by the highway authority, but plainly authorisation should be obtained in advance of works.[224]

---

[220]   A carriageway, as defined by HA 1980, s 329, is a way constituting or comprised in a highway, being a way (other than a cycle track over which the public have a right of way) for the passage of vehicles.

[221]   HA 1980, s 131(1) and (2) In each case, the offence is punishable by a fine not exceeding level 3 on the standard scale (£1,000).

[222]   See *Greenwich London Borough Council v Millcroft Construction* (1987) 85 LGR 66.

[223]   HA 1980, s 131A(1) (works disturbing footpath etc.) An offence under the section is punishable by a fine not exceeding level 3 on the standard scale (£1,000). See also s 134 in relation to disturbances caused by ploughing the soil.

[224]   See e.g. HA 1980, s 135.

Obstruction of highways

27.123   Some obstructions, such as the erection of a building on a highway, may well constitute a trespass. The HA 1980 goes a step further and creates criminal offences out of the creation of actions which, in many cases, will have constituted a trespass. The main provisions are to be found in sections 137 to 155. The main offences as they relate to development works are those in relation to wilful obstruction (section 137), an express offence in relation to the erection of buildings (section 138) and in relation to the deposition of skips (section 139).

Section 137 – wilful obstruction

27.124   If a person, in any way, wilfully obstructs the free passage along a highway, an offence is committed, if there is either no lawful authority or no lawful excuse to do so. This is the basic offence as provided for by section 137 of the HA 1980.

WHAT IS AN 'OBSTRUCTION'?

27.125   Whether something is or is not an obstruction will always be a question of fact for a magistrates' court. *De minimis* obstructions are ordinarily disregarded,[225] but the traditional view is that any stopping on the highway is a *prima facie* obstruction.[226] Land can, however, be dedicated subject to limitations, such as a stile, gate or other structure, which would otherwise be an unlawful obstruction of the highway.[227] In reality, the question is whether such use is unreasonable. It has been suggested that this would depend on the circumstances

---

[225]   Some obstructions can be disregarded on the basis that such obstruction is merely trivial. What is or is not *de minimis* will be a matter for the justices, but seemingly the matter is not as straightforward as it would first appear. See e.g. *Seekings v Clarke* (1961) 59 LGR 268: the pavement involved was 16 feet 4 inches wide and the alleged obstruction, a sunblind in front of a shop, was around 2 feet 6 inches wide, with shelves 1 foot 6 inches wide. This was found to be a substantial projection. See also *Wolverton Urban DC v Willis (T/A SG Willis & Sons)* [1962] 1 WLR 205; *Westminster CC v Alladin Ltd* [1994] COD 488: any encroachment that is more than trivial cannot in law be *de minimis*; *Hinchon v Briggs* (1963) 61 LGR 315. The nature of the obstruction and its duration should be considered: *Nagy v Weston* [1965] 1 All ER 78.

[226]   See *Hirst and Agu v Chief Constable of West Yorkshire* (1987) 85 Cr App R 143. And see *Seekings v Clark* (1961) 59 LGR 268, where it was held that it was perfectly clear that anything which substantially prevents the public from having free access over the whole of the highway which is not purely temporary in nature is an unlawful obstruction. There are, of course, exceptions to that. One possible exception would be on the principle of *de minimis*. And see *Wolverton UDC v Willis* (1961) 60 LGR 135.

[227]   Such obstructions should be recorded on the definitive map. Where such an obstruction is not shown, it will be for the person asserting to show that the land was dedicated to such an obstruction or that it has been authorised by the highway authority pursuant to HA 1980, s 147. See *Rights of Way Circular (1/09)* at para 6.7.

but will include, 'the length of time the obstruction continues, the place where it occurs, the purpose for which it is done, and, of course whether it does in fact cause an actual obstruction as opposed to a potential obstruction'.[228]

27.126   It is not necessary to prove that a member of the public has been obstructed from utilising his right to pass and re-pass over the highway, the question is only whether there has been an obstruction.[229] The law has changed considerably in light of the decision of the court in *Director of Public Prosecutions v Jones*,[230] which provides that the highway may be used:[231]

> for any reasonable purpose, provided the activity in question does not amount to a public or private nuisance and does not obstruct the highway by unreasonably impeding the primary right of the public to pass and repass: within these qualifications there is a public right of peaceful assembly on the highway.

27.127   Thus the way can be used for activities which are incidental to the public's right to pass and re-pass, but not actions which cause a significant impediment on the way. Only unreasonable activities which affect the primary right of the public will thus amount to obstructions at law. It is now plain that holding a meeting on the highway would not *per se* constitute an unlawful obstruction provided it did not obstruct those who were using the highway for passage. However, a right to hold a protest meeting on the highway would not extend to the establishment of a permanent camp for protestors.[232]

WILFUL OBSTRUCTION

27.128   For the purposes of section 147 of the HA 1980, an obstruction must be 'wilful' in order for it to constitute an offence. 'Wilful' in this context is something which is deliberate or intentional.[233] Merely accidental occurrences,

---

228   *Nagy v Weston* [1965] 1 All ER 78 at 80D per Lord Parker CJ. See also *Absalom v Martin* [1974] RTR 145.

229   See *Wolverton Urban DC v Willis (T/A SG Willis & Sons)* [1962] 1 WLR 205.

230   [1999] 2 WLR 625.

231   [1999] 2 WLR 625 at 632 per Lord Irvine.

232   *The Mayor, Commonality and Citizens of the City of London v Tammy Samede* [2012] EWHC 34 (QB); *Manchester Ship Canal Developments Ltd v Persons Unknown, Crane & Others* [2014] EWHC 645 (Ch). In *Ineos Upstream Ltd v Persons Unknown* [2017] EWHC 2945 (Ch), the court continued injunctions restraining persons unknown from a range of activities relating to protests against fracking operators. The injunctions prevented them from substantially interfering with rights of way, from creating obstructions preventing the claimants from accessing the highway from sites with the intention of causing inconvenience or delay, or from walking in front of vehicles to slow them down.

233   *Hirst and Agu v Chief Constable of West Yorkshire* (1987) 85 Cr App R 143. And see *R v Senior* [1899] 1 QB 283

where, for example, a person is unaware that a right of way subsists, will not be 'wilful' for the purposes of the statute. The offence seems to be made out where 'a person without lawful authority or excuse, intentionally as opposed to accidentally, that is, by an exercise of his or her free will, does something or omits to do something which will cause an obstruction'.[234]

LAWFUL AUTHORITY AND LAWFUL EXCUSE

27.129 The term 'lawful authority' is only concerned with the right upon which the obstruction is alleged to have been permitted. A body which grants permission, but has no power to allow such an obstruction, will not be a lawful authority.[235] Where the way itself has been dedicated subject to an obstruction, there will be lawful authority for the continuing placement of that obstruction. Building works which are commenced with the benefit of planning permission will still amount to an unlawful obstruction if the way has not been properly stopped up, as the grant of planning permission does not provide 'lawful authority' to block a highway.

27.130 It is foreseeable that those constructing a highway may seek to show that they have an excuse, either because they were unaware of the existence of the highway or because a mistake was made as to the implications of the planning permission. In either case, it is unlikely a person charged with an offence under section 137 of the HA 1980 could exculpate himself on that basis. The word 'excuse' has been construed to mean 'lawful excuse', thus a mistaken view of the law (e.g. the effect of planning permission) cannot as a matter of law amount to a defence.[236] If, however, the defendant had an honest and reasonable belief in a state of facts, which, if true, would have provided a defence, then this will be an 'excuse' for the purposes of section 137.[237] Thus a mistake as to the effect of planning permission is not a defence, but a reasonable and honest belief that a way had been stopped up may amount to a defence.

---

[234] *Arrowsmith v Jenkins* [1963] 2 QB 561 at 567.

[235] See *London Borough of Redbridge v Jaques* [1970] 1 WLR 1604.

[236] See e.g. *Brook v Ashton* [1974] Crim LR 105, a case in which a defendant charged with an offence under Highways Act 1959, s 121 explained that the dealings between the authority and himself had been so protracted he did not realise he was not permitted to carry out the alteration to his home (which happened to affect an adjoining path). The court found that a mistaken view of the law could not constitute an excuse for the purposes of the statute. See also *Cambridgeshire and Isle of Ely CC v Rust* [1972] 2 QB 426 per Widgery CJ: 'I do not believe at any time one can have lawful excuse for conduct because one is mistaken as to the law; everyone is supposed to know the law, but a mistake of fact ... seems to me to amount to a lawful excuse'.

[237] And see *Dickins v Gill* [1896] 2 QB 310 at 316.

PENALTY

27.131   The appropriate sentence is a fine not exceeding level 3 on the standard scale.[238] Where the obstruction is continuing and it is in the defendant's power to remove the cause of the obstruction, the court may, instead of a fine, or in addition, order the defendant to take such steps so as to remove the cause of the obstruction.[239] If the defendant thereafter fails without reasonable excuse to comply with that order, he is guilty of a more serious offence and liable to a fine.[240]

Section 138 – the erection of buildings

27.132   The construction without lawful authority or excuse of a building or fence, or the planting of a hedge in a highway which consists of or comprises a carriageway is expressly an offence in the HA 1980 by virtue of section 138.[241] As a matter of construction, the offence appears to be one of strict liability. There are powers in relation to the removal of such obstructions pursuant to section 143.

Section 139 – control of builders' skips

27.133   Building materials and skips may also cause obstruction in the development process. The HA 1980 provides expressly that the relevant highway authority may authorise skips to be located on a highway, thus making lawful that which would otherwise be an unlawful obstruction.[242] If no permission is obtained, then naturally an offence may be committed,[243] although there are statutory defences available.[244] Provision in the permission may be made for the

---

[238]   Up to £1,000, see Criminal Justice Act 1982, s 37.

[239]   See HA 1980, s 137ZA.

[240]   The fine would be 1/20th of either of the sum of £5,000, or level 4 on the standard scale, for each day on which the offence is continued, i.e. on each day until the obstruction is removed.

[241]   HA 1980, s 138. A carriageway, as defined by s 329, to mean a way constituting or comprised in a highway, being a way (other than a cycle track over which the public have a right of way) for the passage of vehicles.

[242]   The word 'skip' is expressly defined within the relevant section: HA 1980, s 139(11).

[243]   Punishable by a fine not exceeding level 3 on the standard scale. See HA 1980, s 139(3) and Criminal Justice Act 1982, s 37. It is also considered that such an interference would naturally be chargeable under HA 1980, s 137; in addition, see s 139(5)–(7).

[244]   See HA 1980, s 139(6), which provides that it is a defence to prove that the commission was due to the act or default of another person and that he took all reasonable precautions and exercised all due diligence to avoid the commission of such an offence. See in particular *York District Council v Poller* (1975) 73 LGR 522.

siting of the skip, as well as other conditions.[245] Even where such permission is granted, a uniformed police constable or the highway authority may order the skip to be removed or repositioned. Non-compliance with such an order is also an offence.[246]

Trespass

27.134   The erection of a building, or the depositing, without lawful authority, of some item on the highway will constitute a *prima facie* trespass actionable in the civil courts, since intrusion onto another's land will *prima facie* be a trespass.[247] Whether something is, or is not, a trespass will now have to be considered in light of the decision in *Director of Public Prosecutions v Jones*[248] that use of the highway extends beyond simply passing and re-passing. Where the highway obstructed is maintainable at public expense, it seems that the trespass will be actionable at the suit of the highway authority itself, since the 'top two spits' vest in them.[249] It is unlikely that the owner of the subsoil could bring an action for obstruction himself in relation to things simply deposited on the way. It is suggested the position would be different, however, where such an obstruction, as in the case of the erection of a building requiring foundations to be dug out, were to affect the subsoil.[250]

---

[245]   As to conditions, see HA 1980, s 139(2). Lighting of the skip during the hours of darkness where it is placed on a road will be a necessary condition. See *Saper v Hungate Builders* [1972] RTR 380.

[246]   HA 1980, s 140(2) and (3).

[247]   See e.g. *Ellis v Loftus Iron Co* (1874) LR 10 CP 10 at 12 per Lord Coleridge CJ – such an intrusion would ordinarily give rise to injunctive relief. The cause of action will cover not only deposits and obstructions on the land, but those things which encroach into the airspace above. See e.g. *Kelsen v Imperial Tobacco Co* [1957] 2 QB 334; *Bernstein v Pamson Motors (Golders Green)* [1987] 2 All ER 220. In the case of a highway which is publicly maintainable, however, the interest is limited to 'such property only as is necessary for the control protection and maintenance of the street as a highway', *Tunbridge Wells Corporation v Baird* [1896] AC 434 at 442.

[248]   [1999] 2 WLR 625.

[249]   As to the ownership of the 'top two spits', see HA 1980, s 263; *Tithe Redemption Commission v Runcorn Urban District Council* [1954] 2 WLR 518. For a highway trespass case brought by a council, see e.g. *Hackney LBC v Arrowsmith* [2002] CLY 63, a case concerning the placement of political posters on street furniture, without authority. The borough council sought to recover costs for removing them. The court found a *prima facie* trespass and awarded the costs of removing the posters.

[250]   See *Cox v Glue* 136 ER 987, a case concerning a close in which the owner of the land (A) had agreed to give exclusive possession to pasture cattle to another person (B) for a certain period. The court accepted that 'the possession of the surface may be in one person, and the possession of and the right to the subsoil, in another'. On the facts, A could have maintained an action against a trespasser digging holes in the land so as to affect the subsoil, but not against someone who merely rides over the close, i.e. only affecting the surface, in which that person was not in possession. The reasoning seems to be that a person can claim a remedy where he is in possession

Causing danger to highway users

27.135 The third category of offences created by the HA 1980 are those in relation to the creation of dangers affecting highway users. The relevant offences are contained in sections 161 to 175. The offences created are numerous and cover a very wide range of possible activities including:

(a) the depositing of anything (without lawful authority or excuse) in consequence of which a user of the highway is injured or endangered;[251]
(b) allowing (without lawful authority or excuse) any filth, dirt, lime or other offensive matter to flow onto a highway from adjoining premises;[252]
(c) the carrying out of building operations in or near a street where an accident takes place causing serious bodily injury, or which could give rise to such an accident;
(d) the mixing of mortar on a highway (otherwise than on a receptacle or plate) or any other substance likely to stick to the surface of the highway or which would solidify in a drain.

27.136 As in the case of the offences elsewhere in the HA 1980, many of the offences so created here appear to be of strict liability. Some of the offences listed above are more novel than others. The creation of an offence relating to the depositing of 'anything' which in consequence injures 'or endangers' a person, is likely to cover a particularly wide array of conduct. The accidental leaving of a pile of bricks across a footpath on a proposed development site would seem to be caught by the express wording of the section.

Public nuisance

27.137 It is beyond the scope of this book to consider the law of public nuisance to any great extent, and a separate text should be consulted by those who seek an in-depth analysis. Public nuisance is both a criminal offence at common law and a civil wrong. It is said that public nuisance is incapable of an exact definition, but a public nuisance arises in the case of either an act or an omission which interferes with 'or obstructs the public in the exercise or enjoyment of rights common to all Her Majesty's subjects'.[253] Other definitions in the context of

---

of the land, but not, for example, where he has granted to another an interest, such as a term of years, and the reversion is not affected. See also *Cooper v Crabtree* (1828) 20 Ch D 589 (the reversioner was not entitled to pursue a trespass where the reversion was unaffected by the annoyance caused to his tenants).

[251] HA 1980, s 161(1).

[252] HA 1980, s 161(4).

[253] See *R v Rimmington; R v Goldstein* [2005] UKHL 63, [2006] 1 AC 459; Richardson, J, *Archbold: Criminal Pleading Evidence and Practice 2016* (Sweet & Maxwell, 64th edn, 2015).

highways law have included, 'any wrongful act or omission upon or near a highway, whereby the public are prevented from freely, safely and conveniently passing along the highway'.[254]

27.138   Acts which are caught by such a wide definition will inevitably include many of the offences now expressly created by the HA 1980. Obstructions and activities generally that are such as to affect the safety of highway users may well come within the definition, as would the following:

(a)   obstruction of the highway where parked vehicles significantly restrict the free passage of traffic;[255]
(b)   causing the closure of a highway, where a person threatened to jump off a bridge;[256]
(c)   allowing the dispersal of mud, dust and dangerous contaminants into the air, so as to affect the users of a highway;[257]
(d)   allowing waste to accumulate on a piece of land so as to be injurious to public health.[258]

27.139   The nature of use of the highway is such that there is a balancing act of the rights of users of the way and those of adjoining landowners. Thus:[259]

the law relating to the user of the highway is in truth the law of give and take. Those who use them must in doing so have reasonable regard to the convenience and comfort of others and must not themselves expect a degree of convenience and comfort only obtainable by disregarding that of other people. They must expect to be obstructed occasionally. It is the price they pay for the privilege of obstructing others.

27.140   The law in this area is very much about the balancing of competing interests, and the question in most cases will be whether one user's action is unreasonably interfering with the rights of the public to use the way. The mere fact there is an obstruction will not give rise to the automatic conclusion that a public nuisance has been committed, and the knowledge of the person causing the nuisance that such a nuisance exists, whether that person has a way of abating the

---

[254]   *Jacobs v London County Council* [1950] AC 361 at 375.

[255]   See e.g. *Attorney-General v Gastonia Coaches* [1977] RTR 219. Sixteen coaches, owned by the defendant, were parked in residential roads near to the defendant's office. The parking of these vehicles was found to interfere with the free passage of other traffic. The court found that a public nuisance has been committed, and was prepared to make a monetary award in respect of the emission of exhaust gases, excessive noise and obstruction of private driveways.

[256]   *R v Dallinger* [2012] EWCA Crim 1284.

[257]   *Corby Group Litigation v Corby DC* [2009] EWHC 1944 (TCC).

[258]   *Attorney-General v Tod Heatley* [1897] 1 Ch 560.

[259]   *Harper v Haden & Sons* [1933] Ch 298 at 320.

nuisance and what actions he has taken will all be relevant to the question of liability in finding 'fault'.[260]

27.141　As far as civil liability is concerned, an action can only be brought when an individual suffers special damage, over and above the inconvenience incurred more generally by members of the public. In the context of highways law, owners of properties fronting the highway who run businesses which suffer pecuniary loss as a result of the obstruction will be able to claim damages.[261] Unlike private nuisance, however, there is no need for a claimant to have an interest in the land affected by the nuisance.[262]

27.142　Persons suffering injury as a result of a public nuisance can bring a claim for compensation alleging public nuisance as the cause of action, but causation as between the obstruction or danger created and the damage suffered would need to be proved.[263]

Criminal law

27.143　There is a considerable overlap between the offences created by the HA 1980 and the common law offence of public nuisance. Where an alternative charge is available to that of public nuisance, it is envisaged that the statutory offence will be charged as a matter of good practice.[264] A prosecutor must prove both that the act complained of is capable of constituting a public nuisance and that the defendant knew or ought to have known that a public nuisance had arisen. Seemingly, the offence can be committed by either an omission or by an act of commission,[265] but to be a 'public' nuisance it must 'materially affect the reasonable comfort and convenience *of life of a class of* Her Majesty's subjects' (emphasis added).[266] 'The sphere of the nuisance may be described generally as

---

[260]　*Wandsworth London Borough Council v Railtrack Plc* [2001] EWCA Civ 1236, [2002] WLR 512.

[261]　See *Fritz v Hobson* (1880) 14 Ch D 542, but see *Winterbottom v Lord Derby* (1867) LR 2 Ex 316. See also M Jones, A Dugdale and M Simpson, *Clerk & Lindsell on Torts* (Sweet & Maxwell, 21st edn, 2015) at 20-01.

[262]　See *Colour Quest Ltd v Total Downstream UK Plc* [2009] EWHC 540 (Comm).

[263]　*Dymond v Pearce* [1972] 1 QB 496.

[264]　*R v Rimmington; R v Goldstein* [2005] UKHL 63, [2006] 1 AC 459.

[265]　For omissions, see e.g. *Attorney-General v Tod Heatley* [1897] 1 Ch 560, in which an unused parcel of land, owned by the defendant, became injurious to the inhabitants of the local parish where dead dogs, cats, vegetable refuse, fish, offal, rubbish and all kinds of filth had been thrown onto the land by others. The court found a public nuisance was made out.

[266]　See *R v Rimmington; R v Goldstein* [2005] UKHL 63, [2006] 1 AC 459:

　　'in my opinion ... any nuisance is "public" which materially affects the reasonable comfort and convenience of life of a class of Her Majesty's subjects. The sphere of the nuisance may be described generally as "the neighbourhood"; but the question whether the local community within that sphere comprises a sufficient number of persons to constitute a class of the public

the "neighbourhood"; but the question of whether the local community within that sphere comprises a sufficient number of persons to constitute a class of the public is a question of fact in every case'.[267]

27.144   As regards to intention, it does not have to be proved by the prosecution that a person intended to create a nuisance or that he simply ignored the accumulation of what would amount to a nuisance, it is enough to show that the defendant knew or ought to have known of the nuisance.[268] As a criminal offence, the matter is triable either way, and a person convicted of an offence will be liable to a financial penalty and/or imprisonment. In cases where the nuisance is alleged to be continuing, the court (notwithstanding the criminal context) is able to order abatement of the nuisance.

STOPPING UP AND DIVERSION ORDERS

Introduction

27.145   As has been indicated, the grant of planning permission does not of it itself obviate the need to make an application to formally extinguish an existing public right of way. Nor does mere disuse of a highway end the public's right to use the way as a means of passage, hence the aphorism 'once a highway always a highway'.[269] There must, therefore, be recourse to some formal procedure to either stop up or divert the right of way. Before such an order is made, the highway must inevitably be left unobstructed.

27.146   The process of obtaining an order to stop up or divert a right of way can add considerably to the delay of concluding development works. Formerly, the target time frame in which to deal with stopping up applications from receipt to decision was around 13 weeks,[270] although in cases where the making of an order is contested and the matter listed for inquiry, that period is likely to be considerably longer.

---

is a question of fact in every case. It is not necessary, in my judgment, to prove that every member of the class has been injuriously affected; it is sufficient to show that a representative cross-section of the class has been so affected for an injunction to issue.'

[267]   *Attorney-General v PYA Quarries Ltd* [1957] 2 QB 169 at 184.

[268]   *R v Shorrock* [1994] QB 279.

[269]   There is no concept of abandonment of a highway in English law, thus although the highway might appear to be disused, such rights will continue to endure until they have been stopped up. See *Dawes v Hawkins* 8 CBNS 848 at 858 per Byles J, which is the earliest case in which the maxim is used.

[270]   See the Consultation Paper, *Stopping up and Diversion Orders: Reform of the Application Process for Local Highways* (Department for Transport, July 2012) at para 4.2.

27.147   The Growth and Infrastructure Act 2013[271] has made new provision to allow applications for stopping up under sections 247 and 257 of the TCPA 1990 to be received in advance of planning permission.[272] In all cases, those dealing with a planned development are well advised to identify the rights of way likely to be affected at an early stage and to liaise with the planning and highway authorities, local groups and other affected individuals so as to identify any possible conflict arising from the proposed development.[273] In cases where there is likely to be significant and lengthy negotiation between the developer and the planning authority, and where there is a reasonable expectation that planning permission will eventually be granted, any proposals for stopping up or diverting a public highway could be considered alongside the discussions on the proposed development.[274] Notices and a draft of the order should be included, as far as that is possible.[275]

27.148   There are number of statutory provisions which enable the stopping up and diversion of existing rights of way. The relevant sections are disorganised and spread across a number of different statutes. It is beyond the scope of this book to consider fully all of the relevant sections, but the main provisions are considered. Alternative means by which such rights may be extinguished (e.g. by destruction) are considered at the end of this chapter.

27.149   The reader should note that the provisions of section 53 of the Countryside and Rights of Way Act 2000 (not currently in force) will, by operation of statute, extinguish some unrecorded rights of way from the cut-off date on 1/1/2026. Predominantly, this relates to rights of way not recorded on the definitive map which were created before 1/1/1949.

Effect of stopping up and diversion

27.150   The effect of an order stopping up a highway is to extinguish the public's right to pass and re-pass over the defined route. In the case of publicly maintainable highways, the top two spits[276] vest in the highway authority.[277] Thus when an order stopping up the highway takes effect, the highway authority's interest will determine and re-vest in the original landowner.[278] In cases where the

---

[271] Sections 11 and 12.

[272] TCPA 1990, s 253.

[273] *Rights of Way Circular (1/09).*

[274] *Rights of Way Circular (1/09)* at para 7.9 *et seq.*

[275] *Rights of Way Circular (1/09)* at para 7.10.

[276] I.e. the top two spade depths, see *Tithe Redemption Commission v Runcorn Urban District Council* [1954] Ch 383 at 407 per Lord Denning.

[277] HA 1980, s 263(1).

[278] *Rolls v Vestry of St George the Martyr* (1880) 14 Ch D 785.

land is not maintained at public expense, the land over which the highway formerly ran will simply be freed from the burden of the right of way. Notably, the stopping up of public rights of way will not affect private rights also existing over the land formerly subject to the highway.[279] In some cases, the way may be stopped up entirely, or with a reservation of a lesser right, for example a bridleway might be stopped up, but a footpath reserved.[280]

27.151 Diversions normally involve the stopping up of an existing right of way and the creation of a new way over another piece of land. In some cases, those seeking to divert may attempt to utilise an existing right of way. There is conflicting case law as to whether a diversion should necessitate the creation of a new way or whether an existing way can, in fact, be utilised. The answer seems to depend partly upon the provision under which the right is diverted.[281]

Stopping up and diversions – development provisions

TCPA 1990, section 247

27.152 In the context of development, the provisions of the TCPA 1990 provide a key provision for the stopping up or diversion of an existing right of way. Section 247 provides that the Secretary of State may authorise by order the stopping up or diversion of any highway (outside Greater London) if he is satisfied that it is necessary to do so in order to enable development to be carried out in accordance with a planning permission under Part III or by a government department.[282]

27.153 In the case of a London borough, the council of that borough may similarly make an order on the same grounds where the right of way exists either in that borough or in another borough and consent for the making of the order is provided by the council for that borough.[283] In either case, the entity making the order is empowered to make such provision as it considers expedient for the provision or improvement of the highway (notably, including diversion and stopping up of any rights of way), and it may direct that any highway provided or improved shall be maintainable at the public expense.[284] Notably, an order can be

---

[279]   See e.g. *Walsh v Oates* [1953] 2 WLR 835 at 839.

[280]   See in particular HA 1980, s 116(4), which expressly provides that a lesser right may be preserved.

[281]   See S Sauvain, *Encyclopedia of Highway Law and Practice* (Sweet & Maxwell, looseleaf) (*Highway Law and Practice*) at 9-13–9-16; consider in particular *Welch v Nash* (1807) 8 East 394; *De Ponthieu v Pennyfeather* (1814) 5 Taunt 634.

[282]   TCPA 1990, s 247(1).

[283]   TCPA 1990, s 247(2A).

[284]   TCPA 1990, s 247(3)(a).

made in relation to 'any highway'. It is therefore one of the few provisions which allows for an order to be made in respect of highways accessible by vehicles.

Guidance – timing the application

27.154   An application for an order under section 247 of the TCPA 1990 can now be made in advance of planning permission, and the Secretary of State or council may publish in advance notice of the draft of such an order.[285]

27.155   Care should be taken to ensure applications are not left too late. The wording of the TCPA 1990 is that the Secretary of State (or council) can make an order if 'he is satisfied that it is necessary to do so in order to enable development *to be carried out*' (emphasis added). Once work is completed, the availability of an order pursuant to this section is precluded.[286] The courts have made it clear that this is a process 'with a beginning and an end; once it is begun, it continues to be carried out until it is completed or substantially completed'.[287] This section cannot therefore be used by a developer who unknowingly builds upon a right of way and has either completed or substantially completed the development.

27.156   Attempts to circumvent this rule by demolishing part of the works after they had been built, so as to give rise to an argument that, 'the works are not substantially completed' have failed.[288] The reasoning seems to be that, 'when a discrete and substantial part of a planning permission is completed in accordance with that permission, then that part of the permission has been completed and achieved, and is spent in so far as that aspect of the permission is concerned.[289] Thus in *Hall v Secretary of State for the Environment, Transport and the Regions*,[290] it was found that the destruction of one corner of a garage (up to 2 metres) which had previously been constructed and so encroached upon a public footpath, but was then demolished to enable an application for an order, had been substantially completed when it was first constructed.

---

[285]   TCPA 1990, s 253(1).

[286]   The key case in this area is *Ashby v Secretary of State for the Environment and Another* [1980] 1 WLR 673.

[287]   *Ashby v Secretary of State for the Environment and Another* [1980] 1 WLR 673 at 682 per Stephenson LJ.

[288]   *Hall v Secretary of State for the Environment, Transport and the Regions* [1998] JPL 1055.

[289]   *Hall v Secretary of State for the Environment, Transport and the Regions* [1998] JPL 1055 at 1061; but see also *Calder v Secretary of State for the Environment* [1996] EG 78 (CS), note that the decision was made in relation to the similar provision under TCPA 1990, s 257.

[290]   [1998] JPL 1055.

Guidance – when will the application be successful?

27.157   The Secretary of State cannot make an order unless he is satisfied that it is necessary in order to enable the development in question to be carried out. Even where he is so satisfied, a discretion is retained and the Secretary of State may decide not to make an order. There is no guidance in the TCPA 1990 as to how this discretion should be exercised. The Department of the Environment, Food and Rural Affairs (Defra) has repeatedly stipulated that the developer should not consider that an order will automatically follow the grant of planning permission.[291]

27.158   Nonetheless, there have been a number of cases which have provided the following principles on how an application should be approached:

(a)   The determination to grant planning permission and the decision to stop up or divert a highway, are two distinct decision-making processes which inevitably require different considerations. It is not for the Secretary of State for Transport to reconsider the merits of a planning permission.[292]

(b)   However, considerations as to whether to stop up or divert a highway may overlap with the considerations made in deciding to grant planning permission. The Secretary of State can and should consider the loss to the general public as a whole of the extinguishment or diversion of the right of way, as well as to the owners of the properties which adjoin the highway subject to the proposal.[293]

(c)   The Secretary of State should consider the business and financial loss of closure of the highway on adjoining landowners.[294]

(d)   Road safety is a matter of key importance, and the Secretary of State must be able to take it into account when he exercises his discretion. This is the

---

[291]   *Rights of Way Circular (1/09)* at para 10.1; *KC Holdings (Rhyl) Ltd v Secretary of State for Wales and Colwyn BC* [1990] JPL 353. The section confers a discretion only and it is not incumbent on the Secretary of State where planning permission has been granted to make an order stopping up or diverting a highway.

[292]   *Vasiliou v Secretary of State for Transport and Another* (1991) 61 P & CR 507 at 515–516 per Nicholls LJ. See also *Network Rail Infrastructure Ltd v Secretary of State for the Environment, Food and Rural Affairs* [2017] EWHC 2259 (Admin), where the decision of a planning inspector was quashed in that he had erred in his application of the merits and necessity tests in *Vasiliou*.

[293]   *Vasiliou v Secretary of State for Transport and Another* (1991) 61 P & CR 507. See in particular at 515 per Nicholls LJ.

[294]   *Vasiliou v Secretary of State for Transport and Another* (1991) 61 P & CR 507. Concerns were raised that to consider the effect on trade would be to reconsider considerations raised at the planning stage. The court concluded that the effect on the restaurant in *Vasiliou* should have been considered, but what remains unclear is the extent to which it would be entitled to reach, for example, a different conclusion from that of a planning authority, see at 515–516. Note the lack of provision for compensation within the HA 1980 for the stopping up of a highway.

case irrespective of whether it has already been considered at the planning stage.[295]

(e)   Some proposed developments are of greater importance than others, from a planning perspective. The Secretary of State should consider this factor.[296]

(f)   Where works have begun before an application is made and part of the highway has been obstructed, such obstruction should be ordinarily disregarded. The decision should not be taken to refuse to make such an order so as to punish the developer. Penalties are a matter for the criminal law.[297]

27.159   In recent times, negative conditions at the planning stage have been imposed so as to prohibit any development until an order stopping up or diverting the right of way has been maintained.[298]

27.160   The Defra guidance in *Rights of Way Circular (1/09)* has stressed that the Secretary of State will only expect to exercise his power under section 247 of the TCPA 1990 in exceptional circumstances.

27.161   The Secretary of State can make an order under section 247 of the TCPA 1990 where planning permission has been granted or, for example, where an application for planning permission is before him, either on appeal or following call-in and it is considered expedient to invoke the concurrent procedure under section 253. Otherwise, he will expect to exercise his power only in exceptional circumstances, for example in relation to a development of strategic or national importance.[299]

Cost and contributions to compensation

27.162   A theme running through all of the legislation which empowers the making of diversion or stopping up orders, is the incidental powers in relation to costs. In respect of section 247 of the TCPA 1990, powers to order any person or authority to pay or make contributions to the cost of doing any work or to repay or make contributions in respect of any compensation paid by the highway authority in respect of restrictions imposed under section 1 or section 2 of the

---

[295]   *R v Secretary of State for the Environment, Transport and the Regions ex parte Batchelor Enterprises Ltd* [2001] EWCA Civ 1293 at [9] per Keene LJ.

[296]   *Vasiliou v Secretary of State for Transport and Another* (1991) 61 P & CR 507 at 515 per Nicholls LJ.

[297]   *Ashby v Secretary of State for the Environment and Another* [1980] 1 WLR 673 at 682 per Goff LJ.

[298]   See *Grampian v City of Aberdeen DC* [1984] JPL 590, but compare *Jones v Secretary of State for Wales* [1990] JPL 907.

[299]   *Rights of Way Circular (1/09)* at para 10.1.

Restriction of Ribbon Development Act 1935 have similarly been included.[300] An order being made at the suit of a developer may therefore incur incidental expenses from either compensation or costs attributable to the making of such an order.

Procedure

27.163   The procedure for making an application under section 247 of the TCPA 1990 is contained in the provisions of section 252. The Act has been amended to reflect the changes made by the Growth and Infrastructure Act 2013, and now the section 252 process (as set out below) can be commenced and a draft order published, notwithstanding the fact that planning permission has yet to be granted.[301]

27.164   Before making an order, a notice stating the general effect of the proposal, specifying a place where a copy of the draft order and any relevant map may be inspected for a period of 28 days and stating that any person within that period may object to the making of the order, must be advertised in one local newspaper and in the *London Gazette*.[302] A copy of the notice, draft order and map should be served on every local authority in whose area the highway runs, a number of specified undertakers and any relevant National Park authority.[303] The notice must similarly be erected and displayed in a prominent position at the ends of the highway proposed to be stopped up.

27.165   Where objections are received following the notice above being provided, a local inquiry will be held, unless (in the case of objections received by parties other than a local authority, undertakers or a transporter), the public inquiry may be dispensed with by the Secretary of State if such an inquiry is considered 'unnecessary'. A slightly different procedure applies in relation to a London borough[304] and in respect of Wales.

27.166   Immediately after the order has been made, the Secretary of State shall publish the notice (in the same way as set out above) stating that the order has been made and where a copy of the notice may be seen at all reasonable hours.

---

[300]   TCPA 1990, s 247(4).

[301]   TCPA 1990, s 253(1).

[302]   TCPA 1990, s 252(1).

[303]   See TCPA 1990, s 252(2).

[304]   TCPA 1990, s 252(4)(b) and (5A).

TCPA 1990, section 257

27.167   Section 257 of the TCPA 1990 is similar in wording to section 247. It empowers a 'competent authority'[305] with a discretion to make an order to authorise the stopping up or diversion of a footpath, bridleway or restricted byway if it is satisfied that it is necessary to do so in order to enable development to be carried out in accordance with a planning permission or by a government department or in relation to works certified under section 293A.[306] Such an application can be made now in advance of planning permission being granted.[307]

27.168   The section also empowers the authority to create an alternative highway to the one being diverted or stopped up if it is satisfied 'that it should do so',[308] and it may provide for the preservation of any rights of statutory undertakers and, in the normal way, require a contribution to the costs of carrying out the works.[309] Developers may therefore be required to make payment where an order is made under this section.

Guidance

27.169   The grounds for making the order are similar to that specified in section 247 of the TCPA 1990. Once again, no guidance in the Act is provided as to how that discretion should be exercised, but it is submitted that the same considerations as those set out above in relation to orders made by the Secretary of State and London boroughs will be relevant, including those which relate to the timing of the application. Note that the order is made 'in order to enable development', thus development which is completed or substantially completed will be outside of the remit of section 257.[310]

27.170   The Defra guidance in respect of section 257 of the TCPA 1990 suggests that whilst a discretion is retained to grant an order stopping up or diverting a right of way affected by development works, even where planning permission has been granted, where an authority decides to refrain from making an order, it must have a good reason for not making or not confirming an order.[311] As in the case

---

[305]   In the case of development authorised by planning permission, the competent authority will be the LPA which granted such permission. See TCPA 1990, s 257(4) for the full definition.

[306]   This relates to development works that are of national importance and which are necessary to be carried out as a matter of urgency. TCPA 1990, s 293A(1).

[307]   For which, see TCPA 1990, s 257(1A).

[308]   TCPA 1990, s 257(2)(a).

[309]   TCPA 1990, s 257(2).

[310]   See *Hall v Secretary of State for the Environment, Transport and the Regions* [1998] JPL 1055.

[311]   *Rights of Way Circular (1/09)* at para 7.15.

of section 247, an application may be made in advance of planning permission being granted.

27.171 Section 257 of the TCPA 1990 only applies to footpaths, bridleways or restricted byways and thus, unlike section 247, it does not empower an authority to stop up roads over which there is vehicular access. The same orders could be reached via the section 247 process, but Defra has stressed that the Secretary of State will 'expect to exercise his power only in exceptional cases' under section 247, such as where the development site is of strategic or national importance.[312] The appropriate order to be sought is therefore an order under section 257 where that is available.

Procedure

27.172 The procedure to obtain an order pursuant to section 257 of the TCPA 1990 is contained in Schedule 14 to the TCPA 1990 and the Town and Country Planning (Public Path Orders) Regulations 1993;[313] both should be consulted fully, but the procedure is summarised in brief. The process is different to that under the section 247 provisions. As with most stopping up or diversion orders, there are two stages to the making of an order: the initial making of the order by the authority; and the confirmation of the order, either by the Secretary of State (in the case of opposed orders) or by the same authority where such an order is unopposed.[314] It is likely that the authority itself retains a discretion as to whether it will refer the order in the case of orders which are strongly opposed by the local community to the Secretary of State; an authority will not be duty bound to submit such an application.[315]

27.173 Notice provisions are provided before such an order can be confirmed. A notice in a prescribed form stating the general effect of the order and that the order is about to be submitted for confirmation, naming a place where a copy of the order can be viewed and specifying times within which representations or objections may be made, should be printed in one local newspaper and the notice should be served upon a class of people.[316] A notice containing such information and a plan with such a notice must also be erected in a prominent position at the ends of the way to be stopped up or diverted, as well as at the council offices in

---

[312]   See *Rights of Way Circular (1/09)*.

[313]   SI 1993/10, and see Rights of Way (Hearings and Inquiries Procedure) (England) Rules 2007 (SI 2007/2008).

[314]   TCPA 1990, Sch 14, para 2.

[315]   See e.g. *R (Hargrave) v Stroud DC* [2002] EWCA Civ 1281, which relates to an application for an order under the s 119 process.

[316]   See TCPA 1990, Sch 14, para 1(2)(a)–(c). See also Sch 14, para 1(6), where the Secretary of State may direct that it shall not be necessary to serve the order on those specified within para 1(2)(b)(i).

the locality of the land and at such other places as the local authority may consider appropriate.[317]

27.174   Where objections to the making of the order are received, a local inquiry will normally be held, but if the objections are raised by a person other than a local authority, the matter may be dealt with in the alternative by giving that person an opportunity for being heard by a person appointed by the Secretary of State. In the case of statutory undertakers objecting to the creation of a new way, the application may be subject to the special parliamentary procedure.[318]

27.175   The Secretary of State cannot make an order until notice as above has been provided, a local inquiry has been held or, alternatively, hearing the objections through a person appointed by the Secretary of State.[319] After confirmation, further notice must be given of the order having been confirmed.[320]

TCPA 1990, section 248

27.176   In addition to sections 247 and 257 of the TCPA 1990, there are powers given to the Secretary of State (or where the highway is in a London borough, to the council for that borough) under section 248 to stop up or divert a highway for what are effectively reasons of road safety. The power exists, first, either where planning permission has been granted already for the construction or improvement of a highway or where such permission has yet to be granted, but the Secretary of State proposes to construct or to improve such a highway. The second condition to the making of an order is that another highway crosses or enters the route of the highway to be constructed, or will otherwise be affected by the proposed construction.[321]

27.177   Once the above grounds exist, the Secretary of State or council may make the order if they consider it 'expedient' to do so, in the interests of the safety of the users of the new or improved way or to facilitate the movement of traffic on that way.[322] In making an order, the Secretary of State or the London borough may make such provision as appears to be necessary or expedient for the improvement of any other highway.[323]

---

[317]   TCPA 1990, Sch 14, para 1.

[318]   See TCPA 1990, Sch 14, para 3(5). Note also the provisions of Sch 14, para 5 (not discussed fully here), which further protect statutory undertakers.

[319]   TCPA 1990, Sch 14, para 3(6).

[320]   TCPA 1990, Sch 14, paras 7 and 8.

[321]   TCPA 1990, s 248(1).

[322]   TCPA 1990, s 248(2).

[323]   TCPA 1990, s 247.

TCPA 1990, sections 251 and 258

27.178 Where land has been acquired or appropriated for planning purposes and is being held by the local authority for those purposes, the Secretary of State may by order extinguish any rights of way over the land if he is satisfied either that an alternative right of way has been or will be provided or that the provision of an alternative way is not required.[324]

27.179 The procedure to be followed before such an application is made is provided for in section 252 of the TCPA 1990 in relation to the various notices that must be served.

27.180 An identical power is given to local authorities under section 258, subject to the caveat that in cases of opposed orders, the order will not take effect until confirmed by the Secretary of State, or confirmed by the same authority in the case of unopposed orders.[325] An order shall not be confirmed unless the body confirming it is also satisfied of the grounds for making the order.[326]

27.181 The procedure for an order under section 258 of the TCPA 1990 is set out in Schedule 14.

Other development provisions

27.182 In addition to the above provisions, further powers are granted under the TCPA 1990 to stop up or divert highways. It is not necessary to consider these fully. They include the power to temporarily stop up or divert a footpath, bridleway or restricted byway for mineral workings,[327] and powers for a local authority to apply to the Secretary of State to extinguish rights of way by vehicle (with the reservation of lesser rights) to improve the amenity of the area.[328]

PROVISIONS UNDER THE HA 1980

Section 116 – judicial orders

27.183 Unlike the other provisions which relate to administratively made orders, section 116 of the HA 1980 empowers a magistrates' court (at the suit of a highway authority) to make an order to stop up, or divert any highway (other than

---

[324] TCPA 1990, s 251(1).

[325] TCPA 1990, s 259.

[326] I.e. that it is satisfied that an alternative right of way has been or will be provided, or that the provision of an alternative right of way is not required. See TCPA 1990, s 258(1).

[327] TCPA 1990, s 261.

[328] See TCPA 1990, s 249.

a trunk road or a special road) if it appears to two or more of the Justices that the highway is unnecessary or can be diverted so as to make it nearer or more commodious to the public.[329] Such an order may provide for the stopping up of all traffic, or otherwise subject to the reservation of a footpath, bridleway or restricted byway.[330] It can also be used by applicants to reduce the width of an existing highway.[331]

27.184 Any person who desires a highway to be stopped up or diverted, but is not authorised by section 116 of the HA 1980, may request the highway authority to make such an application. Where it refuses to do so, it is bound by the principles of administrative justice and must consider all of the relevant factors in making its decision.[332] If the authority makes an application, it may make provision for the recovery of costs incurred in connection with the matter.[333]

Stopping up in cases where the highway is 'unnecessary'

27.185 Whether the right of way is unnecessary for the purposes of section 116 of the HA 1980 is a question of fact for the court. A gloss should not be added to the statutory words and it is a matter for the court to weigh up all the relevant factors,[334] but the following guidance has been provided:

(a) The court, when it considers the question, must have in mind 'for whom is the highway unnecessary?'.[335] If it is for the public, the court will then consider the purpose for which the public use the right of way. If a way is used primarily for recreational purposes, that is a consideration which they can take into account.[336]

(b) The question should always be considered in light of the circumstances prevailing at the time of the application. The intention to construct a new

---

[329] HA 1980, s 116(1).

[330] TCPA 1990, s 116(4).

[331] Note the definition of 'highway' within HA 1980, s 328 means 'the whole or part of a highway'.

[332] An authority declining to make an application will be subject to judicial review on the basis that the decision is, for example, *Wednesbury* unreasonable or that it has failed to consider all of the relevant factors. See *Spice v Leeds City Council* [2006] EWHC 661 (Admin), but note that the authority is not under a duty to make the order just because a party has shown that it has a 'good arguable case'.

[333] HA 1980, s 117.

[334] *Compton v Somerset County Council*, 23/3/1982, unreported per McNeill J; see *Ramblers Association v Kent County Council* (1990) 60 P & CR 464 at 471 per Woolf LJ.

[335] *Ramblers Association v Kent County Council* (1990) 60 P & CR 464 at 471 per Woolf LJ.

[336] *Ramblers Association v Kent County Council* (1990) 60 P & CR 464 at 471 per Woolf LJ.

highway at some point in the future does not enable an argument that a highway should be stopped up now.[337]

(c) Where there is evidence of use of the way, *prima facie*, it 'will be difficult for a Justice properly to come to the conclusion that a way is unnecessary unless the public are or are going to be provided with a reasonably suitable alternative'.[338]

(d) In deciding whether such an alternative way is reasonable, the court should have regard as to whether it is suitable for the purpose for which the public were using the existing highway.[339] It should also disregard activities which are unlawful or which do not relate to the public's right to pass and re-pass.[340]

(e) In considering the application, there is nothing to stop a magistrate from taking into account the surrounding social circumstances which may affect the motive (on either side) for the making or opposing of an application.[341]

Diversions under section 116

27.186   The relevant test for a diversion is whether it appears to the Justices a highway can be diverted so as to make it nearer or more commodious to the public. This will be a question of fact for the Bench to determine, but the wording 'commodious' is said to bear its normal meaning, which will include 'a flavour of convenience, roominess and spaciousness … older definitions also include a flavour of utility'.[342] Note the wording is that the way is either nearer *or* more commodious, thus an applicant need not prove both to make a successful application.

Procedure

27.187   Largely, the procedure relating to section 116 of the HA 1980 is contained in Schedule 12. If an authority proposes to make an application under section 116, it must give notice of the proposal (where applicable) to the council for that district and/or the council of the parish, or, in the case of Wales, the Welsh council for the area and the council of the community in which the highway is situated.[343] If within two months from the date of service any of the notified councils refuse to consent to the making of the application, then the application

---

[337] See *R (Hertfordshire County Council) v Department of Environment, Food and Rural Affairs* [2006] EWCA Civ 1718 at [55]; *R v Midgley* (1864) 5 B & S 621.

[338] *Ramblers Association v Kent County Council* (1990) 60 P & CR 464 at 471 per Woolf LJ.

[339] *Ramblers Association v Kent County Council* (1990) 60 P & CR 464 at 471 per Woolf LJ.

[340] *Westley v Hertfordshire County Council* (1996) 160 JP 813, 'unnecessary' within HA 1980, s 116 means unnecessary for use as a highway, i.e. to pass and re-pass.

[341] *Maille v Manchester City Council* (1997) 74 P & CR 443 at 451.

[342] See *Gravesham Borough Council v Wilson and Another* [1983] JPL 607.

[343] HA 1980, s 116(3).

shall not be made. In other words, the local council has a right of veto of the continuation of an application under section 116. Similarly, the written consent of every person having a legal interest in the land over which the highway is to be diverted must be provided at court before an order can be made.[344]

27.188   Further provisions as to notice must be complied with, including service on adjoining landowners and occupiers, any statutory undertakers and, where the road is a classified road, on the applicable council.[345] Such notice should be given at least 28 days before the application to apply to the court is made, specifying the time, date and location of the place where the application will be made.

27.189   Notices must also be erected on the site involved in a prominent position at the end of the highway[346] and in the *London Gazette* and another local newspaper.[347] Compliance with the notice requirements is taken seriously and failure to provide notice in pursuance of the relevant provisions of the HA 1980 will deprive an applicant from being able to pursue an application in the magistrates' court.[348] Previous cases have suggested that courts have been strict in policing adherence to the service of notice, but it is suggested in *Ramblers Association v Kent County Council*[349] that as long as there is substantial compliance with the Schedule 12 requirements, then that is satisfactory for the purposes of section 116. Nonetheless, those dealing with applications under Schedule 12 should look carefully at the procedural requirements involved to ensure the application is not refused on that basis

When to use this section – tactics?

27.190   On the face of it, there may be advantages to pursuing an application before a magistrates' court, not least that the application might be dealt with more expeditiously, but those considering proceeding should consider both the cost implications and the comparative formality of the process. Unlike orders obtained through sections 118 and 119 of the HA 1980 (outlined below), an application made to a magistrates' court carries with it the potential adverse cost orders that

---

[344] HA 1980, s 116(8).

[345] See HA 1980, Sch 12, para 1.

[346] HA 1980, Sch 12, para 2.

[347] HA 1980, Sch 12, para 3.

[348] Note that HA 1980, s 116(6) provides expressly: 'a Court shall not make an order under this section unless it is satisfied that the applicant authority has given the notices required by Part 1 of Schedule 12 to this Act'. See also the judgment of Woolf LJ in *Ramblers Association v Kent County Council* (1990) 60 P & CR 464, 'the requirement of subsection (6) are in my view, mandatory ... a Magistrates' Court has no power to dispense with the requirement'.

[349] (1990) 60 P & CR 464 at 470.

might usually be made against an unsuccessful party at court.[350] It is for that reason, together with the comparable formality of having to make a case in a court context, that the Ramblers Association have argued for the discontinuance of the magistrates' court in the role of stopping up and diverting highways.[351] The right of veto over which a local parish council can bring to an end the furtherance of an application under section 116 similarly makes the process unsuitable in many developments where the proposed works and consequential effect on the highways are controversial or locally unpopular.

Section 118 – public path extinguishment orders

27.191   Section 118 of the HA 1980 empowers a council[352] to make a 'public path extinguishment order' in respect of a footpath, bridleway or restricted byway (other than a trunk road or special road). The section therefore does not enable a council to extinguish rights over a way over which there is vehicular access, but the section is potentially of use where section 247 or section 257 is no longer available to a developer, but where the developer proposes to construct an alternative highway (see below).

27.192   An order under section 118 of the HA 1980 can be made if it appears to the council that it is expedient that the footpath, bridleway or restricted byway involved should be stopped up on the ground that it is no longer needed for public use.[353] The process of making such an order has two stages: first, the making of an order by the council; and, secondly, the confirming of that order, either by that council (where the order is unopposed) or by the Secretary of State in the case of opposed orders.

The initial stage

27.193   The two stages have different tests and should not be confused. At the initial stage, the council need only consider that it is 'expedient' that the way should be stopped up, on the ground that it is not needed for public use. Temporary circumstances preventing or diminishing the right of way will be

---

[350] Applications under HA 1980, s 116 can be treated as a complaint for the purposes of Magistrates' Court Act 1980, s 64(1), allowing the court jurisdiction to make an order for costs. See *Lincolnshire County Council v Brewis* [1992] COD 430.

[351] Ramblers Association, 'Public rights of way', www.ramblers.org.uk/policy/england/rights-of-way/public-rights-of-way.aspx.

[352] Which would include county, district and unitary councils. It would also, within Greater London, include London borough councils and the common council. It further includes the Broads Authority, for which, see Norfolk and Suffolk Broads Act 1988, Sch 3.

[353] HA 1980, s 118(1).

disregarded.[354] What is a 'temporary circumstance' for the purposes of section 118 of the HA 1980 will depend on a variety of factors, but the overarching question must be whether the obstruction is likely to endure.[355] It will only be in rare cases that an unlawful obstruction of the land will be considered to be something other than temporary.[356] A seemingly permanent obstruction (such as a tree or hedge) may be considered to be a 'temporary' obstruction because legal steps could be taken to remove it.[357]

27.194   Where proceedings for a public path creation order, public path diversion order or rail crossing diversion order are commenced prior to the confirmation of a public path extinguishment order under section 118 of the HA 1980, the council or Secretary of State (at both stages) can consider the extent to which the order would provide an alternative way. It has been suggested that public path creation agreements may also be taken into account.[358]

Confirmation of the order

27.195   Once the above grounds are made out, if the order is opposed, it will be for the Secretary of State to confirm the order. The council retains a discretion whether to submit such an order and is seemingly under no duty to submit the order for confirmation.[359] The order will not be confirmed (whether opposed or unopposed) unless the Secretary of State/council is satisfied that it is expedient to do so having regard to the extent that it appears to them that the way, apart from the order, would be likely to be used by the public. Regard *must* be given to the effect that the order would have on land served by the way, taking into account

---

[354] HA 1980, s 118(5).

[355] *R v Secretary of State for the Environment ex parte Stewart* (1980) 39 P & CR 534 at 539.

[356] *R v Secretary of State for the Environment ex parte Stewart* (1980) 39 P & CR 534 at 539. Unlawful obstructions are liable to be removed in any event, but if the contrary position were adopted it would have the implication that blocking the highway would be the easiest way to ensure success under HA 1980, s 118. Plainly, this cannot be the law. Also consider *Wood v Secretary of State for the Environment* [1977] JPL 307, now doubted.

[357] *R v Secretary of State for the Environment ex parte Stewart* (1980) 39 P & CR 534. The case also considered whether an electricity substation could be considered a 'temporary circumstance'. The court ruled that it could; if indeed the station did obstruct the highway there could be no justification for it remaining. Accordingly it was also a 'temporary' obstruction.

[358] See *Hertfordshire County Council v Secretary of State for the Environment, Food and Rural Affairs* [2006] EWCA Civ 1718: agreements are less certain in nature than public path creation orders, but it has been suggested (albeit *obiter*) that future events, such as an existing and unconditional public path creation agreement, may be taken into account.

[359] See *R (Hargrave) v Stroud DC* [2001] EWHC 1128 (Admin).

the provisions available for compensation.[360] Thus there are two main considerations at the confirmation stage.

27.196   When considering whether to confirm the order, the council or Secretary of State must also have regard to the right of way improvement plan prepared by any local highway authority whose area includes land over which the way exists.[361] It must also disregard, as at the initial stage, temporary circumstances and it may take into account the extent to which concurrent proceedings for a public path creation order, public path diversion order or rail crossing diversion order may provide an alternative route.

27.197   The two stages are different and should not be confused, and it has been suggested that at the confirmation stage, the test is not so much one of need, as it is of expediency, although regard is directed to the extent of the way's likely use 'but for the order'.[362]

Procedure

27.198   The procedure for the making and confirmation of the order is contained in Schedule 6 to the HA 1980 and the Public Path Order Regulations 1993.[363] The same procedure is followed in cases of orders made under section 119 for a public path diversion order.

Section 119 – public path diversion orders

27.199   Under section 119 of the HA 1980 a council[364] is empowered to make an order diverting a footpath, bridleway or restricted byway in its area, where it appears expedient that the way, or part of the way, should be diverted 'in the

---

[360]   HA 1980, s 118(2). The reference to compensation is a reference to s 28 as applied by s 121(2). But note that the mere availability of compensation does not obviate the need to consider the effect on adjoining landowners. See e.g. *Jenkins v Welsh Assembly Government* [2010] EWCA Civ 1640.

[361]   HA 1980, s 118(6A). A 'Rights of Way Improvement Plan' is a requirement brought in by Countryside and Rights of Way Act 2000, s 60. Every local highway authority (other than an inner London authority) should now have prepared and published such a plan, dealing with the current issues affecting the use, maintenance and management of the rights of way within their area, together with a statement of action they propose to take for the management and securing of an improved rights of way network.

[362]   See *R v Secretary of State for the Environment ex parte Cheshire County Council* [1991] JPL 537.

[363]   SI 1993/11.

[364]   Which, as in the case of an order under HA 1980, s 118 would include county, district and unitary councils. It would also, within Greater London, include London borough councils and the common council. And it would include the Broads Authority, for which, see Norfolk and Suffolk Broads Act 1988, Sch 3.

interests of the owner, lessee or occupier of land crossed by the ... way, or of the public'.[365] Notably, the section only confers a discretion, thus where the council is of the view that it would be expedient in the interests of the public/occupier, it can still decline to make an order.[366]

27.200   The process for making an order is much the same as it is for other diversion orders. The council may make and confirm the order where it is unopposed, but opposed orders will need to be submitted to the Secretary of State. Once again, the council retains a discretion as to whether to submit such an application and is not obliged to do so, even where it was originally considered expedient to make the order.[367] When deciding not to proceed, a formal resolution should be made.

27.201   The order itself may be made following representations from an owner, lessee or occupier of land crossed by an existing path. Where that is the case, a council is authorised to enter into an agreement to recoup expenses from the party concerned, which may reflect: (a) the costs of bringing the new way into a fit condition for public use; (b) expenses which may be charged by the highway authority (where the council making the order is not the highway authority); and (c) compensation.[368]

Conditions for making the order

27.202   The relevant test is simply whether it is expedient that the line of the path should be diverted with regard to the interests of: (a) owners, occupiers or lessees of land crossed by the highway; or (b) the public. The word 'expedient' is said to

---

[365]   HA 1980, s 119(1).

[366]   An example might be where there is public opposition to the making of such an order. The discretionary nature has been recognised by the court in *R (Hargrave) v Stroud District Council* [2002] EWCA Civ 1281, see in particular [15] per Schieman LJ:

'on the face of it ... the authority has a discretion as to whether or not to make an order. I do not consider that the mere fact that it is expedient in the interests of the owner that the line of the path should be diverted means that Parliament has imposed on the authority a duty to make such an order once it is satisfied that this condition precedent has been fulfilled.'

But obviously such a discretion must not be exercised irrationally or take into account factors irrelevant to such a determination.

[367]   See *R (Hargrave) v Stroud DC* [2002] EWCA Civ 1281, in particular [33] per Buxton LJ, and note in particular 'the process of inquiry is a continuing one, and indeed the local authority not only may, but ought to retain an open mind on whether or not it can support the propositions originally put before it in the light of local reaction'. See also *Ramblers Association v Secretary of State for the Environment Food and Rural Affairs* [2012] EWHC 3333 (Admin).

[368]   HA 1980, s 119(5). In the case of compensation, the act envisages a situation where the diverted track may extend over land not owned by either the council or the owner of the land over which the existing track subsists. See s 28 in respect of compensation, and see the Local Authorities (Recovery of Costs for Public Path Orders) Regulations 1993 (SI 1993/407).

expand the range of circumstances that the local authority may consider when exercising its discretion. Its determination is thus not solely based on restricted grounds, but can include other considerations, including the statutory considerations that a Secretary of State is obliged to consider when deciding whether to confirm the order.[369]

Conditions for confirmation

27.203   When it comes to confirmation of the order, there are three stages to the process. These should not be conflated.[370] The Secretary of State or council may not confirm the order unless he/it is satisfied, first, that the original conditions as set out above are made out (i.e. that it is expedient to divert the way with regard to the interests of owners, occupiers and lessees or the public). The second stage is that the confirming body must also be satisfied that the path or way will not be substantially less convenient to the public than the existing way. Lastly, he/it must be satisfied that it is expedient to divert the way with regard to the effect the diversion would have on: (a) public enjoyment of the way; (b) other land served by the existing way; and (c) the effect any new right of way would have upon the land over which the new right is created, taking into account the provisions as to compensation.[371]

27.204   The determination as to whether the diversion will be 'substantially less convenient' will include considerations as to the length of the way, the difficulty of walking it and the purpose for which the way is used.[372]

27.205   Once again, the council or Secretary of State must have regard to any material plan of a rights of way improvement plan prepared by the local highway authority whose area includes land over which the order would create or extinguish a public right of way.[373]

27.206   Unlike in section 118 of the HA 1980, there is no express reference to discounting temporary obstructions affecting the existing right of way, although it is suggested that such obstructions should be ignored in a determination as to whether the replacement route is substantially less convenient to the public.[374]

---

[369]   The factors that should be considered when considering whether to confirm the order are set out in HA 1980, s 119(6).

[370]   See *Young v Secretary of State for Food and Rural Affairs* [2002] EWHC 844 (Admin).

[371]   HA 1980, s 119(6).

[372]   *Young v Secretary of State for Food and Rural Affairs* [2002] EWHC 844 (Admin) per Turner J.

[373]   HA 1980, s 119(6A).

[374]   See *Rights of Way Advice Note 9*.

What the order may contain

27.207   Where the council makes an order, it may extinguish existing rights, either in whole or in part as appears 'requisite', and may additionally create from a date it specifies a new footpath, bridleway or restricted byway to such an extent as is requisite to effect the diversion.[375] If works are required on the new way, the council may specify a date from which the way is to have effect and may decide to extinguish the existing way once the works have been completed, where it proposes to stop up an existing way.[376] Where a diversion order is made, the order may provide for limitation or conditions on the way, whether or not an existing way was subject to such limitations.[377]

27.208   Where a highway is diverted, the termination point of the way must be on another highway and must be onto another point on either the same highway or a connected highway which is as substantially convenient to the public.[378] The crossing of one highway over another will not necessarily be the point of termination.[379] It has been suggested that section 119 of the HA 1980 does not allow a wholesale diversion along an existing right of way.[380]

Procedure

27.209   The procedure is reflected in Schedule 6 to the HA 1980 and the Public Path Orders Regulations 1993.[381]

Other provisions under the HA 1980

27.210   In addition to the orders that can be made under the sections that are dealt with above, there are a number of provisions within which powers are conferred to order the stopping up or diversion of existing rights of way. Many of these provisions have been inserted by the Countryside and Rights of Way Act 2000. The following sections are included for fullness but it is unlikely in the context of development works that a thorough working knowledge of these provisions will be necessary.

---

[375]   HA 1980, s 119(1)(a)–(b).

[376]   HA 1980, s 119(3).

[377]   See s 119(4).

[378]   HA 1980, s 119(2).

[379]   *R v West Dorset District Council ex parte Connaughton* [2002] EWHC 794 (Admin).

[380]   See *Highway Law and Practice*, at [2]-10286/1 (Local Government Library); see *R v Lake District Special Planning Board ex parte Bernstein* (1982) *The Times*, 3/3/1982; *R (Ramblers Association) v Secretary of State for Defence* [2007] EWHC 1398 (Admin).

[381]   SI 1993/11.

Sections 118A and 119A – stopping up and diversion of rights of way crossing railways

27.211   Schedule 2 to the Transport and Works Act 1992 inserted further provisions for the stopping up and diversion of rights of way, where the highway crosses a railway otherwise than by a tunnel or bridge.[382] The provisions in relation to stopping up and diversion are contained in separate sections of the HA 1980, but the provisions are similar in nature and both provisions apply only in relation to footpaths, bridleways and restricted byways.[383]

27.212   Sections 118A and 119A of the HA 1980 (section 118A in respect of stopping up and section 119A in respect of diversion) both empower a council to extinguish or divert the right of way in circumstances where it appears expedient to do so in the interests of the safety of members of the public using, or likely to use, a way which crosses a railway.[384] In considering whether to confirm such an order, the Secretary of State (or the council in the case of unopposed orders) will consider all of the circumstances and in particular, whether it is reasonably practicable to make the crossing safe for use by the public and what arrangements have been made for ensuring that, if the order were confirmed, appropriate barriers and signs are erected and maintained.[385]

27.213   The *Rights of Way Circular (1/09)* states:[386]

> This provision enables all the relevant factors to be taken into consideration, which may include the use currently made of the existing path, the risk to the public of continuing such use, the effect that the loss of the path would have on users of the public rights of way network as a whole, the opportunity for taking alternative measures to deal with the problem, such as a diversion order or a bridge or tunnel and the relative costs of such alternative measures.

27.214   The right of way may be extinguished on the crossing itself and/or for as much of the rest of the way as is considered expedient. The *Rights of Way Circular (1/09)* makes it clear, however, that particular care should be taken to avoid the creation of a cul-de-sac that would encourage trespass on the railway.[387]

27.215   Rail operators are able to request the making of such an order and it is usually for the operator to justify the need for an order to be made. The Rail

---

[382]   HA 1980, ss 118A(1) and 119A(1).
[383]   HA 1980, ss 118A(1) and 119A(1).
[384]   HA 1980, ss 118A(1) and 119A(1).
[385]   HA 1980, ss 118A(4) and 119A(4).
[386]   *Rights of Way Circular (1/09)* at para 5.49.
[387]   *Rights of Way Circular (1/09)* at para 5.48.

Crossing Extinguishment and Diversion Orders Regulations 1993[388] prescribe the particulars and form upon which such a request should be documented.[389]

27.216   The inevitable costs provisions have been added to the relevant sections, thus where an order is made on representations from the operator of the railway crossed by the path, the council may require the expenses incurred in connection with the maintenance of barriers and signs to be defrayed by the rail operator.[390] In the case of a diversion, a requirement may similarly be made in relation to the payment of compensation and the costs of bringing the new path into a condition for public use.

Section 119D – diversion of highways for the protection of Sites of Special Scientific Interest

27.217   Section 119D of the HA 1980 provides that a council may divert a highway if it is adjacent to, or contiguous with, an SSSI, and it is of the opinion that the use of the highway is causing, or that continuing use is likely to cause, significant damage to the flora, fauna or geographical or physiographical features by reason of which the SSSI is of special interest.[391] Such an order will not be confirmed by the Secretary of State, or, in the case of an unopposed order, by the council unless it is satisfied that it is expedient to confirm the order having regard to: (a) how the diversion would affect public enjoyment of the right of way as a whole; (b) how the new order would affect other land served by the existing right of way; and (c) how the new right of way would affect the land over which the diversion is intended.[392]

27.218   Such an order may be made only on application by 'the appropriate conservation body', which would be either Natural England or the Natural Resources Body for Wales (although the provision is not currently in force in Wales).[393] The order can be made in relation to footpaths, bridleways, restricted byways and BOATs where they are shown on the definitive map.[394] It also includes a highway which is shown on a definitive map and statement (DMS) as a footpath, bridleway or restricted byway but over which the public have a right

---

[388]   SI 1993/9.

[389]   See in particular reg 2 which specifies the form to be used. Applications which do not use the appropriate form or are not in a form to substantially the same effect or which fail to supply the required information cannot be accepted as validly made. See also *Rights of Way Circular (1/09)* at para 5.46.

[390]   HA 1980, ss 118A(5) and 119A(8).

[391]   HA 1980, s 119D(1).

[392]   HA 1980, s 119D(9).

[393]   HA 1980, s 119D(12).

[394]   HA 1980, s 119D(2)(a).

of way for vehicular and all other kinds of traffic.[395] The section does not, however, apply to a trunk road or special road.

27.219 Where the test is made out, an order may be made to extinguish as much of the way 'as appears to be requisite for the purposes of preventing damage to the SSSI.[396] Where a new way is created by an SSSI diversion order, the costs may be defrayed by requiring the conservation body to enter into an agreement to make contribution towards any compensation which may become payable and any expenses which may be incurred in bringing the new site of the highway into fit condition for the public.[397]

27.220 Separate provision has been made for the procedure governing an application made under this section, for which the reader should see both section 119E of the HA 1980 and the Highways (SSSI Diversion Orders) (England) Regulations 2007.[398]

Further provisions

27.221 Further provisions which enable the stopping up and diversion of highways are currently on the statute books, but a discussion of all these provisions is beyond the scope of this book and in most cases not strictly relevant to the theme. Nonetheless, the following, non-exhaustive list is provided for completeness. A separate text should be consulted in relation to the following provisions:

(a) sections 8 to 9 of the Land Powers (Defence) Act 1958 – this empowers the Secretary of State to use section 209 of the TCPA 1971 to stop up or divert where the land is to be used for various defence purposes;
(b) section 15 of the Open Cast Coal Act 1958;
(c) section 32 of the Acquisition of Land Act 1981 – this concerns land acquired, or proposed to be acquired by compulsory acquisition or by agreement;
(d) section 48 of the Civil Aviation Act 1982 – this relates to the safe and efficient use of land (for civil aviation purposes) vested in the Secretary of State;
(e) section 294 of the Housing Act 1985 – this relates to housing authorities that acquire land under section 290 of the same Act;

---

[395] HA 1980, s 119D(2)(b).
[396] HA 1980, s 119D(3).
[397] HA 1980, s 119D(8)(b)–(c).
[398] SI 2007/1494.

(f)   section 118B of the HA 1980 – special extinguishment order (for crime prevention);

(g)   section 119B of the HA 1980 – special diversion order (for crime prevention);

(h)   section 249 of the TCPA 1990;

(i)   section 261 of the TCPA 1990.

Temporary diversions

27.222   There are also powers to temporarily divert rights of way. These include:

(a)   section 14 of the Road Traffic Regulation Act 1984 – temporary closures for repair works;

(b)   section 135A of the HA 1980 – this is an important provision added by the Countryside and Rights of Way Act 2000, which provides for the temporary diversion of a way, where works of a prescribed nature are likely to cause a danger to users of a footpath or bridleway;[399]

(c)   section 135(2) of the HA 1980 – authorisation of works disturbing a footpath, bridleway or restricted byway in an agricultural context.

Alternative ways by which highways might be extinguished

Physical destruction

27.223   It is possible that a public right of way may be destroyed by physical destruction of the land over which the public right of way exists. Such an event may occur where, for example, a way exists over a coastal formation and the cliff simply falls into the sea by process of erosion.[400] Where the land itself over which the way pertains has been destroyed, there is no right to deviate so as to create a new path, nor does it seem that there is a duty on the highway authority to prevent erosion.[401] Thus where a river wears away a path which runs alongside the bank, the highway does not automatically move inland.[402] The position is different in the case where there is a temporary obstruction over the land, where, in such a

---

[399]   Note the limitation that the diversion may not take place if the period or periods for which the way is diverted amount in aggregate to more than 14 days. See also the supplemental section: HA 1980, s 135B.

[400]   *R v Thomas Bamber* (1843) 5 QB 279, 114 ER 1254; *R v The Inhabitants of the Parish of Paul* (1840) 174 ER 298.

[401]   See the *obiter* in *R (Gloucester County Council) v Secretary of State for the Environment, Transport and the Regions* (2001) 82 P & CR 15 at [89] per Hallett J.

[402]   *R (Gloucester County Council) v Secretary of State for the Environment, Transport and the Regions* (2001) 82 P & CR 15 at [80] per Hallett J. See also the *dicta* in *R v Oldreeve* (1868) 32 JP 271 per Willes J.

case, the public would have a right to deviate from the way which has been so obstructed.[403]

27.224   Where a way has been destroyed and, as consequence, members of the public deviate but have no right to do so, rights may of course arise over time by way of implied dedication.[404] Where, however, the land is not destroyed, but the way is simply rendered unpassable, the way may be found to endure. For example, where a landslide carries away part of the surface of the highway and earth, stones and other debris are deposited, but the track of the highway is otherwise intact, it may be said that the highway itself has not been destroyed, although in need of repair.[405]

27.225   There may, additionally, be cases in which a public right of way ceases, where the highway itself loses its character of being a highway, for example where, by formal process, both ends of the highway are stopped up, in which case it ceases to be accessible.[406]

Adverse possession

27.226   There can be no claim for adverse possession of highway land.[407] To succeed in such a claim, the person asserting adverse ownership would have to show that he has dealt with the land as an occupying owner might. Such physical

---

[403]   *R v Oldreeve* (1868) 32 JP 271 per Willes J:

'if there is a public way over a man's field, and he puts an obstruction upon it, then the public … are entitled to go round a reasonable distance into his field by the side of the way, and use that as a temporary way until he removes the obstruction. But if the obstruction is caused by the actions of the elements, then no such right accrues to the public.'

Note that the right to deviate in respect of temporary obstruction has been held even for a period of 50 years. See *Dawes v Hawkins* (1860) 141 ER 1399. See also *R (Gloucester County Council) v Secretary of State for the Environment, Transport and the Regions* (2001) 82 P & CR 15 at [57] per Hallett J.

[404]   Or statutory presumption.

[405]   *R v Greenhow Inhabitants* (1876) 1 QBD 703, 41 JP 7.

[406]   *Bailey v Jamieson* (1876) 1 CPD 329 per Denman J: 'I think we are compelled to hold that this is a case where that which formerly was a highway, but which, though it has not been stopped up by statutory process, has, by reason of legal acts at either end, ceased to be a place which the Queen's subjects can have access, loses its character of a highway'. And see *Kotegaonkar v Secretary of State for the Environment Food and Rural Affairs* [2012] EWHC 1976 (Admin).

[407]   The leading authority is *R (Smith) v the Land Registry* [2009] EWHC 328 (Admin). See also *Bromley v Morritt* (1999) 78 P & CR D37. Although *obiter*, clear reference was made by Mummery LJ in relation to a claim for adverse possession of a highway:

'in my judgment, this appeal does fail. On the judge's findings of fact the land enclosed by the fence and wall was part of the public highway. As a matter of law, an adverse possession or squatter's title cannot be acquired to land over which a public right of way exists. The only question is the exercise of discretion to make a mandatory order.'

use of the land would almost certainly amount to an unlawful obstruction of the highway and thus a criminal offence.[408] As a matter of public policy, it is therefore not possible to either obtain the legal title to highway land (the top two spits of which vest in the highway authority) by adverse possession subject to a public right of way, nor is it possible to extinguish the right of way by adverse ownership.

ASCERTAINING AND RECORDING RIGHTS OF WAY

Introduction

27.227   Certain rights of way (footpaths, bridleways, restricted byways and BOATs)[409] are recorded on what is known as the definitive map and statement (DMS) which surveying authorities[410] are now obliged to keep and maintain under continuous review.[411] The purpose of the map and statement is to record the rights of way open to the public and, broadly speaking, where such a way is recorded, the map and statement taken together will be conclusive evidence that, at the relevant date, such a highway existed, unless and until there is a review.

27.228   Those seeking to develop land are well advised to consult the definitive map to ascertain where such rights exist over development land, but should be aware that the map itself may not provide the full picture, as such rights may arise but have yet to be recorded.[412] Those seeking to develop land should always consult with the surveying authority to ascertain whether they have reason to believe that there are additional rights which may have accrued over the development land.

---

[408]   *R (Smith) v the Land Registry* [2009] EWHC 328 (Admin) at [14] per HHJ Pelling QC (sitting as a Judge of the High Court).

[409]   RUPPs were also recorded. Note that not all highways are therefore recorded on the definitive map. In *Suffolk County Council v Mason* [1979] AC 705, Lord Diplock said that:

'the only classes of users of highways who are intended to be benefited by the recording of public rights of way are those who may conveniently be referred to as ramblers and riders; they go on foot and horseback ... the only kinds of highways with which the relevant provisions of the Act are concerned are those which are exclusively or mainly, used either by ramblers alone or both riders and ramblers.'

[410]   A surveying authority is, depending on the area, the county council, metropolitan district council or the London borough council. In the case of Wales it will include the county borough council. See WCA 1981, s 66(1).

[411]   WCA 1981, s 53(2).

[412]   E.g. such rights may have arisen by implied dedication of the land.

What is the DMS?

27.229   Those seeking to consult the DMS may find that there is more than one map and statement kept by the authority for their area (although provision is now made for consolidation)[413] which is largely a result of the historical background in which the maps came about.

27.230   The term was originally introduced by virtue of the National Parks and Access to the Countryside Act 1949, which required the council of every county in England and Wales to 'carry out a survey of all lands in their area over which a right of way … is alleged to subsist' and not later than three years thereafter, prepare a draft map.[414] The section empowered the council to show on a map, footpaths, bridleways and RUPPs.[415] The survey was optional in county boroughs, which were then abolished following the Local Government Act 1972 (LGA 1972).

27.231   Changes were subsequently made by the Countryside Act 1968, the Wildlife and Countryside Act 1981 (WCA 1981) and the Countryside and Rights of Way Act 2000. It is beyond the scope of this book to consider the full history of the statutory law surrounding the definitive map, for which a different text should be consulted,[416] but the net effect of the various statutory and administrative changes seems to be that one surveying authority may have inherited more than one map compiled under different procedures. This is reflected in the current definition of the 'definitive map' which is said to be:

(a)   the latest revised map and statement prepared in definitive form for that area under section 33 of the National Parks and Access to the Countryside Act 1949; or
(b)   where no such map and statement have been so prepared, the original DMS prepared for that area under section 32 of the National Parks and Access to the Countryside Act 1949; or
(c)   where no such map and statement have been so prepared, the map and statement prepared for that area under section 55(3) of the WCA 1981.[417]

---

[413]   WCA 1981, s 57A.

[414]   National Parks and Access to the Countryside Act 1949, s 27.

[415]   National Parks and Access to the Countryside Act 1949, s 27(1)–(2). Note that RUPPs will be automatically reclassified as 'restricted byways' from 2/5/2006, which is when the Countryside and Rights of Way Act 2000 came into force.

[416]   In particular, the reader is directed to *Highway Law and Practice* at 12-01 *et seq.*

[417]   WCA 1981, s 53(1).

27.232　The definitive map itself is based on an Ordnance Survey map on a scale of not less than 1:25,000.[418]

Inclusion of rights on the DMS

27.233　Inclusion of a right of way on the DMS is conclusive evidence that, at the relevant date (as defined below), such a right existed; in most cases such a right is without prejudice to any other right that might exist. Thus the map is conclusive of the lesser, but does not preclude the greater existing. In the case of a:

(a)　*footpath* – inclusion on the map is conclusive evidence that there was at the relevant date a highway and that the public had a right of way on foot, without prejudice to any question whether the public had at that date any other right of way;

(b)　*bridleway* – inclusion on the map will be conclusive evidence that there was at the relevant date a highway and the public had a right of way on foot and a right of way on horseback or leading a horse, without prejudice to any other right that might exist;

(c)　*restricted byway* – the map will be conclusive evidence that at the relevant date a highway as shown on the map existed and that the public had at that date a right of way on foot, horseback or leading a horse, together with a right of way for vehicles other than mechanically propelled vehicles,[419] without prejudice to any other rights that might exist;[420]

(d)　*BOAT* – the map will be conclusive evidence that there was at the relevant date a highway as shown on the map and that the public had thereover a right of way for vehicular and all other kinds of traffic.

27.234　Where the statement contains particulars as to the position or width of the way, or contains particulars in relation to any limitation or condition upon the way, that too will be conclusive evidence of the way's width and position at the relevant date. The relevant date for the purposes of the definitive map in most cases will be the date specified in the statement, but where a way is shown as a result of a modification order, the relevant date will be the date specified in the order.[421]

---

[418]　Wildlife and Countryside (Definitive Maps and Statements) Regulations 1993 (SI 1993/12).

[419]　Note that a 'mechanically propelled vehicle' does not include an electrically assisted pedal cycle of a class prescribed for the purposes of Road Traffic Act 1988, s 189(1)(c) – WCA 1981, s 56(1A).

[420]　The terms are set out in full at WCA 1981, s 56(1).

[421]　WCA 1981, s 56(2). See also s 56(3).

27.235 It may be subsequently claimed that a greater right than that which is included in the statement exists, or that, by error, the map wrongfully included a way at the relevant date. In each case, the rights are expressed to be without prejudice to 'any question [as to] whether the public had at that date any right of way [other than the right provided for in the DMS]'. Such rights may naturally change over time so as to expand, for example, to include rights by other modes of travel. The mere fact that the definitive map is said to be conclusive that such a right exists at the relevant date does not preclude rectification of the map where evidence comes to light from before the relevant date that the right has been erroneously included.[422] Thus although a way being recorded on the map is conclusive that such a right exists at the relevant date, the right may subsequently be erased or downgraded on the basis of evidence that emerges either before or after the relevant date.

Roads used as public paths

27.236 'Roads used as public paths' or 'RUPPs' were formerly recorded on the definitive map and may still be discovered on some older maps. A RUPP was defined as 'a highway, other than a public path, used by the public mainly for the purposes for which footpaths or bridleways are so used'.[423] Where such a right was included on the definitive map, such a right was not to be conclusive that any vehicular rights existed, only that 'the public had thereover at that date a right of way on foot and a right of way on horseback or leading a horse'. Once again, such rights were expressed to be 'without prejudice to any question whether the public had at that date any right of way'.[424]

27.237 The Countryside Act 1968 brought in a duty to re-classify such rights of way as footpaths, bridleways or BOATs.[425] The position is now that such rights

---

[422] *R v Secretary of State for the Environment ex parte Simms* [1991] 2 QB 354, overruling *Rubinstein v Secretary of State for the Environment* (1989) 57 P & CR 111. Note that evidence which exists prior to the relevant date specified on the definitive map can be considered when making a modification order to the definitive map. See *R v Secretary of State for the Environment ex parte Riley* (1989) 59 P & CR 1; *Mayhew v Secretary of State for the Environment* (1992) 65 P & CR 344.

[423] National Parks and Access to the Countryside Act 1949.

[424] National Parks and Access to the Countryside Act 1949, s 32(4).

[425] As to the considerations which were to be taken into account in such a determination, see Countryside Act 1968, Sch 3, para 10. And see subsequently s 54. A 'byway open to all traffic' 'means a highway over which the public have a right of way for vehicular and all other kinds of traffic, but which is used by the public mainly for the purpose for which footpaths and bridleways are so used'. In deciding to re-classify a RUPP as a BOAT, it has been suggested that s 66 should be applied literally to include current usage. The court, however, takes a purposive approach. See *Masters v Secretary of State for the Environment, Transport and the Regions* [2000] 2 All ER 788; *R v Wiltshire County Council ex parte Nettlecombe Ltd* [1998] JPL 707; *Buckland v Secretary of State for the Environment and the Regions* [2000] 1 WLR 1949.

will automatically be reclassified from 2/5/2006, with the coming into force of the Countryside and Rights of Way Act 2000, as restricted byways. Any reclassification orders that are pending will be processed to their conclusion.[426]

Effect of the Natural Environment and Rural Communities Act 2006

27.238 Following the commencement of the Natural Environment and Rural Communities Act 2006 (NERC 2006) on 2/5/2006, no public right of way for mechanically propelled vehicles will arise unless it is:

(a)   created (by an enactment or instrument or otherwise) on terms that expressly provide for it to be a right of way for such vehicles, or
(b)   created by the construction, in exercise of powers conferred by virtue of any enactment, of a road intended to be used by such vehicles.[427]

27.239   Existing rights of way for vehicles which have gone unrecorded on the definitive map, or were recorded on the definitive map only as a footpath, bridleway or restricted byway[428] will be extinguished unless they fall within one of the listed exceptions.[429]

27.240   The net effect of the changes brought by this statute are that, as far as new applications for definitive map modifications are concerned post-2/5/2006, rights of way by vehicles will simply have been extinguished where such rights are not so recorded on the map and the case is not one to which the listed exceptions apply. Pending applications at the time of commencement still have to be processed to conclusion and the reader should note the transitional provisions where the application is for a modification order to show a BOAT on the definitive map.[430]

27.241   Where unrecorded vehicular rights are simply extinguished and the existing right of way was reasonably necessary to allow a person with an interest in land to obtain access to that land, or part of that land, NERC 2006 provides for the creation of private rights of way.[431]

---

[426]   See Countryside and Rights of Way Act 2000, s 48(9).
[427]   See NERC 2006, s 66.
[428]   See NERC 2006, s 67.
[429]   See NERC 2006, s 67(2) and (3).
[430]   See NERC 2006, s 67(3).
[431]   See NERC 2006, s 67(5).

27.242   NERC 2006 itself does not affect those rights of way already recorded on the DMS, but plainly applicants seeking a definitive map modification to show vehicular rights that have arisen may now find that such rights have been extinguished and they will be unable to seek such a modification to the DMS.

Conflicts between the map and statement

27.243   There may be times where there is conflict between the definitive map and the statement. There is no guidance as such in the WCA 1981 as to which should take priority. Seemingly, both the definitive map and the statement are capable of being relevant as to the existence or non-existence of the right of way in a review.[432] The guidance that has been provided comes from Pitchford J in *R (Norfolk County Council) v Secretary of State for the Environment, Food and Rural Affairs*:[433]

> the correct approach to interpretation of the definitive map and statement must be a practical one. They should be examined together with a view to resolving the question whether they are truly in conflict or the statement can properly be read as describing the position of the right of way. If they are in conflict, then the map must take precedence since the discretionary particulars depend for their existence upon the conclusiveness of the obligatory map. Unless the statement can properly be interpreted as describing the same footpath as that shown on the map, then the statement cannot be regarded as conclusive evidence of the position of the footpath shown on the map. The question whether the statement does describe the position of a footpath shown on the map is, I accept, a matter of fact and degree. That the statement purports, by reference to the same footpath designation number, to specify the position of a footpath similarly designated on the map is some but, in my view, inconclusive evidence that it in fact does so.

27.244   In cases of real dispute, it therefore seems that the map will take precedence, but there is not an automatic presumption in favour of the map:[434]

> [64]   Where the map and statement conflict as to the position of a public right of way I can see no basis for the application of an evidential presumption in favour of one at the expense of the other … the fact-finder starts from the position that both the map and the statement were prepared following the correct procedures. Save perhaps in the case of demonstrably false particulars in the statement, the natural inference is that the surveying authority was at least attempting conscientiously to record the position of the footpath shown on the map. What is required at review is, in my judgment, simply a consideration which (or which other) route, on a balance of probability, is correct, if any, in the light of all the relevant

---

[432]   *Kotarski v Secretary of State for the Environment, Food and Rural Affairs* [2010] EWHC 1036 (Admin).

[433]   [2005] EWHC 119 (Admin) at [38] per Pitchford J.

[434]   [2005] EWHC 119 (Admin) at [64] per Pitchford J.

evidence, including the terms of the map and statement. The judgment being exercised in a case such as this is whether, under section 53(3)(c)(iii), any particulars in the map and statement require modification unless it emerges that either a new footpath should be added or the footpath shown on the map should be deleted altogether. It may, by an examination of the documents together and an inspection on the ground, be a straight forward task to identify the mistake or inaccuracy in the preparation of the documents. It would be inappropriate in such an exercise to impose what would be an artificial presumption in favour of one document or the other simply because, until modification, it is treated as the primary document.

Modifications to the DMS

27.245   It is inevitable that as rights of way are stopped up and new tracks are created, the definitive map itself will need to be modified. Section 53 of the WCA 1981 provides that the statement must be kept under continuous review and that the surveying authority must, as soon as is reasonably practicable after the occurrence of any of the listed trigger events, modify the map. The following events are the trigger events as specified in section 53(3)(a)–(c):

(a)   the coming into operation of any enactment or instrument, or any other event, whereby—

   (i)   a highway shown or required to be shown in the map and statement has been authorised to be stopped up, diverted, widened or extended;

   (ii)   a highway shown or required to be shown in the map and statement as a highway of a particular description has ceased to be a highway of that description; or

   (iii) a new right of way has been created over land in the area to which the map relates, being a right of way such that the land over which the right subsists is a public path or a restricted byway;

(b)   the expiration, in relation to any way in the area to which the map relates, of any period such that the enjoyment by the public of the way during that period raises a presumption that the way has been dedicated as a public path or restricted byway;

(c)   the discovery by the authority of evidence which (when considered with all other relevant evidence available to them) shows—

   (i)   that a right of way which is not shown in the map and statement subsists or is reasonably alleged to subsist over land in the area to which the map relates, being a right of way such that the land over which the right subsists is a public path, a restricted byway or, subject to section 54A, a byway open to all traffic;

   (ii)   that a highway shown in the map and statement as a highway of a particular description ought to be there shown as a highway of a different description; or

(iii) that there is no public right of way over land shown in the map and statement as a highway of any description, or any other particulars contained in the map and statement require modification.

27.246 The recording of a right of way on the definitive map is not a way of creating new rights, but a way of reflecting those that are currently in existence. Any person is empowered to apply to the surveying authority to modify the definitive map in the case of the trigger events specified in section 53(3)(b) or (c) of the WCA 1981.

27.247 The trigger events listed in section 53(3)(b) and (c) of the WCA 1981 relate to events which have occurred since the definitive map was prepared and are fairly clear in scope. Such events may have resulted in a right of way coming into existence where none had existed before, or the upgrading of an existing right of way.[435] A highway remains a highway until it has been formally stopped up. No modification should be made until the final order has been confirmed by the appropriate body.

27.248 Section 53(3)(b) of the WCA 1981 relates to rights which may have arisen either by the section 31 statutory presumption or at common law. That much seems clear from the wording of the phrasing 'expiration ... of any period'. Seemingly, a dedication at common law could take place in less than the statutory 20-year period as prescribed by section 31.[436]

Discovery by the authority of evidence

27.249 It is suggested that section 53(3)(c) of the WCA 1981 is unlike the preceding sections in that, rather than being concerned with events that have arisen since the definitive map was made, section 53(3)(c) is 'concerned with the correction of mistakes as the result of newly discovered information, which was previously unknown, and which may result in a previously mistaken decision being corrected'.[437] The power of correction is said to cover three situations:[438]

---

[435] Glidewell LJ in *R v Secretary of State for the Environment ex parte Simms* [1991] 2 QB 354:

'I agree with the suggestion made to us in argument, that s 53(3)(a) and (b) relate to events which have happened since the definitive map was prepared. These events may have resulted in a right of way coming into existence where none existed before, or the upgrading of an existing right of way to a right of a wider sort, e.g. by express dedication under paragraph (a)(iii) or by prescription under paragraph (b).'

[436] See in particular *North London Railway Co v St Mary, Islington* (1872) 27 LT 672, where a period of 18 months was held to be sufficient to create a right of way at common law.

[437] *R v Secretary of State for the Environment ex parte Simms* [1991] 2 QB 354 at 387–388 per Glidewell LJ.

[438] *R v Secretary of State for the Environment ex parte Simms* [1991] 2 QB 354 at 388 per Glidewell LJ.

(i) the addition of a right of way not shown on the definitive map ... (ii) the upgrading or downgrading of rights of way shown on the map, ... (iii) the deletion of a right of way which the latest information proves should not have appeared on the map at all ...

27.250   Notwithstanding that a recording of a right of way on the definitive map is conclusive evidence that such a right existed at the relevant time, seemingly this section can be used to downgrade or otherwise correct an error on the definitive map.[439] The starting point nonetheless appears to be that where a right of way is shown on the definitive map, it will be presumed that such a right does exist, thus: 'Evidence of some substance must be put in the balance, if it is to outweigh the initial presumption that the right of way exists. Proof of a negative is seldom easy, and the more time that elapses, the more difficult the task of adducing positive evidence'.[440]

---

[439] *R v Secretary of State for the Environment ex parte Simms* [1991] 2 QB 354; see *Rubinstein v Secretary of State for the Environment* (1989) 57 P & CR 111, now overruled.

[440] *Trevelyan v Secretary of State for the Environment, Transport and the Regions* [2001] EWCA Civ 266 at [38] per Lord Phillips MR. See also *R (Macintosh and others) v Secretary of State for the Environment, Food and Rural Affairs* [2006] EWHC 2703 (Admin). *Trail Riders Fellowship v Secretary of State for the Environment, Food and Rural Affairs* [2017] EWHC 1866 (Admin), where an inspector's decision was quashed as she had wrongly treated the HA 1980, s 36(6), list of streets maintainable at public expense as being conclusive when it was only intended to identify, and not precisely delineate, a given street in contrast to the accuracy and precision of a DMS. The practical effect of the inspector's decision was that a mechanically propelled vehicle could no longer lawfully travel the whole length of a lane from one end to the other. The lane in question fell within the definition of street for the purposes of s 36(6) and local authorities were required to keep a corrected and up-to-date list of the streets within their area which were maintainable at public expense. The claimant contended that the DMS should be modified to show the whole of the land, not as a restricted byway, but as a BOAT. The inspector concluded that by taking the historic documentary evidence into account, public carriageway rights existed over the land. However she also concluded that between two points the historic carriageway did not follow the slightly bowed course or alignment over a bridge marked with magenta on the map with the list of streets but a more straight course over another bridge slightly to the west. That led her to conclude that the true historic right of way was not shown on the list of streets, albeit that the slightly bowed alignment marked in magenta clearly was. The court held that whilst the purpose of NERC 2006 was to extinguish existing, but unrecorded public rights of way for mechanical vehicles, Parliament clearly intended to make exceptions to those which were shown either in a DMS, which might be expected to be accurate and precise, or in a list of streets which might not be. The admitted historic and continuous right of way was so shown in the list of streets and it was perverse that over one section of its length it was automatically extinguished because of imprecision in the magenta line on the map, which was part of, but not the whole of the list of streets. In other words, although the court agreed with the inspector that she could have regard to what the local authority said was its list of streets, the error made by her was that she actually treated the precise alignment of the magenta line on the street map as conclusive, even though a list of streets was not required to include any map at all. The inspector had made an error which was founded on a clear error of law and that error had created a perverse result and her decision was quashed. The case is important for the distinction between a DMS and the effect of a list of streets kept by a highway authority under HA 1980, s 36(6).

27.251   The discovery that there was an inconsistency as between the definitive map and the statement is capable of being a 'discovery' of evidence which would trigger a modification order under this provision.[441] Such evidence does not have to be new evidence, just evidence which is discovered.[442]

Definitive map modification orders

Procedure

27.252   Any person is empowered under the provisions of section 53(5) of the WCA 1981 to apply for an order modifying the definitive map where either of the events set out in section 53(3)(b) or (c) are made out.

27.253   Such an application must be made in the prescribed form[443] accompanied by a map drawn to the prescribed scale (not less than 1:25,000)[444] and showing the way or ways to which the application relates, together with copies of any documentary evidence which the applicant wishes to adduce.[445] Minor departures from these requirements will not invalidate an application,[446] but it has been suggested that the requirements in paragraph 1 of Schedule 14 to the WCA 1981 must otherwise be strictly complied with; the omission of a signature from the application is not *de minimis*, nor is the omission of providing a map, although the defect could be remedied by the sending of a signed letter, noting the defects and asking the council to treat the application as bearing the date of the letter, shortly after submission of the form.[447] It was suggested by Dyson LJ that where, however, the form is left unsigned for a substantial period of time, that will not generally be regarded as a minor departure,[448] but the correctness of this has been

---

[441]   *Kotarski v Secretary of State for the Environment and Rural Affairs* [2010] EWHC 1036 (Admin).

[442]   See *Mayhew v Secretary of State for the Environment* [1993] COD 45.

[443]   See Wildlife and Countryside (Definitive Maps and Statements) Regulations 1993 (SI 1993/12), Sch 7.

[444]   Wildlife and Countryside (Definitive Maps and Statements) Regulations 1993, reg 2.

[445]   WCA 1981, Sch 14, para 1.

[446]   *R (Warden and Fellows of Winchester College) v Hampshire County Council* [2008] EWCA Civ 431, [2009] 1 WLR 138 at [54] per Dyson LJ.

[447]   *Maroudas v Secretary of State for the Environment, Food and Rural Affairs* [2010] EWCA Civ 280.

[448]   *Maroudas v Secretary of State for the Environment, Food and Rural Affairs* [2010] EWCA Civ 280:

'the lack of a date and, in particular, the lack of a signature are important omissions. The signature is needed to prove that the application is indeed that of the person by whom it is purportedly made. If the application form remains unsigned for a substantial period of time, I would not regard that as a minor departure from the statutory requirement that it should be signed.'

But see the criticism of the decision in *Maroudas* in *R (Trail Riders Fellowship and another) v Dorset County Council (Plumbe intervening)* [2015] UKSC 18, [2015] 1 WLR 1406.

questioned and the better view seems to be that, where the defect, such as a signature, has been remedied to the satisfaction of the authority and waived by them, such a strict approach should not be adopted.[449]

27.254 As far as the map is concerned, there is no provision that such a map must be produced by the Ordnance Survey or any other commercial or public authority, or that it must contain the same features that an Ordnance Survey map would.[450] The crucial point is that any map submitted must show the way to which the application relates and must be on a scale of not less than 1:25,000. For the purposes of the Regulations it would not matter that such a map provided with the application had been digitally derived from a map with a scale of 1:50,000, as long as when presented the scale was at least 1:25,000. The word 'drawn' can be construed to include new techniques for the creation of maps.[451]

27.255 The applicant who seeks such an order must then serve notice on the owner or occupier of any land to which the application relates, save where, after a reasonable inquiry has been made, the surveying authority are satisfied that it is not practicable to do so. In such a case, the authority may direct that the notice will be served by affixing it to some conspicuous object on the land and addressing it to him. The applicant must then certify that he has complied with the provisions as to service.[452]

27.256 As soon as is 'reasonably practicable' after the applicant has certified compliance with service of notice, the authority will investigate the facts giving

---

[449] *Maroudas* in *R (Trail Riders Fellowship and another) v Dorset County Council (Plumbe intervening)* [2015] UKSC 18, [2015] 1 WLR 1406 at [65] *et seq* per Lord Carnwath; see in particular [79].

[450] *Maroudas* in *R (Trail Riders Fellowship and another) v Dorset County Council (Plumbe intervening)* [2015] UKSC 18, [2015] 1 WLR 1406; see in particular [26] per Lord Clarke.

[451] See *Maroudas* in *R (Trail Riders Fellowship and another) v Dorset County Council (Plumbe intervening)* [2015] UKSC 18, [2015] 1 WLR 1406. The case concerned five applications for modification orders which were accompanied by a map created by a computer software programme. The map was digitally encoded and originally derived from an Ordnance Survey map drawn to a scale of 1:50,000. The maps were enlarged and were all presented within a scale of 1:25,000. One of the questions before the court was whether the map had been 'drawn' to the prescribed scale in circumstances where it had been digitally derived from an original map with a scale of 1:50,000. The court found that as long as the map when presented was at a scale of 1:25,000, the map itself was not required to be based on an Ordnance Survey map and that the word 'drawn' did not mean 'originally drawn':

'It ... should be given a meaning which embraces later techniques for the production of maps. For practical purposes, when a computer is used to translate stored data into a printed map, it can properly be said that the computer and the printer are, on human command, "drawing" the map which emerges to the scale which has been selected' (per Maurice Kay LJ (in the Court of Appeal), as endorsed by Lord Clarke – see [30] of the Supreme Court judgment).

[452] WCA 1981, Sch 14, para 2.

rise to the application and must consult every local authority in whose area the land/alleged right of way runs.[453] Where the surveying authority fails to deal with the application within 12 months, the applicant may make representations to the Secretary of State who may direct the authority to determine the application by a set date.[454]

27.257 Once the authority has determined the application, it will serve notice upon the applicant and on any other person who was originally served with notice of the application, i.e. the occupier or landowners so notified by the applicant.[455] An appeal can be made where the authority declines to make the order. Appeals are to the relevant Secretary of State. Such appeals are time limited to a period of 28 days from the date of service of the authority's notice that it is not proposing to make an order.[456] Where, on appeal, the Secretary of State does believe that an order should be made, he will give directions to the authority as appear necessary, which may include a direction as to the time within which an order is to be made.[457] The form of such orders is also prescribed by regulations.[458]

Orders modifying the DMS

27.258 Where an authority seeks to make an order to modify the definitive map, there are further procedural requirements which are set out in Schedule 15 to the WCA 1981. That Schedule should be consulted fully, but in brief the requirements of that Schedule are as follows.

27.259 As with most orders relating to public rights of way, the order itself does not take effect until it is confirmed. Where there are no objections to the order, the authority itself may confirm the order in the usual way.[459] Where such an order is opposed, the confirming of the order will be a matter for the Secretary of State.[460]

---

[453] WCA 1981, Sch 14, para 3.

[454] WCA 1981, Sch 14, para 3(2).

[455] WCA 1981, Sch 14, para 3(3).

[456] WCA 1981, Sch 14, para 4(1).

[457] WCA 1981, Sch 14, para 4(2).

[458] See Wildlife and Countryside (Definitive Maps and Statements) Regulations 1993.

[459] But note that it may not confirm such an order where objections have been raised, even where such objections are irrelevant or outside the grounds which can be taken; such an order should still be referred to the Secretary of State. See *Lasham Parish Meeting v Hampshire County Council* [1993] COD 42.

[460] See WCA 1981, Sch 15, paras 6 and 7.

27.260 Before making the order, the authority has to give notice in the prescribed form[461] in at least one local newspaper circulating in the area and by serving the notice on certain persons, including every owner and occupier of the land so affected and every local authority in whose area the land runs. The notice must also be displayed in a prominent position (with a plan) at the ends of the way affected by the order, at council offices in the locality and at any such other place as the authority may consider appropriate within 42 days before the expiry of the time in the notice.[462] Service of notice on the owner or occupiers may be dispensed with, but where the authority does so, it must, then, address a notice to the 'owners and any occupiers' by affixing a notice to some conspicuous object on the land.[463]

27.261 The notice itself must include a description of the general effect of the proposed order, stating that it requires confirmation, naming a place where a copy of the order can be inspected and specifying the time and the manner in which such objections may be raised.[464]

27.262 Where objections are made in relation to some, but not all of the proposed modifications, the authority can effectively separate the proposed modifications into separate orders.[465] The unopposed part of the order can simply be confirmed by the authority as unopposed. Note that where an order is opposed but the grounds for opposing it are not lawful grounds, the surveying authority must still refer the matter as an opposed order to the Secretary of State.[466] Opposed orders will be submitted to the Secretary of State for confirmation, who will either cause a local inquiry to be held or allow a person raising an objection an opportunity to be heard by someone appointed by the Secretary of State.[467]

27.263 Following that process, the Secretary of State may then confirm the order with or without modifications.[468] The decision itself may be given by the

---

[461] See WCA 1981, Sch 14, para 1, and see Wildlife and Countryside (Definitive Map and Statements) Regulations 1993.

[462] WCA 1981, Sch 15, paras 3(2) and (5).

[463] WCA 1981, Sch 15, para 3(4).

[464] Although the period may not be less than 42 days from the date of the first publication of the notice. See WCA 1981, Sch 15, para 3(1).

[465] WCA 1981, Sch 15, para 5.

[466] See *Lasham Parish Meeting v Hampshire County Council* (1992) 91 LGR 209. As for the provisions in relation to the submission of unopposed orders, see Wildlife and Countryside (Definitive Maps and Statements) Regulations 1993, Sch 4, para 3.

[467] WCA 1981, Sch 15, para 7. As for the procedures for hearings, see Rights of Way (Hearings and Inquiries Procedure) (England) Rules 2007 (SI 2007/2008). Note that an inspector is not limited only to the grounds of objection and other issues may arise. See *Marriott v Secretary of State for the Environment, Transport and the Regions* [2001] JPL 559

[468] Note the restrictions on the power to make such modifications, WCA 1981, Sch 15, para 8.

Secretary of State or by some other person appointed by him. As soon as is reasonably practicable after a decision to confirm an order is made, the authority must give further notice describing the effect of the order and naming a place where a copy of the order as confirmed may be viewed free of charge.

Further challenge

27.264 Where an order has not been made, there is no statutory basis for review and accordingly remedy lies to the High Court in judicial review proceedings. Such an application must be brought within the three-month time limit. Where an order has been confirmed, the statute provides for statutory review. A person aggrieved by the order who desires to question its validity may do so on the ground that it is not in the powers available under section 53 or section 54 of the WCA 1981, or otherwise that any of the procedural requirements in Schedule 15 have not been complied with. Such an application is to the High Court and must be made within 42 days from the date of the publication of the notice or following confirmation of the order.[469] In the result, any legal challenge must be based on an error of law, either substantive or procedural.

27.265 Note that the grounds themselves are tightly circumscribed. The High Court is empowered to quash the order or any provision either generally or in so far as it affects the interests of the applicant,[470] but only where it is satisfied that the order is not in the powers of section 53 or section 54 of the WCA 1981, or that the applicant has been 'substantially prejudiced' by a failure to comply with the requirements.[471] The grounds are therefore either that there was some sort of procedural irregularity which was significant enough that the applicant was 'substantially prejudiced' or that the order was otherwise unlawful because it was not in the powers of section 53 or section 54. It is not for a court to simply re-examine the facts and to substitute its own decision.[472] The grounds upon which such an appeal could be brought are in many ways similar to that for judicial

---

[469] WCA 1981, Sch 5, para 12(1).

[470] It must affect the 'interests of the applicant'. For an order which did not affect the interest of the applicant, see *R v Secretary of State for the Environment and Hereford and Worcester County Council ex parte Badman*, 13/2/1966, unreported.

[471] WCA 1981, Sch 15, para 12(2).

[472] See *R (Elveden Farms Limited) v Secretary of State for the Environment, Food and Rural Affairs* [2012] EWHC 644 (Admin) at [2]:

'The claimant sought to ... found an approach that this court could examine the facts before the relevant inspector and substitute its own decision from that analysis of the facts, if, of course, the court disagreed with the earlier factual analysis ... such an approach is one that is open to the Court of Appeal when it is dealing with an appeal from a judge, but that approach is not apposite when Parliament has directed that the court is not the initial decision maker and the initial decision maker is the Secretary of State or an inspector appointed by the Secretary of State.'

review. They will include, for example, that the inspector had failed to take into account relevant factors,[473] that the inspector failed to provide adequate reasons for his conclusions[474] or that the decision was *Wednesbury* unreasonable.[475] However, *Wednesbury* challenges are notoriously difficult as the court will avoid descending into the merits of the decision.[476]

FINANCIAL PROVISIONS

Agreements under the HA 1980, section 278

27.266 Part XIII of the HA 1980 deals with financial matters. The most important provision, as far as development works are concerned, is section 278, which allows highway authorities to enter into agreements with developers for the execution of highway works at the developer's expense.[477] The powers provided to the authority are wide ranging and may include provision for the payment of a sum to reflect maintenance of the works, as well as any other consequential provision as appear to the highway authority to be necessary or expedient.

27.267 Recovery of such monies is also expressly dealt with. Where expenditure remains outstanding, it may be declared to be a charge on the land and registrable as a local land charge.[478] The authority is additionally enabled to direct that any means of access afforded by the works to which the agreement relates shall not be used until the sum is paid, and it provides for recovery as against any person having an interest in any estate or land for the benefit of which any means of access or facility is afforded.[479]

27.268 The availability and importance of section 278 agreements has changed since the introduction of the Community Infrastructure Levy (CIL), which came into being on 6/4/2010. The purpose of the CIL is to ensure that costs incurred in supporting the development of an area can be funded (wholly or partly) by owners

---

[473] See *R (Elveden Farms Limited) v Secretary of State for the Environment, Food and Rural Affairs* [2012] EWHC 644 (Admin) at [88]–[90].

[474] *R (Elveden Farms Limited) v Secretary of State for the Environment, Food and Rural Affairs* [2012] EWHC 644 (Admin). See also *Martine v Secretary of State for the Environment and Kent County Council* [1996] 3 CL 422.

[475] Such a ground is, of course, very difficult to establish. For a recent case in which irrationality was raised, see *Trail Riders Fellowship v Secretary of State for the Environment, Food and Rural Affairs* [2015] EWHC 85 (Admin).

[476] See also *R (Roxlena Ltd) v Cumbria County Council* [2017] EWHC 2651 (Admin).

[477] HA 1980, s 278(1).

[478] See HA 1980, s 278(8). See also Local Land Charges Act 1975.

[479] HA 1980, s 278(5).

or developers of land.[480] CIL is discussed elsewhere in this book, but the reader should note that section 278 agreements cannot be required under a planning condition for works that are intended to be funded through CIL and are thus on a charging authority's regulation 123 infrastructure list.[481] Such a restriction does not apply to agreements made with the Minister, a strategic highways company or Transport for London.[482]

27.269   Where such agreements are made between a developer and the highway authority, planning permission will have been granted and changes will be required to existing road infrastructure as a result of the development works. Section 38 agreements may be entered into at the same time so as to adopt newly constructed ways on the development land.[483]

27.270   Highway authorities are authorised to enter into such an agreement where they are satisfied that 'it will be of benefit to the public'. There is no clear guidance laid out in the HA 1980 as to what the authority must take into account but, at the very least, it is bound to involve a consideration of the road safety implications of the proposed scheme, which will have already been considered at the planning stage.[484]

Relationship between section 278 agreements and planning permission

27.271   The legal relationship between the role of the planning authority in determining whether or not to grant planning permission and the role of a highway authority in determining whether or not to enter into a section 278 agreement has been considered by the court in *R v Warwickshire County Council*.[485] In the *Warwickshire* case, planning permission for the construction of a supermarket with associated parking and a suitable means of access to an adjoining highway had initially been refused. One of the reasons given was that, having consulted the highway authority with regard to the proposed highway works, the proposal was considered to be 'detrimental to the interests of highway safety'. Planning permission was later granted on appeal subject to conditions, including that certain specified highway works would be undertaken. To satisfy this condition, a section 278 agreement would be required, which the highway authority refused to enter into, citing once again that the council was of the view that the proposed

---

[480]   Planning Act 2008, s 205(2).

[481]   Community Infrastructure Levy Regulations 2010 (SI 2010/948) (CILR), reg 123.

[482]   CILR, reg 123(2B).

[483]   For which, see paras 27.78–27.82.

[484]   See *R v Warwickshire County Council* (1998) 75 P & CR 89 at 90.

[485]   (1998) 75 P & CR 89. This was the issue formulated for the court in the *Warwickshire* case.

access arrangements were unsafe. Judicial review was then sought of this decision.

27.272   On review, that court found that, following a successful appeal by the developer in relation to planning permission, the relevant highway authority had no option other than to co-operate in implementing the planning permission. It asked the following question:[486]

> is it reasonable for a highway authority, whose road safety objections have been fully heard and rejected on appeal, then, quite inconsistently with the Inspector's independent factual judgment on the issue, nevertheless to maintain its own original view? In my mind there can be but one answer to that question: a categoric 'no'.

27.273   The reasons for the judgment were:

(a)   The site access and associated highway works, together with the road safety problems which they raised, were central to this particular planning application and had been considered in full detail at the planning stage.
(b)   The planning permission was granted following appeal to the Secretary of State and not merely by the LPA.
(c)   There were no new facts nor were there any changes in the circumstances following the inspector's determination of the appeal. The highway authority's continued refusal was based upon identical considerations as were raised in objecting to planning permission.

27.274   The point seems to be that, if there has already been a determination and a decision reached by the LPA, and there has not been a change in circumstance since that decision has been made, a local highway authority cannot go behind it and reach a differing conclusion. The situation would plainly be different where there had been a change of circumstances.

---

[486]   (1998) 75 P & CR 89 at 95.

Chapter 28

Gypsies and Travellers[1]

INTRODUCTION

28.1   This chapter is divided into two parts:

(a)   Dealing with illegal and unauthorised encampments: a summary of the powers available to local authorities, the police and landowners.

(b)   Planning issues (including national planning policy).

ILLEGAL AND UNAUTHORISED ENCAMPMENTS[2]

Introduction

28.2   Local authorities and the police have extensive powers to deal with illegal and unauthorised encampments and the nuisance which they can cause. In deciding whether to take action such bodies should always consider:

---

[1]   The term 'gypsies and travellers' is difficult to define as it does not constitute a single, homogeneous group, but encompasses a range of groups with different histories, cultures and beliefs including: Romany gypsies, Irish travellers, and Scottish gypsy travellers. There are also traveller groups which are generally regarded as 'cultural' rather than 'ethnic' travellers. These include new age travellers and occupational travellers, such as showmen and waterway travellers (House of Commons Briefing Paper Number 08083, 8/5/2018, 'Gypsies and Travellers').

[2]   In the periodic Ministry of Housing, Communities and Local Government (MHCLG) 'Count of Traveller caravans: July 2017' (as reported in the House of Commons Briefing Paper, 'Gypsies and Travellers', Number 08083, 8/5/2018), it was noted that there were 3,721 caravans on unauthorised sites. Of these, 2,197 caravans were on land owned by travellers and 1,524 caravans were on land not owned by travellers. The number of caravans on unauthorised sites increased by 7% from July 2016 to July 2017. However, the proportion of traveller caravans on unauthorised sites has fallen from 23% in July 2007 to 16% in July 2017. MHCLG classifies unauthorised sites as being either 'tolerated' or 'not tolerated', examples of which, in the case of the latter, are where enforcement notices have been served (including temporary stop notices), where the results of a planning appeal are pending, where an injunction has been sought or where the compliance period has been extended. According to this classification, in July 2017, 1,532 caravans were on a tolerated unauthorised site and 2,189 caravans were on a not tolerated unauthorised site.

(a)   the harm that such developments can cause to local amenities and the local environment;

(b)   the potential interference with the peaceful enjoyment of neighbouring property;

(c)   the need to maintain public order and safety and protect health – for example, by deterring fly-tipping and criminal damage;

(d)   any harm to good community relations;

(e)   that the state may enforce laws to control the use of an individual's property where that is in accordance with the general public interest.

28.3   Any prudent authority should plan for such eventualities and, if warranted by the circumstances, should always act swiftly. Clearly local agencies should work together and, in mitigation of the risk which they face, should consider:

(a)   identifying vulnerable sites;

(b)   working with landowners to physically secure vulnerable sites where possible;

(c)   preparing any necessary paperwork, such as applications for possession orders or injunctions, in advance;

(d)   working with private landowners to inform them of their powers in relation to unauthorised encampments, including advance preparation of any necessary paperwork;

(e)   developing a clear notification and decision-making process to respond to instances of unauthorised encampments;

(f)   the prudence of applying for injunctions where intelligence suggests there may be a planned encampment and the site of the encampment might cause disruption to others;

(g)   working to ensure that local wardens, park officers or enforcement officers are aware of who they should notify in the event of unauthorised encampments;

(h)   working to ensure that local wardens or park officers are aware of the locations of unauthorised campsites or other alternatives;

(i)   identifying sites where protests could be directed/permitted.

Local authority powers (including private landowners where mentioned)[3]

Temporary stop notice

28.4   Town and Country Planning Act 1990 (TCPA 1990), section 171E stops any activity that breaches planning control for a period of 28 days. This gives the local planning authority (LPA) time to decide whether further enforcement action,

---

3   See 'Dealing with illegal and unauthorised encampments: A summary of available powers', published jointly by the Department for Communities and Local Government (DCLG), the Home Office and the Ministry of Justice on 27/3/2015, on which this section is largely based.

such as issuing an enforcement notice, possibly with a stop notice, should be taken. The penalty for non-compliance is a fine of up to £20,000 on summary conviction or an unlimited fine on indictment (section 171G). New guidance states that it may be appropriate in some circumstances for an LPA to issue a temporary stop notice where the breach of planning control has occurred on land owned by a third party, including the local authority or another public authority.

Injunctions to restrain breaches of planning control, trespass and nuisance

28.5   If a local site is particularly vulnerable and intelligence suggests it is going to be targeted for unauthorised camping, causing disruption to others going about their day-to-day lives, local authorities could consider applying to the courts for a pre-emptive injunction preventing unauthorised camping or protests within a defined area (see TCPA 1990, section 187B), arising from an actual or apprehended breach of planning control. In cases of urgency, application should be made for an interim injunction. Such injunctions are common in cases involving encampments or works within Green Belts or on Green Spaces. In such cases it is open to the court to make orders against persons unknown for limited periods prohibiting the stationing of caravans and/or preventing development occurring within a given area without planning permission. It is also possible to obtain a time limited borough-wide final injunction preventing travellers from encamping on any Green Spaces or on industrial sites (see Chapter 14, 'Injunctions restraining breaches of planning control'). The remedy of an injunction, particularly an interim injunction against persons unknown, is clearly available to a private landowner wishing to prevent or put a stop to trespass/ nuisance occurring on his land.

Licensing of caravan sites

28.6   The Caravan Sites and Control of Development Act 1960 prohibits the use of land as a caravan site unless the occupier holds a site licence issued by the local authority. A caravan site includes anywhere a caravan (including mobile or 'park' home) is situated and occupied for human habitation including touring sites and single sites. However, it does not include sites where caravans are kept for storage only (driveways, retailers, storage parks) or where a caravan is used as additional accommodation for an existing dwelling. Violation of licensing terms brings a £100 fine for a first offence, and a £250 fine for any subsequent offence.

Power of local authority to control use of movable dwellings

28.7   Section 269 of the Public Health Act 1936 gives the local authority powers to control the use of movable dwellings and to license the use of land as a site for

such as a dwelling. If the land is to be used for more than 28 days in total in any calendar year, planning permission must be obtained. A site which is used for more than 42 days consecutively or 60 days in total in any consecutive 12 months, must have a site licence for the area concerned. The local authority may also decide to license tented areas on existing sites which operate within the 28-day planning allowance period. Violation of licensing terms brings a £2 fine per day.

Possession orders

28.8   A possession order under Part 55 of the Civil Procedure Rules (CPR) can be obtained by both local authorities and private landowners who require the removal of trespassers from property including land. The claim must be issued in a County Court which has jurisdiction over the affected land/property. A claim can be issued in the High Court in exceptional circumstances where there is a risk of public disturbance and harm to persons or property that requires immediate determination. Local authorities should also be prepared to advise private landowners about their rights to recover land from trespassers through the courts or using common law powers. It is also possible that local authorities may be called upon to assist other government bodies such as the Highways Agency.

28.9   The ordinary possession order may be used in relation to the use of any land and in the case of any type of squatter or trespasser. The landowner may also claim damages for trespass and costs. A possession order may be secured quickly against trespassers (a minimum of two days' notice before a hearing can take place if the property is non-residential, or five days for residential property), but not as quickly as an interim possession order, and is not backed up by criminal sanctions, unlike the interim possession order.

Interim possession order

28.10   If trespassers have occupied premises (rather than open land), a local authority or a private landowner may also apply (under Section III of the CPR, Part 55) for an interim possession order, which is an accelerated process for regaining possession of property. Once the court has granted such an order and it has been served, trespassers who fail to leave within 24 hours of service of the order or return to the premises within the currency of the order are guilty of an offence under section 76 of the Criminal Justice and Public Order Act 1994.

28.11   The interim possession order has the obvious advantages of speed and being backed up by the criminal law. It is, however, not a final order, and there is a return date at which the court will decide whether to make the order final. If the court decides that the interim order was not justified, the landowner may have to pay damages. The interim possession order is also more restricted in that it may only be used where the property is or includes a building, not open land, and may not be used where the landowner also wishes to bring a claim for damages and an occupation rent.

Local byelaws

28.12 Section 235 of the Local Government Act 1972 (LGA) enables a local authority to make byelaws for the good rule and governance of the whole or any part of the district or borough and for the suppression and prevention of nuisances. Section 150(2) of the Police Reform and Social Responsibility Act 2011 enables local authorities to attach powers of seizure and retention of any property (which could include tents and sleeping equipment) in connection with any breach of a byelaw made under section 235 and enables the courts to order forfeiture of any such property on conviction for contravention of any byelaw. Local authorities could use this byelaw as a pre-emptive tool to prohibit encampments if they consider it has an area at risk of encampment protest. This will save having to obtain costly injunctions after any encampments have been set up. Local authorities should consider this option as part of their local risk assessment and mitigation plan. Westminster City Council has already introduced such a byelaw which came into force for a specified area around Parliament Square on 30/3/2012.

Power of local authority to direct unauthorised campers to leave land

28.13 Where people are residing in vehicles (including caravans) on land then section 77 of the Criminal Justice and Public Order Act 1994 gives local authorities in England and Wales power to give a direction to leave the land. The power applies only to land forming part of a highway and on any other unoccupied land or on any occupied land without the consent of the occupier.

28.14 It is an offence to fail to comply with such a direction. If the direction is not complied with, the local authority can apply to a magistrates' court for an order requiring the removal of vehicles and any occupants from the land (section 78). Responsibility for eviction lies with the local authority. Officers or agents of the local authority may use reasonable force to evict. It is usually recommended that the police attend such evictions in order to prevent a breach of the peace. Note that this power does not apply to other campers, i.e. those sleeping under canvas.

Obstructions on the public highway

28.15 If tents are erected on the public highway, so as to constitute a nuisance, the highway authority may serve a notice requiring their removal under section 149 of the Highways Act 1980 (HA 1980). If the recipient fails to comply, the highway authority can apply to the magistrates' court for a removal and disposal order. The key issue is the need to demonstrate that tents, etc. deposited on the highway are clearly obstructing the highway.

28.16 The HA 1980 provides other grounds on which highway authorities may take action in relation to protest activity on the highway. Under sections 1 and 263 the freehold title of the surface of a highway maintained at public expense is vested in the highway authority. This means that, in some circumstances, it could seek a possession order through the courts.

28.17 It is the duty of the highway authority to protect the rights of the public regarding the use and enjoyment of the highway and to prevent its obstruction. Not only is it an offence under section 137 to wilfully obstruct the highway without lawful authority or excuse, but it is open to the highway authority to seek an injunction in relation to protests which restrict public use of the highway.

28.18 Normally a highway authority would try to persuade individuals causing an obstruction to desist from such conduct, but if it is obvious that these parties are not going to back down then it is the duty of the authority to take steps to prevent those obstructing free passage along the highway. As with section 149 of the HA 1980 (removal and disposal orders), if the objects, e.g. tents, are causing a danger then there is a provision for their immediate removal. The power would not be effective where the obstruction is only temporary and formal proceedings are likely to be frustrated by the voluntary removal of the object before any court proceedings can bite.

Planning contravention notice

28.19 Section 171C of the TCPA 1990 enables an LPA to serve a planning contravention notice. This may be used where it appears that there may have been a breach of planning control and the LPA requires information about the activities taking place on the land or to find out more about the occupier's interest in the land. This is a useful procedure and enables the recipient of such a notice to respond constructively to the LPA about how any suspected breach of planning control may be satisfactorily remedied.

28.20 These notices enable LPAs to take actions quickly following complaints and may be sufficient to reach a solution to the problem without taking further formal action. Penalty for non-compliance is a maximum of £1,000 on summary conviction (section 171D). A second conviction for continuing non-compliance can be penalised by a daily fine. A false or misleading response to a planning contravention notice (either deliberately or recklessly) is subject to a maximum fine of £5,000.

Enforcement notice and retrospective planning permission

28.21 Section 172 of the TCPA 1990 gives LPAs the power to issue an enforcement notice which requires steps to be taken to remedy the breach of planning control within a given period. Such steps can include demolition and restoration of a site or alterations to a building. There is a right of appeal to the Secretary of State against an enforcement notice (section 174). If the notice is upheld, the penalty for failure to comply is a fine of up to £20,000 on summary conviction or an unlimited fine on indictment (section 179). A person convicted of failure to comply with an enforcement notice also faces the very real prospect of a confiscation order under the Proceeds of Crime Act 2002, which can be very costly in those cases where, for instance, dwellings have been sub-divided for rental without planning permission. Enforcement notices should be clearly expressed and should enable recipients to know: (a) exactly what activity, in the LPA's view, constitutes the relevant breach of planning control; and (b) what steps the LPA require to be taken, or what activities are required to cease, in order to remedy the breach.

28.22 If an enforcement notice has been issued, the LPA may decline to determine a retrospective planning application which would grant planning permission for any of the matters specified in the enforcement notice (section 70C of the TCPA 1990, as inserted by section 123 of the Localism Act 2011 (LA 2011)).

Stop notice

28.23 Section 183 of the TCPA 1990 has the effect of quickly stopping any activity which is in breach of planning control where there are special reasons which justify this step, for example, to prevent further environmental damage or to stop the construction of an unauthorised building. A stop notice may only be served with or after an enforcement notice relating to the same activity. Penalty for non-compliance is a fine of up to £20,000 on summary conviction or an unlimited fine on indictment (section 187).

Breach of condition notice

28.24 Section 187A of the TCPA 1990 allows a breach of condition notice to be served where there has been a failure to comply with any condition or limitation imposed on a grant of planning permission. The penalty for non-compliance is a fine of up to £2,500 on summary conviction.

Power of entry onto land

28.25 Sections 196A, 196B and 196C of the TCPA 1990 provides authorised officers of the LPA with a power of entry to enable them to obtain information required for enforcement purposes. This may be without a warrant at any reasonable hour (with 24 hours' notice for a dwelling-house), or with a warrant if access has been or is expected to be refused, or in case of an emergency. Wilful obstruction of an authorised person is an offence. The penalty is a fine of up to £1,000 on summary conviction.

Clean-up powers

28.26 Fly-tipping or the illegal deposits of controlled waste on land (i.e. in the absence of an environmental permit contrary to the Environmental Protection Act 1990 (EPA 1990), section 33) give rise to an offence which may be prosecuted by the Environment Agency (EA) (in more serious cases) or local authority.

Removal of waste from land

28.27 Local authorities are obliged to remove fly-tipped waste from public land but on private land it is the responsibility of the landowner to remove waste and to dispose of it lawfully. Section 59 of the EPA 1990 allows local authorities and the EA to require owners or occupiers of land to remove waste which they have caused or permitted to be deposited illegally. A default power exists enabling the EA or local authority to enter land to clean up the waste for which the landowner may be charged. This is an effective power where a person is in occupation of the land, or where a landowner is refusing to take steps to prevent fly-tipping or has otherwise allowed the fly-tipping to take place on the land. However, the power cannot be used against the offender unless he is the owner or occupier of the land or where there is doubt over whether the deposit is an illegal deposit.

Power to remove items abandoned on land

28.28 Section 6 of the Refuse Disposal (Amenity) Act 1978 provides local authorities with the power to remove anything (other than a motor vehicle) which has been abandoned without lawful authority on any land in the open air or on any other land forming part of a highway provided that they have given notice to the occupier of the land and no objection has been received within 15 days. The local authority may be entitled to recover their costs of removal from the person who deposited the articles.

Harm to public health

28.29 Local authorities have certain duties and powers to control statutory nuisances under sections 79 to 81 of the EPA 1990. A statutory nuisance is variously defined and can include any premises or land which are in such a state as to be prejudicial to health (i.e. where it is injurious or likely to cause injury to health) or a nuisance (i.e. where the matters of which complaint is made give rise to an unacceptable interference with the personal comfort or amenity of the nearby community).

28.30 The statute requires local authorities to inspect their areas for statutory nuisances and to take such steps as are reasonably practicable to investigate complaints of statutory nuisances made by residents. A local authority has a duty to serve an abatement notice if it is satisfied that a statutory nuisance notice exists, or is likely to occur or recur. The abatement notice should generally be served on the owner of the land if the person responsible (e.g. a tenant or occupier of the land) cannot be found or if the nuisance has not yet occurred or recurred. If the abatement notice is not complied with, the local authority has the power to take further steps to deal with the nuisance itself but is not obliged to take those steps. In doing so, the local authority may do whatever may be necessary in the execution of the notice and may be able to recover expenses from the landowner, if necessary through a charge on the land. A local authority also has the power to take criminal proceedings against a person who fails to comply with an abatement notice if it considers that doing so is in the interests of the inhabitants of the area. If the local authority considers that the criminal procedure is inadequate (e.g. in an emergency) then it has the power to seek an injunction in the High Court to deal with the statutory nuisance.

28.31 The foregoing powers are effective in tackling statutory nuisance arising from the unlawful occupation of land (e.g. to deal with noise, smells, the accumulation of rubbish or other noxious material, fumes or dark smoke). However the statutory nuisance regime cannot be used to require people who are responsible for causing the statutory nuisance to move themselves from an encampment, even if they are occupying the site unlawfully.

Power to require proper maintenance of land

28.32 Where it appears to the LPA that the amenity of a part of its area, or of an adjoining area, is adversely affected by the condition of land in its area, it may serve on the owner and occupier of the land a notice requiring steps for remedying the condition of the land to be taken within such period as may be specified (see section 215 of the TCPA 1990).

28.33 Any person on whom a notice has been served may appeal to a magistrates' court (with a further appeal to the Crown Court) on various grounds:

(a) that the condition of the land does not adversely affect the amenity of any part of the LPA's area, or of any adjoining area;
(b) that the condition of the land is attributable to, and as such results in the ordinary course of events from, the carrying on of operations or a use of land

which is not in contravention of Part III of the TCPA 1990 (control over development);

(c)   that the requirements of the notice exceed what is necessary for preventing the condition of the land from adversely affecting the amenity of part of the LPA's area, or of any adjoining area; and

(d)   that the period specified in the notice as the period within which any steps required by the notice are to be taken falls short of what should reasonably be allowed.

28.34   Where an appeal is brought, the notice to which it relates shall be of no effect pending the final determination or withdrawal of the appeal. This procedure is probably of limited effect in practice in view of the defence that the activities in respect of which complaint is made do not constitute a breach of planning control. Provision is made for penalties for non-compliance by an owner or occupier of land with a notice served under this part (section 216). Where the notice has come into effect and the required steps have not been taken, the LPA has a power to go onto the land in order to clean it up itself and it can recover its reasonable expenses from the owner of the land (section 219).

Power to deal with accumulations of rubbish in the open air

28.35   The Public Health Act 1961 gives local authorities powers to deal with accumulations of rubbish in the open air. In particular, section 34 creates a power for local authorities to remove rubbish on land in the open air which is seriously detrimental to the amenity of the neighbourhood. For the power to be exercised a number of conditions must be met:

(a)   There must be rubbish which is defined as rubble, waste paper, crockery and metal, and any other kind of refuse (including organic matter); however, any material accumulated in the course of a business will not count as 'rubbish'.

(b)   The rubbish must be on land in the open air in the local authority's area.

(c)   The presence of the rubbish must be seriously detrimental to the amenities of the neighbourhood.

(d)   The local authority must have given 28 days' prior notice to the owner and occupier of the land requiring the removal of the specified rubbish.

(e)   The recipient of a notice has the right to serve a counter-notice stating that they will remove the rubbish themselves. If a counter-notice is served the local authority must not remove the rubbish unless the person who served the counter-notice fails to take or complete the steps in the counter-notice within a reasonable time.

(f)   The recipient of the notice may appeal to the magistrates' court on the grounds that the authority should not take action under section 34 (for example, if they allege that the rubbish is not seriously detrimental to the amenity of the neighbourhood) or if the steps proposed in the notice are unreasonable. If an appeal is brought against the notice, the local authority must not remove the rubbish unless and until the appeal is finally determined in its favour or is withdrawn.

28.36 This power could be used to deal with the accumulation of rubbish on land arising from an unlawful occupation. The power does not extend to removing material accumulated for, or in the course of, a business. It follows that where unlawful occupants are carrying on a business, careful consideration will need to be given to whether items which the local authority wishes to remove fall within this exclusion. This power cannot be invoked to remove occupants from an unauthorised encampment.

Seizure of motor vehicles

28.37 Since 6/4/2015, where a vehicle is suspected of having been involved in the commission of an offence relating to the illegal deposit of waste or other waste offences (e.g. breach of duty of care, carrying controlled waste while unauthorised to do so or operating an illegal waste site), a local authority or the EA or Natural Resources Wales may seize a vehicle and its contents in accordance with the provisions of the Control of Pollution (Amendment) Act 1989/EPA 1990 and the Control of Waste (Dealing with Seized Property) (England and Wales) Regulations 2015.

28.38 This power can be used where a vehicle is suspected of having been involved in the commission of an offence but there is insufficient information concerning who has committed the offence. It can also be used to 'flush out' owners where it is unclear who is the registered keeper and to disrupt and prevent illegal waste activities, reducing the impact of waste crime on the environment.

Powers of the police

Power to direct unauthorised campers to leave land

28.39 Should trespassers refuse to comply with a request to leave land, sections 61 to 62 of the Criminal Justice and Public Order Act 1994 gives the police discretionary powers to direct trespassers to leave and remove any property or vehicles which they have with them. The power applies where the senior police officer present at the scene reasonably believes that two or more people are trespassing on land with the purpose of residing there, that the occupier has taken reasonable steps to ask them to leave, and that any of the following have occurred, namely: (a) that any of the trespassers have caused damage to land or property; (b) that any of the trespassers have used threatening, abusive or insulting words or behaviour towards the occupier, a member of the occupier's family or an employee or agent of the occupier; or (c) that the trespassers have between them six or more vehicles on the land.

28.40 Failure to comply with the direction by leaving the land as soon as reasonably practicable is an offence. Similarly it is an offence for a trespasser who has left the land in compliance with an order to re-enter it as a trespasser within three months of the direction being given.

Power to direct trespassers to move to an alternative site

28.41 Police have power under sections 62A–E of the Criminal Justice and Public Order Act 1994 to direct both trespassers and travellers to leave land and remove any vehicle and property from the land and move to where there is a suitable pitch available on a caravan site elsewhere in the local authority area.

Offence of squatting in a residential building

28.42 This offence arises under section 144 of the Legal Aid, Sentencing and Punishment of Offenders Act 2012, which came into force on 1/9/2012. The offence is committed where a person occupies a residential building as a trespasser, having entered as a trespasser (knowingly or when he/she ought to know that they are trespassers), and is living in the building or intends to live there for any period. Although the offence does not cover squatting in non-residential buildings or on land, squatters who have broken into those premises, removed items or caused damage might well be guilty of other offences, such as criminal damage or burglary, and should be reported to the police.

Reform?

28.43 It has often been claimed that local authorities are not making best use of the planning enforcement powers available to them. In March 2015, the DCLG, the Home Office and the Ministry of Justice published their summary of the powers that public bodies have to help them deal with illegal and unauthorised sites.[4] A joint ministerial letter, issued alongside the summary of powers, urged council leaders, police and crime commissioners and police chief constables to make full use of their powers:

> It is vital that communities see that the law applies to everyone and they should be confident that local agencies are able to deal effectively with issues such as unauthorised encampments that can cause local concern. We are clear that the response to unauthorised encampments requires a locally driven, multi-agency

---

4   'Dealing with illegal and unauthorised encampments: A summary of available powers', published jointly by the DCLG, the Home Office and the Ministry of Justice on 27/3/2015.

response, supported by local authorities and the police. There are sufficient powers for local authorities and the police to take action; and Ministers have already reminded local councils of the need to act swiftly to stop unauthorised encampments starting in the first place. Public bodies should not gold-plate human rights and equalities legislation. Councils and the police have been given strong powers to deal with unauthorised encampments and when deciding whether to take action, they may want to consider for example: (a) the harm that such developments can cause to local amenities and the local environment, (b) the potential interference with the peaceful enjoyment of neighbouring property, (c) the need to maintain public order and safety and protect health – for example, by deterring fly-tipping and criminal damage, (d) any harm to good community relations, (e) that the state may enforce laws to control the use of an individual's property where that is in accordance with the general public interest.

28.44 In a House of Commons debate on gypsies and travellers and local communities on 9/10/2017, a number of MPs voiced concerns that, in spite of a range of enforcement powers already in place, unauthorised development and encampments remained a significant issue. In the debate the Minister of State for Communities and Local Government, then Alok Sharma, said that Members' views had been heard 'loud and clear'. He announced a review of the effectiveness of enforcement against unauthorised development and encampments, but said this was not a reason for local authorities and the police not to use their existing powers:

> We want to seek views on whether there is anything we can do to ensure that existing powers can be used more effectively. Let me be clear, however: this is not a signal to local authorities and the police that they should wait for the outcome of such a consultation. They have the powers to act, and we expect them to act.

28.45 In April 2018, the Government launched a consultation on powers for dealing with unauthorised development and encampments. The Minister of State for Housing, Dominic Raab, set out the rationale and scope of the consultation in the ministerial foreword:

> Recent debates in Parliament have addressed the topic of unauthorised traveller encampments, and Members of Parliament have voiced their constituents' concerns regarding the impact on both settled and nomadic populations. I was deeply troubled by these concerns, particularly by the widespread perception that the rule of law does not apply to those who choose a nomadic lifestyle, and the sense that available enforcement powers do not protect settled communities adequately. Unauthorised encampments can cause settled communities significant distress, and they perpetuate a negative image of the travelling community, the vast majority of whom are law-abiding citizens. Unauthorised encampments also have a detrimental effect on the life chances of those who live within such encampments, and their children, who may not benefit from the same opportunities as everyone else. This document serves to show that the Government is listening: we want to understand more about the

nature of the issue, and to hear views on the effectiveness of enforcement powers against unauthorised development and encampments. I welcome suggestions as to whether existing measures should be strengthened, and how public authorities can use the powers available to them more effectively. I look forward to hearing your views.

28.46 The consultation, carried out jointly by the Ministry of Housing, Communities and Local Government, Home Office and Ministry of Justice, seeks views on what more can be done to ensure local authorities, the police and landowners can deal with unauthorised encampments and developments efficiently. It covers: (a) local authority and police powers; (b) court processes; (c) planning enforcement; (d) government guidance; (e) the provision of authorised sites; and (f) impacts on the travelling community. The consultation was open until 15/6/2018. Responding to the launch of the consultation, organisations representing the travelling community have urged the Government to address the shortage of permanent and transit traveller sites.

PLANNING ISSUES

Planning policy for traveller sites

28.47 The following is taken from current national planning policy updated by the Department for Communities and Local Government (DCLG) on 31/8/2015:

Introduction
1. This document sets out the Government's planning policy for traveller sites.[5] It should be read in conjunction with the National Planning Policy Framework. Guidance on the Framework can be found at: http://planningguidance. planningportal.gov.uk/.

2. Planning law requires that applications for planning permission must be determined in accordance with the development plan, unless material considerations indicate otherwise. This policy must be taken into account in the preparation of development plans, and is a material consideration in planning decisions.[6] Local planning authorities preparing plans for and taking decisions on traveller sites should also have regard to the policies in the National Planning Policy Framework so far as relevant.

3. The Government's overarching aim is to ensure fair and equal treatment for travellers, in a way that facilitates the traditional and nomadic way of life of travellers while respecting the interests of the settled community.

---

5   See Annex 1 for the definition of traveller for the purposes of this statement.

6   Planning and Compulsory Purchase Act 2004, ss 19(2)(a) and 38(6) and TCPA 1990, s 70(2). In relation to neighbourhood plans, under s 38B and C and para 8(2) of the new Sch 4B to the 2004 Act (inserted by LA 2011, s 116 and Schs 9 and 10) the independent examiner will consider whether having regard to national policy [it is] appropriate to make the plan.

4. To help achieve this, Government's aims in respect of traveller sites are:

(a)   that local planning authorities should make their own assessment of need for the purposes of planning

(b)   to ensure that local planning authorities, working collaboratively, develop fair and effective strategies to meet need through the identification of land for sites

(c)   to encourage local planning authorities to plan for sites over a reasonable timescale

(d)   that plan-making and decision-taking should protect Green Belt from inappropriate development

(e)   to promote more private traveller site provision while recognising that there will always be those travellers who cannot provide their own sites

(f)   that plan-making and decision-taking should aim to reduce the number of unauthorised developments and encampments and make enforcement more effective

(g)   for local planning authorities to ensure that their Local Plan includes fair, realistic and inclusive policies

(h)   to increase the number of traveller sites in appropriate locations with planning permission, to address under provision and maintain an appropriate level of supply

(i)   to reduce tensions between settled and traveller communities in plan-making and planning decisions

(j)   to enable provision of suitable accommodation from which travellers can access education, health, welfare and employment infrastructure

(k)   for local planning authorities to have due regard to the protection of local amenity and local environment

5. To benefit those engaged in planning for traveller sites, specific planning policies for traveller sites are clearly set out in this separate document. The Government intends to review this policy when fair and representative practical results of its implementation are clear.

6. The Government still intends to review in the future whether Planning Policy for Traveller Sites should be incorporated within the wider National Planning Policy Framework. This will be considered as part of any wider review of the Framework.

Using evidence
Policy A: Using evidence to plan positively and manage development
7. In assembling the evidence base necessary to support their planning approach, local planning authorities should:

(a)   pay particular attention to early and effective community engagement with both settled and traveller communities (including discussing travellers' accommodation needs with travellers themselves, their representative bodies and local support groups)

(b)   cooperate with travellers, their representative bodies and local support groups; other local authorities and relevant interest groups to prepare and maintain an up-to-date understanding of the likely permanent and transit accommodation needs of their areas over the lifespan of their development plan, working collaboratively with neighbouring local planning authorities

(c)   use a robust evidence base to establish accommodation needs to inform the preparation of local plans and make planning decisions.

Plan-making
Policy B: Planning for traveller sites

8. Local Plans must be prepared with the objective of contributing to the achievement of sustainable development. To this end, they should be consistent with the policies in the National Planning Policy Framework, including the presumption in favour of sustainable development and the application of specific policies in the Framework, and this planning policy for traveller sites.

9. Local planning authorities should set pitch targets for gypsies and travellers as defined in Annex 1 and plot targets for travelling showpeople as defined in Annex 1 which address the likely permanent and transit site accommodation needs of travellers in their area, working collaboratively with neighbouring local planning authorities.[7]

10. Local planning authorities should, in producing their Local Plan:

(a)   identify and update annually, a supply of specific deliverable sites sufficient to provide 5 years' worth of sites against their locally set targets[8]

(b)   identify a supply of specific, developable sites, or broad locations for growth, for years 6 to 10 and, where possible, for years 11–15[9]

(c)   consider production of joint development plans that set targets on a cross-authority basis, to provide more flexibility in identifying sites, particularly if a local planning authority has special or strict planning constraints across its area (local planning authorities have a duty to cooperate on planning issues that cross administrative boundaries)

(d)   relate the number of pitches or plots to the circumstances of the specific size and location of the site and the surrounding population's size and density

(e)   protect local amenity and environment.

11. Criteria should be set to guide land supply allocations where there is identified need. Where there is no identified need, criteria-based policies should be included to provide a basis for decisions in case applications nevertheless come forward. Criteria

---

[7]   See Annex 1 for definitions of 'pitch' and 'plot'.

[8]   To be considered deliverable, sites should be available now, offer a suitable location for development, and be achievable with a realistic prospect that development will be delivered on the site within five years. Sites with planning permission should be considered deliverable until permission expires, unless there is clear evidence that schemes will not be implemented within five years, for example they will not be viable, there is no longer a demand for the type of units or sites have long term phasing plans.

[9]   To be considered developable, sites should be in a suitable location for traveller site development and there should be a reasonable prospect that the site is available and could be viably developed at the point envisaged.

based policies should be fair and should facilitate the traditional and nomadic life of travellers while respecting the interests of the settled community.

12. In exceptional cases, where a local planning authority is burdened by a large-scale unauthorised site that has significantly increased their need, and their area is subject to strict and special planning constraints, then there is no assumption that the local planning authority is required to plan to meet their traveller site needs in full.

13. Local planning authorities should ensure that traveller sites are sustainable economically, socially and environmentally. Local planning authorities should, therefore, ensure that their policies:

(a)   promote peaceful and integrated co-existence between the site and the local community
(b)   promote, in collaboration with commissioners of health services, access to appropriate health services
(c)   ensure that children can attend school on a regular basis
(d)   provide a settled base that reduces both the need for long-distance travelling and possible environmental damage caused by unauthorised encampment
(e)   provide for proper consideration of the effect of local environmental quality (such as noise and air quality) on the health and well-being of any travellers that may locate there or on others as a result of new development
(f)   avoid placing undue pressure on local infrastructure and services
(g)   do not locate sites in areas at high risk of flooding, including functional floodplains, given the particular vulnerability of caravans
(h)   reflect the extent to which traditional lifestyles (whereby some travellers live and work from the same location thereby omitting many travel to work journeys) can contribute to sustainability.

Policy C: Sites in rural areas and the countryside
14. When assessing the suitability of sites in rural or semi-rural settings, local planning authorities should ensure that the scale of such sites does not dominate the nearest settled community.

Policy D: Rural exception sites
15. If there is a lack of affordable land to meet local traveller needs, local planning authorities in rural areas, where viable and practical, should consider allocating and releasing sites solely for affordable traveller sites. This may include using a rural exception site policy for traveller sites that should also be used to manage applications. A rural exception site policy enables small sites to be used, specifically for affordable traveller sites, in small rural communities, that would not normally be used for traveller sites.[10] Rural exception sites should only be used for affordable traveller sites in perpetuity. A rural exception site policy should seek to address the needs of the local community by accommodating households who are either current residents or have an existing family or employment connection, whilst also ensuring that rural areas continue to develop as sustainable, mixed, inclusive communities.

---

[10]   Small rural settlements have been designated for enfranchisement and right to acquire purposes (under Housing Act 1996, s 17) by SI 1997/620–25 inclusive and SI 1999/1307.

Policy E: Traveller sites in Green Belt

16. Inappropriate development is harmful to the Green Belt and should not be approved, except in very special circumstances. Traveller sites (temporary or permanent) in the Green Belt are inappropriate development. Subject to the best interests of the child, personal circumstances and unmet need are unlikely to clearly outweigh harm to the Green Belt and any other harm so as to establish very special circumstances.

17. Green Belt boundaries should be altered only in exceptional circumstances. If a local planning authority wishes to make an exceptional, limited alteration to the defined Green Belt boundary (which might be to accommodate a site inset within the Green Belt) to meet a specific, identified need for a traveller site, it should do so only through the plan-making process and not in response to a planning application. If land is removed from the Green Belt in this way, it should be specifically allocated in the development plan as a traveller site only.

Policy F: Mixed planning use traveller sites

18. Local planning authorities should consider, wherever possible, including traveller sites suitable for mixed residential and business uses, having regard to the safety and amenity of the occupants and neighbouring residents. Local planning authorities should consider the scope for identifying separate sites for residential and for business purposes in close proximity to one another if mixed sites are not practical.

19. Local planning authorities should have regard to the need that travelling showpeople have for mixed-use yards to allow residential accommodation and space for storage of equipment.

20. Local planning authorities should not permit mixed use on rural exception sites.

Policy G: Major development projects

21. Local planning authorities should work with the planning applicant and the affected traveller community to identify a site or sites suitable for relocation of the community if a major development proposal requires the permanent or temporary relocation of a traveller site. Local planning authorities are entitled to expect the applicant to identify and provide an alternative site, providing the development on the original site is authorised.

Decision-taking

Policy H: Determining planning applications for traveller sites

22. Planning law requires that applications for planning permission must be determined in accordance with the development plan[11] unless material considerations indicate otherwise.[12]

---

[11]   Planning and Compulsory Purchase Act 2004, s 38(1): this includes adopted or approved development plan documents, i.e. the Local Plan and neighbourhood plans which have been made in relation to the area (and the London Plan).

[12]   Planning and Compulsory Purchase Act 2004, s 38(6) and TCPA 1990, s 70(2).

23. Applications should be assessed and determined in accordance with the presumption in favour of sustainable development and the application of specific policies in the National Planning Policy Framework and this planning policy for traveller sites.

24. Local planning authorities should consider the following issues amongst other relevant matters when considering planning applications for traveller sites:

(a) the existing level of local provision and need for sites
(b) the availability (or lack) of alternative accommodation for the applicants
(c) other personal circumstances of the applicant[13]
(d) that the locally specific criteria used to guide the allocation of sites in plans or which form the policy where there is no identified need for pitches/plots should be used to assess applications that may come forward on unallocated sites
(e) that they should determine applications for sites from any travellers and not just those with local connections

However, as paragraph 16 makes clear, subject to the best interests of the child, personal circumstances and unmet need are unlikely to clearly outweigh harm to the Green Belt and any other harm so as to establish very special circumstances.

25. Local planning authorities should very strictly limit new traveller site development in open countryside that is away from existing settlements or outside areas allocated in the development plan. Local planning authorities should ensure that sites in rural areas respect the scale of, and do not dominate, the nearest settled community, and avoid placing an undue pressure on the local infrastructure.

26. When considering applications, local planning authorities should attach weight to the following matters:

(a) effective use of previously developed (brownfield), untidy or derelict land
(b) sites being well planned or soft landscaped in such a way as to positively enhance the environment and increase its openness
(c) promoting opportunities for healthy lifestyles, such as ensuring adequate landscaping and play areas for children

---

[13] *Flintshire CC v Jayes* [2018] EWCA Civ 1089, where the Court of Appeal found that the judge had erred in quashing the temporary grant of planning permission to continue using a site as a gypsy caravan site where the adverse impact of refusal, namely forcing the families on site, including 11 children, to live by the roadside with consequent disruption to education and access to healthcare, was sufficient to outweigh countervailing considerations including the identified planning harm. In the result, a temporary grant to use the land as a gypsy site for five years in 2011 was allowed to remain in place. This was a case where a refusal of temporary planning permission would have been a disproportionate interference with the European Convention for the Protection of Human Rights and Fundamental Freedoms 1950, Art 8 rights of the resident families.

(d)   not enclosing a site with so much hard landscaping, high walls or fences, that the impression may be given that the site and its occupants are deliberately isolated from the rest of the community.

27. If a local planning authority cannot demonstrate an up-to-date 5 year supply of deliverable sites, this should be a significant material consideration in any subsequent planning decision when considering applications for the grant of temporary planning permission.[14] The exception is where the proposal is on land designated as Green Belt; sites protected under the Birds and Habitats Directives and / or sites designated as Sites of Special Scientific Interest; Local green space, an Area of Outstanding Natural Beauty, or within a National Park (or the Broads).

28. Local planning authorities should consider how they could overcome planning objections to particular proposals using planning conditions or planning obligations including:

(a)   limiting which parts of a site may be used for any business operations, in order to minimise the visual impact and limit the effect of noise
(b)   specifying the number of days the site can be occupied by more than the allowed number of caravans (which permits visitors and allows attendance at family or community events)
(c)   limiting the maximum number of days for which caravans might be permitted to stay on a transit site.

Policy I: Implementation
29. The policies in this revised Planning Policy for Traveller Sites apply from the day of publication. This replaces the version published in March 2012.

30. The implementation policies set out in the National Planning Policy Framework will apply also to plan-making and decision-taking for traveller sites. In applying those implementation provisions to traveller sites, references in those provisions to policies in the National Planning Policy Framework should, where relevant, be read to include policies in this planning policy for traveller sites.

Annex 1: Glossary
1. For the purposes of this planning policy "gypsies and travellers" means:

> Persons of nomadic habit of life whatever their race or origin, including such persons who on grounds only of their own or their family's or dependants' educational or health needs or old age have ceased to travel temporarily, but excluding members of an organised group of travelling showpeople or circus people travelling together as such.

---

[14]   There is no presumption that a temporary grant of planning permission should be granted permanently.

2. In determining whether persons are "gypsies and travellers" for the purposes of this planning policy, consideration should be given to the following issues amongst other relevant matters:

(a)   whether they previously led a nomadic habit of life
(b)   the reasons for ceasing their nomadic habit of life
(c)   whether there is an intention of living a nomadic habit of life in the future, and if so, how soon and in what circumstances.

3. For the purposes of this planning policy, "travelling showpeople" means:
Members of a group organised for the purposes of holding fairs, circuses or shows (whether or not travelling together as such). This includes such persons who on the grounds of their own or their family's or dependants' more localised pattern of trading, educational or health needs or old age have ceased to travel temporarily, but excludes Gypsies and Travellers as defined above.

4. For the purposes of this planning policy, "travellers" means "gypsies and travellers" and "travelling showpeople" as defined above.

5. For the purposes of this planning policy, "pitch" means a pitch on a "gypsy and traveller" site and "plot" means a pitch on a "travelling showpeople" site (often called a "yard"). This terminology differentiates between residential pitches for "gypsies and travellers" and mixed-use plots for "travelling showpeople", which may / will need to incorporate space or to be split to allow for the storage of equipment.

Shortage of traveller sites

28.48 It is widely acknowledged that there is a national shortage of suitable permanent and transit traveller sites.[15] There has been a long-term policy and

---

[15]   Data published by the DHCLG from the count of traveller caravans in England which took place in July 2017: 29% of traveller caravans were on public sites (i.e. operated by local authorities and private registered providers of social housing, including housing associations, trusts and co-operatives); 54% were on privately funded sites; 19% were in unauthorised developments on land owned by travellers; and 7% were in unauthorised encampments on land not owned by travellers. Only 315 sites were recorded as being operated by local authority and private registered providers of social housing. The proportion of caravans on all authorised sites (including public sites) has risen from 77% in July 2007 to 84% in July 2017. Caravans on authorised private sites have formed a growing proportion of the total number of caravans over the last ten years, increasing from 38% in July 2007 to 54% in July 2017. However, the action group Friends Families and Travellers (FFT), using Freedom of Information requests in May and June 2016, undertook research to ascertain whether local authorities in South East England were meeting the requirement to identify a supply of specific deliverable sites sufficient to provide five years' worth of sites against their locally set targets. The FFT reported that most local authorities had not identified such a supply: Only ten (out of 66) local authorities had identified a five-year supply of specific deliverable sites. Five local authorities had no identified need for new sites. The research found that up to the year 2033 a total of 1,745 additional pitches were needed in the South East of England. Similar research carried out by the National Federation of Gypsy Liaison Groups in the East and West Midlands, and by the London Gypsy and Traveller Unit in London,

practice failure to deliver and manage gypsy and traveller sites in the United Kingdom. The resulting shortage of sites manifests itself in unauthorised encampments and expenditure on clearing up and eviction. Good quality sites are provided in some areas, but historically a number of councils have ignored the strategic issue and only use reactive enforcement measures against encampments. In other areas there may be sites but they are so poorly managed that they are expensive and unsustainable. Nor has national policy and legislation provided the impetus to deliver sufficient sites and it is often not enforced. There are examples of councils turning down their own applications for sites or including conditions that add expense and delay to site delivery.

28.49 The Coalition Government put in place a package of financial incentives and other support for local authorities to encourage the appropriate development of traveller sites. Measures included:

- £60 million Traveller Pitch Funding to 2015, as part of the Affordable Homes Programme, to provide new or refurbished traveller sites in England.

---

concluded that there had been insufficient progress in identifying a five-year supply of specific deliverable sites to meet the accommodation needs of gypsies and travellers. In September 2016, the specialist publication, *Planning*, reported that some councils had found that the new definition of what constituted a 'traveller' in planning policy had slowed down councils' progress in planning for gypsy and traveller accommodation and had led authorities to revisit their need assessments. The *Travellers' Times* has reported concerns that the new definition could be used by local authorities to reduce the number of traveller sites that they would have to plan for. In a written submission to the House of Commons Women and Equalities Select Committee, the MHCLG reported progress on delivering new traveller pitches: between 2011 and March 2015, the Homes and Communities Agency spent over £43 million delivering more than 500 new pitches and refurbishing nearly 400 more pitches through the Traveller Pitch Funding programme. In addition, under the 2015–18 Affordable Homes Programme, allocations were agreed for 68 new pitches with £4.9 million funding. A report by FFT, published in December 2017, criticised the low uptake of funding for new socially rented pitches since 2015. Their analysis found that only four additional traveller pitches had been created under the Affordable Homes Programme 2015–18. The report concluded that 'the government's mechanisms for creating new affordable pitches for gypsy and traveller families are not working, despite well-evidenced need and demand' and recommended that the Government: (a) should adopt a definition of a traveller in planning terms that incorporates all gypsies and travellers who need a pitch to live on (for example as proposed in the Draft London Plan); (b) should re-introduce targets, and a statutory duty to meet the assessed accommodation need of gypsies and travellers, as formerly existed under the Caravans Sites Act 1968; (c) should ring-fence gypsy and traveller pitch funding for local authorities to produce socially rented pitches (this will require improved communication between DCLG, HCA and local authorities); and (d) should begin to accurately record and monitor figures on actual net increase of gypsy and traveller pitches. The Government's current consultation on powers to deal with unauthorised development and encampments seeks views on whether there are any specific barriers to the provision of more authorised permanent and transit sites, and, if so, what could be done to overcome them.

- A financial incentive to local authorities, through the New Homes Bonus, for the development of authorised traveller site accommodation.
- Promoting good practice examples of positive engagement between service providers and gypsies and travellers.
- Training to support councillors with their leadership role around traveller site provision, including advice on dealing with the controversy that can sometimes accompany planning applications for traveller sites.

28.50 The Government has confirmed that funding for traveller pitches is available through the Shared Ownership and Affordable Homes Programme 2016–2021.

Planning policy

28.51 The Government's planning policies and requirements for gypsy and traveller sites have already been set out above at para 28.47 and were last updated in August 2015. They accompany the March 2012 National Planning Policy Framework (NPPF) and must be taken into consideration in preparing local plans and taking planning decisions. They encourage local authorities to formulate their own evidence base for gypsy and traveller needs and to provide their own targets relating to pitches required. Specifically, the planning policy directs LPAs to set pitch targets for gypsies and travellers and plot targets for travelling showpeople which address the likely permanent and transit site accommodation needs of travellers in their area, working collaboratively with neighbouring LPAs. In a January 2014 Written Ministerial Statement (WMS) the Coalition Government sought to re-emphasise existing policy that:

> unmet need, whether for traveller sites or for conventional housing, is unlikely to outweigh harm to the green belt and other harm to constitute the "very special circumstances" justifying inappropriate development in the green belt.[16]

28.52 On 14/9/2014 the Coalition Government published a consultation on planning and travellers, which proposed to change the definition of 'traveller' for planning related purposes so that it would exclude those who have permanently ceased travelling. This change came into force from August 2015 following the issue of a revised version of planning policy for traveller sites.

28.53 The Coalition Government's 14/9/2014 consultation also proposed to make intentional occupation of land without planning permission a material

---

[16] MHCLG and the Rt Hon Brandon Lewis MP; Written statement to Parliament: Green belt, 17/1/2014.

consideration in any retrospective planning application for that site. The document set out:

> For the avoidance of doubt, this does not mean that retrospective applications should be automatically refused, but rather failure to seek permission in advance of occupation will count against the application. It will, the Government hopes, encourage all applicants to apply through the proper planning processes before occupying land and carrying out development.

28.54 This change in planning policy was introduced by means of a letter from the Government's Chief Planner to planning officers in England. It was later reaffirmed in a written statement to the House on 14/9/2015. The Traveller Movement[17] expressed concern that the changes to planning policy for traveller sites will exacerbate problems around unauthorised sites, lack of site provision and community tensions:

> The Traveller Movement believe that the new measures will do the opposite and make it significantly harder for Gypsies and Travellers to obtain planning permission, adding to the existing chronic shortage of Traveller sites in England. We expect this in turn to result in many community members being forced onto the road, increasing numbers of unauthorised sites and damaging community cohesion; all issues which the new guidance apparently aims to improve. At the heart of these changes lies a deep misunderstanding of the culture and lives of England's Gypsies and Travellers and a failure by Government to meaningfully recognise their ethnic minority status in the planning system.

Will there be further change to planning policy?

28.55 Revisions to the NPPF were published on 24 July 2018, replacing the original version which was published in March 2012. Reference should be made to Chapter 24 where the key changes are summarised.

Recovery of planning appeals in the Green Belt

28.56 The WMS in January 2014 also confirmed that the Secretary of State would continue with his pledge to recover more planning appeals relating to traveller sites in Green Belt land for his own determination. Following a legal challenge (*Moore v Secretary of State for Communities and Local Government*)[18] which found that certain aspects of this policy were contrary to provisions in the Equality Act 2010 and the European Convention for the Protection of Human Rights and Fundamental Freedoms 1950 (ECHR), the Government decided to 'de-recover' a number of

---

[17]   The Traveller Movement, 'Government changes to Planning Policy for Traveller sites', September 2015.

[18]   [2015] EWHC 44 (Admin).

outstanding appeals. In August 2015 the Government subsequently said that it would 'consider the recovery of a proportion of relevant appeals in the green belt for the secretary of state's decision'.

Connors v Secretary of State for Communities and Local Government and *Mulvenna v Secretary of State for Communities and Local Government*[19]

28.57 These important cases (which related to traveller sites in the Green Belt) raised involved issues as to: (a) whether in recovering appeals for his own determination, the Secretary of State had breached the appellants' human rights and the provision on indirect discrimination in section 19 of the Equality Act 2010; (b) whether the judge had been wrong to refuse an extension of time in the judicial review proceedings; (c) whether the judge had been wrong to conclude that the Secretary of State, having recovered and determined the appeals, had become *functus officio*, and was therefore unable to revoke his decisions; and (d) whether the Secretary of State's decisions were a nullity because they had been made pursuant to recovery directions which were unlawful pursuant to *Moore*.

28.58 The appellant travellers appealed against decisions of the Secretary of State to uphold the refusal of planning permission for a material change of use in the Green Belt. The fifth and sixth defendants also renewed applications for permission to seek a judicial review out of time of the Secretary of State's decisions to recover the appeals for his own determination.

28.59 In light of the NPPF (2012), traveller sites in the Green Belt constituted inappropriate development which would only be approved in exceptional circumstances. In the ministerial statements of 2013 and 2014, it was declared that appeals relating to such sites would be subjected to particular scrutiny and that the Secretary of State would consider recovering them for his own determination. In *Moore* it was held that the application of the two ministerial statements in such a way as to recover all appeals, or an arbitrary percentage of them, was unlawful. The appellants had applied unsuccessfully for planning permission to enable mobile homes to be stationed on land in the Green Belt. On the appeals, a planning inspector held that there were special circumstances justifying the proposed developments. The Secretary of State recovered the appeals for his own determination and dismissed them.

28.60 The appeals were dismissed. In relation to the recovery of the appeals, it was held that it was neither irrational nor unfair to express an intention in the ministerial statements to give 'particular scrutiny' to appeals involving traveller

---

[19]   [2017] EWCA Civ 1850

sites; nor was it inherently discriminatory against travellers in comparison with the rest of the population. The Secretary of State's decisions to recover the appeals did not automatically conflict with section 19 of the 2010 Act since they fell to be reviewed by the court in accordance with public law principles and the appellants had failed to demonstrate that the decision-making process had been tainted by unlawfulness. Moreover, since none of the appellants had sought a remedy before the Secretary of State's decision on the appeal in question, their challenges were brought out of time. The policy expressed in the ministerial statements was not susceptible to challenge under TCPA 1990, section 288; nor had there been any breach of Article 8 of the ECHR, since the court's review of decisions made by the Secretary of State on planning appeals on a case-by-case basis was sufficient to comply with that provision and was not displaced by the existence and operation of a national policy for the recovery of appeals. Nor was there any breach of Article 8 of the ECHR, as the Secretary of State had addressed the potential impact of a refusal of planning permission on the rights of the appellants' families, having regard to the best interests of the children. In relation to the public law allegation, the Secretary of State had been entitled to differ from his inspectors in exercising a planning judgment, provided he did so on the basis of proper evidence. In none of the cases had he acted in bad faith, unreasonably or irrationally, nor had he failed to give reasons for his decision.

28.61 In relation to the issue of an extension of time for bringing judicial review proceedings, it was found that the fifth and sixth appellants had failed to take advantage of the remedy available to them by making a timely challenge to the Secretary of State's recovery directions, even though their professional planning advisors had expressed concerns as early as two weeks after the publication of the first ministerial statement (*Gerber v Wiltshire County Council*[20] followed). It was held that the exercise of judicial discretion to permit very late challenges was rarely appropriate and there was no justification for extending time.

28.62 On the *functus officio* issue, it was held that the statutory scheme contained no power for the Secretary of State to review or revoke a decision dismissing an appeal or to revisit a recovery direction once he had made his decision. Such a power would be contrary to the fundamental objective of providing certainty and finality for those affected by planning decisions made under the statutory regime. Lastly, the court reiterated (following *Moore*) that a recovery decision was not a consideration of the substantive merits of a planning appeal, but a procedural step. Therefore, even if the recovery directions were a nullity because of *Moore*, it did not follow that the Secretary of State's determination of the appeals was also a nullity because the statutory framework gave him jurisdiction to determine the

---

[20]   [2016] EWCA Civ 84.

appeals, whatever the lawfulness of the recovery decisions. It followed that the decisions on the statutory appeals were lawful.

Index

Scotland
ancient woodlands 376
community right to buy scheme 465
Forestry Commission Scotland 382
National Trust for Scotland 379
Scottish Natural Heritage 348
Section 38 agreements *see* Highways,
maintenance, adoption of roads
Section 106 agreements *see* Planning
obligations
Section 278 agreements *see* Highways,
agreements under HA 1980, s 278
Secure residential institutions 98, 116
Self builds 221
Sensitive areas *see* Environmental impact
assessments (EIAs), sensitive areas
Sensitive Marine Areas (SMAs) 381
Sewers 85, 118, 120, 553–554
see also Drainage; Pipes and pipe-lines
Shops
GPDO and 109, 110–111, 112–113,
116, 117, 119–120
PSI applications in London 18
shop fronts, appeals relating to *see*
Commercial Appeals Service
use class A1: meaning 95
see also Betting offices; Hot food
takeaways; Pay day loan shops
Simplified Planning Zones (SPZs) 9,
131, 283 n34
Sites of Community Importance 381
Sites of Special Scientific Interest (SSSIs)
355, 373–375
GPDO and 106, 110 n36, 112 n38,
113 n40, 114 n42, 117 n45, 119
n46, n47, 120 n48, 121 n49
hedgerows in 410 n41
highways and 548, 594–595
NPPF and 24 n12, 54 n119, 142 n78,
161 n130, 385, 390
as sensitive areas in EIA context 337
n13, 338 n16
see also Regionally Important
Geological and Geomorphological
Sites (RIGS)
Skips 568–569
Solar energy 393 n15, 395

Spatial development strategy for London
6 n34, 13, 27 n22, 51–52, 450–451
Special Areas of Conservation (SACs) *see*
Habitats, European protected sites
Special diversion orders 548
Special Landscape Areas (SLAs) 381
see also Areas of Great Landscape
Value (AGLVs)
Special nature conservation orders 346
Special Protection Areas (SPAs) *see*
Birds, European protected sites
Sport
ACVs and 467
land use classification and *see*
Assembly and leisure
new facilities in Green Belt 353, 366–
367
playing fields *see* Playing fields
sports and pastimes, and TVGs *see*
Village greens, criteria for
registration
see also Infrastructure projects;
Swimming
Statements of Community Involvement
36 n56, 43
Starter homes 212, 454 n15
Statutory undertakers 85, 227, 348, 375,
471–472
GPDO and 104, 107 n30
highways and 559, 580, 582, 586
railways *see* Railways
see also Infrastructure projects; Public
transport
Stop notices 131, 321–323, 346, 621
CIL and 223–224
temporary stop notices 301–303,
616–617
see also Enforcement notices
Stopping up and diversion of highways
573–596
introduction 523, 544, 573–574, 604
by legal but non-statutory process 597
effect 544, 574–575, 597
temporary stopping up or diversion
583, 596
under HA 1980 577 n294, 583–595,
596